VERDICT ON VICHY

VERDICT ON
VICHY

POWER AND PREJUDICE IN
THE VICHY FRANCE REGIME

MICHAEL CURTIS

Arcade Publishing
NEW YORK

FIRST U.S. EDITION

First published in Great Britain in 2002 by Weidenfeld and Nicolson

Library of Congress Cataloging-in-Publication Data

Curtis, Michael, 1923–
     Verdict on Vichy / Michael Curtis.
         p. cm.
     Includes bibliographical references and index.
     ISBN 1-55970-689-9
         1. France—History—German occupation, 1940–1945. 2. Pétain, Philippe, 1856–1951—Influence. 3. World War, 1939–1945—Collaborationists—France. 4. Vichy (France)—Politics and government. I. Title.

DC397.C87 2003
944.081'6—dc21   2002044055

Published in the United States by Arcade Publishing, Inc., New York

Distributed by AOL Time Warner Book Group

Visit our Web site at www.arcadepub.com

10 9 8 7 6 5 4 3 2 1

EB

PRINTED IN THE UNITED STATES OF AMERICA

To Judy

Count Pozzo di Borgo, a diplomat from Corsica, imagined the triumphant entrance of the famous French statesman Talleyrand into Hell, where he was greeted with great pomp and circumstance. Satan complimented him on all he had done but added: 'Prince, your zeal has slightly exceeded my expectations.'

'Oui, le Vél d'Hiv, Drancy, Compiègne et tous les camps de transit, ces antichambres de la mort, ont été organisés, gérés, gardés par des Français. Oui, le premier acte de la Shoah s'est joué ici, avec la compliçité de l'Etat français.'

'Yes, the Vél d'Hiv, Drancy, Compiègne, and all the transit camps, these antechambers of death, were organised, administered, and guarded by French people. Yes, the first act of the Shoah [the Holocaust] was played out here with the complicity of the French State [the Vichy regime].'

French Prime Minister, Jean-Pierre Raffarin, 21 July 2002,
at the commemoration of the 60th anniversary of the
Vél d'Hiv round-up of Jews on 16 July 1942

CONTENTS

ILLUSTRATIONS

PREFACE

This book to a large extent results from a sudden epiphany reading Serge Klarsfeld's weighty volume, *French Children of the Holocaust: A Memorial*, and being profoundly moved by its 1400 pages of photographs of Jewish children deported from France during the years of 1940–44 to their deaths in the extermination camps in eastern Europe. Only the coldest heart can be indifferent to, or unmoved by, the overwhelming evidence of the consequences of discrimination and persecution in France, and by the absence of moral principle and isolation of Vichy France from true law and justice.

Echoing Sir Philip Sidney, in his sonnet from Astrophel and Stella, 'Fool said my muse to me, look in thy heart and write', I have done both. In doing so, I have benefited from the now considerable literature in both English and French on the four years of the Vichy regime. It is a pleasure to acknowledge intellectual debts to those whose works have been acute, scholarly and influential contributions to the subject, especially Robert O. Paxton, Michael R. Marrus, Jean-Pierre Azéma, François Bédarida, H. Roderick Kedward, Serge Klarsfeld, Denis Peschanski, Vicki Caron, Susan Zuccotti, Richard Golsan and Richard Weisberg.

Vichy France continues to engage the attention of Europeans and Americans. Since Robert Paxton's ground-breaking book, *Vichy France: Old Guard and New Order, 1940–44*, and Marcel Ophul's *The Sorrow and the Pity* thirty years ago, scholarly books, films, and novels have addressed the Vichy regime. Why did a country, the first to grant full civil rights to Jews and with its share of those who resisted the German occupation, descend to policies of discrimination and persecution? Over the last fifty years, the historical record has become increasingly clear, although new material still emerges, such as the definitive government-sponsored Mattéoli report of 2000 on how Jews were systematically robbed of their property through the "aryanization" process.

I have not attempted to provide a comprehensive history of the Vichy years as some works in both French and English have done. Rather, writing as a political scientist, I have concentrated on one central theme: the attitude and actions of French officials and citizens regarding Jews in France. This book assesses people and institutions, official and non-official, and their role during the Vichy years by using up-to-date relevant information and research on a number of subjects. They include the Aryanization process; the acquiescence of French administrators and the judicial system in the multiple laws of discrimination; the indictments and trials of individuals accused of crimes against humanity; the hesitations and difficulties of the judicial system in decision on the trials, thus leaving no definitive or unambiguous ruling on the crimes or on the nature of the Vichy regime itself; the role of Church leaders; the attitudes of prominent personalities in the cultural world, including Jean-Paul Sartre, Simone de Beauvoir, Robert Brasillach, André Dérain and Alfred Cortot.

My own interpretation of people and events in Vichy France stems not only from objective assessment and synthesis of significant research of recent years but also from passionate conviction about these issues. I trust that reaching conclusions on them does not violate intellectual integrity. Those conclusions do not necessitate categorical moral judgment of the motivation, actions, or non-actions of French people. Considering the extraordinary conditions of wartime France, accommodation and collaboration with the enemy and acquiescence in discriminatory policies can be seen either as unwarrantable self-abasement or charitably construed as necessary for survival. As a specific example, it is not easy to evaluate those people, among whom François Mitterrand can be included, who were officials for a time of the Vichy regime but who also, albeit belatedly, established links to or joined the Resistance, either out of genuine conviction or as pliable opportunism.

If some French people exhibited varying degrees of cruelty, hatred, or simple indifference towards the fate of Jews in the country, others were honorable, compassionate and humane, providing shelter and food and, at risk to their own lives, saved Jews. Some of the latter group have been honored by Yad Vashem, the Holocaust museum in Jerusalem, which so far has recognized 19,140 people who were "righteous among the nations"; of this number 2,171 were French people, the third largest of any country.

I am grateful to a number of friends, especially Bernard Lewis, Claire Andrieu, and Roger Errera, who have read all or part of the manuscript and have provided collegial and critical advice, and who cannot be held responsible for the contents of the book. Above all, my greatest debt is to my wife, Judith Kapstein Brodsky, who in her customary warm and generous way has contributed intellectually, artistically and emotionally to the book.

Michael Curtis

ABBREVIATIONS

.

ACA   Assemblée des Cardinaux et Archevêques
AP   *administrateur provisoire*
AS   Armée Secrète
CAR   Comité d'Assistance aux Réfugiés
CDC   Caisse des Dépôts et Consignations
CDJC   Centre de Documentation Juive Contemporaine
CGQJ   Commissariat Général aux Questions Juives
CIMADE   Comité Inter-mouvements auprès des Évacués
CO   *comité d'organisation*
EIF   Éclaireurs Israélites de France
FSJF   Fédération des Sociétés Juives de France
FTP   Francs-Tireurs et Partisans
GMR   Groupes Mobiles de Réserve
GTE   *groupements de travailleurs étrangers*
JOC   Jeunesse Ouvrière Chrétienne
LFC   Légion Français des Combattants
LVF   Légion des Volontaires Français contre le Bolchevisme
MBF   Militärbefehlshaber in Frankreich
MNPGD   Mouvement National des Prisonniers de Guerre et Déportés
MOI   Main d'Oeuvre Immigrée
OJC   Organisation Juive de Combat
ORA   Organisation de Résistance de l'Armée
OSE   Oeuvre de Secours aux Enfants
PPF   Parti Populaire Français
PQJ   Police aux Questions Juives
PSF   Parti Social Français
RNP   Rassemblement National Populaire
SCAP   Service du Contrôle des Administrateurs Provisoires
SEC   Section d'Enquête et de Contrôle
SiPo-SD   Sicherheitspolizei–Sicherheitsdienst
SOL   Service d'Ordre Légionnaire
SPAC   Service de Police Anticommuniste
SSE   Service Social des Étrangers
STO   Service du Travail Obligatoire
UGIF   Union Générale des Israélites de France
Vél d'Hiv   Vélodrome d'Hiver

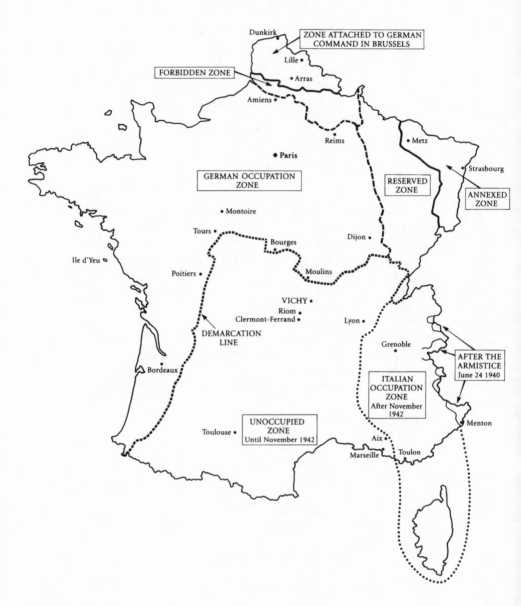

ZONES OF FRANCE

MAIN INTERNMENT CAMPS FOR JEWS
Communists were interned in a number of camps,
including Chibron, Aincourt, Fort-Barraux, and Rouillé.
Gypsies were interned in Jargeaux, La Morellerie,
Montreuil-Bellay, and Sailiers

VERDICT ON VICHY

INTRODUCTION

On 16 July 1995, Jacques Chirac, President of the French Fifth Republic, admitted and apologised for 'the dark hours which will forever tarnish our history'. The timing made it an event of major symbolic significance. It was on this fifty-third anniversary of the major *rafle* (round-up) of 16–17 July 1942 of over 13,000 Jews in Paris, who were arrested and taken to the stadium, the Vélodrome d'Hiver (Vél d'Hiv), that Chirac spoke of 'the criminal insanity of the occupying power [which] was assisted by the French, by the French state ... On that day France delivered those she was protecting to their executioners.' For the French President, the way to defend 'a vision of man, of his freedom and dignity' was to recognise the errors of the past, the errors of the state, and not to hide the dark hours of French history. Over the next two years, Chirac made similar speeches; on 5 December 1997, at the memorial of Jewish martyrs in Paris, he again denounced the 'moral abdication of the Vichy regime' for its co-operation in arrests, round-ups and deportation of Jews.

Chirac was implicitly rejecting the contention of General Charles de Gaulle and his followers that the Vichy regime was an illegal 'parenthesis' for which France now could not be held to account. Chirac's condemnation of France's inglorious past, echoed in similar speeches at the same period, by Prime Minister Lionel Jospin, was in stark contrast to the attitude of his predecessor as President, François Mitterrand. At the annual ceremony of 16 July, held in 1997, Jospin made clear the sombre truth. The Vélodrome d'Hiver *rafle* was 'decided, planned and carried out by the French. Politicians, administrators, police, and gendarmes, all took part. Not one German soldier was needed to accomplish this hideous crime.' A total of 13,152 Jews were arrested and most were put for a short period in the Vél d'Hiv by 4500 French police and gendarmes in actions co-ordinated by Jean Leguay, the delegate in Paris of René Bousquet, head of Vichy's national police force, before being deported and sent to their death. Central in the criticism of these actions of the French police is that they were not obliged to act. Paris was in the zone of

France occupied by the Germans and was not under the jurisdiction of Vichy.

On the plaque at the site of the demolished Vél d'Hiv, the official figures of those interned are given as 4115 children, 2916 women and 1129 men. At a nearby memorial on the quai de Grenelle, an inscription reads: 'The French Republic in homage to the victims of racist and anti-Semitic persecutions and crimes against humanity committed under the authority of the so-called [fait dite] government of the French State 1940–1944.' It ends with the words 'Never forget.' The 'French State' was the name taken to indicate that the Third Republic had been replaced by the regime that established itself in the spa town of Vichy. The regime, henceforth referred to here as Vichy, lasted four years, but the memory of that historical experience has not ceased to evoke passionate and even polemical dispute.[1]

Acknowledgment of French responsibility for Vél d'Hiv and many other acts of persecution against Jews was long in coming. At the fiftieth anniversary of the Vél d'Hiv rafle, Mitterrand still refused to acknowledge that responsibility of the French state for the arrest and deportation of Jews to their death. He had, under pressure, declared in February 1993 that 16 July would be a national day of commemoration. But Mitterrand, a former Vichy official, was still equivocal about the past. Vichy was an aberration: the French nation was never involved, nor was the French Republic. Again, in September 1994, Mitterand explained that 'France is not responsible, nor is the Republic' for the Vichy regime. That regime was 'a minority of agitators who seized the occasion of the defeat to gain power, and are accountable for the crimes'.

Despite Mitterrand's ambivalence, eventual confessions of responsibility were not confined to Chirac, the head of state, who belonged to a generation too young to have been involved in any actions in the war years, or to the Prime Minister. Following Chirac, three groups made similar statements. The French bishops, on 30 September 1997 at Drancy, asked forgiveness of God and the Jewish people for the 'silence' of the Catholic Church about the anti-Semitic activity and laws of Vichy. The police union apologised to the 'Hebrew' [sic] people' for police actions during the war. The French doctors' association, representing 180,000 members, acknowledged that the 'basic values of their profession had been violated when they acquiesced in legislation that discriminated against and excluded their Jewish colleagues' from practising.

The circumlocutions and ambiguities of Mitterrand were disposed of by the lower chamber of the French parliament when on 29 February 2000 the National Assembly unanimously adopted a *proposition de loi* that made clear that the 16 July national day commemorated the victims. Vichy was acknowledged as having participated in racist crimes and anti-Semitism between 1940 and 1944. Contrary to Mitterrand's 1994 statement, implying that Vichy was an unrepresentative group of criminals, the National Assembly acknowledged that France itself was responsible.

For at least twenty years after the end of the war many French people, public officials and private citizens, were reluctant, unwilling and even opposed to subjecting the Vichy regime to critical examination for its actions and legislative enactments, especially those directed against the 330,000 Jews living in France. Many sectors of the French population, including Jews, were quiescent in the immediate post-war years.

Defenders of the regime, supporters of Marshal Philippe Pétain, argued that it was the least bad system for a defeated France, that Vichy had been a shield protecting the country against a worse fate, or that it had been a victim of the Nazis. Another group, the *Vichysto-résistants*, a term used by some French historians to denote early adherents to Pétain who gradually vacillated towards the Resistance as the tides of war changed, were not anxious to dredge up the past. The strong communist movement was not eager to evoke memories of the neutrality of the party, and its acceptance of the Stalin–Hitler pact of 23 August 1939, until the Soviet Union was attacked on 22 June 1941 by Germany. The charismatic General de Gaulle and his supporters, on taking power on 25 August 1944, gave priority to cementing national unity and reconstructing an honourable French identity. In so doing, the myth of a heroic, mass resistance of the French people was created. Vichy had not represented the 'real' France.

Vichy was dismissed as a *de facto* government, not regarded as a legal state; it was a collaboration by a minority of French people. The ordinance of 9 August 1944 published in Algiers by de Gaulle's Free French group, 're-established republican legality on the mainland territory' and declared null and void all the constitutional acts, legislation and rules from 16 June 1940 until the establishment of the provisional government of the new French Republic. In his rhetoric at the Hôtel de Ville in Paris on 25 August 1944, de Gaulle, with a calculated disregard of the reality that the Anglo-American forces had played the major role, proclaimed that Paris had been liberated 'by its people with the help of the armies of France, with the support and help of the whole of France, of the France that fought, of the only France, of the true France, of eternal France'.

France can be genuinely proud of its heroes and patriots, upholding the honour of the nation and struggling against injustice and Nazi oppression. It can salute the 10,000 volunteers who joined General de Gaulle's Free French forces in 1940, and the 70,000 men and women who took part in the Resistance in some form, some 48,000 of whom were awarded the medal of the Resistance. It can honour the brave citizens who hid and protected the persecuted Jews, at peril to themselves, but it must also remember the role of other citizens in aiding and abetting the Shoah, the Holocaust.

The record of Vichy in its persecution of Jews does not reflect credit on France, nor do the political and legal attitudes in the immediate post-war years that were slow to acknowledge that record. In that period, French official intransigence in refusing to reveal or to co-operate in the search for accurate information about the persecution during the Vichy years sometimes amounted to collective amnesia. How can one explain the slowness of the judicial process, the destruction or misplacing of documents, the reluctance of the police to search for those accused of war crimes, the help given by some elements of the Church in protecting war criminals, or the astonishing clemency of the pardon given by the President of the Republic, Georges Pompidou, in September 1971 to Paul Touvier, twice sentenced to death, *in absentia* in 1946 and 1947 by French courts for treason and 'assisting the enemy', or the continuing friendship of François Mitterrand with René Bousquet, Vichy head of police?

Little attention, political or intellectual, was paid to the role of Vichy persecution of Jews. Gaullists, Pétainists, communists all, for different reasons, permitted themselves a blessed act of oblivion.[2] Some who argued, during the Fourth Republic and the first years of the Fifth Republic, that Vichy was 'illegitimate' felt no responsibility or guilt. Others held that the regime, despite its deficiencies, was necessary for the recovery of France after its inglorious defeat in 1940. Still others denied the deficiencies.

> One power has Fate to God himself denied
> To make undone the thing that has been done.[3]

Intellectual and judicial circles, as well as the court of public opinion, appeared to be afflicted by the same voluntary amnesia as the political world. Raymond Aron recalled a conversation with Jean-Paul Sartre soon after the end of the war. Why, they wondered, had there not been a single article saying, 'Welcome to the Jews on their return to the French community'? The underlying reason for the silence was that people had blotted out what had happened.[4]

The French were slow to admit that France was the only occupied country whose government remained on its national territory, which accepted its military defeat as final, which broke with its past, creating a new regime that changed from a democratic to an authoritarian system, whose legal government and police worked and acted in support of German demands, and which transformed itself from the great independent power status of the past to one of collaboration with the enemy.[5]

It was difficult for the French to accept responsibility for their part in genocide, to accept the reality that the 10,000 Jews deported from the unoccupied zone which Vichy administered were the only Jews killed in the Holocaust who came from an area without any German military presence at the time, or to appreciate French complicity given that the three German police battalions in the whole of France together only numbered between 2500 and 3000 men. Charges brought in the courts in the immediate post-war period concentrated on political and military activity of French personnel, such as treason or collaboration with the enemy, not on actions relating to the Holocaust or to persecution. Buchenwald, the concentration camp, not Auschwitz, the death camp, symbolised Nazi barbarism for the French, suggesting lack of knowledge or wilful misunderstanding of objectives of a Germany intent on the Final Solution. The fine eloquent film *Nuit et Brouillard*, by Alain Resnais, portrays the symbolic emphasis; the camps appear as prisons, brutal to be sure, but not extermination camps.

A significant illustration of this early concentration on the political and military aspects of the war and on treason and collaboration of French persons to the almost complete neglect of the French role in the persecution and extermination of Jews was the decision by de Gaulle as immediate post-war Prime Minister to honour Oradour-sur-Glane, the small town in the Limousin, where a company of the German Waffen-SS on 10 June 1944 slaughtered 642 men, women and children, and then burned the whole village.[6] The village, left in its ruined state, was made a national preserve, a memorial for the country, in 1946. In contrast to the preservation of Oradour as a memorial is the destruction of the Vél d'Hiv stadium. No doubt by chance, but with superb irony of history, that site is now occupied by offices of the Ministry of the Interior. Only in 1993 was a monument erected close to the site as a memorial to the French Jews who were deported.

Equally revealing in this early post-war concentration on political and military activity and on treason were the charges brought against Marshal Philippe Pétain at his trial in July 1945. He was tried for plotting against the Republic, for intelligence with the enemy, and for collaboration. For Charles de Gaulle, a major criticism of Pétain was that he had signed the armistice with Germany, thus admitting and accepting defeat. It took almost forty years before trials in the courts, as well as historical analysis, concentrated not so much on the armistice and on issues such as hostages, obligatory work rules or actions against the Resistance, as on the persecution of Jews by Vichy, on its co-operation with Nazi objectives and on the concern for equal rights and civil liberties.[7]

In earlier court cases, even when persecution of Jews was involved in the trial, more attention was given to atrocities committed by Germans than to the role of Vichy.[8] This was understandable. Part of the dilemma for French people in coming to terms with the conduct of the war years was that the country was simultaneously partly occupied, with a population subjected to German control, and partly governed by a regime with pretensions of being autonomous.

France took part in the Nuremberg International Military Tribunal starting in November 1945 to hear charges of war crimes committed by German officials. However, the country maintained a discreet silence about the complicity of French agencies in infamous deeds, the participation, willingly or reluctantly, of officials, police, magistrates, temporary administrators of Jewish assets, and professional groups in discriminatory activities. This silence was for some years accompanied by the myth, the visionary fancy, of a strong resistance movement supported by a majority of the French population.[9] By this Vichy was minimised, and the Resistance was equated with the nation as a whole. France became full of RMS, resisters of mid-September 1944, a month after Liberation.

The Gaullist political position during 'les trentes glorieuses' of 1945 to 1975, thirty years of increasing affluence, minimised the wartime divisions in France, holding that collaboration with Germany was limited to a small number of people, and said little about the Vichy persecution of Jews. Fifty years later, specious defences of de Gaulle's attitude were offered by old colleagues. At the trial of Maurice Papon in November 1997, Claude Bouchinet-Sereulles, a close associate in wartime London, explained that the General had never written about the Holocaust because 'his pen did not lead him in this direction'. The influential Olivier Guichard, director of de Gaulle's office in London, acknowledged that 'the General did not want France to be on trial' after the war. To this end, de Gaulle had inspired two myths: the Vichy regime did not really exist, and France had won the war, largely through its own efforts.[10] In view of the Gaullist positions that Vichy was merely a parenthesis in French history and that the country needed national unity after the war, it is worth remembering that all three of the prime ministers appointed by de Gaulle while President of the French Fifth Republic had some association with the Vichy system or had lived in internal silence during the life of the regime. This had been anticipated in the Fourth Republic when individuals who had played some role in the Vichy years, such as Félix Gaillard and Jacques Chaban-Delmas, came to be more prominent.

The best-known illustration of French reluctance to discuss the Vichy years with candour and objectivity was the twelve-year delay by the French state television network in airing the documentary *Le Chagrin et la Pitié*, made for television by Marcel Ophuls in 1969. The four-hour portrait of life in Vichy, drawn from archive footage of the period and testimony of those who lived in it, was a devastating picture of wide public support for Marshal Pétain and of the degree and the extent of accommodation and collaboration with the Germans, shattering the myth of a courageous, defiant French citizenry. The film was shown in a small Paris art cinema in 1971, and then on German and Swiss television, before finally being allowed on French television in 1981. By October 1981, over 15 million had witnessed on television this image of Clermont-Ferrand, a middle-sized, provincial town whose inhabitants in the main displayed themselves as weak and timorous and obsessed by their concern for material comfort.

In the academy there was a troubling lack of research or interest by French historians in the early post-war years in the fate of Jews during the Vichy regime. The explanation is complex: the reluctance of historians was due partly to unwillingness to explore the wartime behaviour of administration, judiciary and police, some members of which were politically active in the Fourth Republic; academic timidity prevented research on controversial subjects; relevant archives previously unavailable were a treasure trove found only in 1991, largely through Serge Klarsfeld's activities, in the Office of Veterans' Affairs, where they had, according to him, been deliberately hidden for many years; French historical interest was diverted because of the influence of the *Annales* school, from contemporary affairs to 'la longue durée'.

The political mood, also diverted from the subject, was expressed at the highest level. Explaining his surprising and controversial pardon of the anti-Semitic criminal Paul Touvier, in 1971, President Georges Pompidou at a press conference on 21 September 1972 asked: 'Has not the time come to draw a veil over the past, to forget a time when Frenchmen disliked one another, attacked one another, and even killed one another?' Pompidou's timing, as well as his decision, was poor, and his plea for historical oblivion had the opposite effect, reminding people of, or bringing attention to, the crimes of Touvier and others supposedly committed in the interests of France.

The consequent long-delayed judicial inquiry and indictment of a number of people active in the Vichy period – Jean Leguay in 1979, Klaus Barbie in 1983, Maurice Sabatier in 1998, Paul Touvier in 1991, René Bousquet in 1991 and Maurice Papon in 1992 – for crimes against humanity, occasioned more public interest in a dialogue regarding the treatment of Jews in wartime France. Publication of works by Holocaust deniers, especially by Robert Faurisson, Paul Rassinier and later by Roger Garaudy, former Stalinist turned Islamic fundamentalist, provoked bitter discussion of the Jewish experience. Ironically, Faurisson, the Holocaust denier sentenced in 1981 to pay a symbolic franc in damages to organisations representing former inmates of the death camps, made the Holocaust and anti-Semitism familiar issues.[11]

They were also made familiar by the eruption of anti-Semitic attacks on Jewish cemeteries and synagogues and shops, and by anti-Jewish statements and actions in the 1980s. The most startling event was in Carpentras, the site of the oldest surviving synagogue in France, which dated from the fourteenth century. In May 1990 the Jewish cemetery there was desecrated and a body was exhumed and violated. In immediate response to the desecration of the cemetery, and more generally to the activities of the Holocaust deniers, the Gayssot law was passed in May 1990 making it illegal to contest the existence of crimes against humanity as defined by the statute of the International Military Tribunal (the Nuremberg trials) annexed to the London Accords of 8 August 1945.

Thus, indifference on the part of the French people in the Vichy persecution of Jews diminished, though was by no means ended, for a variety of reasons. From the late 1960s, the combination of political events and judicial processes, intellectual and academic inquiry, and the proliferation of pertinent fiction and films, all contributed to greater awareness of French atrocities. Among the influential films, in addition to Le Chagrin et la Pitié, were Lacombe Lucien (1974) and L'Oeil de Vichy, directed by Claude Chabrol. In the former somewhat ambivalent film, a young peasant drawn to violence becomes an aide to the anti-Semites and the Gestapo even though he is in love with a Jewish girl. The latter film, with its presentation of wartime newsreels and radio broadcasts that aimed at making Marshal Pétain a national hero, implicitly condemned the men of Vichy through their own statements, in which they blame Jews and some others for inflicting defeat on France in 1940 and call for collaboration with Germany to fight against Bolshevism in order to build a new Europe.

In addition, the publication of memoirs and personal accounts by the persecuted or their descendants, or by witnesses of wartime horror, has led to a more open and realistic evaluation of French behaviour during Vichy. Distance in time has not reduced intensity of awareness of that behaviour. In the public arena the dramatic and militant political protests in Paris and elsewhere in France in the summer of 1968, especially by students, critical of the policies and style of President de Gaulle, tended to call into question the Gaullist version of the regime, or non-regime, in France during the war.

An intellectual sea change was brought about by the critical writings on Vichy by foreign historians, the most prominent of whom in the beginning were Robert Paxton and Eberhard Jäckel, both of whom made use of German archives.[12] They were less inclined than most contemporary French historians at the time to accept a benign view of Vichy or to believe that the Vichy leaders might have played a 'double game' against the German occupiers or that they were coerced to collaborate and engage in discriminatory actions. In the subsequent book by Paxton and Michael Marrus, the French responsibility for persecution of Jews became unmistakably clear.[13]

Attitudes, intellectual and political, began changing further as revelations unfolded. One provocative event was the interview entitled 'Only lice were gassed in Auschwitz', published in a major French popular political journal L'Express in October 1978, with Louis Darquier de Pellepoix, the former Vichy commissioner for Jewish affairs, which revealed an unrepentant anti-Semite, living in comfort in Spain. Attitudinal change accelerated during the 1990s. The growing literature and media presentations on the Holocaust; the American television series on the Holocaust broadcast in French; and the presidential decree of 3 February 1993 issued for a national day of commemoration were contributing factors. From the periphery of national attention the question of discriminatory anti-Semitic practices by the French of their own initiative has become more central.[14] In the indictment of Vichy for its actions and legislation, it has become, and must remain, the most important single factor.

For some French historians that factor has become too central, and they contend that too much emphasis has been placed in recent years on Vichy's complicity in persecution of Jews.[15] But today it is not possible to be ignorant of the Holocaust, which after lack of attention or knowledge for some years has now seeped into European consciousness, where it has been inextricably lodged in the discourse about the Second World War.[16] Nor is it excusable to argue that too much emphasis can be put on a nation's complicity in mass murder of its own citizens.

This contention that too much emphasis is now being placed on the anti-Jewish policies of Vichy may, consciously or otherwise, reflect the changed climate in contemporary France, where the Jewish community, larger than in pre-war days and more varied, has become more assertive and less troubled about its identity, and more vocal and active in denouncing both the anti-Semitism of Vichy and the post-war silence about French complicity in the Shoah. Moreover, this objection to the centrality of anti-Semitism in discourse on Vichy can be linked not only to increased visibility of and more effective articulation by Jews in France, but also to the emergence of issues that affect Jews on the French national scene in the last twenty years or so: concern about assimilation of Jews, along with others; French hostility towards, as well as criticism of, the policies of the state of Israel; the prejudices openly manifested by the National Front of Jean-Marie Le Pen; and perhaps the influence of the writings of the Holocaust deniers. It seems misguided, if not disingenuous, to argue as some French historians do that by placing anti-Semitism at the centre of debate on Vichy, other issues pertinent to the war years are being neglected and that German pressure on France is being minimised. It is also fallacious to suggest that putting anti-Semitism at the centre makes discussion of Vichy more like a debate between French Jews and the rest of the nation than a debate between the nation and its own past. One might detect in an argument of this kind echoes of the familiar tactic of 'blaming the victim'. Anti-Semitism, it is now acknowledged, has been a disease of non-Jewish society, and therefore much of the burden in dealing with it and assessing responsibility must be borne by non-Jewish individuals, who in the process need not forget other problems to be confronted.[17]

Another issue that is relevant in the discussion of Vichy is the discourse about the interrelationship of memory and history that has become fashionable in intellectual circles in recent years. What Pierre Nora has called 'lieux de mémoire', sites of memory defined as real or imagined units that have become, through human agency or the effects of time, elements symbolic of a given community, now abound regarding Vichy.[18]

In his *Assassins of Memory* (1992) Pierre Vidal-Naquet suggested that memory is not history because history's mode of selection functions differently from that of memory and forgetting. Nevertheless he integrated memory into his historical analysis and his devastating criticism of the Holocaust deniers. Memory is made even more poignant by the appearance of works such as Serge Klarsfeld's *French Children of the Holocaust: A Memorial*.[19] This book, with its text and photographs of 2500 of the 11,400 children under the age of eighteen who were deported from France to extermination camps between 1942 and 1944, constitutes powerful documentary evidence of the nature of the Holocaust and is a damning indictment of the French participation in, and collaboration with, the Nazi regime in the policy of genocide during the Vichy years from 1940 to 1944. Memory, individual and collective, though imperfect, has been valuable and potent for the record of names, faces and events, and for providing information in the uneven and delayed process of seeking retribution for criminal acts.

Information and analysis of the Vichy regime are now plentiful, and are continually being reinforced by empirical studies, mostly of local areas or particular regions. That has led some, especially Henry Rousso, to believe that the French are obsessed with the memory of Vichy and with the actions of their elders during the Occupation.[20] Certainly, the post-war controversies over the Vichy past, fuelled by the plentiful information and memories, illustrate the painful nature of memories of Vichy and also the difficulty for French people in being reconciled with their recent history in the 'guerre franco-française' that has not fully ended.[21]

History is always being rewritten, partly because of new methods of inquiry, partly because new information becomes available, and partly because of changing political perspectives. History, as the Dutch historian, Pieter Geyl, wrote in *Napoleon: For and Against*, 'is an argument without end'. At one end of the historical argument over Vichy is the claim that it upheld traditional Catholic and right-wing values that were supported by a considerable part of the population. Early histories by Robert Aron and François-Georges Dreyfus contrast the 'good' and 'bad' parts of the regime.[22] For these writers, Marshal Philippe Pétain, the great hero of the First World War, elderly, patient, a believer in wait-and-see, was concerned with the moral regeneration of the country and saw the armistice as an interlude in the war. By contrast, Pierre Laval appears as the harmful or 'evil' genius, the collaborator who saw the armistice as an opportunity for France to participate in the New Order. In this view Laval was the sinister influence on policy, and the Marshal never issued any official proclamation that Jews were enemies of the state.

More recent commentaries do not support this argument. Eberhard Jäckel clearly indicated the extent of Pétain's collaboration with the Germans.[23] Robert Frank, in an essay on poisoned memory, suggests that Pétain's charisma anaesthetised public opinion to the anti-republican and anti-Semitic measures of the regime.[24] More critical assessments of Vichy, from the path-breaking work by Robert Paxton to books by French authors such as Jean-Pierre Azéma and Marc Ferro, hold that the Vichy regime did not resist the occupation, willingly accepted collaboration with the Germans, wanted to change society and the state, and took part in anti-Semitic activity, sometimes under pressure and sometimes on its own initiative.[25] Indeed, although the connotation of the term at that time is open to dispute, the word 'collaboration' was used by Pétain on 30 October 1940 after his meeting a week earlier with Hitler at Montoire when he said: 'It is with honour and to maintain ten-century-old French unity in the framework of the constructive activity of the new European order that I embark today on a path of collaboration ... Follow me: Keep your faith in *la France éternelle*.'

The abundant and rapidly increasing literature and media representations of Vichy and its personnel allow us to assess the regime objectively and to make judgements on the behaviour of people and institutions during the Vichy years. Yet those judgements belie easy generalisations because there were internal conflicts within the regime, differences in motivation of the participants, changes in emphasis and personnel during the four years of the system and varying relations with and pressures from the German authorities. At a minimum, Vichy practised policies of exclusion and persecution of Jews, policies in which anti-Semitism and xenophobia were prominent. This concept of politics stemmed from the intellectual strand in French thought which includes advocacy of integral nationalism, the belief in the organic unity of the French nation, and a long history of anti-Semitism. Foreigners, especially Jews of foreign origin, and other people regarded as undesirable would not be regarded as included in that unity. For some who held this point of view, all Jews would be excluded from that unity. Vichy participated in the round-ups and deportation of Jews, but it is debatable whether most of the leaders of the regime consciously approved a policy of extermination.

Ambivalence in French history and politics is not a new phenomenon. Fifteen hundred years after the baptism, supposedly in Rheims, of Clovis, the founder of the Merovingian dynasty, opinions differ as to whether he should be praised as the father of France, as the man who created the first Christian monarchy in the West, or castigated as an unscrupulous opportunist. Not surprisingly, Jean-Marie Le Pen, the leader of France's extreme right-wing party, anti-immigrant and anti-Semitic, sees Clovis as a symbol of ultranationalism. More pertinently for this subject, the Vichy regime named its highest medal for services to France and to Pétain after the *francisque*, the double-headed axe that Clovis used to kill a soldier. A modern example of this ambivalence is reflected in the personal history, to be discussed later, of François Mitterrand, a quintessential embodiment of the complex political culture of France, with its two, sometimes contradictory, heritages stemming from the Revolution of 1789: a yearning towards liberty and equality on the one hand and towards nationalism, order and French grandeur on the other. Mitterrand's ambivalence about Vichy and his lack of candour about his own past reflect both the divisions, past and present, of the French and the reluctance of former officials and citizens to acknowledge the degree of their complicity in the Holocaust. Confession may be good for the soul, but it does not usually break through the layers of self-interest or complacent indifference to the fate of others. Pragmatic and personal interests for many French people in the post-war years had higher priority than assertion of moral values or concern for justice. For French people in the war years, living under an authoritarian regime and with fear of the Nazis, it is readily understandable how difficult it was to manifest those ethical principles or protest against injustice.

It has long been recognised that of the 40 million French people alive in the war, 40 million were Pétainists and 40 million were Gaullists. Clearly, wartime France was not a country of heroic resisters, risking life and liberty, gallantly defying Nazi demands or attempting, subtly or otherwise, to sabotage them. In spite of the myth to the contrary, the Resistance movement was small and was operational in a significant way only in 1943–4. It is more probable that a majority of the population, undergoing the French crisis of identity, accepted Maréchalisme: that is, attachment to the person of Marshal Pétain as the necessary head of the country.

The myth of a heroic Resistance movement, cultivated by the media and intellectuals in post-war years, has been dispelled in many works over the last two decades. Relatively few, such as the writers René Char and Paul Eluard, were courageous in defying the Occupation in their work. On the part of prominent writers – André Gide, Paul Claudel, François Mauriac, Jules Romains, Roger Martin du Gard, even André Malraux until nearly the end of the war – the rule was silence or inaction. This silence was even more deafening in the case of Jean-Paul Sartre and Simone de Beauvoir, who so strongly influenced the climate of intellectual opinion after the war, because of their claim not only that they took part in the Resistance in a significant way, but that their courageous defiance inspired their conduct in peacetime.[26]

Yet if France was not a hotbed of resistance, nor was it a land of infamous collaborators or supporters of anti-Semitic persecution. Most citizens, especially at the beginning, were passive or opportunistic, uninvolved in the crimes and atrocities in their country. Some, though disliking foreigners and anti-Nazi refugees, were troubled by the increasing extent of persecution but remained convinced of the need for the authoritarian Pétainist regime to replace the weak democratic republic with which they were disillusioned, to preserve the unity of France, to maintain order and discipline, and to make internal changes. Two problems arose from this formula. The first was that Vichy, instead of creating *une union sacrée* as in the First World War, began by excluding part of its population from the unity. The other difficulty was that Vichy policy meant putting the French administration and police at the service of the Nazi cause, and being a party to anti-Semitic laws and persecution of Jews.

After fifty years of historiography on France the direct responsibility of Vichy for its anti-Semitic policies and for its contribution to the Final Solution is no longer an open question. No doubt Pétain himself and Vichy officials in general genuinely believed their actions would both protect and make manifest the existence of French sovereignty. More specious was the claim by Pétain that Vichy was in reality a shield against further German demands. Neither of these arguments can justify or excuse the increasingly severe policies of discrimination and persecution of Jews along the inexorable path to deportation. Nor can they explain away the reality that Vichy actively took the initiative in those policies and was not a passive instrument of the Nazis.

The case made in early post-war hagiography of Pétain that he was an essentially 'good' person faced with the 'evil' Laval was never very compelling.[27] It appears true that Pétain did not propose or support any programme of extermination of Jews, but he did nothing, apart from an occasional half-hearted attempt to save an individual Jew whom he considered meritorious, to prevent the flow of policies that led to that extreme end.

Even admitting this ignorance or misunderstanding of German intentions for the Final Solution, Pétain was aware of the rhetorical vituperation and action by his supporters against the 'enemies' of France. He was a believer in stern measures against Jews for the welfare of France. Insisting at first that these measures be directed against foreign Jews only, he soon acquiesced in their extension to Jews, including some personally known to him, of French nationality whose families had long been in France. Unlike the situation in other European countries occupied by the Nazis, the very existence in France of an indigenous leader rather than one imposed by the conquerors, who was seemingly acceptable, at least at first, to the majority of the population, endowed Pétain's policies and attitudes with a legitimacy that enhanced obedience to the law, in the process enlisting the obedience or gaining the acquiescence of the general population in persecution of Jews.

The attitudes and policies of Pétain and the Vichy leaders can usefully be compared with those of the leaders of other European countries defeated by the Nazis. The closest equivalents to the Vichy attitude to Germany were the clerical rule by Father Josef Tiso in Slovakia and the authoritarian rule by General Milan Nedic in the Serbian part of the old Yugoslavia. Leaders of a number of countries – Norway, Belgium, Holland, Greece, Poland, part of the old Czechoslovakia – formed governments in exile in London; no significant political figure in the home countries participated in collaboration. The Scandinavian countries exhibited two extremes; at one end was the infamous leadership of a hitherto minor figure in Norway, Vidkun Quisling, whose name is now synonymous with betrayers of one's country as a result of his help to the Nazis; at the other extreme was the honourable and dignified conduct of King Christian in Denmark, who refused to be a collaborator. If Pétain was not a Quisling, he was not a King Christian either.

Not surprisingly, information about the actions, not to mention motivation, of the participants in the Vichy regime remains incomplete. Archives, as with those of the Germans controlling the Drancy camp, were destroyed; some documents were shredded after the war to prevent embarrassment; some records, as with those of the French internment camps, have disappeared; some, as with account-ing documents, were not well preserved; some, such as the archives of the *Domaines*, have not been found; some German records on France were taken to Moscow.

Yet, if 'the past is a foreign country' in L. P. Hartley's famous phrase, enough of the true reality of Vichy has been revealed over the last thirty years in scholarly works and dramatic presentations. Not everyone is comfortable with the emergence of truth,

> The woundless and invisible thought that goes
> Free throughout time as north and south wind blows

in Swinburne's optimistic lines, but systematic research has provided a more objective picture of Vichy than that provided by the writings, some *apologias*, in the first twenty years after the end of the war.[28]

The most recent example of this objective analysis is the long, meticulously documented report of April 2000 written by eleven distinguished historians and professionals, members of the Mattéoli Commission set up in January 1997 by the Gaullist Prime Minister Alain Juppé, and confirmed by his Socialist successor, Lionel Jospin, a few months later. The Commission was headed by Jean Mattéoli, a non-Jewish former Minister of Labour, the President of the Economic and Social Council, and an honoured Resistance fighter, who had survived his deportation to the camps of Neuengamme and Bergen-Belsen.

The Commission's task in Juppé's instructions, was 'more than a moral obligation, it is a national obligation'. It was not a full-scale inquiry into the activities of French citizens and officials during the Vichy years. It was focused on the policies and mechanisms used in confiscating and stealing the assets of Jews and in eliminating Jews and Jewish influence from the national economy. Its picture of legal and administrative misdeeds in the elimination of that supposed influence portrays the discriminatory actions of Vichy in depriving Jews of personal freedom and occupations and in the commission of crimes against humanity. The sheer scale of the spoliation of Jewish property and assets, the detail with which the spoliation was pre-scribed, and the willingness, indeed sometimes enthusiasm, of the French authorities and professional groups to administer the spoliation, provides evidence for a severe indictment of the Vichy regime.

Equally, that objective evidence is useful in France's never-ending conflict between the desire to forget and the need to remember.[29] The town of Vichy has been slow to erect any memorial to those who perished because of the policies of the Vichy regime or to notice the injustices planned there. Little reminder exists of the local round-up of Jews from the town in 1942. Street names in the town now memorialise French heroes: Foch, de Gaulle, Lyautey. Pétain is not noticeable except on the cover of old pastille boxes produced during the war and still available, if rare, in antique shops.

Some light, if not a spotlight, is still needed to look afresh at France's wartime record. A small indication of this need was the attempts to ban or prevent the showing of a film, *Terrorists in Retirement*, a documentary made in 1984 about young illegal Jewish refugees in Paris who carried out dangerous assignments in fighting the Nazi occupiers, but who were betrayed by local Communist Party members and turned over to the Gestapo in 1943. The protests of the Communist Party, part of the government coalition from 1982 to 1984 while Mitterrand was President, held up the showing of the film until the charges of censorship overcame them. Does France still need a reminder that if its citizens in the war were not docile culprits, they were not for the most part active heroes either? Does France still need to examine the extent to which the Vichy regime and its own citizens were participants in the implementation of the Shoah? Two years after President Chirac offered his apology on 16 July 1995, he gave the answer at a gathering of Jewish leaders on 2 March 1997: 'We must pursue the duty of memory to its conclusion. We must ensure that the role of Vichy and its representatives is fully brought to light.'

CHAPTER I

THE JEWS OF FRANCE

The Jewish presence in France goes back nearly 2000 years, to the Roman province of Gaul, to the Garonne valley and to the area along the confluence of the Rhine and Rhône. In the Middle Ages a small number of Jews lived in different areas, mostly in Provence and Languedoc but also in Limousin, Burgundy and the Île de France, in spite of continuing hostility and mistreatment. Though Jews were able to enter professions and to trade, their situation was precarious. French kings regarded them as people to be exploited for revenue or used as a scapegoat to explain political or economic failures.[1] Their status varied in different regions, from toleration in an area north of the Loire and in Champagne to hostility in other places.

The First Crusade in 1096 led to considerable violence against Jews in Metz and Rouen, irrelevant to the struggle against the Muslim infidels in Jerusalem. Accusations resulted from growing Christian hostility: Jews were responsible for spreading disease, defiling the Christian Host and poisoning wells and rivers. The first accusation of ritual murder came in Blois in 1171. After the declaration of the Fourth Lateran Council, convened by Pope Innocent III in 1215, calling for Jews to be identified and excluded from society, the Council of Narbonne in 1227 ordered Jews to wear a distinguishing badge. King Louis IX, regarded as Saint Louis, implemented this in 1269 by a decree that Jews must wear a *rouelle*, a piece of fabric, on their clothing.

Discrimination and persecution from the beginning of the Jewish presence included various forms of restrictions and extortions, banning of ownership or seizure of property, heavy taxation, brutal attacks, pressure to convert to Christianity and to listen to sermons, physical segregation and expulsion. Jews were massacred in a number of places and expelled from various provinces in the country during the twelfth and thirteenth centuries. In 1306 Philip IV, the Fair, unfairly ordered the expulsion of Jews, and in 1394 Charles IV ordered them out of his domain. After Provence became part of the Kingdom of France in 1481, Jews were within twenty years expelled from that area.

In spite of the persecution by the French kings, some Jewish cultural life continued in other parts of the country. In the eleventh century a northern French Jew, Rashi, in Troyes founded a Talmud school and wrote commentaries on the Bible and the Talmud. His pupils continued these commentaries and glosses on interpretations. These northerners were rivals of the Jews in Provence, who thrived in Marseille, Narbonne and Lunel until their expulsion in 1498. The southern Jews, especially the ibn Tibbon family, played an important role in transmitting philosophical and scientific knowledge from the east to the west, and helping translate works in Arabic by Jewish and Muslim scholars. The most important of these was the work by Maimonides, *Guide to the Perplexed*.

In early modern history Jews came into France from different places.[2] Sephardic Jews entered the country from Spain and Portugal, settling in the south-west, especially in Bordeaux and Bayonne.[3] By the 1648 treaty of Westphalia, Alsace became part of France, thus adding a different group of Jews, Ashkenazis, to the French population.

On the eve of the French Revolution about 40,000 Jews lived in the country.[4] They can be categorised in four groups.

The most integrated group consisted of the Sephardim in the south-west and the Provençal communities of the south, descendants from the *marranos* supposedly converted in Spain. Sometimes also referred to as 'Portuguese Jews', they became a part of the local upper class and served the government, as did the Gradis family.[5] If in legal trouble, these Sephardim resorted to the French court system rather than to the rabbinical one. In 1723, in return for a substantial payment, the *marranos* were officially tolerated and their privileges confirmed. The 4000 Jews in the south-west obtained citizenship on 28 January 1790, the first Jews to be emancipated. A second group, some 2500 'Papal Jews', protected by the Pope, who ruled the area, were in the *Comtat Venaissin*, centred in Avignon and Carpentras.

The largest number, 70 per cent of the total, lived in Alsace, about 25,000, and in Lorraine with its 5500 'German' or 'Teutonic' Jews. They were in Metz, the largest Jewish city in the country in the eighteenth century, in Nancy and Thionville, but excluded from Strasbourg. They were scattered in small towns and villages. These Ashkenazis, facing legal restrictions on residence and mobility and sometimes, as in Colmar, heavy taxation, were prevented from owning land, and worked in traditional Jewish occupations: pedlars, second-hand dealers, pawnbrokers and clothing goods makers. Living in close-knit communities, virtually autonomous corporations, they were highly organised with their own system of jurisdiction and were devoted to the Jewish tradition and the synagogue.[6] Their villages resembled the shtetls of eastern Europe.

In 1789 deputies from Alsace to the newly recalled National Assembly, which was divided on the Jewish question and on granting civil rights to Jews, opposed emancipation of Jews. The decree of 27 September 1791, however, emancipated all Jews, and those in Alsace became citizens.[7] At the same time, their life was changed with the establishment of state-sponsored religious organisations which reduced the significance of their autonomous organisations on the one hand, while enlarging opportunities in economic and social life, including commerce, industry and the military, on the other. Emancipation did not end hostility against them. Anti-Jewish violence erupted in Alsace in 1793 when cemeteries were sacked, sacred tablets destroyed and synagogues closed.

In spite of the hostility, the Alsatian Jews were devoted patriots. Affected by the loss of the two provinces, Alsace and Lorraine, to Germany after the French defeat in 1870, that patriotism was displayed when over 15,000 Jews, about a third of the Jews in the two provinces and about half of the total number of Jews in France at that time, who wanted to remain French, left the area. They also welcomed, as did the French population as a whole, the return of the two provinces to France after the First World War.[8] Ironically, in view of events in the 1890s, among these fervently patriotic Jews who wanted to remain French was the family of Alfred Dreyfus.

The Alsatians who left after 1870 largely went to Paris. A small number of Jews, about 1000 in 1789, lived in Paris, mostly in the Marais district. During the next century the Jewish population, though remaining at about one-quarter of 1 per cent of the population, became increasingly urbanised with Paris as the great magnet. By the end of the nineteenth century, almost the whole of the Jewish population of 85,000, out of the total French population of 39 million, was urbanised, compared with about one-third of the general population. Paris contained at least 60 per cent of Jewry in France, most working in the tertiary sector, commerce and the liberal professions, and in banking. Of the 440 individual owners of financial establishment in Paris, almost a quarter were Jews.

Emancipation

Emancipation had not come easily; even non-Jewish advocates thought it required the end of Jewish distinctiveness, the 'melting' as the Abbé Grégoire put it, of Jews into the national mass, or their conversion to Christianity.[9] Enlightenment ideas, particularly tolerance and reason, naturally attracted Jewish leaders and thinkers. In Alsace, one of those leaders, Cerf Berr, in 1780 asked Moses Mendelssohn, the key figure in the Haskalah movement, advocating modernity for Judaism and the departure of Jews from their geographical, social, professional and linguistic ghettos, to write a memorandum arguing for emancipation. Mendelssohn passed on the task to Christian Wilhelm von Dohm, military counsellor to the King of Prussia. The translation by Mirabeau into French of Dohm's work was published in 1782, just ahead of a royal decree of January 1784. The decree abolished the *péage corporel*, a corporal tax on Jews 'which ranks them alongside animals ... and seems to debase humanity'.

Before the French Revolution numerous legal and social restrictions had been imposed on Jews, and to a lesser degree on Protestants. In 1787 civil equality was granted to Protestants. In the same year an essay competition on the question, 'Are there any ways of making the Jews of France happier and more useful?' resulted in awards to winners including the Abbé Grégoire, who proposed economic emancipation of Jews and the elimination of restrictions on them. After the Declaration of the Rights of Man, adopted on 26 August 1789, which ended discrimination, it took another two years before Jews enjoyed full civil rights. It took almost another hundred years before, in October 1870, Algerian Jews numbering about 35,000 were granted citizenship by the decree of Adolphe Crémieux, the Minister of Justice.

With many barriers removed, Jews began to participate in the economic, political and cultural life of the nation, in the arts and music, in journalism and publishing, and in politics, starting at the local level and then nationally, with the first Jewish deputies to the legislature being elected in 1842. The funeral in 1858 of the Jewish actress Rachel, of the Comédie-Française, symbolised the new role of Jews in French life with the attendance not only of prominent Jews such as Adolphe Crémieux, but also of her two sons, one descended from Napoleon, and the other from General Bertrand.

Crémieux had links to both the state service and the Jewish community. Coming from a family long settled in France, and with a distinguished career as lawyer, parliamentary deputy, political liberal and Minister of Justice, he was also a defender of the rights of Jews as full and equal citizens and a leading person in the Jewish Consistoire Central in Paris and in the Alliance Israélite Universelle in 1864.

If in Alsace various factors fostered continuation of a traditional Jewish lifestyle and occupational distribution, with acculturation being measured 'in generations, not years', and with tension between tradition and modernity, increasing numbers of Jews in Paris and other large cities such as Lyon and Marseille were affluent and integrated, for the most part, into the French bourgeoisie.[10]

The heterogeneous Jewish community responded to emancipation and to the possibility of changes in patterns of behaviour in different ways. Some adhered to the traditional communal autonomy and the *Kehillah*, Jewish life and culture. Others, beginning in the 1830s, sought a new Franco-Jewish identity, advocating a concept of regeneration or modernisation, which entailed socio-economic change, a more secular educational system, the end of some religious rituals, and the unification and centralisation of French Jewry.[11] For this latter group, engaged in processes of acculturation and assimilation, the culture of France, the spiritual home, became more significant than group identity. The French Revolution was the new exodus for the Jewish people, who now had access to the universal rights of humanity. Vichy was to betray those rights and tread them under foot.

Native and Foreign Jews

In his 1893 book *Israël parmi les Nations*, Anatole Leroy-Beaulieu took the integration of Jews for granted. However, increasing Jewish immigration, mostly from eastern Europe, seen by some French people as a foreign invasion, slowed the process. By 1914, over half of the Jewish population in Paris, the magnet, were non-citizens. The Paris population displayed a double image. One consisted of the native Jews, earlier immigrants, now affluent, well placed, influential, with a bourgeois style of life. Politically, at least until the First World War, they were generally republican moderates attached to the 'religion of the French Revolution'; few supported parties of the left until the 1920s.[12] Contrasted to the native Jews were the new immigrants, non-citizens, poor, mostly from Poland, concentrated in the traditional artisan trades of textiles, furs, garments and shoemaking. Many speaking Yiddish, some speaking Ladino (Spanish-Jewish) or Chuadit (Portuguese-Jewish), they were more likely to hold more radical political and economic views, such as those of the Bund, anarchists, Bolsheviks and Mensheviks, than were the native Jews.

The two groups were separated by both a wide social and economic gap, and a geographical one.[13] The natives mostly lived in the richer western sections of the capital, while the new eastern Europeans lived in the central and eastern sections, the so-called Pletzl, the third and fourth *arrondissements*.[14]

France, before and during the Vichy years, had long seen the Jewish population as divided into two parts: the French citizens, 'Israelites', and the foreign 'Jews'. The first group, assimilated, acculturated, integrated into French life and loyal to France, proud of their past as veterans in the First World War, were self-defined as adherents of the Mosaic Law. The foreign-born Jews differed from the French Jewish population in their way of life, religious practice, language, use of Yiddish and attachment to Jewish tradition. The two groups also differed economically and by class. The French Jews were middle to upper class; they were professionals, commercial and business people, and intellectuals. They were assimilated into the secular educational system of the Third Republic, blending their Jewish inheritance and French patriotism. For this assimilated community, the Dreyfus affair was not so much a Jewish issue as a struggle between forces of justice and order. It saw the blatant anti-Semitism at the time as a temporary phenomenon 'due to passing circumstances' and limited to a few people.[15] Foreign Jews were often manual workers, artisans or small tradesmen dealing in clocks and watches, jewellery, furniture and the like.

The two groups also differed on the questions of Jewish identity, the Jewish role in the Diaspora and, later, on the response to the Nazi regime. Moreover, each group had its own institutional structure.[16] The distinction between the citizen and the 'foreign' Jew was crucial, and was literally to be a matter of life and death in the wartime years and the Vichy regime.

Linguistic differences also separated them. The newer immigrants, Ashkenazis from central Europe, spoke little French or French with an accent and also, especially in the older generation, Yiddish. Sephardim from Mediterranean countries spoke French with a different accent but spoke no Yiddish. Native Jews, the leaders, coming from families long resident in France, spoke the language with no accent.

Generally, native and foreign Jews reflected different views on the place of Jews in the general society, on the meaning of Jewishness and on self-definition. Established, assimilated, bourgeois citizens referred to themselves as 'Israélites' or French people of Jewish origin or of the Mosaic persuasion.[17] Distinguishing themselves from poorer Jews, they rejected the idea of a specific Jewish destiny, had little interest in Zionism, were conversant with French culture, were epitomised by the half-Jewish Marcel Proust, and articulated their patriotism and devotion to the Third Republic and its institutions, and to French republican ideas in general. Non-citizens, especially from eastern Europe, were more likely to define themselves as 'Jews', to observe religious practices, to be bound by ethnic ties, to have a Yiddish culture, and were more supportive of socialist or, to a lesser degree, Zionist movements.

The self-definition of native Jews was perhaps expressed most eloquently by Marc Bloch, in his pungent book *Strange Defeat*. He wrote, 'By birth I am a Jew, though not by religion, for I have never professed any creed, whether Hebrew or Christian ... I was born in France. I have drunk of the waters of her culture. I have made her past my own.' In his testamentary instructions to his family, Bloch again repeated that he was born a Jew and never denied it, yet 'I have ... felt that I was above all, and quite simply, a Frenchman ... I can declare that I die now, as I have lived, a good Frenchman.'[18]

He was a good Frenchman but also a tragic one with his expulsion from his university career and from his position as co-editor of the prestigious journal, the *Annales*, and finally his arrest, torture and execution by being shot in 1944. Equally poignant was the fate of Jacques Helbronner, prominent leader of the Jewish community before and during Vichy, who said at a meeting in June 1933, 'French Jews are French before being Jewish.' His destiny was to be arrested and deported as a Jew to his death in Auschwitz.

Some of the native Jews did minimise or dissociate themselves from their Jewish heritage. An example was the secularist Paul Grunebaum-Ballin, a former president of a section of the prestigious *Conseil d'État*, who refused, even after the start of Vichy anti-Semitic legislation, 'categorically to consider myself a French Israelite, a French Jew. I am a Frenchman who is not of the Jewish race because there is no Jewish race ... Nor am I a Jew by religion.'[19] Prominent Jews descended from rabbis – Bloch, Marcel Mauss, Robert Debré, Claude Lévi-Strauss – were assimilated intellectually into French culture. The composer Darius Milhaud defined himself as a 'Frenchman from Provence of the Israelite persuasion'.[20]

Of course a sharp categorisation of this kind needs qualification. Some prominent Israelites spoke of their adherence to the Jewish people as well as of their devotion to France. Léon Blum, early in his career, on 11 January 1923 explained in the Chamber of Deputies his Frenchness and his right to consider himself perfectly assimilated, but also that 'I feel that I am a Jew. And I have never felt the slightest contradiction, the slightest conflict between these two areas of my consciousness.' Later, in his important Luna Park speech of 6 September 1936, Blum, the first Jewish Prime Minister, asserted 'I am a Frenchman who is proud of his country, proud of his history, nourished as much as anyone else on its tradition despite my race.'[21] A later Jewish Prime Minister, Pierre Mendès-France, a supporter in London of General de Gaulle's resistance to Vichy, declared 'I am deeply aware that I am Jewish and my children know it too.'

The self-perception of these eagerly patriotic native Jews as French Israelites stemmed from the emancipation during the French

Revolution, the first such emancipation in Europe, with its principles of liberty, civic equality, religious tolerance, individual citizenship with corresponding rights and obligations, and a universalist, rationalist, secular culture, which challenged particularist loyalties. The tension between the universalism of a wider society and Jewish particularism, still an issue in varying degrees in contemporary politics, can be observed in the celebrated speech of Count Stanislas de Clermont-Tonnerre in the debate in the Constituent Assembly on 23 December 1789.[22] Supporting the proposal that Jews can be granted citizenship, he asserted: 'To the Jews as a Nation, nothing; to the Jews as individuals, everything ... They must not form a political corps or an Order in the state; they must be citizens individually.' The Abbé Grégoire, conscious of the problem, also spoke of the need for Jews to acquire 'healthy ideas' that would make them forget their *esprit de corps*.[23]

If the French nation was 'the locus of identity, a symbol of membership and allegiance', could the Jews with their own historic identity fit in? For the next two centuries the cohesiveness of the Jews was to arouse criticism as a distinct entity threatening the national identity. Rousseau had admired the endurance of 'a swarm of unhappy fugitives' turned by Moses into a political body, a free people that had lasted 5000 years. He was one of the few to praise rather than condemn, as was done by critics from all parts of the political spectrum, the concept of a homogeneous Jewish separate nation within the French nation. The ambiguity inherent in the situation was symbolised early after emancipation, when a celebration was held by the Jews of Metz in a synagogue in October 1792 in a civic festival for the republican victory at Thionville, during which the 'Marseillaise' was sung in Hebrew.[24]

Napoleon and the Jews

Napoleon was not an admirer of the Jews: 'They are the carrion birds of humanity ... they must be treated with political justice, not with civil justice. They are surely not real citizens.'[25] He decided to improve them. They needed civic rectitude and order, French and secular learning, 'useful professions', and adaptation of ritual to appropriate French standards.[26] He imposed a number of restrictions on commercial activities by Jews in money lending and commerce. Intermarriage was the way to end the Jewish people. By his 'infamous' decree of 17 May 1808 Jewish shopkeepers had to apply to the local prefect for an annual trading licence and for permission to trade in some economic fields.[27] Jews were not allowed to settle in Alsace or to move without special permission. Nor could they use Hebrew in commercial transactions. Further, limits could be put on immigration of Jews into France. Not until the end of the Napoleonic empire was freedom of religion guaranteed, by decree of 1 April 1814.

Napoleon insisted that Jews be governed by French rather than by Rabbinical law. In July 1806 he therefore brought together an Assembly of French Notables chosen by his government to answer questions on the relationship between Jewish law and civil law, on the jurisdiction of rabbis and on the loyalty of Jews to France. He then convened a Great Sanhedrin, two-thirds of which consisted of rabbis, to deal with these questions and replies to them. As a result Napoleon promulgated decrees in 1808 on the organisation of the Jewish religion.[28]

Did the Sanhedrin speak truth to power? Historians disagree on the degree to which it appeased Napoleon.[29] It did declare that Jews in France 'cannot but consider themselves Frenchmen in France, and they consider as equally sacred and honourable the bounden duty of defending their country'. It also proposed the use of the term 'Israelites' for co-religionists instead of 'Jew', which suggested a nation rather than a religion.

One of the decrees of 1808 set up a state-supervised system of consistories, thirteen by the decree of 11 December 1808, for Jews throughout the country in *départements*, the administrative areas, with over 2000 Jews. A synagogue was also established with each consistory, each of which was led by a rabbi and laymen chosen by Jewish notables and approved by civil authorities. Jews under a particular consistory financed the local synagogue in the *département* until 1831 when rabbis and cantors were paid as state functionaries.

The functions of the consistories were to act as liaison between the local Jewish population and the government, to supervise the practice of the Jewish religion, to maintain order in the synagogue, to oversee the moral and socio-economic welfare of Jews, to collect dues, to administer educational services, and to integrate Jewish values with French values, and loyalty to France and its culture.

At the apex of the system was the Central Consistory in Paris, headed by the Chief Rabbi, who was obliged to have a priest-like mitre; it was the co-ordinating body in charge of general affairs, administering the rabbinical school and approving the choice of rabbis. The first Chief Rabbi was David Sintzheim, German born, who had been the Alsatian delegate to the National Constitutive Assembly in August 1789, where he called for emancipation of Jews in eastern France, and also protested against acts of violence against Jews in Alsace and Lorraine.

Jews in French Society

Though liturgical and other differences remained between Sephardim and Ashkenazis, Judaism became part of French religious pluralism. The state-imposed institutional framework meant adherence to values of religious tolerance and civic equality, educational reform and promotion of French patriotism in Jewish schools, and acceptance of civil law as the norm with Jewish law restricted to religious ritual. With the consistories dominated by affluent laymen rather than rabbis, the way was open for the transformation of Jews into assimilated Israelites.

In light of the fate of Jews in Vichy France it is salutary to recall that Jews in France were the first in Europe to obtain the rights, privileges and responsibilities of citizenship. They benefited from the principles of universality of liberty and equality embodied in French law. Juridical inferiority was finally eliminated in 1846 when the Cour de Cassation ended *more judaïco*, the obligation for defendants and witnesses to take an oath in a synagogue. At the same time, the diminution though not the end of prejudice and the growth of assimilation, together with the embracing of secular schools, free, compulsory and public, also meant a gradual process of less rigid attachment to Judaism. Emancipation meant changing sufficient social, economic and religious behaviour to function in a modern society.

This process was fostered by organisations other than the consistories, the most significant being the Alliance Israélite Universelle set up by Adolphe Crémieux in 1860 originally to 'reconcile Judaism with the modern world', to combine Jewish identity for those 'attached with [their] heart to the ancient religion of [their] fathers' with French culture, support of universal reason and the principles of 1789. The Alliance was created for the greater emancipation and moral progress of Jews and for relief of those who suffered, for civic equality and for strengthening self-improvement. Yet, through its influential school system it became a potent force for instilling French culture inside and outside the country, for furthering French interests, and for embodying French humanism. It was the first Jewish movement that transcended national boundaries by its international network.[30]

Like the rest of society, Jews varied in religious adherence, in socio-economic class and in occupational distribution. At one extreme were the artisans and pedlars, the immigrant working class mostly from eastern Europe, many living in the Marais district in Paris, the Pletzl. By 1872, a quarter of all Jews in Paris were foreign born; by 1939, a majority of Jews in France were foreign born.

At the other extreme were the wealthy and well regarded, a few of whom received aristocratic titles, such as Rothschild, Hirsch, Horace de Günzberg and Cahen d'Anvers. Financiers and commercial entrepreneurs, Bamberger, Reinach and Péreire with his Crédit Mobilier, were prominent in Paris society, as was Mme de Caillavet, a fashionable hostess and mistress of Anatole France. Similar success stories were evident in a variety of fields: Meyerbeer at the Opera; Adolphe Franck at the Sorbonne; Michel Lévy in publishing; and others in the business of textiles, mines and railroads. Jews were present in intellectual and academic disciplines, in the *Grandes Écoles*, the University, even the military General Staff. By 1895 there were already five Jewish members of the prestigious Institut, and at least five army generals. In one year, 1897–8, twenty Jews were admitted to the prestigious École Polytechnique, and four to the equally important École Normale Supérieure.

During the Third Republic, about fifty prefects or deputy prefects in administrative *départements* were Jews; the Hendlé family served in these posts for three generations. Jews rose to become senior judges, presidents of the courts of appeal, members of the two houses of the legislature and cabinet ministers.

A prominent role in French public life was played by those whom Pierre Birnbaum has called 'state Jews' or 'fools for love of the Republic'.[31] They served and defended the republic, and the principles of the French Revolution, in distinguished positions – political, administrative and military – without, in most cases, converting to Christianity. In the Third Republic, between 1870 and 1936, fifty-two Jews became deputies, senators or ministers, a number of whom, starting with Crémieux in 1870, were Ministers of the Interior.

In administrative and judicial posts, Jews were admitted to the Conseil d'État, the Grands Corps and all branches of the judiciary. Some fifty were prefects, deputy prefects or presidents of Conseils de Préfecture. Another twenty-five were army generals; some families, such as the Brisacs in Metz, evolved into dynasties of generals for about a century. Often forgotten was the fact that in the First World War, over 40,000 Jews served in the forces, of whom 7500 died and 3800 received citations.[32] Of the 12,000 foreign Jewish volunteers, 2000 were killed. Paradoxically, in that war the Jewish Jules Moch, later to become a prominent politician and Minister of the Interior, received a fourth medal from Marshal Pétain personally.[33]

Moreover, the state Jews did not change any obvious Jewish names. Many of them combined strong devotion to universal republican ideas and fervent patriotism with strong ties of Jewish association and identity. Some were active in Jewish communal life; many married

Jewish women, formed Jewish social networks and were buried as Jews. One interesting fact, brought out by Birnbaum in his collective biography, is that the religious affiliations of those appointed to civil and military positions were noted in their dossiers and, in the case of Jews, the religion of their wives. Nevertheless, little discrimination occurred in appointments or promotions. The only qualification to this generalisation is that Jewish officials were normally not sent to very conservative, especially Catholic areas, such as Nord and Brittany. Otherwise, even the Dreyfus affair was not a significant obstacle to advancement of the state Jews.

A sad commentary on the fate of the distinguished Jews in public service is that a larger proportion of them than of French Jews as a whole was deported to concentration camps during the Vichy regime. One noticeable example was Lucien Vidal-Naquet, prominent de-Judaised lawyer, who was forbidden to practise law in 1942, and who in May 1944 was first sent to Baumettes and Drancy, and then deported to Auschwitz.[34] A few state Jews did try to get exemption from the anti-Semitic legislation, but most saw it as lacking moral validity. Vichy betrayed 'the fools for love of the Republic'.

Successive waves of immigration in the twentieth century from Russia, Poland, central Europe, Greece, Turkey, and Germany and Austria increased the Jewish population up to the eve of the Second World War, and internal migration continued to increase the urban population. In 1914, 25,000 immigrant Jews lived in Paris; twenty-five years later there were 200,000, half of whom were immigrants, and only 20,000 of these were alive to return after the liberation of France in 1944. The years of largest Jewish immigration were between 1921 and 1930 when almost 15,000 families were admitted into France. The largest number came from eastern Europe and Russia.

In the *département* of the Seine, including Páris, the largest Jewish occupation continued to be the traditional peddling or dealing in second-hand merchandise: hosiery, needlework, ready-made clothing. In commerce, Jews were in furniture, antiques, leather goods, furs and textiles, and in banking and financial houses. About 12 per cent of doctors were French Jews, and another 3 per cent were eastern European Jews. Some 10 per cent of dentists were Jews.

Estimates suggest that by 1939 Jews in metropolitan France numbered approximately 330,000, about 0.8 per cent of the total population of 43 million. About 90,000 were born in France, and the rest entered the country at different times. Some 15,000 fled from Alsace-Lorraine and 40,000 from the Low Countries at the beginning of the war, and in October 1940, 6500 were expelled by the Germans from the Palatinate and Baden. Over 60,000 Jews, including foreigners, enlisted in the army; between 10,000 and 15,000 became prisoners of war after the defeat of France.

Other calculations of the Jewish population provide virtually the same results. Of the 330,000 living in France on the eve of the war, 42 per cent were foreign, and another 15 per cent were naturalised citizens and children born to foreign parents in France. Foreign Jews constituted 6 per cent of all foreigners in the country. The naturalised Jews or those born to foreign parents were 10 per cent of the total number who had acquired citizenship; about 40 per cent of the 15,000 French citizens deprived of nationality by Vichy were Jews.[35] In the overseas protectorates Jews numbered 200,000 in Morocco, 120,000 in Algeria, 80,000 in Tunisia and 30,000 in Syria. Early actions by Vichy in 1940 stripped Algerian Jews of French citizenship, and extended racial laws to the Maghrib, the three North African countries.

The census ordered by the Germans in the occupied zone in October 1940 counted 148,000 Jews in Paris. By then, thousands had fled the capital. About 180,000 Jews were now living in the unoccupied zone, mostly in large cities such as Marseille, where only 40,000 had lived in 1939. Included in the total are those who left the north, Jewish families from the Low Countries who were deported by the Nazis when they conquered the area, Alsatian Jews and those from the Baden area. The census taken by Vichy in the unoccupied zone in July 1941 accounted for only 130,000, suggesting that many Jews had evaded the census.

With their different origins and backgrounds, Jews in France in 1939 were clearly not a monolithic entity constituting one or even two communities, but rather a 'plural group whose boundaries are and were truly indefinable'. Some intermarriage took place among individuals of the major groups, French and foreign, but social, economic, class and political differences continued to separate them. That separation sometimes led French Jews to assume an attitude of condescension towards the foreign born.[36]

As was the case in earlier years, immigrant behaviour patterns, philosophical outlook and political activism still differed markedly from those of native Jews. The more recent immigrants created a variety of their own institutions, synagogues, self-help organisations, mutual aid societies and welfare bodies, providing sick benefits, pensions and burial arrangements. They started Yiddish newspapers and theatres, and provided educational instruction in Hebrew and in Jewish history. As early as 1913 a Federation of Jewish Societies was started in Paris, grouping twenty-two other societies, and asserting that 'the Jewish immigrant is a source of activity and precious good will' and should participate in management of communal works.

Politically, immigrants were active in the Bund, the Jewish political party established in Russia in 1897, in other left-wing movements, in labour unions where Yiddish-speaking sections were affiliated with existing unions in the Confédération Générale du Travail, and in Zionist organisations such as Hovevei Zion, though there were never more than 10,000 Zionist members. Like the native Jews, immigrants also participated in the French army in the First World War, volunteering though not legal citizens.

Significant differences continued to divide native and foreign Jews on questions of self-identity and assimilation. Natives, as had been the case in earlier periods, supported the French Revolutionary ideals, the universalism of enlightenment and justice, and stressed characteristics of national pride, Frenchness and integration into the general community. They generally supported the secular public school system and textbooks, separation of Church and State, and public education for girls. They were active in social issues: Pierre Laroque in social security, Paul Cahen-Salvador in economic planning, Paul Strauss in public health, Émile Durkheim in the League of Rights of Man and Citizen.

Foreign Jews were more likely to see Jewish identity as self-defence against a hostile world. They valued qualities familiar in the shtetl and sheltered ghettos of eastern Europe, were more infused with traditional liturgy and Yiddish culture, and were generally more religious with a strong sense of community. With their traditional memories and habits, the eastern Europeans were criticised as retarding the assimilation process and increasing the xenophobia and anti-Semitism of non-Jews.[37] To some extent this was a self-fulfilling criticism. The consistories, in which successful native Jews were important, restricted membership of foreign Jews; the Central Consistory in Paris did not allow foreigners to sit on its board until 1939.

On political issues, native and foreign Jews also differed on the appropriate response to the increasing persecution by the Nazis of Jews in Germany and to their threat to Jews elsewhere. The response of native Jews was focused on relief programmes and was generally passive about specific Jewish actions in both national and international matters.[38] Leaders of the Paris Consistory objected when foreign Jews in France linked opposition to anti-Semitism with resistance to Nazism, thus bringing in the Jewish question. Instead, these leaders proposed that the struggle against anti-Semitism in the 1930s could best be waged by a kind of First World War type of *union sacrée*, a national coalition which might even include association with right-wing groups, such as the two led by Colonel François de la

Rocque, the Croix de Feu and its successor the PSF, and patriotic organisations. To counter the perception of Jews as troublesome left-wing agitators, a specifically Jewish patriotic group, the Union Patriotique des Français Israélites headed by Edmund Bloch, was established in June 1934. This group called for Frenchmen to band together in a 'total union of hearts and minds'; it was also a forum for declaration of Jewish loyalty to the nation.

If native and foreign Jews differed on political activity, they also disagreed about help to Jewish refugees, especially those from Germany. Jewish leaders in France in the 1930s faced a cruel dilemma on the question of Jewish refugees. Native French Jews were reluctant to help immigrants partly because of their unwillingness to become involved in politics, and partly because they shared, to a certain extent, the French animus against foreigners. They called for a restrictive policy, and for caution about the distribution of relief or the opening of French borders. At its harshest, as in the speech of Jacques Helbronner, vice president of the Central Consistory, in March 1936, refugees whom he termed 'riffraff', the rejects of society, the elements who could not possibly have been of any use to their own country' should not be allowed to stay in France. He lobbied the government to close the French borders to refugees from Germany.[39]

On the other side, a more liberal position was expressed by Raymond-Raoul Lambert, general secretary of the Comité National, who remarked of Helbronner that 'the fate of foreigners does not in the slightest move him'.[40] Lambert favoured entrance of more refugees and work permits for them. By 1939 the Jewish organisations had agreed, by necessity, on a more liberal approach.

A short-lived group, the Comité Central d'Assistance aux Émigrants Juifs, was set up in April 1933 to co-ordinate Jewish aid programmes for refugees. Two months later, it united a number of other groups to create the Comité National Français de Secours aux Refugiés Allemands, Victims de l'Antisémitisme. Noticeably, this Comité, avoiding any appellation of Jewish, was headed by prominent Jewish and non-Jewish individuals in Paris. It would not harass government leaders; on the contrary, it wanted to limit immigrant involvement in French affairs so that government officials would not be alienated.[41] Though this Comité was recognised as the sole body representing Jews on the refugee issue, it foundered because of internal friction, and was dissolved in July 1935. On these issues Jewish leaders faced two problems. One was the fear by many in France that admitting more refugees into the country might aggravate France's economic crisis. The other was that, in a climate where part of the political elite favoured a policy of appeasement towards Hitler, a call for challenge of Nazi aggression would be seen as advocating war with Germany. *Mourir pour les juifs!*

By contrast, foreign Jews were more vocal in calling for a Jewish response to the Nazis' persecution. The immigrants, however, were handicapped not only by internal friction within the Jewish community, but also by the increasing anti-foreign legislation of the 1930s which, among other things, imposed quotas and threatened immigrants with expulsion. Quotas imposed in 1934 and 1935, the result of xenophobic attitudes, affected the employment of aliens in certain trades, the ability of aliens to start new businesses, and their opportunity to become citizens. Foreign Jews were denounced in contradictory fashion; they might be Hitler's agents, or they might be warmongers instigating war against Hitler. Many of them were disappointed that left-wing organisations, if ideologically opposed to Nazism, were not helpful to any extent. In particular, the abolition of the Jewish subsection of the Communist Party in 1937 indicated that the party would not be concerned with Jewish affairs unless it were in the interests of the Soviet Union. At the outbreak of war, foreign Jews, mostly Poles and Czechs, joined the French army. German and Austrian Jews were interned as enemy aliens, though some joined labour-battalions or the French Foreign Legion. Foreign and French Jews alike were about to enter a sad future.

CHAPTER 2

ANTI-SEMITISM IN FRANCE

It needs no postmodern discourse or rejection of grand meta-narratives to appreciate that historical causation has pluralistic explanations. France, like other societies in the nineteenth and twentieth centuries, was infected with the virus of anti-Semitism, the baffling obsession that defies consistent, coherent, rational explanation without falsifying reality, and that springs from deep, inner emotions and unacknowledged prejudices.

Is this anti-Semitism an explanation of the legislation and actions of Vichy? Indeed, was the persecution of Jews the defining characteristic of Vichy? A troubling question is whether French political culture was so imbued with anti-Semitic beliefs that it laid the basis for, and acquiesced without much hesitation in, overt discrimination.[1] A case can be made that the anti-Semitic discriminatory exclusionary laws, decrees and actions of the Vichy regime have their roots in the prejudicial rhetoric, publications and movements hostile towards Jews which were prevalent over the twentieth century, and in the xenophobic legislation of pre-Second World War France.

Certainly French political culture has been puzzling. The liberal, democratic republic and society based on legal equality and open to talent, thus allowing Jews to rise to positions of power and eminence, was uncharacteristically influenced by and succumbed to xenophobia and to anti-Semitic beliefs and policies. The paradox in France is that Jews experienced the most radical emancipation of any country, but also encountered opposition to that emancipation.[2] Explanations abound, some pertinent and others based on perceptions of reality or on sheer prejudice against Jews or refugees who immigrated into the country.

Some explanations were political: fear of becoming involved in war with Germany; political deadlock and a weak governmental authority; political and economic scandals, particularly the Stavisky affair in 1934; the growing prominence of Jews in economic affairs and in the political world, especially the rise of Léon Blum, the first Jewish Prime Minister, which led to the provocative slogan 'Better Hitler than

Blum'; the violence of the boisterous right-wing political groups; the attraction, for a minority, of Nazism, Fascism and Communism.

Other explanations touched on economics: the stagnation in the economy; the poor state of the agricultural community, which accounted for almost half of the total population; the fall in the French birth rate after the First World War, which led to more foreign workers being needed. Foreigners became the scapegoats to explain everything: the supposed decadence of France; the internal problems of economic competition and diverse ways of life, especially those of Jews; and they would be blamed for the defeat of France in 1940.[3]

An argument of this latter kind not only distorts or even reverses the true nature of the interrelationship of phenomena, but also has the inauthentic ring of historical inevitability. The French collapse in 1940 had nothing to do with Jews; it was a military defeat, largely explicable in terms of the inadequacy of French military commanders, demoralised soldiers and obsolete and defensive strategic doctrines.[4] No doubt the memory of the First World War and its massacres was ever present during the inter-war years, as was the accompanying corollary, that war was a horror to be avoided and the massacres must not recur.[5] The war memorials throughout the country, marking public spaces in every town, were reminders of the abomination of war. Yet, at the same time, these memorials, as Prost has suggested, were in the same way as other *lieux de mémoire*, pillars supporting the Third Republic.[6] Bloch, in his influential book, held that the roots of defeat were not simply military but also lay in French culture and society.[7] Yet the chimerical decadence was not responsible for the defeat. The reality is the reverse: the defeat led to specious explanations as to a cause. That of decadence was an illustration of cognitive dissonance. Not only did Bloch ignore the role of the European countries, the Soviet Union and the United States in the geo-political and military drama. He also ignored the internal factors, the economic and demographic ones, which left France in a militarily weaker position than Germany.[8]

In France, as in other western countries, prejudicial expressions and overt hostile actions directed against Jews have emanated not only, if mostly, from the political right, but also from other parts of the political spectrum. Rationales for the varied arguments for anti-Semitism, whether based on economic, political, racial, religious or personal premises, are not always consonant with real underlying motives for the deep obsession. Contradictory images appear to enhance rather than constrain that obsession: the 'revolutionary Jew' on the one hand and the 'rich Jew' on the other were both used to fuel the myth of a Jewish-dominated world conspiracy that would destroy the true nature of French society.[9]

Stereotypes based on religion saw Jews as founders of anti-Christian sects including Freemasons, as people who sought to be masters of the world, as guilty of ritual murder. In reality, Jews were rarely Freemasons; nevertheless, they were regarded as a challenge, because of their parochial and separate community, to the French Catholic Church and its values. The other stereotypes were no more valid than that of freemasonry.

The economic argument concentrated on Jews as capitalists and controllers of international finance. Individuals such as Léon Halévy, Oline Rodrigues and the Péreires were held responsible for objectionable changes in the industrial and commercial system, as destroyers of the mythical, idyllic French pastoral society. Contradictory arguments were made. Jews were too powerful in the economy and in the control of public policy; at the same time, they condemned the bourgeois system and espoused radical and revolutionary causes. Jealousy or fear of Jewish competition was displayed in a French society and economy that had a structure, legally if not fully implemented in practice, based on merit independent of social, religious or ethnic particularisms.[10]

Cultural anti-Semitism, influenced by nineteenth-century writers, especially Gustave Le Bon, focused on the misrepresentation that Jews lacked understanding of the arts and sciences or could not contribute to a true civilisation. This led to the false premise that Jews were 'the other', supposedly self-alienated from mainstream society, ignoring attempts of Jews to assimilate. Overlapping this view was the racial argument. The distinguished historian Ernest Renan had argued that Jews, whom he regarded as the Semitic race, 'are not merely a different religious community, but ... ethnically an altogether different race',[11] one inferior to the Aryans or the Indo-Europeans. Later writers concluded that Jews were mercantile, cunning, intransigent and greedy, as compared with the noble Aryans with qualities of enthusiasm, heroism, honesty and disinterestedness. The latter constituted the true France, which should be an organic society, rooted in religion, race and nationalism. Jews were cosmopolitans – a term to be adopted by Stalin – who promoted universal rights, civic and legal equality, and open access to public and private positions. They were viewed as having no national loyalty to France or concern for its best interests. Jews were rootless people, incapable of being part of what Maurice Barrès, in his influential phrase, called 'the cult of the land and the dead'.

To all this was added the sexual fear of Jews, exemplified in a curious way. Sometimes it was symbolised by the Jewish heroine Judith, who was excluded from the community because of her depravity and disloyalty. Yet sometimes, Jews were identified with women or seen as bisexual or lacking virility.[12]

In spite of the principles of legal equality of 1789, Jews continued to encounter discrimination over the next century. This took many forms: the 1793 loan of 9 million francs forced on the Jewish population of Strasbourg; the 1806 decree granting a moratorium of one year for debts owed to Jews; the three decrees of 1808 signed by Napoleon, including the 'infamous' one putting Jews outside the common law for ten years; the 1840 Damascus affair in which the French consul there, introducing anti-Semitism into the Middle East, instigated and encouraged the local Christians to proclaim that an Italian monk and his servant who had disappeared had been killed by Jews for ritual purposes to get their blood for the next Passover service; the 1848 anti-Semitic riots in Alsace; the 1882 crash of the Union Générale bank, with the Rothschilds being accused of bringing about the failure of this Catholic bank; the 1886–9 anti-Semitic rhetoric by some leading supporters of General Boulanger, though not by the General himself; the 1889–93 Panama Canal scandal, in which several Jewish businessmen were involved and were attacked; the Dreyfus affair, starting on 15 October 1894 with the arrest and quick conviction of the Jewish Captain Alfred Dreyfus on the charge of treason and espionage for Germany, and ending, at least legally, in July 1906 with the acknowledgement of his innocence. Only in February 1998, almost a century later, did the French army formally acknowledge that Dreyfus has been convicted of 'a crime of high treason he did not commit'.

The Dreyfus Affair

The Dreyfus affair polarised French society; the anti-Dreyfusards were to become, in their old age, supporters of Vichy, while the supporters of Dreyfus became victims under the Vichy regime. For some, Vichy became the belated triumph and revenge over Dreyfus.[13] The division in the French population over the affair was crucial then and in the Vichy years. The affair led to the political moderates and the left of centre being in power up to the Second World War and to the identification of the Republic with the political left. This identification was clear when a large peaceful demonstration of workers took place at Longchamps in June 1899.[14]

On the other hand, the anti-Republican right, grouping all adversaries of the Republic, politicians, press and the Church, used and disseminated anti-Semitism in their utterances and publications. It became a dominating factor in some of the constituencies in the 1898 election.[15] Equally as virulent as Édouard Drumont's newspaper La Libre Parole was La Croix, the journal of the Assumptionists, an order committed to anti-Semitism. This clerical involvement through a paper with a large circulation and many subscribers who were parish priests also had the unintended consequence of the secular radicals shifting to the Dreyfusard side.

The powerful anti-Dreyfusard combination almost won: Zola was convicted at his trial in February 1898, and Dreyfus was found guilty a second time in September 1899. For much of the 1890s those who have been characterised as 'moderate anti-Dreyfusards', and are a herald of future behaviour under Vichy, constituted what might be called a 'silent majority', people who refused to recognise the existence of the affair and upheld the decisions of the military authorities. That silence might help explain why the affair lasted so long.

Of books and articles on the Dreyfus affair there is no end. With its share of heroes, particularly Colonel Marie-Georges Picquart and Émile Zola, 'a moment in the conscience of mankind', and its villains, such as Major Hubert-Joseph Henry and Major Ferdinand Walsin-Esterhazy, the affair was a pivotal event, divisive in character and with a unique intellectual and political impact on French life.

All analysts agree on the pertinence of anti-Semitism in the unfolding events of the affair starting in 1894, though scholars differ on its priority and centrality.[16] Some argue the centrality was crucial. Others give greater emphasis to factors such as nationalism or *raison d'être*, and thus imply that an anti-Dreyfusard position was not inevitably an anti-Semitic one. Inconvenient details blur easy generalisation. The nationalist literary critic Ferdinand Brunetière was pro-Dreyfus. Some inclined to anti-Semitism, such as Georges Sorel and Paul de Cassagnac, Director of L'Autorité, were convinced of Dreyfus' innocence.

Yet a general symbiosis linked anti-Semitic and anti-Dreyfusard opinions. This is clear from the rhetoric, or 'clan language', used by both supporters and opponents of Dreyfus.[17] In his celebrated article, 'J'Accuse', asserting the innocence of Dreyfus, in *L'Aurore* on 13 January 1898, Zola wrote that 'France, the great [and] liberal cradle of the rights of man, will die of anti-Semitism if it is not cured of it.' The rhetoric and arguments for discrimination during the Vichy regime echoed those of the anti-Dreyfusards, refusing to admit the innocence of the colourless, rich, bourgeois, Jewish protagonist even after the miscarriage of justice was evident with the confession by the real traitor, Esterhazy, in an interview published in *Le Matin* on 18 July 1899.

The attack on Dreyfus, the Alsatian who with his family opted for French nationality in 1872 after the loss of the two provinces of Alsace-Lorraine to Germany in 1870, and on his supporters, was relentless. Principles of truth and justice, which would mean a verdict of innocence for the victimised captain, were regarded as merely Jewish and Kantian ideas, which in the view of anti-Dreyfusards led to the degradation and humiliation of man. More important than individual rights were traditional institutions, the army, magistracy and church, without which justice and truth could not exist.

Arguments made by influential writers such as Édouard Drumont, Charles Maurras and Maurice Barrès justifying the condemnation of Dreyfus, heralded those used fifty years later to defend the actions of the Vichy regime and to exonerate it. This continuity between arguments used in pre-war France and in Vichy is apparent. The most widely read of the three writers was Drumont (1844–1917), Catholic and royalist, who in 1886 published his vitriolic *La France Juive*, arguing that Jews had virtually conquered France. As a premature national-socialist appealing to workers as well as to the political right, Drumont wrote: 'in reality it was the Jew that the bourgeoisie worked for and, above all, made others work'.[18] He saw Jews as spies, traitors and ridden with disease. As a loyal Catholic, he thought his religion required that Jews be driven out of France and removed from Aryan society.

The phenomenal success of Drumont's work – 100,000 copies sold in the first year – was surprising because earlier anti-Jewish writings such as the monomaniacal *Le Juif, Le Judaïsme et La Judaïsation des Peuples Chrétiens*, by Gougenot des Mousseaux in 1869, and the explosive pamphlets, such as *Le Juif, Voilà L'Ennemi!*, by the Abbé Chabauty, had aroused little interest.

Drumont's book and general influence lasted for a century. The longest-lasting French anti-Semitic publication was his daily newspaper, *La Libre Parole*, started in 1892, claiming a circulation of 200,000 within two years, lasting until 1924 and then reappearing in 1928 under the editorship of Jacques Ploncard d'Assac and Henry Coston. Writers in the May 1936 edition of the paper, celebrating the fiftieth anniversary of *La France Juive*, denounced the newly formed Popular Front coalition and the Jewish Prime Minister, Léon Blum, as 'the direct victory of Judeo-Masonry', now in control of the country. On the fiftieth anniversary of *La Libre Parole*, on 20 April 1942, Coston wrote that France's military defeat had brought 'a truly French government finally to take the revenge on Israel that Drumont proclaimed half a century ago'.[19] As late as 1963 a group, Les Amis de 'La Libre Parole', was formed to honour Drumont, who was not only a journalist but also a member of the Chamber of Deputies elected in 1898 in Algiers on an anti-Semitic platform.

During the Dreyfus affair, Drumont constantly attacked Jews who, like Dreyfus, could be seen as probable spies working for Jewish financiers and the cogs of a vast conspiracy to destroy Christian values.[20] Already in control of finance, administration and the tribunals, they would be the masters of France when they commanded the army. It was an ironic twist that Drumont, the self-proclaimed patriot who had insulted and fought duels with offended Jewish officers, used as a witness in his duel of 1 June 1892 the real culprit and the arch-traitor Ferdinand Esterhazy, the dishonourable rogue without scruples or moral principles.

Maurice Barrès (1862–1923) had started his career as a journalist and writer supporting General Boulanger and sprang to fame with his polemical defence of the conviction of Dreyfus and his attack on Dreyfusards as 'intellectuals', a noun he coined as a derogatory term for those who believe that society rests on logic and do not understand that antecedent necessities are stronger than individual reason. Dreyfusism was an 'orgy of metaphysicians', of abstract reasoning, which ignored the true needs of France. In one article Barrès, stressing the racial aspect, wrote that 'so many naturalised people, no matter their personal merit or good intention, could not be part of the French community of race, blood, and history, could not feel as we do, especially the national questions'.[21] Barrès spoke of the 'antisémitisme de peau' and of the 'cellules germinales' of Jews; the guilt of Dreyfus was obvious 'from his genes, his race, the shape of his skull'. Barrès played the racial card: 'From his race I deduce that Dreyfus is capable of treason.'[22]

Barrès welcomed the anti-Semitic movement; no one could complain when aware of the enormous power of Jewish nationality which threatened the French state.[23] The enemy common to all social classes was the Jew, who was neither a worker, nor a peasant, nor an honest small shopkeeper.

Later, in his book *Scènes et Doctrines du Nationalisme*, published posthumously in 1925 after his successful career as a writer and minor politician, Barrès rehearsed the arguments used thirty years earlier by the anti-Dreyfusards: anti-intellectualism; anti-individualism; anti-Protestantism; anti-parliamentarianism; the cult of the army; the decadence of liberalism, of democracy, and of modern art; the usefulness of Catholicism for national unity; social discipline; xenophobia; nationalism, from which Dreyfus, 'apatride ... sans patrie', was excluded; and above all, anti-Semitism.

In the affair, Barrès and others who upheld conviction criticised the intellectuals and artists who publicly defended Dreyfus, including Zola, Halévy, Monet, Proust and Durkheim. The Ligue des Droits de l'Homme, established on 24 February 1898, which these writers supported, was categorised as an aristocracy of intelligence, which regarded itself as superior to the common people. Another group of defenders was the Comité de Défense contre l'Antisémitisme, which included prominent people such as Zadoc Kahn, Salomon Reinach and Bernard Lazare.

Barrès' condemnation of fellow intellectuals was disingenuous in view of the quick reaction to this Ligue by the creation in January 1899 of the Ligue de la Patrie Française, a counter-group of literary and academic anti-Dreyfusards, one of the many nationalist organisations with anti-Semitic doctrines or overtones, the common denominator in all these organisations.

Already the Ligue des Patriotes, the nationalist group pressing for *la revanche* against Germany to recover the provinces of Alsace and Lorraine, had been established in 1884 by the fiery demagogue Paul Déroulède, who called for a system with a strong leader who consulted the people. The new body, the Ligue de la Patrie Française, headed by Jules Lemaître, well-known historian of literature, with François Coppée as president of honour, included Barrès as a director, Jules Verne, Vincent d'Indy and Charles Maurras.

Charles Maurras and the Action Française

The best-known and most influential anti-Semitic organisation was the Action Française, formed in 1898 by Maurice Pujo and Henri Vaugeois as a result of the Dreyfus affair. It was dominated by Maurras (1868–1952), the deaf poet from Provence, the virulent polemicist in politics and literature, who remained the major counter-revolutionary writer during the Third Republic and was to be the theorist inspiring, at least for the first year of Vichy, some of its most important figures.

Though Maurras preferred the restoration of the monarchy as a major priority, his theme of 'integral nationalism', rejecting the whole heritage of the French Revolution, was the rallying banner for those with disparate views: reactionaries, anti-parliamentarians, royalists, Catholics, nationalists, xenophobes and anti-Semites.

The Action Française was both a political and a literary movement. The daily paper of the same name started in 1908 and reached a considerable part of the bourgeois, student and Catholic world. In the mid-1930s the organisation claimed some 60,000 adherents. The paper, employing gifted writers, was relentless in its vituperative attacks, on both a general and personal level, on Jews, sometimes inciting violence. With his identification of the 'four confederated foreign states' of 'la France seule' – Protestants, Freemasons, *métèques* and Jews – Maurras combined xenophobia and intolerance, with relentless anti-Semitism. Though condemned by the Vatican in 1926 for its anti-religious but not for its anti-Semitic opinions, the Action Française remained influential, calling in print for the downfall of the Third Republic and taking physical action, being constantly involved in street brawls and demonstrations, especially in February 1934 when an attempt was made to attack the Chamber of Deputies itself.

A key concept for Maurras was 'politique d'abord', political realism or reason of state, which in the affair meant that Dreyfus, guilty or not, had to be sacrificed in the national interest, and Jews removed from public offices.[24] His disregard for the truth and indifference to ethical values were constantly displayed, including his eulogy for Major, later Colonel, Henry, the forger and perjurer who fabricated the documents implicating Dreyfus and who had committed suicide; Maurras greeted him as 'ce serviteur héroique des grands intérêts de l'État, ce grand homme d'honneur'.

The Dreyfus affair, which gave rise to the Action Française, was never forgotten by Maurras or by his movement. It remained an allegory, a symbol of a false regime. Maurras, remarked the literary critic Albert Thibaudet, 'kept the affair going for five acts and indeed never let it die'. For some years the paper Action Française kept a daily calendar of events of the affair on its front page, just above the important racing news. It was the supreme example of Jewish dominance and treachery.

On the Jewish question, Maurras took the same unrelentingly hostile and dogmatic position throughout his long life, towards Jews in general and also individual Jews. In a typical early statement in 1889 he attacked 'Israelites [who] are in no way individuals but, citizens and families, they form within the state another state which hopes to dominate the first'.[25] This is the key to his anti-Semitism, and later to that of the Vichy regime, for its more moderate personnel at least. Anti-Semitism should not be focused on religion or even on race. Indeed, Maurras denounced Joseph-Arthur Gobineau, who had elevated the Aryan race in the human hierarchy, as 'inept, false, lying'. Anti-Semitism for Maurras was a matter of national defence if the French were to remain masters in their own house in the face of the Jewish threat. For Vichy this would be state anti-Semitism.

Maurras attacked indiscriminately, no matter now eminent the Jewish individual: he opposed the election of Henri Bergson to the Académie Française; he protested against a proposal to appoint Einstein to the Collège de France; he instigated violence to get a play by Henri Bernstein withdrawn. Maurras inspired the assassination attempt against Léon Blum on 13 February 1936 with his remarks that

Blum 'will be the first to be killed ... he must not be missed ... now, there is a man to be shot in the back'.[26] An individual Jewish whipping boy was always there to be thrashed. In the 1930s Maurras viciously attacked the Jewish leader of the socialists and Prime Minister, writing of 'the sickening spectacle of the tribe of Blums settled at the summit of the French state'.[27] In 1941 he still spoke of 'the existence of a state within the state, the Jewish state in the French state'. He applauded the discriminatory Statut des Juifs of 2 June 1941 by Vichy, which went 'straight to the root of the matter, to the community'. The desirable state, he argued, should be in the service of a political anti-Semitism.

In his unco-ordinated, if always strongly enunciated political philosophy, Maurras mixed a *mélange* of themes: political federalism and a strong central state; elitism and populism; anti-capitalism and modernism; traditionalism and Gallicanism; inequality and social reform. Yet if his general stance was as a counter-revolutionary and anti-republican, Maurras attracted a wide spectrum of the French right: traditionalists, conservatives, monarchists, Bonapartists, Orléanists, populists and all those troubled by the presence in France of foreigners, especially Jews. His themes were to be those of Vichy: law, order, hierarchy, authority and corporative society.

It was this broad intellectual and political appeal that helped persuade moderates such as Joseph Barthélemy and Jacques Chastenet to join the Vichy administration of which Maurras was the mentor, at least for the first two years. Vichy for him was 'the divine surprise', and Maurras himself, though anti-German, was to remain faithful in support of Vichy, though not as extreme as his Fascist disciples, such as the writers Robert Brasillach and Lucien Rebatet. Maurras gave Vichy a modicum of intellectual respectability. His daily paper, however, appearing in Lyon during the war, was constantly critical of the slow pace of the Vichy National Revolution.

Anti-Semitism beyond the Political Right

These exponents of different expressions of the political right, the populist Drumont, the nationalist Barrès, the royalist Maurras, all shared anti-Semitism as the common denominator in their political outlook. All of these expressions influenced and underlay the views and politics of Vichy, though the exact impact varied with different officials and at different times.

Yet attitudes and behaviour during the Vichy years can only be fully understood by recollection that anti-Semitism was not confined to the political right in France. Other groups and individuals in the political spectrum, challenging the existing political and economic system, liberal values, cosmopolitan concerns and internationalist foreign policy, also advocated prejudicial or discriminatory policies.[28]

A particularly virulent strain of anti-Semitism, influencing Karl Marx during his stay in France from 1843 to 1845, stemmed from the early socialist and Utopian socialists of the nineteenth century, such as Charles Fourier, Pierre Leroux, Pierre-Joseph Proudhon and Alphonse de Toussenel.[29] Fourier was concerned about Alsatian Jews who did not value productive labour in agriculture and industry. The Utopian socialists generally saw Jews as destroyers of their imaginary pastoral paradise. Toussenel, in his very successful book of 1844 Les Juifs, Rois de l'Époque, used both theological and economic arguments in his denunciation of Jewish control and the international financial conspiracy, concentrating on Jewish bankers, especially the Rothschilds and Jewish railway builders. Proudhon, a more vituperative writer, concluded after his diatribe against Jews that 'Satan, Ahriman, was incarnated in the race of Sem'. Jews must be either sent back to Asia or exterminated.

During the first years of the Dreyfus affair, the socialists were mainly neutral or indifferent. No moral issue of justice was present for them. Their most notorious statement, a manifesto of 19 January 1898, a few days after Zola's 'J'Accuse' appeared, published by the socialist parliamentary group and inspired by two of its top leaders, Jules Guesde and Édouard Vaillant, declared that proletarians should not enrol in 'either of the clans of the bourgeois civil war'. The affair was a convulsive struggle, hypocritical and fraudulent, of two rival bourgeois parties. Only in August 1898, after some hesitation, did the leader of the party, Jean Jaurès, who had been defeated in the parliamentary election in May, begin to publish articles in the socialist newspaper La Petite République, holding that Dreyfus was innocent.

A long-held perception is that the population of rural France, unlike Paris, was indifferent to the guilt or innocence of Dreyfus.[30] This is belied both by the record of physical violence and political appeals. Anti-Semitic violence occurred in a number of towns in 1898, in Nantes, Bordeaux, Marseille and Besançon. With slogans of 'Death to the Jews' and 'La France aux Français', hundreds of thousands, including many youngsters, took part in demonstrations, moving from protest to the sacking of synagogues and Jewish shops, and the beating of individuals.[31]

Politically, anti-Dreyfusard candidates, of different parties, used anti-Semitic themes in the 1898 election in appeals to the rural as well as to the urban population.[32] Opinions about Dreyfus seem to have affected local issues. Twenty-two anti-Semitic candidates were elected to the Chamber of Deputies, thirteen from rural and five from urban areas, and four, including Drumont, from Algeria.

The unfortunate reality of the prevalent anti-Dreyfusard and anti-Semitic attitude of the Catholic Church is generally accepted. However, the views that Catholics were the only social group which was cohesive in an anti-Dreyfusard position and that Catholicism was the unifying factor inspiring anti-Semitism in the affair have been challenged in recent years by those denying the existence of a monolithic Catholic bloc. To some degree such a generalisation needs qualification. If about 300 members of the clergy contributed to the subscription for the widow of the duplicitous Colonel Henry following his suicide the day after his arrest for forgery in August 1898, this was only a small number of the 50,000 priests at the time. By comparison, although the Minister of War, Charles Freycinet, forbade members of the armed forces to contribute, almost one-third of the subscribers came from the military, including five generals and the future Marshal Maxime Weygand, and thirty generals in the reserves.[33]

Drumont's *La France Juive* was enormously successful, but the book by the liberal Catholic Anatole Leroy-Beaulieu, *Israël parmi les Nations* published in 1893, also went through fourteen editions. Another liberal Catholic, Paul Viollet, member of the Institute, who believed as did Leroy-Beaulieu that Dreyfus was innocent, joined the Ligue des Droits de l'Homme, founded in February 1898, and set up a small Comité Catholique pour la Défense du Droit in February 1899, composed of Catholics only, which denounced the harm caused to France by the two plagues, anti-Christianism and anti-Semitism.

Nevertheless, Catholic anti-Semitism in the affair was not a myth and is very relevant to events fifty years later in Vichy. The important fact, then and more recently, is that the official Church was silent. It did not choose the path of truth and equal justice, or the principles of universality. Those who took the silence of the clerical hierarchy as implicit approval, engaged in verbal violence as did *La Croix*, issued by the Augustins of the Assumption, which called itself the most anti-Jewish paper in France, *La Libre Parole* with its claimed 300,000 subscribers, and the ultramontanist journal, *L'Univers Catholique*.[34] By contrast, those Catholics who were not anti-Semitic had no important organisation or literary organ and were less well known to the general Catholic community.

The secular Zola, in his 'Lettre à la France' of 6 January 1898, wrote that the Church had inflamed anti-Semitic rage among the people. Sorel thought the Church had committed a great error by its anti-Dreyfusard position.[35] More majestically, Charles Péguy, himself a devout Catholic, in *La Revue Blanche* of 15 September 1899, declared

'It was an evident fact' that the guilt of Dreyfus had been simulated, imagined and cultivated by the Jesuits and the majority of Catholics who had committed 'une injustice sacrée'.

The Catholic papers endlessly repeated the same charges. Jews were the perfidious race responsible for deicide and ritual murder; they had been punished by dispersion. They had inspired discrimination against Catholics in the laic educational system and through the anti-clerical laws. The promoter of the law legalising divorce was a Jew, Alfred Naquet. The first defenders of Dreyfus were Protestants, Jews and Zola, a man loathed in Catholic circles. Jews were, together with Freemasons, plotting to de-Christianise France, which as the oldest daughter of the Church sought to integrate the nation and the Catholic religion.

The Christian Church was inextricably linked with the anti-Dreyfusard camp and with defence of the army. In Péguy's words, the honour of the army became 'a saintly formula'.[36] The future Marshal, Louis-Hubert-Gonzalve, was one of the few senior military figures to believe that Dreyfus was innocent, saying that anti-Semitism 'tient la corde' (pulls the strings). To the end, whether through stubbornness or anti-Semitic beliefs, the army was adamant in the affair. At the second military trial held in Rennes in September 1899, five officers out of seven found Dreyfus guilty with extenuating circumstances, and sentenced him to ten years' imprisonment, despite Esterhazy's confession. The civilian president, Émile Loubet, pardoned him a week later.

The affair ended for Alfred Dreyfus but not for the country. Vichy, aware of its symbolic significance, expunged all references to Dreyfus' innocence from school textbooks, and made his name synonymous with villainy. In 1941 the Vichy regime also removed the works of Georges Clemenceau from public libraries, the ultimate homage to the courageous and outspoken Dreyfusard. Ironically, Pétain largely owed his Marshal's baton to Clemenceau, prime minister in the First World War.[37] Two unrelated events in 1944 were reminders of the affair. The successor to Darquier and the third head of the Commissariat Général aux Questions Juives was Charles du Paty de Clam, son of the general who conducted the first examination of Dreyfus which led to his trial. Almost at the same time Madeleine Lévy, granddaughter of Dreyfus, was deported to and killed in Auschwitz. Forty years later, the tomb of Dreyfus in Montparnasse was desecrated.

The Political Ligues and Parties

Before 1880 political movements advocating anti-Semitism had little mass appeal. With the economic depression in the decade, the crash of the Catholic Union Générale bank in 1882, the political and financial scandals in the Third Republic, the anxiety about the future of France, which had already lost Alsace-Lorraine and which was troubled by internal divisions, weak governments and inability to make decisions, the extent and character of immigration into the country, the criticism of the wealth and influence of Jews, and the turmoil of the Dreyfus affair, new groups, extreme and extra-parliamentary in nature, began to dwell on anti-Semitic themes. The *ligues* were a new departure in French politics. Political parties are interested in capturing power. The *ligues* by contrast, populist in character, grouped individuals making demands on a specific issue and mobilised the masses to affect policy by direct action rather than by parliamentary methods.

Édouard Drumont, following his astonishing literary success, set up the Ligue Antisémitique later led by Jules Guérin; it sought to eliminate Jewish power in French society by breaking windows, pillaging Jewish shops and instigating violence against Jews in Algeria, 30,000 of whom had been granted citizenship by the Crémieux decree in 1870. In 1889 another group, the Ligue Nationale Antisémitique de France, was founded and led by the Marquis de Morès. The vice president of the group called himself a national socialist. In January 1899, the Ligue de la Patrie Française was formed; it claimed a membership of 40,000.

The *ligues*, small but militant, affected the climate of opinion in the years before Vichy. They called for change in the weak parliamentary system and for greater executive authority. All wanted strong leadership capable of taking action, to end divisions and disorder, to reduce unemployment, to create a powerful France and, above all, to reduce or eliminate the power and influence of those, especially Jews, whom they saw as undesirable or a threat to the real France. With their vituperative, abusive rhetoric, their constant resort to violent action, and their military-style uniforms and parades, many of them took on the appearance of fascist groups, though they differed in substance and policies from those groups, except in the case of the PPF, le Parti Populaire Française.

In 1936 the *ligues*, whose paramilitary bodies had already been forbidden, were dissolved by the Popular Front government, which saw them as a threat to a democratic republic. The only militant group that remained surreptitiously was the Cagoule (Comité Secret d'Action Révolutionnaire), an offshoot of the AF and founded in 1935 by Éugène Deloncle, which gloried in street fighting and attempted a coup in November 1937. Only at the end of his life was it revealed that François Mitterrand had been associated with the Cagoule as a student, selling its newspaper in the *Quartier Latin* in Paris and participating in its demonstrations, though apparently not a member of it.

The divisive Dreyfus affair was the first major battle in what has been called the 'Franco-Française' war, still not fully ended, which came to a height in the controversy over the Vichy regime. As in Vichy, the affair witnessed the clash of perceptions about the nature of the desirable social, economic and political conditions of France and the struggle between adherence to authority and the decisions of traditional institutions regardless of content on the one hand, and the universal principles of freedom, equality and human rights stemming from the Revolution on the other hand.

After the First World War, France experienced a dramatic increase both in the outpouring of books, pamphlets and articles of an anti-Semitic nature, and in the number of parties or groups condemnatory of or using Jews as scapegoats for political and economic problems. Increased unemployment caused by the world economic crisis was seen as due to manipulations of international Jewish finance. These anti-Semites argued that the flood of refugees from eastern and central Europe increased competition for jobs, caused internal problems and endangered peace with Germany.

Right-wing organisations in the inter-war years attracted veterans of the First World War, those fascinated and influenced by the rapid ascent to power of fascism in Italy and then Nazism in Germany, and those hostile to Marxism and internationalism. By the mid-1930s, a more frequent and more intense anti-Semitic ideological rhetoric and political activity were manifested. In an inadequate response, a Jewish defence group, l'Union et Sauvegarde Israélite, warned of the growing anti-Semitism, both political and personal.

The Action Française became larger and more influential. Organisationally, the AF continued its demonstrations and engaged in street fights and personal physical attacks, reaching a peak with the riots on 6 February 1934 outside the Palais Bourbon, by which it attempted to achieve the downfall of the Chamber of Deputies housed there, as well as the downfall of the Third Republic in general. Associated with it in the riots were a number of other groups, some financed by the *parfumier* François Coty, such as La Solidarité Française led by Jean Renaud, a commander of colonial infantry, Le Françisme, the Croix de Feu and the Jeunesses Patriotes (JP).

The Jeunesses Patriotes, founded in 1924 by Pierre Taittinger, elected in 1919 to the Chamber of Deputies from Paris, appealed to veterans, called for national unity, criticised political parties as divisive, and viewed social demands as betraying the country.

Organised into groups, the JP aped the fascist movements in its dress code of uniforms, berets and insignia, and in its exaltation of the leader.

A third group, Le Faisceau, founded by George Valois on the symbolic date of 11 November in 1925, explicitly referred to the Italian model. Its organ, Le Nouveau Siècle, advocated fascist-like policies such as an economy based on corporatism and anti-capitalism. The organisation resorted to violence in the streets and associated with paramilitary groups, the Legions, led by a former pilot, André d'Humières. This in turn led to a new group, Le Françisme, founded in 1933 by Marcel Bucard, a First World War hero. Le Faisceau ended in 1928, short of funds after donors realised that Valois took his anti-capitalist rhetoric seriously. Bucard gave his group an anti-Semitic slant in 1936. One intriguing aspect of these various fascist groups was interconnection through their financial sponsors, mainly François Coty and Marcel Bucard.

Other bodies, often small and short-lived, emerged from time to time, all with anti-Semitic motifs. The Ligue Franc-Catholique, established in 1927 and headed by Canon Schaeffer, replaced the former Ligue Anti-Judéomaçonnique founded in 1913 by Mgr Jouin. It was a small group of extremist aristocrats, haute-bourgeois and ecclesiastics. The former *ligue* was reorganised by Dr Georges Cousin, a deputy from Paris. In 1934 two other groups were founded: the Parti Français National Communiste by Pierre Clementi and the Grand Occident by Lucien Pemjean. The Rassemblement Antijuif de France was set up in 1938, and led by Louis Darquier de Pellepoix, soon to become a notorious figure in Vichy. The Parti National Populaire Français Antijuif of Dr Molle of Oran became the Ligue Nationale Populaire in October 1931.

The largest of the right-wing organisations was the Croix de Feu, set up, with the financial support of François Coty, originally in 1927 as a veterans' group. From 1930 it was controlled by Colonel François de la Rocque (1885–1946), an ex-military man with business connections, who expanded its membership beyond veterans and claimed 200,000 adherents in 1934. A charismatic, though aloof and dignified person, he demanded absolute obedience. In the February 1934 riots he instructed his followers, now a mass movement, not to break through the police barriers guarding the building or to become unruly. La Rocque never characterised his organisation as fascist, but viewed himself as a disciplined nationalist calling for a republic with a strong executive, authoritarian in character and socially minded, upholding 'Christian civilisation'.

With the dissolution of the *ligues* in 1936, La Rocque transformed the Croix de Feu into a political party, the Parti Social Français (PSF), which became the largest single right-wing party, claiming 800,000 supporters in 1938, and purportedly aimed to capture power legally through the parliamentary process. Analysts disagree on the appropriate appellation of La Rocque and the PSF; certainly authoritarian but not necessarily fascist. On one side are historians such as René Rémond, holding that La Rocque discouraged the development of fascism in France, and Jacques Nobécourt, arguing that he opposed both Nazism and communism. The other position is taken by Robert Soucy, emphasising his tendency to fascism and the Croix de Feu's street violence and campaigns against 'undesirables'.[38] An interesting intermediate position is that of Kevin Passmore, believing that the Croix de Feu was fascist, representing 'a palingenetic ultra-nationalism' with paramilitary groups, but that the PSF was not and engaged in electoral activity.[39] La Rocque advocated patriotic reconciliation and Christian harmony, but he also called for repression of the usual enemies, Jews, Marxists and Freemasons. As traitors, Blum and Édouard Daladier, former Prime Minister, should be punished.

In the 1930s, La Rocque had welcomed Jews, such as Ernest Mercier, a businessman known as 'the king of petrol and electricity', and Ferdinand Robbe, into his movement. The patriotic Chief Rabbi of Paris, Jacob Kaplan, held ceremonies in his synagogue, especially an important one on 14 June 1936, which La Rocque and members of his party attended. Yet, by the late 1930s he grew increasingly anti-Semitic, denouncing the 'bad Jews', left-wingers and later, during the Vichy years, the unpatriotic Jews and the unwanted immigrants. Always careful not to use anti-Semitic diatribes against Jewish war veterans, he did in his 1941 book, *Disciplines of Action*, attack the prominent role of Jews in French political and financial affairs. He condemned Jews for trying to 'de-Christianise' France, and called for an end to immigration. If less extreme than most other right-wing leaders, he nevertheless indulged in political and cultural anti-Semitism.

La Rocque had an uneasy and ambivalent relationship with Vichy and the German occupiers. Vichy had appropriated the slogan of La Rocque's PSF: 'Travail, Famille, Patrie'. He favoured collaboration, seeing it as a crusade for Christian civilisation, and praised the virility of the Nazi and Fascist regimes.[40] Yet as a French nationalist he wanted partnership, not subservience to Germany. In December 1940 when Vichy abolished all political parties in France, La Rocque changed the name of his PSF to Progrès Social Français. As the tide of war changed, in 1942, La Rocque and some other senior supporters contacted the Resistance; through an underground organisation known as Klan, he supplied British Intelligence with information. His followers were forbidden to join the notorious Vichy Milice or the French Volunteer Legion against Bolshevism. After invading the south of France, the Germans banned the PSF; in March 1943, La Rocque and 152 of his group were arrested by the Gestapo and deported to a German political prison.

A more openly fascist party, the Parti Populaire Française (PPF), was founded in 1936 by Jacques Doriot (1898–1945), who had switched political affiliation. He joined the Communist Party as an ex-serviceman in 1921, became mayor of Saint-Denis in 1931 and then a Communist member of the Chamber of Deputies before leaving his party in 1934. The PFF soon claimed a membership of about 100,000 drawn, in spite of a programme that favoured big business, from the lower middle and working classes, from some young intellectuals, and from a significant number of militants who came to it from parties of the left. Though Doriot tried to restrain his more exuberant followers, the PPF, became more overtly anti-Semitic and fascist. This was clear in 1938 when the PPF, seeking to increase its political support especially in Algeria, not only used anti-Semitic rhetoric but also engaged in physical assaults on Jewish businesses. In the Vichy regime, Doriot became an eager collaborator, a promoter of the Légion des Volontaires Français contre Bolchevisme, which La Rocque had shunned. He also became a full member of the anti-Semitic posse with his talk of 'the Jew with his will to universal domination', the Pluto-Judeo-Bolshevik coalition, and of the need for a racist national revolution.

During the early 1930s another group, a network of Comités de Défense Paysanne headed by the demagogue, anti-Semitic and anti-communist populist Henri Dorgères (real name Henri August D'Halluin) was set up to give voice to supposed peasant bitterness over the decline in commodity prices, high taxes and the insufficient representation of peasants in the public world.[41] Forgotten was the reality that in 1935 the French government was spending nearly 50 per cent more on supporting the wheat market than on national defence. Dorgères went beyond the specific rural grievances to call for an authoritarian state, a corporative system and an end to the Third Republic. The *comités*, claiming adherents from 150,000 to 200,000 and even, incorrectly, half a million in 1937, also engaged in both physical and verbal violence.

Its militia of Greenshirts, set up in 1935 and largely limited to the north and the west, with its belligerent call, 'Haut les fourches' (Raise the pitchforks), was involved in armed confrontation. Equally violent were Dorgères' inflammatory rhetoric and his writing in the network of small papers he controlled in the north and west. Intermittently anti-Semitic, the *comités* can be placed somewhere between a far-right-wing group and a fascist one. On one hand, Dorgères seemed to favour an organic conception of society; on the other, he glorified violent action as the method of change and was supported by uniformed young men prepared to engage in such action.

At the age of forty-two, Dorgères volunteered for military service, winning the Croix de Guerre. In the Vichy regime he became a member of the National Council, and one of the nine directors-general of the Peasant Corporation, though few of its members were his previous supporters.

In June 1933 François Coty, who had financed the Croix de Feu and other right-wing groups, set up another one, the Solidarité Française (SF), after a dispute with La Rocque a year earlier. Coty, who owned a mass daily, *L'Ami du Peuple*, used its editorial staff as the managers of the SF, and appointed as its leader Jean Renaud, former army officer in Indo-China, who was a powerful speaker. The SF quickly recruited members, claiming 315,000 within a year, though probably far fewer. It played a prominent role in the riots on 6 February 1934 in the Place de la Concorde. Emphasising French nationalism, it attacked the usual enemies, Jews, Marxists and liberals. In an interesting variation, the SF also recruited North African Arabs living in Paris by offering them some material rewards of money and clothing, in return for which they aroused anger against Jews and foreigners.

With its use of militants, uniforms and salutes in fascist style, its praise of Mussolini and Hitler, its defence of 'national socialism', its physical assaults on Jews and its invective against them as a menace to society, the SF was fundamentally an anti-Semitic body. Its leader, Renaud, opposed immigration of Jews, 'the scum of the ghettos of Europe', and warned of the influence of Jews in France who threatened to poison French culture and politics by their control of the press, literature, cinema and politics. Again, the spectre of a 'Judeo-Masonic-Bolshevik' conspiracy that threatened France was raised. Renaud's solution was close to that to be implemented by Vichy: restrictions on Jewish immigration, deportation of recently arrived Jews, quotas on employment of Jews in professional occupations, and sending home all foreign workers.

A still puzzling aspect of mid-twentieth-century politics is the fact that attraction to fascist ideas or movements was not confined to those associated with the political right, but also embraced individuals who started on the political left. In most western European countries similar ideological shifts occurred, illustrative of what Philippe Burrin termed 'the fascist drift'.[42] They reflected discontent with liberal democracy and cultural criticisms of the Enlightenment and Marxist materialism.[43] If it is too strong to argue, as Zeev Sternhell has done, that by 1940 French political culture was saturated with fascist ideology, which Sternhell links with left-wing ideology, a better case can be made that the Vichy regime embodied a synthesis of anti-liberal socialism, anti-individualism, a populist nationalism and anti-Semitism. In this the revolutionary right joined with the ex-revolutionary left in the call for an authoritarian system and for class collaboration. In France, disillusioned leftists illustrated this political stance, particularly Doriot, who quickly moved to the political right, but also Marcel Déat and Gaston Bergery. Leaders of small movements, the latter two soliciting larger support, appealed to the left with concepts of nationalism and strong leadership and anti-Semitism.

Unhappy with the traditional socialist party, Déat formed a neo-socialist group within it. In 1941 he founded the Rassemblement National Populaire (RNP), the Popular National Rally, urging more collaboration with Germany, criticising Pierre Laval for not being sufficiently fascist, advocating a kind of fascist socialism, and calling for the end of class struggle, for a totalitarian regime and for a new kind of person. That new necessary person would be a defender of Aryanism, opposing the intrusion of Jewish 'parasites' into European culture.[44]

Gaston Bergery, former member of the Radical Party, founded the Front Commun in 1933, with a socialist programme, and called for a syndicalist rather than a parliamentary system. His fascist style of operation included propaganda, chants, lighting, emblems and flags to emphasise the message. Within a year the group merged with the Third Force led by George Izard. In 1940, Bergery became a member of the Vichy National Council, and then Ambassador first to the Soviet Union and then to Turkey.

An Anti-Semitic Duo

The link and continuity between the pre-war anti-Semitic rhetoric and militant actions of individuals and groups and the policies of discrimination and persecution in the Vichy regime is illustrated by the careers of two persons who became important figures in the regime, Xavier Vallat and Louis Darquier de Pellepoix. With them, verbal confrontation left the streets and erupted in the halls of legislative bodies.

Xavier Vallat (1891–1972), originating from a rural, profoundly Catholic family in the south of France, inherited his strong anti-

Semitic beliefs from his schoolteacher father. He fought bravely in the
Second World War, losing an eye and a leg; his life was saved by Jewish
medical attendants at the battlefront. In 1919 he entered the Chamber
of Deputies; he represented the Ardèche region and became active
as a fiery speaker in extreme right-wing organisations. A strong
personality, he remained a Catholic, xenophobe and royalist, beliefs
and attitudes that reinforced and sustained his anti-Semitism throughout his turbulent life.[45] For him, except for some distinguished, old
French Jewish families such as that of Robert Debré, Jews could not be
assimilated, and they should be seen as outsiders, people of two
nations, the first of which for them was the nation of Jews, who
formed a state within the state. In light of the ultimate fate of Jews in
the Holocaust, Vallat's policies were comparatively 'humane',
confined to ridding France of Jews but not to exterminating them.
Vallat always claimed his anti-Semitism was not related to that of the
Nazis; it came from French history and tradition, from the line of
kings, from Voltaire, Renan, Taine, Proudhon, Drumont and the
Catholic Church.

That may have been true, but this intellectual heritage can hardly
be blamed for Vallat's vitriolic language. In a notorious speech in the
Chamber of Deputies on 6 June 1936, Vallat attacked Prime Minister
Léon Blum, declaring 'for the first time, this ancient Gallo-Roman
country will be governed by a Jew ... I say ... that to govern a peasant
nation such as France, it is better to have someone whose origins,
however modest, are deep in our soil, than to have a subtle
Talmudist.'[46] Perhaps a harbinger of the future, in the debate all the
deputies of the political right and most of the centre remained silent
during Vallat's remarks. The anti-Semitic parliamentarian also got 150
votes when he challenged Édouard Herriot for the presidency of the
Chamber of Deputies.

A milder, more subtle, form of Vallat's argument had been made a
few days earlier by Le Temps on 2 June 1936 when it wrote obliquely
of Blum: 'For the first time in the history of our ancient land, a leader
invested with political power has spoken to the French nation without
claiming to be the representative of the entire nation.' Blum was more
viciously attacked by the journals of the political right and by
Catholic publicists. Among the countless diatribes in 1936 from
journals such as Je Suis Partout, Contre-Révolution and Le Charivari
are a few choice specimens: 'We are on the eve of having a Judeo-
socialist government in the person of Blum'; 'Blum was appointed as
Prime Minister in the interests of the Jewish nation'; the Jews around
Blum were 'an administrative sub-structure to the republican state ...
sacred, consecrated, circumcised'.

Vallat had picked on the most successful Jewish politician as the object of his rhetorical vituperation. Léon Blum, the cultivated free-thinking intellectual, the sophisticated literary and theatre critic, republican patriot, leader of the Socialist Party, high official in the Conseil d'État, was accused of being an outsider, a stranger to the French race and to French customs. Blum received numerous death threats and was wounded in a violent street attack.[47] The Vichy regime disgraced itself and the judicial system when it put Blum on trial in Riom in February 1942 and he and other Jewish individuals were attacked as agents of the 'Anglo-Saxon powers', which were controlled by 'Jewish financiers'.

Vallat became General Secretary for Veterans' Affairs in the Vichy government, quickly merging the various veterans' organisations into the Légion Française des Combattants in August 1940. Within a year, on 23 March 1941, he was appointed to a crucial position, the head of the newly created Commission Général aux Questions Juives (CGQJ). Vallat was now the incarnation of French state anti-Semitism, and proud of it.

As such, Vallat detested Nazi fanaticism on the Jewish question, and annoyed the Germans by the rather light sentences given to violators of the anti-Jewish laws. He refused to attend the anti-Semitic exhibition 'The Jews and France', organised by the Nazis in Paris. In a confrontation with SS officer Theodor Dannecker in Paris in February 1942, he had the temerity to yell at the 27-year-old Nazi, 'I have been an anti-Semite far longer than you.'[48] A few weeks later he was dismissed from the CGQJ.

After Liberation, Vallat was tried in the High Court of Justice in December 1947; he defiantly protested against the judge, whom he called a 'naturalised Jew and communist'. He was condemned to ten years in prison, a light sentence because of his anti-German attitude, and to 'national indignité'. Like so many other Vichyites, he was liberated after two years and amnestied in 1954. In his memoirs, Le Nez de Cléopâtre and Feuilles de Fresnes, and his articles in Aspects de la France, he reiterated his anti-Semitic views and hatred of Jews, expressing no regrets or remorse about the Vichy persecution. His last article in 1969 completed the anti-Jewish, anti-Dreyfusard circle. It was an attack on the reissue of the book L'Antisémitisme, Son Histoire et Ses Causes, by Bernard Lazare, the first person to become a prominent Dreyfusard.

Vallat's implicit argument of 'France for the French', a paramount theme of Vichy, was made more emphatically in a less well-known motion proposed in the General Council of the Seine on 4 June 1936 by Louis Darquier de Pellepoix (1897–1980). Darquier (his real name, to which he fraudulently added the aristocratic title), the son of a doctor, had been a courageous soldier in the First World War and something of a misfit after that. Active in the violence of the *ligues*, he gained his fifteen minutes of celebrity by being wounded in the right-wing riots of 6 February 1934 in the Place de la Concorde, and becoming chair of an association of people injured in the riots. Darquier used his seat on the Paris City Council, as well as his position as a journalist, to hurl verbal onslaughts against Jews. His motion of June 1936 proposed that, because of the growing influence of Jews in France, there should be both a complete annulment of all naturalisations granted since 11 November 1918 and a statute that would specifically regulate the right of Jews to vote and to hold public office.[49]

Anti-Semitic invective was foremost in all of Darquier's publications, especially in *La Vieille France* and *L'Antijuif*. In the former he explained on 26 August 1920, 'It is not rats, it is Jews imported en masse by the Alliance who are infecting Paris with bubonic plague, typhus, cholera.'[50] Darquier received funds from Nazi Germany for both his organisation, Le Rassemblement Antijuif de France in 1938, and his new paper *La France Enchaînée*, 'defence organisations against Jewish invasion'. Again he argued there that France was a 'Jewish plutocracy', that Jews were comparable to syphilis and that for a cure 'the microbe has to be destroyed ... the limb has to be amputated'. In 1937, Darquier argued that the Jewish problem must be resolved urgently either by expelling Jews or by massacring them. At that time he prescribed what would be the essential features of the 3 October 1940 Statut des Juifs.

On 21 April 1939 the Marchandeau decree was issued; it imposed penalties on those who incited hatred and included anti-Semitism. With poetic justice the decree was quickly invoked against Darquier; he was sentenced to prison for three months for inciting racial hatred. With perverse logic, the Vichy regime, in an early action, abrogated the decree on 27 August 1940. It also rewarded Darquier, who became the second head of the CGQJ, replacing Vallat on 6 May 1942.

Darquier never relented. He survived the aftermath of the war and avoided any punishment by living in exile in Spain. His views never changed; he had learned nothing and regretted nothing. The interview he gave, published in *L'Express* of 28 October–4 November 1978, dramatically illustrated the anti-Semitic obsession. Titled 'Only lice were gassed in Auschwitz', he held that it was a Jewish invention that 6 million Jews had disappeared. 'The photographs of piles of underwear in concentration camp warehouses were faked ... the Jews always lie. The Jews who immigrated into France before the war ... these half-breeds ... wanted our ruin.' Darquier, in his interview, with unamusing irony, had the temerity to say, 'I set myself one goal ... to make the situation of French Jews as comfortable as possible.'

Expressions of Anti-Semitism

A range of publications, both daily and weekly papers, printed anti-Semitic theses, either systematically or more sporadically. The most significant daily, *L'Action Française*, with brilliant writers such as Maurras, Léon Daudet and Maurice Pujo, had a circulation in the mid and late 1930s that varied between 45,000 and 72,000. The larger *L'Ami du Peuple*, owned by François Coty, was intellectually poorer than the AF, but claimed a million readers in 1930 and 460,000 in 1936. Other dailies, publishing occasional anti-Semitic articles, were *Le Jour* with 250,000 readers, *Le Matin* with 313,000 in 1939, *Le Journal* with 410,000 and *La Liberté*, the organ of the PPF.

The most prominent of the anti-Semitic weeklies were *Candide*, *Gringoire* and *Je Suis Partout*. *Candide*, managed by popular historian Pierre Gaxotte, with writers of the calibre of Lucien Rebatet and Louis Bertrand, followed the themes of AF, and in a more lively fashion. In the 1930s its readership increased to about 465,000. *Gringoire*, owned by Horace de Carbuccia and directed by Henri Béraud, had a circulation of some 650,000 in the late 1930s. Anglophobic, admiring Mussolini and Franco, favouring appeasement with Hitler, *Gringoire* violently attacked Jews in general, and Léon Blum in particular. The pro-fascist *Je Suis Partout*, with a constellation of talented writers including Robert Brasillach, Lucien Rebatet and Pierre-Antoine Cousteau, had a circulation varying between 40,000 and 80,000, which rose to about 300,000 in 1944. Its special issues, violently anti-Semitic, of April 1938 and February 1939, were sufficiently successful to be reprinted on a number of occasions. In the latter issue, Rebatet returned to Dreyfus. Whether the latter was guilty or not, he was a calamity for France. The fight against the anti-militarist and anti-clerical Dreyfus clan had to continue.

The writers in this abundance of anti-Semitic papers and journals, though engaged in rivalries and personal ambitions to become the leading figure, presented similar points of view on the question of Jews. Most were young, with well-known older anti-Semites such as Maurras, Daudet, Urbain Gohier and Lucien Pemjean being a small minority. Some of the talented writers were in their twenties in the 1930s. Most of these writers came from the north or Paris, the latter group interacting with militant activists. Most came from middle-class families and were well educated. Activists included doctors, such as Céline and Cousin, lawyers, teachers and ecclesiastics, such as

Mgr Jouin and Canon Schaeffer. They were influenced by the work of important literary figures such as Drieu La Rochelle, Marcel Jouhandeau, Paul Morand, Jean Giraudoux and Robert Brasillach.

A strong bond between the militants in anti-Semitic groups and like-minded literary personnel was military service in French forces in the First World War, in which some were wounded and a number had meritorious records. Nostalgically, many sought to recreate the camaraderie of the war years or to engage in heroic action. Some had difficulty in post-First World War France in finding a suitable job and felt *déclassé*. They felt insufficiently rewarded for their sacrifices in the war, and found a solution to their discontent in anti-Semitism.[51]

But why anti-Semitism? One is aware of fear, jealousy and even hatred of Jews, psychological personal frustration, nostalgia for the past glories of France, and concern for a traditional form of civilisation and way of life, which was supposed to be endangered by Jews. Whether one considers these factors specious or relevant, it is still bewildering to witness the virulence of some of France's renowned writers in their denigration of Jews.

Louis-Ferdinand Céline portrayed Jews as monsters, defective hybrids; Georges Bernanos wrote of a Jewish conspiracy; Drieu La Rochelle of the Jew who incarnates everything that is undesirable; Jean Giraudoux, later to become for a short time Minister of Information and Propaganda, wrote of the hordes who invaded France from Polish and Romanian ghettos and recommended creation of a Ministry of Race. Even the cautious André Gide, a generation earlier on 24 January 1914, confided to his diary that 'it is enough for me that the qualities of the Jewish race are not French qualities'. The best that can be said of these writers is that, whatever else they proposed, they did not envisage extermination.[52]

The activists in anti-Semitic organisations were more varied than their literary counterparts: some were honest and genuine believers in their prejudicial opinions and beliefs, while others had committed crimes of various kinds or were opportunistic adventurers. A number, both personally or on behalf of their organisations, received funding from Nazi Germany. Among these were Marcel Bucard, Darquier, Jean Boissel, Jean Luchaire, Fernand de Brinon and the information agency Prima. Doriot's PPF received funds from Mussolini, though not necessarily from Germany. In addition, Le Service Mondial, the anti-Jewish press agency in Erfurt, was in touch with, and sent documentation to, many French anti-Semitic bodies and people, and saw that their articles were published. Darquier was assisted financially by this organisation.

For the most part, the literary and militant anti-Semites were more measured in France than in Germany; legal action rather than pogroms or violence was the way to deal with the Jewish problem. Many suggestions were made for such actions. The Jewish population in France was held to be too high. Consequently, frontiers should be closed to Jews, especially refugees. Jews given French nationality should lose it, and be given a separate 'Jewish nationality'. All naturalisation of Jews since 1914 should be re-examined. Jews should not only be excluded from government; they should have no political rights, no vote, not be elected, not hold public office. The liberal professions should be closed too, or open only in limited numbers. Property could be confiscated. Mixed marriages should be discouraged. Some even argued that Jews should be expelled, to Madagascar or Palestine.

Mainstream organisations, concerned about the scarcity of jobs and competition from new refugees, advocated discriminatory action. Part of the labour movement opposed granting work authorisations to refugees because they would work for sub-standard wages.[53] Professional groups, lawyers, doctors, merchants, were all anxious to protect themselves against Jewish competition. A law of 19 July 1934, modified in 1936, imposed a delay of ten years on naturalised foreigners before they could hold public office, including membership in the bar. The medical profession, doctors and dentists, was also subject to anti-Semitic regulations. A waiting period, of five years for public practice and four years for private practice, was required for newly naturalised doctors who had not completed their military service; foreign Jews who were not naturalised were completely barred. Even then, the medical associations could be consulted on applications to practise from naturalised foreigners. The Chambers of Commerce, themselves, pressed for more restrictions on naturalisations.

The discriminatory legislation against foreigners had as its main target the recent Jewish immigrants, symbolic embodiments of economic liberalism and political tolerance. The governments of the 1930s, and into 1940, succumbed to pressure from the professional groups who were worried about that liberalism and economic competition. Not surprisingly, members of those groups and occupations that had sought protection from foreigners rather than face competition were the same people to be given advisory or executive roles by the Vichy regime on the issues of work permits and naturalisations.

Politicians arguing a policy of appeasement and concessions to Hitler, such as Foreign Minister Georges Bonnet, who on 6 December 1938 signed a declaration with his German counterpart, Joachim von

Ribbentrop in Paris, that 'peaceful and good neighbourly relations between France and Germany constituted one of the essential elements for general peace', thought that Jews were a danger to that peace. French governments in the 1930s, especially in the two years before the war, fluctuated in their attitudes and policies on refugees. Policies of exclusion and discrimination, especially towards Jewish refugees, adopted in the last years of the Third Republic anticipated the more severe ones of the Vichy regime.[54] Naturalised and foreign individuals were carefully identified and subjected to surveillance, and a central service of identity cards was set up. Already in 1933–4, Prime Minister Daladier spoke of refugees as the 'Trojan horse of spies and subversives'. They could be sent to 'assigned residences'. Five years later, in 1938, his government restricted entry of immigrants and increased police surveillance over those already in France. French police in May 1938 were given power to fine and even imprison illegal immigrants and instructed to send back Jews trying to escape from Germany. Special border police were given this task. Undesirable foreigners without residence or work permits could be expelled. More internment camps were set up.

The Minister of the Interior, Albert Sarraut, in May 1938 ordered the police not to renew identity cards of foreign merchants and artisans wanting to remain in France. A month later, on 17 June 1938, another decree regulated the number of foreigners who could engage in commerce and industry. To start a business, foreigners needed a *carte de commerçant* from the police, and this required consultation with local Chambers of Commerce, which were able to set quotas on the number of foreigners to be allowed into a specific commercial area. A law of 5 April 1935 had obliged foreign garment workers to get an artisan's card, which had to be approved by local craftsmen's associations.

In November 1938, naturalised foreigners were forbidden to vote until they had been citizens for five years. Prefects in certain *départements* of France were given power to expel foreigners with improper papers. Foreigners who had been naturalised could be deprived of French nationality if they were 'unworthy of the title of French citizen'. Foreigners lacking residence or work permits could also be expelled or confined to detention centres. At first those confined in detention centres in 1938 were mostly Italian anti-fascists, Spanish republicans, fighters of the International Brigades in Spain, and later German Jews. For its own reasons the Communist Party was hostile to the refugees; its daily, *L'Humanité*, used the slogan 'France for the French'. As a consequence, communist Jews in 1938 formed their own organisation, the Union des Sociétés Juives.

Yet at the same time a decree of April 1939 allowed foreigners to enlist in the forces: in peacetime, in the army or the Foreign Legion; in war, in the army or the *prestataire* or non-combatant labour service. Government policy was inconsistent, even incoherent. On the one hand, it interned foreigners again after the April decree. On the other hand, it allowed Czechs and Poles to join their own national units in the army, and other nationals to join the Foreign Legion. Thousands of foreigners wanted to volunteer, but Prime Minister Daladier decided on 8 September 1939 that they could enlist only in the Foreign Legion. Confusion continued. At the very same time, in September 1939, all males aged from seventeen up to fifty and, a few days later, up to sixty-five who had come from 'Greater Germany' were ordered to report to assembly centres. All others, men and women, from the assembly centres had to report to police headquarters or city halls to obtain new identity papers and could not leave their neighbourhood without police permission. The outbreak of the war added to the confusion. On 9 September 1939, Albert Sarraut, Minister of the Interior, issued a decree that naturalised foreigners could be deprived of citizenship if suspected of being a danger to the natural security of France. Another decree of 17 September allowed the police to arrest all politically suspect foreigners, and to expel them or put them in an internment camp.

About 18,000 people, 13,000 German and 5000 Austrian refugees, were detained in some eighty internment camps, where they were badly treated. Though some of these 'enemy' nationals were released, many were regarded with suspicion, partly because of the fear of Nazi spies being disguised as Jewish refugees, and partly because of the Nazi–Soviet pact of 23 August 1939, which made communists automatically suspect. Not only were refugees interned; all males of military age had to disembark from neutral ships taking them out of the country. Nevertheless, the government did allow the internees to join the Foreign Legion or *prestataire* service. In the Legion they were put in special units, the Régiments de Marche des Volontaires Étrangers. The tension remained between official and military anti-Semitism and the need for military reinforcements.

With the German invasion in May 1940, another round of arrests and internment of refugees began: German males from seventeen to sixty-five, and for the first time, females up to fifty-five were detained. Some 8000 Germans, of whom 5000 were Jews, were arrested in Paris, many in the provinces, and the 10,000 who had fled from the Low Countries. At that point, some 70 per cent of those interned in camps in southern France were Jews. The over 30,000 foreign Jews who had enlisted were put in the camps or in a Foreign Labourer Group (GTE).

Was all this discrimination and callous indifference to human suffering due to anti-Semitism? Can these last policies of the Third Republic be seen as a prelude to Vichy? Without doubt anti-Semitism, present in so many elements of French society and politics, played a distasteful role. Yet, if the official attitude to Jews in France was ambivalent at best, if the lot of Jewish refugees declined in the period before the German victory, if the talents of the gifted refugees were not used and if conditions in the internment camps bordered on the inhumane, these were also partly the consequence of poor organisation, bureaucratic confusion and muddle, explainable by fear of German or even communist spies and general xenophobia, as well as persecutory intention against Jews. Refugees suffered horribly in 1939 and 1940. Yet the distinction between these conditions and those to be suffered under Vichy is more significant than the resemblance. Republican France did not set the stage for Vichy. That was a drama of a quite different order.

CHAPTER 3

VICHY: THE FRENCH STATE

On 10 May 1940 the German *Wehrmacht* launched its offensive in western Europe, starting in the Low Countries and the Ardennes, and defeating France in thirty-nine days. Marc Bloch, in *Strange Defeat*, explained that the defeat astonished the country and its allies, all of whom were confident of military success because of their superiority in weaponry. But as Ernest R. May has recently pointed out, Germany won its 'strange victory' largely by technical advantages: its war planning was more imaginative; it had better field commanders, especially General Heinz Guderian and General Erwin Rommel; it had good communications; and it was prepared to be innovative on the battlefront.[1]

In advance of the German troops who captured Paris on 14 June, the French government, including Prime Minister Paul Reynaud, and the two chambers of the legislature left the capital on 10 June for Tours and then Bordeaux. Unable to overcome the internal political turmoil, or to change the defeatist attitude of some military leaders, especially General Maxime Weygand, who in May had replaced General Maurice Gamelin as supreme commander, or to handle the panic among the threatened French population, 6 million of whom were on the road, Reynaud unexpectedly resigned on 16 June.

His replacement on that day was Marshal Philippe Pétain, who had been the deputy prime minister for a month; Pétain accepted the position, modestly stating: 'Je fais à la France le don de ma personne pour attenuer son malheur.' (I give to France the gift of my person to attenuate her misfortune.) That *malheur* could only be ended by peace and social order. Bewildered France sought scapegoats to blame for unexpected events.[2] Pétain attributed the defeat to 'moral laxness' and to the fact that France had too few children, too few arms, too few allies. But the soldier and hero of the First World War remembered the four and a half million Frenchmen killed or wounded in that war. He was equally aware that in the six weeks, May to June 1940, the country had lost about 125,000 who were killed, and suffered another 200,000 casualties. Another 1.6 million were prisoners of war. Even if there was no threat of moral collapse, or any lack of moral fibre in the French, Pétain and his new government, which included a number of senior military men, were unwilling for France to suffer further casualties.

France had options. A legal government could leave for its empire in North Africa, or for Britain, to continue the war after having lost a battle. It could capitulate but still continue to fight outside France. It could ask Germany for an armistice. Pétain, pessimistic, defeatist, and mistrustful of France's ally, Britain, spoke of the need to cease combat. So did Weygand, head of the army, who thought resistance was useless and that Britain would soon collapse; he spoke of the British condition, 'le cou tordu comme un poulet' (the neck twisted like a chicken's). Both argued an armistice was necessary to save France, to ensure the integrity of the French Empire and to retain the French fleet.

In his telegram of 17 June 1940 to the British Ambassador in France, Foreign Secretary Anthony Eden saw the danger: 'We cannot contemplate that France ... will add shame to disaster ... Lesser nations, under dire stress, have refused to bow to the dictate of the invader. They have been defeated, but they do not capitulate. Does Pétain think he is reserving any better fate for the French people than by asking them to continue the struggle?'[3] Eden was understandably bitter in view of the Anglo-French agreement of March 1940 that neither country would sign a separate armistice or peace agreement with Germany. Churchill himself, in indirect contact with Pétain, encouraged the French to maintain a maximum of passive resistance to the enemy. He also derided Weygand's gibe with his reference to British courage; 'some chicken, some neck'.

Nevertheless, Pétain did not want to continue the struggle and sought an armistice, which was signed on 22 June 1940 in the forest at Rethondes, the same site used for the armistice ending the First World War in 1918.[4] In his speech of 25 June, written or edited by Emmanuel Berl and justifying the armistice, he called for a new order, inviting his people to 'an intellectual or moral revival first of all'. It was really the first demonstration of weakness. No other country invaded by the Nazis, not Poland, Norway, Denmark or the Low Countries, had asked for an armistice. It was Vichy's original sin.

For Hitler, acting with calculated moderation, the armistice achieved his objectives. France was out of the war; it would have a government that would keep order and prevent resistance against German forces; it would help, if not join, the continuing war against Britain. He did not insist on occupation of all of France, an edict that would have risked a French government going to North Africa and continuing the war; he also allowed France to retain its fleet and empire.

German policy in the conquered countries varied, from total occupation as in the lands east of Germany, Poland, the Baltic states and parts of the Soviet Union, to indirect rule through willing collaborators, either by the existing administration as in Norway, Belgium and the Netherlands, or by a satellite government such as the brutal Ustasha regime in Croatia, or by a partly autonomous regime as in Slovakia and France. In the latter countries the German Nazis, for the most part, did not favour the holding of power by or promotion of local Nazis.[5]

For their part, the French leaders, appeasers, advocates of a policy of conciliation, mostly Anglophobic – a sentiment to be strengthened by the British destruction of the French fleet at Mers el-Kebir on 3 July 1940 when 1300 sailors were killed – believed Britain would be defeated by Germany. Some leaders even accepted the idea of a New Order led by Germany and welcomed the Nazi attack on the Soviet Union on 22 June 1941. Pétain himself spoke of the need for France to 'liberate itself from those friendships and enmities regarded as "traditional"'.[6] That 'liberation' almost immediately became collaboration with Germany.

It also meant a humiliating armistice. France was to send war materials to Germany. The French military were essentially demobilised and disarmed; they became a small number of 100,000 without tanks or heavy artillery. Among the other provisions was Article 19, which called on a French government to 'surrender upon demand' all Germans named by Germany who were living in France, its colonies, protectorates and mandated territories. Pétain hoped, in a specious defence of this edict, that Germany would confine its demands to 'warmongers' of German nationality. No agreement was reached on the 1.6 million French prisoners of war who were obliged to remain in and work for Germany. No peace treaty was ever signed. In Turin, on 25 June, a second armistice agreement was signed with Italy, which had entered the war only two weeks earlier. In return, France was allowed to retain 'sovereignty' with a government, military force and an empire.

In his radio address from London on 26 June 1940, General de Gaulle, the self-appointed leader of the Free French movement, which would not accept the armistice as valid, assured Pétain, M. Maréchal: 'Yes, France will rise again. It will rise in liberty ... in victory ... The day will come when our arms will be triumphant on the national soil.'

During the fighting in the First World War, a number of *départements* in north-east France, with about 10 per cent of France's territory, 12 per cent of France's population and producing a considerable amount of France's industrial output, were occupied and administered, in an oppressive manner, by the German army for four years.[7] The 1940 armistice went much further. France was divided into two major zones, and later, by other arrangements, into a number of other areas.

The larger of the two zones, the 'occupied' or 'northern' zone, about three-fifths of the whole country (25 million people) and including the Atlantic and Channel coasts, Paris and Bordeaux, was put under the direct rule of the German military authorities, who could exercise all rights in the zone. All French authorities and officials would comply with regulations of the German military commanders. This co-operation or collaboration was limited to fulfilling the technical details of the armistice, on disarmament, the security of German forces and the costs of occupation. To cover these costs a war indemnity was imposed of 20 million marks (400 million francs) a day. Since the exchange rate of the German mark was deliberately manipulated and increased by Germany, the actual cost was substantially higher in French currency. The amount was lowered to 300 million francs a day on 10 May 1941, and increased to 500 on 11 November 1942.

The smaller zone, 'free' or 'unoccupied' or 'southern' (14 million people), would be governed by a French authority, which could choose its seat of government including Paris.

The disputed provinces of Alsace and Lorraine, recognised before the war by Germany as within the French border, were soon annexed by Germany and ruled under German law by Gauleiters. As a consequence, 70,000 in the provinces were expelled to the unoccupied zone, and another 140,000 Frenchmen there were conscripted into the German army. Three other small zones in the north, termed 'attached', 'reserved' or 'prohibited' or 'forbidden', were ruled by the Germans. A seventh zone, in south-eastern France, was under Italian occupation.

Rejecting Paris and other probable places such as Lyon, Marseille, Toulouse, Perpignan and Clermont-Ferrand as the seat of government, the political elite moved to Vichy, the small, sleepy spa in central France close to the demarcation zone line. The improbable choice stemmed partly from availability of hotel space for housing and offices, and partly because it was near the Auvergne country home of Pierre Laval, the quintessential embodiment of manipulative politics and intrigue in the Third Republic, soon to be ended. In this resort town of 20,000 where people came to take the sulphurous waters and where the working class, except for the bellboys and maids, was absent, each ministry had its own hotel. Marshal Pétain in the Hôtel du Parc faced the main casino where those seeking cures for rheumatism and liver ailments often spent the night.

On 23 June 1940 the Marshal, now Prime Minister, appointed Laval as his deputy. Convinced that Britain had lost the war, and arguing that a new governmental system more authoritarian than the Third Republic was needed to negotiate with Germany, to bring unity and security, and to safeguard the sovereignty of France, Laval was the main protagonist for change. With ceaseless manoeuvring and incessant machinations, the defeatist Laval, aided by Gaston Bergery, a fellow ex-radical socialist, was persuasive in his lobbying of deputies and senators and in his call for an authoritarian, hierarchical and national system to replace the French parliamentary democracy that he held responsible for the defeat of France.[8]

In a state of political crisis and confusion, the National Assembly – the two chambers of the Senate and Chamber of Deputies – met in the Grand Casino in Vichy on 10 July 1940, and gambled away its existence. It voted to give Pétain *pleins pouvoirs*, full executive and legislative powers, and authority to revise the existing constitutional laws, which in fact was never done in any comprehensive way. Whether the 10 July law was constitutionally illegal in the light of the 1875 constitutional law, or invalid because the country was under foreign occupation, or unacceptable because it denied the deeply rooted idea, habit and affection for republicanism, is still a matter of heated contention. What is not contentious is that no official institution resisted or challenged the introduction of the new political provisions in any way similar to the actions of the Brussels Free University in its strike in 1941.[9]

'The divine surprise', in the words of the counter-revolutionary Charles Maurras, had occurred.[10] After sixty-five years, the democratic, republican regime, which had survived so many economic and political crises, including the Dreyfus affair, and constant governmental instability, ended, and a new system calling itself *l'État Français*, based on the concepts of *Travail, Famille, Patrie*, began on 12 July.

Though the exact figures are sometimes misstated, the vote on 10 July was overwhelming for change: 570 for, 80 against and 20 abstentions, with over 250 of the total 932 not attending. Some in the last group wanted to continue the war. Twenty-seven members of parliament, including Édouard Daladier, Pierre Mendès-France, Jean Zay, Yvon Delbos and Georges Mandel, wanting to set up a government in exile as other western European countries defeated by Germany had done, sailed on 21 June on the ship *Massilia* to North Africa. Four of them decided to join General Charles de Gaulle and the Free French in London. The others were arrested by order of Pétain, and were denounced as traitors by Vichy propaganda. Of the eighty who dissented, twenty-two were imprisoned, ten were deported and five died in concentration camps.

Strikingly, parliamentarians of all political points of view voted in favour, including 54 per cent of socialists and 66 per cent of radical moderates. Of the Communist members, sixty-one did not vote, but eight of the fourteen who did voted for the change. However, a political split is noticeable. The political left made up 91 per cent of the 'no' voters and 80 per cent of the abstentions, while only 5 per cent of the right did not vote 'yes'. During the years of Vichy, about a third of the parliamentarians supported the regime, while the rest engaged in either symbolic opposition or acts of resistance. At Liberation in 1944, an honour jury decided that 321 were ineligible for public office and 182 were excused because of links to the Resistance.[11]

How are we to explain the overwhelming vote for change and the establishment of a new, authoritarian system that the Germans did not demand? Confusion, fear, desire to maintain municipal and local offices, belief it was a provisional arrangement, distress over the military débâcle, especially among the 100 parliamentarians who had served in the forces, eagerness for a New Order for France, all were motivations. Alternatives were disliked or feared: continuation of a Third Republic that was incapable of governing effectively and blamed for losing the war; a possible coup by General Weygand's troops stationed nearby; an insurrection by the PPF, the fascist group led by Jacques Doriot; control by Germany over the whole territory of France; a fascist system, more on Italian than on German lines.

Above all, the providential man, the person whom Pierre Cot and Laval, in 1934, had called 'the best republican general', had appeared. Pétain would save France again, as he had done in the First World War when he halted the German advance on Paris at Verdun in 1916 and ended the mutinies in the French army in 1917. He would unite the country, restore and be the guarantor of social order, prevent a German takeover of the whole country, resist German demands, maintain the integrity of the French Empire, and link the occupied and unoccupied zones. Gertrude Stein, the American writer living in France esteemed for her writing but not renowned for her political wisdom, waxed ecstatic, calling Pétain 'the heroic father of France, the embodiment of the French nation'. This *apologia*, for some literary critics, has led to discussion of the possible links between Stein's modernism, 'apolitical' aesthetics, and right-wing politics.[12] Politics soon took the form of myth as Pétain began a series of rhetorical variations on favourite themes: the chaos of pre-war France to be avoided; the suffering imposed on France and its people; and the necessary work to reconstruct the country along the right path.[13] In spite of his age Pétain was seen as the only person who could speak for France and had the prestige to rule.

The myth took hold, just as over a century earlier it had done for Napoleon, of the indispensable ruler, the individual who would lead France out of its difficulties. Even those who had devoted themselves to republican values succumbed to a coup, as Emmanuel-Joseph Sieyès had done in bringing Napoleon to power, in the belief that there was no better alternative.[14] Vichy France had the dubious honour of being the only country defeated by Germany which had a government run by its own citizens, which established a new regime and which collaborated with the Nazis. Moreover, unlike other defeated countries, France was a historic great power, and one whose boundaries largely, apart from disputed Alsace-Lorraine, remained intact, if much of it was controlled by the Germans. Through actions of its own, France became powerless despite the pretence of maintaining its national sovereignty.

The Start of Vichy

After its vote on 10 July the National Assembly vanished into the dustbin of history. France was left without a national legislative body. A National Council was eventually appointed on 22 January 1941 to help Pétain prepare a new constitution, which was never completed; former parliamentarians made up 77 of its 213 members. Of the 932 former parliamentarians, about 100 became active collaborators and another 200 gave general support to Vichy. The Council was in reality an ineffectual consultative body.

The existing President, Albert Lebrun, never officially resigned, but simply left the political stage. The new regime, the French State, came into existence by the four constitutional acts of 11 and 12 July 1940, and defined the authority of the head of the state, a title Pétain gave to himself. Constitutional Act No. 1 fused the functions of the head of state and the head of government in one person. Constitutional Act No. 2 gave Pétain both executive and legislative powers. Constitutional Act No. 4 allowed him to name his successor. Later, Constitutional Act No. 11 of 18 April 1942 declared that the effective direction of internal and external policy was in the hands of the newly created 'head of government', in fact, Laval. Constitutional Act No. 12 of 17 November 1942 gave the head of government authority, under his own signature, to promulgate laws and decrees. In an improbable reincarnation of Louis XIV, Pétain would embody a concentration of political power: appointing and dismissing ministers, exercising legislative power in the Council of Ministers, promulgating and executing laws and decrees, appointing civil and military officials, granting pardons and amnesties, commanding the armed forces, conducting diplomatic relations and negotiating treaties, and exercising judicial power. The qualification that Pétain could not declare war without the assent of the legislative assemblies was hardly meaningful since the two chambers of the Third Republic were suspended indefinitely, although they were legally preserved.

In the new system there would be no separation of powers, no countervailing legal institutions, no elected assemblies, no general departmental councils, no President of the Republic. In this strong, hierarchical and authoritarian system, the head of state was to be the key legal figure and in theory an absolute monarch. Curiously, very belatedly, Pétain's plenitude of power was challenged by Laval of all people. At his trial after Liberation, Laval argued that the 11 July 1940 law was improper because the Constitutional Act of 10 July had invested both the Marshal and the government with constituent power, though no constitutional act could be passed without Pétain's approval and signature. Certainly, Constitutional Act No. 1 stated that 'The National Assembly gives all powers to the government of *the Republic* [my italics] under the authority and signature of Marshal Pétain.' Yet Constitutional Act No. 11 of 18 April 1942 made Laval head of government, having the right of choosing ministers and having 'effective direction of internal and external policy'. Pétain could not remove a minister without consulting Laval. In effect, for a time the relationship between the two leaders was a premature form of what in the Fifth Republic has been called 'cohabitation'. Constitutional Act No. 12 of 19 November 1942 gave Laval power to promulgate laws and decrees. Pétain largely confined himself to personal appearances in the southern zone.

Vichy, the French State, had replaced the 'Jewish, Masonic, Bolshevik' republic of the Popular Front led by Léon Blum and the Third Republic. Indeed, some ministers and their subordinates associated with the Republic were charged in the new Supreme Court set up on 30 July 1940 with having been responsible for the defeat of France and having betrayed their duties. On this charge, prominent personalities, including Blum, Edouard Daladier and General Gamelin, were put on trial at Riom on 19 February 1942, proceedings that proved to be counterproductive for Vichy.

The Providential Leader

Vichy began with veneration of the new leader. The historian Jean-Pierre Azéma has provided a useful distinction between attitudes of *pétainisme* and *maréchalisme*.[16] The former denotes belief in and support for the ideas and policies of the so-called National Revolution of Vichy, enthusiasm for which was never fulsome and which sharply declined after a year or so. The latter term signified admiration and esteem for the persona and character of the 84-year-old Marshal, *le chef, le père* of his country, who appeared most of the time in uniform. He stood erect, a handsome old man with bright blue eyes and a beautiful white moustache.

Personal appearances by Pétain in many towns in the unoccupied zone brought out thousands of people. In Lyon in November 1940 everyone in the crowd wanted to touch his coat; his journey was like 'the entry into Jerusalem'.[17] As late as 26 April 1944, Pétain was welcomed enthusiastically by a large number, perhaps a million, on his visit to Paris, his first to the city since the defeat of France. He received some 2000 letters a day. Pétain benefited, in a way similar to Hitler, from the distinction made by the population between the 'good' leader and his 'bad' advisers and associates.[18] As with Hitler, few orders came directly from him, with rare exceptions; Pétain tried persuasion by appeal to *mes amis, mes enfants*.[19]

New laws and decrees began with the royal phrase, 'Nous, Philippe Pétain, Maréchal de France'. Coins, postage stamps and banknotes contained the words 'L'État Français' and a profile of the Marshal. His image was to be found on prints, posters, photographs, postcards, pipes, paperweights, pastille tins and calendars, and in school classrooms. As symbolic embodiment of France his bust replaced that of Marianne.[20] Historic parallels were invoked: Pétain was patriotic like Joan of Arc, brave like Seigneur de Bayard, *le Chevalier sans peur et sans reproche*, a commander of troops like King Henri. The official standard of the head of state remained the *tricolore* but it now included seven golden stars below a double-headed axe, the *francisque*, supposedly the weapons of the Franks, founders of the organically French nation.

The cult was reinforced by a later constitutional act of 27 January 1941 which decreed that all members of the government, all high officials and dignitaries of the state must take an oath to the chief of state, 'swear allegiance to his person' and be personally responsible to him.[21] This requirement of an oath of loyalty was extended to the army and magistracy, creating an obvious dilemma for the supposedly impartial courts. Later, on 14 October 1941, the oath was required for all public servants, and then for the prefects.

The man called to greatness had come from a rural, farming background in northern France and was to remain, at least verbally, attached to his roots. For a man who was listed 403 out of 412 in his military training, he had a surprisingly successful career after a slow start. He had become Marshal of France two weeks after the armistice in 1918, member of the prestigious Institut de France in 1919, and of the Académie Française in 1931, succeeding Marshal Foch. He had been vice president of the Supreme War Council, inspector-general of the armed forces, briefly Minister of War in 1934, and the creator of the defensive Maginot Line, since he was opposed to aggressive strategies based on tank and support aircraft, tactics favoured by Charles de Gaulle. He was appointed Ambassador to Spain in 1939, and then in May 1940 recalled by Reynaud to become his deputy prime minister to boost French morale. Cincinnatus had returned to Paris at the age of eighty-four.

A certain paradoxical quality ran through Pétain's life and public persona. The military man who appeared faithful to the Third Republic, the republican general, was crucial in its abolition. The hero who symbolised resistance to Germany in the First World War called for collaboration with the hereditary enemy and refused to leave Vichy when the Germans took over the southern zone of France in November 1942. He was a defeatist, deluding himself there was no obstacle to international collaboration and that France must liberate herself from 'traditional friendships'. The defender of the French African Empire saw it lose its value with the arrival of German troops in Tripoli and German experts in Morocco. The proponent of National Revolution saw traditionalists and nationalists lose power to technocrats and pragmatists. The saviour of his people saw the loss of Alsace and Lorraine, 30,000 shot, 60,000 deported and 76,000 Jews sent to their death. The saviour of France gave a talk in 1941 at the opera between the fourth and fifth acts of *Boris Godunov* which to William Leahy, the American Ambassador, sounded as though it had been written by Hitler. The man who heralded the family as the most important social unit and emphasised the cult of youth was a philanderer who kept trunks full of love letters, did not marry until sixty-four and had no children. The person educated by Jesuits and Dominicans who relied on Catholics for political support was essentially secular.[22] The unideological individual of the political non-extreme right became the proponent of elaborate social and political change. The aloof private person became the centre of adulation and a cult object. The elderly restorer of traditional communities also introduced organisations to foster a new kind of youth. The honest, upright soldier claimed that, as head of state, he played a 'double game', privately resisting the German occupiers. The embodiment of power implied at the end that discriminatory acts of the regime were performed by others. The honoured general of the First World War never understood the ideological dimensions of the Second World War, the world conflict or the true nature of the Nazi regime. The man of the past whose strategic and political ideas had been crystallised by his experiences in the First World War could not recognise that Hitler was a modern version of Attila, not Bismarck. The national hero on 22 June 1942 expressed his wish for a German victory in the war. The would-be saviour who constantly invoked the sacred law of national unity presided over a repressive regime that divided the nation. The leader of a discriminatory regime delivered speeches on the virtues of simple, peasant life written by Emmanuel Berl, a half-Jewish Paris intellectual, the husband of the Jewish popular singer Mireille, who later fled France to avoid persecution. The leader concerned about the 1.6 million French prisoners of war in Germany himself became on 20 August 1944 a virtual prisoner in Sigmaringen, former home of the princes of Hohenzollern and the place chosen personally by Hitler for Pétain, who shared the town with, among other people, the scoundrels of the Milice.

The career of the 89-year-old Pétain, wearing uniform at his trial, ended tragically on 15 August 1945 when he was found guilty of intelligence with the enemy. He was condemned to death – the twelfth French Marshal to be so condemned – deprived of civic rights, including loss of rank and honours, and accorded national degradation. The death sentence was commuted two days later by Charles de Gaulle, his former pupil, colleague and rival, to life imprisonment. Pétain died in a fortress on the Île d'Yeu, off the Atlantic coast, at the age of ninety-five, in 1951.

De Gaulle's action can be construed either as magnanimity or political realism. On 2 August 1940 de Gaulle had been condemned to death *in absentia* by Vichy for desertion, and he was stripped of French nationality on 8 December 1940. Nevertheless, in 1968 on 11 November, President de Gaulle laid a wreath on the tomb of Pétain, paying homage to 'the victor of Verdun'; his presidential successors followed this gesture until 1992.

Pétain deceived himself to the end. Like his heroine, Joan of Arc, whom he termed 'the martyr of national unity',[23] he would save the nation, even if it meant sacrifices and suffering, especially against the perfidious British. Indeed, the British Ambassador to France, Sir Ronald Campbell, reported to London that Pétain was 'a character of transparent simplicity, tinged with a vanity which was in itself relieved by a devastating candour'.[24] At his trial in 1945, Pétain objected that the High Court of Justice, which was trying him, did not represent the French people. On the contrary, he declared that he had been the heir to a catastrophe for which he was not responsible, he had been begged to take power, and he had used this power as a shield to protect the French people, while de Gaulle had been the sword of France; for France's sake Pétain had sacrificed his personal prestige. He congratulated himself that he had preserved an unhappy but living France; he had saved the French Empire, and he represented traditional French and Christian civilisation, which resisted the excesses of tyrannies. About Jews he said nothing.

In fact, Pétain had welcomed the call to power, believing he would restore the former glory of France, 'eternal France', recompose the national soul, regroup organically French society, restore cohesion, reform the internal political and social system, and maintain French sovereignty. Neither an extreme ideologue, nor a personal dictator making unilateral decisions, nor the leader of a single, monopolistic political party, Pétain's political approach rested on a few basic principles: family, duty, property and patriotism. He delivered moral sermons rather than imposed ideological concepts. He was obsessed by the need for order and discipline.

What was Vichy?

How should the Vichy regime be classified in terms of comparative analysis? It does not fit into the classic tripartite typology of the political right in France, legitimists, Orléanists and Bonapartists, formulated by René Rémond.[25] Nor is it an obvious example of indigenous French fascism.

For some years controversy about fascism in France has been acute, even reaching the French courts in libel cases. The concept of fascism, so often used polemically or as a pejorative insult, has been notoriously difficult to define, either as a set of ideas or in assessing a given political system. The fundamental difficulty stems from the particularistic variations and historical specificities of parties, movements, individuals or states designated as fascist. Each fascist country had it own particular style. German Nazism with its racial and anti-Semitic emphasis is clearly different from Fascist Italy with its basis in the role and power of the state.

How did fascism arise, intellectually or politically? At one extreme is the view that fascism stems from the political left. It is seen as derived from the radicalism of the French Revolution, populist and plebeian.[26] Essentially, anti-bourgeois and anti-establishment, it was a mid-twentieth-century form of neo-socialism. The strongest proponent of this view, Zeev Sternhell, argues that fascism as a set of beliefs originated in France at the turn of the century and was a radical leftist rather than a right-wing ideology. Critics of Sternhell may accept that conservative French thought was permeated to some extent by fascist ideas, but still insist that fascism is not native to France or that it was marginal and limited to a few intellectuals and political mavericks.[27] Whether one accepts or denies the perspective that France was the birthplace of fascist concepts, different French writers did advance a radical ideology combining emphatic nationalism with a variety of forms of socialism and new social relationships, a kind of cultural revolt against the liberalism, rationalism and humanism of the Enlightenment.

Was Vichy a fascist system because of the intellectual current flowing through it? Pétain himself at one moment seemed to imply this when writing in, or having his name appended to, an article in *Revue des Deux Mondes* of 15 September 1940 that when France examined 'the principles which have assured the victory of her adversaries ... she would be surprised to recognise throughout them her own works, her purest and most authentic tradition'.

Analysts from different political perspectives have made similar, seemingly plausible arguments. For Sternhell, the fount of fascism is to be found in French writers in early twentieth-century France. For the influential *littérateur*, Thierry Maulnier, 'our political theorists, from Maurras to Sorel, have been the guiding lights of contemporary revolutions'.[28] The German historian Ernst Nolte argued, controversially, that the Action Française was an archetype of fascism because of its similar themes: exalted nationalism, anti-Marxism, anti-capitalism, corporatism, hierarchy, state definition of individual rights, elitism, ties of family, anti-democracy, cult of the leader and a New Order.[29] For some French intellectuals – Emmanuel Mounier, Bertrand de Jouvenel, Jules Romain, Drieu La Rochelle – fascism was intermittently a magnetic attraction.[30]

At the other extreme of the discussion on the origin of fascism is the more traditionally accepted view that fascism, including Nazism, is the product of the radical right, fundamentally anti-left in its origin, and welcome to conservatives if their economic and social interests are threatened.[31] Fascism, in the Marxist view, might thus be considered as an attempt by the middle class to hold down or suppress the political and economic aspirations of the working class.

Disputes over the origin, intellectual or political, of fascism do not prevent more general agreement on the nature of a fascist political system. The 'ideal-type' of such a system would include a call for a unified society, in which class struggles were eliminated or overcome, and reconciliation between employers and workers would exist. Stress on unity meant on the one hand heightened nationalism, and, on the other, elimination of those organisations, parties and trade unions that might challenge that unity, and the removal of those individuals and groups that were 'outsiders', incapable or not worthy of being part of the national community.

Institutionally, the system would be marked by a dominant, often charismatic, leader, by a single political party which sought a mass membership, by paramilitary groups, by highly organised demonstrations, parades, insignia, uniforms and ceremonies inducing enthusiasm, by mobilisation of all citizens from children on, by resort to violence against 'enemies', by the use of terror and concentration camps, by discrimination against those regarded as undesirable, by an ideology regarded as the fount of truth, past, present and future, by a hierarchical political structure, and by the claim for the leading party or the state to exert control over all aspects of life and for individuals and groups to be subordinated to that control.

By criteria of this kind Vichy was not a totalitarian system, monolithic bloc or reactionary static polity. Some resemblances to the Nazi and Fascist systems are apparent. Vichy did emphasise national unity, it did limit and control public political criticism, it did censure papers and journals, it did ban critical political parties, it did end independent organisations of workers and employers, it did dissolve the lodges of Freemasons. It did have official news agencies – Havas-OFI, Radio Diffusion Nationale, Radio Vichy, a single film company – and used meetings, the cinema and posters for propaganda purposes. It had no freely elected legislative body or local councils. It did try to enrol people, especially youngsters, in para-official or paramilitary organisations: the most prominent were the Légion Française des Combattants, the Compagnons de France and the Jeunes du Maréchal. The Légion according to General Emile Laure, its inspector-general, was to be a great assemblage of Frenchmen knowing only one order, duty.

The list of similarities can continue, intellectually and organisationally. Vichy was critical of both capitalism and socialism. It engaged in and initiated discriminatory measures and actions; it excluded whole categories of people, for political, ideological or racial reasons, from membership in the French community, which would be reborn with desirable values.[32] The 'enemies' – Jews, foreigners, Freemasons, communists – would be purged. Vichy helped the Nazis implement the Holocaust, the 'Final Solution'.

Like the Nazi and Fascist regimes, if to a lesser degree, Vichy intervened, or mostly envisaged intervening, in many areas, in industry, agriculture, urban affairs, law, education, and the family, to change society. It combined anti-industrial nostalgia with some economic planning, tradition with science, order with movement, gerontocracy with technocracy.[33] It did not advocate a simple return to the past. It called for national reconciliation of classes and for a corporative system, based on *comités d'organisation*, that would overcome class divisions.

The Vichy system concentrated power, at least legally, in Pétain, the self-appointed head of state. It emphasised the concept of leadership through key executive officials and technocrats. It created exceptional courts to render swift and imperfect justice. It established special police units to harass and hunt down Jews and resisters. Vichy resembled Nazi Germany in the way its style of governing mirrored that of Hitler, who in a highly modern state without any central co-ordinating body acted as a 'head of government largely disengaged from the machinery of government'.[34]

Yet, the differences between Vichy and the totalitarian systems were even more apparent. Vichy had no overarching ideology resembling a secular religion, which purportedly would explain the past, understand the present and determine future policy. Pétain's homilies, mixtures of traditionalism and populism, were brief, grand-fatherly messages to his people. Vichy did not employ techniques or rely on mystique to garner support for political policies. It did not attempt mass mobilisation for desired ends. Its strong scouting movement emphasis was not the equivalent of the Nazi or Fascist youth movements and Vichy had no one youth movement. Though it tried, with modest success, to create a single powerful veterans' organisation, it did not have a one-party system in which that party dictated ideas and actions. Pétain rejected the manifesto calling for a single mass party written in July 1940 by Gaston Bergery and signed by seventy other supporters of Vichy.

The Vichy leader, though the recipient of loyalty, was not the unique, automatic initiator of crucial policies. The system did not assert, or try to assert, total control over all areas of life or impose aesthetic controls over art and films. It did not orchestrate any series of dramatic extravaganzas or demonstrations intended to induce support, instil fear or whip up emotions. It was not a reactionary regime, nor did it envisage a restoration of the monarchy, nor was it a Catholic polity. It had no coherent ideology calling for a future modernised society or for a new, more desirable form of personality. Vichy maintained some symbols of the republican tradition: Bastille Day, the 'Marseillaise', the tricolour flag. It did not introduce or promulgate a new constitution, through it made some organisational changes. Not until 1944 did French fascists enter the government, under strong pressure from the Germans.

It is too strong to argue that French political culture was saturated
in 1940 by fascist ideology. The appeal of fascism for some literary
intellectuals and activists was not a serious threat to the Third
Republic or a credible political alternative after the defeat. Indeed, it
was the French fascists in Paris, above all Marcel Déat and Jacques
Doriot, who were critical of Pétain for not implementing an ideological
or totalitarian regime. If Pétain had any kind of model system in mind,
it was more akin to a corporative regime or to Salazar's *Estado Novo*
in Portugal.[35] A corporative system is one in which, theoretically,
producers, employers and workers are represented by corporations
which regulate output in the interests of all concerned under the
effective guidance of the state.[36] The Portuguese constitution under
the Estado Novo (1933) stated that 'in the corporate organisation, all
branches of the nation's activities shall be represented through their
association in the corporative organisation ... the state shall promote
the formation and development of the national corporative economic
system'. According to Salazar, the constitution was not based on a
totalitarian conception, but 'established the moral law and justice as
limits to its own sovereignty'.[37] To create such a corporative system in
Vichy, professional associations were set up as autonomous entities,
starting in October 1940 with doctors, pharmacists and dentists and
then embracing other professions. In theory, they regulated themselves, making their own rules and conditions of entry. In practice, the
corporativist concept was not always implemented. The National
Revolution was the attempted extension of the concept to the
population as a whole.

The Vichy Mixture

Vichy took on different colourations during its four-year existence as
a result of the varying military balance between Germany and the
Allies in the war, the demands made on France, and the Franco-
German relationship. Different individuals and groups played
important roles at particular times, a diversity that led some to define
the regime as a 'pluralistic dictatorship'.[38] Certainly, this diversity of
individuals and groups embraced a very wide array of political
positions, past and present. It could be expected that Vichy would be
approved and supported by the various parts of the diverse political
right whose common theme was anti-communism. Included were
traditional conservatives; financial and industrial groups; authori-
tarians such as Xavier Vallat and Jean Ybarnégaray; counter-
revolutionaries led by Charles Maurras and including Raphaël Alibert
taking revenge on the Popular Front of 1936, military leaders such as

Weygand, General Léon Huntziger and Admiral Darlan; Catholics, conservative or hostile to the past secular regime, such as Georges Lamirand, Jean le Cour Grandmaison, President of the National Catholic Federation, and General de la Porte du Theil; a host of anti-republicans; classical humanists such as Thierry Maulnier; and the rather small number of devoted fascists such as Jacques Doriot, Jacques Benoist-Méchin, Paul Marion and Joseph Darnand; and Nazi sympathisers such as Fernand de Brinon.

Yet support for and approval of Vichy went far beyond these anti-parliamentary, anti-democratic, and anti-leftist groups and personnel, many of whom shared prejudicial opinions, anti-Semitic beliefs and attitudes, as well as confidence in Pétain as the desirable leader. That additional support and approval came from pacifists, the main-stream left, neo-socialists, communists, syndicalists, nationalists, technocrats and engineers and some Protestants.[39] Authentic members of the mainstream left who supported Vichy included Charles Spinasse, former socialist Minister of the Economy, and Paul Faure, former head of the Socialist Party. The most prominent of the syndicalists, who included Georges Dumoulin and Pierre Vigne, was René Belin, former leading figure of the CGT, the main trade union, who was to become Minister of Labour in July 1940. Others coming from or originally part of the left were neo-socialists such as Marcel Déat and Adrien Marquet, former communists such as Angelo Tasca, and former radicals such as Gaston Bergery, a former member of the Chamber of Deputies. Moderate radicals included Pierre-Étienne Flandin, former minister in the Third Republic, Joseph Barthélemy, renowned jurist, deputy and journalist, and Lucien Romer, journalist with Le Figaro. Most shared a policy of pacifism, and all were anti-communist.

Another important group of supporters or adherents were the technocrats, who for a time were to play an important role in Vichy; they included Pierre Pucheu, Jean Bichelonne, Jacques Barnaud and François Lehideux. The technocrats were the indispensable cogs in the Vichy regime; they ensured rational, if perverse, administration. Jacques Benoist-Méchin became secretary of state of the Council of Ministers, dealing primarily with Franco-German collaboration. Jacques Barnaud, close to the Worms bank and founder of the journal Nouveaux Cahiers, became head of the ministerial cabinet of Réne Belin, Minister of Labour. Paul Marion became head of information services. François Lehideux, close to the car manufacturer Léon Renault, became Minister of Industrial Production in August 1941.

One of the key figures in this group was Pierre Pucheu (1898–1944), born poor in Algeria, a successful businessman and an expert in metallurgy. Believing that France needed a strong national state and social programmes to deal with unemployment, and rejecting both capitalism and socialism, Pucheu was attracted first to La Rocque's national volunteers and then to Doriot's PPF, which was financed by industry and banks. Pucheu left it in 1938 on finding it was also financed by Mussolini.

In Vichy, Pucheu became Minister of Industrial Production and then Minister of the Interior from July 1941 until April 1942. In that position he imposed harsh controls on Jews, communists and anarchists, and fostered the creation of the Special Sections of the police. His most notorious action, on 20 October 1941, was to select hostages, supposedly the most dangerous interned communists, who were to be executed by the Germans; he sent the list to General Otto von Stulpnagel, the military commander.[40] By the end of Pucheu's tenure, over 40,000 French people were imprisoned, and another 30,000 had been killed by the Germans or their Vichy accomplices. On Laval's return to power in April 1942, Pucheu resigned and left France for North Africa. Arrested in Casablanca, he was tried by the French Committee for National Liberation, sentenced to death 'by the French people' and executed in March 1944. The conundrum remains: why did gifted administrators such as Pucheu lose their moral compass and go so wrong?

Negative combinations in politics, as de Tocqueville once observed, are more potent than positive ones. The heterogeneous supporters of Vichy agreed on little except the need to break with the past, create a new kind of society and struggle against communism. At some moments especially at the beginning of the Vichy regime, personal friends of Pétain were influential; the most notorious was the sinister Dr Bernard Ménétrel, the *éminence grise* who fed him prescription drugs. Some of Pétain's friends, though not his best friends, were Jewish, especially Jacques Rueff, former Vice-Governor of the Bank of France, and the apparently half-Jewish Ludovic-Oscar Frossard.

In the summer of 1940, the most important of these friends was Raphaël Alibert (1887–1963), an early adviser and key figure in formulating the first anti-Semitic laws. Catholic, a well-known professor of constitutional law, a prominent legal personality as *maître des requêtes* between 1923 and 1934, Alibert was active in both business and politics, where he suffered electoral defeats due, he thought, to his enemies.[41]

From 1936 Alibert was a close associate of Pétain, visiting the Marshal, then French Ambassador in Madrid, in October 1939 to suggest that Pétain become prime minister. When the latter was recalled to Paris to join the government, Alibert became director of his political cabinet in May 1940 and was appointed Minister of Justice in July. Alibert, who argued strongly against the government moving to North Africa to continue the war, assisted Laval in drafting the 10 July 1940 constitutional law, granting *pleins pouvoirs* to Pétain, and other constitutional documents. Although he preferred a monarchy, Alibert was satisfied by notions of authority, order, respect and discipline. Disliked by others in Pétain's entourage, Alibert, convinced of his own indispensability, was regarded as megalomanic, quarrelsome, hot-headed and indiscreet. He was a relentless anti-Semite, 'a maniac of anti-Semitism', largely responsible for the first Statut des Juifs of 3 October 1940, about which both Laval and Darlan were hesitant. For Alibert, unlike Laval, this strong discriminatory anti-Semitic legislation was not only desirable in itself, it also demonstrated that France could act as a sovereign state exercising control over people in its territory.

A month later, on 20 November 1940, the Minister of Justice issued a circular demanding a list of Jewish magistrates, who would be dismissed. A revealing comment on Alibert's policies came from a fellow anti-Semite, Xavier Vallat. Alibert, he said, was only adhering to a policy that found its source in a long national tradition, and also its justification in the position taken throughout the centuries by the Church with regard to the Jewish problem.[42] The wine of power was too heady for Alibert, who saw himself as Pétain's successor. However, he was forced out of office in January 1941, and entered the Conseil d'État. After the war he hid abroad and was condemned to death *in absentia* and to confiscation of property in March 1947, but he was amnestied in February 1959.

Assisting Alibert in the anti-Semitic measures, but later disclaiming his role, was Marcel Peyrouton, with good credentials as a traditional republican, a more open person than Alibert, an individual with a Scottish mother, a public official father and an association with freemasonry, which he was soon to repress. In July 1940, Peyrouton became Minister of the Interior, and signed and collaborated on racial measures, though he claimed not to be anti-Semitic himself. His actions belied this. His ministerial circular of 7 November 1940 called on prefects to provide in their *départements* a list of police officials who were considered to be Jewish. He advocated that the 3 October 1940 Statut be applied with rigour, that Jewish doctors be barred from hospitals, and that there be a strict interpretation in Paris of the bans on Jews in other professions and public positions. This was typical of his authoritarian inclinations, which were manifested in his belief that France should be governed without interference from elected officials, and in his consequent role in the abolition of both municipal and *départemental* councils.[43] France could be governed as if it were a colonial country.

Not surprisingly, the German military occupiers, concerned more with rational and efficient management of the country than with ideological conformity to Nazism, preferred in their northern zone to deal with such traditional intermediaries rather than with the extreme Paris fascists or the strong proponents of the National Revolution, who had little contact with the population at large. They were willing to rely on competent former officials of the Third Republic, including socialists, and even the Communist Party in the summer of 1940, to facilitate administrative orders.[44]

Assessment of Vichy has to reflect the changes in personnel and in direction of policy over time due to internal political differences, external pressure from the Germans, and the decline in public support for the regime. At the beginning Vichy was an authoritarian state with overtones of the Salazar regime in Portugal and that of Franco in Spain. By the last year, 1944, the regime had become subject to control by extremist ideologues, more sympathetic with Nazi views and oppressive behaviour and more violent towards Jews, resisters and communists. An embryonic fascist system was in the making.

Critics of the Third Republic always focused on its political instability and constant changes in ministerial positions. Yet Vichy was little different. A few changes of officials, such as the dismissal or resignation of Weygand in September 1940 and Xavier Vallat in May 1942, and the return of Laval in April 1942, resulted from German pressure, but most changes stemmed from the acrimonious internal rivalries in Vichy.[45] Pétain remained head of state for the whole of the regime and in 1940 was also the acknowledged head of government with Laval as deputy head from 12 July 1940 until 13 December. After a brief interregnum, François Darlan replaced Laval on 23 February 1941, remaining as Deputy Prime Minister and also Foreign Minister, Defence Minister and Dauphin to the head of state. Bringing technocrats and experts to replace the traditional right-wing officials in government positions, Darlan remained until 18 April 1942 when he in turn was replaced by Laval. Darlan and Laval were both political opportunists, not ideologues, who made the fatal mistake of assuming that Germany had won the war. By December 1942, Pétain had virtually handed over all legislative and political power to Laval. A year later Laval had to bring extremists into the government, with Joseph Darnand becoming Minister of the Interior.

Why did these extremists emerge? Pétain was the French Micawber, always waiting for something good to turn up. His 'new France', his 'New Order' with the National Revolution was supposed to be incomparably better than the previous Republican regime. The early optimism began to fade as problems accumulated, the National Revolution remained a pious aspiration, and the mood of the country, and of Pétain himself, darkened: 'The present is indeed dark,' Pétain confessed on 12 August 1941. The 'evil wind' was blowing through France.[46] Controls over the lives of citizens and continuing discrimination led many to reconsider support for Vichy. Nationalists found subjection to Germany intolerable. Anti-German sentiments were stronger than approval of the National Revolution. With the German entrance into the previously unoccupied zone in November 1942, and the growing Allied military successes in North Africa, France, by the end of 1942 totally occupied, its empire decreasing and its fleet scuttled, could hardly make a pretence of being a sovereign state. Few could now doubt the disparity between the grandiloquent claims of sovereign authority and the sordid realities of the political world and Hitler's dream of making Europe a collection of colonial dependencies.

By 1944, active support of Vichy was limited to extremists and militants of the political right, who saw Jews and Freemasons as the main enemies of France. Their chief spokesmen and activists were Joseph Darnand, Philippe Henriot, Marcel Déat and members of the Milice, not publicly criticised by Pétain until 6 August 1944. They dominated the last year of Vichy, controlling the maintenance of order, the penal administration and the media, especially the radio, and performing acts of violence and assassinations against Jews and members of the Resistance. Collaborators wielded the instruments of power. Others left Vichy or were dismissed. For them collaboration had not brought the promised or hoped-for results.

The heterogeneous *mélange* of people and groups supporting Vichy was indicative of an inherent ambivalence as Vichy evolved through different periods. In broad terms, four stages can be observed: traditional orientation from July 1940 to February 1941; influence of technocrats under Darlan from February 1941 to April 1942; virtual dictatorship and increasing repression under Laval from April 1942 to August 1944; final collapse and phantom government from September 1944 to April 1945.

During those periods the ambivalence wavered between behaviour pattern, personnel, and policies reflecting traditional values embodied by Pétain himself, and counter-revolutionary and fascist concepts on one side. On the other were the modernists, technocrats, senior officials, prefects, captains of industry, proposing new solutions for political and economic problems.

Anti-capitalist rhetoric might be voiced but rarely did it lead to action. Administrative regionalism was advocated but centralisation of power became more pronounced. By a law of 17 July 1940 all state officials could be dismissed by ministerial decree; 35,000 were dismissed. Prefects were given increased power including the nomination of mayors in towns with under 50,000 inhabitants. An oath to Pétain was taken by senior officials and legal personnel.

The Political Leaders

Pierre Laval (1883–1945), born in a small village in the Auvergne, began his career as a lawyer defending trade unionists and individuals of the political left. In 1914 he was elected by a Paris working-class area to be a socialist member of the Chamber of Deputies. Belonging to the pacifist wing of the Socialist Party, he urged a negotiated peace to end the First World War, and was one of the fifty-three deputies who voted in 1919 against the Treaty of Versailles, which ended it. His name typified his politics: a palindrome that worked both ways. Laval was a political weather vane, perpetually mobile, but always resting on the same base, himself, the Talleyrand of Aubervilliers. His political career reflected personal ambition, shrewd bargaining and relentless intrigue, and an absence of any real set of principles, except perhaps a pessimistic pacifism, a dislike of Britain, a dread of war and an aspiration for Franco-German reconciliation. Quickly leaving the Socialist Party, he moved to the centre right, becoming mayor of Aubervilliers in 1923, retaining this position throughout his life, and becoming a deputy from the town the next year, and a senator from the area in 1927.

Though mistrusted by almost everyone in the political world, the ugly, short, dishevelled, chain-smoking, swarthy, saturnine Laval, nicknamed the 'Jamaican' and always wearing his trademark white tie, was one of the indispensable *ministrables* of the inter-war years, serving in eighteen ministerial positions after 1925, twice as Prime Minister, in 1931–2 and 1935–6, when he also acted as Foreign Minister. In the latter position, eager to reach a *rapprochement* with Italy and to avoid war, he advanced a policy of appeasement when he agreed, together with the British Foreign Minister Samuel Hoare in December 1935, to approve Mussolini's annexation of part of Ethiopia. At his end, accused of being a war criminal, he sardonically replied that he would rather be a criminal of peace.[47]

In June and July 1940 Laval was a crucial player, pressing for an armistice and organising the machinations to change the political system. To his inherent pacifism was added the argument that Germany had won the war and that France must adapt to this reality and play a strong role, helped by its navy and its empire, in the new German-dominated Europe. On 12 July the seemingly indispensable Laval was appointed Pétain's dauphin, successor, as well as his deputy head of government. Palace intrigue and political infighting in Vichy, however, led to his dismissal in December 1940.

Largely because of German pressure, Laval returned to office on 17 April 1942 as head of government. He was now the real effective political power, taking over a number of ministerial portfolios in the regime, but it was his unfortunate destiny to lead Vichy in a period of increasing subjugation. He acquiesced in German demands for French workers to be sent to German factories. In his most infamous speech, on 22 June 1942, calling for French volunteers to go to Germany, Laval expressed his hope for a German victory in the war. Though not apparently anti-Semitic himself, and though he had taken no part in drafting anti-Semitic legislation, he ratified the arrangements for the arrest and deportation of both French and foreign Jews to their death.

After the Allied landing in France, Laval was sent to Germany, tried to enter Switzerland and then fled to Spain, from where he returned to France. After a speedy, six-hour trial, Laval was found guilty of high treason and complicity with the enemy and sentenced to death. Failing in an attempt to poison himself in prison, he was executed on 15 October 1945.

Defenders or hagiographers of Pétain, who admire the Marshal for putting the needs of the state before his own personal interests, see Laval by contrast as the symbolically designated villain. Yet, even if Laval was a self-interested manipulator, this argument essentially denies or mitigates the responsibility of Pétain for the actions of the regime. Laval himself always believed he had kept France out of further hostilities and that the occupation by Germany would have been even more cruel without him. Differences between Pétain and Laval were those of degree; the Marshal remained the key to the system.

Pierre-Étienne Flandin (1889–1958) was a stopgap Foreign Minister in Vichy for about two months. A lawyer, leader of a conservative centre group in the Third Republic, he was a deputy from 1914 to 1940, a minister several times, and Prime Minister in 1934–5. In July 1940 he was unenthusiastic about Laval's proposal to abolish the Third Republic, preferring that Pétain replace the then President, Albert Lebrun, in that role, but in the end he did vote for the new system. He was appointed Foreign Minister on 13 December 1940, pledged to continue political and economic collaboration with the Germans, but had little influence and soon resigned. His main contribution was persuading Pétain in January 1941 to create a National

Council.[48] In 1946 the French High Court acquitted him of treason, but convicted him on a lesser charge. His sentence of five years of 'national degradation', however, was commuted because of his help to the Resistance in the latter part of the war.

Flandin was a typical republican politician gone wrong. A more enigmatic figure was Laval's successor, Admiral François Darlan (1881–1942), a short man with an irregular nose. This patriotic republican, left of centre politically, had opposed the pre-war policy of appeasement, had supported the Anglo-French alliance, and had cordial relations with the Royal Navy. He rose to the political top in Vichy, and collaborated with the Germans, not because of any Nazi sympathy or inclinations, but in what he perceived was the interest of France because Germany would win the war against Britain.

Originally a radical socialist and a Freemason from a small town in south-western France, son of a *notaire* and minor political figure, Darlan's career was largely spent in ministerial offices, not on the sea – he was known as the *amiral au mouillage* (the admiral at anchor) – dealing with and constantly urging the case for French naval supremacy. Promoted in 1937 to the rank of Admiral of the Fleet, Darlan was Commander-in-Chief of the Navy during the war. After appointment as Pétain's Minister of Marine Affairs in June 1940, Darlan faced the crucial decision on the disposition of the French fleet. He had promised Churchill it would not fall into the hands of Hitler. But unwilling for it to go to the former British ally, he sent it to North Africa. Churchill, fearing the worst, ordered its destruction on 3 July 1940 at Mers el-Kebir in Algeria. For Darlan this put an end to his friendly relations with the British navy and also put him on the path towards accepting Vichy.[49]

Darlan acted as deputy head of government and heir apparent from 10 February 1941 until 18 April 1942, after which he became head of the Armed Forces and High Commissioner in North Africa. Not an ideological adherent of fascist or extreme right views, Darlan can best be understood as a military man, if one with luxurious personal tastes and extravagant demands, concerned above all to defend and maintain French sovereignty and French maritime power and to retain the French Empire.

During his tenure, Darlan met Hitler twice. He embraced collaboration in the military as well as in the general political area. After meeting with Hitler on 11 May 1941 in Berchtesgaden, Darlan broadcast that only with a victorious Third Reich would the French nation be saved and able to play an honourable, even important, role in the Europe of the future. Two weeks later, on 27–8 May, he signed the Protocols of Paris, three military and one political agreements.

The first, confirming an earlier agreement, allowed the German Luftwaffe to use airfields in Syria. The second allowed the Germans to use the port of Bizerte in Tunisia and the Tunis–Gabès railroad to supply Rommel's army in North Africa. The third authorised access for German ships or submarines and commerce in the port of Dakar. The 'political' accord dealt with German concessions on food, prisoners of war and demarcation lines in North Africa. Darlan approved a Franco-German aircraft production deal. He offered naval intelligence to Admiral Erich Raeder in January 1942. With his detestation of Britain, he allowed Germany to use in Syria, still under French mandated rule, airfields and military supplies that had been made in France, to help the seizure of power by the pro-Axis Iraqi nationalist Rashid Ali against the British in April 1941. In response in June the British, accompanied by some of General de Gaulle's forces, attacked Syria and defeated the Vichy troops there. Darlan's policy had lost Vichy another part of the French Empire.

On coming to power Darlan dismissed a number of people, including Raphaël Alibert, Marcel Peyrouton and Jacques Chevalier, who had been part of the clique responsible for overthrowing Laval in December 1940. In their place he substituted individuals with administrative backgrounds, technocrats, people from the worlds of business, finance and the military. With them Darlan attempted to strengthen administrative control in a number of ways: by national control over municipal police forces, by setting up regional prefects and by centralising control over information and youth organisations. The appointment of technocrats or experienced administrators to political positions was to become familiar in the early years of the Fifth Republic, but at this time it was a novel departure from the practice of the Third Republic. At the time some in Vichy talked of the Synarchie, a supposed secret economic society, in which people from the business world and the Worms bank were influential, which was set up for technocrats to take over power. In reality it was a kind of pressure group for technocrats such as Jacques Rueff and Jean Bichelonne, to influence policy. Darlan's star began to fade when in late 1941 he failed to get a peace treaty of co-operation from Germany, and when growing action by the Resistance led to greater German reprisals.

On the Jewish question, Darlan's stewardship can be held ultimately responsible for the second Statut des Juifs of 2 June 1941, for the participation in the Aryanisation process and for the creation of the Commissariat Général aux Questions Juives (CGQJ) on 29 March 1941. He can claim credit for trying to protect Jewish veterans and Jewish families long resident in France, and for resisting the

German demand that Jews wear the yellow star on their clothing. Yet German Ambassador Otto Abetz reported, 'Darlan has shown himself ready to let the French government bear the responsibility for the founding of a central *Judenamt* while Pétain showed a certain amount of vacillation.'[50]

Darlan remains an ambiguous and perplexing figure. Dismissed from his leadership position in Vichy on 18 April 1942 he switched to the Allied side in November 1942 when, claiming to have assumed authority in North Africa in the name of Pétain, he ended resistance to the Anglo-American landing there and spoke of French participation in a renewed war against Germany. The puzzled American commanders, and for a moment President Roosevelt, recognised him as the *de facto* head of the French government, though six months earlier he was still prepared as military commander to oppose such a landing. Was he politically naive, a technocrat out of his depth, or an ambitious, intriguing manipulator who had no strong allegiance to people or policies, or a sincere, pragmatic patriot who was misguided in his perception of national interest and pragmatic policies? Even his end is puzzling. Was his assassination on Christmas Eve 1942, a month after he switched sides, by a young disgruntled royalist carried out for personal reasons, or was it prepared by political opponents, perhaps Gaullists, or perhaps emissaries of the Comte de Paris, the pretender to the French throne? Whatever the truth, the haunting problem remains: why did apparently sincere former republicans like Darlan, even if ambitious careerists, support Vichy and collaborate with the Germans?

The Vichy System

With Pétain's self-appointment on 11 July 1940 as head of the French State with plenitude of executive, legislative and partly judicial powers and the right to designate his successor, and with the suspension of the two chambers of the existing legislature, the Third Republic was ended. Authority, as Pétain himself said, no longer emanated from below but from him: 'The only authority is that which I entrust or delegate.' That authority was patriarchal: 'In 1917 I put an end to rout. Today, I wish to save you from yourselves.'[51] He was not to acknowledge that his mission as guarantor of national cohesion and as saviour was limited to freeing his people from the evils of free elections, which would not take place in Vichy, representative institutions, trade unions, employers' organisations, political parties expressing dissent, free press and parliamentary deputies, whose salaries were stopped. Political leaders would be appointed, not elected. Pétain chose the members of the two ministerial councils that conducted affairs: a full council consisting of all members of the government, and a smaller one of ministers who met every morning.

The Third Republic had long relied on executive decrees and ordinances to supplement parliamentary legislation. With the elimination of the traditional legislature, executive authorities and administrative officials in Vichy regulated life and behaviour by different kinds of text and in all areas of life. The different texts included laws, decrees, communications, ordinances, decisions, declarations, *arrêtes, rectificatifs, circulaires, accords, traités,* conventions and protocols. Not surprisingly, the number as well as the power of officials increased, from 650,000 in 1939 to about 900,000 in 1944.

By comparison with the militant individuals in the Légion and later in the Milice, the administrative officials were a relatively moderate element. Yet they were politicised, collaborating with political leaders and with the Germans, interested in the outcome of policy, and committed by the oath of loyalty to Pétain, made mandatory in January 1941. What is most disconcerting was the approval or acquiescence of the administration, police and judiciary in the discriminatory, anti-Semitic regulations. No senior official quit his job because of the arrests and deportation of Jews. No member of the Conseil d'État raised serious objections about the Statuts des Juifs.

Executive authority of both the prefects and the police was expanded. The increased role of the prefects partly resulted from the dissolution of the elected general departmental councils on 12 October 1940 when they were replaced by appointed administrative councils and their powers were transferred to the prefects of their areas. The 163 existing municipal councils of middle-sized and large cities were replaced by 'municipal delegations'. On 16 November 1940 a decree provided for prefects, administrative authorities or ministers to name mayors, usually chosen from conservative local notables, for all towns of between 2000 and 10,000 people. The municipal councils were chosen by the mayors, but could be suspended by the prefects. Most of those chosen came from local business, small industry and finance, and the liberal professions, the 'notables' of the country.[52] Socially conservative personnel were now in positions of power. On 19 April 1941, eighteen regional prefects were appointed and given powers over the distribution of food supplies and economic organisation as well as being responsible for the maintenance of order and oversight of the police.

Four days later, on 23 April 1941, the French police force started on the path of centralisation, headed by the Direction Générale de la Police Nationale. A cardinal feature, symbolising French sovereignty, was that public order would be maintained by French police. The national force consisted of the Sûreté Générale and the Gendarmerie, created in 1790 as a soldier-police force to keep order; it was linked to the Ministry of Defence. The local forces were municipal units, large city units such as those in Lyon and Marseille, which were state controlled, and a separate Paris police force.

By the new law of 23 April, all police personnel were to become agents of the state. The regular municipal forces were regrouped into regions. A National Police School to train police officials was established in August 1941. The Ministry of the Interior, assisted by the secretary-general of police, now had authority over the police force. At the same time, the regional prefects, who were to co-ordinate the maintenance of order as well as other matters, became the real heads, aided by the superintendent of police, of the force in their sectors.

These regular police, like the administration and the population in general, adapted themselves to circumstances, enforcing laws and decrees, and reconciling in their own fashion French national interests, the maintenance of order and co-operation with German authorities. Officials believed still faithful to the Republic were dismissed. Yet some distinction can be drawn between the different regions of France. In Paris co-operation with the Germans was active; in the east, the police were more likely to be repressive than in Brittany and the south, where some passive resistance was exhibited after November 1942.

Beyond the regular police were other special units which competed with them, concerned with the fight against 'enemies', primarily Jews, communists, Freemasons and members of the Resistance. The mobile reserve groups, *groupes mobiles de réserve* (GMR), were concerned with public security, which really meant finding dissidents. The CGQJ and the unit looking for Freemasons got their own police unit. The Service de Police Anticommuniste (SPAC) was set up by Pierre Pucheu. Already, in March 1940, the 'special brigades' of the prefecture of police in Paris had been created to look for militant communists. In the autumn, a unit with the innocuous name Service des Contrôles Techniques began to intercept postal and telephonic communications.

This diffusion of police power made it difficult for the central authority to absorb most of the police forces. On 18 April 1942, Laval appointed René Bousquet, the golden boy of administration, as head of the national police. Bousquet tried, for personal reasons as much as for those of public order, to concentrate power. As a result, in June 1942, sections of political affairs were set up in each regional police unit, and the Gendarmerie was detached from the armed forces. However, repressive bodies dealing with Jewish affairs remained, being renamed *sections d'enquête et de contrôle*. The SPAC became the Service de Répression des Menées Antinationales (SRMAN).

Bousquet believed his control of the police force would symbolise the existence of French sovereignty. That force would willingly on its own initiative take part in repressive activities and arrests on behalf of the Germans. The German authorities were aware of the reality. On 23 July 1942, after the Vél d'Hiv round-up, SS police chief in France, Karl Albrecht Oberg, wrote to Bousquet: 'Je vous confirme bien volontiers que la police française a réalisé jusqu'ici une tache digne d'éloges' (a task worthy of praise).[53]

In May 1942 Bousquet met Reinhard Heydrich, a meeting with ominous overtones. Would Bousquet deliver the 40,000 Jews that Theodor Dannecker, head of the Gestapo Jewish office in France, had promised Adolf Eichmann he would get from France in June 1942? The so-called accords that Bousquet reached with Oberg in July 1942 were the Rubicon of Vichy policy, a tragic choice. Bousquet's administrative activity was accompanied by a complete lack of moral principle. The Germans agreed to allow the French police an 'autonomous' existence with full control over internal order in the occupied zone, but at the price of France agreeing to arrest Jews for deportation and to hunt for resisters.

In the authoritarian Vichy system, justice for the most part was conducted in the regular courts, which were formally correct and applied the law in a formally competent way.[54] This acquiescence in the texts allowing persecution and discrimination constitutes the severest indictment of the legal profession. Judges and lawyers alike betrayed the whole concept of the rule of law, of impartial and equal justice.

Vichy went even further. Some twenty-six laws were issued establishing nine new categories of 'exceptional Tribunals', special sections to deal with political opponents, and special criminal courts to punish terrorists. Pétain was given power to pronounce penalties against officials who had left their positions less than ten years earlier. They could be condemned and imprisoned, as were Paul Reynaud and Georges Mandel in August 1941. The best-known and potentially very important body was the Supreme Court of Justice set up on 30 July 1940 with judges appointed by Pétain to punish those responsible for the defeat of France. By Constitutional Act No. 5, of the same date, the state was given authority to try officials held responsible for the defeat. In July 1941 the farcical trial of prominent republicans Blum, Mandel, Reynaud, Daladier and Gamelin took place in Riom. After courageous speeches by the defendants, and criticism of Pétain for his own responsibility for the poor military condition of France in the war, the trial was indefinitely suspended.

Of the other jurisdictional bodies, the most active were the *sections spéciales*, created by a law dated 14 August 1941, and in fact set up after the assassination of a German officer in the Paris metro a week later. They were attached to military tribunals in the unoccupied zone and to the courts of appeal in the northern zone. Their function was to punish alleged 'terrorists', sentencing the victims without appeal to prison or to death. Even more, the law was retroactive, another cardinal violation of the rule of law. The Minister of Justice, Joseph Barthélemy, whose conscience appears to have been infinitely flexible, signed the law supposedly under strong pressure from Pucheu, Minister of the Interior, who argued that 'national security' was more important than 'juridical scruples'.[55] The *section spéciale* of Paris, with non-professional magistrates appointed to it, had a forbiddingly large competence, to punish those who had the intention to cause disorder, to disturb internal peace, public tranquillity or international relations, or generally to harm the French people.

The Call for a New France

Even before the formal creation of the Vichy regime, Marshal Pétain on 25 June 1940 spoke of the need for change: 'C'est à un redressement, intellectuel et moral que, d'abord je vous convie.' New economic, social, political and cultural forms and moral principles would replace the outmoded or failed capitalism, class struggles, cultural liberalism, democratic republic with elected officials, individualism, and the false idea of natural equality.

De Gaulle, in his peculiar oracular terminology, once spoke of France as 'both a fact, a product of history, and a value derived from and embodied in her culture'. France had existed for twenty centuries; France had witnessed Vercingétorix, the first 'résistant de notre race'; Clovis, as he merged Roman Gaul and Christianity; and the Capet monarchy, which established the boundaries of France. For de Gaulle, France could not be France without grandeur.[56] More prosaically, Pétain spoke of a new, united, regenerated France, ordered and disciplined, incorporating the natural communities of society in a more exclusive France from which outsiders would be rejected. Society had primacy over individuals; families, professions, regions and religion would be its basis. Social and professional elites would replace the false idea of equality. Character was more important than intellectualism. Rural France expressed the true values of the nation.[57] This fantasy of a new society would produce the desirable French person. This would come about through youth movements, which would regenerate the nation, through new educational programmes, through a new political culture, through a propaganda and information process to form a new conception of man, and through appropriate economic policies.[58]

Pétain was not a dogmatic ideologue: his political outlook was grounded in a few orthodox principles – family, property, work, unity, duty, order, patriotism – but it was eclectic in character and reflected a mixture of intellectual sources, consciously or otherwise. Those sources included criticism of industrial society (Le Play), social Catholicism (La Tour du Pin), populist nationalism (Barrès), counter-revolutionaries (Maurras), corporativists (Bouvier-Ajam), philosophical personalists (Mounier), advocates of strong executive power (Tardieu), and the solidarity of veterans.

Pétain had remained silent during the Dreyfus affair, had said little in general about politics, and was not clearly identified with any particular intellectual heritage or any political party or organisation. His words may not have suffered from 'sumptuous emptiness',[59] but they had a broad appeal across the political and social spectrum to peasants; the Church; Catholic intellectuals; veterans; traditional conservatives; technocrats; modernisers; the military; members of the former *ligues* and fascists; some on the political left who saw him as the most republican of military men and a non-clerical; anti-Semites; and all those who remembered him as the hero of Verdun.

Verdun was a crucial factor in explaining the appeal of Pétain. The site of a ten-month battle in 1916 when the French army defended a salient in the German lines, the battle, 'a complete war in itself', in the words of Paul Valéry, took a toll in French casualties: 61,200 killed, 216,000 wounded, and 101,000 'missing'. Pétain was the commander, employing a defensive strategy to minimise casualties rather than take the offensive, and rotating troops in the front line every two weeks. Whatever the value of this strategy it meant that a considerable part of the French army had come under Pétain's command, and that many in the inter-war years and in 1940 looked on his as a leader who protected his men.

In the new system, the French Revolutionary triad of *Liberté, Egalité, Fraternité* was replaced by Pétain's *Travail, Famille, Patrie*. Pétain originally thought of the new social order as 'national renovation', but it was soon termed National Revolution. The term had already been the title of a book by Georges Valois in 1924 and had been used by Laval on 8 July 1940 in his report on and suggestions for constitutional reform. The National Revolution would rebuild society and reconstruct the national soul.

In the new France, national identity would be associated with the peasant way of life, the family, Catholicism and the absence of undesirable persons. To foster the desirable society a new educational system was essential. Pétain had long been critical of the existing pattern of education. His declaration on 15 August 1940 in *Revue des Deux Mondes* made clear that the school system would no longer be neutral 'between France and anti-France'. Left-wing teachers were removed from schools, teacher training colleges were closed, the teachers' union, SNI, was ended in October 1940, and the syllabus was revised at all school levels.[60]

In reaction against the republican laws on secular education passed between 1882 and 1905, Catholic schools were re-established and subsidised, and the clergy allowed to teach. By a law of 6 January 1941, religious instruction was permitted in public schools. For a time, a crucifix could be placed in schools as well as in town halls. In April 1942 religious orders were more able to seek legal recognition. However, with Jérôme Carcopino, renowned classical scholar, and then Abel Bonnard as Ministers of Education, the principle was re-established of a secular rather than a Catholic-dominated school system in order to assert the primacy of state institutions and policies of the state, especially about youth. Vichy did not want to introduce confessional conflict. Schools would be concerned with building character, instilling discipline and respect for society and the country.

At first, during 1940 and 1941, teachers in the state schools were obliged to be careful about their instruction. They were expected to uphold the values of Vichy and to instil qualities of discipline and patriotism. Surveillance over their performance took both official and unofficial form. Priests might denounce the state teachers. Thousands, perhaps millions, of letters were sent by citizens to the police or to the prefects, all of whom took part in the surveillance process. The Légion Française des Combattants from August 1940 also acted as a body of vigilantes.[61] The official education authority, the Inspection Académique, working through local bodies, passed on directives from Vichy, and provided detailed instructions for the syllabus to be used. Teachers mostly conformed to the new instructions and the expected behaviour towards the regime.

By the latter part of 1942 the crusade to promote Pétainism had halted or slowed down. With the decline of confidence in the regime, denunciations of teachers decreased. The official inspectorate hesitated about implementing certain parts of Vichy's educational policies. It protected teachers and students from many demands by the state, including service in the Service du Travail Obligatoire (STO) in

Germany. The teachers, docile at first because of the pressures on them, the monitoring of their conversations and letters, and the burdens of extra-curricular activity, as well as sympathy by some for the values of the regime, were less likely to be subjected to ideological control at the local level from 1942 on.

In Pétain's organic conception of society, nature did not create society from individuals; it created individuals from society. The initial cell of society was the family, the essential unit, the foundation of the social structure. Family interests must be protected and women 'honoured'. Women were encouraged to stay at home. France also needed an increase in the birth rate; large families would be given certain privileges and family allowances.[62] Divorce laws were made more stringent and subsidies were provided for women in the home. Mother's Day was now celebrated. Abortion was made illegal, and in February 1942 a capital offence.[63] A Vichy law of 1940 restricted the ability of women to work in the civil service and denied them further promotion to senior positions. By 1942 about 14 per cent of women in senior posts had been dismissed, but the 1940 law was then suspended.[64]

Irrespective of the pious rhetoric about the family, Vichy was faced with the reality that the number of single women had sharply increased because of the absence of prisoners of war and the men who worked in Germany. Vichy had wanted to restrict the employment of women, but female labour was needed by 1942.[65] At first, women were involved in charity networks and in assisting prisoners of war. By 1942, almost a quarter of all French workers in Germany were women; by 1944 about 50,000 women worked there. Women entered the Resistance in larger numbers, protesting against rationing, and objecting to workers going to Germany.

For Vichy, the new French society must establish other priorities. Popular traditions and folklore were encouraged.[66] France must once again become an agricultural and a peasant country: *rétournez à la terre* was to be a policy, not a mere literary slogan. The earth was a solace, a fatherland, in which French people must be rooted and must re-establish contact with the soil, the essence of eternal France. The hard-working peasant would replace the despised *faubourien*, the working-class Parisian.

Popular culture and films had to reflect this. Representations of *le petit peuple* in films of the 1930s as endangered but jovial *poilus*, militant strikers, plebeian tricksters and *faubouriens*, reflected the growing political and economic strength of workers and the lower middle class.[67] They must be replaced by less demoralising spectacles. For Vichy the myth of craftsmen and peasants imbued with proper values of life and behaviour existing in an idyllic image of rural areas prevailed over the reality of an industrial and commercial urban society. It did not, however, prevent the reorganisation of the Paris metro in 1942. Yet Vichy did try to implement the myth. Vichy refused to recognise that rural life had changed. Peasants had become more prosperous, more bourgeois; they were provided with material objects and services. No clear demarcation existed between peasants and those living in small towns.

Politically connected with this return to the land would be the revival of meaningful old provinces of France, which had been replaced after the French Revolution by the artificial administrative *départements*. This could not be done, but in December 1940 the Corporation Paysanne, a national council with regional and local associates, was set up as an autonomous administration of agricultural activities concerned with the production and transmission of crops, and the cultivation of small plots of land. State credits were promised to farmers willing to take over abandoned land. In May 1941 a grant was made available for the return to the land by families with at least one child, in return for a promise to remain there and work on the land for at least ten years; only 1500 families took advantage of this. They were not enough to replace the 55,000 farmers who had been killed in the war and the half-million who were POWs.[68]

Not surprisingly, the Corporation Paysanne, whose powers were unclear, was in practice more protective of large-scale producers than of small farmers. A striking example came in 1943 when, because more workers were needed to go to Germany, exemption from the STO was removed from many of the small farmers. Attempts by Vichy to establish a harmonious relationship with farmers was unsuccessful partly because of the problem of food supply, and partly because of dislike of officials.

The Corporation Paysanne was a major example of what was supposed to be rational organisation of production based on corporative institutions. Class struggle would be overcome by a harmonious conjunction of authority and liberty. In essence, authority must not degenerate into tyranny, and liberty must not lead to licentiousness. The joys of overcoming difficulties by work should be preferred to the easiest pleasures; the spirit of sacrifice should be stronger than the spirit of enjoyment.[69]

Sacrifice certainly came from workers with the abolition in August 1940 of national trade unions, as well as business organisations. They were replaced by Organisation Committees (COs). A Labour Charter was formulated in 1941, which theoretically provided for equal representation of workers and employers, but in reality it did not protect workers' rights; strikes were forbidden, and workers' participation was limited.[70]

Youth in Vichy

The new desirable society required a new kind of youth and youth culture. Vichy did not set up a single body on the lines of the Hitler Youth or the Italian GIL. Instead, in addition to a Ministry of Youth, Family and Sport, set up on 12 July 1940 with cabinet ministerial rank, and the Ministry of Education, over sixty organisations were engaged in training youth in the right values of discipline, courage, loyalty and practical ability. This would be done by changing the school system, and by 'healthy collective experiences' in youth groups.[71]

Schools must be purged of the old teaching corps. Teachers had to sign a document attesting that they were neither Jews nor Freemasons. Different educational methods would be used for youngsters. Sport was particularly important. Yet, if the sports activities would foster health and service to the country, it was not wholly disinterested. Some of the activity was accompanied by anti-Semitism. The review La France au Travail exhorted sports instructors to show an example and be 'racists'.[72]

The emphasis on sport was demonstrated by the appointment of Jean Borotra, the former tennis champion, as the Minister of Youth from 1940 to 1942. On 6 September 1940 the youth section of the ministry was transferred to the Secrétariat Général à la Jeunesse (SGJ) in the Ministry of Education. The SGJ was responsible for overseeing training programmes at all levels for youngsters after they left school, and for maintaining liaison with the various youth movements.

At first, the SGJ was headed by Jean Ybarnégaray and Georges Lamirand, director of Renault factories and a pragmatic supporter of Pétain. After April 1942 until it was closed on 31 December 1943 its leader was Georges Pelorson, a prolific writer and somewhat curious individual who claimed to be a literary modernist and a friend of Samuel Beckett, Henry Miller and James Joyce, though a collaborator and extreme right-winger.[73] Soon after his appointment Pelorson set up the équipes nationales, grouping youngsters from twelve to fifteen, and having them participate in civic and social activities in which they would undergo a 'virile and strong' training. He also supported Jeune France, which had been set up first in the unoccupied zone in November 1940 and then in the occupied zone in January 1941.

Pétain wanted maisons de la jeunesse to be set up throughout

France to foster future elites for the country. This was not done, but three organisations were particularly important, at least for a while, in the training of youth: the Uriage school, the Compagnons de France and the Chantiers de la Jeunesse.

The École Nationale des Cadres, housed in a château with a medieval setting at Uriage, was an austere school founded in October 1940 and directed by Pierre Dunoyer de Segonzac, a Catholic, royalist and military man, for training a cadre of future leaders, intellectually, physically and morally to renew France. A few months earlier a new form of the publication, *Esprit*, combined intellectuals from the political right and the anti-communist left. Its editor, Emmanuel Mounier (1905–50), whose personalist, communitarian philosophy was a *mélange* of concepts, Christian and revolutionary but neither Marxist nor fascist, critical of both capitalism and parliamentary democracy, influenced the new Uriage school, intellectually and personally.[74]

Mounier and his fellow intellectual, Hubert Beuve-Méry, later to found the paper *Le Monde* after the war, influenced the tone of Uriage with its strong personalities, authoritarianism, Catholicism and hierarchical character, and is exclusion of Jews and communists from the national community. The central school and its regional associates saw its mission as preparing for the renaissance of the national community by military strength but mostly by training pupils, the future cadres of the new society which would exemplify the right values. It would mould *moines chevaliers* (knight-monks), authoritarian, Catholic, traditionalist persons.[75] Though Uriage was always loyal to Pétain, it was also anti-German; it was closed at the end of 1942 after internal disputes in Vichy about it. Some of the group then joined the Resistance. Even on the eve of their belated passage to the Resistance, the cadres of Uriage decided to create an 'order' to perpetuate the spirit of the community. The purpose of the new group would be to stigmatise those who were deceived by 'international interests whether capitalist, Jewish, Freemason, or communist'.

Les Compagnons de France was a major youth organisation, subsidised by Vichy and banned in the occupied zone. Led at first by Henri Dhavernas and largely modelled on the Boy Scout movement, it was set up in August 1940 to help reconstruct the country. Organised in groups of fifty, youths aged between fifteen and twenty underwent training in healthy living, physical labour, communal living and indoctrination in the values of the new society. Wearing a uniform of berets, blue shirts and shorts, the Compagnons worked long hours on the land and in road construction and sports projects. The indoctrination, influenced by the communitarians of the Uriage school, and expressed in lectures and in a considerable number of publications, was critical of capitalism and liberal democracy.

By June 1941, there were 679 camps, all in the unoccupied zone and mostly in rural areas.[76] Their communal activities included saluting the colours, singing around the campfire, drama performances, art and pottery. The routine included physical fitness, vocational training and practical activities. The ideal of self-sacrifice was implemented by socially useful tasks. The Germans, wary of any seemingly military or organised collective Vichy institutions, banned the Compagnon camps from the occupied zone. In February 1941, after 30,000 Compagnons had completed their training, Dhavernas was replaced by Guillaume de Tournemire, who directed over 200 companies of the youth members, who graduated at a rate of 500 a month. After the German entrance into the unoccupied zone, the group began losing membership. As a result of divisions within the group over finance and policies, including anti-Semitism, which was criticised by some, it was dissolved in January 1944. Tournemire, who had allowed Jewish youths to enter the camps under false names, joined the Resistance together with some Compagnons.

Les Chantiers de la Jeunesse was started in July 1940 and headed by General Joseph de La Porte du Theil, who had been an active figure in the Boy Scout movement and who used the Boy Scout motto, 'Be prepared.' It was originally intended as an emergency measure to find work for six months for men who had been demobilised or were of draft age. Over 92,000 had been called up for military service in June 1940, but the war ended before they were part of a military unit. In a sense the Chantiers replaced conscription.

The Chantiers became a mandatory body under the authority of the Secrétariat Général à la Jeunesse, and a substitute for military service, for which it provided training. In January 1941 the Chantiers began to provide semi-military training and communal living for young men of twenty years old for eight months. The Chantiers supported Vichy but not the policy of collaboration. The fact that the young men wore uniforms of green and saluted the French flag every morning troubled the Germans, who forbade the group from their zone. The style was military: hierarchical organisation, short hair, cold water ablutions and strong discipline.

The Chantiers established camps for 2000 youngsters, divided into groups in which individuals of all classes were mixed together to work on public projects such as deforestation and agricultural work. The overall objective of the group was to revive the spirit of duty, to instil desirable values of health, honesty, honour, work and obedience, and to encourage harmonious comradeship as well as competition.

Significant in all this was indoctrination in the Vichy policy of return to the soil, and in the general principles of the National Revolution.

Because of the increasing German demands for factory workers, the Chantiers from 1943 became the body from which the young men were taken to work in Germany under the Service du Travail Obligatoire (STO). In January 1944, after over 300,000 had passed through the organisation, its leader, La Porte du Theil, was arrested and deported, and imprisoned in Germany. After the war he was charged and found not guilty in the French courts in 1947.

From Veterans to Extremists

Vichy did not have or want a single political party. Only a small group of extremists, mostly fascists in Paris, favoured such a development. Instead, Pétain and associates thought the voice of public opinion could be appropriately expressed and French energies be regrouped through a unified veterans' organisation. In the First World War, 8 million men had been mobilised; of these 5.5 million were still alive in 1940 and 3 million of them belonged to various veterans' organisations, some conservative such as the Union Nationale des Combattants, and others more radical.

At the beginning of Vichy the existing veterans' organisations were dissolved with the creation of the Légion Française des Combattants (LFC), open to veterans of both world wars, that would promote the ideals of the National Revolution, co-operate with officials and be the link between the government and the people. In an elaborate ceremony the Légion was officially set up, by a law of 29 August 1940, with echoes of the legendary Arveni leader, Vercingétorix. Pétain, in his position as Marshal of France, was the honorary head, and François Valentin, a former member of the PSF of La Rocque, was chosen as leader. Though it was banned in the occupied zone and though some of the old veterans' organisations objected to it, the LFC reached a membership of 1.7 million, mostly older men from the rural areas. Eligibility for membership was widened to include all men over twenty in the unoccupied zone in 1942 when its influence began declining. The organisation became a useful mechanism through which jobs might be obtained, as well as a body to support the National Revolution, which was done through the oath of allegiance, propaganda and organised receptions. It also became increasingly involved in collaboration, leading some members to leave the organisation, and causing tensions and ruptures within it as a result of political differences of its members and the relationship with political leaders.

The more militant and extreme members of the LFC not only supported collaboration but also formed a new body to engage in more aggressive action. From his native Alpes-Maritimes, Joseph Darnand (1897–1945) emerged as the key figure. Darnand had been a courageous hero in both world wars; besides losing an eye and a leg in the first, he staged a daring raid behind the German lines in January 1940. Escaping from a POW camp, he became head of the Nice office of the LFC, gaining over 50,000 adherents. His very success and his eagerness for action led him to set up in December 1941 a paramilitary organisation, the Service d'Ordre Légionnaire (SOL), still nominally under the Légion, to act against the 'enemies' of Vichy. Self-defined as anti-Semitic and anti-democratic in its 21-point programme which members had to accept, it condemned Jews, Freemasons and communists and proclaimed a struggle 'For French purity and against Jewish leprosy'. Though Laval as head of government disliked the group and Darnand personally, he saw the SOL as useful, in view of possible manoeuvres by Doriot's PPF and Déat's RNP, to help maintain order.

On 30 January 1943 the SOL was transformed into the Milice Française, a kind of praetorian guard with an official leadership by Laval but directed by the increasingly powerful Darnand.[77] It was an autonomous unit detached from the Légion. Members took an oath of allegiance similar to that of the SOL: 'I swear to fight against democracy, against Gaullist insurrection, and against Jewish leprosy.' The Milice, like its predecessor the SOL, gloried in its militancy, its discipline and hierarchical order, its marching songs, rhetoric, dress (a uniform of dark blue trousers, khaki shirts, black ties and berets), and symbolic sign of the ram to denote strength. Its slogan was 'For those who brought about our defeat, no punishment is harsh enough.' To be a member of the Milice, an individual had to be French by birth and not be a Jew or belong to a secret society. The given task was to repress all anti-government agitation and propaganda, and to guarantee the functioning of public services.

Hope by Vichy that the Légion would be the major instrument for the implementation of the National Revolution now ended for good. Figures may be inexact, but probably only between 10 and 15 per cent of the Légion joined the SOL, and less than 5 per cent, nearly all of them young veterans of the Second World War, entered the Milice and were prepared to fight for Germany. The director-general of the Légion, François Valentin, switched sides and went over to de Gaulle.

Regarded as the link between the Paris activists and fascists and Vichy, the Milice maintained order by fighting the *maquis*, the word from Corsica that signified the Resistance, and tracked down Jews, communists and those French people who refused to work in Germany. Within six months of its creation, the Milice claimed a membership of over 30,000, mostly from young working-class men, more interested in the job and the excitement than in ideology.[78] Eager to combat the Allied invasion of North Africa in November 1942, Darnand called for an African phalanx to fight alongside Germany.

In July 1943, Frenchmen were given permission by Laval to join the Waffen SS. Members of the Milice, about 300 at the beginning, began enlisting in the Charlemagne division to fight on the eastern front, putting on Nazi uniforms. Darnand, together with eleven of his supporters, took an oath of loyalty to Hitler in October 1943 and was given the rank of SS Obersturmführer. In return, the Milice was given German machine guns to expand its military activity. Darnand called himself a man of the Marshal, but he was now an extreme collaborationist. Armed by the Nazis, he was essentially their agent. The Milice co-operated with Klaus Barbie's notorious Section 4; the most familiar collaboration is that of Paul Touvier, who became head of the regional information branch office and who ordered the execution of seven Jews in the town of Rillieux-la-Pape in June 1944. The Milice was the ugly face of fascism in France, incorporating both a military and bellicose style and a programme and quasi-ideology.

At first the Milice had a leadership school commanded by Pierre-Louis de La Ney du Vair, a Catholic royalist who had been active in the SOL, and who lived in the Château Bayard of the Uriage group. The courses at the school, either two to three weeks or six months, intended to train a civilian and military elite, were attended by young people between eighteen and twenty-five, most from the upper middle class. La Ney du Vair was soon replaced by a more aggressive person, Jean de Vaugelas.

In January 1944, Darnand was appointed Minister for Order, and in June, Minister of the Interior. The extreme Milice had captured power. Its adherents were appointed to official positions: superintendents of police, directors of prisons, propaganda units, broadcasters, even prefects and special tribunals. Though the regular police were not sympathetic to the Milice, Darnand now controlled 45,000 gendarmes, 6000 *gardes mobiles* and 25,000 in the *groupes mobiles de réserve*. The Milice had become a state within a state. It was central to the process of repression. France was now on the threshold of becoming a fascist state.

The Milice ruthlessly used violence against political opponents and anyone suspected of being part of the Resistance. It assassinated well-known figures: Georges Mandel, Jewish associate of Georges Clemenceau and former cabinet minister in the Third Republic; Jean

Zay, former Education Minister; and Victor Basch, Jewish President of the League of the Rights of Man, and his wife. Its most notorious action was to assist German forces in March 1944 in their attack at Glières in Haute-Savoie on Resistance fighters, of whom 155 were killed by the 12,000 Germans and units of the Milice.

The unit of the Milice in Lyon was headed by Joseph Lécussan, a navy captain who was a specialist in hunting Jews.[79] It was he who arrested and killed eighty-year-old Basch. He was also the organiser of the *rafle* of seventy Jews on 21–2 July 1944, in his capacity as both head of the local Milice and regional delegate of the CGQJ in Toulouse. This round-up was a reprisal for the hanging of thirteen of the Milice by the *maquis*; innocent Jews were sent to Bourges and twenty-six of the men were pushed into wells.[80]

Extremists by 1944 controlled the propaganda outlets, the only Paris radio station, Radio-Paris, and the national station, Radio-Vichy, where Philippe Henriot delivered twice daily vituperative broadcasts attacking Jews, the *maquis* and communists. Next to Darnand, Henriot was the most influential figure in the Milice movement. A fervent Catholic and pacifist, he had been elected as a right-wing deputy from the Gironde in 1932, had voted for the appeasement Munich agreement in 1938 and was an early supporter of Pétain. His highly skilled, violently anti-Semitic and anti-communist daily broadcasts led to his appointment as Minister of Information and Propaganda in January 1944 after it was clear that he was having a considerable impact on public opinion. Disturbed by this impact the Resistance assassinated him on 28 June 1944.[81] His funeral was commemorated as an important state occasion, including a service by Cardinal Suhard of Paris at Notre Dame, and his coffin was on display at the Hôtel de Ville where it was visited by over a quarter of a million people.

After the Allied landing in France, Darnand fled to Germany in September 1944, joining Pétain and Laval in the town of Sigmaringen. Even there he conducted military operations against resistance fighters in northern Italy. On being returned to France after the war, he was condemned by the High Court and executed in October 1945.

Pétain shared the same town in Germany with Darnand, but their political paths had diverged. At the very end of the regime Pétain, on 6 August 1944, wrote to Laval, denouncing the *néfaste* action of the Milice, whose odious and inadmissible deeds he had known for several months. Pétain now complained that the Milice threatened the prefects, the official police, made arbitrary arrests, collaborated with the German authorities and police, delivered French prisoners to the Germans, insulted the population, burnt farms and even villages as reprisals, arrested and tortured innocent victims, and committed murder. All this produced an atmosphere of police terror unknown in France. Pétain deservedly received a strong rebuke in reply. 'For four years,' wrote Darnand, 'I have received your compliments and felicitations. You encouraged me ... now that the Americans are at the gates of Paris you say that I am a blemish on the history of France.'

The Vichy regime spluttered to an end in August 1944 in confusion. Pétain hoped to reach an accord with de Gaulle. Laval, the arch-intriguer, wanted to preside over a new transitional government. Both were forced to leave for Germany. In Sigmaringen, the small German town near Lake Constance, the humiliated Vichy leaders postured and presided over a non-existent polity with the grandiose title of *Délégation Française pour la défense des intérêts Français*. The trauma of an unprecedented defeat from which France had suffered for four years had ended with the would-be upholders of French honour and sovereignty as virtual prisoners, with an indigenous quasi-fascist group of extremists, and with an aggravation of the internal strife within France. De Gaulle, as head of the provisional government in November 1944, haughtily dismissed Vichy, remarking that 'The form of the French government was and remains the Republic. The Republic has never ceased to exist.'

CHAPTER 4

THE NEW ANTI-SEMITIC LEGAL SYSTEM

The French origin of the anti-Semitic legislation is now clear; it was the result of the logic of the National Revolution, the policy of collaboration with the Nazis and the long heritage of French anti-Semitism. It is equally clear that it stemmed from a deliberate autonomous French government policy rather than from a response to German pressure.[1] The best that can be said of Vichy policy is that it tried to draw a distinction, with some success, between French and foreign Jews; the latter could be sacrificied to save the former. Of the Jews deported from France, 24,500 (32 per cent) were French and 56,500 (68 per cent) were foreign. About 13 per cent of French Jews, compared with 41 per cent of foreign Jews, were deported or died in French camps.[2] If some ambiguity existed about the fate of French Jews, there was none about the foreign Jews.

Within weeks of taking power the Vichy regime began initiating anti-Semitic policies for the whole of the mainland territory and the overseas possessions of France.[3] German occupation authorities, the Militärbefehlshaber in Frankreich (MBF) concurrently issued their own discriminatory ordinances against Jews applicable in their zone, the occupied or northern zone; they also began, as did other German organisations, pillaging activities in the zone.

At the very beginning, a Vichy law of 22 July 1940 provided for a committee to start a 'systematic review' of all naturalisations granted since 1927 because of the danger to peace and public order. Though the law did not specifically refer to Jews, or appear to be aimed at them, a total of 17,000 people with French nationality, of whom 6000 were Jews, became stateless persons. The text referred to 'all acquisitions of French nationality', which could therefore apply not simply to those born abroad, but also to foreigners married to French nationals and to children born in France to foreign parents.

A day later, on 23 July, a decree authorised cancellation of the citizenship and confiscation of the property of 446 French nationals who had left metropolitan France between 10 May and 30 June 1940 without a valid reason or official authority. The decree applied to some well-known non-Jews, such as General Charles de Gaulle, General Catroux, General de Larminat and Eve Curie, but it was mostly relevant to Jews, the Rothschilds, Jean Zay and Pierre Mendès-France. By leaving the country these people were labelled as 'Jews before they were French'. A few weeks later, the Vichy 27 August 1940 law repealed the Marchandeau decree of 21 April 1939, which, because of the virulent attacks on Jews, banned anti-Semitic publications and made racist remarks and attacks on religion in the press a misdemeanour. The abrogation thus legitimised anti-Semitic utterances and expressions of racial hatred.

The Nazi regime recognised the significance of the Vichy initiatives. A telegram from Ambassador Otto Abetz in Paris, dated 1 October 1940, to Foreign Minister Ribbentrop read: 'The solution of the Jewish problem in the occupied territory requires, besides other measures, a regulation as soon as possible of the citizenship status of the Reich German Jews who were living here at the beginning of the war.'

Those other measures came quickly. In 1846, repeal of provisions for different legal oaths needed for Christians and Jews ended legal discrimination against a religious or ethnic group. This was nullified by Vichy laws and regulations. The crucial starting point for any further discrimination was the legal definition for the first time in French politics of the word 'Jew' in the Statut des Juifs of 3 October 1940. The definition, repudiating the honoured republican principles of equality of citizenship and separation of Church and State, was the start of a series of legislative enactments that collectively created a new branch of French law, a 'Jewish civil status'.[4] Paradoxically, this new law was directed against Jews, but it also allowed them legal opportunities to challenge the civil status assigned to them.[5]

The new branch of law, flowing rapidly and widely from the now inferior legal status of Jews, relentlessly reduced or eliminated their individual freedoms, and their access to occupations, professions, wealth and economic possessions. In little over a year, between October 1940 and December 1941, 109 anti-Jewish laws and decrees had already been published by Vichy in the *Journal Officiel*, an act that declared them to be in effect. The new law had its experts, its doctrinal controversies and legal issues.[6] It involved civil law, dealing with questions of the definition of a Jew, criminal law, which allowed punishment of infractions, and resort to the courts up to the Conseil d'État, which made final decisions on contentious issues, including exemptions from the provisions of the laws; on this last issue there were in fact only thirty-two rulings in a two-year period.

In the four years of Vichy, 168 discriminatory texts on Jews were issued and Jews were thus injected into every branch of the legal system, and in all subjects, especially those of individual rights and property. Sometimes touches of black humour were present. The second Statut des Juifs of 2 June 1941 allowed some Jewish officials, dismissed under the law and who were soon to be deported and exterminated, to keep their pension rights. Prisoners of war were allowed to work for two months before being dismissed.

The legal system accepted and did not question the legitimacy of the new laws, and applied them with technical expertise. Its passive acceptance of discrimination was even more telling because jurists did uphold principles of republican law in cases that did not involve Jews. French judges, lawyers, and law professors accepted the anti-Semitic legislation almost unanimously, or discussed it in a seemingly neutral fashion. A few honourable jurists, principally Pierre-Henri Teitgen, François de Menthon, René Capitant and René Courtin, opposed the measures and played some role in the Resistance.

Some prominent constitutional law professors played an active part in support of the regime. Most jurists, however, took a neutral position. Law professors and legal journals commented in supposedly objective fashion, with scientific detachment on the anti-Semitic laws, thereby confirming their discriminatory nature and exclusion of a whole people. Using this 'scientific' analysis or 'neutral discourse' or 'purely technical legal method', no article in the law journals or in legal manuals expressed reserve on the legality or legitimacy of the new laws, which broke with the 200-year tradition of legal equality.

The most celebrated and contentious of these articles, to become the subject of suits in the courts of the Fifth Republic, was that by Maurice Duverger, who later claimed it was the first synthesis of the new laws published in the most serious French law review.[7] Written with rhetorical skill and apparent neutrality, this article by an aspiring jurist maintains an ambiguous impersonality by its constant use of the indefinite pronoun. Duverger does not make clear his own position. Rather 'on estime que les juifs et les naturalisés sont inaptes, d'une façon générale, à assurer le bon fonctionnement de ces services'. Or, 'on a estimé que les juifs, comme les naturalisés, ne présentaient pas en général cette aptitude' (a political aptitude to exercise a public function). Or, 'on a jugé les juifs plus dangereux politiquement que les naturalisés'. Therefore the public interest required stricter regulation of them. The 'neutral', dispassionate and measured tone of the law review articles not only did not challenge the new laws but also, in accepting them as normal, treated them as equally appropriate for study as any other part of the legal code.

Vichy needed the existing judges and jurists, who remained in place in the new regime, to give legitimacy to the new legislation and to the regime itself. Judges were not coerced, nor were external controls imposed on them. The legal officials did not directly take part in deportation and extermination, but their deferential attitude in accepting the law starting with exclusion of Jews in 1940 was the first step in the inexorable logical chain to the Final Solution. By accepting and implementing the legislation, they implicitly accepted the formula of Jews as a separate species, a 'race' different from citizens of France, in their determination of the term 'Jew' and their acquiescence in confiscation of property. They did this, for the most part, seemingly without the dictates of racial hatred or ideological militancy, but on the basis of objective criteria and obedience to the law.

The haunting question remains: could they have done otherwise? Vichy at the beginning, in 1940, removed 209 magistrates, forty-one of whom were reinstated, out of a total of 3420. If jurists did not approve the new laws, they could have resigned, the most honourable if not the easiest or most practical solution. They could have delayed the implementation or given favourable interpretations on behalf of the victims, or required adequate proof of the facts. In the jurisdictional disputes between the ordinary courts and the CGQJ, some leeway was available to limit racial persecution. On the contrary, the ordinary courts did not try to help Jews; nor did magistrates protest racial and religious laws in any serious way. They did not challenge *ex post facto* laws, putting the burden of proof about an individual's true religion on the person being challenged. The French courts routinely sent copies of all verdicts and sentences to the Gestapo.[8] A significant commentary on all this was that only 363 magistrates were dismissed after the war.

At all levels the French legal system legitimised discrimination. The study, among other legal matters, of the Paris Bar Association by Robert Badinter, later a Minister of Justice, is a devastating indictment of self-interested opportunism and prejudice.[9] The Bar acted quickly on the law of 10 September 1940 excluding individuals, almost all of whom were Jews, from practising if they did not possess French nationality. Other Jews were then excluded from it. The Bar remained silent when some of the Jewish members were arrested by the French police and deported. Paris lawyers took part in framing the original definition of 'Jew' in October 1940. They eagerly acquiesced, whether to eliminate competition or because of anti-Semitic inclinations, in the *numerus clausus* regulation. Not until March 1943 did the Bar express some criticism of events. Even after the war, the Bar refused to consider reparation payments for Jews prohibited from practising law during the war.

At the highest level, the record of the Conseil d'État is not admirable. As an institution it claimed not to have been consulted on the laws of exclusion of Jews. Yet some of its members who were seconded to ministerial cabinets lent their juridical knowledge and experience to the elaboration of the laws. The members of the Conseil played a large role in applying the texts, giving advice on interpretation and judgements on the decrees and regulations stemming from the laws. The Conseil decided on the procedures for removing Jews from public offices and on the individuals claiming exemption from the anti-Semitic laws; few exceptions were approved. The Conseil did not try to limit the excesses of the regime; it even in 1943 tried to expand the number of denaturalisations. It continued its work undisturbed, providing no help to Jewish colleagues. It saw that exclusion and discrimination took place in the proper manner, and were therefore legitimate. A new area of legal specialisation had been created and in 1941 the Conseil set up a special commission on anti-Jewish laws. Its members took the oath of allegiance to Pétain.

Why did the French legal profession sanction discriminatory laws? Why did it help in excluding Jews from the profession or restrict their number? Why did it legitimise anti-Semitism? No doubt latent anti-Semitism became overt. Many French lawyers believed that Jews were too influential in society, and specifically in the Bar. Two of the five presidents of sections of the Conseil d'État were Jewish, and therefore had to go. Few protests were made at the imposition of the *numerus clausus* for Jews. Even the supposedly moderate Joseph Barthélemy, in his self-serving memoirs, asserts that 'at the outbreak of war, Jews had an excessive place in France ... [they were] so well placed in top positions that they had the air of a governing race of an autochtonous and inferior population'.[10]

Mercenary and opportunistic factors were also involved. Jurists might, with the elimination of Jews and because of the new laws, make more money, have more legal work, be promoted and exercise more authority. They took advantage of litigation over Jewish property, and possibly became temporary administrators of that property. They became members of the special courts designed to try those suspected of 'endangering national security', and which denied normal legal rights to those brought to court.

In all this they had no clear moral compass or guidance, a lack that was reinforced by the general silence of the Catholic Church and of the Pope, who said nothing, even in October 1943 when 1200 Jews were arrested in Rome and imprisoned just outside Vatican City. Perhaps they genuinely shared a fear of communism, but this does not excuse the lack of opposition to racial laws.

Perhaps the most specious explanation for this lack was that of obedience to the law. Many jurists defended themselves on the premise that 'it is the law; it must be obeyed'.[11] This is the positivist argument that French courts for two centuries had not engaged in any form of judicial lawmaking or usurping of the legislative function. The courts and the legal system were concerned only in applying the legal rules in an impersonal, neutral way. No moral beliefs or extra-legal considerations were relevant. Courts could not make regulatory decrees or interfere with actions of executive and administrative bodies.

Yet, even if jurists adopted a legal approach to legal texts, they could not be oblivious to the consequences of those texts, and to the reality that Jews in France were deprived of the equality on which the law rested.

CHAPTER 5

FROM DEFINITION TO DETENTION

The path to legal inequality was set: definition, census, discrimination, exclusion, persecution, Aryanisation, arrest first of foreign and then of French Jews, and internment. The Germans added general internment and deportation from France to the extermination camps in eastern Europe.

The new civil status of Jews defined in the 3 October 1940 Statut des Juifs was published soon after the German ordinance of the MBF of 27 September 1940. This ordinance, imposing some restrictions on the rights of Jews, defined them as those who belonged or had belonged to the Jewish religion or who had more than two Jewish grandparents.

The October Statut, an instrument of the new French State, ended the old state, the tolerant legally egalitarian state, of Clemenceau and Waldeck-Rousseau.[1] The draft of the Statut, mostly written by Raphaël Alibert, was examined by Pétain's cabinet for two hours on 30 September 1940. According to Paul Baudouin, Foreign Minister in Vichy for a short time, the Marshal was the most severe person there, insisting particularly that Jews be barred from the legal and teaching professions, though it is not clear that Pétain had any consistent view on this subject.[2] Whatever Pétain's real view or attitude, his own *chef de cabinet* from July 1940 to April 1942, Henri Du Moulin de la Barthète, made clear in an interview on 26 October 1946 that 'Germany was not at the origin of the anti-Jewish legislation of Vichy. That legislation was spontaneous and autonomous.'[3] Similarly, Xavier Vallat, in prison after the war, agreed that the Pétain government was not a 'servile plagiarist of the Nazis ... [its anti-Semitism] never went beyond the just limits set by the Church in order to protect the national community'.[4]

The singularity of the Holocaust is that abstract ideology motivated its perpetrators, rather than the pragmatic concerns of other genocides in history.[5] If Vichy did not intend to eradicate every Jew in France, as did the Nazis, it contributed to that end by treating Jews in an abstract manner, irrespective of personal differences.

Who is a Jew?

The German ordinance of 27 September could be expected. The Vichy measure was a surprise. The first country to emancipate Jews abandoned the revolutionary, egalitarian principles stemming from 1789.[6] For the first time in France a legal identity was given to a whole people. The Jews were defined by Vichy as those persons who had three grandparents of the 'Jewish race' or two such grandparents if the spouse was also Jewish. The law, applicable to the whole territory of France, Algeria and the French colonies and protectorates, enumerated the public and professional positions access to which would be prohibited or restricted. Jews were excluded from political office, judicial appointments, diplomatic and prefectorial posts, and the senior branches of public services. They could not be officers or heads of enterprises in which the state was involved. They could not be managers or directors in the press, radio, cinema or theatre. A quota, *numerus clausus*, usually of 2 per cent, was imposed for positions in the liberal professions. Exceptions to these prohibitions and restrictions would be made in individual cases by the Conseil d'État for those Jews who, in the literary, scientific and artistic worlds, had rendered exceptional services to the French state. Minor public offices were still open for veterans of the First World War and for those decorated in the Second World War. The Statut would be strongly enforced in Algeria as a result of the particular ethnic, political and economic situation there.[7]

Commentary on the 3 October Statut by juridical analysts was essentially cold, unfeeling and positive. One commentator even pointed out that one of the decrees allowing exemption was illegal because it had not been properly published in the *Journal Officiel*. An initial difficulty for interpretation and application of the Statut was that 'race' was not legally defined in French law, thus causing confusion in implementation. To deal with this and other issues a second Statut des Juifs, largely framed by Xavier Vallat, the first head of the recently created Commissariat Général aux Questions Juives (CGQJ) was issued on 2 June 1941, after careful drafting in a number of cabinet meetings and consultations with Joseph Barthélemy, Minister of Justice.

The new definition of 'Jew' in the 2 June 1941 Statut interrelated 'race' and 'religion' in a complicated way. Jews were now those people who, *irrespective of religion*, had at least three grandparents of Jewish race, or two if the spouse was also Jewish. Grandparents who adhered to the Jewish religion were considered to be of 'Jewish race'. If an individual abandoned the Jewish religion, that person could claim to be non-Jewish if the abandonment occurred before 25 June 1940 and if the person had only two grandparents of 'Jewish race'. Non-Jewishness would mean adhesion to another of the 'religious denominations recognised by the state before the law of 9 December 1905'. The explanation for this double definition by Vichy officials, especially Vallat, was that 'Jewish influence', stemming from a 'spirit' formed by both race and religion, had to be ended. Indeed, discriminatory measures of all kinds and in all spheres of life followed the definition.

Who took the lead in formulating definitions? Chronologically, the German ordinance of 27 September 1940 was issued first, but this might have been done to pre-empt the French law, about which the Germans had become aware. This is suggested by the German memo of 13 October 1940 that the German ordinance should be published first to be a 'conscious step designed to ensure that the treatment of the Jewish question emanated from the German authorities'.[8] Moreover, not only can Vichy claim priority in formulating a definition, but also its formula was more extreme and harsher than the German. It was broader than the German which, at first, was based only on religion, and which did not count the spouses of Jews as Jews. The Germans recognised the significance of the Vichy formula at once. Later, this was acknowledged when, in a memo of 1 July 1942, SS Hauptsturmführer Theodor Dannecker wrote, 'The French definition [of Jew] being broader, it will now serve as a basis in all doubtful cases'.[9] The German ordinance of 26 April 1941 had already imitated Vichy by incorporating 'race' in a new definition.

Terminology became even more discriminating and virulent for some in Vichy. The second and more extreme anti-Semitic head of the CGQJ, Darquier de Pellepoix, in a letter of 9 September 1942, revealed he was disturbed that some Jews were called 'Israélites', by themselves or by others. He saw this as a Jewish device to pretend there was only a religious problem. To correct this, Jews henceforth must be called 'Jews'. A Monsieur Lévy must be referred to as 'the Jew Lévy' and Monsieur Dreyfus as 'the Jew Dreyfus'.[10]

Vichy took the initiative in framing the definitions without subjection to German pressure. On 13 July 1940 Pétain decreed that only men of French parentage might belong to the ministerial cabinets. This discriminatory attitude found disingenuous explanation. Maurice Duverger, writing of the two Statuts of 3 October 1940 and 2 June 1941 and of 'the incapacity of access of Jews in the French administration', argued that the two laws did not 'have the character of reprisals, but measures in the public interest'.[11]

French responsibility is clear. No document has yet been found indicating direct pressure on Vichy by the Germans to pass the Statuts or to remove Jews from official positions. The law of 3 October 1940 was planned by Raphaël Alibert, Minister of Justice, disciple of Charles Maurras and notorious anti-Semite. The June 1941 law was agreed to by his successor, Joseph Barthélemy, an advocate of order rather than an ideological anti-Semite, yet one who believed that 'Jews did not dissolve in the French community'. It was Vallat, however, who proposed and co-ordinated the legislation.

State anti-Semitism had begun, purportedly based not on an 'anti-sémitisme de peau', but on the inability of Jews, because of their unsociable and particularistic nature, to be in accord with the interests of the state. The Statut of 2 June 1941 not only redefined 'Jew', but also extended the application of the prohibitions in the first Statut to an increasing number of occupations and areas of the national economy, and to the start of the Aryanisation process. The whole public administration, including subsidised enterprises and local communities, was now barred to Jews, ending the limits in the first Statut, which essentially restricted the prohibitions to public positions of influence or authority. Exemptions might be made for those Jews who had eminent military careers. Provisions of numerus clausus for professions, including doctors, laywers and architects, were set at 2 per cent of the total number of non-Jews; for university students it was 3 per cent.

How Many Jews?

Having defined 'Jews', the next step was to count them, an action never previously taken in France. In the Third Republic, census-taking had not allowed questions on religion or maternal language, though the regime did try to identify foreigners. No official number of Jews living in France was therefore available.[12]

In this area, the Germans were first, ordering on 27 September 1940 in the occupied zone a census of Jews who, in alphabetical order, had to register as such with French prefectures in the area where they lived, giving details of their occupation, nationality and residence. The great philosopher Henri Bergson, the first Jew to become a member of the Académie Française, registered as 'universitaire, philosophe, prix Nobel, juif'.[13] A file, a fichier, was started in each prefecture. The census was kept by a French official, André Tulard, who remained unpunished after the war. Like others his self-defence was that he had merely done his bureaucratic duty. The police were given the task not only of establishing the fichiers but also of finding those Jews who had not registered and verifying issues required by the prefecture.

Jews who had fled from the occupied zone were forbidden by the Germans to return. Not only did Vichy comply with this order and allow the use of French police for this singular pupose, it also issued its own ministerial circular of 27 October 1940. Prefectures in the occupied zone were to go beyond simply recording voluntary registrations by Jews as the 27 September ordinance required, and were to initiate active checks and punish recalcitrant individuals.

On 2 June 1941, the day of the crucial second Statut des Juifs, another Vichy law extended the census of Jews to the whole of France, Algeria and French overseas possessions. Individuals defined as 'Jews' had to register, and also to declare their property holdings with French prefectures and sub-prefectures. Both the persons and their property could now be easily tracked.

Violation of the order to register could be punished by fine and imprisonment. Prefects had authority to impose detentions. A typical example of Vichy insistence on the order was the instruction by the general secretary of the police in the Vaucluse to prefects on 19 July 1941 indicating 'how important it is that this census, a measure of public order, be carried out carefully and supervised with all the means at your disposal', with the help of the lists he had sent them.[14] The master list of Jews in the Vaucluse was in fact updated three times after the initial list of 1 July 1941. Individuals signalled by a mayor or by the police as being or presumed to be Jewish and who had not participated in the census were reported by prefects to the Ministry of the Interior, or to the Commissariat Général aux Questions Juives (CGQJ).

The CGQL was created on 23 March 1941 to prepare and propose legislative measures concerning Jews, including a rigorous definition of a Jew which was generally acceptable to policy-makers, the Church and public opinion, and to participate in the Aryanisation process, dealing with the sale or liquidation of property and assets owned by Jews. It was responsible for nominating the provisional administrators of Jewish enterprises after the 2 June 1941 law on the subject of taking over Jewish firms. The CGQJ could intervene in the activity of every ministry, including the police, when it was pertinent.

Originally a unit under the deputy head of government, the CGQJ was transferred in September 1941 to the Ministry of the Interior. Its numbers grew as it undertook more functions, including direct control on 19 June 1941 over the Service du Contrôle des Administrateurs Provisoires (SCAP), which had been set up in autumn 1940 in the occupied zone to prevent seizures of property by the Germans. The CGQJ could thus name a trustee for all industrial, commercial or artisanal enterprises and for real estate and movable property that was confiscated. As a result, it clashed over jurisdictional issues related to Aryanisation with other units, particularly the Ministries of Finance and Industrial Production and the *comités d'organisation* (COs), which were concerned with sectors of economic activity.

The CGQJ was the virtual ministry of state anti-Semitism under Vallat and his successor Louis Darquier de Pellepoix, appointed on 6 May 1942, an even more virulent anti-Semite than Vallat and more agreeable to the Germans. One illustration of this was the letter of 27 June 1942 from the German Embassy in Paris to the head of the Security Police and the SD in France concerning the handing over of 50,000 Jews to be deported: Darquier would 'be given complete freedom of action according to the laws already promulgated'.[15]

Even before identifying and counting those legally considered to be Jews, the Vichy regime, as well as the German occupiers in their zone, began issuing the extensive legislation and decrees and ordinances that excluded, isolated and marginalised Jews, and which cumulatively posed a threat to their very life. From exclusion the road led to extermination.

The Question of Citizenship

First was the question of citizenship and French nationality. Were Jews to be regarded as members of the French community? Early steps to limit citizenship were taken by the Vichy laws of 16 July 1940 and 22 July 1940. The first, amending the crucial law of 10 August 1927, which facilitated obtaining French nationality, dealt with forfeiture of 'the quality of being French'. This would be implemented by decree issued on advice of the Conseil d'État. The law was significant not only in itself but also because it was pertinent to two other laws issued in the same week. That of 12 July, on the composition of ministerial *cabinets*, included the phrase that only persons born of French parents could hold these positions. By the law of 17 July 1940 public employment would be limited to those of French nationality, defined as those born of a French father.

The law of 22 July 1940, introducing a different procedure, set up a commission concerned with revision of 'all acquisitions of French nationality' since 10 August 1927. This broad category might include wives and children born in France to foreign parents. Withdrawal of nationality would be pronounced by decree after advice from the commission and a report of the Ministry of Justice. The Conseil d'État was not mentioned.

The law of 22 July 1940 could not be applied in an equitable manner because of the large number of people involved whose dossiers could not be examined. The figures are disputed and there is still no completely accurate number available. Nevertheless, between January 1927 and December 1940 about 913,000 persons acquired French nationality. Of these, between 485,000 and 650,000 were naturalised.[16] The figure of those who lost nationality is either 15,154, a figure based on those who were mentioned in eighty-eight official decrees published in the *Journal Officiel*, or 17,000, an unofficial calculation. About 6000 of these were Jews. Jews were 5 per cent of the total naturalised between 1927 and 1940. About 40 per cent of those who were denaturalised during the war were Jews. Over a quarter of the Jews who had acquired French nationality in the thirteen pre-war years lost it by the laws of 16 and 22 July. The latter fact touched on the contentious defence of Vichy that it had tried to save French Jews. Yet its very actions in the first month of its existence, through which it transformed legally naturalised Jews into foreigners, imperilled them.

A sterner regulation was issued for North Africa. On 7 October 1940 a law abrogated the Crémieux decree of 24 October 1870, which had granted full citizenship and political rights to indigenous Algerian Jews. The Crémieux decree provoked a violent response from the 'colons' of Algeria, the white Frenchmen who not only engaged in hostile activity at that time, as they continued to do, but also elected deputies to the Chamber of Deputies in 1885 and 1889 on an anti-Semitic platform. Seventy years after the decree, Jews and their descendants who had been beneficiaries of it now lost all political rights and citizenship. In 1940, about 120,000 Jews lived in Algeria, while about 200,000 lived in Morocco and 80,000 in Tunisia. After the 7 October law about 100,000 Algerian Jews lost citizenship.

Since Algeria, a French colony where most Jews lived in a few cities, became part of Vichy France after the armistice of June 1940, the 3 October 1940 Statut des Juifs was applied there. So was the other anti-Semitic legislation, which indeed was maintained even after American forces landed in North Africa. After the assassination there of Admiral Darlan, high commissioner of the area, Jews were subjected to even harsher treatment until Darlan's successor General Henri Giraud, under American pressure, ended the racist laws.

In Morocco, a protectorate, Jews who were more dispersed geographically than in Algeria were subject to the second-class citizenship of *dhimmi* (protected people), but were less likely to experience anti-Semitism in practice than in Algeria. The Vichy laws were applied with less severity, largely affecting those Jews in urban areas. Nevertheless, some 4000 Jews were imprisoned in labour or concentration camps.

In Tunisia, where about half of the Jewish population lived in the city of Tunis, the Jewish experience was similar to that in Morocco, until November 1942 when the Germans invaded the area and put 5000 Jews in labour camps. Tunisia was the home of 80,000 Jews, most of whom were descendants of people who had lived in the area for 2000 years; they were subjects of the Bey. In addition, 5000 Italian Jews, descendants of those sent as colonists two hundred years earlier, were subjects of Italy, and yet another 5000 Jews were French subjects. The Vichy laws were applied relatively mildly by Admiral Jean Pierre Esteva, resident general in Tunisia since July 1940. Ordered by Vichy not to oppose the invasion by the Axis countries in Tunis and Bizerte, he could not prevent the arrest of some of his senior officials. Yet he did release political prisoners, evacuate men and material to Algiers, and help Jews and Allied soldiers escape from the advancing Nazi forces. His record was mixed, partly because of the influence on him of Georges Guilbaud, ex-communist member of the PPF and a fervent collaborator. Esteva's own fate was to be condemned *in absentia* in Algiers in March 1943 for collaboration with the enemy, and to be condemned for treason in March 1945. Sentenced to life imprisonment and to military degradation, he was released in 1950 because of ill health.

In Vichy, discussion of denaturalisation continued, and was interrelated with other dire issues. At the meeting on 2 September 1942 of Laval and Oberg, agreement was reached that Vichy would give to the Nazis all Jews who had acquired French citizenship since 1933, which the Germans had proposed, though no action was taken. Differences were in the degree of persecution. René Bousquet, head of the national police, proposed denaturalisation of Jews who had acquired citizenship since 1 January 1932; Darquier wanted the date of 10 August 1927. A draft law supporting Darquier's position was proposed in July 1943, but it did not go into effect since Laval, who signed it, withdew his support of it in August, and Pétain disapproved of it.[17] The Marshal accepted the principle of denaturalisation but opposed indiscriminate application. By contrast, the German occupiers pressed for a further law on denaturalisation, since that would allow many more Jews, no longer considered French, to be arrested by the French police. Like Darquier, Roethke proposed the date of 1927; he estimated that 50,000 Jews had entered France between 1927 and 1932. Protests by prominent French Jews went unheeded. In June 1941 a group of them wrote to Pétain on behalf of 'We Israelites', informing him that they did not regard themselves as an ethnic minority or as a political community. They called on 'the venerated leader' to avoid the tragic consequences of the cruellest decisions being made.

Exclusion of the Jews

For the venerated leader and others, Jews, whether French nationals or not, were all seen as 'anti-France' and increasingly excluded from French life as restrictions were put on movement, individual rights, occupations and professions, and property before their lives were endangered. Jews were not allowed to travel outside their area of residence without special permission.

In the occupied zone Jews were banned from public places open to others: cinemas, theatres, museums, libraries, swimming pools, public gardens and parks. An ordinance of 26 April 1941 prohibited them from most economic activities and professions. Another, on 13 August 1941, ordered confiscation of radios, which had to be deposited with French police officials. By order on 10 December 1941 of the French prefect of police, Jews living in the Seine *département* had to register any change of address and were subject to periodic checks. A week later the prefect of police ordered all Jews arriving in Paris from the provinces to report to the police.

The chronology of persecution continued. Jews were forbidden to possess telephones and bicycles. A German ordinance of 7 February 1942 forbade them to be outdoors between 8 p.m. and 6 a.m., a prohibition enforced by French police. Women could go only to the Rothschild hospital to bear children. Jews on 10 February 1942 were forbidden to change their names and had to register all Jewish family names changed since October 1870. In July, they were limited to shopping between 3 and 4 p.m. and were obliged if they travelled in the Paris metro to use the last car. In early 1943 Jews were forbidden to reside in fourteen *départements* of France, and on the Spanish and Italian frontiers. Foreign Jews by an order of 16 March 1943 had to report any move; the Ministry of the Interior could determine their residence in a particular locality.

The most public form of humiliation came on 29 May 1942 with the German order that all Jews over the age of six wear the yellow star inscribed with the word 'Juif' on their clothing in a prescribed fashion. The Nazis thought that over 100,000 would collect the badge, but in fact only 83,000 did. This order, and the sight of Jews wearing the badge, was the first action to ignite considerable sympathy for the victims on the part of the population and also clerical figures. As a consequence Vichy refused to impose a similar order in the unoccupied zone.

Vichy did, however, on 6 November 1942, order, purportedly as a measure of internal security, all foreign Jews to remain in their residences unless they got permission to move. It still refused to impose the yellow star, but on 11 Decemberr 1942 it ordered the word 'Juif' or 'Juive' to be put on identity cards and ration books in red letters. Later, on 9 August 1943, Jews in the *département* of the Seine were ordered to report to the prefecture of police to get an identity card in good condition.

Could Jews leave France? At first Vichy appeared to be anxious to get rid of Jews peacefully, perhaps to Madagascar or to Spain or Portugal if they could get transit visas from those countries.[18] To speed exit of refugeees, Vichy set up a special internment camp at Les Milles in autumn 1940 for those holding entry visas for other countries. For a variety of reasons, both internal and external factors and administrative disorganisation, this policy had only qualified success; about 1400 refugees were able to leave France with the assistance of the Jewish emigration organisation, HICEM.

Laval declared his desire in stark terms. Jews were coming to Vichy at an alarming rate. They would foment trouble and give the place a bad name. He would get rid of them. How? At first he supported emigration, but then, partly under German pressure in spring 1942, he agreed to deportation. Some discussion of exit visas in October 1942 by Bousquet, who agreed to 500 for children, and by Laval, who agreed to only 150, ended unsuccessfully. Visas were not provided and those already given for emigration were cancelled. Jews became invisible. Mayors were ordered to erase from their registers the names of all Jews, French citizens or not, who had been arrested, interned or deported. They ceased to have legal existence.

For those who remained, censorship was imposed in both zones of the country. In the occupied zone, lists of books, known first as 'liste Bernhard' and then 'liste Otto', were issued by the Germans in 1940 banning undesirable works, 'those which systematically poisoned French public opinion'. Over 1000 books were forbidden, including those written by 600 French authors of Jewish origin, and by communist writers. Other lists in 1942 and 1943 added about 1000 more books and some 700 authors. The 1943 list includes 739 writers 'de langue française'. At the same time the Germans published lists of authors whose works should be promoted, and some publishers were happy to comply. In all, over 2 million books had been seized and destroyed by 1944.

Besides Jews, others such as gypsies were subjected to persecution and discrimination. On 13 August 1940 Masonic lodges were dissolved. In September and October, partly because of the Stalin–Hitler pact of August 1939, communists were suppressed and rounded up in the Paris region. National professional organisations were dissolved in November.

But for Jews the worst was yet to come. Occupational discrimination started early in the regime. In public offices it was immediate. By a decree of 18 July 1940, no one would be employed in the civil service whose father had not been born French. The Statut of 3 October 1940 ended positions for Jews in the press, cinema and upper civil service. Jews were banned from public offices and positions: head of state, member of government, council of state, the court judges, all elected bodies, diplomatic officials, prefects and sub-prefects, all grades of police officials, members of the teaching profession, officers of the armed forces, heads of enterprises receiving subsidies from the state. The only exceptions were for Jews who were veterans of the First World War or who were cited in the Second World War, or Jews who had rendered exceptional service to the state in the literary, scientific, and artistic fields. Jews were forbidden to work in many fields – insurance, ship-owning, art, antiques and any occupation involving speculation – or to own anything except a home or business. On 6 June 1942 they were banned from the theatre and cinema, and from vocal or instrumental concerts. The law of 17 November 1941 prohibited the Jewish owners of property placed under 'temporary administration' from being employed in their own companies and generally from occupying executive posts in any corporate enterprise. Even Jewish prisoners of war were to vacate their positions two months after their return from captivity. No Jew could be a member of the financial, administrative or medical staff of the armed forces.

Starting with the Vichy law of 2 June 1941, prohibitions and restrictions were put on Jewish membership of the liberal professions. On 21 June 1941 a quota of 3 per cent was imposed on university admission and examination. By a number of implementing decrees, a *numerus clausus*, almost always 2 per cent, was imposed on one profession after another. Some of the more important were lawyers and public officials on 16 July 1941, doctors and architects on 24 September 1941, pharmacists and midwives on 26 December 1941, dentists on 5 June 1942, and performers on 6 June 1942. Within a year, from June 1941 to June 1942, Jews were excluded, wholly or virtually completely from almost all professions. To their discredit, the professional organisations, except the architects, acquiesced and even supported this discrimination, partly for reasons of personal advantage.

In Algeria a quota of 14 per cent, then reduced to 7 per cent, was imposed on Jewish students at primary and secondary schools. A regulation of 21 July 1942 by the prefect of Algiers forbade Jews from being milkmen. The stated reason was that the 25,000 Jews in Algiers consumed a total of 5000 litres of milk a day while the 270,000 Europeans and Muslims there consumed only 7000 litres a day.

Exceptions from these prohibitions were allowed for Jews who had rendered exceptional services to the French state. Thus, some Jewish magistrates were regarded as 'honorary judges'. These included for a time Jacques Helbronner, Cahen-Salvador (Section President of the

Conseil d'État) and Julien Reinach. In a personal letter to Pétain, Henri
Bergson honourably refused any claim to favoured treatment. Similar
exemptions were granted by the Germans in a few cases concerning
the wearing of the yellow star and permission to travel. Among the
fortunate few were Mme de Brinon, née Franck, wife of the Vichy
Ambassador in Paris, the countess Bertrand d'Aramon, née Stern, and
the Marquise de Chasselout-Laubat.

CHAPTER 6

THE ARYANISATION PROCESS

Within weeks of taking power, the Vichy regime began initiating anti-Semitic legislation and discriminatory measures and actions for the whole of French territory and overseas possessions.[1] German occupation authorities, the Militärbefehlshaber in Frankreich (MBF), concurrently issued their own discriminatory ordinances applicable in their zone, the occupied or northern zone, and also engaged with other German units in pillaging activities.[2]

By these measures Jews began to be excluded from national economic life. Their links to the economic and social fabric of the country were severed as they were deprived of occupation, assets and properties, and means of subsistence by both German and Vichy measures. Exclusion began on 3 October 1940 in Vichy with prohibition or restriction of Jews in various professions: civil service positions, from which 3500 were dismissed, press and cinema. All professions regulated by law were virtually closed to Jews by the law of 2 June 1941 and the succeeding implementing decrees, and by other laws.

Crucial in this perverse path of prohibitions, deprivation of normal status and deportation from France were the policies and process of 'Aryanisation', the neologism borrowed from Nazi Germany to define the complex and increasingly extreme edicts for removing 'all Jewish influence from the French economy', and liquidating or transferring Jewish property to Aryans.[3]

Numerous Vichy laws and decrees, and German ordinances, laid down the substance and the methods for the transfer to Aryans, non-Jews, of the assets of Jews – in manufacturing, commerce, property development, craft trades, real estate, property rights, leasehold rights, movable assets, equity, shares and bonds – or for the disposition of those assets by officials appointed for the task.

At the outset, certain features of the complex Aryanisation process can be noted: its extensive range in both the nature of assets and numbers of people affected; the considerable participation for the most part of both governmental and non-governmental French individuals and organisations; the paradoxical emphasis on legal procedures and formulas for much of the policy; the rapidity of its introduction first in the occupied and then in the unoccupied zone; the unevenness and some slowness in implementation; the movement along parallel and sometimes overlapping tracks of the German and Vichy policies; the variations in completion of the process between geographical regions and economic sectors and at different times between 1940 and 1944; and the changes in behaviour and attitudes of French people and professional groups during that period.

A useful and working, if incomplete, distinction can be drawn between two general forms of deprivation of Jewish assets: on one hand, spoliation by legal enactments of businesses, property, assets and French shares deposited in financial institutions and accounts; on the other hand, theft and pillaging, especially by the Germans, of works of art, gold, currencies, foreign securities, furniture, music and contents of apartments. Yet, if a legal if not moral distinction can be made between the two, the reality was that they merged in their impact on Jewish possessions. Aryanisation was not simply spoliation; it was also an attack on private property, a limitation of the rights of citizens, a break with an equitable social order, a civil theft by law, in which Jews lost and others, people and institutions, gained.

Even now, over sixty years after the events, the full picture of Aryanisation is not available because of the sheer extent of the process and because some relevant archives and other written documents have been destroyed or are missing. Nevertheless, many details, data and information concerning the complex process and administrative mechanisms have emerged in the reports of the non-partisan study mission set up in February 1997 by the then Prime Minister, Alain Juppé, a Gaullist, and confirmed in October by his socialist successor, Lionel Jospin.

No completely exact calculation of the various forms of expropriation, spoliation and theft of the property and wealth of Jews can be made for a number of reasons. More precise information is available about the policies in the occupied, northern than in the unoccupied, southern zone. The value of the assets taken in the whole of France was larger than the amount registered by the CGQJ, the Caisse des Dépôts et Consignations (CDC), other state agencies and the notaires. Sales and liquidations of Jewish assets were often not made at a fair price; the CGQJ for the welfare of the French economy wanted, though it often failed, to obtain a high price. A considerable part of the proceeds of the transactions went on deductions and expenses of lawyers, temporary administrators and accountants. Much of the process was unfinished at the time of Liberation in 1944.

Nevertheless, approximate, if not completely exact, calculations based on official documents show the magnitude and impact of the process. The extent can be seen in the following figures. The value of Jewish assets seized in France was 5.2 billion francs at 1940s prices. Over 50,000 Jewish-owned companies or properties were seized, though less than half of the started procedures for disposing of them were completed by the end of the regime. Sales and liquidations of companies and properties accounted for 3.2 billion francs of the total figure.

The estimated number of Jewish security and currency accounts that were frozen was 67,962, comprising 37,124 deposit bank accounts, of which 15 per cent were company accounts, 26,582 savings bank accounts, partly national savings bank and partly ordinary savings bank, and 4256 post office chequing accounts. Securities accounts amounted to 6 billion francs, and current accounts to 1.2 billion. About 6000 safe deposits were frozen.

In the occupied zone, Jews had 22,088 individual cash accounts. Of the Jewish population, 16 per cent had frozen savings bank accounts, 18 per cent had frozen regular bank accounts and 3.4 per cent had frozen post office cheque accounts. The majority of deposits were small. Only 2 per cent of savings accounts and 19 per cent of regular bank accounts had balances over 10,000 francs. In all, assets of 53,000 Jews were frozen. Of the 75,721 Jews deported from France, 7400 had assets that were frozen. Cash deposits in the internment camps amounted to 39 million francs.

Beyond this there was extraordinary pillaging. Several million books were stolen from Jews. Over 40,000 Jewish apartments were looted by German occupiers, and their contents shipped in 20,000 trainloads to German cities. About 100,000 art objects belonging to Jews were stolen, some 61,000 of which were recovered and returned to France after the war; of these about 45,000 were returned to their owners. A considerable amount of money and valuables was taken from Jews in internment camps. Cash, jewellery, stocks and bonds amounted to some 215 million francs, mostly from those in the Drancy camp. Property was also taken from internees in the provincial camps outside Paris.

Of the more than 50,000 dossiers of Jews found after the Liberation concerning Aryanisation, 42,000 stemmed from the occupied zone – 31,000 from the *département* of the Seine and 11,000 from other *départements* in that northern zone – and 8000 from the unoccupied zone. The degree of Aryanisation varied according to region, economic sector, size of the enterprise and time of the activity.

In general, Aryanisation was started and advanced and completed to a greater degree in the northern than in the southern zone. Larger businesses naturally took longer to handle than smaller ones. Assets took longer to sell than to liquidate.

Economic sectors varied considerably. Aryanisation was highest in the sectors of tailors, milliners and street traders in the Seine area, and weak in real estate, where it was only 20 per cent. It was particularly high – over 70 per cent – in sectors of clothing manufacturing, furs, shoes and leather goods, and considerable in haberdashery and underwear (51 per cent). It was low in banking and insurance (17 per cent), food and commerce.[4]

In the sector of clothing and shoes, many small shops were liquidated, and their equipment and raw materials sold; all the same, nearly a third of small tailoring firms survived. Real estate was almost at the bottom, partly because Aryanisation in the sector began late, and partly because of the need for legal deeds. This was a time-consuming process for notaries, who were sometimes slow to co-operate and were not happy about forced sales.[5] Notaries were criticised by SCAP and the CGQJ for raising technical obstacles. Equally, real estate agents, uncertain about the future of Jewish property, were not enthusiastic about sales.

The Aryanisation programme varied through time as well as in the different geographical regions and economic sectors. In the first year and a half it proceeded rapidly in both zones. As the military balance began changing with the Anglo-American successes in North Africa in late 1942, shattering the image of German invincibility and a German-controlled western Europe, less zeal and more caution were displayed by French governmental organisations and individuals, except for extreme anti-Semites, especially in the banking sector and by notaries in implementing Aryanisation or discriminatory orders. On the other hand, looting by the Germans became more frequent during that period of change.

As with so many other features of the Vichy regime, judgement of the Aryanisation programme is still immersed in political and historical controversy. Debatable questions remain: who was responsible for the policies; when were the policies devised and for what purpose; how was the programme implemented? Relative degrees of responsibility are involved in the overlapping jurisdiction and sometimes concurrent legal measures emanating from the German occupiers and from Vichy. Initiative by Vichy in framing and implementing those measures is undeniable, though sometimes they were imitative of the Germans, and in various ways constraints on the Vichy regime were formidable. Even accepting the presence of the German constraints, the complicity and willingness of so many governmental and non-governmental personnel in the formulation and implementation of Aryanisation are sufficient evidence to justify an indictment of Vichy.

Already, on 20 May 1940, after conquering the Low Countries, the German High Command issued orders about abandoned enterprises or property (not all of which was owned by Jews) that it considered vital for food supply of the population. In occupied France, as in the other countries, trustees, called by the Germans management commissioners (MCs), were chosen to administer any property left unattended by those who fled the zone. Jews, however, were not specifically mentioned until the ordinance of 18 October 1940.

On the very day, 14 June 1940, that the German army entered Paris, pillaging began. Within two days the Devisenschutzkommando (DSK), Currency Protection Commando, part of the administrative empire of Goering, and of his four-year plan, not only seized the Jewish-owned Banque Lazard, but also froze foreign and French securities held in foreign currencies in safes rented in banks in the occupied zone. This was a first step in fulfilling the German desire to control assets in a French economy that would be further weakened by an overvalued mark to the detriment of the French franc, and by the payment, soon to be imposed, of the indemnity of 400 million marks a day on France.[6] Later to come was looting of gold and foreign currencies belonging to Jews 'residing on enemy territory'.

The Process Begins

The Aryanisation process was launched by the MBF, the German occupiers, with ordinances of 27 September 1940 and, more important, 18 October 1940. They ordered all Jewish businesses in the occupied zone to be registered and identified, with a notice in German and in French to that effect. Such businesses were so identified if they had a Jewish owner or manager, or if over one-third of the board of directors was Jewish. People affected had to declare their ownership at the nearest French prefecture of police. By the same ordinance, any legal contract with a Jew made after 23 May 1940 could be declared void.

The Vichy representative or pseudo-ambassador, so-called general delegate, to the MBF in Paris, at that time General de la Laurencie, ordered French prefects in the occupied zone to assist in implementing the German ordinances. The MBF instructions for the appointed management commissioners for the appropriated Jewish enterprises, to dispose of them by selling to non-Jews or by liquidation, were distributed by French prefectures in the German occupied zone.

Some Vichy officials were troubled by these ordinances. For them the decrees exceeded the limits of German authority granted by the armistice of 22 June 1940, since they were not required for any security need. The French saw the appointment of the MCs to manage property as an abuse of power. Above all, in what was to be a constant theme, French officials expressed the apprehension that the Germans would gain control of significant sections of the French economy. They held it was for Vichy to decide whether an enterprise should be sold, liquidated or used in its existing state.

Nevertheless, the French regime and officials in general were not unduly troubled by the principle of Aryanisation as such, but rather by two possible consequences of the programme: disregard of proper legal authority on which action must be based and, above all, infringement of the sovereignty of France. Vichy legalised, implemented and even paralleled some of the German measures. It accepted the Aryanisation policy, extended it to the unoccupied zone and initiated its own measures to deprive Jews of their assets and property.

Vichy amplified the German ordinance on abandoned property of 20 May 1940 by its own law of 10 September 1940, applying it to enterprises whose heads were for any reason not capable of exercising their functions, though Vichy did not immediately call for the sale of the properties. The law also introduced, as agent for implementing the Aryanisation process, the position of the *administrateur provisoire* (AP), temporary administrator, the title that Vichy preferred to the German MC, who would manage the property and businesses of people who were not capable for any reason of managing them. At this early stage, the AP was to be nominated by the Ministry of Industrial Production.

Vichy responded to the German ordinance of 18 October 1940 with its own circular of 27 October 1940, imposing registration on those Jewish businesses that still carried on activities in the occupied zone, but had transferred their main offices to the unoccupied zone. These businesses were also put under the management of a temporary administrator.

A number of German ordinances were further issued over the next year. The MBF order of 12 November 1940 was expressly aimed at 'suppressing definitively Jewish influence in the French economy'. The options were stark. Jews could decide to sell 'freely' their properties to non-Jews. Some Jews did as a result sell their enterprises, occasionally to friends or well-meaning people, but usually cheaply to avoid total loss. If they did not sell, the appointed MCs could sell the properties, after MBF authorisation, or could liquidate them.

A second German ordinance, of 3 March 1941, focused on the protection and transport of art objects, many of which were soon to be stolen, in the occupied zone. The important ordinance of 26 April

1941 banned Jews from most careers and professions, forbade almost all economic activity for them, and denied them the income, which was frozen, from the sale of their stolen property. Landlords could evict Jews from their houses or apartments for non-payment of rent.

By the important ordinance of 28 May 1941, the MBF forbade all commercial transactions for Jewish businesses for which MCs had not yet been appointed. Interestingly, in this complex relationship of German occupiers and Vichy, the May ordinance explicitly referred to the role to be played by the French Service du Contrôle des Administrateurs Provisoires (SCAP) in its implementation.

SCAP had been set up by Vichy on 9 December 1940, specifically to supervise the work of the APs, temporary administrators, introduced on 10 September. Even the extreme anti-Semite, Xavier Vallat, head of the CGQJ, was troubled at the beginning that the policies of genuine, ideological anti-Semitism that he embodied might be discredited by 'regrettable profiteers' and looters, including some APs, who were already abusing the confiscatory legislation. The new body, SCAP, headed for a few months by P-E. Fournier, former governor of the Bank of France, implemented the German ordinance of 28 May and appointed APs, though the Germans (MBF) claimed veto power over the nominations in the occupied zone.

Placed at first in the Ministry of Industrial Production, the SCAP was then attached from 19 June 1941 to the CGQJ, to which it reported on the extent and nature of Jewish assets, although ultimate authority supposedly rested with the relevant ministries. In May 1942 the SCAP was fused with the existing Direction de l'Aryanisation Économique (DAE), the Management Department of Economic Aryanisation, a unit of the CGQJ; as a result one director was in Paris and another in Vichy with this extension of authority to the whole of France. Complicating the untidy and sometimes internally contentious administrative structure, the SCAP continued to operate in the occupied zone as a separate unit for a time.

The Role of the CGQJ

The fundamental governmental implementer and deviser of political anti-Semitism in all its aspects was the CGQJ. Its first head, Xavier Vallat, regarded the legal exclusion of Jews from the economy as an essential part of a policy of anti-Semitism; he was the stimulus behind the Vichy measures of 2 June 1941 and 22 July 1941. The CGQJ played an increasingly important role in the management and liquidation of Jewish assets, and the freezing of bank account deposits and other money, a role that was reflected by the decree of 20 October 1941.[7]

Employees of the CGQJ increased from 250 in July 1941 to over 1000 in 1944. In October 1941 it was reorganised and its role became more aggressive with the creation of the Police des Questions Juives (PQJ) as a unit within it. Not a part of the regular police, and including rogues and pimps from Pigalle in Paris, the PQJ, though it had no legal power to make arrests, specialised in hunting down Jews, both searching and stealing from them, and acting as guards in the internment camps, where they stole jewellery, watches, rings and money. A brutal, violent, and corrupt group, it was transformed on 5 August 1942 into the Section d'Enquête et de Contrôle (SEC), the Section for Enquiry and Control, a more neutral name, set up by Laval after his return to power.

In spite of its supposed respect for legality, the PQJ and the SEC were only the more extreme forms of typical behaviour by the parent CGQJ organisation. It engaged in spying on inhabitants, intercepting mail, monitoring telephone calls, preventing music by Jewish composers from being performed, and asking the police to rid the town of Vichy of Jews.

The activity of the CGQJ was aided by numerous citizens, mostly covertly, by denunciations of Jews, letters about them from creditors or concierges, and messages to and from the temporary administrators. Clearly, self-interested individuals profited from the liquidation of Jewish property. Acts of support for Jews were rare, and active opposition to the process was even rarer.[8]

The 62,000 dossiers compiled by the CGQJ now available portray the drama of the requisitioning and spoliation of the assets of thousands of Jews, whose names and addresses are carefully listed. Where property was concerned, the name of the AP (provisional administrator) was also listed. Letters to the unfortunate victims came from SCAP, referring to the German ordinances of 18 October 1940 and 26 April 1941. The dossiers of property and enterprises were methodically divided into three groups: the Paris and Seine region, broken down into economic sectors; the rest of the northern or occupied zone; and the unoccupied zone. It is thus possible to compare the degree of Aryanisation in the different geographical zones.

Who can be held responsible for this ongoing Aryanisation programme? German policy and actions interacted with Vichy legislation and behaviour. It was French prefects who identified Jewish properties in the occupied zone, and French authorities and personnel who managed those properties and who carried out the census of Jews in the occupied zone. The Germans skilfully allowed Vichy to act by legal methods, and to participate in the process that ended with the deportation of Jews from France.[9] The crucial reality is that Germany did not have sufficient personnel of its own to carry out the anti-Semitic policies in France. The repeated Vichy rhetoric insisting on French sovereignty was not unwelcome to the Germans, who saw the political usefulness of Vichy's involvement in the anti-Semitic policies. An early memo of 1 November 1940 by Dr Elmar Michel of the Economic Bureau of the German High Command clearly noted that if French authorities participated in the anti-Semitic measures, 'We thereby gain shared responsibility by the French and we have at our disposal the French administrative apparatus.'[10] On 12 December 1940, the German occupiers instructed the prefects in the occupied zone to appoint the temporary administrators; after the law of 22 July 1941 this authority was given to the SCAP.

The Germans were conscious of the political dilemmas and internal conflicts within the Vichy regime, of which they were made aware by members of that regime who expressed their concern. This concern was strikingly articulated by Vallat, head of the CGQJ, who reported to Dr Best of the MBF in Paris that Pétain himself had asked him to stop abuses in implementing Aryanisation because it might provoke justifiable counter-propaganda.[11]

The Vichy explanation and defence of its collaboration with the German occupiers on Aryanisation policies and of its own initiatives related to those policies was grounded in a number of economic and political arguments. The Vichy regime, as we have seen, was early concerned that whole sectors of the French economy might fall under German control unless it acted to forestall this possibility. At the same time it also hoped to use Aryanisation to rationalise the economy and to reduce unemployment, and therefore evaluated action on Aryanised assets and enterprises in the context of its effect on a particular economic sector. On the one hand, small commercial enterprises that were too numerous and too archaic could be eliminated.[12] On the other hand, some concentration of resources, as with cotton mills, was acceptable.

The political argument for maintaining French sovereignty by acting independently and unilaterally and on its own initiative was a constant refrain of the Vichy regime. So was insistence on adherence to the law, *ordre moral*, honesty, the fight against theft, partly for reasons of political expediency. Vichy wanted to reassure the French public that private property had not been taken illegally. The whole basis of the 'National Revolution' would be discredited if French actions were seen as taking the form of pillage and theft rather than of legal processes. Adherence to legal formality would help check the emergence of a critical public opinion about discriminatory actions and policies. Such adherence would also justify the behaviour of public officials and private executives who felt, or claimed to be, bound by an administrative ethos, obedience to legal, if bureaucratic, rules, even if the chief policy-makers were prejudiced and self-seeking individuals.

This emphasis on the legality of Vichy actions, and the accompanying virtual absence of expressions of disquiet or moral qualms about the discriminatory, persecutory nature of anti-Semitic legislation on economic matters, has overtones of surrealistic farce. Cognitive dissonance might charitably explain the requirement that managements and accounts of expropriated Jewish businesses and property be strictly and diligently done in accordance with legal regulations. The pillar of anti-Semitism, the CGQJ, constantly illustrated this bizarre situation by its rules for discriminatory actions. One example was an order of 6 October 1941 by which the CGQJ could legally determine the fee for the AP after it approved the management accounts. It carefully fixed the time limit of appointment of an AP for a maximum of six months, the time allowed for completion of a particular process of disposal of assets. The functions and behaviour of APs were laid down in detail. Crucial to the whole process was the card index of Jews, assembled from many *fichiers* of future victims; the *fichier* compiled by the Paris prefecture of police in October 1940 is the best known.

Perhaps the greatest paradox in the Aryanisation process is this dissonance between the volume of the juridical anti-Semitic legislation and the sordid reality of spoliation and theft. Vichy issued 220 legal texts on the process, including 71 *arrêtés* (official orders), 71 decrees, and 67 laws. The Germans issued 28 ordinances and official notices. Both Vichy and the Germans realised the need for legislation to justify their actions. A German memo of 26 August 1940 stated that the transfer of Jewish enterprises into German hands must seem to be following the norms of private law.[13]

Following norms did slow down the Aryanisation process for Vichy.[14] The CGQJ, conforming to the text of the law of 22 July 1941, would only, at least in theory, approve the sale of Jewish property if it helped eliminate Jewish influence and if the sale price was appropriate. Auditors in August 1941 were instructed to check the management of companies by APs to ensure that regulations were being followed.

In similar fashion, lawyers were not happy about forced sales because of the likelihood of disputes about the relevant laws, and often advised caution. They, like others, were aware that sales and liquidations were sometimes carried out by inappropriate procedures or disregarded the right of private property. Some lawyers retained loyalty to their Jewish clients; one even refused to give the address of his client to officials. It seems clear that lawyers slowed down the Aryanisation process, even if they did not oppose it openly.

Some initial misgivings were expressed about economic Aryanisation, propelled by Vallat, first head of the CGQJ, who had largely been responsible for the second Statut des Juifs of 2 June 1941. An individual who claimed to be a moderate, the Minister of Justice, Joseph Barthélemy, was disturbed: 'I do not want our country to appear as the refuge of barbarism.'[15] In the Vichy Council of Ministers he spoke of the exceptional nature of the dispossession of Jews from a legal point of view. This action, he held, was contrary to the general rule of French law. French citizens, as far as the right of ownership was concerned, were placed in 'a situation inferior to that of foreigners residing in France'. Nevertheless, Barthélemy did co-sign the important discriminatory law of 22 July 1941, accepting it, he said, for reasons of general politics.[16]

The Laws on Aryanisation

The extraordinary volume of laws and decrees created an exceptional judicial category for Jews; these laws and decrees were accepted with varying degrees of enthusiasm and passive compliance, but also caused alarm for some French citizens. The sanctity of private property was challenged by the legislation, and consequently some criticism was directed at a policy that deprived individuals of their assets without their consent.

The very significant, indeed crucial, Vichy law of 22 July 1941 was formulated after considerable discussion with the German authorities. It extended to the whole of France, apart from the *départements* of Alsace-Moselle which were annexed by Germany, the objectives of economic Aryanisation already stated in the German order of 8 October 1940. This law was the cornerstone of Vichy policy on the subject. For the first time, Vichy legalised in its unoccupied zone a framework, reiterated in many forms, for Aryanisation, the systematic disposing of Jewish assets in order to 'eliminate all Jewish influence from the French national economy'.

The July law, which deprived Jews of legal rights over their property, set up a specific Aryanisation procedure for three categories of assets.

The first category included businesses, companies, shops, buildings and real estate rights, rental and vacation homes, which belonged to Jews. Only residences for personal use were exempted. The rest would be managed by the APs.

The second category was of stocks and shares, corporate equity belonging to Jews, which, except for those owned by companies being managed without decision by APs, were placed under the control and responsibility of the Domaines, a unit in the Ministry of Finance, which was the management department of the State Property Authority.

In the third category were bank account balances and all sums of money belonging to Jews, which were frozen or deposited by order of the CGQJ.

Aryanisation of businesses, shops, buildings and real estate belonging to people identified as Jews was put in the hands of the APs. Paradoxically, this device of temporary administration had been used in pre-war France for official intervention when owners of enterprises were legally incompetent; but it was now applied for exactly opposite reasons, to dispose of enterprises that were healthy and viable, and for purposes not of economic improvement, but of discrimination.

By its law of 10 September 1940, Vichy had introduced the position of the temporary administrator (AP), who would manage industrial or commercial enterprises whose owners for any reason found it 'impossible to exercise their functions'. The decree of 16 January 1941 amplified this law, defining the method of appointment and the functions of APs.

Nominated by the relevant Vichy minister after consulting a *comité d'organisation* (CO), APs were at first appointed by the Ministry of Industrial Production. The COs were semi-public, industry-wide professional groups set up on 16 August 1940 to represent people in their occupational activity. The COs not only suggested individuals they thought appropriate and competent to implement Aryanisation processes, but sometimes also recommended which particular Jewish enterprises should be managed.

A decree of 16 January 1941, amended in August, gave APs broad powers for the Aryanisation process: disposing of the whole or parts of an enterprise by selling or liquidating Jewish enterprises, subject to approval by the Ministry of Industrial Production. This need for approval was removed by a law of 2 February 1941. The APs worked with the banking system in their selling and liquidating; the proceeds of the transactions were deposited in blocked accounts at the Caisse des Dépôts et Consignations (CDC) by the law of 22 July 1941. Before that law, they were to be paid to the legitimate owner.

The APs became responsible for legal acts for disposing of Jewish assets, without, after a brief time, obtaining permission of the rightful owners. Any business arrangement made without the consent of the AP would be considered void. On appointment, the APs estimated or assessed and then reported to the CGQJ the value of the assets, determined the nationality of the owner and made proposals for appropriate action.

The APs could choose what steps to take. One was to do nothing, either by negligence, or by complicity with the Jewish owner, or by delaying a decision. The other path was decision to sell or to liquidate part or all of the property, either definitively or after endorsement by Vichy and, in the occupied zone, by the Germans. The funds from the transactions stayed with the notaries or the APs until the action was completed and until approval of the action was given by the CGQJ. If a Jewish business, such as a retail or craft shop, was small, it might not be worthwhile for APs to spend time to sell or liquidate in any prolonged way. The APs might therefore ask the CGQJ for the business to be closed and for any materials or implements to be sold. Some small businesses were left alone, but their owners, usually foreign Jews lacking French contacts and easily identifiable, were among the first victims of the mass arrests in 1942.

Aryanisation of the larger and more considerable enterprises touched on many sectors of French economic life: newspapers, banks, industrial and commercial enterprises. A few of these can be mentioned. Among the newspapers were the *Tribune Républicaine* and the *Mot d'Ordre* of Marseille. The banks included Lazard Frères, Eugene Lévy, the Banque d'Escompte, Hirsch and Maurice Rueff. Included in the industrial and commercial sector were the Société Gazo-Industrie, Bloch Aviation and chain stores such as the Établissements Sudarski.

Proceeds of sales or liquidations by APs did not go directly to the Jewish owners. The usual procedure was that they were deposited in escrow in two accounts at the CDC. After paying off debts, liabilities and the fees and expenses of APs, 90 per cent of the proceeds were deposited in frozen accounts in the names of the Jewish victims, and the other 10 per cent in accounts of the CGQJ, to which the APs reported on their management accounts. In theory, though not always in practice, the victims were allowed monthly withdrawals from their frozen accounts for subsistence needs.

A tax was also deducted from the proceeds, collected by the APs and paid to the German Treuhand und Revisionstelle (official escrow and audit agency), of an amount equal to a monthly fee for the AP. The Germans were unsatisfied by the amount they received. On 2 December 1942, the MBF ordered 'the devolution to the German Reich of the assets of Jews now possessing or having possessed German nationality'. Later, on 15 September 1943, the Germans claimed the assets of Jews originating from Poland and Czechoslovakia. Therefore, part of the funds of Jewish refugees that were seized in France went to Germany.

Though in fact considerable corruption ensued, the APs were expected to behave properly and honestly, and could be held accountable before judicial tribunals as well as being supervised by the CGQJ. Generalisation is not possible about the actual behaviour of the

7834 APs appointed.[17] Some were honest and competent; others were guilty of theft or misappropriation. Some were people of principle, diligently performing their job in what they saw as the public interest; others exaggerated their expenses or did favours for friends who acquired Jewish property cheaply, and used the position as an office of profit. During his tenure as head of the CGQJ, Vallat was aware of the greed of some officials, and got auditors to oversee the management and accounts of APs. Some cases were managed by a succession of APs because of the length of time needed, or because of resignations or dismissals.[18] The rate of turnover of APs varied between one-fifth and almost 40 per cent in different parts of the country. By the same token, some efficient APs handled a number of enterprises, even up to twenty. By April 1944, APs had been appointed to manage 42,227 Jewish enterprises; of these about 17,000 had been sold to Aryans, non-Jews.

The Aryanisation process was slow and largely unfinished because of the extraordinarily large number of over 50,000 dossiers, which imposed a heavy workload. It was also uneven, geographically and economically, in its results. Much depended on timing. The earlier an AP was appointed, the more likely the action would be finished.[19] Those APs appointed before 1942 completed their work in 85 per cent of the cases. The proportion of completions fell after that time, rose for a time in 1943, and then fell again. In the Seine *département*, sales and liquidations were completed in 75 per cent of actions started in 1940–1, but varied and dropped for actions started later. In the rest of the occupied or northern zone, the completions were fewer. In the unoccupied zone the rate of completions was about 43 per cent. The difference between the two zones can largely be attributed to timing. By July 1941, over one-third of Jewish enterprises were in the hands of the APs in the Seine area; by mid-1942 almost all enterprises in the Seine area had APs. In the unoccupied zone, little over half were being managed by APs in 1942.

The Aryanisation process varied economically, socially and by nationality. It was likely to affect poorer Jews – foreign immigrants, who worked as tailors, second-hand dealers and small artisans. By contrast, French Jews – wealthier, more professional and more assimilated, with useful contacts in French society – were more likely to survive, economically as well as physically.

The Slow Process

Apart from the sheer volume of work involved in Aryanisation, the process was slow and intricate, going through a bureaucratic maze and shifting legal, formal requirements. For technical reasons alone delays occurred, caused by the need to publish relevant activities in the *Journal Officiel* for the individual dossier to be assembled. Agreement had to be reached on appropriate procedures for sales or liquidations among the officials and organisations, including the APs, the DAE and the COs.

Nomination and approval of the APs took time, as did confirmation of their activities. Other delays occurred between authorisation of a sale and the sale itself. In the occupied zone, sale or liquidation of Jewish property was confirmed by the CGQJ if the property was valued at less than 200,000 francs. If the value was higher than 200,000 francs, the dossier went back to the MBF, which, together with the CGQJ, examined it. In spite of its ideological bent, the CGQJ was careful not to compromise the process by improper acts or non-adherence to the rules, which not only could be challenged in court, leading to annulment of the decision, but also might offend public opinion.[20]

The CGQJ would approve sales if it thought they would help eliminate Jewish influence in the economy, and if the price of sales was normal, and not the result of friendship or favouritism or connivance between the purchaser and the victim. That meant research to ensure that the purchasers were true 'Aryans', by examining their genealogy and baptism certificates, and by assurance that they were not under Jewish influence or connected with Jewish individuals.

Indeed, before the CGQJ was established, some businesses in September and October 1940 were sold and 'Aryanised' through sales to non-Jewish friends of Jews, who then left for the unoccupied zone, sometimes taking information about the businesses with them and thus causing delay. Other Jewish owners used the resources of the law to challenge the process in the courts; one procedure was to ask the courts to decide that they or their children were not Jewish according to the Vichy definition. Poor Jews and recent immigrants had little opportunity to go to the courts, but the better-established French Jews, with friends and contacts, might be able to do so.

The CCQJ tried to overcome these obstacles by persuading lawyers to refuse to help the victims, but it was not always successful. In particular, the notaries, who were needed to draw up title deeds, were careful, sometimes advising clients not to buy Jewish property. Some of these potential Aryan clients refused to buy because of possible legal problems.

A second category of Aryanisation concerned stocks, shares and corporate equity held by Jews. By German ordinances of 26 April 1941 and 28 May 1941, and the Vichy law of 22 July 1941, shares and equities belonging to Jews were frozen. The only exceptions were securities and bonds issued by the French state and publicly owned bodies and local authorities, and all foreign securities, which were blocked for all people at the German request. In the occupied zone the CGQJ was given the task of making a list of securities held by Jews.

The temporary administrators (APs) at first had shares and equities under their administration. The Vichy Law of 22 July 1941 designated the Domaines, the French State property management agency, a unit in the Ministry of Finance, as the administrator of those assets.[21] The Domaines could manage or dispose of those assets without consent of their owners. It was made aware of the assets by the CGQJ, by the APs and by information from prefectures.

From December 1941, shares and equities were frozen in banks, stockbroker accounts and notarial offices in the occupied zone. About 9500 Jews had their securities frozen; approximately 43 per cent of all stocks and shares were placed under the temporary administration of the Domaines. Many of the archives on the activities of the Domaines are missing, and the full record of the number of stock certificates it held or sold is therefore not available. However, the nature of its behaviour is clear.

The stock certificates could be sold either on the stock market or directly to financial establishments, including the CDC, which bought some 200,000 securities for a total of 650 million francs. The proceeds from the sales were mostly deposited in accounts in the names of the Jewish owners at the CDC. Two factors are significant about the work of the Domaines. It was not compelled to sell the equities and was aware that stock prices might fall if there were substantial selling. It also sought to keep assets in French, albeit non-Jewish hands, to prevent the Germans from obtaining them.

The Domaines sold about a third of the shares for which it was the temporary administrator between 1941 and 1944. Jews could not buy securities, and could receive revenue from the sale only if it was under 6000 francs a year. For its work, the Domaines took a 2 per cent deduction for administrative costs. The rest of the revenue was divided in the usual way: 90 per cent to a frozen account of the victim at the CDC, and 10 per cent to the CGQJ account. After covering its administrative costs, the CGQJ put the rest in what was said to be a fund for destitute Jews, but what in reality were funds for the Union Générale des Israélites de France (see p. 142). In March 1944, the levy going to the CGQJ was increased to 20 per cent.

Stocks and transferable securities were more important in the Seine area than in the unoccupied zone because of the location there of the main stock exchange in France. Yet, even in the northern zone, some of these Jewish assets, in blocked accounts, were not touched, partly because some were still under a temporary administrator, and partly because the Germans were more interested in gold, currency and stocks in foreign currency, than in French securities.

Another form of economic discrimination was through control of bank accounts and deposits belonging to Jews. The German occupiers had already, in May 1940, set a favourable exchange rate for the mark, thereby reducing the value of the franc by half and causing difficulties for the French banking system. They soon took over administration of banks in Paris that they considered 'enemy property'. These included a number of British banks, such as Barclays and Lloyds, and others, including the Royal Bank of Canada. Properties and bank accounts of 'enemy citizens' were frozen by an ordinance of 23 May 1940. Foreign securities held in the occupied zone, and safe deposit boxes with currencies, gold and foreign assets in them, were frozen on 14 June 1940. Transfer of funds between the occupied and unoccupied zones would be allowed only if individuals had correct identity papers and a permit to travel. At this time, only French francs and French securities were not frozen.

By these measures the German occupiers acquired considerable powers over the French banking system. For a time a German banker, Carl Schaefer, was appointed as commissioner to the Bank of France and head of the banking supervisory office for the occupied zone. After the Vichy laws of 13 and 14 June 1941 his role became less necessary for the control and organisation of the banking profession; the banks were now subject to the supervision of Vichy as well as to the Germans.

Vichy responded to the early German initiatives in two ways. One was the law of 23 July 1940, which instituted the withdrawal of nationality from French citizens who fled France between 20 May and 30 June 1940. The other action, a little later, was to set up in June 1941 the Association Professionnelle des Banques, a mandatory organisation for all banks, which passed on instructions from both the Germans and Vichy to their members, kept in touch with the MBF and provided advice. The advice touched on complex issues: the freezing of assets, the accommodation with German and Vichy authorities, the surveillance of expenses and withdrawals by their Jewish clients.[22]

Specifically anti-Semitic rules on bank holdings began in autumn 1940. The German ordinance of 18 October 1940 defined 'Jewish' companies and targeted individual bank deposits. Any action disposing of assets belonging to Jews and spouses could be declared null. These assets had to be reported to French prefectures or, in Paris, to the prefecture of police.

French banks were now cautious about the accounts of their Jewish clients, sometimes suspending loans, forbidding mortgage loans, avoiding deficit accounts and refusing any withdrawal or transaction that involved substantial sums of money or sales of securities by Jews on the stock exchange. The chairman of the Crédit Lyonnais, in a circular of 6 February 1941 to its branch members, wrote that 'the main aim [of the bank] must be to avoid placing ourselves in any position possibly indefensible in the eyes of the German authorities'.[23]

Jews could play no role in banking. About 5 per cent of banks, with 3 per cent of cash deposits, had been owned or controlled by Jews. The Vichy law of 2 June 1941 banned Jews from the banking profession, a ban reinforced when Jewish bank tellers were dismissed after the head of the bankers' union insisted on 'an extremely rigorous interpretation' of the June law.[24]

Further restrictions were put on the assets of Jews in the occupied zone. The German ordinance of 26 April 1941 ordered the takeover of equity and shares belonging to companies or persons said to be Jewish. These equities and shares, of which the CGQJ had made a list, could be sold by the temporary administrators. The ordinance was immediately implemented by French banks. A Vichy law of the same date, but not officially published until a year later, authorised the freezing of certain bank accounts. By May, Jewish shareholders were not free to handle their own assets.

The Germans took a major step on 28 May 1941 when they ordered the freezing of the assets, accounts and savings bank books of individual Jews and Jewish companies in banks and other places; this would be implemented by the SCAP. Jews in the occupied zone with several bank accounts were forced to consolidate them into one account. Withdrawals were to be allowed up to 15,000 francs a month for 'unavoidable subsistence expenses'.

The French banks were made aware of the German ordinance several days before its promulgation through a circular of 21 May from the director of the Office de Surveillance des Banques. This advised them, in anticipation, to limit withdrawals by Jewish clients, and to regard legal transactions by Jews, as defined in the ordinance of 18 October 1940, as null and void.[25] Many of the individual banks acted immediately to examine and possibly refuse transactions by their Jewish clients, and also to freeze safe deposit boxes belonging to Jews. French financial institutions, the National Savings Bank and the Post Office Current Accounts Office, laid out the procedures for identifying those accounts held by Jews. Even in the unoccupied zone where Jewish assets were not frozen, these two kinds of account were carefully identified.

By mid-1941, Jews who had assets in the occupied zone had no free access to them, but only authorised withdrawals could be made, no matter where they lived, since assets left by those who had fled could not be transferred to the unoccupied zone.

The German ordinance of 28 May 1941 limited financial transactions of Jews to no more than 15,000 francs, but this did not entail total blockage of accounts. Taking the ordinance as the basis for its own directives to banks, stockbrokers and notaries on individual deposited assets, the CGQJ imposed severe restrictions. Assets from sales of Jewish property would go into a blocked account, and limits were put on the way in which the account could be used. French bankers, not German controllers, were now responsible for overseeing the assets of their Jewish clients.

By the German ordinances in the occupied zone, Jews could make withdrawals of up to 15,000 francs a month under control and from the one consolidated account only. The CGQJ instructed banks on 2 October 1941 that the withdrawals must not exceed one-twelfth of the individual's income or one-twelfth of the rent multiplied by seven; these were lower figures than the German. In a circular of 9 October 1941 banks were ordered not to exceed the permitted ceiling for 'subsistence expenses', and to examine other authorised expenses for 'usual activity'.[26] On average, the permissible withdrawal when agreed to by the CGQJ was 5000 francs a month, a third of the German amount. No Jewish account would be unblocked if the Jewish owner or his company had gone to the unoccupied zone. Even the wages owed to dismissed Jewish employees were put into blocked accounts. It is difficult to calculate the total of the frozen balances on all the individual accounts.

In the unoccupied zone, deposits were not frozen for those Jews who had originated in that zone, except for assets of businesses being managed by APs. But assets of refugees living in the south whose deposits had originally been made in the occupied zone were frozen by the CGQJ on 13 October 1941, even if the assets were now in the unoccupied zone.

The German Devisenschutzkommando (DSK) on 14 June 1940 ordered that all safe deposit boxes and the valuables and foreign assets in them be frozen. In spring 1941, these boxes, whose owners were absent, were forced open, and gold and foreign securities in them taken. An uneven policy ensued. In summer 1941, when the banks had to declare the existence of the boxes to the CGQJ, and when the policy distinction between securities in foreign and in French currencies was ended, Jews lost access to their French assets. The next restriction was more severe when the MBF on 22 December 1941 ordered that Jews could no longer have access to their boxes. Banks were later ordered to supply the DSK with an inventory of gold, foreign currency and foreign securities belonging to Jews. Yet these regulations changed again in 1942 when individuals were allowed access to their boxes, if accompanied by an official.

The Billion-Franc Fine

In what they pretended was retaliation for attacks against their occupying forces, the MBF issued an official notice signed on 14 December 1941 that attacks by individuals 'in the pay of the Anglo-Saxons, Jews or Bolsheviks' would be punished not only by the deportation of the 'Judeo-Bolshevik criminals' but also by the execution of 'one hundred Jews, communists and anarchists', and by a billion-franc fine imposed on the Jews in the occupied territories.[27]

The order came one month before the Wannsee conference of 20 January 1942 when the Nazi leadership formulated the 'Final Solution', which would lead to the murder of 6 million Jews. It was to be followed in three months by the first convoy, of 1112 Jewish men, on 27 March 1942 from France to the extermination camps.

The Germans had already in the pre-war period imposed a heavy fine on Jews when in November 1938 the atrocities by the Nazis took place on *Kristallnacht*. In France, the MBF imposed the billion-franc fine in December 1941, as well as two smaller ones on Jews in Tunisia: 20 million on 21 December 1942 and 3 million on 15 February 1943.[28]

How was this large amount of 1 billion francs to be paid to the Germans? Two weeks earlier, on 29 November 1941, Vichy had created a new body, the Union Générale des Israélites de France (UGIF), to represent all Jews in France, thus replacing almost all existing Jewish organisations. The new body was to be financed by assets of the dissolved organisations, by contributions of its members, and by some funds from the CGQJ.

The German ordinance of 17 December 1941 designated the UGIF as the body responsible for collecting and paying the fine. In reality, the objective of the fine was, as in November 1938, to steal Jewish wealth; in this case by confiscating some of the proceeds of the sales of Jewish business and property, and by taking advantage of bank accounts and securities owned by Jews.

Immediately after the 17 December ordinance the MBF outlined the payment arrangements of the fine, and ordered the French banks to notify it of the assets, the nominal value of the securities and the safe deposit boxes belonging to Jews. Almost 300 banks and financial institutions, eighty-nine stockbrokers and two notarial offices informed the Germans of their Jewish holdings.

Since the UGIF did not have sufficient funds of its own to pay the fine, the Vichy regime, together with the banking system, organised a complex instalment plan for the payment, the first quarter, 250 million francs, of which was demanded by the Germans by 15 January 1942. To pay this first instalment of the fine, the UGIF was allowed a loan to which twenty-nine banks contributed, some under pressure from the CGQJ.[29] The rate of interest was set at a moderate 3 per cent.

Vichy had tried to avoid having the shares belonging to Jews and held in escrow put on the open market. In this unusual situation in late December 1941, it now encouraged French banks to buy directly from the Domaines, and allowed the CDC, which also acquired securities held by the Domaines, to use some of these funds to help pay the first instalment. The hastily devised, complex Vichy plan was aimed more at protecting French economic interests by preventing Germans from confiscating shares in case of default of payment than at aiding the Jewish victims.

In the complex arrangements for payment of the fine, French governmental and financial institutions and professional bodies and the UGIF all played a part after the MBF notice of 14 December 1941 of the imposition of the fine. Within two weeks the French bodies had agreed on a formula. The official organs included the CGQJ, the Domaines in the Ministry of Finance, the Treasury Department and the CDC. The professional groups were the Standing Committee for the Organisation of the Banking Profession, and the Professional Association of Banks.

The Vichy law of 16 January 1942 provided for a 'guarantee fund' resulting from levies on 'all assets belonging to Jewish companies or private individuals in the occupied zone'. The fund was opened at the CDC in the name of the UGIF.

The CGQJ called for 50 per cent of deposit account balances over 10,000 francs and amounts owned by Jews which were in frozen accounts to be transferred from banks and savings banks to the CDC. These accounts, numbering about 2350, represented about 10 per cent of private accounts in the occupied zone. As usual, 10 per cent of the Jewish accounts went as a levy to the CGQJ and the rest to the UGIF.

To this 50 per cent deposit was added further money from stockbrokers and notary publics who sent to the CDC a levy of 100 per cent on balances over 10,000 francs. The banks also transferred 80 per cent of accounts if the balance was over 250,000 francs; there were thirty transfers of this kind. The banks joined with the Ministry of Finance and financial institutions in arrangements for payment of the fine. The banks were fully repaid, with interest, for their loans by funds from Jewish accounts. The rest of the three instalments was largely paid through funds coming from the Domaines and major banks trading securities, which were advanced as loans to the UGIF. About 14 per cent of the payment of the fine came from Jewish deposits at the CDC while 86 per cent came from securities sold by Domaines. Funds for the other three instalments in reality came from the sale of Jewish assets managed by the APs, escrowed equity and frozen balances and securities.

The billion francs went to the Reichskreditkasse, connected with the German Reichsbank, but curiously, part of it, at least 10 per cent and probably more, went to a group called the Comité Ouvrier de Secours Immédiat, which also got revenue from the fine imposed on 21 December 1942 on Jews in Tunisia.[30] Formed in March 1942 under the auspices of the German Ambassador Abetz, this group supposedly provided aid to victims of the Anglo-American bombing of the Paris area and in Normandy. It also provided support for French collaborationists, especially adherents of Doriot and Déat.

The economic plight of Jews became increasingly severe, as were the discriminations in general and the steady deportation to the death camps. By the law of 29 November 1941, UGIF was set up to be the representative of Jews to public institutions. It had been the instrument through which the billion-franc fine had been paid. Its role continued and on 28 August 1942 a decree called for Jews to provide 'voluntary contributions of six million francs a month to support it'.[31]

Since the total of these contributions was far from reaching this sum, another decree of 11 May 1943 allowed Jews to deduct them from frozen accounts, as well as already authorised contributions to pay debts to the state and public institutions. An individual tax on Jews was established. All Jews of both sexes over eighteen were subject to a tax of 120 francs in the occupied zone and 360 in the unoccupied zone, to be paid into the post office account of UGIF. This regulation had a menacing quality about it, since individuals had to provide information about themselves, including name, address, age and nationality. To indicate their payment, individuals were given a special card by UGIF, which was attached to an official identity card. The CGQJ insisted that the tax be paid from permitted 'subsistence allowances' rather than from frozen deposit balances.

In addition to this tax, the 11 May order imposed a levy of 5 per cent for the benefit of the UGIF from every withdrawal by Jews from banks. The amount raised was not substantial, reaching about 181 million francs, since enforcement by banks was weak.

Friction over Aryanisation

Conflict over the Aryanisation process was not uncommon, between the German occupiers and Vichy, and among the Vichy institutions and personnel. On the one hand, collaboration was a continual, daily act. On the other hand, the CGQJ, a powerful bureaucratic organisation with over 1000 employees, competed for control over Aryanisation in the occupied zone with the Germans, in MBF headquarters in the Hotel Majestic in Paris, who could veto the appointment of APs as well as the latter's decision to sell or liquidate property and enterprises, after ensuring satisfactory completion of transactions. A small group of MBF officials was even present in the CGQJ organisation.

Both the German MBF and the CGQJ disliked the idea of APs managing property without disposing of it, or delaying a decision. On other issues they might disagree. Both preferred decisions to sell rather than liquidate. The Germans wanted sales without competition to speed up the process. The CGQJ, however, wanted sales by competitive bidding or public auction. By this method a higher price would result, the value of property owned by non-Jews would not be reduced, and the economy of the country would benefit. Only if a sale was not possible or might have undesirable consequences would the CGQJ favour liquidation.

Within the Vichy camp, differences were registered on similar questions of sale or liquidation. On one side, the Ministry of Industrial Production and the *comités d'organisation* (COs), responsible for reconstruction of particular sectors of the French economy, wanted to limit or eliminate competition. They therefore favoured liquidation over sale.[32] By contrast, the CGQJ preferred sale. Its objective was to eliminate all Jewish influence in the economy, more than to ensure the welfare of a particular sector in the economy.

Aryanisation in France was devised and implemented both by the German military authorities and by a profusion of interrelated French governmental authorities and non-governmental professional bodies and individuals. The major, propelling official body was the CGQJ. Other agencies played significant roles: the Ministry of Finance, the Treasury and Property Registration Departments, the Caisse des Dépôts et Consignations, the Conseil d'État, the Domaines, the stamp duty office, French prefects, police and gendarmes. The Commissaire aux Comptes, created by the Vichy decree of 16 January 1941, which was attached to the Court of Appeals, verified data obtained from the APs and reported to the Ministry of Finance or other relevant ministries.[33] The APs were the largest number of people in any group involved in the process.

Professional groups, especially lawyers and bankers, played an indispensable role. Notaries, a uniquely French body, part public and part private, were active in a number of ways. In all, 179 notarial offices participated in some aspect of Aryanisation. They drew up the legal deeds for sale or liquidation of Jewish businesses and property. They put proceeds in escrow at the CDC. They held deposited assets of both funds and securities belonging to Jews. A few also acted as temporary administrators of Jewish property. The *comités d'organisation*, were given interim and final reports by the APs on Aryanisation of a particular economic sector with which they were familiar.

The CDC was set up in 1816 to receive, manage and restitute money and securities entrusted to it by law or by court decision. It became a central participant in the whole process of Aryanisation as the legal and official holder of escrow and public accounts. It was the agent for money, securities and valuables obtained from the APs, banks of deposit, notaries and internment camp account clerks. It managed deposit accounts for various official departments. It played a key role in assembling the funds by which the billion-franc fine was paid.

The holdings of the CDC came from a number of sources. They resulted from sales and liquidations of Jewish businesses and properties by the APs after debts were settled. Those funds were transferred by order of the CGQJ to the CDC. Theoretically, but in reality infrequently, Jews could withdraw some funds for 'absolutely unavoidable subsistence costs'.

The CDC obtained the proceeds from sales of securities by the Domaines; it opened escrow accounts in the name of the Jewish owners and closed them after the sales were made. It received 50 per cent of the balance of deposit accounts of 10,000 francs or more in the occupied zone. It also got 100 per cent of the Jewish deposit accounts held by notaries in the occupied zone.

The CDC held the money confiscated from those interned at Drancy and the provincial camps. It handled the 10 per cent levy, which was transferred to a deposit account in the name of the CGQJ at the CDC. This levy served two purposes. One was to provide the 'guarantee fund' to help indigent Jews. The other was to pay the cost of companies being administered by the APs which were in deficit. In March 1944 the levy was increased to 20 per cent.

The question of the nationality of the Jewish owner of assets became important. The German authorities had ordered the seizure of assets in December 1942 of Jews of German origin; in September 1943 the order was broadened to include Jews from Poland and Czechoslovakia. On 15 March 1944, the CGQJ ordered that assets belonging to foreign Jews were no longer to be held at the CDC. That money, owned by Jews from Germany and central and eastern Europe, was to be paid to the Reichskreditkasse in Paris; about 590 accounts were in this category. Already, the funds of 'enemy Jews', mostly from the United States, Britain, the Soviet Union and Brazil, had been paid into the *Anderkonto 13,* an account with about 200 deposits at Barclays Bank in Paris. It therefore appears that most of the funds deposited in the name of Jews at the CDC came from French, not foreign, Jews.

Belatedly in the 1990s, over fifty years after the events, the chief executive officers of the CDC began reconsidering its role in economic Aryanisation and in the spoliation of Jewish assets. It confessed to some weaknesses and even misconduct. A particularly troubling fact was that Henri Deroy, then executive officer of the CDC had been the Vichy Secretary-General of the Ministry of Finance from 16 July 1940 until 1943.

The CDC, which was consulted about the law of 22 July 1941 on companies, assets and securities belonging to Jews, does not appear to have raised objections to its crucial role in economic organisation. It strictly applied the law and impartially carried out orders of the Ministry of Finance or the CGQJ. The Vichy anti-Semitic policy was not challenged by the CDC, which implemented it in traditional bureaucratic form.

Pillaging

Aryanisation was to a large extent based on laws, decrees and ordinances, both French and German. The 'legal' process, for both economic and ideological reasons, meant dispossessing Jews of their assets, companies, industries, workshops and immovable property, and freezing their securities, bank accounts and credits. It meant forced deductions from those accounts to pay the billion-franc fine imposed by Germany, and the obligatory financing of UGIF.

However, confiscation, looting and pillaging were theft, not in accordance with the Vichy 'legal' process. Peculation by some APs during their management of Jewish properties was illegal behaviour, as was stealing of money and personal valuables by French police and guards from Jews in the internment camps where they were imprisoned before deportation from France.

Yet, though French personnel engaged in this practice to a certain extent, theft was largely a German operation, about which Vichy was concerned because the properties stolen or pillaged were French, even if they belonged to Jews.[34] From the start of their occupation, the Germans sought gold and valuables, irrespective of the religion of their owners, but soon their organised pillaging was targeted at Jews and legalised for them by their ordinances. The pillaging was widespread, including apartments, furniture, works of art, music, pianos, libraries, gold, money, bank deposits and foreign negotiables.

A number of German agencies engaged in this activity mostly for economic reasons, but some for ideologically anti-Semitic motives. Among the latter were purportedly research groups. Hitler's Institute for Research on the Jewish Question wanted to take objects for a museum at Linz, his home town. Close to this was the Research Institute into Jewish Issues directed by the anti-Semitic ideologue Arthur Rosenberg, who was also active with other agencies. One of these was the Devisenschutzkommando (DSK), part of Goering's bureaucratic empire, which started as early as 16 June 1940 to block currency and securities in foreign money in the occupied zone. Other agencies participated, and to some extent competed, in the activity. One was the German Embassy in Paris under the Ambassador, Otto Abetz, who was familiar with the French cultural world. Another was the MBF.

Rosenberg was involved with the most active groups and with the infighting among them. Any original ideological pursuit of the 'enemies' – Jews and Freemasons – was soon accompanied by looting of the 'cultural treasures' of Jews. The Einsatzstab Reichleiters Rosenberg (ERR) was the overall agency instructed to take libraries, archives, works of art and musical instruments belonging to Jews. Yet Rosenberg, who had the position of Minister of the Reich for the occupied territories in the east, insisted that the removal of furniture be in the hands of his ministry, not in those of the ERR, which could not cope with the volume of work. As a result, a separate unit, the Dienstelle Westen (DW), Administration for the West, was set up in March 1942 as a branch of the ministry with personnel separate from the ERR, to operate in France, Belgium and Holland; it was headed in France by Kurt von Behr. Other units included the Möbel Aktion (Furniture Action) and the Sonderstab Musik under Herbert Gerigk.

German pillaging continued until the last days of the occupation. Even after rail traffic had halted as a result of the retreat of German forces from France in 1944, trucks kept going to Germany carrying stolen goods. In March 1944 the pillaging was about to be extended to the former unoccupied, southern zone, which from the end of 1942 was under German control, but was limited because of the changing military situation.

Economic and aesthetic motivation for the theft of artefacts owned by Jews was mixed with an ideological struggle against 'Jewish art' and culture and the desire to obliterate Jewish memory. To this end, significant documents of Jewish history and society were taken, including libraries and archives of Jewish organisations, the holdings, 40,000 volumes, of the Alliance Israélite Universelle, the libraries of the Federation of Jewish Associations of France and of the Rabbinical School, and of the Rothschild family, including 760 boxes of the bank's archives.

Residences belonging to Jews who had been interned or had fled from the occupied zone were pillaged in that zone by the Germans, who to a lesser extent did the same in the southern zone after they occupied it in November 1942. Though different German units were involved, and the main one was the DW, it was primarily the Möbel Aktion that seized movable objects.[35] The contents of apartments, especially those in the Paris *arrondissements* where poorer Jews lived, were removed; included were furniture, clothing, household linen, dishes, books, musical instruments and art objects. Much of the contents was ostensibly for distribution to German citizens left homeless in their cities by Anglo-American bombing raids, invariably referred to as 'Jewish bombing'. But the Germans also seized family papers and photographs of no interest to German citizens, but important for the obliteration of Jewish memory. An unknown number, perhaps millions, of books were taken. The French police did little to check the pillage.

By July 1944, over 69,000 apartments had been pillaged in France, Belgium and the Netherlands, and their contents sent in 674 trains with 27,000 rail cars to Germany. In Paris alone, 38,000 residences were looted. To increase the number of objects available, the German authorities forbade the sale of Jewish goods by auction, a transaction favoured by Vichy. In all, about 80 per cent of stolen goods were shipped to Germany.

The Sonderstab Musik (SM), part of the main agency, the ERR, was set up in summer 1940, specifically to seize musical libraries and instruments, manuscripts and scores from Jewish homes and organisations. Part of the theft included 8000 pianos, many of which were sent to Germany. As late as 21 July 1944, twenty-one wagons containing forty-three pianos left Paris by train for Germany. At the Liberation in 1944, over 2000 were found stored in the Palais de Tokyo in Paris. Possessions of Jewish musicians who emigrated from France or had gone to the southern zone were seized; one prominent victim was the celebrated harpsichordist and pianist Wanda Landowska, whose instruments and works were stolen. The SM also had an ideological role. It collected and sent to Germany all manuscripts and correspondence concerning German composers. It also conducted the offensive against 'degenerate music', of which Darius Milhaud was the best-known symbol; Jewish music would be forbidden.

Vichy also initiated a similar offensive in the musical realm. The profession of musician was not banned to Jews, but they needed special authorisation to perform. Even if they obtained this permission, the performance could not take place in a publicly subsidised hall and could not be broadcast.

Diffusion or performance of works by Jews in the theatre, cinema or in spectacles was forbidden. To evade this ban some Jewish composers such as Norbert Glanzberg, composer of some of the songs sung by Edith Piaf, sold their works directly to the singers who performed them. Vichy also had difficulty in compiling a list of Jewish composers because it was not always clear which people, such as Paul Dukas who died in 1935, or Reynaldo Hahn or Jacques Ibert, should be considered Jews.

Musical publishing houses belonging to Jews were put under temporary administration. Jews did not receive publishing royalties, and all money due to them was supposedly put into a frozen account. This discrimination was enforced by the Société des Auteurs, Compositeurs, et Éditeurs de Musique (SACEM), which withheld royalties from its Jewish members for a time, and would only pay creditors or concessionaries if they signed a declaration that they were non-Jewish. SACEM eagerly executed French laws and German ordinances concerning Jews for a time.

Adolf Hitler, the Austrian artist *manqué*, had long wanted to acquire works of art and documents belonging to Jews, more for political and ideological reasons than for aesthetic ones. For the Nazis, art was to be 'de-Judaised', as were music and other forms of cultural expression. With the fall of France in June 1940, some Jewish art collectors and dealers left the occupied zone, often making arrangements about their holdings.

The Germans quickly began the seizure of art objects owned by Jews. The German Ambassador in Paris, Otto Abetz, was entrusted in a memo by Foreign Minister Ribbentrop on 3 August 1940 to be, among other functions, the responsible person to seize art treasures.[36] Abetz used the secret police to steal some of the best collections of Jewish collectors and art dealers and put them in a place he chose.

However, the embassy was soon supplanted by the ERR as the confiscator of Jewish collections. Most of the art, certainly at the beginning, came from a small number of important collectors; the largest four were the Rothschilds, David David-Weill, Alphonse Kann and the Seligmann family. Other collections included those of Lévy de Benzion, Wildenstein, Paul Rosenberg, Kraemer, Pregal Auxente and Walter Strauss.[37]

In all, about 100,000 art objects were stolen. About 61,000 works found in Germany were returned to France after the war. Possibly about one-third of the privately owned art in France was shipped to

Germany. The leading individual looter was Goering who, on twenty-one occasions, visited the Jeu de Paume in Paris where many of the stolen works were housed for a time. His private train carried art objects from February 1941 until 27 August 1944, two days after the Allied forces entered Paris, to his private home at Carinhall as well as to other places. A few art objects were not stolen but were bought by the Germans in the flourishing art market in Paris and in auctions at bargain rates and with overvalued marks.

An indelible stain tarnishes the Vichy regime: the sordid internment camps and the deportation from them of so many to their death. The role of French officials, police and gendarmes is now well known. Less familiar, and still not fully documented, are the details of irregular behaviour in the camps.[38]

To their discredit, French personnel were not immune from theft and pillaging, if at a much lower, though disquieting, level than the German occupiers. Some irregularities occurred during the arrests by French police of Jews, but most took place in the camps in which Jews were interned.

About 80,000 Jews were interned in Drancy: of the 75,000 deported from France, 67,000 left from it. After the most dramatic police round-up of Jews, the Vél d'Hiv, on 16–17 July 1942, women and children, 4000 of whom had been separated from their parents in the Pithiviers and Beaune-la-Rolande camps, were also sent there. Drancy was in most cases the last stage in France on the road to extermination. The camp was administered by the prefecture of the Seine *département* in which it was located, and was guarded by the French gendarmerie, whose commander was appointed by and under the control of the prefecture of police. The prefecture for the Seine area was responsible for food, accommodation and services, and the police and gendarmerie for maintaining order and searching internees. These searches took place on the arrival and deportation of the victims. They were done by the French police, particularly the Police aux Questions Juives (PQJ), set up on 19 October 1941, controlled by the head of police and answerable to the Ministry of the Interior for a short time, and then to the general secretary of the national police, before being transformed into the Section d'Enquête et de Contrôle in August 1942 and attached a few months later to the CGQJ.[39] The PQJ terrorised the internees and stole currency, watches, jewellery, clothing and suitcases to such an extent that few items survived.

On 2 July 1943, Drancy was officially taken over and administered by the notorious SS Obersturmführer Alöis Brunner, an assistant of Adolf Eichmann, and the man who had supervised the brutal deportation of Jews from Salonika to extermination, and the Nazi who after the war found refuge in Syria.[40] Yet even then, though French police were no longer present inside the camp, having been replaced by the brutal SS, and no French administrative officials were now responsible, French gendarmes still guarded the perimeter of the camp, which was now a concentration camp.

At Drancy the interned were searched on arrival and all money, securities and jewellery taken from them. Meticulous, if complicated, records were kept by the camp cashier, a man named Maurice Kiffer, who was appointed on 29 September 1941 by the prefecture of police. He deposited the money of the internees in individual accounts, gave them receipts and recorded the balance; some 7000 accounts were recorded. The internees were allowed to withdraw 50 francs on which to live. Some of the jewellery and valuables were stored by order of the prefecture of police in a safe rented from the Bank of France. Some of it was used to finance the deportation costs from the camp to Auschwitz.[41]

At first, the money was deposited in the City of Paris Municipal Savings Bank, which was responsible for all receipts and expenses of the City. Two factors changed this arrangement. The bank raised technical questions about the deposits, which it felt unable to handle. The increasing number of Jews arrested and interned in 1942 altered the situation. On 6 February 1942 the CGQJ designated the CDC as the depository of the funds. By the summer, transfer of funds was being made to the CDC. Deposits were made in two ways: a single withdrawal account in the name of the Jewish owner, and an escrow account also in the name of the holder. From the individual accounts, 10 per cent was taken by the CGQJ. In reality, with so many thousands entering Drancy after the Vél d'Hiv arrests, and staying only for a short period before deportation, little time was available to give receipts to the newly interned or to open accounts for them. Most of the Jewish assets disappeared.

Beyond this formal spoliation of Jewish assets came brutal rapaciousness. Part of the property of the interned victims was stolen by the French police units that arrested, interned and guarded them. Though some French officials viewed this behaviour as distasteful, it can at best be regarded as semi-official sanctioned theft by Vichy, made more poignant because so many of the victims were to be exterminated.

The relatively modest amount of property and assets deposited by the internees is explicable by a number of reasons. The main factors were the considerable theft from the internees and from packages sent to them by the motorised reserve of the gendarmes and by the PQJ; the extensive black market in the camp run by the police, who charged exorbitant prices for necessities, foodstuffs, bread, tobacco and blankets, transactions which reached scandalous proportions; and the fact that a majority of the internees were poor and usually foreign Jews.

The situation changed when Brunner and the Nazi SS took over Drancy on 2 July 1943. Money, securities and other effects of the internees were supposedly recorded in 'search registers', but these have not been found. It is known that the SS searched the incoming Jews, and either sent their money or possessions to Germany or stole them when they fled the camp on 22 August 1944. The French cashier, Maurice Kiffer, remained at the camp, but was no longer the depositor of funds, but rather the liquidator of the Drancy accounts of the previous period at the CDC.

More is known about Drancy than about the provincial camps in which Jews were interned. Following the law of 24 October 1940, which authorised prefects to intern foreign Jews from Belgium and Holland who had fled the German military advance, as well as those from central and eastern Europe, over 60,000 were interned in different camps in the unoccupied zone at different times. The conditions in the camps run by Vichy, especially those of Milles, Gurs and Le Vernet, caused the death of over 2500 internees.

Of the total of 75,700 Jews deported from France, 36,500 were arrested in the provinces, compared with 39,200 in Paris. Of those in the provincial camps, deposits of 24 million francs in French currency and 11 million in other currencies have been traced, probably less than one-tenth of the true total. Deposits aside, money and jewellery were often stolen by the police who transferred the internees from the provinces to Paris.

Widespread Involvement

In this dismal story of economic discrimination against Jews, Aryanisation, spoliation and theft, many agencies were involved. Among the official bodies were the Ministry of Finance and its relevant departments, the Domaines, the stamp duty office and the CGQJ. Prominent among the non-official bodies were the French banks. To their discredit, the banking system and its legal advisers willingly participated in the Aryanisation process, at least until late 1942 when it became less eager to help the work of the temporary administrators, especially in implementing the 5 per cent levy on every withdrawal by Jews in 1943. More than a hundred banks operated in France during the years of occupation, in addition to other financial institutions that took deposits, including the Caisse d'Épargne, the French national savings body, the post office and insurance companies.

Familiar questions about the role of the banking community spring to mind as they did in the cases of lawyers and bureaucrats.[42] How responsible were the banks in furthering the process of spoliation, theft and discrimination? Should they have resisted or temporised implementing the discriminatory ordinances of both the German occupiers and the agencies of the Vichy regime? Was their essential acquiescence in unjustifiable, if technically legal, orders the outcome of inherently anti-Semitic prejudices or, more neutrally, a passive acceptance, a conservative adherence to orders and rules?

Ascertaining motivation for behaviour is rarely easy, and in the case of the banks it might charitably be seen as equivocal in character. At best, bankers can be seen, during the occupation, in shades of grey, the typical colour of their suits, rather than in black or white. Their actions have to be considered in the context of relevant reality: the strong pressures of the German occupiers, the Vichy authorities, especially the CGQJ, and professional associations; the quandary of how to behave in a dictatorial or authoritarian system; the changing behaviour over a three-year period, during which professionalism and the natural caution resulting from the changing military balance began to condition the previous willingness to conform.

No doubt, some self-interest was involved. The banking system used the Aryanisation process to eliminate competition of Jewish-owned or managed banks.[43] Jewish day traders had been eliminated early from the stock market. If the banking system did not, with rare exceptions, try to add to the severity of the anti-Semitic economic restrictions on Jews, it also did not publicly oppose or criticise them. On the contrary, banks obeyed German ordinances and Vichy laws and instructions which initiated similar orders as well as taking account of the ordinances.[44] They, including branches of American banks in Paris, complied in 1941 with instructions to declare their Jewish accounts in the occupied zone. They implemented orders to block Jewish accounts. They ratified instructions of the Banking Association in May 1941 advising caution on withdrawal rights for Jews.[45] They accepted the precise instructions of the CGQJ about the amount and conditions of withdrawal by Jews from their accounts. They decided the monthly sums to be allowed, after ascertaining if the demands for withdrawal could be seen as of 'exceptional character or absolute necessity' or 'usual business', or 'unavoidable subsistence expenses'.

The haunting questions remain. How could the French banks and insurance companies so willingly undermine Jewish deposits and betray professional secrets?[46] How could they so readily act so contrarily to the principles of the Republic of non-differentiation between people? Some deluded themselves that it was the Germans who imposed the discriminatory Aryanisation measures and that Vichy only brought 'legality' to the process.[47] Many in the banking and insurance worlds were unwilling to acknowledge that hundreds of thousands of French people were involved in the Aryanisation process and the implementation of spoliation. Were their consciences salved by the fact that this implementation was couched in functional and technical language and not in terms of anti-Semitism?

CHAPTER 7

DETENTION BY VICHY

Detention of unwelcome persons did not start with Vichy.[1] Thousands of people had been interned in pre-war France. Most, about 465,000, were Spanish republicans, who had fled their country after Franco won the civil war in February 1939, and members of the International Brigades who had fought in Spain. Camps for the interned, sometimes euphemistically called *centres d'acceuil* or *centres d'hébergement*, were located in the area of Roussillon, such as Argèles or Saint-Cyprien in Poitiers. The camp at Poitiers, like the others, was run by a small number of French gendarmes when it held Spanish refugees and gypsies. When in 1941 Jews were housed there, the local prefect refused to employ any more gendarmes and recruited extra civilians to join the existing police to guard the camp.[2]

Increasing immigration by refugees from Nazi Germany and from Austria after the *Anschluss* on 15 May 1938 led France to impose restrictions in the 1930s on immigration and on opportunity for foreigners to work. A rising wave of xenophobia and anti-Semitism, increasing anxiety about the menace of war with Nazi Germany, and the violence expressed in the nationalist press against the flow of Jewish refugees, help explain the regulations issued by the last two governments of the Third Republic, under Édouard Daladier and Paul Reynaud, aimed at 'undesirable foreigners'. Two decree laws of 2 and 14 May 1938 were directed at foreigners who were to be located in 'assigned residences'. A third decree of 12 November 1938 provided for assignment of individuals seen as dangerous to national security or as undesirables, to residences or to internment camps. Following another decree of 21 January 1939 the first camp was set up in Rieucros in Lozère to house refugees seen as undesirables.

At the outbreak of war with Germany on 3 September 1939, restrictions were put on 'ressortissants de puissances ennemis'. Twenty thousand people who had fled Nazism were interned as possible dangers to security: men were put in Le Vernet-d'Ariège, and women in Rieucros until February 1942 when they were transferred to Brens or La Petite-Rocquette in the Paris area. Ironically, most of the interned Jews were eager to fight for France against the Nazi regime. Arthur Koestler provided a vivid picture of his life as an internee in Le Vernet, a camp with barbed wire and trenches and guarded by gendarmes.[3] People were beaten up daily; some died for lack of medical attention; individuals slept without blankets; food was sparse; heat and lighting were almost non-existent; individuals worked six hours a day; a roll call was taken four times a day.

Besides German refugees a second issue confronted France as a result of the Soviet–German pact of 23 August 1939. Communists were now also on the list of suspects. The Communist Party was banned on 26 September as were all organisations affiliated with the Third International, which might commit hostile acts. A decree of 18 November 1939 was aimed at all 'suspects' whether French or foreign. Internment was again authorised for individuals held to be a danger to national defence and public security. A secret message from the Minister of the Interior, Albert Sarraut, on 14 December 1939 to prefects made clear the need to take action against suspects. Prefects would decide if an individual would be sent to a residence or to internment. They were also responsible for recruiting personnel for the camps; the personnel, voluntary until June 1940, usually came from officers of the gendarmes. Camp administrators reported directly to the prefects.

Without any German pressure, the Vichy regime proclaimed three new laws, of 3 September, 27 September and 4 October, which laid the basis for its own process of physical exclusion. Detention of individuals would take three forms: internment camps; assigned residences with the police restricting Jews to stated areas; and foreign labour battalions.

Internment Begins

On 27 September 1940 a law called for male foreigners between the ages of eighteen and fifty-five, '*émigrés* in excess of the French economy', to be placed in groups of foreign workers, *groupements de travailleurs étrangers* (GTEs). About 60,000 men, a third of whom were Jews, were sent to these GTEs. Containing men who could not return to their country of origin, or who were regarded as not useful for the national economy, or who had illegally crossed over to the unoccupied zone, the battalions had a double function. They were a means of excluding Jews and unwanted foreigners from social and economic life, and they were also a way of exploiting cheap labour to perform manual work. Usually they contained 250 to 300 men controlled by a French administrator. Darlan, in December 1941, ordered that all Jews in

France, whether citizens or not, who entered France after January 1936 would be grouped in GTEs. Minister of the Interior Pucheu went further and called for Jews to be grouped together in units. Some Jews regarded the battalions as preferable to camps, but the GTEs were also an easy target for arrests in August 1942.

Jews from all different occupations and backgrounds were forced into foreign labour brigades, and sent to work on roads, sewers and swamp drainage, and in coal mines. Also, paradoxically, they were sent to help build the Atlantic Wall defences against an Allied invasion.[4] Stringent controls were imposed on the workers, and only rare visits were allowed to families. The fate of the members of the brigades was largely dependent on the camp commandant; one was relatively benign, another was a notoriously harsh anti-Semitic converted Jew. If there were variations in degree, conditions in all the camps were harsh. The labourers slept in rain-sodden wooden shacks, in silos, in temporary structures. Clothing was poor, hygiene virtually non-existent and food inadequate. People worked at least eight or nine hours a day, for poor wages, part of which was deducted for the supposed 'board'.

Probably the worst of these labour brigades was that at St Georges d'Aurac, consisting of 200 German and Polish Jews who were subject to harsh controls, including frequent punishment, and many of whom were ill. This was only one of the places where harsh punishment was given; labourers who complained were sent to special treatments in Aubague, Fort de Chapoly or Auchères. The life of the labourers was made slightly more bearable by the supply of relief funds, and by cultural activities including an entertainment troupe.

With the defeat of France and the introduction of discriminatory legislation, internment camps played an important role in Vichy policies of exclusion and persecution. The argument has sometimes been made that the groundwork for the camps in the Vichy years was laid by actions at the end of the Third Republic.[5] Vichy did inherit internment camps but the difference in their use in the two regimes is crucial. The discriminatory actions before the war and before the defeat of France were precautionary, the result of what was perceived to be a military and political emergency, even if the perception was distorted by a xenophobic mood: Anti-Franco Spaniards at first and then refugees from Germany and Austria were interned. Internment of people who might be harmful was seen as one means of ensuring public security, as was to be the case for both Britain and the United States with their wartime regulations. For Vichy, the mythical danger came from 'anti-France', those people responsible for the military defeat; Jews, Freemasons, communists and foreigners. Repression was a deliberate policy, systematised discrimination against those, mostly Jews but also others such as gypsies, who would be excluded from the normal life of France. The camps were an inglorious illustration of state anti-Semitism.

The law of 3 September 1940 prolonging the decree of 18 November 1939 gave prefects authority to detain people seen as a danger to national defence or public security in 'special camps'. On 27 September, the day on which the GTEs were set up, the police were given authority to deal with registration by Jews. The ordinance of the German MBF on that day called for the registration of all Jews in the occupied zone by 20 October. The Paris police, helped in this task by the large central file of Jews put together by Inspector André Tulard, immediately set up a timetable for Jews to register, in police stations or prefectures, in alphabetical order. The police, keeping surveillance over those who had fled to the unoccupied zone, also ensured they did not return to the occupied zone.

A third law, on 4 October, followed the Statut des Juifs the previous day, which defined a 'Jew' and imposed a whole set of restrictions and discriminatory actions. The new law gave authority to the prefect of a *département* to intern foreigners 'of the Jewish race' in special camps or 'centres d'hébergement', and authorised a commission to organise and administer the camps. The prefect could also assign Jews to a 'residence forcée'; such a residence would in fact be under police surveillance and located in remote villages. The two laws of October were the essential foundation of state anti-Semitism. French administrative officials could now group Jews in camps in the unoccupied zone, as in the rest of France, distinct from the earlier ones, which essentially housed Spanish refugees.

In the unoccupied zone, new camps, such as Rivesaltes, Noé and Récébédou, were opened; others, such as Gurs, which had been set up in spring 1939 supposedly for six months, but which in fact lasted until the end of the war, were expanded. Rivesaltes, a camp of mud, rats and other vermin, lasted until November 1942 when it became a military camp. Noé, started in January 1941 to house Spanish republicans and German Jews, was theoretically a 'hospital camp', but its wretched sanitary conditions resulted in many of its inmates suffering from cachexia and tuberculosis.[6] Expansion of the camps was essential to handle an immediate problem not of Vichy's making. On 22 October 1940, Germany expelled its Jews from the areas of Baden, the Palatinate and the Saar to the unoccupied zone of France. Of the 7700 new refugees, 6500 were put in the badly equipped camp of Gurs, and the other 1200 in Saint-Cyprien. The Germans also, on 4 October 1940, demanded the internment of gypsies. It is noticeable that almost all the internments were until spring 1941 in the unoccupied zone, with few in the northern zone. By then 40,000 Jews were in camps in southern France, a number reduced to about 10,000 by July 1942 after people had been liberated and allowed to emigrate.[7]

On 5 August 1942 a circular from the national police to all departmental prefects in the unoccupied zone called for mass internments. Following this directive during August, by decision of the Minister of the Interior, transfers took place from the camps in the unoccupied zone to those in the occupied zone of Jews who had entered France after 1 September 1936 and who might be in internment camps, groups of foreign workers, brigades in surveilled residences or elsewhere. The minister instructed prefects to take severe police measures to prevent any incidents. All foreign Jews who had entered France from 1936 on were to be sent to the occupied zone.

Originally in mid-1940 about fifteen camps were set up in the occupied zone, but for convenience the Germans closed most in order to herd Jews into a smaller number of camps. The most important were Beaune-la-Rolande (Loiret), Pithiviers (Loiret) set up by the Germans in 1940 to intern POWs, and above all Drancy, set up in August 1941. Vichy administered the three camps. A fourth camp, Compiègne (Royallieu), 50 miles north of Paris, was originally a prisoner-of-war camp. In 1941 it became a concentration camp controlled by the Gestapo, who imprisoned political opponents as well as Jews; by mid-1941 over 1200 were interned. The first two deportation convoys leaving France for the extermination camps came from Compiègne, the first in part and the second wholly. On 27 March 1942, 1120 were deported, consisting of French Jews arrested in Paris and sent from Compiègne, and foreign Jews from other camps. The second convoy on 5 June 1942, with a thousand Jews, communists and syndicalists, came from Compiègne.

Beaune-la-Rolande, 60 miles south of Paris, near Orléans, had also been a prisoner-of-war camp. Starting in 1941 and administered by Vichy, though under Nazi control, it became a transit camp for arrested Jews who were sent on to their death. Two convoys left from the camp. The first on 28 June 1942 contained 1038 people, including sixteen adolescents: two days later, all but thirty-five had been killed in Auschwitz. The other, on 5 August 1942, conveyed 1014 adults and children over twelve, though two were in fact only nine years old, to death. Pithiviers, another holding camp, sent six deportation convoys. The first, on 25 June 1942, numbered 1000, all men over eighteen, mostly Jews of Polish ancestry. The last, on 21 September 1942, also numbered 1000 and included 175 children, almost all of whom were born in France. The camps had become the cornerstone for the deportation of Jews.

Vichy had agreed in the notorious Article 19 of the Armistice agreement of 22 June 1940 to surrender people living in France demanded by Germany. General Wilhelm Keitel gave the French assurances that the German demands would be limited to those inciting war or those who had broken the law. Yet Vichy agreed to an elastic interpretation of these demands in its desire to get rid of foreign or stateless Jews, and to German gross violation of the right of asylum.[8] Moreover, Vichy, applying Article 19, authorised in July 1940 a German Commission, the Kundt Commission, to inspect the camps, prisons and hospitals in the unoccupied zone. By an early circular of 14 August 1940, Vichy ordered all German nationals aged between seventeen and sixty-five to be interned. The anti-Semitic character of these regulations soon became apparent in the policies of both Vichy and the German authorities. By its month-long visit in August of thirty-one internment camps in the unoccupied zone, the Kundt Commission became aware of 7500 German subjects, including 5000 Jews in the camps, who could thus be located. A second visit to the camps took place in July 1942 by Theodor Dannecker with the agreement of René Bousquet.

Broadly speaking, camps, never referred to as 'concentration camps', were of three types. One was the *centres de séjour surveillé* and the *centres d'internement* for 'extremists', pseudonym for communists: these included Fort Barraux and, for foreigners, Rieucros and Le Vernet. A second type, the most populated, were the centres of *hébergement surveillé*, such as those at Gurs, Argèles and Rivesaltes, for foreigners without means of existence. Gurs was the most important of this group. Near the Spanish border, with blocks of barracks surrounded by barbed wire and guards with handguns, Gurs contained about 12,000 people by early 1941, including 4300 women and 350 children under fourteen, and over 6500 of those who were evicted from Baden-Palatinate by the Germans on 22 October 1940. In the Gurs cemetery over 1000 Jews are buried. A third type of camp, Les Milles, near Aix-en-Provence, was a transit place for those aliens with visas to emigrate. At first the camps in metropolitan France were under the Minister of Justice. In November 1940 control was transferred to the Minister of the Interior.

The camps in the unoccupied zone therefore accommodated Spanish republicans, foreigners said to be undesirable and anti-French, German or Austrian nationals, almost all refugees from the Nazi regime, and Jews, both foreign and French, who were arrested by French police. Justification for the latter was that Jews might be spies, or supporters of de Gaulle, or communists, and would be security risks. By the beginning of 1941, when some thirty camps existed, about 1000 people were in camps in the occupied zone, and between 50,000 and 60,000, three-quarters of whom were Jews, were in camps in the unoccupied zone. Another 25,000 men were in the GTEs.

At the beginning some people could leave the camps after a few months for medical or family reasons. They could be shifted from one camp to another or to assigned residences. Later, they might be sent for a time to a centre of the Service Social des Étrangers (SSE), which helped open centres in 1941 and which lasted until 1942, to lodge families of internees put in GTEs. The SSE was headed by a Quaker, Gilbert Lesage. The centres were of uneven quality.

On 25 June 1941 Darlan sent a circular instructing prefects that all foreign Jews who had immigrated after 10 May 1940 should be put in camps. The law of 2 June 1941 had already reaffirmed the right of prefects to 'pronounce' internment in a special camp, even if the individual was French. On this subject, no legal distinction between French and foreign Jews now existed.

One interesting example of the change in the nature of camps is Mérignac, near Bordeaux, constructed in 1939 to house 600 to 700 Spanish refugees. In January 1941, it was transformed into an internment camp under the Minister of the Interior and the regional prefecture of the Gironde. Jews arrested in that *département* were put in the camp. The prefect Maurice Sabatier gave authority to his deputy Maurice Papon, the secretary-general, to sign papers dealing with Jews and to lend support to their transfer from Mérignac to Drancy from 18 July 1942 to 13 May 1944. In all, 1560 Jews, including 200 children, were transferred in eleven convoys to Drancy, from where they were deported to Auschwitz. It took over fifty years for Papon to be tried in court and punished for a few of his actions.

Another camp, Poitiers, located in the occupied zone, might be taken as a case study of the interrelations between the German occupation and the French administration, especially of the help given by the French in the Final Solution. The camp was run by a small number of French gendarmes when it originally held Spanish refugees and gypsies.[9] When Jews arrived and it became a concentration camp, civilians were added to the gendarmes to guard the camp. The prefect of the Vienne *département*, Louis Bourgain, from August 1941 until the Liberation applied all orders in the most restrictive way concerning the internment and deportation of Jews.

Between 15 July 1941 and 17 July 1942 about 700 Jews were interned in Poitiers. The German field commander made clear that the camp was installed by the French administration, which was responsible for its surveillance and organisation. Yet Bourgain complied with the German demand for a list of Jews classified by nationality, most of whom had already been deported, as he had already imposed a heavy workload on the internees, also suggested by the Germans. The prefect continued to ask the German authorities about anything concerning the internees. He went even further than the Germans suggested. After a note in December 1941 from the German command, replying to a French enquiry, that there was no obligation to keep French Jews interned in Poitiers, Bourgain did not release any.

Like other departmental prefects, Bourgain was an essential cog-wheel, a pivotal figure in the complex administrative arrangements for the camps under the aegis of the Ministry of the Interior. Their administrative authority was enhanced by the law of 2 June 1941 prescribing a census of Jews; anyone disobeying instructions could be fined, imprisoned or interned in a special camp, even if the individual was a French citizen. French police and gendarmes were required to effectuate the transfer of Jews from Poitiers to Drancy, obeying their superior officers in the departmental prefecture and in Vichy, who acted to facilitate German demands. The French personnel, knowing local geography and population, were able to make arrests and formulate the logistics for deportations that the Germans could not have done.[10] Bourgain, at his trial after the Liberation, was sentenced to five years in prison.

Drancy, the Antechamber of Death

By far the most important internment camp was Drancy.[11] At the outbreak of war Drancy was a dreary, unfinished apartment complex, a collection of buildings forming a square, a suburb of Paris, near a railway freight yard with lines to the east. It is now the symbolic embodiment of French internment camps, the main camp for departure of deportations 'to the East', the antechamber of death, the place from which Jews were sent to 'Pitchipoi', the children's nickname for Auschwitz.[12] The place was requisitioned by the French government at the outbreak of war to intern German and Austrian nationals for a short time. After the Armistice, Drancy served for a year, in irregular fashion, as a prison where the German occupiers first put French POWs, then interned British persons, then other prisoners and foreigners, some from Yugoslavia and Greece, all protected by the laws of war.

On 20 August 1941 it became virtually a concentration camp for Jews. This changeover resulted from the round-up on that day by the Paris police, in the 11th and 12th *arrondissements* of Paris, of Jewish males under sixty; 4232 were arrested, as were another fifty-two Jews, members of the Bar. They were the first Jews to be put in Drancy. As an internment camp it lasted until 17 August 1944, the scene of human tragedy. About 67,000 Jews were interned there and deported, out of a total of nearly 76,000 deported from France, in sixty-seven convoys starting on 27 March 1942 and lasting until 8 August 1944. Less than 3 per cent of the deported returned in 1945. For the Jews who died in Auschwitz, Drancy was their last sight of France.

The first convoy from Drancy to Auschwitz left on 27 March 1942 and a second on 22 June 1942. The first convoy had a contingent drawn partly from the camp and partly from Compiègne. Those chosen then and in the following deportations were men in good health, who could work and could travel, though the choice was rapid, superficial and often incorrect.[13] On 16 July 1942 the nature of the camp changed with the Vél d'Hiv round-up and the consequent arrival of men, women and children. Five thousand foreigners were interned in a single day, under appalling conditions. Three days later deportation began of those arrested. Drancy until the end was a place of permanent terror.

From 16 July 1942 to July 1943, women and children were interned and deportations began in earnest, forty occurring in the year. During these periods a French official, nominated by the prefecture of Paris police, administered the camp, with ultimate control first by SS Hauptsturmführer Theodor Dannecker, and then by SS Obersturmführer Heinz Roethke. Drancy was guarded internally and externally by French police and gendarmes. A commissioner of police was its administration head under the overall control of the German SS leaders, who imposed a rigid discipline; in succession they were Dannecker, Roethke and Brunner.[14] Different French officials performed given functions. The prefecture of police was responsible for the commandant, the inspectors, the auxiliaries, the medical service and the cashier. The gendarmerie was responsible for surveillance. The prefecture of the Seine *département* was responsible for food and equipment. In addition, a parallel Jewish 'administration' emerged which kept files, arranged food packages and was able to maintain some contact with the outside world, including the UGIF, the Jewish representative organisation. Until August 1942 an individual from the UGIF visited Drancy every day.

On 2 July 1943 Drancy became a typical Nazi concentration camp when a small group of the German Sicherheitsdienst (Security Service) headed by SS Hauptsturmführer Aloïs Brunner took over control. Brunner, a physically small and badly built person, was a pitiless murderer who had already liquidated Jews in Austria and 43,000 in Salonika, Greece, who had been Adolf Eichmann's private secretary, and who was to apply his own special brand of cynical brutality and demoralisation of his victims to Jews in France.

Brunner relieved all French administrators of the camp of their functions and internal policing. The French commander of the camp, the police inspectors and the medical personnel all left. No French police were allowed in the camp, though gendarmes guarded the outside and observation posts. Brunner remained to the end, on 17 August 1944, a fanatical anti-Semite whose priority was to exterminate Jewish children and who on the very last day before Liberation obtained three cars on a train to take fifty-one Jews, including the director of the Rothschild Hospital in Paris, to Buchenwald; he used them to cover his escape from France. Brunner had been responsible for deporting over 22,000 Jews from Drancy. In 1954 he was sentenced to death *in absentia* for war crimes. He escaped to Syria where successive rulers allowed him to remain alive and well and unpunished in that country.

Conditions in the camps were catastrophic, the result not only of neglect and inefficiency, but also of active and deliberate ill will. Inmates suffered from gastro-enteritis in all the camps, from typhoid and malaria because of polluted water, and later from hunger. Mortality rates were high. At Gurs alone, in the three months of winter 1940–1, over 1000 died. In all the camps in the unoccupied zone, about 3000 Jews died.[15] Gurs, for example, lacked enough bed space, proper windows, electricity, stoves, toilets and clean water. It stank of manure and urine. The whole camp was mud-ridden for half the year. Without help and food supplied from outside relief organisations, many more inmates would have starved.[16]

Conditions in the camps varied in place and in time, as did the fate of the internees, some of whom were released and later re-arrested. However minimal the differences, conditions in all the camps were appalling. People, in small areas, slept on two-tiered bunk beds, on piles of straw that were filthy and never changed, on sand, or on partial flooring. Some camps had poor ventilation or lighting; others had little or no heating. In rainy weather, some camps became swamps. In warm weather, some were infested with rats and mosquitoes. Water was filthy, and sanitary conditions were poor. Hunger was prevalent; camps spent on average only one-third of the amount of money allotted for food for each detainee. Clothes quickly became difficult to keep clean, and almost impossible to replace. Children, lacking clothing, were wrapped in blankets, and sometimes kept apart from their families.

All this was known early on. A message from the World Jewish Congress in New York to the *London Jewish Times* on 28 October

1941 reads that thousands of Jews in the French internment camps 'will die that winter unless there is a radical improvement in the food situation ... they receive only one–two hundredths of what is required for normal sustenance'.[17] Not only was food bad; medical supplies were inadequate. Other humanitarians were aware of the situation. Donald Lowrie, the American YMCA representative, saw Pétain, and representatives of the Quakers saw Laval, with no success. In his report of August 1942, Lowrie wrote of Laval's 'tirade against Jews in general', as well as the fact that even chaplains were denied admission to the camps, which were surrounded by fully armed national police.[18]

Persecution in North Africa

In addition to the camps in the unoccupied zone in metropolitan France, a number were set up in North Africa where about 15,000 Jews were interned. The Jewish communities in North Africa were subjected to discrimination and anti-Semitic laws as in metropolitan France.[19] Algeria, French territory, and Morocco, a French protectorate, were under Vichy control. General Weygand was high commissioner in North Africa, and General Auguste Noguès remained resident general of France in Morocco from 1936 to 1943. Tunisia, also a French protectorate, was under Nazi control from November 1942 to May 1943. Jews there during this period suffered under a reign of terror directed by the notorious Walter Rauff, head of the security police in Tunisia. Libya was under Italian rule.

Jews in the area were deprived of civil rights; Algerian Jews were stripped of French citizenship in October 1940. Jews were detained in over thirty camps, fourteen in Morocco and the others in Algeria, administered by officers of the French Foreign Legion who were sympathetic to the Nazis. Jews were sent to concentration camps and labour camps; about 4000 were found held in camps in south Morocco and in Algeria in November 1942 when the Allies took over the area: However, it took some time before they were released and the camps were not officially closed until April 1943. Some Jews were deported to their death, but large-scale deportations or murders did not occur owing to the relatively short occupation period before the military successes of the Allies in 1942–3.

The North African territories were governed by officials loyal to Vichy; the initiatives and measures taken there were French, not German. Anti-Semitic actions, the Aryanisation process, persecution, removal of rights, the *numerus clausus* imposed on the teaching and liberal professions, the work camps, the concentration camps, were all

Vichy decisions. Willingness to implement discriminatory measures derived from different motives. Some officials, as always, were opportunistic. Others bureaucratically applied laws and decrees automatically and obeyed instructions without challenge. A glaring example was General Noguès himself. This resident general was appointed by the Popular Front in 1936 and was a model 'republican general' before he acquiesced in Vichy rule. He opposed the Allied landings in North Africa in November 1942, but then changed sides, remaining in his position until June 1943.

Noguès had to cope with considerable public support for official repression of Jews in Morocco, as in the rest of North Africa.[20] This came from both European settler and Arab anti-Semitism.[21] Anti-Semites in the Magrib approved of the census of North African Jews ordered by Vichy in June 1941, the Aryanisation of Jewish property and the *numerus clausus* in the liberal professions and schools. Though anti-Semitic legislation was implemented more readily in Algeria than in Morocco or Tunisia, even in Morocco by a decree of 19 August 1941 Jews were forbidden to live in the European quarters of urban areas. French fascists and local Arabs attacked Jewish shops and businesses in a number of towns. Noguès set up detention camps, but defended this as necessary to avoid the public anti-Semitism that might lead to instability in the cities where Jews lived. A similar argument was made by Jean-Pierre Esteva, resident general in Tunisia, who approved a Statut des Juifs in November 1940, but who implemented anti-Semitic legislation with less vigour than did Vichy in general or Algeria in particular. He claimed that the legislation was necessary to placate Muslims. French officials and citizens in Tunisia evinced anti-Jewish leanings, but these never assumed the virulent forms they did in Algeria. Partly this was due to fear that strong action against Jews would drive them to the side of Italy, which was anxious to have a stronger position in the country. It was noticeable that anti-Semitic laws were applied more loosely than in Algeria; for instance, the restriction on the number of Jewish doctors was not put into effect.[22]

If Esteva was lenient, other French officials in North Africa were ideologues who supported Vichy but who differed on the wisdom of collaboration, and, sometimes, on the extent of anti-Semitic discrimination. Out of this group came a number of future members of the Resistance, such as Jacques Lemaigre-Dubreuil and Henri d'Astier de La Vigerie.

North Africa was also the setting for the complex, bewildering attitudes of two generals, Weygand and Giraud, both supporters of the Marshal, both anti-German, both anti-Semitic. Weygand was sent to

Africa, after differences with Vichy leaders on collaboration with Germany, as delegate-general in Algiers. He built up an army in Tunis, was kidnapped and imprisoned by the Germans, was placed under arrest after the war, and was finally freed in 1948.

Henri Giraud, commander of the French 7th Army in 1940, escaped from a POW camp; he was a conservative supporter of Pétain but not a collaborator. Leaving France for North Africa, he became civil and military commander after the assassination of Darlan in December 1942. In this position he refused to abrogate the Statuts des Juifs, a position in which he was supported by President Roosevelt.[23] The American President favoured Giraud to be head of the Free French forces, but the General, lacking political skills, was easily outmanoeuvred by the more astute de Gaulle.

Not only were Vichy regulations extended to North Africa, but others were added locally. Jews were eliminated from professions and schools, forced into relocation to ghettos (mellahs), subjected to land expropriation and financial extortions, as well as sent to camps. The Bedeau camp was for Algerian Jewish soldiers. One incidental disconcerting aspect was the unhelpful attitude of the United States. At the Casablanca Conference in January 1943, President Roosevelt thought that the number of Jews in the professions in North Africa should be limited to the proportion of their population to the whole.[24]

In Morocco Jews were detained in camps but not deported. Did the King, who ordered detention, protect his Jews? Historians differ on whether he was powerless to act, whether he co-operated in the anti-Semitic policies, or whether he opposed or delayed implementing them.[25]

Tunisia was another story. While the French had been lenient, once the Germans took over, the situation changed drastically. With SS Obersturmbannführer Walter Rauff in control, at the end of 1942, Jewish property was confiscated, hostages were arrested, over 4000 Jews were deported, 5000 were sent to labour camps, some were murdered, some died of diseases in the camps. The terror included assaults on synagogues, the beating of Jews, and the drafting of 4000 Jewish workers to airports and harbours in various towns. Gas chambers were being prepared there but were not yet operative when Tunis was liberated in May 1943.

The Disgrace of France

With their overpopulation, under-equipment, inadequate food and high mortality rate, the camps are a stain on France. The dishonourable names still resound: Gurs, on a barren plateau and a sea of mud resembling a scene from *King Lear*; Rivesaltes, 'the Sahara of the Midi', mosquito-ridden, insalubrious, subject to strong north winds; and Drancy.[26]

The internees tried to alleviate their plight, as did outside agencies. They set up a system of voluntary taxation that helped them buy additional food, and engaged in occupational and cultural activities. Workshops provided training in trades and crafts: carpentry, shoe-making, sewing, hairdressing, basket weaving, drawing and languages. Children attended improvised school classes in Rivesaltes without any textbooks or writing implements; in Gurs they were taught by well-known intellectuals. Concerts by interned musicians and singers, lectures and drama performances were given. The younger brother of Léon Blum declaimed by heart the fables of La Fontaine; another detainee recited the poetry of Ronsard.

The internees obtained help from social workers, medical people and teachers, both Jewish and non-Jewish. Some twenty-four relief organisations participated, including the Oeuvre de Secours aux Enfants (OSE); Secours Suisse; the Organisation pour la reconstruction et le travail (ORT); the American Friends Service Committee (Quakers); religious organisations such as the Comité Inter-mouvements auprès des Évasions (CIMADE), a Protestant group; Amitié Chrétienne (a Catholic group); and the Central Committee of Jewish Relief Associations. Many of these groups joined in creating the Comité de Nîmes (the Comité de Coordination pour l'Assistance dans les Camps). The main funding agency was the American Jewish Joint Distribution Committee, which, like the other agencies, was in touch with the detained. The different agencies helped with particular services, with education, clothing, food, soup kitchens, hygiene and sanitation. They also performed an important psychological role by providing a link with the outside world and protection against the camp administration. Rabbi René Kapel worked to improve living conditions in some of the camps, especially Gurs, and to humanise the departure of the convoys of deportees.[27] The relief organisations and personnel helped the internees but could not save them from death.

Memorials at Drancy now mark the place of the past horrors: a train wagon of the French railway SNCF, which could contain forty people or eight horses, a sculpture and plaques. The official plaque reads, 'The French Republic in homage to the victims of racist and anti-Semitic persecutions and crimes against humanity committed under the *autorité de fait dite* [the *de facto* authority known as] "Gouvernement de l'État Français" (1940–1944). Never forget.' A second plaque placed at Drancy by the UEJF, the Union des Étudiants Juifs de France, in February 1993 is more direct. It reads: 'Here, the French State of Vichy interned many thousands of Jews, gypsies and foreigners. Deported to Nazi camps, almost all were put to death there. We, the generation of memory, will never forget.'

CHAPTER 8

PERSECUTION

At the Wannsee Conference in Berlin on 20 January 1942, presided over by Reinhard Heydrich, the head of the Reich Central Security Organisation and Himmler's deputy in the SS, the 'final solution of the Jewish problem', the extermination of the Jews of Europe, was planned by the Nazi hierarchy. The number of Jews in metropolitan France and its territories was calculated to be about 700,000, suggesting presumably that the figure included 400,000 in the territories of North Africa.[1] A similar, if imprecise, figure was given by Himmler to Hitler on 10 December 1942 when he declared that between 600,000 and 700,000 Jews in France were to be 'abgeschaffen' (eliminated).

Decision and implementation of the Final Solution would be made by the SS leader in each country, but first the Jews had to be arrested. The first mass arrest of Jews in France took place in Paris on 14 May 1941 by French police on orders from the Gestapo's Jewish Affairs Department and with the assent of the CGQJ and the prefecture of police. Over 3700 foreign Jews, Polish, Czech and Austrian, were arrested when they responded to orders to appear in police stations. More arrests in Paris followed on 20 August 1941 by French police over a five-day period, again on orders from the German military authorities and the Gestapo's unit under Dannecker. The 2400-member police force arrested 4230 Jews, men aged eighteen to fifty, of whom over 1000 were French. The myth that Vichy would protect its French-born Jews was dissipated. The men were taken to the newly established Drancy.

A third round-up on 12 December 1941 in Paris was conducted by 360 of the German military police and 200 of the SS force, assisted by Paris police. This time 743 Jews were seized, mostly French middle-class citizens, and sent to Compiègne where they were joined by 300 other Jews from Drancy. Among this group was René Blum, the brother of Léon. The Germans now adopted a policy stating that attacks on German soldiers would be attributed to Jews and their agents. Within days, on 15 December, 100 men, including fifty-three

Jews, fifty of whom had been chosen in Drancy the same morning, were executed in Mount Valérien in the Paris suburbs.

A little more than a month after the Wannsee Conference, Dannecker discussed with Eichmann in Berlin the need for Vichy to help in the deportation of several thousand Jews. Plans were made in March 1942 to deport 1000 Jews from Compiègne and another 5000 from other places to Auschwitz. On 27 March, the first deportation took place, with a convoy of 1112 assembled from Compiègne and Drancy. The convoy was escorted by French gendarmes to the German border; Dannecker decided to accompany the train all the way to the death camp and was escorted by German military police to the same border. Vichy had now escorted French Jews part of the way on the road to death.

The Germans envisaged deportations of 100,000 Jews from France. The lack of protest over, and the participation of Vichy in, the 27 March deportation led the Germans to go further. A second convoy left Compiègne on 5 June, followed by three more from the camps in the occupied zone in the month of June. By mid-July, the first five convoys had taken 5149 Jews to Auschwitz. The Germans wanted more. The haul had been insufficient to fill the trains scheduled for deportation. Victims would therefore have to come from the unoccupied as well as the occupied zone.

On 6 May 1942, Louis Darquier de Pellepoix replaced Vallat, who had become *persona non grata* to the Nazis, as head of the CGQJ. The virulent anti-Semite, who declared in June 1936, 'As long as you will not be rid of those people [the Jews], the national existence of the country will be threatened', and on 11 March 1937, 'The Jewish question must be solved most urgently. Let the Jews be exiled or massacred', was now in a position to forward the process of expulsion and deportation, and the confiscation of the property of Jews.[2] Darquier, together with Laval and René Bousquet, entered into a series of discussions on the process with Nazi counterparts.

Darquier remained the persecutor of Jews almost to the end of Vichy. Among other policy proposals, he suggested the mandatory wearing of the yellow star by Jews in the unoccupied zone, that Jews should be prevented without exception from access to and performance of public office, and that French nationality of all Jews who acquired it after 1927 should be annulled.[3] On the last issue, as on other issues, he was more extreme than Vallat, who had set 1932 as the limit for the denaturalisation law. He was also more extreme than Pierre Laval who successfully resisted the call of Darquier, reinforced by German pressure, to implement this denaturalisation.

Vichy Complicity

Yet Vichy was not Berlin. The Nazis wanted to exterminate Jews; Vichy wanted to exclude them from the life of France. The major French political leaders, Pétain, Laval and Darlan, were not homicidal maniacs or inhumane monsters with perverted values. Their crime was to be accomplices in carrying out actions that resulted in the extreme consequences of those values.

Few political actions are devoid of dirty hands. The Vichy leaders soiled theirs. Vichy complied with German demands; it classified Jews, it isolated them, it discriminated against them, it directed propaganda against them, and it arrested and facilitated their journey to death. The administrative, judicial and police system all collaborated in performing the tasks that the German occupiers could not do for lack of manpower and sufficient information. Adolf Eichmann, at his trial in Jerusalem, said that deporting Jews was a complex affair, involving planning, negotiation, organisation and communication. Vichy assistance was crucial in that complex operation, in committing what Winston Churchill called 'the most bestial, the most squalid of offences'.

There was no banality in the squalid behaviour of Vichy. Its personnel exemplified the generalisation of Raoul Hilberg that the destruction of the Jews required the participation 'of all those agencies that had the means to perform their share of the action at the moment when the need for their contribution arose'.[4] Vichy may have been preoccupied with matters other than Jews, as Marrus suggests, and may in general have enforced rules on the basis of administrative routine, and may not have contemplated the idea of mass murder, yet it did little to prevent or delay the physical extermination of its Jewish population.[5] It can fairly be accused of at least complicity in the policy of genocide.

Did Vichy know of the destruction of Jews and, if so, when did it know? No clear answer can be positively asserted but accumulated evidence suggests that the ignorance proclaimed by Vichy was fallacious. Rumours were rife about the fate of the deported Jews. Officials, like people in general, listened to the BBC broadcasts from London. Church dignitaries were informed by their international contacts of atrocities in eastern Europe. The Allies spoke formally on 17 December 1942 of exterminations by the Nazis. Laval, in particular, was careful to use coded language, as conversations in September 1942 indicate. When pastor Marc Boegner, the Protestant leader, spoke to him about massacres of Jews in eastern Europe, Laval replied that Jews were being employed there in 'farming colonies' or in 'gardening'. A report written by SS Sturmbannführer Herbert Hagen on 4 September 1942, concerning the meeting in Paris between Laval and Oberg about the transfer of Jews from the unoccupied zone, states that Laval, who had been troubled by foreign diplomats asking questions about this transfer, would now reply in the same way as the German authorities. Jews from the unoccupied zone who had been 'surrendered' to the occupying authorities were being transferred to the 'General Government', to the non-annexed part of Poland, for work.

In reality, Laval must have known the truth. His *chef de cabinet*, Jean Jardin, asked Robert Kiefe, secretary-general of the Central Consistory, to give him precise information about the massacre of 11,000 Jews in Poland by toxic gas.[6] This was made known in the paper, *J'Accuse*, no. 2, October 1942, by the Swiss press and by Radio London. In the National Archives, twenty-six cartons of transmissions of radio broadcasts are available, some touching on the subject of the massacres. The French diplomatic archives from 1941 to 1944 show that the Vichy government was kept informed of the annihilation of Jews in Bucharest, Budapest and Sofia.[7]

At his own trial in August 1945 Pétain denied knowledge of the fate of Jews who had been deported. Yet representatives of the YMCA had talked to the Marshal. His secretary, Jardel, replied to Tracy Strong, President of the YMCA, that it was regrettable, but nothing could be done. He ignored the information of Donald A. Lowrie given to Strong on 10 August 1942 about the German plan for a new Europe, leading to 'purification of undesirable elements'.[8]

Perhaps it is a human failing that guilt and responsibility so often remain unacknowledged. Certainly, the ideological anti-Semite Darquier, the second head of the CGQJ, expressed no remorse. In his revealing interview in *L'Express* on 28 October 1978, he insisted that the photographs of bodies of women and children pulled out of the gas chambers in Auschwitz were doctored, part of the thousands of forgeries by Jews after the war. He also put the blame on René Bousquet for organising the great round-up of Jews in Paris, and then elsewhere, and was caustic about his evading punishment except for the unfulfilled five years of 'national *indignité*' given the police chief in 1949.[9]

The record, however, is clear. Darquier, Bousquet, Laval and others all dirtied their hands in co-operating with policies leading towards the Final Solution.[10] The Vichy government did less to stop the deportations of Jews from France in 1944 than did Admiral Horthy in Hungary and Marshal Antonescu in Romania.

Comparison with Other Countries

At this point a revealing comparison can be made between the Vichy actions and lack of actions towards Jews with those in Denmark and Bulgaria, and the Italian occupiers in south-east France.

Denmark is the only country that has a plaque on the wall in the Avenue of the Righteous of the Nations at Yad Vashem in Jerusalem. Many parts of Danish society played a role in saving most of the Jewish population in the country: the Danish resistance movement; underground newspapers encouraging Danes to help the Jews; protests against persecution by the leaders of the Lutheran Church, who suggested providing sanctuary; citizens who hid Jews in their private homes and hospitals; others who helped Jews escape to neutral Sweden. Denmark did not comply with the Nazi order to deport Jews.

This refusal was also partly true of the more complex situation in Bulgaria, a member of the Axis, but one country where until late 1942 anti-Semitic laws were laxly enforced and deportation almost non-existent. But in March 1943, the Commissioner for Jewish Questions, Alexander Belev, a fascist lawyer, approved the arrest and deportation of 20,000 Jews. Fourteen thousand of them had come from Macedonia and Thrace, which were occupied by Bulgaria in the war, and 6000 were native Bulgarians. Over 11,300 of those arrested from the first group were deported and only a handful survived. The native Bulgarians, some of whom had been arrested, were saved by a protest movement led by Dimitâr Peshev, the courageous lawyer and vice-president of the National Assembly, who was assisted by other members of the Assembly, part of the Bulgarian Orthodox Church led by Cyril, Metropolitan of Plovdiv, and ordinary citizens.

King Boris III, influenced by this strong expression of public opinion against the deportation, listening to appeals for compassion, and recognising belatedly that deportations would harm his country's reputation and future, acted in this mixture of self-interest and virtue to block the deportations. The compelling argument of Peshev could have been a rallying cry in other countries, especially in Vichy: the deportations, he wrote, were 'in violation of the Constitution, the ordinary rule of law, common decency and basic human sympathy ... To remain silent was a breach of conscience, both as a deputy and as a human being.'[11]

In his honest, sober writings Primo Levi spoke of infinite gradations of responsibility and moral ambivalence.[12] By comparison with Vichy, and of course with Nazi Germany, the record of the response of Italy to the persecution of Jews is admirable. Perhaps as many as 15,000 Jews in France owe their lives to Italian action and non-action.

Fascist Italy has often been likened to Nazi Germany as comparable examples of totalitarian systems.[13] The comparison is valid on a wide range of policies and institutional structures and practices, but on the question of Jews it is less plausible. For whatever reason, whether it was sheer expediency, personal influences of prominent Jews or his

Jewish mistresses, especially the clever writer Margarita Sarfatti, or genuine dislike of anti-Semitism, Mussolini was less likely to exhibit antagonism towards Jews and Judaism or to feel an urgent need to promulgate discriminatory measures against Jews than Hitler.[14] Mussolini, responding indirectly to Hitler in 1933, said, 'National pride has no need of the delirium of race.'

Not until October and November 1938 and the Manifesto of the Italian Race, and the Race Laws, did Mussolini enact anti-Jewish legislation. Signs did appear on shops, 'No Jews or dogs allowed', but implementation of the laws was lax, and uneven in different local areas.[15] The Italian Foreign Ministry at that time could have given lessons to the US State Department on immunity from anti-Semitic beliefs.

Mussolini followed the accepted tradition. Jews had lived in the country for 2000 years, and were for the most part assimilated. They played significant roles: a prime minister, a mayor of Rome, over fifty generals in the army. About 10,000 Jews were members of the Fascist party, a third of adult Jews. Native Jews were joined in pre-war years by 10,000 refugees from Nazi Germany, comprising a total Jewish population of 57,000 in a country of 33 million.

Italy entered the war on 27–8 May 1940 and invaded France. After the Franco-Italian armistice on 24 June 1940 a small area of south-east France, around the town of Menton, remained in Italian hands. Italy opened consular offices in a number of towns in the Vichy zone as well as in the German-occupied zone, including Paris. When the Germans invaded the unoccupied Vichy zone on 11 November 1942, the Italian army also went into southern France, taking control of the area east of the Rhône. As a result an Italian occupation zone consisting of seven whole *départements*, most of two others and part of one other was created.

In reaction to the armistice between the Anglo-American military command and the Badoglio government that had replaced the Mussolini regime, the Germans on 9 September 1943 took over the zone. About 5000 foreign Jews had been placed in supervised residences in the Italian zone and another 5000 were free in the Côte d'Azur.[16]

The Germans were well aware that Italian military commanders and diplomats were not sympathetic to this Nazi style of anti-Semitism. Those commanders in the Italian-occupied Balkans disapproved of Jews being handed over to Germany and its puppet regimes. They thwarted plans for Jews to be taken by the Ustasha, the Croatian fascists: they were able to change Mussolini's mind on the subject to some extent. Italian diplomats used their own bureaucratic methods to the same end. The 15,000 Jews who survived in what was pre-war Yugoslavia were almost all saved by those diplomats and military men.

The Italian occupiers in France adopted similar tactics by insisting on their rights as legal authorities. Differences with the Nazis were apparent. Martin Luther, the German Under-Secretary of State, warning of Italian opposition to their policies, wrote a memo on 22 October 1942 to the Minister of Foreign Affairs recognising that Italy had failed to tackle the Jewish problem and that this failure was creating an increasingly intolerable situation.[17] The telegram from the Foreign Minister, Joachim von Ribbentrop, to the German Embassy in Rome on 13 January 1943 was equally direct:

> There are considerable differences between the official Italian and German positions on how to handle the Jewish question. Whereas we have recognised Jewry as a disease that threatens to corrupt the body politic and hinder the reconstruction of Europe, the Italian government tends to think of Jews as individuals and reserves preferential treatment for individual Jews or certain groups of Jews. The Italian government also protects Jews abroad if they hold Italian citizenship, especially if they are influential in the economy.

Ribbentrop was correct. Italy was concerned, as a manifestation of its sovereignty, to defend and be protective of all its citizens, including Jews, in the occupied areas. The argument for sovereignty was even more pronounced after the Germans took over the Vichy zone in November 1942 and the Italian zone including all or most of ten *départements* was created. Italy claimed control over all issues in its zone, even though Vichy officials were still there.[18]

Beyond the matter of sovereignty, a mixture of motives was apparent. Certainly, the Italians exhibited a more humane attitude than did the Germans. They tried to protect foreign in addition to Italian Jews. They also had geopolitical and economic interests. They were making the case for annexing or continuing to rule those south-eastern areas of France that the two countries had long disputed.

Believing that Jews made useful contributions to the Italian economy in the Mediterranean area, the Italian government looked unfavourably on the Vichy policy of Aryanisation and its attempt to confiscate the property of the 5000 Italian Jews in the area that it occupied. The Italian attitude was similar in Tunisia. In November 1942, after the German landing which was an attempt to prevent the Allied invasion, the Italians successfully protected the 5000 Italian Jews there, though, unlike their policy in southern France, they did not similarly try to protect non-Italian Jews.

The Italian record is blemished, but on the whole good. The Italians tried to sabotage the Final Solution in Croatia, Greece and France. A meeting between Mussolini and Ribbentrop in February 1943 produced an ostensible agreement that Jews would be expelled from the Italian zone in Croatia, but the Duce reneged and nothing was done. Italy refused to yield on the Italian Jews in France. It rejected all German proposals to deport them 'to the east', though it consented to some social and economic restrictions. It also rejected the Vichy call for all foreign Jews to be transferred out of the Italian zone.

The Germans remained puzzled about Italian behaviour and tried to find explanations. One possible explanation concerned Signor Vitetti, Director-General of the Italian Foreign Ministry, who was married to an American Jewess with connections to Standard Oil and who spent a considerable part of her time in Switzerland. Was this the reason that the American Minister in Berne could send such well-informed reports on German and Italian personnel, obviously based on information from an important Italian, to Washington? Italian officials, trying to protect their nationals, and soon non-Italian Jews, challenged both German and Vichy demands. Indeed, that very protection made it more difficult for Vichy to surrender French Jews.[19]

After the major *rafles* in July and August 1942, the Italian consul in Paris, Gustavo Orlandini, intervened with the German authorities to free Italian Jews who had been arrested. The Italian Consul in Nice, Alberto Calisse, assisted by the Roman Jewish banker Angelo Donati, who had been in the Italian Chamber of Commerce in Paris before the war and the director of the Banque France-Italie, and who spoke for the Italian Jewish community, insisted that all foreign Jews, not only Italians, should be exempted from Vichy measures. Calisse and other Italian officials argued that the Vichy and German regulations on Jews should in practice be disregarded in Italian-held territory. Rebuking Laval, Calisse declared that Italy would apply the same legislation to Jews in the Italian zone as was applied in Italy itself.[20]

Italy followed the same policy in North Africa.[21] Its ambassador in Berlin, Dino Alfieri, on 2 September 1942 asked the German Foreign Office to delay the application of racial laws in that area. In this he was successful, as was also his stand that the German high command in Tunisia not take any measures against Jews of Italian nationality without prior consent of the Italian consul-general. Even after the Germans took control of Tunisia in 1942, the Italians were still able to save the lives and property of the Italian Jews, probably about 5000.

On 20 February 1943, as a result of the assassination of two German officers in Paris and consequent German demands for deportation of 2000 Jews as a reprisal, the French police made mass arrests in the unoccupied zone. The Italians, however, refused to allow the police to do so in their zone. In the Isère *département*, the Italians prevented the arrest of over 200 Jews. In Annecy the Italian Fourth Army forced the release of Jews who had been arrested and imprisoned there. In Grenoble, Italian troops blocked railroad tracks to prevent departures. The Italian military made the police chief in Lyon annul an order for the arrest of several hundred Jews.

Knochen, Roethke, Eichmann and Ribbentrop were all disturbed by Italian behaviour. A letter of 25 February 1943 to the Foreign Ministry, drafted by Eichmann and signed by the head of the Gestapo, Mueller, complained that the Italian authorities were taking the side of the Jews. Knochen and Roethke both wrote of Italian 'sabotage' of the anti-Semitic laws, and Italian protection of the Jews. Knochen pointed out that 'the best of harmony prevails between the Italian troops and the Jewish population'.[22]

Unlike the French, the Italians were active in that sabotage and harmony, especially after the deportations began. When Marcel Ribière, prefect of the Alpes-Maritimes (the area of the Riviera), tried to enforce Vichy ordinances expelling foreign and stateless Jews, some of whom had lived there since 1938, from the Mediterranean coast to the Ardèche district, the Italian Consul in Nice, Alberto Calisse, blocked it, saying that only the Italians could deal with Jewish questions in their zone.[23] He also refused to implement the law of 11 December 1942 ordering the stamping of the word 'Jew' on identity cards and ration books. He made clear that any French policeman who detained a Jew would be arrested. He also protected the synagogue in Nice from demonstrations.

Knochen correctly feared an influx of Jews in the Italian zone. For a time the Côte d'Azur was indeed virtually a promised land for Jews in France. Individual Jews tried to move to the area, and Jewish organisations, conscious of the greater tolerance there, moved some of their main offices and documentation centres to the Italian zone after the arrests in Marseille in January 1943. The Mouvement de Jeunesse Sioniste (MJS), the Zionist Youth Movement, set up a group in Nice, engaging in clandestine activity, producing forged identity papers, as well as rescuing children.

People were also moved for safety. Roethke indicated that the Italians had transferred about 2000 Jews to hotels in the spa town Mégève, in the Alps.[24] Foreign Minister Ribbentrop remarked that Italian military authorities did not sufficiently appreciate the Jewish problem and that they had annulled in their zone measures taken by the French authorities. To discuss the impasse he met in Rome on 25 February 1943 with Mussolini, who typically, and untruthfully, denied that Italy was annulling the anti-Jewish measures. As a result of the German pressure, Mussolini sent the next month a senior official, Guido Lospinoso, to Nice as 'Inspector of Racial Policy'. The new inspector became an invisible man. When Eichmann invited him to Paris he did not consider a meeting appropriate at that time. He refused to meet Knochen in either Paris or Berlin.

Lospinoso did, however, meet with Father Marie-Benoit, who persuaded him to allow about 30,000 Jews to cross into the Italian zone, and who met with the Pope to discuss a plan. The banker Donati had been appointed as Lospinoso's adviser on Jewish affairs. Donati's idea was to transport the Jews in the Italian zone to northern Italy or to North Africa. Italian ships and American Jewish financing were needed, as was the assent of the Anglo-American allies. But the Italian–Allied armistice, prematurely revealed by General Eisenhower, brought the Germans into the Italian zone. The plan had failed, but the memory of Italian courage lives. Not a single Jew was handed over to the Germans by the Italian army.

Vichy and the Germans

In contrast to these three countries, Denmark, Bulgaria and Italy, two of which were part of the Axis alliance, Vichy and its personnel were involved in the handing over to the Germans of Jews from both the occupied and unoccupied zones. Arrests and deportations of Jews followed from the German demands and from the complex and equivocal relationship – cordial, cautious, suspicious, at different moments – between Vichy and the German occupiers, first in the occupied zone and then in the whole country after November 1942. Vichy had to deal with a number of German authorities, some of which were competitive with each other and involved in normal internal bureaucratic friction.[25] None was benign, but they did differ in their eagerness to fulfil the French contribution to the Final Solution.

The Militärbefehlshaber (MBF), the German military command in Paris, located in the Hotel Majestic, the professional military force authorised by the 1940 armistice agreement to maintain order, protect the security of the occupying forces and supervise the French prefects, had some dedicated Nazis among its administrators. The main administrator, Werner Best, was a fanatical anti-Semite who had run the administrative and personnel sections of the Gestapo in Berlin, had commanded an *Einsatzgruppe* in Poland, and would be civil governor of Denmark. Elmar Michel was the chief economic adviser. The MBF was divided into military and civilian units and into geographic sectors.

Unlike the administrative staff, the MBF commanders were not fanatical or enthusiastic Nazis: some were Bavarian Catholic aristocrats. Neither they nor General Walter von Brauchitsch, Army Commander-in-Chief, nor General von Rundstedt, the senior German commander in the west, allowed their troops to participate in activity related to the Final Solution. The first MBF commander, General Otto von Stülpnagel, opposed efforts to remove Jews from French society, and was critical of the actions of the SS and their French collaborators in the bombings of Paris synagogues in October 1941 and in the German confiscation of art owned by Jews. This criticism led Hitler and Himmler to remove from the MBF military authority over Jewish matters and over the police. For this function SS General Karl Oberg was appointed head of the SS and German police in France. Stülpnagel resigned in February 1942 and was replaced in July by his cousin, General Karl-Heinrich von Stülpnagel. The latter was to be hanged in August 1944 for taking part in the failed plot on 20 July 1944 to assassinate Hitler. The military successively lost control over foreign policy issues, art, diplomacy and police.

The German Embassy in Paris was headed from 1940 to 1944 by Otto Abetz, who had studied art in Paris and cultivated French right-wing intellectuals and cultural personalities before the war and after the defeat of France, who had married a Frenchwoman, and who claimed to be a francophile working for Franco-German reconciliation. In reality, Abetz, a member of Ribbentrop's private office, fostered antiwar sentiments among French pacifists and fascists. Expelled from France in June 1939 for subversive activity, Abetz returned exactly a year later as ambassador. Significantly, France was the only occupied land to which Germany sent an ambassador. However, since only an armistice, not a peace treaty, had been signed between France and Germany, Abetz was accredited to Paris, not to Vichy. Abetz became a central figure in facilitating policies of collaboration with French individuals and groups and with the Vichy regime. The Embassy also exerted pressure on Vichy's internal affairs; the most notable example was its success in pressure for Laval's return to power in April 1942. The Embassy had its own Jewish Affairs section, headed for a time by Karl-Theodor Zeitschel, which kept contact with similar sections in the MBF and the German police. It also kept contact with the Vichy delegate, or ambassador, in Paris; at first, for a very short time, this was Jacques Benoist-Méchin, and for most of the time Fernand de Brinon, a devoted pro-Nazi sympathiser.

Opinions about Abetz differed widely. Some found him brutal, cynical and arrogant, others courteous and sophisticated. A non-fanatical but devoted Nazi, he skilfully fostered division among

French political groups and played on themes of pacifism, a new European order and a 'France of the left' to influence public opinion. He became particularly friendly with Laval, his main interlocutor, as well as the extremist Déat, in Paris. Competing with the MBF and the German security forces for influence, Abetz also corrupted complaisant French politicians, intellectuals and journalists, supervised the theft of French archives and personal papers of Republican politicians and organised the pillage of *objets d'art*. Abetz would be condemned in July 1949 by a French military tribunal to twenty years' imprisonment, but was freed in 1954.[26]

The Einsatzab Rosenberg was the organisation primarily concerned with requisitioning *objets d'art* of Jews in France.

The German authorities most pressing in their demands on Vichy officials were the security forces, a complex structure. In their own country, the German police contained units performing different functions. One part, SiPo, concerned with security, was divided into two sections: Kripo was the criminal police, and Stapo, or the state police, was an intelligence service. Hitler in 1933 set up his own Nazi security service, the Sicherheitsdienst (SD), and in 1936 instructed Himmler to merge Kripo, Stapo and an expanded SD to be known as SiPo-SD, which was directed by Reinhard Heydrich. Adolf Eichmann was the specialist for Jewish affairs in that office. A special department had been set up by Himmler, the Reichssicherheitshauptamt (RSHA), which included the SiPo-SD, the SS Security Police and the Gestapo, and which was headed by Heydrich. Outside Germany, the RSHA acted through 'Advisers on Jewish Affairs', usually attached to the Security Police, who received their orders from Berlin.

On the occupation of France, Heydrich set up a Paris office of the SiPo-SD, headed by the thirty-year-old SS Obersturmbannführer Helmut Knochen, a student of English literature who had written a dissertation on Coleridge, an 'intellectual' Nazi, a 'practical' rather than a violent anti-Semite. As commander of the SD and Security Police in the occupied zone between 1940 and 1944 with thirteen provincial units under him, he worked closely with the Vichy authorities, especially the police chief, René Bousquet, and pressed strongly for Jews to be denaturalised and arrested. In March 1942 his authority was expanded when the secret police unit of the MBF was transferred to the SD. One of the provincial units, that in Lyon, was headed by Klaus Barbie for the latter part of the war period. Knochen was served by subordinates, the most important of whom was Kurt Lischka, a law school graduate who had joined the Gestapo in 1935 rather than a law firm, and who had organised the atrocities of *Kristallnacht* in November 1938. SS Obersturmbannführer Lischka, head of the SiPo-SD in Paris was recalled from France on charges of stealing from victims who were arrested.

On 1 June 1942 SS Brigadeführer Karl Oberg, an associate of Heydrich, became head of the German police and the SS in the occupied zone. He was thus responsible for security until the Germans withdrew from France. He maintained a working relationship with Bousquet and the French police, though he could not speak French. Oberg's personal adviser was SS Sturmbannführer Herbert Hagen, who had been head of the anti-Jewish section of the SD in Berlin before the war and was head of the SiPo-SD in Bordeaux from 1940 to 1942. In 1980, both Hagen and Lischka got prison sentences, twelve years and ten years respectively.

The 27-year-old frenetic SS Obersturmführer Theodor Dannecker, who joined the SS at the age of nineteen, was head of the Jewish Affairs Bureau of the Gestapo, the RSHA Bureau IV B4-J, in Paris from 1940 until July 1942. A subordinate of Eichmann, Dannecker was the key figure, at the beginning of the occupation, involved in, and the architect of, anti-Semitic activities. Though his unit had only thirty men, he was largely responsible for the creation of the CGQJ, the arrest of Jews in Paris and the first deportations. He insisted that all Jews over six years old wear the yellow star of David on their clothing. He was also an original proponent of sending Jews to the island of Madagascar.

That plan was not feasible. Instead, Dannecker met twice with his chief, Eichmann, in June 1942, once in Berlin and once in Paris, to discuss deportation of all Jews from France. Since this was also not immediately feasible, the alternative was to deport 40,000 in the next three months.

The overlapping functions of these German units and the strong personalities of their leaders led to friction and differences of opinion and policies, which alternated with co-operation among them. An early disagreement centred on public and private art treasures, particularly those belonging to Jews. In spite of the prohibition by the military administration on the removal of art from the Louvre, Ambassador Otto Abetz disregarded it, sending important works to Germany.

Similar differences appeared on the Jewish question. The fiery zealot Dannecker wanted immediate deportations of Jews. Oberg was concerned with maintaining order in France, a concern which might require a slower policy and concessions to placate French public opinion. The SS wanted to maintain co-operation with the Vichy authorities. As a result of friction, Dannecker was replaced, though he continued in office for a while, by a new leader, SS Obersturmführer

Heinz Roethke, on 1 July 1942. Dannecker's well-deserved fate was to hang himself while under arrest in an American military prison in Germany in 1945. Roethke, a former theology student, became the Grand Inquisitor of the Gestapo and SS in France.

Roethke too had policy differences with the others. He proposed in September 1942 to arrest over 5000 leading rich and influential French Jews in Paris. He was opposed by Oberg and Knochen who, warned by Laval of the adverse effect on public opinion of such arrests, vetoed it. Even Himmler agreed with the opposition. Instead, 1500 Romanian and then several hundred Greek Jews were sent to death. Nevertheless, 3000 French Jews would soon be arrested.

Yet, despite the friction and differences among the German authorities, co-operation on the Jewish question did take place. The German Embassy played its part in this co-operation, though it had views of its own. A telegram from Otto Abetz on 1 October 1940 states that the solution of the Jewish problem in the occupied territory of France required, among other matters, regulation of the citizenship status of German Jews in France. This would be merely the first step towards the solution of the entire problem. Later, Dannecker reported on 'the genuinely friendly support which our work' received from Abetz and other officials. Abetz had placed a large sum of money at the disposal of the lawyer in charge of the Jewish question for the financing of the anti-Jewish Institute. In another report, dated 22 February 1942, Dannecker referred to the weekly meetings attended by people from different groups: military commands, administrative, police and economic sections, the Embassy, the ERR.

From the beginning of the Occupation those meetings discussed the Jewish question, and the role of Vichy in the matter. Lischka in January 1941 made clear that the French would be involved to avoid reactions by the French people against the Germans. The French police should act independently and on its own initiative. Two years later, in April 1943, Oberg informed Knochen that the best results were obtained where strict co-operation existed between French and German police.[27] Bousquet had helped this co-operation by creating the Sections des Affaires Politiques (SAP), which collaborated with local commanders of the German police. Bousquet's force regularly kept SS Geissler, permanent representative of Oberg in Vichy, informed of French plans.

Bousquet's force was not the only police unit implicated in the machinery of persecution. The CGQJ had one force; the Police for Jewish Affairs was created by Pierre Pucheu, Minister of the Interior, in November 1941, and dealt with Jewish issues on a national basis and in the Paris area. Other units, SPAC, the anti-communist police service, and the SSS, dealing with secret societies, also participated in the persecution.

The French police appeared to be an instrument of Germany. Hundreds of them supervised the first mass round-up of Jews, over 3700 foreigners, in Paris on 14 May 1941. They had reported for examination of their status by the police; most were Polish Jews aged between eighteen and forty, the others were Czech and Austrian. Three months later, on 20 August 1941, the Jewish Affairs Department of the Gestapo issued orders for a second round-up directly to the prefecture of police in Paris without participation of the Vichy government. The Paris police, who went to every metro station in the 11th *arrondissement*, arrested 4232 Jews, men aged eighteen to fifty, over 1000 of whom were French, including prominent lawyers. For the first time German authorities ordered the collective arrest of French Jews by French police. The arrested Jews were all sent to Drancy.

With one exception, French police would be the organisers and executors of the round-ups.[28] The exception was the round-up of 12 December 1941 carried out in Paris by German military police and the SS, assisted by the French. About 750 middle-class French Jews – professionals, intellectuals and business people – were arrested and sent to Compiègne, not to Drancy, before being deported to Auschwitz on 27 March 1942. Again, the Gestapo showed that it made no distinction between French and foreign Jews.

Vichy did not oppose deportation of Jews in principle. The information it gathered on individual Jews, the census it conducted of the Jewish population and its carrying out of the first round-ups in 1941 were fulfilling German demands. Yet Vichy had the possibility of limiting and even cancelling those demands.[29] The French police assisted in murder. When on 15 December 1941 the Nazis shot 150 hostages in Mont-Valérien, the police had selected forty-four immigrant Jews in Drancy, suspected of being communists, to be included in the list.

French policy at first seemed to be clear on the issue. Vichy was reluctant to arrest French Jews in the occupied zone, and it would arrest only foreign Jews in its own zone. Whatever the intention, the performance was not clear. Vichy raised no objection to deportation of foreign Jews. However, it declared that it would protect Jews of French nationality, and insisted that it would be French police, as a demonstration of French sovereignty, that would make the arrests of foreign Jews. The protection of French Jews was spasmodic, constantly uncertain. French Jews were arrested by French police, interned and deported. In the first deportation on 27 March 1942, about half of the victims were French Jews.

In spring 1942 a new cast of *dramatis personae* appeared on the stage of collaboration. Laval had come back to power on 16 April. He appointed René Bousquet as head of the French police two days later. Oberg became head of the German police and SiPo-SD in France. Knochen and Hagen were promoted. Darquier replaced Vallat as leader of the CGQJ.

A series of meetings in May, June and July between French and German officials discussed the collaborative relationship and the functions to be performed. What was crucial was the disparity in the numbers available for these functions. The Germans in France had about 60,000 men to maintain order or to anticipate an invasion, but only three battalions of police, between 2000 and 3000 men, to make arrests. By contrast, the French police numbered about 120,000, including 30,000 in Paris. Its role was vital in facilitating the Final Solution. The French police made the arrests in both the occupied and unoccupied zones for three years. It organised the transfer of the arrested to internment camps and to their deportation. It maintained lists of Jews, and the special police unit in the Paris prefecture of police had an elaborate card file index of 150,000 Jews, controlled by André Tulard, available for the arrests.

Without action by the French police and authorities, German intentions could not have been realised. The Vichy regime was the only regime claiming autonomy and sovereignty which freely surrendered its Jewish population in areas that were not occupied, as well as those that were, to the Germans. Moreover, it handed over those Jews at a time when Germany was preoccupied elsewhere, not only fighting its war with the Anglo-Americans on one front and with the Soviet Union on the other, but also transferring 275,000 Jews from the Warsaw ghetto to Treblinka. Collaboration on Jewish affairs began early. In January 1941 an SS officer was delegated to the Paris prefecture of police. Later in the same year a special anti-Jewish police unit was set up which the SS found valuable for its records and files.

How many Jews could be transported from France? Adolf Eichmann at first called for 5000 in 1942, and then increased the number to 100,000 aged sixteen to forty from France, to be combined with another 15,000 from Holland and 10,000 from Belgium. Dannecker, who had originally suggested the figure of 100,000, which would include French Jews, realistically reduced it to 40,000 for the moment because of the lack of transport. In mid-June 1942 he knew that Vichy would put 'several thousand Jews from the unoccupied zone at our disposal for evacuation'.[30]

Bousquet had already made this clear in his meeting in Paris on 6 May 1942 with Reinhard Heydrich, Oberg and Knochen. Did Bousquet realise he was doing the bidding of the Gestapo in his desire to assert the independence of the French police? Bousquet assured Heydrich and Oberg that the French police would act in the same spirit as the German police and would lend support to the SS in the struggle against anarchists, communists and terrorists.[31] In return, the German leader agreed that in the occupied zone the French police would not be subordinated to the German security forces under Oberg.

The latter spoke repeatedly of the close collaboration between German and French police, of the 'common work' they did. His gesture was to promise better equipment for the French police, to authorise *groupes mobiles de réserve*, and allow the setting up of police schools to increase the efficiency of the French force. Bousquet agreed to use that force to ensure the security of the army of occupation, to maintain order and to exchange information with his counterpart. He also surprised the Germans by suggesting that Jews interned in the occupied zone for over a year could be sent to Drancy and then to a 'destination in the east'.

At the beginning of his tenure as police chief Bousquet wanted to limit the tasks of the French police to the obligations charged to the French government by the Armistice Agreement of June 1940. He also wanted French authorities to be the judges of French nationals accused of offences, whether people were arrested by French or German police, if the offence was not against the occupation forces. Yet Bousquet had gone far beyond the providing of information for the benefit of the SS. The French police were put at the service of the German Reich, becoming virtually agents of the Gestapo. Orders from the Germans were given to Leguay, Bousquet's deputy, for delivery of the first 10,000 Jews. Dannecker on 29 June 1942 made clear that he needed at least 2500 French police for the forthcoming operation.

French and German officials met in different combinations. At a meeting on 25 June 1942 between Dannecker, who had been officially replaced as head of the Gestapo's Jewish office in Paris by SS Lieutenant Heinz Roethke, and Jean Leguay, Bousquet's deputy police chief, the arrest of 22,000 Jews in Paris and the suburbs was discussed; Leguay also agreed to removing Jews in the unoccupied zone, starting with 10,000. Dannecker proposed that 40 per cent of the arrests should be of naturalised French Jews. Vichy disagreed and Laval even reneged on the arrest of the 10,000 from the unoccupied zone, though clearly Vichy wanted to remove foreign Jews from their area. The dispute brought Eichmann himself to Paris on 29 June to meet Dannecker. They agreed that all Jews in France, starting with those in the occupied zone, would be deported. The country would be purged of all Jews.

Another meeting on 2 July between Bousquet and the Gestapo and SS leaders in Paris led to a compromise after differences had been expressed. Bousquet reported Laval's view that the French police should not make arrests in the occupied zone, and should arrest and transfer only Jews of foreign nationality. The French had no objection to the arrests themselves, but the Germans should make them in Paris. The Germans, without the necessary manpower to do this, agreed that French Jews would be provisionally excluded from arrest in return for Bousquet's agreement that the French police would arrest foreign Jews in both the occupied and unoccupied zones in the numbers wanted by the Germans. Essentially, this would mean 22,000 foreign Jews in Paris, and then others in the rest of France. The Bousquet–Oberg Accord of 2 July was based on perverse logic: Vichy police collaboration in return for illusory sovereignty and autonomy of the French police.

The Vichy Council of Ministers agreed with the arrangement the next day. Two conclusions could be drawn. Vichy imagined that French independence and sovereignty would be manifested by the use of French police and gendarmes. The regime would also distinguish, as Laval put it, between French Jews and 'the refuse sent to us by the Germans themselves'.[32] In fact, the regime would arrest French Jews in the occupied zone. Laval had agreed that French Jews in the occupied zone would only be deported if the number of deported foreign Jews fell short of the German quota.

A particular example was the arrest of Roger Masse, a POW, Knight of the Légion d'Honneur and decorated with the Croix de Guerre, and member of a distinguished French family. Pétain had taken a special interest in his fate, but Eichmann, to whom the case had been referred, refused to delay Masse's deportation to and his death in Auschwitz. Pétain had not replied to and had failed to protect this well-known lawyer who, after the Statut des Juifs of October 1940 had written to the Marshal asking whether he could retain or must return his military medals and those of his forebears.

At a meeting in Paris on 4 July 1942, Laval astonished his German counterparts by proposing that, in addition to German demands for the arrest of Jews aged between sixteen and forty-eight, children under sixteen in the unoccupied zone who were arrested should also be deported, either with their parents or alone if their parents had already been deported. The children in the occupied zone did not interest him. The proposal was referred back to Eichmann in Berlin, who assented two weeks later. Laval's feeble excuse was that the decision to arrest and deport the children was taken for humanitarian reasons.

Vél d'Hiv

Meanwhile, a committee had been set up of officials of both countries to make arrangements and work out the logistics of the great round-up, the *rafle* of 16 and 17 July, the best-known single event in persecution of Jews in France and the symbolic representative incident of the persecution to follow. Postponed from 14 July because of Bastille Day, this two-day *rafle*, code-named *Vent Printanier*, is usually referred to as the round-up of the Vélodrome d'Hiver, Vél d'Hiv, the bicycling arena in western Paris where about two-thirds of those arrested were temporarily interned.

At 4 a.m. on 16 July 1942, 9000 French police and gendarmes, assisted by bands of PPF youths, in Paris and its suburbs, provided with lists by the prefecture of police and index cards containing names, addresses, occupations and nationality of 28,000 Jews, were ordered to arrest Jews of both sexes, the males aged from two to sixty and the females aged from two to fifty-five. No one was exempted; the list included UGIF card holders, furriers who worked for the Germans (*Ausweis*), companions or widows of non-Jews, pregnant women and those with infants, wives of POWs, and Jews of nationalities other than those to be arrested. A fleet of fifty Metropolitan Company buses was used to transport the arrested to the Vél d'Hiv. No German took part in the operation.

The toll was smaller than expected: 13,152 in all, of whom 4100 were children and about 6000 were women, were arrested; 15,000 escaped the *rafle* for a number of reasons. The lists themselves were partly inaccurate. More important was the fact that rumours in the days preceding the *rafle*, stemming from leaks by officials in the prefecture of police and from police superintendents, allowed people to escape the trap.[33] Some underground communists, the Jewish Amelot group as well as the UGIF, apparently had some advance knowledge. UGIF prepared clothes and bedclothes for 7000 people but did not spread the rumour of arrests for fear of panic.[34] Yet, the fact that so many were arrested indicates the dilemma for Jews. Some did not take the rumour of mass arrests seriously. Jewish veterans thought they were safe. Poorer individuals with few non-Jewish contacts had no prior information and, in any case, found it difficult to hide. Vichy officials implemented the operation and its aftermath with cold indifference and impersonal language. One revealing illustration of this coldness was that of the regional prefect writing to the prefect of the region of Chalons-sur-Marne on 18 July, describing Jews in an impersonal fashion as 'des personnes intéressées de ma région'.

This was the first time that women and their children had been arrested together. Single individuals and families without children or with grown children were taken to Drancy the same day. Those with children aged between two and sixteen were sent to the Vél d'Hiv, where conditions were atrocious with few latrines, little water and almost no medical attention. Some children were taken from their mothers and put in a hospital. Several people committed suicide. Darquier proposed that the children be placed in homes in Paris and the suburbs run by the UGIF and other groups. The French police wanted immediate deportation. Roethke, awaiting a reply from Eichmann, kept the children together, sending them to the Pithiviers and Beaune-la-Rolande camps in the Orléans region together with their parents. The remarkable part of this story is that the French police, led by Leguay, Bousquet's deputy, and the leading Paris police prefecture officials, were more insistent on the children being deported than either Darquier, the ideological anti-Semite, or the Germans.

The two camps of Pithiviers and Beaune-la-Rolande were emptied of their 928 interned people, who were deported on 17 July to make room for those coming from the Vél d'Hiv. Gradually the internees of the two camps were sent to Drancy from where, starting on 19 July 1942, deportations took place over the next two weeks. People went to Drancy in buses guarded by French police and French inspectors of police. By the end of July, 4996 had been deported from Drancy.

Children aged between two and twelve were separated from their parents, who were deported directly from the two camps in the Loiret in trainloads of about 1000 to their extermination. On 29 July, Eichmann telephoned his approval of deportation of the children. They were sent in August to Drancy together with adults who were not their parents. The children, who were brutally treated, arrived in a pitiable condition, with torn clothing, lacking shoes, and suffering from diarrhoea. They were housed over 100 to a room, lying on filthy straw mattresses or on the cement floor. By the beginning of September, all had been deported to their death in convoys of 500 children and 500 adults. Jews arriving in Drancy had been mixed with children from the two camps in the Loiret so that in every convoy half would be children, on the pretence that families were travelling together.

Over 13,000 Jews had been arrested in the two days of Vél d'Hiv, but 20,000 and even 28,000 at one point had been anticipated. The disappointed Germans made clear to Vichy that more should be found and that French Jews must be included at the final stage of operations.[35] Vichy kept up the pretence, or might for a time have been genuinely deceived, about deportees being sent to work camps in the east. The Germans were clear. Three days after Vél d'Hiv, Dannecker wrote to Knochen, 'The Jewish community must have understood that all Jews in the camps are doomed to total extermination.'[36]

The Jewish community might have understood, but did Laval? The obsessive dissembler, speaking to American Quakers from the Nîmes Commission on 6 August 1942, stated that foreign Jews had always been a problem in France and that he was glad to get rid of them, but he gave no indication of their fate. Instead he asked the Quakers why the United States did not take these Jews. He agreed to deportation because 'the population of Hebrew stock has reached an excessive proportion ... [the Jews] form a manifestly dangerous element ... they engage in the black market and in Gaullist and communist propaganda'.[37] Criticism of France by the United States and other countries was hypocritical: why didn't they take Jewish refugees or grant transit visas? Laval had neither interest in nor sympathy for the fate of Jews who he callously remarked were already far too numerous in France. He pointedly referred to the 'high moral tone' of certain governments regarding their fate, remarking that these governments had consistently refused to admit Jewish refugees over their own border. The ever-cynical Laval told the American Chargé in France, S. Pinkney Tuck, on 11 September 1942 that the only concrete offer he had received so far was from the Dominican Republic, which was willing to take 3000 Jewish children.

Continuing Round-ups

French officials were responsive to German demands for more Jews. Darquier, in a letter of 23 July 1942 to Laval, suggested the arrest of all 'cosmopolitan Jews', which would include those naturalised since 1 January 1927, a subject that became an obsession with him.[38] Laval proposed denaturalisation of those who had become citizens since 1933. The French were still not happy about the pressure to arrest Jews of French nationality.[39] This discomfort had led to some leaks about future arrests. To remedy this situation Roethke suggested, 'it seems essential that the French police, at any rate the officials involved, should be informed about them at the last moment'.

New round-ups of Jews, based on the census ordered in December 1941, and including people in the camps, labour battalions and surveilled residences, began in August 1942. The camps in the un-occupied zone were closed to any release; even those with exit visas could not leave.[40] Bousquet had instructed prefects in the zone that emigration visas should henceforth be annulled. Laval too, in September, refused to allow certain Jews to leave France, saying, incorrectly and deliberately misleadingly, that Jews of military age should not be given exit visas.[41]

In any case, exit was difficult. A potential emigrant had to have a valid entry visa for the destination country, reserved passage on a ship out of France, or a transit visa for a country bordering France. This led to a bureaucratic nightmare. To get a transit visa, a refugee had first to book a passage on a ship, but reservations were valid only for three weeks. A number of steps had to be completed; by that time validation of the visa might have expired.

Instructions and telegrams flowed from René Bousquet and his associate director of the national police, Henry Cado, to regional prefects. On 22 August 1942 Bousquet ordered regional prefects to be responsible for arrests and transfers for deportations: they should 'break all resistance' and indicate the officials who were causing difficulties; they should take severe action and impose controls in verifying the identity of people; they should 'liberate' their regions of all foreign Jews.[42]

Cado's secret telegram of 5 August 1942 instructed prefects that foreign Jews who had entered France after 1 January 1936, wherever they were located – in camps, GTEs or residences – would be arrested and transported to the occupied zone before 15 September 1942, with some exceptions at first. The latter included persons over sixty, children under two, pregnant women, veterans, those wounded in the Second World War, half-Aryans, and Jews with an Aryan husband or wife. Cado and the Vichy authorities asked the prefects to provide two copies of a list of Jews with their vital statistics. Moreover, no emigration would be permitted even for those with a proper visa. A few days later, the exemptions of 5 August were cancelled, and Cado expanded the eligible categories of future victims to include single Jewish men who had entered France between 1933 and 1935.[43]

The camps were raided and some were emptied; the 3904 Jews in Gurs were transferred in two weeks of August 1942 to Drancy. Another 1200 were taken from the GTEs, the labour battalions. People were transported by freight cars, thirty to a boxcar: this was more economical because freight cars took fewer guards than did passenger trains. From Drancy the convoys left in rapid succession for Auschwitz. Eichmann on 13 August 1942 had ordered that no convoys must be made up only of children.[44] They must be accompanied by adults: the solution was to mix the two groups at Drancy.

Bousquet, insisting on 30 August that only the national police could give orders, took the initiative in the continuing repression and in the calls for intensified action. Indicating the disparity between the number of foreign Jews in a given area and the number arrested, he instructed the prefects to use all police and gendarmerie to check and search people and residences. At no time did he seek to protect foreign Jews. He even tried at that time to get the army to accompany the convoys from France, but the army hierarchy refused all participation in the process of arrest and deportation. Another telegram from Bousquet on 11 September 1942 informed prefects that some police commissioners were giving certificates to people stating that they did not belong to the Jewish race so they would not be arrested. Those certificates could only be given by the CGQJ.

Bousquet delivered the interned foreign Jews in the unoccupied zone, starting with the German refugees. Vichy personnel interacted on this delivery. The prefects in their *départements* gave the police the names of foreign Jews, aged eighteen to forty, who had entered France between 1933 and 1935 and who were currently living in those *départements*. In each prefecture a representative of the CGQJ was present to witness the procedure. Laval had promised the Germans 10,000 foreign Jews living in the unoccupied zone. Each *département* would furnish its quota of the expected number.

One case study reveals the eagerness of some officials to implement instructions.[45] The prefect of Vaucluse, Henri Piton, wrote on 24 August 1942 a 'secret and urgent' memo to the gendarme unit commander in Avignon telling him to arrest all the foreign Jews on an enclosed list. The arrested would be assembled and driven to Les Milles, the nearby camp, in two buses he was providing. The memo also refers to the 'competent division chief' who prepared arrangements for the arrests; this reference confirms the fact that in every prefecture a first division, second bureau (D1B2) unit was set up to organise anti-Semitic action.

On the days of 26 to 28 August 1942, foreign Jews were arrested throughout the unoccupied zone and sent to Drancy. They were taken from those interned in camps, especially Les Milles, Gurs, Rivesaltes and Le Vernet, and from personal residences and homes. In a night raid on an OSE home near Limoges, the gendarmerie took seventy children whose parents had arrived in France after 1936; all but one died in Auschwitz.[46]

For objective observers the conduct of Vichy was clear. The evidence, wrote Donald A. Lowrie on 7 October 1942 to Tracy Strong, General Secretary of the YMCA in New York, 'suggests rather strongly that the Vichy authorities have not been reluctant to turn over people specially sought by the Germans'. Some who might have been considered safe were threatened with arrest and deportation. They included Turkish Jews in France because of 1935 Turkish legislation that limited the citizenship of persons resident abroad, and 2000 Polish Jewish families who held Paraguayan passports. Over 1000 Jews of Greek nationality were arrested in Paris; an additional deportation transport was needed for them.

Again, the Germans were not satisfied. Laval had suggested 10,000, Bousquet at one point promised 12,000, but only 7000 had been caught. For Vichy the hunt for Jews became a routine operation as much as an obsession. All foreign Jews, whatever their date of entry into France, were by Bousquet's telegram of 5 September 1942 to be arrested if they did not have proper papers.[47] The net widened to include Jews not only from Germany, Austria, Poland, Hungary and Czechoslovakia, but also from the Baltic countries and from the Balkans. Bousquet reminded the prefects that Jewish children aged two to sixteen, whose parents were subject to arrest, should be arrested at the same time. Youngsters aged sixteen to eighteen should be sent to the occupied zone if they were not accompanied. Children taken from homes or centres would be sent to Rivesaltes and then to Drancy for deportation, as adults were.

The hunt, the arrests, the reporting of the numbers of victims, the transfers and the deportations, all were performed with pitiless efficiency. The police made the arrests; the gendarmes escorted the trains of the deportees to the German frontier. On one recorded occasion, 9 February 1943, the thirty-three gendarmes on the train that day prevented the escape of eleven individuals from the train, and were warmly thanked by the German officer in charge.[48] By the end of 1942, 42,000 had been deported in forty-three convoys to Auschwitz.

Bousquet made arrests easier by ordering the prefects in the unoccupied zone to apply rigorously the law of 9 November 1942, which forbade Jews to move freely or to leave their residence without police authorisation. Two other factors helped the arrests. One was the employment of the special police force, created by Leguay, to make arrests. The other was the enforcement by prefects of the 11 December 1942 law, which obliged Jews to acknowledge themselves on identity papers and ration cards.

Arrests of Jews continued. In January 1943, French police in Rouen, acting on German orders, conducted round-ups for several days between the 13th and 16th, as reprisals for an attack on a German officer. These led to arrests of 222 Jews, of whom 170 were French. All were sent to Drancy. French Jews were now being arrested and deported.

A larger, more organised *rafle* took place in Marseille, a town where collaboration by French officials happened daily and where Aryanisation proceeded with dispatch.[49] Himmler was responsible for the overall operation to 'cleanse' Marseille of 'undesirable elements', primarily

Jews and 'anti-social people', particularly criminals, by arrests and by dynamiting the Vieux Port (old port). In telexes of 4 and 18 January 1943, Himmler instructed Oberg, whom he had sent to oversee the operation, that French independent action must be respected and that the French police and Garde Mobile must participate to the largest extent in the operation.[50] The national police chief, Bousquet, met with Oberg on a number of occasions, on 13, 14 and 23 January 1943, to discuss the round-up and deportation of Jews from the city, the role of the French police in the arrest of 'undesirables', and the part of the Vieux Port to be dynamited. The destruction of the Vieux Port thus became linked with the anti-Semitic persecution and the French contribution to the Final Solution.[51] The photograph taken at the Marseille town hall on 23 January 1943 of a smiling, nonchalant René Bousquet, together with fellow Vichy officials, the regional prefect of Marseille and the deputy attached to the city administration, along with German officers including Colonel Griese, SS commander of the German police in Marseille, is one of the most potent symbolic representations of collaboration and anti-Semitic persecution. At their trial in September 1954, the two Nazis Knochen and Oberg stated that, in the Marseille operation as in other activities, Bousquet had 'eased' things for them.[52] The two Nazis were sentenced to death by a tribunal in Paris on 1 November 1954, but the sentences were not carried out. Knochen was pardoned in 1962 and Oberg in 1965 by the French President.

Among the Vichy officials involved in the Marseille operation, some of whom willingly took part in the identification, persecution and arrest of Jews, were Lemoine, the regional prefect, who instructed French police to arrest, among others, all Jews they could find; Barraud, the prefect delegate to the city; the local French police chief, Maurice Rodellec du Porzic; and his deputy, Robert-Stephane Auzanneau. Directed for a time by Bousquet himself, about 12,000 French police in uniform and in civilian clothes from all over the country took part in the round-ups between 22 and 27 January 1943, checking identities of 40,000 people, detaining about 6000 people and arresting over 2000 referred to as 'disturbing elements' in the old port quarter that the Germans had marked for destruction. Some 1640 including about 800 Jews were deported, of whom 585 were French.

Whole Jewish families, not warned of the imminent danger by Jewish and other organisations in spite of the obvious concentration of police and gendarmerie in the Marseille area, were arrested. The Germans congratulated Bousquet on his co-operation. Later, on 3 August 1943 Bousquet met Heinrich Himmler in Paris. The SS leader was sufficiently impressed to call the French police chief 'a precious collaborator' and thought he would play an important role in French policy.[53]

However, the changing military situation, with Germany suffering defeats and increasing casualties, inspired second thoughts and began to instil some defiance in Vichy. In March 1943, Pétain was expressing his incomprehension at the deportation of French Jews, and Bousquet had ordered the police not to participate in their evacuation.[54] In that month for the first time, the French police refused to escort a train deporting French Jews.[55] Laval opposed, and Pétain refused to sign, a law in August 1943 removing French nationality from Jews naturalised after 10 August 1927. The Marshal's refusal was based on the law's collective character. It blocked the German plan for the wholesale deportation of French Jews.

Another agreement between Bousquet and Oberg was signed on 16 April 1943. By it German police would be limited to protecting German soldiers while the French police would generally undertake all other functions. Also, French citizens arrested by Vichy would be judged only in French courts unless German property was involved.[56] Both sides recognised that German intervention in security and legal procedures would be counter-productive if the Vichy authorities were seen less as working in the interests of France than as being auxiliaries in the German insistence on the Final Solution.

Vichy was not totally submissive to German demands. It did remain 'neutral', with the agreement of Hitler, in the continuing war, not so much playing a double game as acting in what it conceived as French national interest. Vichy did not impose the yellow star, as the Germans wanted, in the unoccupied zone; it did not forbid mixed marriages; it did not ban Jews from public places; it did not establish ghettos. It did not abrogate citizenship of Jews naturalised after 1927.

Vichy did not provide the Germans with the lists of French Jews until 25 January 1944, a period in which extremists were powerful in the government. The Faustian bargain continued. In March 1943 Vichy refused to convey French Jews from Drancy to the border, but was willing to deliver foreign Jews to Germany in order to prevent or reduce the number of deportations of interned French Jews. To that end the French police in February 1943 arrested 1600 foreign Jews, who were all deported, including children. Pétain, like the police chief in the film *Casablanca*, expressed surprise at events. In his case the surprise was that Jews of French nationality were being deported while so many non-French Jews were available. A small victory: the French police had not automatically fulfilled the German demand. Roethke had to ask Berlin for reinforcements to do the deporting, and also sought permission to use firearms if the prisoners tried to escape.

Were these incidents evidence of cynical Machiavellian machinations by Vichy authorities, examples of belated righteous behaviour or prudence now that the Allies were winning? Laval allowed the police in the occupied zone to act in accordance with German demands, yet he asserted that he did not want French Jews arrested. He ignored the fact that in March and June 1942 they were already interned in Drancy and Compiègne. Among the internees who were sent to Auschwitz were 150 veterans, fourteen from the First World War; sixty-five of them were French and forty-seven naturalised after 1936.

In February 1943, Bousquet, according to Roethke, acquiesced in the deportation of French Jews by Germans from Drancy, but said the French police would not help in the escorting or transfer. In fact, he did give way, and French police did co-operate in the deportations. Over 1400 police and gendarmes arrested 1600 Jews; a shameful display of authority since 1200 of them were over sixty years old and twenty-two children were under ten. Older people who had been previously spared were taken because they had nowhere to hide. The children were taken from children's homes in the Paris area where they had been placed by the UGIF.

The arrests of French Jews in Marseille in January 1943 occasioned some concern, cautious though it was, on the part of the Catholic hierarchy. On 1 February 1943, Cardinal Gerlier wrote to the Chief Rabbi of France that 'the painful measures taken against such a large number of French Jews can only be the result of confusion provoked by such a large operation'.[57] There could be no confusion about the arrests a week later. On 9 February 1943 the Gestapo arrested in Lyon eighty-four members of the staff of the UGIF, the Federation of Jewish Societies in France, and the Sixième. A day later, on the night of 10–11 February French police arrested forty-eight children in UGIF centres in Paris, as well as patients in hospitals, elderly people in residences and people at home. A large proportion of the 1569 foreign Jews arrested were elderly or under twenty.[58]

In November 1943 both Laval and Bousquet hardened their position. Laval allowed the police to execute measures against foreign Jews but insisted that, from that moment, French Jews would not be arrested. Similarly, Bousquet, in the same month, used an astonishing argument: 'For the police services the fact of being an Israelite does not constitute a presumption of responsibility, either politically or in common law.'

Bousquet's change of attitude reflected growing criticism by French people and the Church of the arrests and deportations. In some ways Vél d'Hiv in July 1942 can be seen as a turning point as people became aware of the extent of the arrests and consequent deportations of Jews, regardless of age, sex or state of health of the individual. Some who found Vichy behaviour distasteful secretly gave warnings of impending round-ups to Jews or Jewish organisations that might be affected. The Germans were aware that informers might help Jews escape. Roethke reported that rich and influential Jews might receive advance information about round-ups.

Yet after the occupation by German military forces of all of France in November 1942, in response to the Allied landings in North Africa, ending the division of the country into occupied and unoccupied zones, the round-ups continued with varying success. Nearly half of the Jews who were marked for arrest escaped capture, and some of those arrested avoided deportation because of legal exemptions or the work of humanitarian organisations.[59]

Round-ups were most successful when the prefecture complied with or was eager to implement orders. One such prefecture was that in Bordeaux. German raids in Nice in September 1943 and in Bordeaux in December were not as successful as hoped; the latter raid produced 108 arrests, a fifth of the desired number, though seventy-nine of them were French Jews. In that month Joseph Darnand replaced René Bousquet as head of the national police, which now joined the Germans in arresting French as well as foreign Jews.

The Germans got agreement from the prefecture of the Gironde in Bordeaux, after both Laval and Darnand had assented, that French police would undertake a major *rafle* in the city on 10 January 1944. Maurice Papon, responsible for Jewish affairs as well as other matters in the prefecture, ordered the French police to arrest 473 Jews; 228 were found. Together with another 364, including fifty children, they were sent to Drancy. Papon had played a key role in the arrest and deportation of French Jews.

Any possible moderation by Vichy ended with the dismissal of Bousquet in December 1943 and the ascent to power of Darnand, head of the infamous Milice. Pretence of the independence of the French police was implausible. The police actively hunted Jews; on 27 January 1944 several hundred searched the Poitiers area, deceptively referring to Jews as 'potential terrorists'. They collaborated in Gestapo raids and in the arrest of French Jews in a number of towns, including Nancy, Bordeaux, Toulouse and Orléans, and in the Ardennes and Languedoc. In early 1944, 4500 Jews from the provinces were sent to Drancy.

Atrocities continued to the very end of the Vichy regime and the German occupation. On 21–22 July 1944, seventy Jews were arrested by order of Joseph Lécussan, regional delegate of the CGQJ at Toulouse and head of the local Milice. They were executed on the spot. The same day raids took place on the children's homes of the UGIF in the

Paris area. Of the 350 children in the homes, 250 were arrested and sent to Drancy, and almost all went on to Auschwitz on 31 July in a convoy that also included fifty staff members of the UGIF itself. Other staff members had already been arrested on 22 December 1943 in Marseille, and the office there was closed. Wives of prisoners of war, and of political prisoners in French camps and prisons, were all given to the Germans.

As late as 2 August 1944, Darnand's office ordered the prefect of police in Paris to provide the Gestapo with a list of all Jews in the Seine *département*. The prefect delayed, thus preventing another mass arrest before the liberation of Paris. The final deportation convoy from Drancy, the sixty-seventh, organised by Brunner on 17 August 1944, took fifty-one Jews to Buchenwald. The last one from France left from Clermont-Ferrand on 22 August 1944 for Auschwitz with a small number of people.

The figures convey part of the horrors of the Vichy years. Of the estimated 330,000 Jews living in France in June 1940, 75,721 were deported. Only 2654 returned from the extermination camps. The approximate figure of 75,000 was 22.9 per cent of the total Jewish population. Of that total, 24,669 were French native or naturalised citizens. They represented 32 per cent of the total victims, 7 per cent of all Jews and 14 per cent of French nationals. The other 51,052 deported were foreign or stateless. They constituted 68 per cent of the victims, 15 per cent of all Jews and 31 per cent of the estimated 165,000 foreign Jews.

Since lives depended on the distinction among the French Jews because of the abrogation of naturalisations, another set of figures is revealing. Of the estimated 170,000 or so French Jews, about 110,000 were native, 90,000 had arrived in France before 1933, and about 65,000 were naturalised, 55,000 of whom had arrived after 1933.

Between 6 June 1942 and 17 August 1944, 67,000 were deported from Drancy. The 11,400 children deported all died. About 1000 Jews were executed or murdered by the Milice or the Gestapo. Another 3000 died of illness or hunger in French internment camps. Nearly 10,000 were sent to death from other French camps.

The total of Jews who died is about 77,000. Of the victims, 8700 were over sixty, 6000 under thirteen and 2000 under six. Looking at the figures chronologically, 42,500 were deported in the summer and autumn of 1942, over a quarter of whom came from the unoccupied zone. About 22,000 were sent in 1943 and 12,500 in 1944. Of the total of 11,400 children under sixteen, about half came from each sex. Of the overall total, some 54 per cent were men, and 46 per cent women. The main death camp was Auschwitz, to which 70,000 were sent; the others were Majdanek, Sobibor and Buchenwald. Jewish leaders were not spared.[60] Of the sixty rabbis in the Central Consistory in 1939, seventeen were deported and two others were shot. Some of the major lay leaders, including Jacques Helbronner, who claimed to have seen Pétain often, and Raoul-Raymond Lambert, were sent to death.

The death of Jews is, of course, only part of the Vichy story. The regime witnessed or was responsible for 150,000 hostages shot, internment of 70,000, sending almost 700,000 workers, both men and women, to Germany as conscript labourers, as well as the 77,000 Jews murdered or dead.

Only 77,000? Only 22.9 per cent of the Jewish population? It is no defence of Vichy to compare these figures with comparable ones in neighbouring countries. The Netherlands lost 75 per cent, and Belgium 42 per cent of its Jews.[61] A number of factors explain the disparity: the changing military situation after 1942, which led to more caution on the part of the French; the geographical extent of France and its sizeable mountainous areas, which made it harder to round up Jews; the unavailability of German police; the scarcity of rolling stock causing transport shortages; the greater assimilation of native Jews in the general population; the fact that Jews now lived a more clandestine life and changed identities; the lower percentage of foreign Jews than in the Low Countries; the growing sense of shame among non-Jews as knowledge of the atrocities and the wearing of the yellow star by Jews made them conscious of the problem; the help by righteous individuals, both secular and religious; the resistance groups and Jewish organisations that hid people; and the delay of the Italians in implementing discriminatory measures.

CHAPTER 9

RESPONSE TO PERSECUTION

The figures tell the story of Vichy's mistreatment of children living in France and its role in their deportation to death. Of the 11,402 children deported from France, barely 300 survived. Of those who died, 8000 were born in France and 2000 were under six. Jewish children in 1939 numbered 70,000, about 21 per cent of the total Jewish population. Some 13 per cent of the children lost their lives. About 12 per cent of all Jews deported and murdered were under 16. A recent work, *French Children of the Holocaust: A Memorial* by Serge Klarsfeld, with its collection of photos and commentaries on 2500 of the children is a fitting commemoration of these victims of the Nazi genocide. Several hundred more children died in the French internment camps or were killed in France; in all, 11,600 children were lost. Of the eighty-four convoys that went to the extermination camps from France, that of 21 August 1942 from Drancy to Auschwitz is particularly memorable because it contained the largest number of children carried in any convoy, 614 out of a total of 1000 people.

Originally, the Germans had wanted those children under sixteen of Jews arrested to be put in the charge of the UGIF. Only people aged sixteen to fifty were to be deported, and thus the hostility aroused by taking children would be avoided. Later perhaps, according to Dannecker, they might be sent. It was Laval who on 4 July 1942 proposed that children should be arrested and taken with their families from the unoccupied zone. His rationale, as Laval explained to the cabinet in Vichy on 10 July, was that for 'humane' reasons children should accompany their parents. Dannecker asked approval from Eichmann in Berlin to agree to the transport of children; it took two weeks before Eichmann sent a positive reply. A later statement by Bousquet was equally hypocritical and as callous as Laval's proposal remarks. Opposing the sending of 5000 Jewish children to the United States, the police chief said, 'We will not let the children cross the Atlantic while their parents are left in Poland.'[1] In fact, only 311 children were able to emigrate legally between May 1941 and July 1942.

Until Vél d'Hiv the French police had not arrested children. In the
rafle of 20 August 1941 a few youngsters had been picked up, but this
was mainly in error. The order for Vél d'Hiv was to arrest only foreign
Jews, but the over 4000 children gathered were almost all born French.
Before the Vél d'Hiv *rafle* only a handful of youngsters had been
deported in the first five convoys from 27 March to 28 June 1942.
Starting with convoy five on 17 July 1942, the number of deported
children increased. Between 14 August and 9 September, twelve
convoys left Drancy with some 5000 children taken from both zones.
Leguay had decided at the beginning of August 1942 that parents must
not leave in the same convoys as their children; the latter stayed for a
week or more in the camps of Pithiviers and Beaune-la-Rolande before
being transferred to Drancy. No one spoke any longer about reunion of
families in the east.

In the latter part of 1942, 1032 Jewish children under six, 2557
between six and twelve, and 2464 from thirteen to seventeen were
deported.[2] None survived, nor did any child arrested in Vél d'Hiv. This
was the worst time. In a few weeks over 6000 of the eventual 11,400
children deported were sent to their death. The news reached London:
the Secretary of the British Cabinet, the well-informed Sir Maurice
Hankey, called it 'really filthy work'.[3]

Organisations of Rescue

To counter the behaviour of Vichy, organisations both Jewish and
non-Jewish tried to ameliorate the life of the children in the camps, and
to rescue them from internment and deportation.[4] Some children were
able to escape, through their own initiatives, through planning by their
parents, or through the efforts of helpful policemen or neighbours.
Serge Klarsfeld has told his own moving story of his narrow escape
from arrest and death because of his father's sacrifice.[5] Most children
who survived were rescued by a variety of humanitarian organisations
and by courageous French people of generosity and goodwill.

These organisations provided assistance and comfort for those
interned in the camps and tried with little success to gain release of
children as well as providing general relief for refugees and others. In
November 1940 representatives of twenty-five organisations, French
and international, religious and secular, Jewish and Christian, formed
an umbrella group for national and international relief agencies, the
Comité de Coordination pour l'Assistance dans les Camps (Committee
of Co-ordination for Aid in the Camps), known as the Nîmes
Committee, after the town where they met. Its function was to collate
information and statistics about the interned, partly obtained by

visiting the camps, and bringing this evidence to the attention of Vichy authorities to obtain amelioration of conditions in the camps and even release of the internees.

Directed by Donald A. Lowrie of the YMCA, the Committee was active from November 1940 to March 1943; it concentrated on saving children. Through its efforts, 204 children were released from the Rivesaltes camp in March 1941 to the Quakers and the OSE. In August 1942, Lowrie, on behalf of the Nîmes Committee, appealed to Pétain to stop the deportations: the Marshal replied that they were regrettable but 'nothing could be done'.[6] At the same time, Quakers appealed to Laval to allow 1000 children who had obtained visas for the United States to be released, but he refused. Attempts to gain emigration of children by visa to the United States, using legal means and negotiations, largely failed. Only 311 in all were able to leave France, though five organisations worked on the issue.

The task of Jewish organisations broadened and more relief work was necessary as Vichy and German discrimination grew. The arrests and deportations, especially of children in 1942 steered the organisations into secret, and then resistance activity as well as the continuation of their relief work. Rescue of children was now paramount, a major part of the effort of the Jewish community.

Organisations, non-Jewish as well as Jewish, began engaging in clandestine activity. The main Jewish groups were the OSE, EIF, MJS and OJC, the militant unit. Through their efforts – hiding children in institutions, private families and special 'homes' set up for them; fabricating false documents; arranging escape out of the country; and armed resistance – many children were saved. How many were saved by Jewish organisations? Perhaps 8000 to 10,000, while other children were saved by their families or by non-Jewish institutions or families.

The Oeuvre de Secours aux Enfants (OSE) was founded in Russia in 1912 at the time of Tsarist anti-Semitic outbreaks and pogroms; it was concerned with the health and welfare of Jewish children and with the distribution of food. It moved to Germany in 1923 and then to France in 1933, where it was headed by Andrée Salomon and Joseph Weill. Its main objective in the inter-war years was to help children of German and Austrian refugees fleeing the Nazis, particularly those separated from their families. It provided educational, medical and social help, and distributed food.

Officially, it continued in the Vichy years to provide health care and food for children, and social services for those in internment camps. By 1940, with new headquarters in Montpellier, the OSE had opened seven houses for children in the unoccupied zone, in the Haute Vienne and La Creuse, as well as two in the occupied zone. By 1942 it had fourteen houses and was supervising over 1400 children.[7] In them children were taught trades: sewing, shoe repair and carpentry. They were kept in one place for short periods of time.

One residence that has become well known, as the result of a film on the subject directed by the daughter of a survivor, is the Château de Chabannes, a school in the Creuse region in rural France.[8] Over 400 children were taken in by the director, Félix Chevrier, and two local schoolteachers and were taught a number of subjects, including French. This safe haven lasted until the end of 1942 when, with the Nazis approaching, the children were dispersed, some to private homes, some to the Resistance, some to the OSE, and some to Switzerland where the OSE had an office. Chevrier was justifiably proud that only six of the children were sent to concentration camps, four of whom died there. He was a heroic figure, protecting the children by putting them in the hospital or sending them on long walks when the police came to the Château or deliberately misidentifying them to mislead the authorities.

Unofficially, the OSE joined the secret child rescue networks, which included organisations of non-Jewish women, some belonging to the Red Cross; they engaged in making false identity papers and ration cards to help children. By 1944 the OSE had closed its children's centres in the southern zone, occupied by the Germans since November 1942, because the organisation anticipated German raids on them; it placed the children in religious residences or with non-Jewish families. The OSE disguised the real identity of children by removing any revealing family photos or mementoes. Jewish children had ostensibly been transformed into Christians, an issue that was fraught with difficulty and personal anguish after the war. This loss of Jewish identity has become a meaningful subject of post-war fiction and films as well as scholarly analysis.

In April 1943 the OSE began smuggling children out of France. It had suffered great disappointment when the exit visas for 500 children whom it had brought together in Marseille, and who were to enter the United States, were revoked by Bousquet in November 1942. No similar legal arrangements were possible after the Allied landing in Algeria in that month. Together with other groups, the OSE tried to smuggle youngsters into Switzerland. People with different experiences and from varied occupations joined in this illegal activity: schoolteachers, local officials, pastors, priests and escorts, who were paid to take the children to the Swiss border. Stratagems helped in rescuing the children. One heroic figure in the story is Jean Deffaugt, mayor of Annemasse. He helped design a sign at the railroad station of his town marked 'Exit for Vacation Camps', when it was in fact the indicator for passage to Switzerland. Games, especially soccer, for youngsters, some in scout uniform, were organised near the border, thus allowing children to slip across when it got dark. Some French customs officials and police were helpful in not noticing what was happening.

In this rescue operation, the Quakers played a significant role, smuggling refugee children out of the Gurs camp and leading them to safety in Switzerland, in co-operation with the OSE. The clandestine network was essentially organised as a unit within the OSE by Georges Garel, a Jewish engineer from Lyon, a resister and man of exceptional courage. Working together with Joseph Weill, an Alsatian physician, and Andrée Salomon, he planned the underground forging of false identities, finding safe places, houses, religious and secular institutions, charitable organisations, friendly doctors and officials that might help in placing children among families and social organisations. He recruited young non-Jewish assistants to help with the social activity, procured ration cards, raised funds and organised escapes to Spain and to Switzerland. Each assistant was responsible for a certain area, usually a geographical *département*, and some belonged to the Red Cross.

The most dramatic success of the underground network was the saving of 168 people, including 108 children, on the 'night of Vénissieux'. It was the culmination on 29 August 1942 of three days of efforts to save people from being taken from the internment camp of Vénissieux to be sent from Lyon to Drancy for deportation. The OSE and Amitié Chrétienne, led by the Jesuit Father Pierre Chaillet, acting on the suggestion of the Abbé Glasberg, a converted Ukrainian Jew, removed the children from the camp, taking them first to the headquarters of the EIF, the Jewish scout movement, in Lyon and then dispersing them.

Heroic figures emerge in this story of the rescue of children. One honourable figure in the safeguarding of children was Sabine Zlatin, who founded and was the superintendent of the children's home in Izieu. In association with the OSE she had organised the rescue of children interned in the camps of Agde and Rivesaltes. Seeking refuge in the Italian zone in 1943, Zlatin took over the farmhouse, funded by the OSE, in Izieu and supervised forty-four Jewish children. On 6 April 1944 all the children and seven adults in charge (except Zlatin, who was away at the time looking for other accommodation) were arrested by the Gestapo of Lyon under the direction of Klaus Barbie. All were deported: two children and one adult were shot; forty-two children and five adults were gassed in Auschwitz. Barbie, the 'butcher of

Lyon', escaped justice until France obtained his extradition from
Bolivia; in 1987 he was found guilty of crimes against humanity and
sentenced to life imprisonment. He died in prison in 1991.

Another heroine was Andrée Salomon, thirty-four years old in 1942,
who worked in a number of the camps, and managed to arrange the
escape of a number of adults and children by using fake documents.
Working in the network organised by Georges Garel, Salomon helped
disperse the children to suitable hiding places, set up facilities for
visitors to see them, and supervised the operation.

Through people like Zlatin, Salomon, Garel and many unsung
heroes and heroines, the OSE network saved about 5000 children.
Other organisations saved another 5000, and about 45,000 were saved
by non-Jewish families or by parents who hid the children. What made
non-Jews risk their lives or face penalties to rescue Jewish children?
One must assume a mixture of motives: on one side benevolence,
charity and abhorrence of persecution; on the other, mercenary
factors, since families were usually paid for the room and board of the
children. Men who took children across the border to safety in
Switzerland were also paid about 300 francs for each child. Most of the
funding came from the American Joint Distribution Committee.
Saving children in this way was made more perilous after September
1943 when German forces controlled the Savoie départements,
formerly occupied by the Italians.

The Éclaireurs Israélites de France (EIF), the Jewish scouts and
guides movement, was founded in 1923 by Robert Gamzon, and had
about 3000 members. In the Vichy years it set up homes for youngsters whose parents had been interned or deported, or who had placed
their children with the EIF for safety. It started farm schools in the
unoccupied zone, advocating return to the land, promoting loyalty
to France, and teaching trades as well as Jewish history, thus also
promoting commitment to Jewish tradition by youngsters aged
between nine and sixteen. As persecution unfolded in 1942, the
EIF began placing children with non-Jewish organisations and
individuals.

Like other Jewish organisations, it began engaging in clandestine
activity. A special section was established, known as the sixth division,
La Sixième, the Service Social des Jeunes, which concentrated on
saving children from deportation. The members forged identity cards,
ration books, birth certificates and military papers. Of the sixty-eight
young Jewish men and women involved in the work, twenty-six were
arrested and four shot.

Overlapping the EIF was the Mouvement de Jeunesse Sioniste (MJS),
which in May 1942 unified two youth movements and set up a

clandestine group, the Éducation Physique, which, like the Sixième, was active in producing false documents for those being pursued. The different militant bodies in the EIF and the MJS also formed the Organisation Juive de Combat (OJC), a body of about 400 fighters in June 1944; this group had links with both communist and non-communist resistance units.[9]

Non-Jewish rescue organisations, both secular and religious, were also active in the struggle against persecution. The most prominent were the Quakers, who housed refugees, as did the Secours Suisse, with its eight houses for children in the unoccupied zone, the YMCA, Amitiés Chrétiennes and the Comité d'Inter-mouvements auprès des Evacués (CIMADE). CIMADE was created in September 1939 by a coalition of different Protestant groups to help those transferred from Alsace and Lorraine to the Dordogne and Haute-Vienne. In the Vichy years it aided hunted Jews. Under the direction of Madeleine Barrault, CIMADE helped set up schools in the camps, especially Gurs, found places for people to live outside the camps, and organised escape routes to Switzerland.

Amitié Chretiénne, in some ways the Catholic counterpart to the Protestant CIMADE, founded in 1941 in Lyon to help Jewish victims, worked in the camps and in clandestine activity. It officially ended in late 1943, but its adherents and other Catholic groups continued their resistance activities individually or through other groups, organising channels of escape. Convents such as the Grande-Chartreuse, and presbyteries such as Villeurbanne, were notable in this activity.

A particularly courageous and energetic individual, an unsung heroine for many years, was Germaine Ribière, a Catholic from Limoges who left her studies to give her full time and energy to save Jewish children.[10] In touch with sympathetic clergy, she worked in the camp of Récébédou in May 1942. In one unusual incident in January 1943 she forestalled a Gestapo trap to arrest Jews who were trying to get forged papers at the CIMADE office in Lyon to help them escape, by pretending to be a cleaning woman on the premises, and thus having the opportunity to warn Jews who had arrived.

The task of the clandestine organisations and the courageous individuals who worked with them was not easy. Some of the Jewish children were relatively new immigrants, spoke little French, could not easily assume a false identity, and might be religiously observant. Nevertheless, both Catholic and Protestant groups and personnel helped in aiding and trying to rescue the victims, as did women as well as men.

Considerable help in the comforting and aid given to the persecuted was provided by young women, mostly non-Jewish, who were often termed 'social assistants'. They went into the camps to help children, sought out families of welcome, and visited children in their new family settings. Though not as physically militant in guerrilla activity as men, these women operated in propaganda work, producing underground papers, and in organisational networks, finding and running safe homes.[11]

Rescue work was not, of course, confined to the children. Brave and courageous individuals emerged to defy authority and uphold civilised behaviour in the extraordinary circumstances of wartime France. Some tried to help Jews and refugees; others concentrated on saving the political and cultural elite. A fascinating example of the latter group is Varian Fry.

Among the papers of Fry is an epigram by Ralph Waldo Emerson: 'There are men for whom a crisis comes graceful and beloved as a bride.' Fry himself, a Harvard-educated classicist and editor, impeccably dressed in outfits from Brooks Brothers, and a sophisticated political observer, became at thirty-two an improbable heroic person in the face of the crisis; he engaged for a year in Marseille in saving by legal and by clandestine means the lives of over 1500 distinguished artists and intellectuals who were in danger from Germany and Vichy.[12]

Fry had been sent to Marseille in August 1940 by the Emergency Rescue Committee, which was based in New York, with a small amount of money and a list of 200 well-known cultural personalities whose situation in France was thought perilous and who might be helped to escape to the United States. His general assignment was to assess the refugee situation, but he soon went far beyond this as thousands sought his help. With a small, highly dedicated team of helpers, some of whom, like Albert Hirschman, were later to become distinguished figures themselves, Fry began clandestine operations, using false documentation, to get the imperilled celebrities out of the country.

Not only were the Vichy authorities annoyed by his extra-legal activities, but so were the United States Consulate in Marseille and the State Department in Washington. The only sympathetic American official was Hiram Bingham; the State Department was anxious to have Fry expelled from France. The Department's position was that 'the Government does not countenance any activities by American citizens desiring to evade the laws of the governments with which this country maintains friendly relations'. Later, Fry was to refer to this policy as 'treason'. American Ambassador to Vichy Admiral William Leahy refused to renew Fry's passport and informed Vichy that the State Department did not approve of his activities and would not oppose Vichy's actions against him.

The United States Consulate in Marseille was reluctant to provide exit visas for the remarkable cultural individuals seeking them: the refugees were 'liable to become a public charge' on the United States, and many of them were likely, it said, to be communists or even Nazi spies. The fact that many of the refugees were Jews remained unspoken. The Consulate held up the visas, both quota visas and the 'special danger' visas, on some technicality. Among the long list of 'public charges' smuggled out of France, usually through Spain, by Fry's team were Marc Chagall, Max Ernst, André Breton, Marcel Duchamp, Heinrich Mann, Hannah Arendt, Franz Werfel, Jacques Lipchitz, Lion Feuchtwanger, Wanda Landowska, Golo Mann, André Masson and Max Ophuls. To deal with the human miseries he confronted, Fry said a mixture of cynicism, irony, idealism, a little naivety and orneriness was needed. At his funeral, Lipchitz spoke of Fry as 'un cheval de course attelé à un chariot rempli de pierres' (he was like a racehorse hitched to a wagon load of stones).[13]

Fry had played a dangerous double game, charity official by day and clandestine rescuer by night. In August 1941 he was arrested on orders of the Vichy Ministry of the Interior with the approval of the United States Embassy, escorted to the border and sent to Lisbon.

After his expulsion from France, Fry had an unadventurous and modest post-war career as a part-time journalist, worked for a film company and corporations like Coca-Cola, and taught classics in a girls' school. He died in 1964 aged fifty-nine in a house lent to him by the artist Louise Bourgeois. Unacknowledged in his own country, Fry was awarded the French Legion of Honour just before his death, and was posthumously recognised in 1985 as a righteous non-Jewish person; he was the first American to be so recognised at Yad Vashem in Jerusalem in 1996. Only at the end of 2000 was Fry honoured by his own country in a belated homage. A small plaque, written in both French and English, was put outside the United States Consulate in Marseille honouring him, and the square in which it is located was renamed 'Place Varian Fry'.

The Dilemma of Jewish Organisations

A frequent, and misguided, occurrence in making political judgements is to blame the victim. In the heated post-war dispute about the activity of Jewish organisations under Nazi rule in Europe, Gershom Scholem, in his open letter to Hannah Arendt, questioned whether 'our generation is in a position to pass any kind of historical judgement' on Jewish behaviour during the Nazi period.[14] Arendt had made some provocative and troubling comments about the *Judenrate* (the Jewish Councils set up by Nazis in eastern Europe): 'To a Jew this role of the Jewish leaders in the destruction of their own people is undoubtedly the darkest chapter of the whole dark story.'[15]

The tone of her utterance might have been unduly emphatic and the seeming shifting of responsibility from perpetrator to victim unwarranted, yet the controversial issue remains; if the Jewish population had been unorganised and leaderless, would the number of victims have been fewer? In a more moderate form, the dilemma was expressed by Primo Levi in his concept of a 'grey zone' in which the victims were also collaborators. Whether that grey zone was the space occupied by official Jewish organisations and some Jewish leaders in the France of Vichy is still a matter of dispute. One is obliged to ask a difficult question. In the extraordinary circumstances of discrimination, persecution and murder of a people, what kind of response and behaviour on the part of that same people and its leaders was appropriate or possible?

The response was never a unified one, at least not until almost the very end. The divergent perspectives and objectives of French Jews and foreign, immigrant Jews, which was already present in pre-war France, persisted in the Vichy years. Organisations of French Jews had as their first priority the continued existence of French Judaism. Not only were foreign Jews excluded from those organisations; their fate as immigrants was of secondary importance. The traditional bodies of French Jewry, especially the Consistory, tended to believe that an understanding could be reached with Vichy, which would recognise the rights of French Jews, and overcome Vichy's initial mistakes and subjugation to German demands.

This belief, or more properly delusion, of French Jews stemmed from their conviction that their rights would be respected and their loyalty to France would be understood. The great historian Marc Bloch was typical in this regard, holding that all Jews domiciled or resident in France were obligated and affiliated to the country. The prominent social scientist Raymond Aron, who spoke of the 'uncompromising patriotism' of French Jews, mistakenly believed that the Statut des Juifs had been imposed by the Germans.

Attitudes of this kind have to be put in the context of divisions within the Jewish community. Whereas foreign Jews were grouped into two communal bodies – the Union of Jewish Societies in France, small and linked to the Communists, and the Federation of Jewish Societies of France, about seventy to eighty bodies, with Zionist inclinations – French Jews rejected the idea of separate Jewish political organisations. They put their faith in the defence of the rights of man.

They believed that the extreme right wing was not inevitably anti-Semitic: after all, La Rocque attended a service once a year between 1934 and 1936 at a synagogue in Paris to commemorate the Jewish deaths in the First World War. Some Jews supported the Action Française. A few even formed an extreme right-wing organisation, the Union Patriotique des Français Israélites, founded by Edmond Bloch: its 1936 manifesto declared that love of France was more significant than attachment to Judaism.[16]

For many French Jewish leaders the distinction between Jewish Frenchmen (*Israélites Français*) and foreign Jews (*Juifs Étrangers*) remained real until they became aware of the increasing severity in the implementation of laws against all Jews. Protests were then made against the 'measures taken against Jews in France as a whole'. Appeals were made to the historic principles of France. The record of Jewish patriotism and sacrifices on the battlefield was emphasised. Jewish adherence to the law and to obedience was pronounced. The genealogy of old French Jewish families was traced. The contribution of Jews to all aspects of French life was publicised. Obedience to the law continued to be reaffirmed.

French Jewish religious and secular leaders alike were anxious about the new Vichy regime and were, for the most part, careful in their attitude. These French Jews felt bound to the France of their ideal, the France of emancipation and the rights of man. Optimistically, they believed that their past contribution to France would save them from major harm. Raymond-Raoul Lambert, General Secretary of the Committee of Assistance to Refugees, writing of his family roots in France for over a century, said he and his children could not imagine 'life in any other country – this would be an uprooting worse than amputation'.[17]

These French leaders deluded themselves for a year about Vichy and about Pétain personally. Chief Rabbi of France, Isaiah Schwartz, though encountering some obstacles in performing his pastoral function, referred to Pétain, who in fact refused in August 1940 to meet with him, as 'above suspicion'.[18] He thought 'it would be unjust to say that we are dealing with a deliberate policy of hostility' towards Jews. The rabbinate assured Pétain that it was exhorting its flock to serve country and family and to be loyal to the Marshal.[19] In spite of the discriminatory laws and the increasing anti-Semitic attacks in the media as a result of the abolition of the Marchandeau decree on 27 August 1940, Jewish leaders were uncertain if Vichy was pursuing a policy of anti-Semitism or if it was obeying 'the orders of the occupier in order to avoid still graver measures'.[20]

French Jewish leaders were quiescent about the first Statut des Juifs of October 1940. The distinguished Jewish lawyer, senator and former government minister, Pierre Masse, wrote to Pétain on 20 October 1940 that he would 'insist on obeying the laws of my country, even if they are dictated by the invader'. Similarly, Raymond-Raoul Lambert regarded the Statut as a 'demand by the Germans', though he did write in his private diary, after the Statut of 3 October 1940, that 'racism has become the law of the new state ... I still cannot come to terms with this negation of justice and scientific truth.'[21] Jacques Helbronner, prominent lawyer and then Vice-President of the General Consistory, remained silent about the blows that Jews were receiving because otherwise it might damage the 'work of patriotic resurrection' by Pétain.[22]

The leaders were naively self-deceived about responsibility for the anti-Semitic legislation and actions. They tended, for tactical reasons as well as from genuine belief, to argue that the discrimination was due to German pressure, or to the extremists of the Action Française, or to some fanatical anti-Semites in Vichy.[23] Russian Jews during the pogroms around the beginning of the twentieth century used to say, 'If only the Tsar knew.' Similarly, the deluded French leaders wrote to Pétain for protection. The head of state, whom some Jewish leaders had met, would redress the injustices being imposed.

French Jewish bodies never evaluated Vichy's policy towards Jews correctly. They believed that Vichy persecution was an understandable part of its desire to get better terms from the German occupier. They accepted the law and the myth. The Consistory made little protest: it turned down, almost unanimously, a motion in its council for Jews not to present themselves to police stations to have their identity cards stamped with the word 'Jew' in December 1942. It accepted the myth that Jews were being sent to 'settlements' in eastern Europe, though it knew better. The French Jewish organisations largely limited themselves to charity and relief work for immigrant Jews. They hoped to change Vichy policy by personal persuasion. Helbronner, who became President of the Central Consistory, claimed to have spoken to Pétain on twenty-seven occasions. Helbronner had known Pétain since the First World War, when he was an official in the Ministry of War; he was sometimes called *le juif du Maréchal*. Helbronner had also known Cardinal Gerlier as a fellow law student and remained friendly. Whatever impact he may have had, Helbronner himself was arrested in October 1943 and deported with his family on 23 November to death in Auschwitz.

The Central Consistory, the body dating back to Napoleon's regime, was entrusted with supervision of ritual and religious affairs and with the preparation of Jews for French citizenship. It adopted a low profile for almost three years of Vichy. In pre-war France, with a membership of 7000, it had not welcomed German Jewish refugees or supported a boycott of German goods. Its politics then, and under Vichy, was one of cautious timidity, its self-deluding view was that the persecution of the regime was only temporary, even though between October 1940 and November 1941 sixty laws or decrees about Jews had already been issued.

The Consistory insisted on loyalty to the country and obedience to the law. Its declaration on 22 October 1940 affirmed, 'we are neither a racial minority nor a political minority, but a religious community'. Two months later it reiterated that Jews should submit to regulations imposed by the law and regulations of France. It remained in Paris for a time before moving to Lyon, and was reluctant in both locations to become involved in relief activity for Jews. Reflecting the position of native French Jews, some of whom even met with Pétain, the Consistory did not want to be identified with foreign Jews or seen as an ethnic group.[24]

Chief Rabbi Isaiah Schwartz was one of those who appealed to Pétain personally. On 22 October 1940 he wrote to the Marshal, 'French Israelites have accepted as a motto: Religion-Fatherland. Always devoted to this ideal we draw our courage and hope from the love of God and the lessons of the Bible, the sources of the spiritual life of the French people.' Schwartz spoke for many of the French Jews in the Consistory, who might protest privately to Vichy officials, but would not make public protests. President of the Consistory Jacques Helbronner persisted in the belief that intercession with Pétain would ameliorate the plight of Jews. For him and the Consistory generally, the discriminatory law ordering the census of Jews was 'in servile imitation of the occupying authority'; members of the Consistory retained their faith in the destinies of eternal France to righting the violations. Only a few discreet protests came from its members or the rabbinate; among the few who raised their voices in protest was Rabbi Jacob Kaplan, who expressed objections to the census law to Vallat and who spoke in his synagogue against the discriminatory laws. Kaplan's attempt to persuade Vallat that to attack the Jewish religion was to attack the founders of Christianity was answered brutally. Vallat, first head of the CGQJ, replied that the anti-Semitic laws did not signify governmental anti-Semitism, but simply the application of reason of state.[25]

Only in August and September 1941 did the Central Consistory acknowledge that the anti-Semitic measures were 'not totally the imposition of the occupying authorities'. Jewish leaders still maintained their illusion about Pétain's role; they were also comforted by the importance given by Vichy to religious observance. Jewish religion and rituals were not at first affected, nor were synagogues, by any official action. Sympathy was expressed by Christian dignitaries at bomb attacks against synagogues in Paris and Marseille in 1941. Some normal relations continued. The French Jewish Scouts (Éclaireurs Israélites de France, EIF) was not only acknowledged as a significant part of the scouting movement, but also was approved for its emphasis on 'return to the land'.

The French Jewish leaders, whose patriotism was an important part of their identity, were troubled, as were so many in Vichy, by the large number of Jewish refugees, 'foreign elements who had not been assimilated into the French national spirit', elements that caused an understandable anti-Semitism. The fate of foreigners, Lambert said of Helbronner, did not move him in the slightest.[26] The latter had indeed lobbied the government in pre-war France to close the borders to Jewish refugees from Germany.[27] Still some leaders did not take this view of the refugees, or accept that Vichy was benevolent and that its anti-Semitic laws were justified by objective factors of excessive immigration. The Consistory represented and spoke only for French Jews: it kept its distance from the groups concerned with providing social assistance for foreign Jews. Among the more important of these were the Comité d'Assistance aux Refugiés (CAR), HICEM, OSE, ORT, the FSJF and the AIP. Some of these groups were created by immigrant Jews. An important supplier of funds and advice was the American Jewish Joint Distribution Committee (Joint), which moved its office from Paris to Marseille in 1940.

Not until the deportations of July 1942 did the Consistory protest to Vichy about the increasing persecution. In August it protested the cancellation of the right of asylum long traditional in France. It suggested that Vichy must be aware that Jews being deported were not being sent to 'work camps'.[28] It also complained about the exclusion of Jewish youngsters from the Chantiers de la Jeunesse, the youth service corps. Only in January 1943, when 2000 French Jews were arrested in Marseille by French police and the Gestapo, did its legalistic approach begin to change. And only belatedly in 1944 did the Consistory admit the plural nature of the Jewish community.

The UGIF

Before then Vichy had tried to establish a unified overall organisation of Jews. The Union Générale des Israélites de France (UGIF) was created by a law of 29 November 1941 as 'un établissement public autonome doté de la personnalité civile' to 'assure the representation of the Jews with the public authorities, particularly for questions of public aid, medical assistance and social reconversion'.[29] Formulated by Vallat, head of the CGQJ, the law was a response to and was drafted in prolonged and sometimes conflicting discussion with Dannecker, head of the Gestapo's Jewish Office. Dannecker had long pressed for a single committee for Jewish charitable organisations in the occupied zone. One was created in January 1941 called the Co-ordination Committee of Jewish Relief Organisations, but it did not wholly succeed, and a compulsory representative body of Jews was created to replace it. The UGIF absorbed the other Jewish organisations, except the religious bodies and the Consistory. The Consistory was not required to, and did not, join the UGIF but it did try to influence the composition of its leaders, and was kept informed of issues by its President, Albert Lévy, and the Secretary-General, Raymond Raoul Lambert. It did not, however, take part in any of the activities of the UGIF. The Co-ordination Committee, although essentially replaced by the UGIF, did continue relief activity in the occupied zone. Membership in the UGIF was compulsory for all Jews, French and foreign; they were required to pay dues to it.

Yet it was never a fully representative body. The Consistory was allowed to remain independent, but in any case opposed the principle of a central representative body because it incorporated all existing organisations, including those of the immigrants, which the Consistory did not regard as being on an equivalent level. The rabbinate thought the existence of the UGIF would create a division between the spiritual and the social character of French Judaism. Both the Fédération des Societés Juives de France (FSJF) and the Comité de la Rue Amelot (Amelot) refused to join the board, not wanting to collaborate with a body extending governmental controls over Jews, though the relief activities of the FSJF were subsumed within the UGIF. The Jewish communists and the Bund also found it unacceptable to collaborate with Vichy. Even the Central Commission of Jewish Relief Associations, COPJA, set up by French Jews in June 1940, opposed the creation of the UGIF.

However, despite these objections, the UGIF was established with separate boards operating in the two zones, with two government representatives on the boards. The UGIF in the occupied zone, with offices in Paris, was more centralised and open to German demands and official pressure than its counterpart in the unoccupied zone, which had a more federative structure. The UGIF faced criticism from the start, not least on the validity of a Jewish body created by Vichy and the Germans. Its inherent problem was that it was a body precariously poised between the Jewish population and public power, but incapable of stopping or even minimising persecution. Critics saw it as a transmission mechanism between Vichy and the Germans on the one hand and the victims on the other, rather than as a brake on the actions of the CGQJ. In stark terms, was it the only way to wring compromises out of the regime, or a trap by which it lent support and help to the regime?

No one can doubt the indispensable work of the UGIF when it took over the functions of the previous Jewish bodies, essentially those of social welfare. It supplied food and clothing, provided medical care and gave subsidies to indigent Jewish families.[30] It ran hospitals, homes for the elderly and orphanages. Its branch in the unoccupied zone incorporated most of the main Jewish social service agencies. Branches in both of the two zones sheltered children in the residences they ran, especially in and around Paris: they placed 1000 children in homes. The UGIF supported technical education and trade schools. It distributed funds coming from the Joint in New York to Jewish groups and relief agencies in France. It helped agencies pursue their clandestine activity to some extent. The EIF operated within its framework; the UGIF helped the OSE as it became involved in underground activity.

The UGIF was faced with overwhelming problems from the beginning. It had to handle and be responsible for the payment of the billion-franc fine imposed on the Jewish community by Germany on 17 December 1941. It had to manage supplies for Drancy: food, nursing staff, medical supplies. It had to collect shoes and blankets for 7000 persons. It provided equipment and food for those to be deported by the convoys and to pay transportation costs. It soon, on 28 August 1942, was ordered to raise the sum of 6 million francs a month from Jewish families for its own operations.

The creation of the UGIF originated from German pressure on Vichy, but it was not a *Judenrat* appointed by the Nazis.[31] Its leaders were, however, approved by the CGQJ. All were honourable French citizens. The Vice-President, André Baur, was a successful banker who came from a rabbinical background and had been President of the Paris Reform synagogue. Raymond-Raoul Lambert, one of the two leaders, had previously served as Secretary-General of the Comité d'Assistance aux Réfugiés d'Allemagne (CAR). He was descended from an old French Jewish family from Metz, had served bravely in the First World War, and was a captain in the Second World War. Albert Lévy, leader of the CAR, became President of the new body. Marcel Stora, gifted administrator, became general administrator in the unoccupied zone. Georges Edinger, a former company director, was a director of UGIF in Paris. Robert Gamzon, founder of the Jewish scout movement, was a member of the UGIF council.

At a court hearing by Jewish organisations after the war, examining charges against the UGIF, its leaders were found not guilty of criminal actions. Many of them had been arrested and deported to Auschwitz: Lambert, arrested in September 1943, was deported three months later; Baur went on convoy 66, on 20 January 1944, to Auschwitz.

The activity of the UGIF was not criminal, but can it be considered collaboration? It was obliged to co-operate in different ways. In the occupied zone it provided goods on demand by the Germans to be used for those Jews being deported. It supplied food and assistance for those arrested in the Vél d'Hiv round-up. It saw itself as a relief organisation and to perform this function it did not want to provoke the Gestapo or antagonise Vichy. It was forbidden by the CGQJ to place children with non-Jewish foster parents. It was ordered by the CGQJ to send out social workers to collect such children and bring them to the UGIF homes or to Drancy. To counteract this order, the UGIF formed a secret Service Social to help the children, and to assist all Jews who lived illegally and therefore could not have access to money. The Service was mostly drawn from the Jewish scout organisation, the EIF, which was dissolved in early 1943.

Both Lambert and Lévy sent telegrams to Vichy to stop deportations that were 'unworthy of the French tradition and capable of harming the reputation of our country among all neutral and Christian countries'.[32] The French Jewish leaders could not accept, in a letter to Pétain in January 1942, that 'French people of the Jewish religion were being excluded from the national community'.

In general the UGIF, especially in the occupied zone, obeyed the law. It delayed informing Jews about the impending round-up of Vél d'Hiv. When it was warned by the Comité Général de Défense des Juifs, an immigrant group, of impending arrests and asked to remove the children from its homes, it did nothing; the Gestapo, in raids on the homes in Neuilly on 20–2 July 1944, took 233 children, all sent to Drancy. The UGIF dismissed its foreign employees in the unoccupied zone in September 1942 when asked to do so. It complied with the order by the CGQJ in October 1942 that its board be entirely French, and dismissed its foreign employees in the occupied zone in November. It also complied with the order to prepare 500 yellow armbands with the words 'Jewish marshal' for the Drancy camp after Brunner took it over. The UGIF safeguarded itself: it accepted for its 815 employees 'certificates of legitimation', official passes to its personnel, thus saving them, at least temporarily, from arrest, internment or deportation. But the safeguards were to no avail. Most, especially those who worked in the Drancy camp, were to suffer the same fate as fellow Jews. UGIF employees were arrested in their office in Lyon in March 1943, and in Marseille in December.

A troubling and contentious question is the degree to which this obedient activity by the UGIF on behalf of all French Jews was counterproductive. The assistance given by UGIF Jewish personnel to needy Jews may have created an unwarranted climate of security and confidence among those Jews. The actual request for help to the UGIF meant that a file was created which could be put to disastrous use. The UGIF files were used by the French police and the German authorities to identify and arrest Jews. Its own offices were useful to the hunters to find both information and individual Jews: Barbie used the UGIF materials to arrest children. It eased the work of the German authorities by being the mechanism for the collection of the billion-franc fine imposed on the Jewish community and for collecting the tax imposed on individual Jews, 120 francs in the unoccupied zone and 320 francs in the occupied zone. The houses used by the UGIF to care for children whose parents had been deported were also easy targets. As late as July 1944, 300 children maintained in Neuilly were seized by Aloïs Brunner, the SS commander at Drancy, and sent to Auschwitz in the last major convoy from France.

The UGIF continued traditional philanthropic activities familiar to Jewish organisations; it devoted its resources to charity. It assumed that French Jews would survive the persecution and belatedly concerned itself with foreign Jews also. It was insufficient and mistaken. In the extraordinary, unique dilemma that French Jewish leaders faced, a fair conclusion is that their judgement was badly flawed.[33] Like other Jewish organisations, the UGIF never entered into or justified collaboration with Germany even though it worked with Vichy.[34] In choosing to do so, the history of the UGIF illustrates the sad dilemma in adopting the politics of the lesser evil. Speaking truth to power was commendable but unsuccessful. The leader of the UGIF in the unoccupied zone, Raymond-Raoul Lambert, tried to balance the provision of aid and relief with efforts to stem persecution and deportation. Lambert, a heroic and tireless figure, pursued this effort with Laval in August 1943, but was arrested with his family by the Gestapo and sent to Auschwitz in December 1943.

Jewish Resistance

Other Jewish leaders tried speaking truth in different ways, drawing attention to the increasingly tragic plight of the Jewish population. In August 1942, Chief Rabbi Jacob Kaplan visited Cardinal Gerlier, Archbishop of Lyon and Primate of the Gauls, asking for help regarding the 10,000 foreign Jews who were to be arrested and deported: Kaplan tried to make the case that they were not being sent to work there but to be exterminated.[35] Similarly, a message from the Consistory to the government on 25 August 1942 informed Vichy of the 'unmistakable intention of exterminating [Jews] ruthlessly and methodically'.[36]

Like French people in general, Jews were reluctant to break the law or to cause difficulties. Georges Friedmann, the distinguished French sociologist, exemplified this attitude when, shocked by the Statut des Juifs of October 1940, he repeated to himself the maxim *Civis gallicus sum* (I am a French citizen).[37] Yet Jews (including the UGIF, which funnelled funds from the Joint to militant Jewish organisations) did engage in resistance activity earlier than non-Jews; furthermore, they joined in larger proportion than the comparable populations. Non-Jews joined for reasons other than survival: opposition to the inhumane policies of Vichy and the German occupiers; bitterness at the sight of others collaborating; the German defeats at Stalingrad and in Libya; and their refusal to be part of the Service du Travail Obligatoire (STO).

A saying attributed to de Gaulle was that 'I appealed to Frenchmen, and Jews responded.' Jews were noticeable early in the Resistance movement, internally and externally. Distinguished Jews such as René Cassin, Jules Moch, Raymond Aron, George Boris and later Pierre Mendès-France joined de Gaulle in London. Internally, Jews were associated with different groups: Libération, Combat, Francs-Tireurs. Some of them were Marc Bloch, Max Heilbroun, head of Galeries Lafayette, Léo Hamon, Jean-Pierre Lévy and Daniel Mayer. All these were loyal republicans, believers in French values and a liberal democratic system. Jews were not only involved in the Resistance, they were among the leading figures. Three of the six founders of Libération were Jews, as was the Secretary-General of Combat. One estimate suggests that some 5 per cent of Libération was Jewish. A different group of resisters were the Jewish communists, especially Solidarité, which followed the Stalinist party line and was closer to the Party than to the Jewish community, as shown by its policy of attacking German communications rather than the trains carrying Jews to their death. Foreign Jews were more active than their French counterparts in the Resistance. Increasing knowledge or suspicion about the real fate of Jews sent 'to the east' sparked them to become involved in the Resistance movement, both 'passive' in rescue operations, and 'active' in urban guerrilla warfare.

By contrast with the organisations of French Jews, those of immigrant, foreign Jews were more realistic in their understanding of the policies of Vichy anti-Semitism and xenophobia. They had no illusions about their sad plight or the intentions of Vichy. From the start, they had to ensure the survival of the thousands of Jews who had no work permits and no employment, and who were subjected to internment or sent to the GTEs. They had to provide soup kitchens, medical facilities, clinics, job retraining, children's homes and activities.

At the outbreak of the war the Fédération des Societés Juives de France (FSJF), led by Marc Jarblum and including over 200 different societies, reflected the needs of immigrants. However, existing Jewish self-help, welfare and relief organisations were unable to cope with the number of refugees and the mass exodus from Paris. To handle and co-ordinate relief, new agencies were formed. Two of the more important ones were the Comité de la rue Amelot, in Paris, and the Commission Centrale des Organisations Juives d'Assistance (CCOJA), headed by Rabbi René Hirschler.

On the day the German troops entered Paris, a number of Jewish immigrant activists belonging to different organisations, the best known of which was the FSJF, decided to form a joint new body, known by its street name, Amelot, to provide relief and soon to engage in rescue missions in the occupied zone. Though reluctant, it joined for a short time the Comité de Coordination des Oeuvres Israélites de Bienfaisance (Jewish Welfare Groups), but left because of increasing Nazi control over the Comité. When the UGIF was formed in November 1941, Amelot remained independent, continuing its relief work and serving meals. Headed by David Rapoport and becoming more actively resistant, it hid children and distributed forged papers. Rapoport was arrested and deported in June 1943. Amelot saved the lives of hundreds, perhaps a thousand, children.

The Commission Centrale, formed in Marseille in October 1940, was primarily concerned with relief for Jews interned in camps. It was soon combined with non-Jewish bodies, such as CIMADE, YMCA, the Quakers, the Red Cross and Catholic groups to form the Comité de Coordination pour l'Assistance dans les Camps, the Nîmes Committee. A later leader, Pastor Pierre Toureille, bravely helped rescue hundreds of refugees. A Calvinist from southern France, Toureille worked with a network of local Protestant pastors to hide families until they could get to Switzerland or Spain.

The leaders of the foreign Jews saw the need for a communal response, unified if possible, to protect the Jewish population. That desired unity was difficult to achieve because of differences between French and non-French Jews, and because of political and ideological differences, primarily between communists and non-communists.

right: Poster of Marshal Pétain, 'Follow me, put your faith in eternal France.'
middle: Hoisting of the Colours: Pétain in Place Stanislas, Nancy, May 1944.
below left: General Charles de Gaulle's first message to the French people, 18 June, 1940.
below right: De Gaulle sentenced to death by the new military tribunal, published 4 August, 1940.

«Suivez-moi. Gardez votre confiance en la France éternelle.»

Pétain outside the Hôtel du Parc, his headquarters to his left is Admiral François Darlan.

Pétain and Pierre Laval outside the Hôtel du Parc.

Pétain and Laval with Cardinals Emmanuel Suhard of Paris and Pierre Gerlier of Lyon, November 1942.

Laval meets Adolf Hitler at Montoire, 22 October, 1940.

Xavier Vallat, first head of the General Commissariat of Jewish Affairs (CGQJ).

Louis Darquier de Pellepoix, second head of the CGQJ (*left*), and Charles du Paty de Clam who replaced him in February 1944.

Jacques Doriot, ex-communist, fascist in military uniform.

René Bousquet, Vichy secretary-general of police (*right*), with French officials and German officers, before destruction of the Port of Marseilles, 23 January, 1943.

Bousquet with François Mitterrand at table dining together.

The infamous handshake depicted in a mural at an anti-Bolshevik exhibition in Paris, March 1942.

LA PATRIE *peut assurer, embellir et justifier nos vies fragiles et chétives. Donnons-nous à la FRANCE: elle a toujours porté son peuple à la grandeur. (Appel du Maréchal - 11 Juillet 1940).*

IMAGERIE DU MARÉCHAL - Image exécutée spécialement pour PATRIE

Top: Vichy Propaganda.
Below left: The reality: the anti-Semitic exhibition, 'The Jew and France'.
Below right: An appeal to join the French Division of the Nazi Waffen-SS.

French police and Germans deporting Jews to their death.

The end of Vichy: the castle of Sigmaringen in Germany.

La République française
en hommage aux victimes
des persécutions racistes et antisémites
et des crimes contre l'humanité
commis sous l'autorité de fait
dite "Gouvernement de l'Etat français"
(1940 · 1944)
N'oublions jamais

Left: Plaque at the site of the camp at Drancy.

Below: The memorial for Varian Fry outside the US Consulate in Marseille.

Representative of these differences are two important groups, Amelot and Solidarité, the communist group.

Amelot started from the premise that Jews must mobilise and essentially depend on themselves. Solidarité argued that Jews must link themselves with other French organisations; it would oppose the anti-Jewish laws, but priority must be given to the fight against the real enemy, Nazism. Amelot stressed self-help based on communal unity. Survival was paramount. Solidarité, ideologically committed to the Communist Party, thought the French population would help in the struggle against the enemy, and sought to draw the immigrant organisations into that struggle rather than deal with immediate discrimination and persecution. The armed struggle must intensify: everything else was secondary.

Organisational differences also separated the two groups. Amelot was pluralistic, internally divided but searching for compromise among its members based on Jewish identity. It was not a disciplined group, but relied on consensus and the goodwill of its associated members. Solidarité was a typical communist organ, monolithic, centralised, disciplined, made up of fighters who obeyed decisions. Even in the internment camps, including Drancy, they formed communist cells.

In spite of their differences, the two groups, like other Jewish organisations, recognised the plight of Jews and the urgency to act. At first, the priority of those Jewish organisations was to ameliorate the living conditions of the refugees from central and eastern Europe, providing not only material assistance but also the cultural and educational reorientation for them to live a productive life in France. With the increasing discrimination and persecution against Jews, the organisations broadened their relief and social work, including medical help and accommodation, all still open and legal activity. With the increase in arrests by the French police and the deportations from France, the organisations, while maintaining their relief work, began their clandestine activity and participation in Resistance movements.[38] Finally, the Consistory began to co-operate with the UGIF in 1943, especially after Helbronner, its President, was deported. To consolidate activity, including resistance, an organisation called the Conseil Représentatif des Juifs de France (CRIF) was formed in January 1944.

Rescue was the essential characteristic of Jewish resistance. The paradox was clear. By obeying Vichy law and German ordinances, non-Jews suffered little or no risk. Jews doing the same would be in peril. The activities of Jewish networks and organisations in resistance, therefore, were to disobey the law by finding hiding places either in private homes or in lay or religious institutions, by forging identity papers and by smuggling Jews out of the country. Manufacture of false papers reached a high level of sophistication as workshops produced birth certificates, identity cards, demobilisation certificates and ration cards. Friendly municipal officials, policemen and priests occasionally helped in the production of these false papers.

All this was necessary to avoid extermination. Early on, the legal method was available for those interned to apply or have others apply on their behalf for release from the camps; only a very small number were successful. More, perhaps about 500, were able to escape from camps in the occupied zone, except Drancy and Compiègne. With the mass arrests in summer 1942, networks were established. A children's rescue network formed by Amelot operated in secret. A system was created of warnings about forthcoming round-ups, which were circulated in some *départements*. When Dr Joseph Weill, responsible for medical and social services of the OSE (Oeuvre du Secours aux Enfants), was informed by Gerhart Riegner, representative of the World Jewish Congress in Geneva, of the extermination programme he immediately asked Georges Garel, an engineer in Lyon already in the Resistance, to form a clandestine network to save Jewish children. The OSE had broken away from the Consistory pattern of providing only relief, instead engaging in illegal assistance and helping foreign Jews.

The clandestine Jewish press was a weapon in the resistance movement. An illegal Jewish communist paper, *Unzer Vort*, appeared in Yiddish in June 1940 and was translated into French as *Notre Parole*. On the eve of Vél d'Hiv, the paper *Solidarité* advised readers not to stay in their residence, to try to hide, and to leave their children with sympathetic French people. The issue of *J'Accuse* of 20 October 1942 revealed the use of gas in the extermination camps to which Jews were deported. Other publications providing information on arrests and deportations were distributed among non-Jews, for teachers and for doctors.

Stratagems for survival were the essence of Jewish activity. This activity, concerned with both physical survival and moral health, was diverse, reflecting the different groups and interests of Jews living in France. Friction between leaders of French and foreign Jews delayed any kind of unified approach until the intensification of anxiety after the Germans moved south in November 1942. Clandestine activity grew, as did the *rapprochement* between the Consistory and foreign Jews. At long last a unity of a kind between the two groups came about in late 1943, with the former accepting the equality of the latter and the validity of a secular Jewish identity. The groups might differ on the urgency of action and the nature of that action, but both were now more militant.

All this diverse activity can be categorised not only as 'passive' or 'active', but also by organisational priorities. One category is of groups that were concerned with Jewish affairs and composed of Jewish resisters, the best-known being Amelot and the OSE. Many of the Amelot leaders were arrested and deported in summer 1943. The Armée Juive, Zionist oriented, with commando groups, operated in different cities in both zones, striking at informers who worked for the Gestapo.[39] This unit established relations with other bodies, the EIF, MJS and Poale Zion, which were eventually brought together in the Organisation Juive de Combat (OJC) (Jewish Fighting Organisation).

Starting as a legal group, an organisation that became an active resister was the Éclaireurs Israélites de France (EIF), the Jewish scout movement that became a clandestine group with the creation in 1942 of a unit, La Sixième. This unit organised a rescue network, essentially for children, which provided false identities, placed children among non-Jews and transported them across the borders. The network co-existed with the other parts of the EIF's activities, primarily education. In late 1943 an underground group, the Compagnie Marc Haguenau was formed, named after the late leader of the Sixième who had committed suicide after capture by the Gestapo. It had links with the OJC and with the Armée Secrète, de Gaulle's adherents. The EIF rescued perhaps a thousand Jews.

Another group engaging in both social and clandestine activity was the Mouvement de la Jeunesse Sioniste (MJS), the Youth Zionist Movement, in the unoccupied zone. Part of the operation to save children, its secret unit, Éducation Physique, worked in collaboration with the Sixième and the OSE, forging needed papers and documents.

Historians still differ on whether a distinct Jewish resistance movement existed separate from other non-Jewish movements.[40] Some groups, which the OJC and the EIF can exemplify, were part of both the Jewish and the wider resistance movement. At the other extreme were organisations the members of which were mainly Jewish but which concerned themselves with broader priorities and issues rather than simply Jewish ones: the Manouchian-Rayman group and the Carmagnole battalion exemplify these.

A disputed question is, in whose interests were the Jewish communists working? The first active armed unit in Paris was the Organisation Spéciale (OS) formed by the Communist Party. Because of the Stalin–Hitler pact, which left the Party neutral for a time, the OS was not so much a resistance group as a defence unit to protect communist leaders. Only after the Soviet Union was attacked by Germany did the party become more active with the Francs-Tireurs et Partisans (FTP) under Charles Tillon.

Jewish communist urban guerrillas carried out attacks against members of the German military using grenades and bombs. Partly because of movies made about them, the best-known unit is the so-called Manouchian-Rayman group, a small unit of communists from central Europe led by the poet Missak Manouchian himself, from Armenia, who carried out assassinations and bombings. The group was part of the larger Jewish communist unit, the Main d'Oeuvre Immigré, set up after Vél d'Hiv, later becoming the group Solidarité, and linked to the Communist party's FTP. Twelve of the twenty-three fighters of the group were arrested and executed by the Nazis in February 1944 after a trial, the most important public trial of immigrant fighters staged by the Nazis.[41] The Nazis made the Manouchian-Rayman group well known by plastering Paris with a red poster containing photographs of the members, who were labelled 'Jewish, Armenian, and other stateless terrorists'. Both the Nazis and Vichy used the term 'Jewish terrorists', to heighten feelings of xenophobia.

An interesting and important aspect of this event was the accusation, probably justified, that the French Communist Party had sacrificed the unit by refusing to help it escape after the French police were shadowing it. Foreign Jews were not given the same protection by the party as French communists. The betrayal by non-Jewish communists of their Jewish colleagues aside, the controversial issue is the nature of activity by the Communist Party as a whole and of its Jewish members in particular. These members of the guerrilla groups attacked a small number of German soldiers, and altered signs in the streets to confuse the occupation forces, but did nothing to prevent or delay the arrangements of Vichy and the Germans for the round-ups of Jews or the deportations from France. They shot officers of the German army but not the *Judenreferenten*, the Nazis responsible for Jewish affairs. The priority of the Communist Party was not the survival of Jews whose existence was in danger. The party never attacked in Paris the institutions or personnel that directly imperilled Jews.

Moreover, concentration on attacks on German soldiers had another consequence. It automatically led the Germans to take hostages – innocent people who had nothing to do with the attacks, but who were Jews and who were then executed. Some Jewish communists may have been ambivalent about adhering to the line of the Party; they may have preferred armed opposition or, out of greater concern for specific Jewish interests, they may have undertaken rescue work.

If no consensus exists on the issue, it is fair to conclude that the Jewish communist groups lacked any meaningful Jewish identity.

CHAPTER 10

BETWEEN THE DEVIL
AND THE DEEP BLUE SEA

The most disagreeable word applicable to all those involved in and with Vichy is 'collaboration'. Assessment of the regime and of individuals and groups within it rests to a considerable degree, second only to support and approval of anti-Semitism and persecution, on whether anti-Semitic actions or legislative measures taken by Vichy can be seen as necessary in the best interests of France, or as betrayal of those interests for personal advantage or for the benefit of the German occupiers.

Collaborators came in all shapes and guises. Many files of the Bureau Central de Renseignements et d'Action (BCRA), the secret service of the Free French movement, have been destroyed. Enough remain in the national archives to reveal that thousands of people of France worked for the Gestapo or German military intelligence. Hairdressers, concierges, butchers, dance hostesses, film actors, private detectives, magicians and *parfumiers* vie with senior officials, journalists and industrialists in their collaborationist activities.

In a moving letter of 13 August 1940 to his wife, Count Helmuth von Moltke, the heroic anti-Nazi major in the Abwehr (the German intelligence service) termed by George Kennan 'a pillar of moral conscience' and 'the greatest man' he met in the Second World War, wrote of the moral débâcle in France. Pierre Laval had invited German Ambassador Abetz to lunch. Moltke comments, 'we [the Germans] could not do such a thing until after the ratification of the peace treaty'. Moltke also commented that 'the individual Frenchwoman tends to prefer the German billeted on her, to her husband, who returns defeated'.[1] His private remarks are even more compelling in view of his fate, arrested for opposition to Hitler in January 1944 and executed by the Nazis on 23 January 1945.

Collaboration was not only morally wrong and politically unwise but also, after the war, was made legally punishable. The ordinance of 26 August 1944 created a new crime of 'national *indignité*', which might be translated in English as 'unworthiness', punishable by degradation or loss of civic rights. It was applied to those guilty of 'having published articles, brochures or books, or made speeches in favour of the enemy, collaboration with the enemy, racism or totalitarian doctrines'. Also guilty would be those who participated in an organisation involved in collaboration: especially in the Legion of Order, the Milice, the group called 'Collaboration' and the African Phalanx.

The problem started right from the defeat of France. Article 3 of the armistice agreement stated that 'The French government will immediately invite all officials and all French administrative services in the occupied territory to conform to the rules of the German authorities and to collaborate with them in a proper manner.' Technical collaboration would quickly become state collaboration, based on supposed reciprocity of interests. For Vichy the intention was to return to order and normality. There is no satisfactory way of assessing or defining correctly the mixture of consternation and morose resignation of the French population in June 1940 and in the subsequent years of Vichy. There was considerable, if not unanimous, support for the armistice, which was supposed to bring national unity and peace, and which was more meaningful than the change of political regime. Support of Pétain was reinforced by the drama of the attack on the French fleet by Britain on 3 July 1940 at Mers el-Kebir.

Collaboration in persecution of the Jews was not the only option for France and the French people. Collaboration was a choice, a tactic, a strategy. Various alternatives were always open: active resistance to the Germans or refusal to implement orders; mild accommodation with German authorities, giving only limited assistance where essential; passive indifference and inaction; slowing down or raising difficulties in implementing orders or fulfilling discriminatory policies; an attitude of *attentisme* or wait and see.

The general problem in discussing alternatives of this kind, especially in the extraordinary unique circumstances of wartime Europe and a fanatical Nazi determination to eliminate Jews, is the attitude to authority, submission and sacrifice of ethical and moral principles, or the willingness to act on the basis of those principles.

Since the end of the Second World War analysts from different intellectual disciplines, mainly social and experimental psychology and history, have tried to understand the motivations of individuals and groups during the Holocaust that led them to become involved in implementing anti-Semitic policies, on the one hand, or to aid the persecuted,[2] on the other. Research on this issue conducted during the post-war period illustrates a troubling aspect of behaviour and helps make attitudes during the war more understandable, if not more excusable.

Three well-known experiments illustrate a similar point. The first is that conducted by Stanley Milgram, which required subjects to administer what they were told were painful or even lethal shocks to innocent people. Between 50 and 65 per cent of the individuals in the different groups were prepared to administer severe shocks.[3] Milgram's conclusion was that hierarchy and authority are inherent in any society, and are the basis for obedience to legitimate authority. A second study conducted by Herbert Kelman and V. L. Hamilton, stemming from the trial of Lieutenant Calley for his role in the killings at My Lai in the Vietnam War, also led to the conclusion that the habit of obedience to orders from duly constituted authorities operating in an apparently legal framework is maintained even if the directed actions would be harmful to other individuals.[4]

A third experiment took place at the Princeton Theological Seminary. After being given the parable of the Good Samaritan to read, students were divided into different groups and told to go to another location; some were told to go directly and quickly; others were instructed to go in a less direct and more leisurely fashion. *En route* the members of each group encountered a 'suffering' person, actually a participant in the experiment.[5] About 60 per cent of the students, ignoring the parable, did not stop to offer help to the 'victim'. Only 10 per cent of those who did stop to help were in the group instructed by orders to proceed quickly to the new location.

Did French people during the war exemplify the conclusion of Kelman and Hamilton that, for most people, obedience was almost always the simplest and most prudent course?[6] Did that obedience, if ideologically justified, permit, as Milgram suggests, individuals to see their behaviour as serving a desirable end?[7] Did that ideology, couched in the form of discrimination against 'enemies of the state', allow obedience to become banal, necessary for the good of France? Why did so many French people engage in what might be called a pre-emptive cringe? How widespread was French *veulerie*, which might be translated as 'cravenness'?

In their different ways, respectable and less respectable, French people, in individual and collective fashion, came to terms with the difficult choices of anti-Semitic collaboration, accommodation and passivity; or resistance, rejection of Vichy values and more active opposition.

How should we explain the behaviour of people living in France in extraordinary times and in abnormal circumstances? Choices by individuals and groups were influenced or determined by various factors: economic benefit, career opportunism, desire for social access, ideological commitment, religious principles and ethical beliefs, personal courage, altruistic instincts, common human decency or its absence, degree of prejudice, former political affiliation, influence by elite groups, religious organisations and the media, chance encounters and obedience to law. Some were positively attracted to the Nazi system and the conquerors, and desired to participate in the new European order dominated by Germany. Others with prevailing negative attitudes, with spite against and envy of Jews or, among the worst elements, with sadistic impulses were willing to obey the orders issued by the authorities to perform administrative or physical acts implementing anti-Semitic persecution. For some, these acts against 'a scapegoat' overcame or compensated for the sense of failure for which individuals did not hold themselves responsible.[8] For others, monetary rewards for denouncing Jews were sufficient incentives for engaging in the Vichy persecution.

Collaboration and anti-Semitism were intertwined, though they could be logically separated. Collaborators were not inevitably anti-Semites, nor were those prejudiced against Jews automatically collaborators. Irrespective of the Jewish issue, some collaborators shared a genuine desire for reconciliation with the old enemy, Germany, or thought Britain was perfidious Albion. Some thought, paradoxically, that collaboration was the only way to ensure the sovereignty of the country. Others saw it as the way to get back the prisoners of war. Yet for many, even if they were not avidly pro-German,[9] including surprisingly the renowned Jacques Cousteau, anti-Semitism in either a virulent or more moderate form was the key to deal with the problems of France. Some officials did realise that anti-Semitism was not a solution to France's problems; nor did they want to help the extermination process. A few protested to the detriment of their career. General Robert de Saint-Vincent, military commander in the Grenoble district, courageously refused to use his troops in August 1942 to hunt down and transfer Jews to the deportation train; he was dismissed. Robert Maulavé, camp commandant at Les Milles, refused to hand over new internees in summer 1942 for deportation; he was dismissed and arrested. Robert Andrieu, a moderate person who succeeded an extremist as police chief in Marseille, refused to deliver hostages to the Nazis; he was arrested.[10] One inspector-general of education, Gustave Monod, disturbed by the Statut des Juifs, resigned his post and became a teacher. René Gillouin, a close associate of Pétain at one point, expressed, if in muted tones, unhappiness about the injustice of the Statut des Juifs. Non-officials in the occupied zone expressed sympathy when the Jewish merchants had to display a notice that their businesses were Jewish-owned. Students in the unoccupied zone expressed solidarity with their dismissed Jewish teachers in Lyon.

Nevertheless, this was not the norm. All prefects in the country followed orders to arrest and transfer Jews to camps and deportation, except the prefect of Corsica, who did not surrender the fifty Jews interned by the Italians in 1943. Individuals who might have been expected to criticise the anti-Semitic policies of the regime were silent or slow to do so. Not until the second Statut des Juifs of June 1941 did non-communist Resistance fighters denounce persecution of Jews. The underground Communist Party changed its position and strategy at different times, especially after the invasion of the Soviet Union by Germany in 1941. However, the main paper of the central party, *L'Humanité*, contained almost no articles on the Jewish question, though some did appear in other communist publications.

Accommodation or Collaboration

Philippe Burrin has introduced the useful term 'accommodation' to supplement that of 'collaboration' in the discussion of Vichy and the behaviour of French people.[11] Both of the terms are significant not only in assessing attitudes of the French towards the German occupiers but also in discerning the support for or indifference to the persecution of Jews. The list of those in all areas of French life, public and private, who can legitimately be regarded as engaging in some form of collaboration or accommodation is distressingly long. Equally distressing is the reality that many of them were well educated and in professional careers; surprisingly, some were products of the École Normale Supérieure, the fount of liberalism and enlightenment. Prominent, internationally renowned persons engaged in accommodation: in different fields were Alexis Carrel and Jean Claude, Nobel Prize winners, the architect Le Corbusier, the dancer Serge Lifar. Celebrities such as Jean Cocteau and the popular playwright-actor Sacha Guitry did not allow the reality of the occupation to interfere with their private pleasures. Nor did that reality prevent the young charming diplomat Roger Peyrefitte from dining with the head of the Paris Gestapo.

Accommodation in both zones of France during the occupation meant adjusting to a new reality with different and varying degrees of constraint, opportunity, activity and complicity. The response of French people was complex. They might drink with Germans in a bar or café, but not socialise in their homes. Local office-holders in cities and rural areas might try to mediate between the occupiers, Vichy and the French people, not supporting resistance but attempting to minimise German response to that resistance. The behaviour patterns were not always predictable: some anti-Semites might join the resistance because of their strong nationalism and dislike of Germans while some anti-Nazis might support Vichy as the lesser evil.

The unpredictability may be illustrated by actions in the principality of Monaco. Prince Louis II in Monte Carlo refused to hand over his friend Edouard de Rothschild or to dismiss Jewish civil servants and the Monaco police did warn some of the last Jews left in 1944 of the former community of 300. Yet the same police also helped arrest 66 central European Jewish refugees of whom 42 were given to the Germans.

In the occupied zone, cultural activity and entertainment continued, combining normality and caution.[12] Collections of haute couture appeared. Restaurants and nightclubs quickly reopened after the armistice. The Opéra, directed by Jacques Rouché, and the Opéra Comique insisted on staying open. Performers appeared before German audiences: Maurice Chevalier, fervent supporter of Pétain, sang at the Casino de Paris, on the German-controlled Radio-Paris, and at events sponsored by the occupiers. The cultural world of France survived and had considerable autonomy. Public expression, books, articles and plays were censored by both Vichy and the Germans. Yet Vichy did not impose any specific form of artistic expression, in spite of its own propaganda efforts. Classical concerts were regular; the great pianist Alfred Cortot became officially responsible for musical issues. Popular singer Charles Trenet soothed his public with escapist lyrics, as in his successful ballad 'Douce France'. Edith Piaf began her career in Paris music halls. Nightclubs entertaining German soldiers flourished. Few performers, writers or artists abandoned their muse to register criticism of Vichy or the occupiers.

Some writers, artists and performers left the country. The great actor Louis Jouvet spent the war years with his troupe in Latin America. Yet the case of the supposedly non-political Jouvet is not without ambiguity. Jouvet had refused to perform for the Germans in Paris in 1940 and left for the unoccupied zone. However, some doubt has been cast on the heroic stature accorded him.[13] He went abroad with financial support from Vichy, and was accused of being a partisan of the regime while in Latin America from June 1941 to February 1945. Nevertheless, Jouvet was supported on his return to France by General de Gaulle. Other actors replaced the departed performers; this was the moment when Jean-Louis Barrault emerged as a shining star with a series of successes at the Comédie Française. The theatre in Paris thrived; political events did not interfere with cultural ones. Subsidised by Vichy, the theatre, not in itself collaborationist in the main, was active with serious new productions, as well as light froth.[14] Among the more important of the high-quality presentations was *La*

Reine Morte by Henri de Montherlant, *Le Soulier de Satin* by Paul Claudel, *Antigone*, with its appropriately ambiguous themes of obedience and defiance, by Jean Anouilh, *Le Malentendu* by Albert Camus, and *Les Mouches* and *Huit Clos* by Jean-Paul Sartre.

In view of Sartre's well-constructed self-image as a courageous fighter for freedom against oppression and discrimination, his productions invite special speculation. *Les Mouches* had its première in Paris in 1943, having been allowed by German censors. A generous literary critic might suggest that the play, based on Orestes' intention to murder his mother and stepfather, the ruler Aegisthus, denounces the passivity with which the French accepted the Vichy regime or implicitly makes a subtle analogy with contemporary affairs and the Marshal in Vichy.[15] Less generously and more probably, the intentions of the play, in so far as they can be deciphered at all, would be, at best, understood by a small intellectual elite.[16]

The Comédie Française in Paris, in its presentations and administration, reflected the nature of accommodation in the cultural area.[17] Its director during the first year of Vichy, Jacques Copeau, fired all Jewish actors in the company before resigning in January 1941. The second director, Jean-Louis Vaudoyer, a cautious *attentiste*, organised poetry soirées devoted to the work of collaborators and dismissed employees who were not supportive of the Vichy regime. He did, however, get some concessions from the Germans, who freed some prisoners of war and exempted some of the theatre's personnel from working in the STO in exchange for facilitating German performances in Paris.

The cinema flourished, with a large increase in ticket sales from 200 million in 1938 to over 300 million in 1943, and production during the Vichy years of 225 films and 400 documentaries.[18] Some of the films have become classics, such as *Le Corbeau*, *Les Visiteurs du Soir* and *Les Enfants du Paradis*, the last of which was not shown until after Liberation. Of the films made, only ten refer explicitly to the war or to the Occupation. Unpleasant realities of life were temporarily buried by films that quenched the thirst for escapism and distraction, portrayed serene images of France, or emphasised healthy life and work.[19] Accommodation in the film world meant diversion and extravagant spectacles.

A law of 13 August 1942 made it compulsory to show newsreels in all cinemas. At that time two existing newsreel companies, one German and one French, merged to form France-Actualités. Not surprisingly, Pétain's face was ever present in newsreels. Films were censored in a number of ways, by changes made in the scenario and during the filming. If few films were propagandistic in character, none was critical of the regime. At best, ambiguity might be present, as in

Marcel Carné's *Les Visiteurs*, which was interpreted in opposite ways by supporters and opponents of Vichy. Most important film directors and some actors, such as Jean Gabin, had left France, usually for Hollywood. Others emerged, often making spectacles or costumed melodramas and a few films with implicit criticisms of bourgeois society. The most striking reminder of accommodation in the film world is the famous photograph of some of France's best-known and most beautiful actresses happily going in a train from Paris to Germany in March 1942. The influential film critic and author Lucien Rebatet had urged that the 'entire French film industry ... will have to be inexorably and definitely closed to Jews'.[20] Yet though Jews were indeed banned, almost all of the industry managed not to be Pétainist during the Vichy years.

Literature and Culture

The literary world was also active.[21] The Académie Goncourt continued its regular meetings at Paris restaurants, giving its first prize after the defeat of the country to a book, *Vent de mars*, sympathetic to Vichy. The books being published were written not only by well-known collaborators such as Pierre Drieu La Rochelle, Abel Bonnard and Abel Hermant, but also by non-collaborators such as François Mauriac, Louis Aragon, Georges Duhamel and Albert Camus. Some of the books, including one by Camus, were altered by the authors to comply with the demands of the censor.

For those who assume that literature and art are inherently antithetical to racial prejudice and hatred, it is disturbing, and mystifying, that writers might be anti-Semites and racists. In pre-war France the assumption was disproved by well-known literary figures such as Charles Maurras and Maurice Barrès, who argued that Jews should be thought of as separate from the French people, the French nation. In the Vichy years the elderly Maurras remained an influential figure, though he was essentially anti-German even if anti-Semitic. The literary field was full of other anti-Semitic collaborators, the best known of whom were Louis-Ferdinand Céline, Drieu La Rochelle, Robert Brasillach, Lucien Rebatet, Thierry Maulnier and Paul Morand.

Was Jean-Paul Sartre correct that a good novel could not be written in praise of anti-Semitism?[22] The various collaborationist writers certainly tried to express their ideas in their fiction as in their non-fiction. Drieu, obsessed by the fear of the decadence of civilisation and concerned to preserve a properly European culture, published *Gilles*, which epitomised a mood of despair. Yet in spite of the fact that his first wife and at least one mistress were Jewish, this dandy, womaniser and collaborator wrote about the 'remarkable comfort of Dachau', of the Nuremberg rally of the Nazis as 'a kind of virile pleasure'.[23] A friend of German Ambassador Abetz, Drieu was silent about the Vél d'Hiv and had no comment on the deportations. He committed suicide at the end of the war.

Lucien Rebatet, critic not only of films but also of painting, music and literature, journalist first for *Action Française* and then *Je Suis Partout*, was the author in 1942 of *Les Décombres*, a best-selling work that made him a literary star. The anti-Semitic work reflected his other racist writings, particularly the two issues of *Je Suis Partout*, which he organised in 1938 and 1939, a considerable contribution to anti-Semitism. His wild attacks in his journalism on Jews and the Jewish presence in France, his praise of German concentration camps, his denunciation of the Vichy racial laws as insufficient, his praise of Hitler, his association with Marcel Déat's political group of collaborators, led many even in Vichy to find him excessive. Condemned to death after the war, he was finally sentenced to five years in prison after a distinguished group of fellow writers asked for mercy on his behalf.

The collaborator in the cultural realm who has become best known because of his political as well as literary commentary is Robert Brasillach. This graduate of the École Normale Supérieure and student of classics was at the age of thirty-five found guilty, in a trial in January 1945 that lasted one day, of treason and intelligence with the enemy, and was executed a few days later. In spite of a plea for clemency by sixty-five well-regarded intellectuals headed by François Mauriac and including Albert Camus, the sentence was carried out.

In a famous phrase, explaining her refusal to sign the plea, Simone de Beauvoir said, 'there are words as murderous as gas chambers'.[24] A more oracular statement by de Gaulle was that 'in literature, as in everything, talent confers responsibility'. Thus, before the war ended, Brasillach, the brilliant writer, novelist and film critic, the precocious literary critic who published a book on Virgil at the age of twenty-one, became the only writer who was executed. He was condemned to death for his words. Some have thought that he became the scapegoat for the Vichy regime, and that his trial was symbolical of condemnation rather than judicially sound.

Brasillach was tried under Article 75 of the French penal code on the charge of treason, for collaboration and helping send people to death by publishing the names of those who violated Vichy laws. He had worked with the German Institute in Paris and with the collaborationist bookstore, the Librairie Rive-Gauche. He was not charged with offences against Jews or encouraging their deportation. Yet he was callous about the fate of Jews. In 1939 he had called for racial laws, removal of citizenship from all Jews. During the arrests and deportations in 1942, he declared, 'we must treat the Jewish problem without sentimentality, we must separate from the Jews *en bloc* and not keep any little ones.'

His praise for Nazism was fulsome and his attack on the Third Republic politicians egregious. Brasillach attacked Léon Blum and other republicans on trial in Riom. His memorable comment on the Third Republic was that it was 'an old syphilitic whore, stinking of patchouli and yeast infection, still exhaling her bad odours, still standing on her sidewalk. In spite of her canker sores and her gonorrhoea, she had taken so many bills into her garters that her clients didn't have the heart to abandon her.' He admired Nazi-like aesthetics in rituals, flags, parades, in virility and male bonding with its homoerotic implication. He was friendly with Nazi intellectuals and propagandists in Paris and agreed to their suggestion to attack writers opposed to collaboration. He prided himself on being a 'rational anti-Semite', and an aesthetic, joyous fascist.

In his paper *Je Suis Partout*, from which he resigned in August 1943 when its writers split between pro-Germans such as Rebatet and others, like Brasillach, who were now conscious that Germany was likely to lose the war, individuals were denounced as enemies; names and addresses of Jews and others were printed; and people associated with the Third Republic were habitually attacked.[25] Brasillach was an easy target if a writer is to be held responsible for his words. Yet a final irony remains in his story. Both the judges and the prosecutors of his case were judicial and administrative officials in the Vichy regime, and therefore were also collaborators. They were less offensive only because they were not fascists, and they apparently gave some aid to the Resistance.

One of Jean-Paul Sartre's magisterial utterances is that 'the writer is situated in his time: each word has its reverberation, each silence also. I hold Flaubert and Goncourt responsible for the repression that followed the Commune because they did not write a line to prevent it.'[26] Alas, many great writers were silent about Vichy: André Gide, Paul Claudel, François Mauriac, Jules Romains, Roger Martin du Gard, André Malraux until the eleventh hour, and Jean-Paul Sartre.

In spite of their implication in post-war writings that they had played a role in the Resistance, Sartre and his companion Simone de Beauvoir were never involved in any real way, other than having written a few articles in underground resistance papers such as the *Cahiers du Sud* and *Combat*, and their being involved in a short-lived group, *Socialisme et Liberté*. They wrote nothing about the ongoing murder of Jews and did nothing to prevent their persecution. Sartre was wholly preoccupied with his literary career and was prepared to make compromises with the authorities to further that end.[27] Barely leaving his table at the Café de Flore in Paris, Sartre began assuming his various mantles; popular author, admired intellectual, sponsor of avant-garde literature, formulator of a new French form of philosophy and potential endorser of resistance. He wrote in *Comoedia*, a collaborationist weekly backed by German money.[28] His play *Les Mouches* and his book *Being and Nothingness* were approved by the German censors. He even, according to one critic, drank champagne with the Nazis at the opening of his play.[29] He was blind to Auschwitz.

Simone de Beauvoir in 1943 published at Gallimard a semi-autobiographical novel *L'Invitée*, with a French translation of an epigraph of Hegel: 'Chaque conscience poursuit la mort de l'autre.' For a time she worked for Radio Nationale in Paris on a cultural programme. In her memoirs she referred to the war years as 'a period so equivocal that the very memory I have of it is blurred'.[30] She did not attend meetings in 1943 of the communist-dominated Comité National des Écrivains. She explained, 'I should have liked to do something, but I shrank from symbolic involvement and I stayed at home.'[31]

Relatively few writers, of whom René Char and Paul Eluard were conspicuous examples, were courageous in defying the Occupation and joining the Resistance. Camus was a genuine resister in the latter part of the war, yet his important works *L'Étranger* and the *Mythe de Sisyphe* were published in 1942, and his play produced in 1944. In the main, writers were careful, taking few risks; equivocal, their words did not offend either Vichy or its opponents.

Some, such as Céline, were violently anti-Semitic or were more unreserved supporters of Vichy.[32] A small number of intellectuals and wealthy individuals, interested in maintaining and enhancing cultural contact between France and Germany, formed a club, Groupe Collaboration, a body to be proscribed in the law on 'national *indignité*' of 26 August 1944. Set up in September 1940, partly financed by the Germans, it was headed by the pro-Nazi novelist and Catholic reactionary Alphonse de Châteaubriant, and included a number of members of the Académie Française. The Groupe published a journal, sponsored lecture tours and broadcast a weekly radio programme in Paris. While maintaining a separate existence, fostering cultural collaboration with the Nazis, it worked with other collaborationist bodies. Châteaubriant also directed the Paris weekly, *La Gerbe*, which ran articles by a stellar cast of writers and politicians, including Fernand de Brinon, Drieu La Rochelle, Louis-Ferdinand Céline and Henri de Montherlant.

A fascinating example of self-reinvention and metamorphosis of reality into myth and legend is the case of the colourful André Malraux, whose remains were transferred to the Pantheon in Paris in 1996 and who had emerged from the war with a self-inflated reputation as a hero of the Resistance.[33] In his earlier years the courageous activist and sublime, if elliptical, writer had engaged in political and aesthetic adventures in China, Cambodia and Spain, but he was also prone to imaginary adventures with the truth. During the war until 1944, his resistance activity was confined to living in southern France with his mistress, oblivious to the fate of his Jewish wife and daughter. In March 1944 he named himself commander of a local Resistance organisation in the Corrère, giving himself the title of colonel, inflating the story of his activities, taking credit for deeds he had not done, and pretending to have been wounded more seriously than he was. Longing to be 'un homme d'état' (a great statesman), he ended up as President de Gaulle's Minister of Information.

On a less elevated level, a considerable flock of collaborators and accommodationists filled the journalistic and publishing worlds. Vichy had its own information and propaganda units and officials engaged in censorship, most of whom were drawn from those worlds. How could, one analyst wonders, a gifted journalist such as Marcel Paÿs act as a regional censor in Limoges for three years?[34] The vast majority of journalistlc and publishing collaborators were not officials, but nevertheless promoted Vichy and co-operation with Germany either for mercenary reasons or because of sympathy with its objectives. Among the more prominent of the collaborationist daily and weekly papers were *Au Pilori*, the most anti-Semitic newspaper in Paris, with its frenetic hate of and obsession with Jews to the point of advocating murder; *Le Cri du Peuple*, edited by Lucien Rebatet; *La Gerbe*, *Les Nouveaux Temps* and *Je Suis Partout*.

Journalists played a key role in the attempt to sway public opinion to support collaboration. A particularly flagrant example, and a central figure, was Jean Luchaire, writer, editor or co-editor of a number of papers before the war, including *Le Matin*, *Notre Temps* and *L'Oeuvre*, and a friend of Otto Abetz. During the war, he founded *Les Nouveaux Temps* and was head of the national corporation of the French press during the Occupation, a prominent propagandist, a proponent of Franco-German reconciliation, an advocate of greater repression of the Resistance, and an ardent critic of Vichy policy for not being sufficiently fascist. Luchaire, who had fled to Sigmaringen in 1944 and then tried to hide in Italy, was extradited, tried in the court of justice in Paris, condemned and executed in February 1946.

A few other writers and journalists can be used to illustrate the widespread spirit of collaboration and anti-Semitism. Paul Ferdonnet, a journalist, worked for the translation service of the German radio, and wrote anti-French texts that were read over Radio Stuttgart. Jean Hérold-Paquis, a political commentator on Radio-Paris who usually ended his broadcasts with the words, 'and like Carthage, England must be destroyed', left Paris in August 1944 with members of the PPF, and worked in Germany for the propaganda station Radio Patrie. Comte Stanislas de la Rochefoucauld was a political commentator of Radio-Paris, but better known as a man about town, married to a beautiful actress. He is most memorable for his remark when arrested in January 1945: 'J'ai eu tort, il est vrai, mais admettez que j'ai failli avoir raison.'

Interrelated with the journalists were the publishers or controllers of journals, some of whom were put on trial after the war for intelligence with the enemy. Again, a few examples: Jacques Bernard was director and administrator of the Paris publishing house Mercure de France, which published over forty books pressing for collaboration; Henri Clerc, mayor of Aix-les-Bains, former radical-socialist deputy and collaborator with pro-Vichy journals, became director of the Franco-German newsreel company, France-Actualités; Jean Rigaud, journalist and administrator of the paper Le Jour, became private secretary to Jacques Lemaigre-Debreuil, Secretary of the Interior in Darlan's cabinet, and was accused of planning a monarchist coup; Georges Zuccarelli, former member of the Radical Party and a Freemason, became in 1940 co-editor of Les Nouveaux Temps; General Mangeot, collaborator with this paper and with Je Suis Partout, the most important pro-German paper, was arrested on the charge of intelligence with the enemy; Albert Lejeune, director of the paper Petit Niçois, was executed on that charge in January 1945.

Major publishers Robert Denoël and Bernard Grasset worked with the occupation authorities.[35] Denoël was partly financed by Germany; Grasset boasted that he was endorsed by the occupation leaders. Conversely, Jewish publishers were taken over; the firm of Calmann-Lévy became Éditions Balzac. Collaboration in the publishing world started even before the meeting of Pétain and Hitler at Montoire. On 28 September 1940 the head of the publishers' syndicate made an agreement with German authorities on who and what was to be censored and banned. The first of a number of 'Otto lists' prescribed the books that were and were not to be published. Some 2500 titles and 850 authors were on those lists. In their place, French publishers, including Gaston Gallimard, put out 250 German books in translation and acceptable French works. Favourite authors, attacking Jews, Freemasons, communists, Britain and politicians of the Third Republic, were published: among them were Alfred Fabre-Luce, Abel Bonnard,

Bertrand de Jouvenel, Paul Morand, Lucien Rebatet, Georges Blond and Marcel Arland, as well as Drieu and Brasillach.

Why did publishers put out these books and ban so many other great ones? Why were they written? Did the authors work out of pride, political conviction, ambition, money, spirit of revenge or cowardice? Should the authors have stopped or continued to publish? On one side is the view that it was necessary to maintain intellectual life. On the other is the view that it would have been more dignified to abstain, thus making it clear the abyss into which France had fallen. Whatever the view of the responsibility of the writer, the reality was that France was the only country occupied even in part which continued to produce and present important cultural work.

It is clear that France had greater freedom in cultural affairs than did other nations under Nazi rule.[36] Some artists were particularly friendly with the German occupiers; among them were Van Dongen, Dérain, Vlaminck, Maillol, Despiau and Cocteau. The artistic world flourished, except that Jews were excluded from all parts of it. A group called Jeunes Peintres Français et leurs Maîtres was organised with the aid of Vichy officials; the group sent exhibitions abroad. The annual Salon d'Automne and other salons continued, though artists had to certify that they were French and not Jewish. Museums and the Grand Palais were open for exhibitions, except that work by Jewish artists could not be shown. Well-known artists – Cocteau, Dufy, Matisse, Bonnard, Braque, even Miro and Kandinsky – had one-man shows. Over seventy galleries in Paris exhibited works.[37]

Jewish refugee artists were interned, and Jewish artists were prohibited from exhibiting. Artists signed a register that they were not Jewish. An office in Vichy devoted to artistic affairs supervised these regulations:[38] Jewish dealers were barred from doing business or forced into exile. Art journals published by Jews folded. Only some curators at French national museums, especially Jacques Jaujard and Rose Valland, curator at the Jeu de Paume, resisted German pressure and played a heroic role in preserving French treasures.[39]

One irony was that Fauvism, regarded by the Nazis as 'degenerate art', became acceptable and fashionable during the war years. Picasso was not able to show his work publicly, yet he produced almost 400 paintings in addition to prints, drawings and sculptures during the Occupation, and his works were sold privately. Why did the painter of *Guernica* continue to live and work in Paris in those years? Picasso did nothing to help his friend, Max Jacob, the poet who had converted to Catholicism in 1915 but who wore the yellow star. Jacob was arrested in February 1944 and died in Drancy from pneumonia. Jean Cocteau and others tried to get him released, but Picasso was silent.

Whether because of fear, hope, personal interest or ideological affinity with the regime, accommodation in all areas of French life was endemic. In the academic world, the École Polytechnique, which had left Paris for Lyon and then Villeurbanne, continued to train would-be future leaders of the Vichy National Revolution and applied the anti-Semitic legislation, though with some ambivalence about collaboration and even some resistance in spite of its code of disciplined obedience. In the musical world, Claude Delvincourt, director of the Conservatoire, did save young men from being sent to Germany by forming the Orchestre des Cadets, but he also excluded Jewish students; the Conservatoire was the only public teaching institution in metropolitan France that totally excluded Jews. In the liberal professions, science, business, the banking world and the administration, renowned individuals, cultivated and highly educated, were prepared to tolerate discriminatory measures against people living in France, to ignore the principles of freedom and equality before the law, to forsake intellectual integrity. Accommodation was inherent in daily complicity in the policies of the regime or in actions that made self-interested use of them.

Examples of this complicity are plentiful, and a few are startling. One is Lucien Febvre's career opportunism, perversely disguised as national interest, which led him to the betrayal of Marc Bloch, his colleague, co-founder and co-editor of the prestigious journal *Annales d'Histoire Économique et Sociale*. Intriguing successfully to remove Bloch from editorial control of the journal, Febvre wrote, 'The *Annales* are a great French journal. And their death will be yet another death for my country.'[40] Febvre himself did not die until 1956, but Bloch, who joined the Resistance at the age of fifty-seven, was murdered by the Gestapo on 16 June 1944.

A more ambiguous example of complicity and a more controversial one in the world of scholarship is Jérôme Carcopino, well-known scholar of Roman history, Director of the École Normale Supérieure and Rector of the Academy of Paris among other positions, Carcopino was an ambitious, elitist educationalist. As Minister for National Education and Youth in the Vichy cabinet between February 1941 and April 1942, he lent his expertise and prestige to proposed changes in educational policy. He also applied the racially discriminatory laws with alacrity: he dismissed almost all Jewish personnel in the national educational system and Jewish candidates for admission to it; he implemented the 3 per cent *numerus clausus* for Jews. At his trial before the French High Court in July 1947, the charges against him were withdrawn on the grounds that he had attempted, even though rarely successfully, to save the lives of some resisters arrested in 1944.

Carcopino ended as a member of the Académie Française in 1955.

Among scientists a particularly flagrant instance of accommodation was Frédéric Joliot-Curie, Nobel prize winner for chemistry and active socialist. Engaged in research on atomic energy, he had begun building a cyclotron at the Collège de France, which was taken over by the Germans. To preserve the use of the laboratory to continue his research, Joliot allowed German scientists to work alongside him, who thus gained invaluable information that might have helped the development of a Nazi nuclear bomb.[41]

Another prominent scientist, Georges Claude, distinguished member of the Académie des Sciences and also a member of the Action Française, was a frequent guest at the German Embassy and an ardent advocate on the radio and in print for stronger efforts to end the Resistance. At his trial after the war he was charged with and found guilty of treason, but not guilty of giving help and information to Germany to build rockets. He was condemned to life imprisonment, but was freed at the age of eighty after a petition from the Academy of Sciences.

An unexpectedly compliant person was Georges Spinasse, writer and former socialist deputy, minister in the two governments of Léon Blum in 1936 and 1938, supporter of granting full powers to Pétain on 10 July 1940, who was given the chair of history at the École des Arts et Métiers. In his role as editor of two papers, L'Effort, a neo-socialist daily in Lyon, and Le Rouge et le Blanc, he urged socialists to collaborate. Notwithstanding this, his lack of extremism on the issue forced him to retire from political activity in 1942. He was arrested but not punished in 1945.

Almost all of the 150 Jewish academics in higher education were dismissed. The decision to dismiss those at the Collège de France, the oldest institution of higher education, was made even before the October 1940 Statut des Juifs, as its administrator Édmond Faral, specialist in medieval Latin literature revealed, acting, he said, to safeguard the institution. No doubt he thought that Marcel Mauss, Émile Benveniste, Paul Léon and Jules Bloch would endanger it.

To safeguard academic institutions, Vichy appointed an unusual number of inappropriate people as well as establishing propaganda institutions. One of the most absurd was Henri Labroue, former right-wing deputy from Bordeaux in the Third Republic, and anti-Semitic writer, who had helped mount the infamous exhibition 'Le Juif et la France' in Bordeaux in March–April 1942 after it had left Paris. He was appointed by the Minister of Education, Abel Bonnard, to a 'chair of Judaism' at the Sorbonne in Paris in November 1942. His 'course' was greeted with derision by students and it was suspended indefinitely.

An Institute for the Study of Jewish Questions was founded in Paris in May 1941, mostly funded by the SS, and headed by a bizarre character, Paul Sezille, a former colonial officer whose philosophy was that 'the Jew must disappear for many future generations'. The pseudo-academic Institute was supposed to study and draw attention to all Jewish matters. It did this by organising meetings addressed by anti-Jewish speakers, covering the walls of Paris with anti-Semitic posters and issuing malevolent anti-Semitic pamphlets.[42] Another unit, the Friends of the Institute, was set up a year later and claimed 31,000 supporters. The Institute was transformed in 1943 into the Institut d'Étude des Questions Juives et Ethnoraciales (IEQJE).

The IEQJE was headed for a while by the well-known 'academic' anthropologist and ethnologist George Montandon, an extreme anti-Semitic who worked for the CGQJ as a scientific expert on race, and who claimed the ability to identify Jews by their physical characteristics. He identified Jews by their poorly arched feet, slightly depressed septum, prominent lips, particular gestures and circumcision, which entailed a very short mucous sheath but with the fraenum intact. The bizarre tests he conducted allegedly confirmed his weird generalisations. Besides these intellectual contributions he also sold fraudulent certificates ascertaining Aryan origin for large sums of money. His 'science' ended with his murder by the Resistance in July 1944.

Other spurious pseudo-academic institutions were set up: the Institute of Anthroposociologie under Claude Vacher de La Pouge on 24 December 1942; and the Union Française pour la Défense de la Race, set up in January 1943, which published books, held conferences, organised expositions and used radio and cinema to reinforce anti-Semitic propaganda.

Members of the liberal professions acquiesced in the discriminatory measures against Jews. Of those professions, only the architects, at least in Marseille, opposed the numerus clausus for Jews.[43] Robert Badinter, a later Minister of Justice, wrote of the prominent role played by the Paris Bar in discrimination. It officially sanctioned and helped execute the discriminatory laws, and aided in the exclusion of Jews from the legal profession.[44] Lawyers and judges distorted legal and constitutional texts to justify anti-Semitic legislation. They debated legal points without challenging the legitimacy of the laws themselves.[45] Michael Benon, a former President of the Chamber of the Court of Appeal in Paris, became for Vichy the President of the Special Court in Paris for the repression of terrorism.

In medicine, the official body of the profession supported denaturalisation of Jews to prevent them from practising. Bankers and chambers of commerce gave anti-Jewish legislation strong support. Insurance companies refused Jews as clients. Municipalities removed Jewish street names: Meyerbeer, Mendelssohn and Heine disappeared.

The Business World

Business interests were prepared to collaborate in many ways. A few relationships can illustrate the extent of collaboration. To take the rubber business, Georges Perret was director of the French rubber industry and on friendly terms with the Germans; Henri Balay, who was chair of a French syndicate of rubber manufacturers and of a rubber-importing group, signed an agreement with the German rubber industry and accepted full control by German authorities;[46] Georges Vigne, a managing director of a commercial bank, was the official backer for the sale of rubber from Indo-China to France, which then went to German factories or to French factories that worked for Germany.

Other business areas exhibited a similar degree of collaboration without being pressed. Jacques Lemaigre-Dubreuil was a director of the Cie des Huiles Lesieur, and a member of the boards of administration of a number of companies, including petroleum groups and the Paris store, Printemps. General Pujo was Minister for Air for three months in Summer 1940. He was president of the board and director of the Compagnie Air-France, and was believed to have given the Germans aviation material belonging to the company, and to have sent aviation personnel into Germany. Two executives of the cosmetics firm L'Oréal, Jacques Corrèze and André Bettencourt, were identified with right-wing activity and seen as admirers of Vichy and of Germany.[47] Some business firms, Renault and Gnome et Rhône, produced military goods for the Germans. Others, Kuhlmann, Rhône-Poulenc, Péchiney, were mixed Franco-German companies. Banks, in particular the Banque Nationale pour le Commerce et l'Industrie, were co-operative. Business leaders met with Wehrmacht officers for bi-monthly lunches at the Ritz.

The French cultural, academic, professional, administrative and business elites helped legitimise, if they did not initiate, the atrocities perpetrated in the name of France. Understanding the circumstances of the war years and the Nazi occupation, it is perhaps too strong to accuse those people of acute craveness. It is also easy to understand, if not forgive, that courage was a rare commodity, though many others did play an honourable role in the Resistance or in aiding persecuted Jews.

For the most part, people were silent about the atrocities,

experiencing emotional numbness, detachment, indifference to the reality of occurring events. The ineffectual Simone de Beauvoir would confess that 'In occupied France, the mere fact of being alive implied acquiescence in oppression.'[48] She acquiesced by reading Hegel, and then Kierkegaard. Remaining passive is not as bad as participating in crimes, but it does discourage disruptive empathy, the willingness to challenge those in power, and it allows evil to triumph. Options were always available to limit the power of the regime by delay and misdirection, if not by outright opposition or public demonstrations. The French people were safe while they were silent.

The French were not unique in their silence. The United States President refused to act to prevent implementation of persecution of the Jews. The former Congressman Emanuel Celler, speaking in October 1975, sadly remarked of Franklin Roosevelt that instead of showing 'some spark of courageous leadership' he was 'silent, indifferent, and insensitive to the plight of the Jews'.[49] Celler could have made even more devastating remarks about the United States Department of State.[50] On an ordinary level in France, the same attitude of indifference was displayed. When Jews, dining in restaurants, were insulted, other diners often remained silent. For many French people the normal attitude was one of *attentisme*, wait and see, a kind of passive collaboration that epitomised silence. As Camus wrote in *The Plague*, 'In this respect our townsfolk were like everyone else, wrapped up in themselves.' Yet Camus's characters were humanists who disbelieved in pestilences, which did not enter their frame of reference: one character denied 'we had been benumbed people'. For French people, even allowing that they could not possibly imagine the Holocaust, the evidence of persecution was overwhelming. Silence might also reflect opportunistic accommodation. Most French people were neither collaborators nor active resisters; it is arguable that the accommodators can be seen as 'functional collaborators'. In his valuable book *La France à l'Heure Allemande*, Philippe Burrin concludes about the ocean of silence in France: 'To be a hero is honourable; not to be one is not necessarily dishonourable.'[51] Yet the dividing line between silence and dishonourable behaviour remains problematical; the 'silent' accommodators or collaborators included over 3 million letter writers betraying Jews or resisters. On the other hand, moral resistance included anonymous letters criticising government actions and policies.[52]

In his moving work *The Drowned and the Saved*, Primo Levi, aware of the limitations and flaws of human beings, still says concerning the Holocaust, 'The true crime ... was that of lacking the courage to speak.' Behaviour of the French people has to be seen in terms of that grey zone, discussed by both Levi and Vaclav Havel, rather than black or white, in terms of gradations of responsibility and moral ambivalence. How strongly should people be condemned or criticised for their silence? In October 1997 the French Church confessed its shame that its silence about persecution had 'cleared the way for a lethal chain of events ... this silence was a sin.' It had taken over fifty years for the Church to reach this point.

Minimum attention to the plight of Jews, if not virtual silence, was also noticeable in the activities of the courageous individuals in France who made up the Resistance movements. Resisters did play an honourable, if sometimes overstated role in the war years, from the moment of the 18 June 1940 broadcast from London of the then virtually unknown Charles de Gaulle. He reminded Pétain and his fellow countrymen and women: 'We have lost a battle, we have not lost the war ... This war is a world war. France will continue from its colonies.' It did continue at least from London when Winston Churchill on 27 June recognised de Gaulle as the leader in Britain of the Free French.

How were people to protest against the German occupation and the acts of Vichy? Actively, as in an early demonstration by students and other people on the symbolic day of 11 November 1940. Passively, by remaining indoors for an hour on New Year's Day 1941 to commemorate those killed by the Germans. Protest was manifested by individuals or small groups in a variety of ways, materially or symbolically.[53] Tracts and pamphlets were issued in clandestine fashion trying to encourage resistance; German telecommunications, equipment and transportation routes were sabotaged; incorrect directions were given to Germans; individuals wore clothes incorporating the colours of the tricolour; anti-German slogans were put on vehicles and in public places; a small group of academics kept in contact with each other in 1940 at the Musée de l'Homme in Paris until they were arrested in 1941 and shot by the Germans the next year.[54] Small grassroots movements combined into larger groups; a limited amount of direct action took place in the occupied zone and there was some political criticism of Vichy as well as of the Nazis in the unoccupied zone.[55]

The Resisters

The groups engaged in resistance were as diverse as the motivations of their members. These individuals might have acted because of patriotism and nationalism, anti-German attitudes, anti-Nazi or anti-Fascist beliefs, defence of republican and democratic ideals, communist ideology (but only after the Soviet Union was attacked by Germany in June 1941), dislike of Vichy authoritarianism, unwillingness to be sent under the STO to work in Germany, growing realisation that the Allies would win the war, and distaste for, and concern about, Vichy anti-Semitic persecution. Visible resistance was largely male; it was urban because of the logistical facilities available and escape routes in town; it attracted immigrants, who constituted two and a half million in 1939 and who were now in danger; and it included a significant number of Jews. The role of women has now been acknowledged in sheltering the pursued, hiding arms, helping POWs to escape, providing false papers, and acting as couriers and liaison agents, and writers and distributors of clandestine newspapers.[56] An exemplary figure was Jacqueline Bernard, who played a major role in the publication *Combat*.

For convenience the resisters can be divided into different groups: Gaullists from 18 June 1940; communists from summer 1941; nationalists separate from these two groups, and those now described as 'Vichysto-résistants'. The latter believed in the Vichy National Revolution, served the regime, then joined or made links with the Resistance, especially after the Allied landing in North Africa, and joined first General Giraud and then to a limited degree General de Gaulle, through organisations called La Chaîne, the Organisation de Résistance de l'Armée, set up by ex-army officers, and the Mouvement National des Prisonniers de Guerre et Déportés (MNPGD), with which François Mitterrand was associated.

Helpful as such a classification is, it does not do justice to the diverse and complex character of resistance groups. They do not lend themselves to easy classification. Seemingly meaningful distinctions between those which were essentially concentrating on political activity and those which were concerned with militant activity are not valid. Nor are distinctions between movements in the occupied zone, supposedly preoccupied with the military struggle against Germany, and those in the unoccupied, southern zone, working on political propaganda. In both zones the groups shifted from political to armed struggle.

A number of movements emerged in both zones.[57] The main ones were, in the occupied zone, the Organisation Civil et Militaire, Défense de la France, Front National, Liberté, Francs-Tireurs et Partisans and Libération Nord, and, in the unoccupied zone, Combat, Francs-Tireurs and Libération Sud.

Small groups also appeared: Ceux de la Résistance in 1942, mainly Catholics concentrating on propaganda; Ceux de la Libération, mainly middle-class individuals of the centre-right; and the Organisation

Civil et Militaire, mainly ex-officers and professionals concerned with intelligence and military leadership.

These resistance groups organised by region in supplying information to the Allies; mounted sabotage and guerrilla actions against the Germans; attempted to paralyse train transport; and made attacks on arms and petroleum depots and on electricity supplies.

The Francs-Tireurs et Partisans (FTP), set up in spring 1942, resulted from the merger of three militant communist groups: the Organisation Spéciale (OS), formed in 1940 to protect communist leaders; the group of young communists, the first to attack German soldiers; and the fighters of the Main-d'Oeuvre Immigrée (MOI).[58] The FTP was the military arm of the communist Front National, which decided that about 20 per cent of its members would take part in it. With the introduction of the abhorred Service du Travail Obligatoire (STO), non-communists joined the FTP for self-protection to avoid work in Germany, as much as to fight the occupation and Vichy. The FTP claimed that in three months of 1943 it carried out 1500 actions; among the 1500 were 158 on train derailments, and 110 on engines and bridges. While keeping its autonomy, the FTP in February 1944 became a part of the Forces Françaises de l'Intérieur (FFI).

The FFI was itself composed of three groups, with mergers taking place between the creation in October 1942 of the Armée Secrète (AS), led by General Charles Delestraint, a strong critic of Pétain, and the agreement with the FTP in late December 1943 leading to the merger of the FFI and the FTP in 1944.[59] The Organisation de Résistance de l'Armée, formed soon after the armistice, was largely Giraudist in outlook. The AS linked other small groups, the *maquis* of the National Liberation movement among them. The FTP kept its own structure within the overall movement.

Combat, a heterogeneous movement, was formed in November 1941, again from the fusion of different organisations. One was the group founded in Lyon by Henri Frenay, a military captain who tried to create a secret army, more a phantom than reality, to fight the Germans, and usually known by its journal *Vérité*. The other main group was Liberté, founded by the Catholic lawyer François de Menthon, and other Christian-Democrats, a highly organised group with both a political and a militant section. The merger led in time to the formation of the Movement of National Liberation.

The merger, however, suffered from internal disputes, conflicts of political outlook, and differences about the authority over the Resistance movement in France of de Gaulle and Jean Moulin, the representative of de Gaulle and the National Committee of Liberation in London, who was the link between resistance outside and inside

France. Frenay, anti-communist and opposed to collaboration, was unhappy about de Gaulle and felt relatively benign towards Pétain, with whom he did break decisively in April 1942. De Menthon, on the other hand, joined de Gaulle in July 1943, becoming responsible for judicial affairs. Frenay became bitter in post-war France about de Gaulle who, Frenay believed, led people to believe that it was he in London who had inspired, organised and directed the Resistance rather than the people living in France.

A few other groups may be mentioned. In autumn 1940 the former naval officer and then journalist Emmanuel d'Astier de La Vigerie formed a group, La Dernière Colonne, which in 1941 became a diverse body, Libération-Sud. It differed from Combat in its politically left leanings and its cordial relations with some of the socialist leaders. In spite of tactical differences, he formed a merger of Resistance movements in the southern zone, together with Frenay and Jean Moulin.

Groups were organised in various cities in the unoccupied zone. In the region of Lyon a Jewish engineer, Jean-Pierre Lévy, with the assistance of journalists and professionals, set up France-Liberté, which became Francs-Tireurs at the end of 1941. In Marseille local socialists led by Gaston Defferre set up a group called Veni. In Toulouse, a group named Libérer et Fédérer was organised by socialist leaders, communist sympathisers and refugee intellectuals.

While applauding the courage and heroism of the Resistance fighters, one is conscious of their mild reaction to Vichy anti-Semitic policies and the relatively little attention given to those policies.[60] For whatever reason, whether because of the rapidity with which the policies were introduced or because of the links that some in the Resistance maintained with Vichy, or because of their own ambiguity on the subject of 'the Jewish problem', the resisters, apart from non-communist Jews, were not vocal on the policies nor did they undertake activities to frustrate them. The enemy was Germany, not Vichy.

Like most of the rest of the population, the resisters did not discern the responsibility of Vichy for anti-Semitic legislation, or the true nature of the persecution, or the need for urgency in protesting against the discriminatory policies.[61] Jean Moulin himself, when reporting to de Gaulle in London in October 1941, did not utter a word on the persecution of Jews.[62] Only in August 1942 in an article in *Combat* entitled 'Les Juifs, nos Frères' (The Jews, our Brothers) did the Resistance focus sharply on the fate of Jews. This change in focus may have been counterpart to that of public opinion, though caution is necessary in ascertaining the true nature of public opinion and in evaluating the behaviour of the French people during the war. Attitudes towards Vichy were diverse, and as time went on, changes of opinion took place, whether for reasons of opportunism or genuine concern or dislike of policies and the course of events, even if no linear evolution of opinion occurred. Pierre Laborie, in a number of works, has indicated the difficulties in framing categorical typologies or sharp outlines about attitudes to Vichy. He warns that reductionist images of those attitudes may not convey the real ambivalence of French people towards Pétain and de Gaulle, perhaps schizophrenic, perhaps indecisive, perhaps adaptable. Nevertheless, it seems fair to conclude that the majority of the French population accepted Vichy, and Pétain in particular, and that they were neither delighted nor revolted by the course of events. Until the latter part of 1942, apart from those by the Protestant leader Marc Boegner and some isolated priests, few protests were registered against anti-Semitic persecution. But with the Vél d'Hiv and other round-ups in 1942, the Aryanisation process and the mandatory wearing of the yellow star by Jews in June 1942 in the occupied zone, more people developed troubled consciences.

However, it should be noted that people also became more critical of the regime because of increasing food shortages and the unequal distribution of produce to urban areas and the occupied zone, to the detriment of more rural areas in the south.

The Case of Mitterrand

Whether for moral or material reasons, ambivalence of French people during the Vichy years was an important, if not prevailing, sentiment. This ambivalence is reflected in the personal history of François Mitterrand, a quintessential embodiment of the complex political culture of France, with its two, sometimes contradictory, heritages stemming from the Revolution of 1789: a yearning towards liberty and equality on the one hand, and towards nationalism, order and French grandeur on the other. Mitterrand's political career was a classic case of opportunism, moving from right to left while always maintaining his availability as *ministrable*, thus being able to satisfy his thirst for power. His version of his own history is selective, at best disingenuous, at worst couched in terminological inexactitudes. Like others officially associated with Vichy he invented a curriculum vitae for all seasons.[63] His enigmatic character and idiosyncratic nature led French political observers to refer to him as Machiavellian or as 'the Florentine'. He was extraordinary because of the diverse elements in his personality: imperious, charming, subtle, analytical, arrogant, untruthful, amoral, cunning, romantic, elegant, realistic, manipulative, cynical.[64] The astute de Gaulle summed him up with a succinct characterisation as the 'Rastignac de la Nièvre', the area that Mitterrand represented. Mitterrand resembled Balzac's ambitious and corrupt figure. Even his Jewish brother-in-law, the actor and author Roger Hanin, in otherwise laudatory remarks, wrote of his refusal to respond clearly and simply to questions.[65] His good friend Pierre Bergé, in a similarly hagiographical work, speaks of Mitterrand's readiness to 'habillé' reality.[66] His close Vichy associate Jean Védrine (father of Hubert, the future Foreign Minister), himself a strong supporter of Pétain, from whom he got the Francisque medal spoke of Mitterrand's too strong 'politique'. In other words a political creature, cold, individualist, interested in his own success, his true reality.

Not until the end of his life did Mitterrand publicly acknowledge some of that reality. As a young man he had participated in at least two right-wing demonstrations in 1935 and 1936, had written for right-wing journals and a pro-fascist paper, had been an admirer of Colonel de La Rocque and joined the National Volunteers, the youth organisation of the Croix de Feu, and perhaps, though it is uncertain, had some relationship with the Cagoule.[67] He contributed to the campaign to oust Léon Blum and the Popular Front government. This contempt for the democratic Third Republic was evident in a letter written on 5 November 1939 to his future sister-in-law that 'what would bother me is to die for the values in which I don't believe'.[68]

Mitterrand did not die in the war, but he was wounded and ended his military service in a POW camp. In December 1942, he published in an official journal, *France, Revue de l'État Nouveau*, a now notorious article about his journey to Germany as a POW. He wrote disparagingly of the Third Republic, *affaissé*, the collapsed regime, the useless men in charge, the institutions emptied of all their substance. Worst was that 'France had exhausted herself', and the French were 'inheritors of these 150 years of errors' (from 1789 to 1939).[69]

After escaping on his third attempt from the German prisoner-of-war camp where he had been interned for a year and a half, he became an official in Vichy. Mitterrand falsely claimed in his *mémoire* that on return to France he joined the Resistance. In fact he started in January 1942 to do work for the Vichy Legion of Fighters and Volunteers for the National Revolution, headed by François Valentin, and then in May 1942 for the Vichy Commissariat to Aid Returning Prisoners of War, headed by Maurice Pinot. In Vichy his useful contacts included the ultra-Catholic Jean de Fabrègues, former secretary of Charles Maurras, and Henri Frenay, the anti-German supporter of Pétain. Mitterrand also maintained contact with French prisoners still in the German camps, which later helped his formation of a resistance group of former POWs, the Rassemblement National des Prisonniers de Guerre (RNPG), after some 350,000 of them, divided in political allegiance, returned to France at the end of 1942.

Mitterrand never wrote forthrightly about his activity in Vichy, essentially that of public relations and information, except to say he had made false identity papers for POWs. He was not clearly attached to any particular political position, nor did he approve of collaboration or involve himself in state anti-Semitism, on which he later claimed ignorance. He did admire the Marshal. On seeing Pétain at the theatre on 13 March 1941, he wrote in a letter of the Marshal's 'magnificent allure, his face is that of a marble statue'.[70] Mitterrand was happy to meet the Marshal, with whom he was photographed, on 15 October 1942. From Pétain he also received in the spring of 1943 the highest Vichy civilian decoration, the Francisque medal, regarded as a mark of service to the personality and work of the Marshal, being number 2202 of a total 2600 awarded. After misplacing, on several occasions, the truth about the medal, he finally confessed that he had been wrong in accepting it and that his acceptance was an error of judgement.

At the time he received the medal, Mitterrand, sensing the winds of change in the war, also established links of a minor kind with the Resistance, slipping into rather than joining it. He is the classic example of the *Vichysto-résistants*. His break with Vichy was his resignation from the Commissariat on POWs and the creation of his network, the RNPG. He slowly shifted support first to General Henri Giraud and then, hesitatingly but with political realism, to General de Gaulle.

As a post-war politician in the Fourth Republic and as President of the Fifth Republic, Mitterrand traded on his slim resistance credentials in achieving power. He called for 'national reconciliation' between supporters of the Vichy regime and those opposed to it or who were its victims. He offered no apology for the deportation of Jews from France. The comment of Jacques Attali, his former political adviser, was apt: for Mitterrand, 'Genocide was only a fact of war, not a monstrosity of human nature.'

Mitterrand himself was no overt anti-Semite, though some of his family and intimates could be so described. Both Hanin and Bergé speak of his warmth towards Jews and of his expressed admiration of their qualities. Yet he was less than forthright about the Jewish plight: 'I did not think about the anti-Semitism of Vichy ... and I did not implement the legislation or the measures being taken.'[71] His mis-stated the truth in remarking in a television interview on 12 September 1994 that he thought the Vichy laws applied only to foreign, not French, Jews.[72]

The self-serving Mitterrand expressed no remorse, no regrets about Vichy. He did not fill out a questionnaire required for Vichy officials indicating that he was not a Jew because he was not a civil servant; he was on contract. He knew nothing about the Vél d'Hiv, just as he had said nothing about relations with the pre-war extreme right. Was it all a game? wondered Elie Wiesel. If it were, the game became even more intriguing when at Mitterrand's funeral mass, the presiding cleric in Notre Dame in January 1996 was the Polish-born Jew, Cardinal-Archbishop of Paris, Aaron Jean-Marie Lustiger.

Mitterrand's ambivalence about Vichy and his lack of candour about his own past reflect both the divisions, past and present, of the French about the war years and also their reluctance to acknowledge the degree of complicity of their officials and fellow citizens in the Holocaust. They also raise the difficult problem of relating moral values and codes of conduct to extreme cases.

During his presidency of the Fifth Republic, Mitterrand argued that new trials of Vichy personnel would do more damage to 'national reconciliation' in a divided nation than 'a tardy justice meted out to a few old men for acts committed half a century ago'. Mitterrand, however, was kind to some old men, and to their memory. Every 11 November, first in 1984 and then from 1987 to 1993, he sent a wreath to be placed on Pétain's tomb on the Île d'Yeu.

More surprising than this tribute was his continuing friendship with former right-wing extremists such as Éugène Schueller and André Bettencourt of L'Oréal, Gabriel Jeantet and Jean Bouvyer. Was it coincidence that Mitterrand's first important position after the war was as 'Director-General of the Éditions du Rond-Point, a publishing house owned by L'Oréal, founded by Schueller?

Most surprising, and not generally known, was Mitterrand's relationship of mutual support and protection with René Bousquet. Mitterrand had supported Bousquet at the latter's trial in June 1949 for 'national *indignité*'. Again, was it coincidence that the government junior Minister of Information who proposed, on the second day of the trial, a general amnesty for those found guilty of collaboration was Mitterrand? Thirty years later, Mitterrand's influence, direct and indirect, helped delay and prevent the planned trial of Bousquet for crimes against humanity.

Mitterrand's lack of veracity, evasion of the truth and manipulation of the judicial process concerning Bousquet disillusioned many besides Elie Wiesel, who claimed a long friendship with him.[73] He pretended to know little or nothing about the Vichy police chief he had known for thirty years and who was a dinner guest not only on formal occasions but also at family meals. He claimed ignorance of

Bousquet's role in the anti-Semitic persecution, a role that was made public in Billig's books of the late 1950s as well as in the public revelations of the 1980s. The 'ignorance' was even more surprising as Mitterrand had worked with Jean-Paul Martin, former aide to Bousquet and Henri Cado, Bousquet's assistant.[74]

Only under public pressure did Mitterrand in February 1993 sign a decree that the victims of racist and anti-Semitic persecution between 1940 and 1944 would be memorialised on 16 July, the anniversary of Vél d'Hiv. Not only did he fail on ethical grounds. In refusing to condemn the Vichy regime, in adhering to half-truths and non-truths rather than forthrightly engaging in a republican discourse concerning France's past, he also, as Claire Andrieu convincingly argued, failed as the guardian of the constitution of the Fifth Republic.[75]

State Collaboration

In July 1940, the Vichy regime set up a representative body in Paris, calling it the Délégation Générale du Gouvernement Français dans les Territoires Occupiés (DGTO). This body, headed briefly by Léon Noël who quickly resigned, then by General Fornel de La Laurencie, and from December 1940 by Fernand de Brinon, represented Vichy to the Militärbefehlshaber (MBF), and maintained liaison with the Direction des Services de l'Armistice, the Directorate of Armistice Services, a unit in the War Ministry of Vichy. This unit was instructed to collaborate with the occupation authorities in a courteous, loyal, dignified and firm manner, and to transmit orders and ordinances from the occupiers as the armistice required.

The armistice agreement appeared to require only technical collaboration, concerned with the disarmament of the French military, the security of German forces on French territory, and the financial and material contributions of France to the costs of the Occupation.

On 16 August 1940 the MBF notified the DGTO that the texts of Vichy laws and orders applicable in the occupied zone must be communicated to the MBF prior to publication. A month later, on 12 September 1940, Vichy agreed to this prior communication, thus submitting draft laws and regulations to be applicable in the occupied zone. No measure could be published in the *Journal Officiel*, which made it official, unless cleared by German authorities within six of days of submission to the MBF. On a number of occasions Vichy policy had to be amended for this reason: in February 1941 on a law on youth organisation, on a banking law and on a number of texts for the occupied zone.

These official requirements were the start of *collaboration d'état*, state collaboration with German authorities in many areas of French life. Collaboration, however, took many other forms and involved institutions, groups, associations and private individuals in a variety of relationships. One distinction can be made at the outset. Though the dissimilarity between the two is not always clear, collaboration by the state or by others, whether resulting from opportunism, fear, personal interest or perceived if self-deluded recognition of necessity, can be distinguished from what has been termed *collaborationisme*.[76] This latter behaviour was typical of those, mostly French fascists, who were ideologically akin to the Nazis and eagerly approved of German policies. These collaborationists came from both the political and the literary worlds. The political extremists adhered to the PPF, the Rassemblement National Populaire (RNP) set up in February 1941 and headed by ex-socialist Marcel Déat, who in March 1944 became Minister of Labour, and Le Françisme, partially funded by Mussolini. The publications involved with *collaborationisme* were *La Gerbe, Je Suis Partout* and *Au Pilori*, which also received some funding from Germany.

Yet, whether people were *collaborationistes*, intellectuals and politicians in Paris favouring a one-party state and a Nazi-like domestic and foreign policy, or *collaborateurs* (collaborators), co-operating with the Vichy regime and the Germans for different reasons, the result was the same: support for, or acquiescence in, discrimination and persecution.

Collaboration is a stronger, more assertive bond of association than the form of cohabitation which, under the 1907 Hague Convention on Laws and Customs of War, is permitted for non-political functions by people in an occupied country. Unlike the situation in other countries, such as Greece, Yugoslavia, Romania and Slovakia, where only individual citizens collaborated, in France, in addition to similar actions by individuals, collaboration was effected both by formal state power and by many organisations in different sectors of society.[77]

For the relatively small number of French fascists, mostly living in Paris, collaboration with the German occupiers logically flowed from their acceptance of Nazi ideology and the policies of discrimination and anti-Semitism. For other French people, and for the French State, collaboration rested on a number of assumptions. Germany would be victorious in the war against Britain, and later the United States in the West, and against communism and the Soviet Union in the East. Germany would create a new Europe in which France would be allotted an honoured place. Germany would provide the peaceful and secure setting allowing Vichy to usher in its National Revolution.

In an incidental remark in his famous essay 'Politics and the English Language', George Orwell remarked that statements such as

'"Marshal Pétain was a true patriot" ... are almost always made with intent to deceive'.[78] Vichy deceived itself about benefits it might gain by a policy of collaboration, including restoration of France to its former glory. Pétain was an empirical illustration of the German poem 'The Impossible Fact' by Christian Morgenstern:

> And he comes to the conclusion:
> His mishap was an illusion,
> For, he reasons pointedly,
> That which *must* not, *can* not be.[79]

Symbolically, collaboration exemplified the Anglophobia exacerbated by the British attack on Mers el-Kebir, and the reconciliation with the old enemy, Germany.

Vichy justified collaboration as necessary to limit harm to France. At his trial in August 1945, Pétain claimed to have been *un bouclier*, a shield protecting France. Whether he was self-deceptive, disingenuous or, at worst, dishonest, he showed a total misunderstanding of the nature of the Nazi system and its objectives, and ignored the realities of life in France.

Collaboration was a French invention, not a German demand.[80] Vichy gave; it did not receive. For the Nazis, Vichy was useful to help Germany prosecute the war against Britain. Even the argument that collaboration entailed a joint campaign against the common communist enemy is irrelevant, since the Soviet Union did not become an enemy until the German invasion of 12 June 1941.

The argument that collaboration was a necessity of life, that the conditions would have been worse in the country without collaboration, is equally untenable in light of the consequences. Not only was honour lost, but the figures tell the real story: 150,000 hostages were killed; almost 700,000 workers were mobilised to send to Germany; the fleet was destroyed; the Empire lost its loyalty; 110,000 were political refugees; 75,000 Jews were deported.

Unfortunately for Vichy, apart from a small number of disingenuous francophiles, such as Otto Abetz, the Germans were uninterested in any kind of real partnership. The Germans, especially Herman Goering, viewed France as a supplier of raw and manufactured goods, the provider of manual labour, the source of high-quality couturiers, the source of funds for the high costs of military occupation, and even the vacation spot for German tourists. Hitler had as one of his major objectives keeping France weak so that it no longer posed any military challenge. France was not a partner but helpful for his purposes, if it was prevented from joining Britain in the continuing war. Collaboration meant that German troops would not be engaged in fighting against France except for resisters. It also meant Vichy would carry the burden of administration and security, thus relieving the strain on German manpower and resources. An immediate sign of Hitler's contempt for France, following re-annexation of the provinces of Alsace-Lorraine, was Germany's expulsion of 7000 people from the area, sending them to Lyon in the unoccupied zone in sixty-one trains.

The official call for collaboration with Germany by the 'new order' or the 'new regime' of Vichy was made by Pétain in his important speech of 10 October 1940. France was ready to seek international collaboration in all areas with all its neighbours. For Germany, the choice was between 'a new peace of collaboration' or 'a traditional peace of oppression'.[81] Two weeks later, the point of no return was reached when Pierre Laval on 22 October 1940, and then Pétain two days later on 24 October, met with Hitler at Montoire, a small place near Tours, to discuss the nature of Franco-German relations. Accepting the dominance of Germany, the French leaders agreed to collaborate but wanted a French role in the new Europe, the return of the 1.6 million prisoners of war, a decrease in the occupation costs (at first 400 million francs a day) imposed on France, and respect for French sovereignty. France was pledged to defend her soil and divergences of opinion, and reduce dissidence in her overseas possessions. In October 1940 Pétain began speaking of 'the spirit of Montoire'. The spirit hardly became material. France was allowed to be 'the protecting power' of prisoners of war, and became the recipient of the ashes of L'Aiglon.

Early post-war commentary spoke of Montoire as a 'Verdun diplomatique'.[82] More accurately, it was a humiliating surrender of France, akin to Sedan. Hitler had not requested the meeting. No German *diktat* had been issued, nor any specific demand with which France had to comply. Montoire, the small town dating back to Celtic and Gallic-Roman times, is now a symbolic reminder of the self-delusion and failure of Vichy.

The famous photographed handshake between Hitler and Pétain at Montoire reflects French obeisance to the occupier rather than an accord between two sovereign powers. Two remarks are pertinent about the meeting. The first is that it took place on French, not German, initiative. The second is that Hitler never saw Pétain as an equal partner. He was primarily interested in a pacific France that could be exploited economically for the German war effort, and in the neutralising of North Africa to prevent a landing there by British forces.

Nor did Hitler view Pétain as a significant figure. In 1943 he allegedly referred to the French leader as an individual who would inflate from time to time.[83] This contempt was always evident. Vichy had accepted French guilt for its part in the war and set up the Riom trial in February 1942. At the virtual abrogation of any real authority by Pétain in November 1943, his attempt to broadcast his intention to restore the legislature and to write a new constitution was blocked by Germany. In November 1942, when the Germans entered and took over the previously unoccupied zone, Pétain issued a feeble verbal protest but offered no resistance and took no action other than allowing the French fleet to be scuttled.

Laval and Pétain both spoke about collaboration on 30 October 1940. Laval explained, 'We will continue to examine in what practical form our collaboration can serve the interests of France, Germany and Europe.' In his radio address of 30 October 1940, Pétain explained that he had not succumbed to a *diktat* of Hitler. He accepted the principle of collaboration, the details of which would be discussed later.

That path of collaboration became more and more elaborate. At the beginning, official contacts were essentially diplomatic or required for administrative purposes. Laval met with German Ambassador Abetz. French officials met with the German military authorities and with the Armistice Commission in Wiesbaden. One of those officials was Maurice Couve de Murville, later to become Foreign Minister and Prime Minister in the Fifth Republic. Couve had worked in the Ministry of Finance in Vichy until March 1943 when he rallied to General Giraud in North Africa, and then to de Gaulle.

From 1941 the French economy was interrelated with German requirements, and military assistance was provided by Vichy in the overseas territories it controlled. This assistance for some took the form of active participation in German uniforms in fighting in the East. Later, collaboration led the Milice to fight, in company with the SS, against the Resistance, and above all to hunt for Jews, who would then be arrested and deported.

Other Collaboration

Collaboration and accommodation went far beyond the activities and policies of the Vichy regime and took a variety of forms: social, cultural, intellectual, political, military and economic. Social relations of all kinds with Germans occurred. At the most intimate personal level, they were sexual. In the First World War, in the northern, occupied part of France,[84] liaisons with German soldiers had resulted in births of some 10,000 children as well as in an unknown number of abortions. Similar liaisons during the Occupation in the Second World War led to some 70,000 births. Among the women involved in this *collaboration horizontale* were celebrities such as Coco Chanel, and movie stars, Danielle Darrieux, Arletty and Vivienne Romance.

At the Liberation, violence, perhaps accompanied by male sexual antagonism, was manifested against the female collaborators. After they were humiliatingly paraded in the streets, their hair was cut off in a *carnival des tondues* in about eighty of the ninety *départements* of France.[85] The French were not original in this violent vengeance. The Germans did the same thing to their women who had been intimate with French soldiers in the Rhineland. The Italians did the same thing, but it went further with the French. The episode is dramatically conveyed in the film written by Marguerite Duras and directed by Alain Resnais, *Hiroshima Mon Amour*, in which the shorn heroine explains, 'Je deviens sa femme dans le crépuscule; le bonheur et la honte.' (I became his woman in twilight, in happiness and in shame).

For Germany, economic collaboration by Vichy was immensely valuable for its own war effort.[86] Official French funds were derived from the large indemnities imposed by the Occupation. The state paid 400 million francs a day in occupation costs, about fifty times the real amount of those costs, and about 30 per cent of the value of French production. The indemnity was lowered to 300 and then raised to 500 million a day. In all, France paid 730 milliard francs.

Products, food and capital went to Germany, hurting France's industry, economy and standard of living. Some industrial sectors were obliged to collaborate in order to survive, to avoid bankruptcy or to prevent the Germans from seizing their assets. Other sectors or individuals willingly participated, anticipating higher profits. The French photographic company Photomaton even volunteered to make the identity cards for Jews in concentration camps. Lucrative contracts to collaborate with Germany in aircraft production were made. Lafarge built airstrips for the Luftwaffe. Chemical companies such as Francolor became Franco-German enterprises. The pro-Nazi André Betencourt, son-in-law of the founder of L'Oréal, who controlled the cosmetics firm until 1994, collaborated fulsomely: in 1941 he wrote 'The Jews, their race is tainted with Jesus' blood for all eternity.'

In all, about 8 to 9 million French people took part in or worked directly on projects for Germany on roads, naval and rail construction, military defences, aircraft and food production. France contributed more than any other European country to the manufacture of German armaments and products. About 40 per cent of the wealth that Germany took from the defeated countries came from France, including the Belgian gold reserves and the copper mine shares in Yugoslavia that France was holding. In 1942, Germany was appropriating about one-third of France's national income; in 1943 half of that income was going to the German war effort. In 1944 France was supplying 18 per cent of German imports. It also provided nearly 40 per cent of French men of working age either in France or in Germany.

The Vichy law of 16 August 1940 introduced the concepts of state planning (*dirigisme*), corporatism and rationalisation into the economic system.[87] This meant that production and distribution in each branch of industry would be managed by *comités d'organisation* (COs) or organisation committees. The COs grouped together firms in the same area of business, arranged distribution of raw materials, and provided leadership and discipline by imposing dues and sanctions. Headed by the top executive of leading companies, the COs collaborated with German industry, closed down Jewish business enterprises and tried to control the markets in their areas. The COs brought together French business people and industrialists with their German counterparts, and helped to place German business with French firms. Joint Franco-German enterprises were set up in neutral countries. The metallurgical enterprises worked with German industry. The economic leaders of the two countries dined together in famous banquets at the Ritz in Paris.

In theory, Vichy controlled the COs, but in practice business had some autonomy and was primarily interested in keeping the economy working, rather than in ideological conformity. The business leaders (*patronat*) were diversified, disrupting traditional industrial structures, and some, the so-called *jeunes cyclists* such as Pierre Pucheu and François Lehideux, were anxious to modernise the French economy so that it could take its place in the new Europe led by Germany. All argued that collaboration would revive the French economy and increase employment. French business leaders acted in accordance with the sensibility of the time, devoid of any moral concern for the consequences of their actions. Few industrialists were punished after the war. A typical case was that of Jacques Barnaud, the banker and businessman who had arranged an aluminium agreement between France and Germany and who supplied rubber from Indo-China. Arrested in October 1944 for intelligence with the enemy, he was released and had charges dismissed in 1949; he then had a prosperous post-war career.

Not all business enterprises were anxious to collaborate. Some succumbed to threat or compulsion or to forms of enticement. Others resisted or delayed or were ambivalent. The Michelin tyre company and the St Gobain glass group resisted pressure. Peugeot, 80 per cent of whose output went to Germany at one point, tried various ways to slow down armaments production, and later, in autumn 1943, agreed with the Resistance plan to sabotage plant machinery.

With the mobilisation in Germany of all resources needed to wage total war from 1942 onwards, greater demands were made on French industry by Albert Speer, newly appointed Minister of Armaments and Production. Germany wanted metallurgy, construction, aeronautical production and material resources. One empirical study of the Nord and Pas-de-Calais regions, which were administered by German military authorities from Brussels, illustrates the mutually advantageous accommodation between the Germans, who wanted to exploit the valuable mineral deposits in the area, and the local population, who wanted work.[88]

The Germans also needed workers. The most disturbing and divisive issues for French people in relation to the actions of Vichy were la relève (relief shift) and the STO. Already, in September 1940, Vichy had tried unsuccessfully to recruit people to work for Germany in return for release of POWs held there. In May 1942 when Germany was short of foreign labour, which had come mainly from the Soviet Union and Poland, Fritz Sauckel, the Nazi leader responsible for increasing the labour supply, ordered that 250,000 more French workers, including 150,000 specialists, be sent to Germany by July. As a result, in June 1942 Laval proposed la relève, his form of bargain to avoid a compulsory labour service. It was agreed that one French prisoner of war would be freed for every three skilled French workers who volunteered to work in Germany. Sauckel refused to agree with Laval's original, starting formula of one POW for every two workers in la relève.

Regional prefects in both zones engaged in propaganda appeals for la relève to recruit workers to work in Germany in an atmosphere of cordial collaboration. Vichy, with lists of salaried personnel and of artisans, appealed to national solidarity and asked for volunteers. The law of 4 September 1942 had called for Frenchmen aged between eighteen and fifty, and unmarried women between eighteen and thirty-five. Those who volunteered probably expected better pay and working conditions in Germany and were disappointed. Workers resisted the forced draft by strikes and preventing train departures.[89] Vichy increased security at departure sites. Noticeably, it was the government that had made the bargain, and hunted down those who resisted the draft.

Not surprisingly, the volunteer supply fell short of the desired 250,000. Laval then, on 16 February 1943, introduced the most unpopular of his proposals, the Service du Travail Obligatoire (STO), the compulsory labour service, which at first called for young men aged from twenty to twenty-two to register to work in Germany for two years. As a consequence, young men went into hiding, draft dodging, or into the Resistance. Only half of the age group was sent. The disappointed Laval enlarged the source of supply to men between eighteen and sixty and childless women from eighteen to forty-five. About 650,000 men and 44,000 women were sent from France to work in Germany, a total number second only to those sent from Poland, and first as a provider of skilled labour.[90] To this number must be added the 900,000 French prisoners of war working in Germany on farms, in factories and on construction sites, and the 2 million salaried French working for Germany in France, making a total of about half the active population, which was helping the German war effort. France had supplied 10 per cent, of whom 6 per cent were women, of the foreign workers in Germany in September 1944. Vichy had facilitated the German war machine. It had also created an increasingly powerful mood of opposition and resistance to the regime.

Vichy remained officially neutral after its defeat, but it did provide military assistance to Germany. The terms of the Franco-German armistice did not require that France allow territory under French control outside occupied France to be used as a base for Germany military operations. Nevertheless, Germans mounted military operations from French territory on a number of occasions. Vichy acquiesced in a German military presence in its North African territories in Morocco and the Maghrib. It allowed trucks and supplies to be sent through Tunisia to the Africa Corps in Libya. It also kept French forces from opposing the German beachhead in Tunisia, thus forcing the Anglo-American forces into months of warfare in that area. The most egregious instance of Vichy's aid to the Germans came in the spring of 1941. At that time General Erwin Rommel was advancing in North Africa, and the Iraqi nationalist, Rashid Ali, in April had revolted against the dynasty and reigning politicians in the country and against the British presence. Hitler hoped to capitalise on the situation. The Germans were therefore interested in supply bases along the Mediterranean littoral. French ships were used to transport munitions and supplies from France to Tunis which were used by Rommel's forces in Libya.

Darlan, then Deputy Prime Minister and Foreign Minister, wanting Germany to sign a comprehensive peace treaty, met with Hitler at Berchtesgaden on 14 May 1941. Two weeks later on 28 May the Protocols of Paris, the agreement between Vichy and Germany, allowed the Germans access to French bases in Africa and the Middle East. Hitler needed these bases to implement his plans to invade Iraq, the Suez Canal area and Africa. In his directive Number 30 dated 23

May 1941, Hitler stated, 'I have decided to push the development of operations in the Middle East through the medium of going to the support of Iraq.'[91] He was aware of the activities of the Arab Nationalist Party and of the Ba'th (Resurrection) party, based in Damascus and allowed by the French to operate in Syria. The members of this group 'were racialists, admiring Nazism ... We were the first to think of translating *Mein Kampf*. Whoever has lived during this period in Damascus will appreciate the inclination of the Arab people to Nazism, for Nazism was the power which could serve as its champion.'[92]

The French authorities in Syria, a mandated territory under Vichy control, allowed the Germans, eager to assist Rashid Ali as well as to gain a foothold in Syria, to use its territory as a military supply base and its airfields there and those in Lebanon to send planes to Baghdad. Vichy instructed Henri Dentz, the French general in charge of the Levant, not to treat the armed forces of Germany as hostile but to oppose with force any intervention by the British.[93] British troops, accompanied by some Free French forces of de Gaulle under the command of General Georges Catroux, attacked Syria in June 1941; a month later the Vichy force there surrendered.

Germany sent about 120 aircraft through Syria to Iraq. It sent supplies to Iraq from the sealed depots in which, under the armistice terms, they had been placed; these included arms, ammunition and vehicles made in France. Fritz Grobba, the German representative in the Middle East and emissary to Rashid Ali, reported that weapons had been obtained from France and sent to Iraq.[94]

For Darlan, hoping he had laid the basis for Germany to agree to a comprehensive peace, the principle of collaboration did not imply a declaration of war against Britain, but it did permit the French military to resist any British attack with force. The French did, therefore, oppose the British forces, which were trying to prevent the Germans from entering Syria. The French Foreign Legion seemed to have 'especial spite against the British and their Free French allies'.[95] The French also conveyed across the desert about 5000 Syrian volunteers to help the Iraq uprising and to supply it with war material.

On the other side of the world, Vichy in 1941 allowed the Japanese to use facilities in Indo-China, which was a French protectorate, thus leading to the capture of Singapore, the Dutch East Indies and Burma.

French Fascists

Some French fascists, sharing a common bond of anti-communism with the Germans, were anxious to fight against the Soviet Union.

The Vichy regime itself in November 1942 not only ordered troops in North Africa to oppose the invading Anglo-American forces, but also offered to create a military unit, the Légion Tricolore, of French troops to join the Wehrmacht in Tunisia. Collaborationist groups, led by Jacques Doriot, Eugène Deloncle and Marcel Déat, set up the Légion des Volontaires Français Contre le Bolchevisme (LVF) in mid-1941. Initially, about 10,000 volunteered to fight in Nazi uniforms against the Soviet Union. About 3600 did actually fight, though poorly because of insufficient training, in 1942 on the eastern front. A reorganised LVF unit served in operations against partisans in eastern Europe. On 23 July 1943 Frenchmen were permitted to join the Waffen-SS; Laval signed official authorisation for individuals to do so. These individuals soon became an infantry division of the Wehrmacht, and continued to fight in it in Germany, even after the liberation of France. In August 1943 Darnand took the oath of loyalty to Hitler, and was given the rank of SS Obersturmführer. Several hundred of his Milice joined the Waffen-SS and fought on the eastern front. Others fought for the Phalange Africaine in Tunisia against the Allied landings in November 1942. A small group, numbering about 200 volunteers trained by Germans, took an oath to Hitler and fought against the British in April 1943.

A number of parties and groups, mostly with small membership in Paris and in Vichy, embracing anti-Semitic and anti-communist views, supported the new regime and a policy of collaboration in different ways. The largest of them were the Parti Populaire Français (PPF), led by the former communist Jacques Doriot, and the Rassemblement National Populaire (RNP) headed by Marcel Déat. All these groups rejected class conflict as an organising principle and instead emphasised individual qualities of leadership, heroism and sacrifice.

The PPF was the largest group and the one that pressed most strongly for a fascist-type system in France. Founded in 1936, it had been a threat to the Third Republic, and it continued to play an active role in France and in Tunisia, where in November 1942 it organised a pro-Nazi group, the Comité d'Unité d'Action Révolutionnaire, and helped purge from the administration there anyone sympathetic to the Allied cause. Under its magnetic leader Doriot, the PPF, located in Paris, with a parallel Mouvement Populaire Français in Vichy, was partly financed by the Germans and assisted them in various ways, including intelligence gathering.

Included among the different sectors of the party was a military-style group, the members of which wore uniforms and gave fascist-type salutes. Doriot, with his newspaper Le Cri du Peuple, which by 1944 had a circulation of 112,000, and his activity in setting up the

LVF, came to belong wholly to the Nazi camp. With a number of his supporters he served in German uniform on the Russian front. Doriot was killed during an Allied air raid on Germany in February 1945.

The PPF worked closely with the Gestapo. In Lyon it collaborated with Barbie and was officially integrated into his unit and given an office at Gestapo headquarters. The most violent of the Lyon group was a man named François Marty, an individual with a distorted face.[96] After fighting alongside the Germans on the eastern front, he returned and formed the Mouvement National Anti-Terroriste, a group of about 200 militants who hunted Jews and communists in hideous fashion.

The RNP, similar to the PPF in ideas, was set up by the former socialist Marcel Déat, a rival of Doriot, in February 1941. Déat had moved to the political right, forming his own party, the Parti Socialiste de France, in July 1933. With the slogan 'Order, Authority and Nation', and its version of democratic 'national socialism', this party soon expressed admiration for the new Nazi regime. In April 1939 the pacifist Déat published his controversial and influential article, 'Mourir pour Danzig?', a polemic against French help for Poland, on which Hitler had made demands.

In Paris, he founded the RNP, together with Eugène Deloncle. It included a paramilitary unit, the Légion Nationale Populaire. A little later, he still tried to set up a single party to support Vichy. The attempt was unsuccessful because of internal differences among the groups. The aim of the party was to create a new social order and 'to obtain the exclusion of the Jews from the life and the economy of France and to protect the interests of the French who have been hurt by the Jews'. The anti-communist Déat, who had previously been neither a racist nor chauvinist, had become a pro-Nazi collaborator supporting the deportation of Jews, to Madagascar if possible. The Anglophobic Déat was obsessed with the desirability of the New Order emerging under German control, founded on national socialist principles. He persuaded himself that France would be a privileged partner in it.

Déat's RNP was not allowed to operate in the unoccupied zone because of its continual criticism of Vichy as lacking revolutionary action. Yet Déat did belatedly enter the Vichy government, because of German pressure, as Minister of Labour in March 1944. He also left for Sigmaringen in summer 1944. His end was ironic. Condemned to death *in absentia* in June 1945, Déat was hidden after 1947 by a Catholic order in a convent in Turin, where he died in January 1955.

Le Françisme or Parti Français, a fascist group set up by Marcel Bucard in 1933 modelled on Italian fascism, was dissolved by the Blum government in 1936, and re-established in 1941, financed by Vichy and the Germans. A small party, it was committed to creating a fascist revolution, stressing anti-Semitism and anti-communism. Bucard, a brave soldier in the First World War, and his party supported Pétain, though they were critical of the National Revolution as being too weak in bringing change, and they sent volunteers to the LVF. Le Françisme participated with the Waffen-SS in the fight against the Resistance, but because of the quarrels among the collaborationist groups, it refused to join the Milice in its military activity. Bucard was condemned to death and executed in March 1946.

The Mouvement Social Révolutionnaire (MSR) was founded in 1936 by Eugène Deloncle from members of the secret, extreme Cagoule (Secret Committee of Revolutionary Action), which had been backed, as was the MSR, by Eugène Schueller, the anti-Semite, who in 1910 invented the hair dye he called L'Oréal and made a fortune. Members of the Cagoule, who wore dark red hoods over their faces, collected large amounts of arms and explosives, took part in violent demonstrations, engaged in torture of political opponents and organised political assassinations, the best known being that of the Rosselli brothers, the Jewish Italian socialists. Dissolved in 1937, the Cagoule re-emerged in 1940 when its members formed the MSR, joining with the RNP for a time, and resumed violence. Its activities included the destruction of synagogues in Paris, seven in one night in October 1941, and the confiscation of Jewish property, both with the help of the SS. The MSR was almost certainly behind the attempts to assassinate Laval and Déat in August 1941.

The MSR was divided into factions. One leader, Jean Filliol, who challenged Deloncle's control, was responsible not only for serving as head of intelligence for the Milice in Limoges, but also for guiding the SS Panzer Division to the village of Oradour-sur-Glane where 640 French people were massacred on 10 June 1944.[97] Deloncle was expelled from his own organisation, arrested by the Germans in December 1942 and killed in January 1944 at his home by unknown assassins, perhaps the communist resistance, perhaps his own former colleagues, or perhaps the Gestapo.

The Ligue Française was another collaborationist, fascist party founded in 1940, after the British attack on the French fleet at Mers el-Kebir, by Pierre Costantini (Dominique Pascal); the Ligue Française remained small with probably fewer than 3000 adherents. Though a disturbed personality, Costantini published a newspaper, *L'Appel*, and helped establish the Légion des Volontaires Français. In June 1944, after the evident failure of his Ligue, he went for a short time to the Russian front. After the war he was arrested but not convicted, being held not accountable for his behaviour.

The Comité d'Action Anti-Bolchevisme was another group, attempting to unite the other collaborationist groups. Formed in July 1941, it tried to attract volunteers into the LVF to fight the Soviets on the eastern front. Some of its members did fight in the Soviet Union between 1941 and 1944. Because of its fear that Doriot and the LVF would become too powerful, Vichy took it over in July 1942, renaming it the Légion Tricolore (LT). The military successes of the Allied landings in North Africa led to the LT being reconverted from an official to a political body, again being named LVF. Part of the group remained as a secret police force. Other adherents, including Alphonse de Châteaubriant and Robert Brasillach, were active as propagandist writers or in organising rallies.

Two groups familiar in the Third Republic, the Action Française and the PSF, continued into the French State. The Action Française, still under the leadership of Charles Maurras, was faced with a dilemma. An authoritarian, royalist and bitterly anti-Semitic organisation, it supported the Vichy regime, 'the divine surprise', and Pétain who was influenced by its doctrines, as were many others on the political right, but it was also anti-German or at least not happy about collaboration with the historic enemy. Some adherents or disciples of the AF were close to Pétain in the first year of the regime, and the early laws of Vichy on anti-Semitism, hierarchy and authority reflected the doctrines of the AF. Maurras kept his distance from the collaborationists in Paris, but he maintained support for Pétain to the end, though his daily paper, also called *L'Action Française*, published in Lyon, was often critical of the lack of Vichy initiative for change.

Maurras himself was unrepentant to the end. At his trial in Lyon in January 1945 on the charge of intelligence with the enemy, he wore the Vichy Francisque in his buttonhole and tried to turn the proceedings into an attack on the Third Republic. On being found guilty with extenuating circumstances and sentenced to solitary confinement for life and to national degradation, he shouted: 'C'est la revanche du procès Dreyfus.' The French Academy did not formally expel him but declared that he was automatically excluded because of his national degradation or unworthiness according to an ordinance of 26 December 1944. He was released from prison for medical reasons in March 1952 and died in the same year at eighty-four.

The Progrès Social Français (PSF) was the title taken in August 1940 by the Parti Social Français, which in 1936 had regrouped the dissolved Croix de Feu, originally a veterans' organisation.[98] Colonel François de La Rocque remained its leader and generally supported the Vichy regime. But he was not close to it, nor, like Maurras, was he comfortable about the policies of collaboration. Some adherents felt sufficiently uncomfortable to switch sides, as did Charles Vallin, who joined de Gaulle in London in 1942. La Rocque himself became ambivalent about Pétain and de Gaulle. He was arrested by the Germans in March 1943 and sent to Buchenwald. After Liberation he was imprisoned by the new French government but died in April 1946 before his trial as a collaborator.

Other groups, militant, fervent, extreme, emerged as proponents of Pétain and Vichy: the Amis du Maréchal, L'Amicale de France and Henry Coston's Centre d'Action et de Documentation. The most important and the most extreme group intimately involved in collaboration with the Germans was the Milice.

The Légion Française des Combattants (LFC) was formed after the armistice, in August 1940, to bring together all veterans who supported the new regime and 'un redressement moral et intellectuel'. Under François Valentin, a former member of the PSF, its membership soon expanded to about 1.5 million, to include anyone who approved of Vichy; these people became Volontaires de la Révolution Nationale. As it became more associated with collaboration, its membership declined.

Under the leadership of Joseph Darnand in the *département* Alpes-Maritimes in January 1942, a paramilitary wing of the LFC was created. This was the Service d'Ordre Légionnaire (SOL), which was to become the Milice Française. Darnand had been a familiar figure in the pre-war Cagoule, essentially a violent fascist group. He became head of the police in December 1943. His main preoccupation was to hunt Jews and communists, his group actively supporting the Gestapo in this objective.

The Milice was small, probably with 30,000 adherents, wore military style uniforms and swore allegiance to a set of twenty-one 'principles' taken from the SOL; one was the fight against 'Jewish leprosy'. It would support the new State, and maintain order.[99] The Milice received arms from the Germans, thus enabling them to act as a force independent of the local police and authorities. It entered the northern zone to engage in activity and joined the German army in action in the Glières. It captured and tortured members of the Resistance and murdered well-known republicans such as Georges Mandel and Jean Zay. As late as summer 1944 it was the protagonist in the ongoing civil war in France, the so-called *guerre franco-français*. At best, the Milice were fanatics; at worst, they were traitors. They were hated: Darnand escaped assassination, but the chief propagandist, Philippe Henriot, did not.

One of the worst of the Milice was Joseph Lécussan, head of the unit in Saint-Amand, an alcoholic, violent anti-Semite and anti-communist. He personally murdered the eighty-year-old Victor Basch, the Jewish President of the League of Rights of Man, and proudly displayed a Star of David cut from the buttocks of a Jewish corpse.[100] Lecussan helped the Gestapo in their attack on Saint-Amand on 20 July 1944, arrested seventy-six Jews and murdered twenty-six of them by throwing them down abandoned wells.[101]

Members of the Milice received comfortable salaries, which they supplemented by theft. Joining the group was an opportunity for some of them to carry arms, to have police records expunged or to gratify sadistic instincts. The case of Touvier is now symbolic of those with material and sadistic motivation. Others were motivated by ideology and joined the German SS to fight for their fascist ideals. Some cases have come to light. Henri-Joseph Fenet joined the Milice and volunteered in October 1943 for the Waffen-SS, fighting in Poland and in Germany; even in Berlin itself in the final days of the war in April 1945. Similarly, Henri Kreis, also in the Waffen-SS, fought in eastern Poland. Both received the German Iron Cross.

What happened to the collaborators? Figures on this are unclear or disputed, but the most reliable ones suggest that some 9000 or 10,000 alleged collaborators were killed after Liberation with little or no formal investigation. The Resistance executed 2400 people before 6 June 1944, then shot those who had fought with the Germans against Liberation forces, some 5000. There followed an explosion of rage and revenge directed against other collaborators, an extra-judicial purge accounting for about 1600 killed.

Five official tribunals dealt with a large number of cases: summary military courts; military tribunals; ordinary courts of justice; 'civic chambers', which determined the new charge of 'national *indignité*' (unworthiness) instituted by ordinance of 26 August 1944; and a High Court of magistrates and jurors created in November 1944 to hear the cases of those who had held official positions after 16 June 1940.

Some 300,000 dossiers were examined, of which 60 per cent were shelved and the cases closed. Of the other 124,000 individuals, 76 per cent were condemned and over 44,000 went to prison for a time. Between 1500 and 1600 of those sentenced to death were executed. About 50,000 were condemned to national degradation.[102]

Many remained unpunished or were indicted or brought to trial many years later by chance circumstances or by assiduous pursuit: Touvier, Papon, Leguay and Bousquet are the best known. Many, such as François Mitterrand and Michel Junot, kept their past activity in Vichy hidden. Junot, Deputy Mayor of Paris from 1977 to 1995, was found only in 1997 to have helped supervise the internment camp of

Pithiviers and to have been a deputy prefect under Vichy. Confronted by this, he excused himself by saying that all he knew was rumours that Jews were being sent to work in salt mines in Poland.

The last surviving minister of the Vichy regime, François Lehideux, died in June 1998 at the age of ninety-five. Lehideux, a socially well-connected former civil servant and Minister of Industrial Production, had, through marriage into the Renault automobile manufacturing family, supplied car parts to the German army, had tanks repaired and provided technical assistance for its war effort. He was arrested but freed shortly after in 1946; charges of collaboration with the enemy were dropped in 1949. Unrepentant to the end, he remarked in an interview in 1997, 'extenuating circumstances justified Vichy policy'.

CHAPTER 11

THE JUDGEMENTS OF PARIS

French courts have been slow in coming to judgement and rendering a verdict on Vichy and its personnel over its persecution of Jews. Immediately after the war, some of the most prominent and visible war criminals brought to trial were charged with treason, intelligence with the enemy and collaboration. It was over thirty years before the focus of the courts was put on Vichy's policy towards Jews with the indictment of several high Vichy officials for crimes against humanity.

Questions arose about whether the legal system could directly address the anti-Semitic attitudes, ideology and actions of Vichy.[1] Could trials have pedagogical value in indicating comparisons with other countries in the nature of persecution, and in bringing into the courtroom victims of that persecution, camp survivors and resisters?[2] In this conjuncture of event and individuals, memory and history could intertwine, though this would not necessarily bring consensus over interpretation of Vichy.[3]

Memory and history entered into the legal uncertainties that marked the trials of Vichy personnel in the 1980s and 1990s. In the topsy-turvy world of post-war French jurisprudence, the courts let the crime fit the punishment. The courts also proved inadequate for analysing in any consistent fashion the ideology and nature of the Vichy regime. At the core of the problem of the trials was a challenging issue, important not only for the French judicial system in dealing with cases arising out of actions during the Vichy years and in assessing the nature of the regime itself, but also now for the contemporary world; that issue is the definition of 'crimes against humanity'. The problem in France was made more complicated and confusing because the definition was changed four times between 1985 and 1997 to meet the specific needs of particular cases.

War Crimes and Crimes Against Humanity

A legal distinction between the concepts of 'war crimes' and 'crimes against humanity' is the necessary starting point. A first reference to the latter was the public declaration on 18 May 1915 by France, Britain and Russia denouncing the massacre of Armenians as 'new crimes of Turkey against humanity and civilisation'. Though it was politically motivated, it had no practical impact. However, during the Second World War, the Allied governments, the United States, Britain and the Soviet Union, spoke, in documents of 27 October 1941 and 27 April 1942, of punishment of war criminals as a major aim of the war against Nazi Germany. The three powers, joined by a liberated France, signed on 8 August 1945 the London Agreement, which created an International Military Tribunal to try major war criminals of the European Axis countries (Germany and Italy).

The jurisdiction of the Tribunal was defined by a Charter, which was the basis of the famous Nuremberg trial of twenty-two major Nazi figures in 1945. Central to it was Article 6, which defined three categories of crime: crimes against peace; war crimes; and crimes against humanity. These new principles of international law were affirmed in general, if not in specific detail, by the 1946 General Assembly of the United Nations. Article 6(c) defined crimes against humanity in this way:

> [N]amely murder, extermination, enslavement, deportation, and other inhumane acts committed against any civilian population, before or during the war, or persecutions on political, racial or religious grounds in execution of or in connection with any crimes within the jurisdiction whether or not in violation of the domestic law of the country where perpetrated.

Objections that *ex post facto* laws, especially on crimes against humanity, had been introduced in trials were offset by the argument of the Nuremberg Tribunal that crimes of the magnitude committed by the Nazis, above all the Holocaust, had never been witnessed before, were contrary to the laws of civilised nations and must be internationally recognised.

Essential differences emerged between 'war crimes' and 'crimes against humanity'. The former were limited to acts by citizens of one country against citizens of other countries, while the latter also included acts against citizens of the perpetrator's own country. Moreover, war crimes had prescriptible limits of time for trial and punishment, while crimes against humanity were to be regarded as imprescriptible. The laws of humanity had become part of the legal system, and practical justice was available to punish violators. The link between the perpetrator of inhumane deeds and the crime was now established in a universal form.[4]

In the relevant post-war trials in France, the 1939 penal code was applied to those charged with treason, collaboration with the enemy, attacks on the laws of the Republic, and acts harmful to national defence. The French courts did not use the Nuremberg criteria, but decided on the basis of a 1944 decree on war crimes, which added the crime of 'national *indignité'*, punishable by national degradation and loss of civil rights. For over twenty years no trial was based on the charge of crimes against humanity.[5]

In 1964 the German government announced that all war crimes would be prescribed by May 1965, twenty years after the end of the war. The French National Assembly, now made conscious of a problem it had previously neglected, and troubled by the controversial issue of atrocities by French soldiers in Algeria in the late 1950s, voted unanimously on 26 December 1964 that crimes against humanity, as defined by the London Charter of August 1945 and defined in the UN resolution of 11 February 1946, were imprescriptible and were to be incorporated into the French criminal code. The law was enacted to deal with Nazi criminals if they returned to France. Questions still remained about the retroactive nature of the new French penal law, applying as it did to crimes committed before 1964, and also about its applicability to French persons as distinct from Nazi war criminals.

The French courts were left to define and elucidate the nature of the crimes. Since 1967, when the statute of limitations was applied to war crimes, all new prosecutions of wartime activity in Vichy have had to be conducted on the basis of crimes against humanity. The changes in the law became pertinent to the cases of Klaus Barbie in 1987, Paul Touvier in 1994 and Maurice Papon in 1997, and would have been applied to Jean Leguay and René Bousquet. The case of Touvier, who had already been pardoned in 1971 by President Pompidou, arose again in 1973 and 1974 for actions during the war. The courts did not reach clear conclusions about the troubling questions concerning the applicability of the 1964 law.

The first to confront the French judicial system was Barbie, the SS head of the SiPo-SD (IV) unit of the Gestapo in Lyon from 1942 to 1944. By chance Barbie had been born in Trier, the birthplace also of Karl Marx and the site of the first pogrom by the Crusaders against Jews in the Rhineland in 1096. His function was to fight the Resistance and get rid of Jews. In May 1947 the French court in Lyon found Barbie, who had fled to Latin America, guilty *in absentia* of war crimes. After his capture in Bolivia and extradition to France in 1983, he was accused of having committed 340 crimes, including seventeen crimes against humanity. Barbie could not again be tried under the now prescriptible war crimes law for killing Jews and resisters. Two of these crimes during his eighteen months of sadism, torture and terrorism, and 'reinforced interrogation' in his headquarters at the Hotel Terminus were particularly notorious: his murder of Jean Moulin, the leader of the Resistance, and the arrest in April 1944 of forty-four children, all under fourteen, in a house run by the OSE in Izieu, a few miles from Lyon. The children were sent to Drancy; all were murdered in Auschwitz.

Barbie was the first person to be charged with crimes against humanity. What exactly were crimes against humanity as distinct from war crimes? In 1976 the Supreme Court of Appeals, the Cour de Cassation, concluded that the 1964 parliamentary law on imprescriptibility did not create a new situation, but authenticated what was a natural situation before the law. Crimes against humanity were not covered by ordinary French rules of prescription, but were 'imprescriptible by their nature'. Political and legal issues intertwined. The French Foreign Ministry in July 1979 confirmed the principle of 'imprescriptibility'. Barbie challenged the validity of the 1964 law but the Court rejected the challenge, holding that crimes against humanity could be prosecuted in France 'whatever the date and place of their commission'. Barbie was indicted in 1983.

The highly complex legal game began. The Indicting Chamber of the Court of Appeals in Lyon in October 1985 held that Barbie could be indicted on some counts, but that actions against members of the Resistance, irrespective of their religion, were war crimes, not crimes against humanity, since they were not based on racial or religious grounds, and were therefore prescriptible. This surprising decision was overturned two months later, on 20 December 1985, by the Court of Appeals, which amended the definition of crimes against humanity in French law.

The Court defined the concept in a long sentence. It read: 'The imprescriptible crime against humanity is constituted ... by inhuman acts and persecutions which, in the name of a state practising a policy of ideological hegemony, were committed in systematic fashion, not only against persons because of their belonging to a racial or religious group, but also against the adversaries of that policy, whatever the form of their opposition.' Two important issues flowed from the new definition. Was Vichy to be regarded as having a policy of 'ideological hegemony'? And crimes against members of the Resistance could now be regarded as crimes against humanity. The perpetrator of a crime against humanity intends to deny the humanity of his victim, and by attacking the individual is also, indirectly, injuring the group to which the victim belongs. By an ironic twist of fate, the term 'hegemony', brought into political parlance by Marxists, first Plekhanov and then Antonio Gramsci, became the test of a fascist regime. Equally ironic was the fact that Barbie's primary lawyer, Jacques Vergès, had made his reputation defending Algerian nationalists, had lived for a number of years in communist Prague, and had accepted the Stalinist repression there.

As a result of complicated legal manoeuvring, Barbie was charged in May 1987 with only one crime against humanity, the arrest and deportation to their death of the forty-four Jewish children taken from a home in Izieu. The Cour d'Assises in the *département* of the Rhône found him guilty in 1987 and sentenced him to life in prison, where he died in 1991.

The Touvier Case

Barbie was a Nazi murderer whose case did not raise important political, as distinct from legal, problems. For France the case of Paul Touvier was more complicated, legally as well as politically, and it was internally divisive, throwing light and heat on a number of aspects of activities during and after Vichy and on the very nature of the regime. Touvier, born in 1915 and educated in religious schools, had an unsuccessful career before the war. He was attracted to extremist groups, the PSF of La Rocque, the Légion Française des Combattants (LFC) of Vallat and the SOL of Darnand. In 1943 he joined the Milice, becoming head of the Second Section, of intelligence, for Savoy and the Rhône, and then was promoted to regional head for the Lyonnais region. In that role he participated in the arrest, torture and murder of Jews in the area.

After the war, Touvier was condemned *in absentia* by the court in Lyon on 10 September 1946, and by the court in Chambéry on 4 March 1947, being sentenced to death for intelligence with the enemy, a war crime. Arrested in Paris in July 1947, he 'miraculously' escaped and evaded capture, as a result of aid from both Vichyites, including the LFC, and some clerical personnel. In March 1967 the penalty of death was prescribed but Touvier was still subject to lesser penalties, confiscation of property and legal incapacity.

When he resurfaced for a short time, his supporters attempted to have these penalties removed and called for President Georges Pompidou to pardon him; the President did so, on 23 November 1971, without informing the country. After the news had leaked out, he explained the unpopular decision at a press conference on 21 September 1972. Pompidou, who himself had stayed in Paris during the war, though not a collaborator, spoke of the need to 'draw a veil over the past, to forget a time when Frenchmen disliked one another'. The time had come for reconciliation and an end to 'the purge and its excesses'. Pompidou's astonishing remarks, in essence pardoning Vichy by implication as well as Touvier, were counterproductive and ignited interest in the Vichy period.

The pardoned Touvier disappeared again in 1972, before a charge of crimes against humanity was filed by the son of a man he had killed. For eighteen years he was hidden by a Catholic network in a number of convents and monasteries, traditional and *intégriste*, such as the Chevaliers de Notre Dame, and was supported by a group led by Mgr Duquaire, the secretary of the primate of Gaul, who thought Touvier had suffered in the same way as Christ and who had intervened with Pompidou on Touvier's behalf; and by Mgr Gonet, one of the secretaries of the episcopate.

Some clerics put the Church above the laws of man, holding that its laws are those of God, that its justice and morality are superior to judgements of the state, which can be mistaken. For them the mission of the Church, the truths of faith, the salvation of souls and the duty of charity were more important than politics and justified shielding a fugitive from legal punishment. Brian Moore in *The Statement*, a fictional retelling of the last days of Touvier, has a Jesuit priest make a pointed, if extreme, remark: 'In the Church, very often, devotion replaces intelligence.' Yet support of and aid for Touvier, surprising because his private, especially sexual, conduct was at such variance with Catholic morality, came from more than counter-revolutionary or fascist clerics or religious figures.[6] Even the distinguished philosopher Gabriel Marcel, a Jew who converted to Catholicism, wrote on Touvier's behalf to President Pompidou on 17 November 1970; he soon regretted his action, calling Touvier 'a scoundrel who lied all along'. In spite of Touvier's unsavoury activities, such as robbery and black market operations, he was able to hoodwink many individuals for a time and get assistance from a diverse number of people prominent in French life, such as Pierre Frésnay, the actor, and Jacques Brel, the singer.

Indeed, Touvier was an unscrupulous thug, a gangster who had committed armed robbery in Paris in 1946; who had stolen money while in the Milice; who took an apartment in Lyon belonging to a Jew to house his mistress, to whom he gave a car and goods owned by Jews; who confessed to being 'violent by nature'; and who was a vicious anti-Semite. He portrayed himself as a misunderstood patriot who had only acted on orders from above.

Touvier was not an important figure in Vichy but he was prominent in the notorious Milice, co-ordinating all the information services for the ten *départements* in the Lyon region, and engaging in action against 'anti-France'. It is a striking commentary on divisions of opinion in France over Vichy and other matters that Touvier could attract support and aid from a number of important political and ecclesiastical figures. The rationales given for this aid were equally specious: Touvier was a good family man; he had a right to asylum; justice was imperfect; the Church must make its own judgement on people; it was time to forget the past.

None of these was true, and while Touvier was in hiding, two citizens brought charges against him in 1973, starting a long legal battle. The complicated juridical debate was to become a revealing commentary on the continuing difficulty in France in coming to terms with, and in evaluating, actions committed by officials of Vichy.

Courts in Lyon and Chambéry declared their incompetence to hear the case. These decisions were then overturned by the Supreme Court of Appeals in Paris which assigned the case to the Indictments Chamber of the Court of Appeals, which in October 1975 declared itself competent to hear the case but also said the statute of limitations had expired. The Supreme Court again overturned this in June 1976.

That court had confirmed that crimes against humanity were now part of the general body of French law. Touvier could therefore be tried in the regular court system. In 1976 the court held that the 1964 law applied to French citizens as well as foreigners, that it was retroactive, that it applied to crimes committed before its enactment, that it was imprescriptible. The Indictments Chamber in Paris, in dismissing the charges, had said that Vichy did not act on the basis of a 'policy of ideological hegemony' and therefore no legal basis existed to charge Touvier. The chamber also ruled that insufficient evidence had been put forward. Since Vichy was not such a state, Touvier had acted as an accomplice of the Gestapo. The Supreme Court, the Cour de Cassation, did not want to rule on the nature of the Vichy system, but, using a subterfuge, it held that a crime against humanity could only have been committed by 'a European Axis country or in complicity with such a country'. Further, the Court held that a single incident would constitute a crime against humanity. The new investigating magistrate formally indicted the absent Touvier in 1981 for crimes against humanity. The 1964 law would now be pertinent to his case, to which the December 1985 Supreme Court decision would apply.

That decision was important not only in itself, but also because it clarified the decision of the Chambre d'Accusation of Lyon, which had distinguished between different kinds of victim. The latter court held that if the victims were 'innocent Jews', the offence was a crime against humanity, but if they were 'combattants de l'ombre', members of the Resistance, it would be a war crime and therefore prescriptible.

The Supreme Court now applied crimes against humanity to 'adversaries of this policy [ideological hegemony against a particular racial or religious collectivity] no matter what the form of their opposition'. Acts against the Resistance were therefore now included in the definition.

Touvier was finally caught and arrested on 24 May 1989 at a Catholic monastery in Nice operated by followers of Mgr Marcel Lefebvre, who had been excommunicated by the Vatican a year earlier. On arrest Touvier regretted nothing and did not renounce his opinions or his allegiance to the Milice. He was the first Frenchman to be tried for crimes against humanity. Both Leguay and Bousquet had been indicted in 1979 and 1991 on similar charges, but the former died of natural causes in 1989, and the latter by assassination in June 1993. The French penal code was changed in July 1991, making a conviction for crimes against humanity subject to life imprisonment.[7]

At the first judicial investigation of Touvier, the Indicting Chamber of the Court of Appeals, the Chambre d'Accusation in Paris in April 1992, supposedly acting on the basis of the 1985 decision, delivered a stunning decision, one of non-lieu or acquittal before trial. It quashed the indictment of crimes against humanity on the grounds that the charge was not pertinent. Even if Vichy had engaged in anti-Semitic legal and administrative practices, and had exhibited nostalgia for tradition and for a Christian and rural France, it had, according to the Court, tolerated divisions and was not a state practising a policy of ideological hegemony. At no time, it said, did the Vichy regime have either the intent or the opportunity to establish any domination or to impose a conquering ideology. By this logic, a Vichy official could not be indicted for crimes against humanity. No official proclamation by Vichy stated that Jews were the enemies of the state. No speech by Pétain contained anti-Semitic language. Darnand, who had sworn allegiance and taken an oath of loyalty to Hitler, was 'an exception' and his Milice, which did exhibit certain anti-Semitic tendencies, were only one of the powers of the Vichy state. The Court even surprisingly held that the ideology of Vichy was a mixture of good intentions and political animosities, ignoring the persecution and the cruelty of the regime.

The Court, the Chambre d'Accusation in Paris, dismissed five of the six charges against Touvier, and held that the sixth, the killing of seven Jewish hostages in Rillieux-la-Pape, was a criminal, improvised act but not part of a concerted plan of extermination or a crime against humanity because Touvier was not involved in genocide based on ideology. Touvier could not be seen as executor of a decision taken by Germany, and therefore could not be convicted for crimes against

humanity. His actions were 'war crimes' and were no longer
punishable because of the statute of limitations.

The dilemma was that Touvier was not a German citizen acting for
the Nazi regime as was Barbie, but a French employee of a Vichy
agency responsible for security in his region. Moreover, was Vichy
being judged as a state 'practising a policy of ideological hegemony'?
For Gaullists, Vichy had never been a genuine state and therefore
Touvier could not have committed crimes against humanity. And if
Vichy was an autonomous state, Touvier could not have been an agent
of the Gestapo. If Vichy was a regime without its own ideological
hegemony, a charge of crime against humanity was not pertinent. A
law of 23 July 1992 included among victims 'those who combated the
ideological system in the name of which crimes against humanity
were perpetrated'. The law was implemented in March 1994 and
therefore relevant for the trials of Touvier and Papon.

Outcry from many quarters, including the then Prime Minister
Pierre Bérégovny, over the April 1992 court decision led the Supreme
Court on 27 November 1992 to quash it partially on appeal. The Court
did not rule or want to rule on the nature of the Vichy regime, nor did
it comment on the Milice apart from its complicity with the Gestapo.
Instead, relying on Article 6 of the statute of the Nuremberg Tribunal,
it ruled that a crime against humanity was committed by 'acting in
the interests of a European Axis country or in complicity with such a
country'. Touvier was therefore sent to trial on only one charge, after
further complications in the courts, of acting on orders of the Gestapo
to kill Jews. A single incident could constitute a crime against
humanity if it were carried out on behalf of a politics of ideological
hegemony.

Touvier was convicted by the Versailles Assize Court on 20 April
1994 of ordering the execution of seven Jews on 29 June 1944 at
Rillieux-la-Pape, as an act of retaliation for the assassination of Philippe
Henriot, the Vichy Minister of Information, by the Resistance in Paris.
The essential legal problem was tricky: did Touvier act on his own or
act on German orders? The court accepted the argument that he had
made the decision, and that this decision constituted a crime against
humanity, and not simply murder, because all the victims were Jews.
Therefore the crime was motivated against members of a religious
group to further the plan of a state practising a hegemonic ideology of
extermination based on political, racial or religious motivations.
Touvier could only be convicted if he had acted on behalf of the Nazis,
not as an official of Vichy.

Though it was never completely clear that he acted directly on
orders from the Gestapo, or was an agent of Gestapo policy, Touvier

was sentenced to life imprisonment, dying in the prison hospital in 1996 aged eighty-one. One malefactor had been justly punished, but the courts had still not dealt squarely with the question of the autonomy of Vichy. They had altered the definition of crimes against humanity to meet changing political objectives. The character of Vichy, however, and its role in the Final Solution were left undecided. The court had not uncovered the historical truth or passed judgement on the regime.

The Papon Case

The case of Papon was even more legally complicated than that of Touvier because he was a Vichy official acting in the name and with the authority of the state and contributing to the Final Solution. Maurice Papon had a charmed career that lasted through three republics and the Vichy regime; his success was attributable to native ability, good connections and a facility to cultivate and be accepted by influential people who could be useful to him. Born on 3 September 1910 at Gretz-Armainvilliers (Seine-et-Marne) of a bourgeois family, Papon was conscious of politics from an early age. His father directed the French society of glasswork makers, and also was mayor of his town from 1919 to 1937 and a member, later president, of the general council of the canton of Tournan-en-Brie. Papon was born into and adopted the republican, radical-socialist, centre-left political views of his family.

Papon studied at the prestigious Parisian *lycée*, Louis-le-Grand, and at the École des Sciences Politiques, concentrating on law and political science. He quickly began his career as an official, assisted by family friend Jacques-Louis Dumesnil, Freemason, former general councillor in the Seine-et-Marne district, and Minister of Air, who brought Papon into his entourage. Papon entered the political and administrative world, as a member of a ministerial *cabinet*, the traditional small group that assists and advises a minister.

In the four years before the war Papon occupied a number of official positions. In 1935 he became an official in the Ministry of the Interior, working under Maurice Sabatier, who was to be so influential in his life. Sabatier, born in 1897 in French Algeria, a specialist in Islamic law and also a man of the centre-left, had early ambitions to become resident-general of Algeria. A prudent, cautious individual, qualities he shared with Papon, Sabatier ascended the official ladder, partly because of his friendship with Pierre Laval.

A year later, again through family friendship with François de Tessan, parliamentary deputy of the Radical-Socialist Party and junior minister, Papon was appointed as a liaison with the Senate and in foreign affairs, where he was introduced to Islamic issues. In 1938 he returned to the Ministry of the Interior, firmly in the political camp of the centre-left. During the war, Second Lieutenant Papon went with his colonial infantry regiment to Tripoli and Syria before being demobilised in October 1940 in Clermont-Ferrand.

With no apparent hesitation the good republican and radical socialist opted to remain in the unoccupied zone, metamorphosed into a loyal supporter of the new Vichy regime. Both of his political mentors and fellow radical-socialists, Dumesnil and Tessan, had already voted to give *pleins pouvoirs* to Pétain on 10 July 1940. Papon rejoined Sabatier at the Ministry of the Interior, becoming in March 1941 a director of the ministerial *cabinet*, and organising the administration of the department.

In retrospect Papon's decision to accept the appointment can be viewed as a pivotal choice. In spring 1941 administrators were purged by Vichy: 94 officials were dismissed, 104 retired and 79 transferred. Only 27 prefects were kept in office. Some senior officials refused to remain; the best-known, Jean Moulin, attempted suicide. Those like Papon (whether senior or junior officials) who remained, implicitly accepted the validity, if not the direction, of the Vichy regime.

After Laval's return as head of government on 18 April 1942, a number of new regional prefects were appointed. One of them was Sabatier, who was given Aquitaine, in the occupied zone. Again, Papon followed him, appointed in May 1942 as secretary-general of the Gironde region located in Bordeaux, and also deputy prefect, exceptional class. At his trial, Papon explained his acceptance of the appointment as a way of getting out of Vichy because his frankness and 'verbal imprudencies' had led to his being suspected of Gaullist sentiments. In reality, as German confidential reports of April, June and July 1943 make clear, Papon was a compliant collaborator, a good negotiator with the Germans if over-evasive, and entrenched with Sabatier who co-operated with the Kommandantur.

Papon's base was in Bordeaux, a town of 200,000 in the occupied zone, though the *département* of the Gironde was divided between that zone and the unoccupied zone. Sometimes referred to as 'the capital of the defeat', the town where the French government made the decision to ask for an armistice and which was supportive of Pétain, Bordeaux was a centre of pleasurable accommodation, especially of wine trade with Germany. It was also an arena of political rivalries within the regional and local administrations, including the mayor, Adrien Marquet, an ex-socialist who supported Laval in 1940. Indeed, the legacy of the bitter infighting helps explain the appointment of

Papon, rather than a local resister, as prefect by the Gaullists after Liberation in 1944.

The German occupiers used both seductive and repressive behaviour in Bordeaux. The first commander, from June 1940 to mid-1942, General von Faber du Faur was relatively benign. He was succeeded by more sinister officials, manipulative and brutal, responsible for the shooting of 285 in the camp of Souge. Associated with them were French *auxiliares*, not friendly with Marquet, the most important of whom were the fierce anti-communist and anti-Gaullist Commissioner Pierre-Napoleon Poinsot, who became Deputy Director of Information at Vichy in May 1944, and Inspector Lucien Dehan, concerned with the Jewish issue.

The overall record of Bordeaux during the occupation is unsavoury.[8] Without counting those killed in the Resistance or civil conflicts, and the casualties caused by the Service du Travail Obligatoire, the number of victims is high: 285 hostages were shot; 900 political deportees never returned from the camps to which they were sent; 1560 Jews, of whom 223 were children, were deported to Auschwitz and their death. In light of this history a Bordeaux restaurant located near the courtroom where Papon was on trial changed its name from 'Le Petit Maréchal' to 'Les Pas Perdus'.

The gods had favoured Papon with advantages: high intelligence, patrician polish, efficient administrative ability, agreeable charm, precision in expression, and iron nerves. Yet among other facets of his character were coolness, lack of emotion or concern for others, a mordant nature, relentless ambition propelling him to ascend the ladder of success, a sense of his own self-importance, a self-righteous refusal to acknowledge wrongdoing, and a skill in evading responsibility for his actions.

At Bordeaux, Papon was the loyal assistant and administrator in the prefecture. The exact nature of his functions was to become a highly disputed matter at his trial. He supervised policies on transport, fuel, German requisitions and general relations with the Germans. He was also responsible for and signed documents of the Service of Jewish Questions. The prudent Sabatier had delegated to Papon responsibility over the most ticklish areas, especially the Jewish question, over which Papon had at least technical authority.

At his trial Papon claimed he was not a temperamental anti-Semite. He was concerned with the interests of the state, not with Jews; he kept good relations with people whom he called 'juifs intéressants'. Whatever his true inner feelings about Jews, his administration of the Service of Jewish Questions, an office of about twelve people under Pierre Garat, a member of the pro-fascist PPF in 1938, obliged him to implement the Vichy discriminatory legislation against Jews. Papon insisted that the real responsibility lay with Garat, who spoke directly to the prefect about decisions, and with the German occupiers, who decided on arrests and deportations.

This Service of Jewish Questions had two essential functions: the implementation of decisions on regulations arising from the Statuts des Juifs and other decrees, especially on the identity and number of Jews; and the process of Aryanisation of Jewish property and goods, which required naming of an *administrateur provisoire* to settle the property. Crucial to these functions was the *fichier*, the card index of Jews that was in his office and was compiled and brought up to date by the Service, which kept in close touch with the CGQJ and the German authorities. With the *fichier* the Service prepared the operations for the arrests of Jews and their transfer to Drancy.

Papon argued that the Service had not exercised police powers, but was merely a bureaucratic body, preparing decisions for the prefect and providing the best conditions of transport for the deportees. Who then was responsible for arrests? Papon denied he had authority to order arrests; he was only part of the transmission belt relaying orders from the prefect. He blamed the *intendant* of the regional police, which was linked with and colluded with German police and was not controlled by the prefecture. The German security police, which had two divisions in Bordeaux, gave direct orders to the French regional *intendant*, as in the transfer of ninety-two Jews from the Mérignac camp to Drancy in the November 1943 convoy. Papon explained that the list of Jews for the round-up by French police and gendarmerie on 11 January 1944 was supplied by the *intendant* of police, though in fact it was kept in his own office.

Papon regularly reported on the Aryanisation process in his area; in 1942, for example, 204 enterprises had been 'de-Judaised', sixty-four buildings had been sold at auctions and 493 were in the process of 'de-Judaisation'. More damning than this record of expropriation of Jewish property was the administration of arrests and deportation of Jews from his region. Starting in July 1942 and continuing, Papon gave his assent to all stages of the round-ups of Jews, signing documents ordering the arrests by French police and gendarmes, and even being concerned with the budgetary expenses of the operations and transfers.

Papon's prefecture had overall responsibility for the nearby internment camp of Mérignac, with a capacity of about 500, to which the victims were taken. It was also responsible for transferring them from the camp by bus and tram, and occasionally by taxi paid by Papon, to the Bordeaux rail station from where they were sent to Drancy.

Between 18 July 1942 and 5 June 1944, eleven convoys left Bordeaux for Drancy, carrying about 1560 people, of whom 130 were under thirteen years of age; already in the second convoy of 26 August 1942, two-year-old children were present. In the penultimate convoy of 13 May 1944, elderly Jews over seventy, who had been taken from hospitals and sanatoriums and retirement homes, made up about forty of the total of fifty. Crucial questions about the convoys were raised at Papon's trial: how many had he prepared and organised; did he know the destination of the convoys, and the destiny of Jews, after they left Drancy?

Papon remained at his post at the prefecture to the end. When challenged years later in 1981 for his failure to resign rather than carry out the discriminatory measures, he blandly replied: 'By character I did not have the taste to desert; by ideology I remained faithful to the instructions given by de Gaulle in London to officials and magistrates to remain in their posts.'

Yet Papon, like other cautious and opportunistic bureaucrats, trimmed in consonance with the changing tide of the war. An unbridled careerist, he accepted five promotions, and declined others, particularly after the German retreat in the Soviet Union, the Allied invasion of North Africa and the increased role of the Resistance. Papon refused a promotion to become prefect of Lot, a more politically exposed position. He entered into some contact, though no action, with members of the Resistance. On 25 May 1944 he gave up control over the Service of Jewish Questions.

The most brilliant demonstration of his opportunism was to convene, two days before the liberation of Bordeaux in June 1944, a meeting of heads of local police with Gaston Cusin, former senior official, designated by Michel Debré on behalf of General de Gaulle to be Commissioner of the Republic of Aquitaine.[9] Papon made the police available for the use of Cusin. Cusin, in turn, declared that Papon had sabotaged certain measures of Vichy. As a result Papon was appointed in August 1944 to the post of director of the *cabinet* of the Commissioner of the Republic and soon as prefect of Landes.

Overnight, the ex-radical socialist, the ex-Vichyite, became a Gaullist. Ignored were the views of members of the local Resistance in Bordeaux, that Papon had genuinely approved the policies of Pétain and was devoted to the Marshal and to the Laval government, and had believed that the Resistance was contrary to the best interests of France. In contrast, the Gaullist Cusin held to his own version of the past: Papon had tried to prevent the use of anonymous letters, had provided useful information about communists, and had tried to sabotage the STO. The version was accepted, or pretended to be accepted, by de Gaulle himself: a photograph of September 1944 is an emblem of the mutually useful entente, with Papon close to de Gaulle on a balcony in Bordeaux.

Papon was not the only Vichy official in the Gironde to survive and to benefit from the Gaullist leniency and desire for political and administrative stability. Papon's subordinate, Pierre Garat, was promoted to be deputy prefect of Blaye. A purge committee investigated his superior, Maurice Sabatier, the prefect whose region had a proportionally large number of deportations, in December 1944. Sabatier, another cautious career opportunist, who was rumoured to have a wife at least partly Jewish, left few traces in official documents on issues such as forbidding Jews to hold public positions in administration. Cusin spoke of him as a technician of 'haute valeur', but the more knowledgeable purge committee set up to investigate Vichy supporters was less enthusiastic. It did not condemn Sabatier but recommended he be put on half pay and transferred to a non-political administrative post. He was sent to help administer the French zone in post-war occupied Germany. Later, he was awarded the Conseiller d'État Honoraire and became *grand officier* of the Légion d'Honneur.

The seemingly indispensable chameleon Papon continued to advance. Cusin's successors in Bordeaux, Jacques Soustelle, former head of Special Services of Free France (DGSS), and Maurice Bourgès-Manoury, head of the military resistance in the southern zone and *compagnon* of the Liberation, both confirmed Papon in his post. Three resisters and prominent members of de Gaulle's entourage had thus given their *imprimatur* to the ex-Vichy official.

In autumn 1945, Papon returned to the Ministry of the Interior as deputy director of Algerian affairs and soon as *chef de cabinet* of the Deputy Minister. Papon in effect was becoming a colonial administrator for Morocco and Algeria, following a series of appointments between 1949 and 1958. In succession, he was prefect of Corsica in 1947, prefect of Constantine in 1949, secretary-general of the Paris prefecture of police in 1951, envoy to Morocco in 1954, member of the *cabinet* of the Minister of the Interior and adviser on Algerian affairs, again prefect of Constantine, and inspector-general of administration in a special mission for the region of eastern Algeria in 1956. He was virtually the proconsul for the Fourth Republic in the area. In the hostilities that had begun there, Papon was responsible for the police and acted harshly to repress violence.

Once again political events furthered his career. Demonstrations outside the National Assembly in Paris on 13 March 1958 led to the dismissal of the prefect of the Paris police; Papon was appointed to the vacant position by Bourgès-Manoury, then Minister of the Interior. Papon's political astuteness and tactical skills were again displayed when, sensing that the Fourth Republic was doomed because of events in Algeria, he turned down a ministerial appointment on Algeria in the new, and short-lived, government formed by Étienne Pflimlin in May 1958.

At the dawn of the Fifth Republic, de Gaulle, the new head of government, who ordered him to 'tendez Paris', reappointed Papon as prefect of the Paris police. Now an enthusiastic Gaullist, Papon remained in his post until January 1967. For nine years he dealt severely with the attackers who killed over sixty policemen during the violent demonstrations, rounded up Algerians in large numbers, imposed a curfew on 'Français musulmans d'Algérie' between 9.30 p.m. and 5.30 a.m., set up interrogation centres, tolerated some torture and conducted searches of hotels where immigrants lived.

On the fateful day and night of 17 October 1961 the demonstration in Paris on behalf of the Algerian FLN (the Front de Libération Nationale) led to a state of disorder during which an unknown number of the demonstrators were shot and thrown into the Seine by the police. Over 11,000 Algerians were arrested and taken to detention centres. Papon successfully blocked any serious inquiry about the event, blatantly minimising the number of casualties and justifying the massacre on political grounds. The full truth of the event is still disputed. One author, Jean-Luc Einaudi, concludes that 140 people were killed.[10] An official report, the Mandelkern report, of May 1998 states the number as between thirty and forty.

What is relevant here is that Papon lied about his role, not only at the time but also before the Cour d'Assises at his trial in Bordeaux in October 1997. He was a survivor. Papon survived the counter-demonstration by the OAS (the Organisation de l'armée secrète), wanting to keep Algeria French; the riots and the deaths in that incident in February 1962 he dismissed as an unfortunate 'bousculade' (skirmish). He survived the kidnapping in Paris and the assassination of the leader of the Moroccan opposition, Mehdi Ben Barka, in 1965.

His career as an official was over in 1967, but the next year he was elected, the first of three times, to the National Assembly as the deputy from Cher. He was now a member of the Gaullist UDR (Union des Démocrates pour la République), which made him national treasurer of the party. In the National Assembly he became president and then rapporteur of its committee on finance. With a kind of inevitable logic he was appointed in May 1978 Minister of the Budget by the new Prime Minister, Raymond Barre, in the presidency of Valéry Giscard d'Estaing. The Gaullist had now become an equally enthusiastic Giscardian. Papon had by now served three republics, the Vichy French State and three presidents of the Fifth Republic.

In 1981 his extraordinary luck finally ran out when his past caught up with him. *Le Canard Enchaîné*, a weekly celebrated for its revelations, published incriminating documents, found by a journalist whose father had been arrested in Bordeaux in October 1942, deported and killed in Auschwitz; the documents were signed by Papon and showed his role as a collaborator. Papon asked for and obtained a committee of honour, convened by the Comité d'Action de la Résistance and composed of respected members of the Resistance, presided over by Daniel Mayer. Its quick report on 15 December 1981 was ambivalent and balanced. It recognised that Papon had performed some services, soon to be shown to be insignificant, on behalf of the Resistance, but stated that he was involved in acts contrary to the conception of honour and which shocked French sensibility, though they should be regarded in the context of the wartime period. It concluded that he should have resigned in July 1942. Papon refused to resign, to ask pardon or to express public regrets: 'I carried out my duty at the peril of my liberty and my life.'

The judicial case against Papon began with complaints in December 1981 and again in May 1982 made by lawyers on behalf of families whose members had been deported from Bordeaux. The case was to take fifteen years and the legal issues were again highly complicated.[11] After a judicial inquiry began in July 1982, Papon was indicted in January 1983 for crimes against humanity. The indictment, however, was annulled on 11 February 1987 by the Cour de Cassation on complex, technical grounds, though some suspected for political reasons. On 8 July 1988 he was again indicted, as was his former superior Sabatier three months later. The latter died in April 1989 before proceedings began.

At this point, as thousands of documents in the archives of the Gironde *département* were being examined, President François Mitterrand, whose early career as a Vichy official had not yet become public knowledge, asked that the proceedings against Papon be halted in the interests of 'civil peace'. For his part the defiant Papon counter-attacked, comparing himself with Captain Dreyfus, also unjustly accused of offences he had not committed, and seeing his plight as 'a long Calvary'. Papon may not have been explicitly anti-Semitic, but his characterisation of his main opponent, Serge Klarsfeld, as someone paid by 'an American organisation constituted by German Jews, naturalized as Americans' raises doubts.

Delay continued, though new charges were brought in 1990 and 1992. In July 1995 the Cour d'Appel of Bordeaux took up the case and concluded that it should go to the Cour d'Assises. On 18 September 1996 the three judges of the Chambre d'Accusation (the Indicting Chamber) of the Court of Appeals in Bordeaux sent the indictment for complicity in crimes against humanity to the Court of Appeals of the Gironde, a decision that was upheld by the Cour de Cassation on 23 January 1997.

In refusing to dismiss the case, the Indicting Chamber rejected Papon's claim to have been a resister or to have saved Jews. Unlike Mitterrand, he was not one of the *Vichysto-résistants*, officials who made contact with the Resistance after November 1942, the Allied landing in North Africa and the German entrance into the unoccupied zone. No proof emerged that Papon was in the organised Resistance movement, though he may have provided some occasional aid. The Court held that French people knew of the fate of Jews after deportation from France and the unlikelihood they would return to France.

The Chamber spoke of Papon's role in the arrest, sequestration and deportation of Jews which led to their death. It held that Papon's knowledge of Nazi intentions to exterminate Jews was 'clear, reasoned, detailed and continuous', and that this constituted premeditation even if he was unaware of the exact conditions or technical means of that extermination. Papon could have refused to obey illegal orders. Unsurprisingly, Papon declared that the Court's conclusion was 'scandalous', providing an opportunity for communists, leftist groups and foreigners to smear France by linking Vichy with the Holocaust.

Papon's case was different from that of Touvier. Papon had apparently not acted on the basis of anti-Semitism or ideology, but simply in his own career self-interest, indifferent to the fate of victims. His defence argued he had not adhered to Nazi hegemonic political ideology and so he could not be charged for complicity in crimes against humanity on the basis of the Court's 1994 ruling. However, was Papon guilty of knowing the fate of the deportees sent to 'the east' and therefore tacitly approving of the Nazi objective? Was he in effect an agent of the Germans? To fit this entangled issue the Supreme Court of Appeal in January 1997 changed the relevant legal definition, ruling that it was not necessary for proof of complicity in crimes against humanity to require adherence to 'ideological hegemony' by the perpetrators of those crimes. It returned to the Nuremberg definition, which did not require that the accused adhere to this policy or belong to any of the organisations declared criminal at Nuremberg. For the Court it was enough that Papon had facilitated the preparation and consummation of the crimes against humanity.

Finally, on 8 October 1997 the trial began in the Bordeaux Court of

Assizes. Papon was, and will remain, the highest-ranking French official and only the second French citizen to be tried for crimes or complicity in crimes against humanity in the war years. He came to judgement in an atmosphere that had changed. The Church had officially apologised for its role in the anti-Semitic persecution, as had a number of professional organisations. Papon's condemnation of the trial as 'falsified history, a masquerade unworthy of a law-abiding state' had less salience in this changed atmosphere.

Why Papon? Was it he or the Vichy regime on trial? If Papon was acquitted, would Vichy too be acquitted? Papon referred to himself as 'the designated guilty man, a necessary symbol. Not a man but a myth.' His defence was that he was only doing his job. Other potentially designated guilty persons were not available. Maurice Sabatier had died in April 1989 before being tried in court. Réne Bousquet and Jean Leguay were also indicted. The latter died in July 1989 before trial, and the former was assassinated on 8 June 1993. Papon, eighty-six years old when the trial started, was clearly the last person of any consequence who could be tried for acts committed during the war.

Papon was on trial; but simultaneously, for those seeking justice, so was Vichy in that thirty-seven persons in their individual capacities as survivors and witnesses of the persecution in France, and fourteen associations, human rights and Jewish groups, were plaintiffs, charging Papon with crimes against humanity and complicity in those crimes. The court, three judges and nine jurors, their ages ranging from thirty-one to sixty-one were faced with 760 questions, the depositions of many witnesses, lists of deportees who testified about arrest and deportations of Jews from the Bordeaux area, and commentary and analysis by distinguished historians. Memory and history had truly come together.

Not surprisingly in view of the wealth of information and disputed history, the trial took six months, the longest criminal trial in French history. The Barbie trial took less than eight weeks, and the Touvier trial less than six weeks. Ironically, the determined prosecutor, Marc Robert, in the Papon case had a few years earlier acquiesced in the pressure by François Mitterrand to delay the trial of René Bousquet on similar charges; Bousquet was a much more important official than Papon, but an old friend of the President.

Papon's trial ended on 2 April 1998 with a mixed result. Papon was found guilty of complicity in the arrests and detention of Jews, but not of complicity in extermination. Papon's defence went beyond the usual argument that he was obliged to obey orders. He disclaimed responsibility for the arrests and deportation of Jews, insisting that the police power was wielded by the prefect who made the decisions, even if he, Papon, signed documents including arrest warrants in the prefect's name. He claimed to have saved 139 Jews from deportation, warned some Jews about the police round-ups in Bordeaux, protected the town rabbi, provided some comforts for those transported from Bordeaux to Drancy, and given help to the Resistance. He tried to save 'interesting' Jews, usually war heroes. He persisted in claiming ignorance of the ultimate murder of the deported from Drancy, though he knew they faced a 'cruel fate'. If he organised the transport of the arrested first to the camp of Mérignac and then to Drancy, it was in obedience to his official superiors and the German authorities.

Papon was unyielding to the end. The arrogant, ambitious, well-groomed, highly articulate careerist expressed no remorse, no regret and no emotion except in his own defence. Evidence about him was a mass of 'lies, insults and infamies' drawn from the gutter of the media to poison public opinion. In conversation with the historian Michel Bergès before his trial, Papon spoke not only of 'the communist strategy against the *réparable* Gaullist that I was', but also of 'l'action occulte' of American organisations that manipulated the topic of the deportation or spoliation of Jews.

The evidence against Papon was compelling. The *procureur général*, Henri Desclaux, did not find any instance of 'sabotage' by Papon to prevent or delay that deportation. Even small details, such as the bill paid by his office for bringing two Jewish children of five and two by taxi to the police station in Bordeaux, show his involvement. On the question of deporting some Jews in July 1942, Papon wrote: 'Objet: refoulement de juifs étrangers.' When asked by Jean-Louis Castagnède, the chief judge at his trial, to explain *réfoulement*, Papon replied that it was ambiguous and a term used by police administration.

In essence, Papon was found guilty of complicity in crimes against humanity only for the illegal arrest of thirty-seven persons and the 'arbitrary sequestrations' of fifty-three people, and for his actions regarding four of the ten convoys that took Jews from the Mérignac camp to Drancy between July 1942 and January 1944. Though the prosecutor called for twenty years and others expected life imprisonment, Papon was given the relatively light sentence of ten years. It was another compromise decision: on the one hand, he had no personal adherence to objectives sought by the Nazis; on the other, he was part of the collective process of criminality. For the Court, facilitators of crimes against humanity were as guilty as those who originate and execute the crimes.

From the first public revelations about Papon in Vichy, it took seventeen years before judgement and at least partial conviction. With all the evasions, concealments and obstructions put forward by his defence and aided by the improbable alliance of influential ex-Vichyites and Gaullists, Papon, the man supposedly dedicated to law and order, made a mockery of the French judicial system. Justice was delayed and might have been completely denied but for a few dedicated people who appreciated the importance of the revelations in the accurate official documentation of Papon's activities for Vichy.

Papon's cynical disregard for the law and contempt for his accusers persisted even after the verdict. During the six-month trial, and while on appeal, Papon was free from prison except for three days at the beginning. In a week that coincided with Yom Kippur, Papon conspicuously dined and drank *grands crus* at a three-star restaurant in the area, and stayed for at least two nights in a four-star hotel. At the beginning of his trial, arguing that he should not be kept in custody, he said, 'having served the law all my life, I am not going to start betraying it at my age'. On 11 October 1999 he betrayed it by fleeing France rather than turning himself in for at least one day, as required by law, before his hearing by the highest appeals court. The Court automatically confirmed his ten-year sentence because his non-appearance lost him the right of appeal.

Contrary to logic, Papon had been allowed to keep his passport after conviction, and had used it to flee to Switzerland; he believed that country did not recognise the law of crimes against humanity. After fascinating collaborative detective work, he was arrested in a hotel in Gstaad and returned to France. He had not appreciated that the Swiss Minister of Justice would not shelter an individual convicted of complicity in crimes against humanity in a country already sensitive about its own wartime record about Jews, and the holdings of Jewish assets by its banks and private citizens.

At his arrest in Gstaad, Papon had a considerable amount of French, Swiss and United States money, three passports, one of which was not in his name, and driver's licences in different names. Clearly, he had been aided in breaking the law, probably by a secret network of retired military men and some Resistance figures close to conservative Catholic organisations, and by a shadowy group called Résistance, Verité, Souvenir. These individuals, some of whom were lawyers and former ministers, including Guy de Beaufort, a Resistance fighter who had once cleared Papon, still viewed Papon as unjustly convicted and as a scapegoat.

Certainly Papon himself felt he was unjustly treated and tried other means to escape his fate. His appeal to President Chirac for a plea for pardon based on medical grounds was rejected on 7 March 2000. The Minister of Justice, Marylise Lebranchu, refused to consider an early release for him because Papon had expressed neither regret nor remorse; Papon refused such expression 'for a crime I did not commit and for which I am in no way an accomplice'. In June 2001, his appeal to the European Court of Human Rights for release from prison was also rejected. The Court refused to accept his argument that his sentence of ten years violated the European Convention of Human Rights of 1950, which outlawed 'inhuman or degrading treatment or punishment'. Unsuccessful in evading his punishment, Papon still continued to evade the spirit of the law. In 2001 he was organising his insolvency by selling or giving his children valuable properties to avoid paying legal costs and damages resulting from his trial.

Is the Papon trial the last episode in the history of Vichy, and the end of the Vichy syndrome? Papon was not the victim of a vendetta but a man belatedly brought to justice for inexcusable actions in allowing innocent people to be sent to their death in Auschwitz. Like so many others, including François Mitterrand, he expressed no apologies for his actions. His last public statement, a letter of 19 October 1999 in *Sud-Ouest*, was a long revealing exercise in self-pity. In this letter, written to explain his flight from France, he argued that exile was the only course compatible with honour. He would return when 'republican legality' had been restored. The judicial system was guilty of bad faith, of biased accusations, of using selected documents, and of being 'under influence' of unnamed persons. On the other hand, he had acted in the name of honest and faithful officials of the Republic, and in the name of the Resistance. He even blamed the *procureur général* at his trial in Bordeaux for the death of his wife in March 1998 as a result of his indictment. The prosecutor, Marc Robert, compared Papon with Pontius Pilate, who 'simply handed over the Jews and washed his hands'. In his turn Papon compared himself and his sufferings to Jesus.

Papon was neither a martyr nor an innocent scapegoat. Rather the record of his activities as an official and the documentation of his trial provide an opportunity to examine a number of relevant issues about the Vichy regime and attempts to deal in post-war years with those who participated in it. These issues include the question of crimes against humanity; the nature and degree of responsibility of officials, administrators and judges for their activities; and the extent to which an individual may be punished for those activities.

Much ink has been spilled over Hannah Arendt's phrase 'the banality of evil', in her book on the Eichmann trial in Jerusalem.[12] It is an inadequate term for official behaviour and abdication of responsibility for monstrous actions. Papon was not an Eichmann, a sadist ideologically involved in carrying out the Final Solution. He claimed not to have been anti-Semitic, though some language and references at his trial suggest otherwise in a moderate fashion. He was a facilitator, not a perpetrator, as was the senior official, Bousquet. He was not a Nazi sympathiser but an uncritical cog in the machinery of collaboration and the process that led to genocide. He was indifferent, not barbaric; a professional eager to advance and doing nothing to harm his career. He personified those senior and middle-level officials, intelligent and urbane, who had no personal animosity towards their victims.

Why did this middle-level bureaucrat remain in office in Vichy? He defended himself in heroic style: 'I preferred to dirty my hands in the frightful collective and human dramas.' Staying in one's position, he declared, sometimes took more courage than resigning. For him 'the administration remained the only bulwark against the occupiers. He spoke of the 'dramatic friability' of the period of the Occupation, the demands of the Germans and the absence of loopholes.

The essential problem remains. Were Vichy officials able to act, wholly or in part, in an autonomous fashion in making decisions, or were they subject to German *imperium*? No categorical answer is available on this particular question, since much depends on a variety of factors: the zone and the geographical area where officials were located; the real political sympathies of the bureaucrats; the time factor; the state of public opinion and the Church; the precise issues and the personalities involved. Interestingly and unexpectedly, the historian Michel Bergès, who had at first been critical of Papon, changed his mind and in his book *La Vérité n'Interessait Personne*, appears to accept the importance of German pressure on the prefecture of Bordeaux.

The Papon trial showed that the vicissitudes of the Vichy syndrome and sharp internal differences about the nature of the regime, the role of officials and the appropriate punishment for participants in the system had not yet ended. One particularly revealing cross-current in the trial was the heated defence by adherents of the Gaullist legacy of de Gaulle's attitude towards Vichy actions and personnel. This evidence was not without ambivalence. Philippe Seguin, then the feisty leader of the Gaullist party, the RPR, argued that Vichy was a usurping regime and had not represented the true France, which did not have to blush for what happened between 1940 and 1944. He also warned that the trial was taking place in 'a climate of collective atonement and self-flagellation'.

A fellow Gaullist, Pierre Messmer, former Prime Minister and Defence Minister, urged French people to 'stop hating each other and to begin to forgive themselves'; he also criticised President Chirac for apologising for Vichy's treatment of Jews. Chirac had gone too far in saying that the French people must recognise the worst as well as the best in their country and must take responsibility for the whole of its history, the Vichy government and the Resistance fighters and those who saved Jews. Olivier Guichard, one of the grand barons of Gaullism, recounted the pertinent few, terse words of de Gaulle in 1958, 'Papon a rendu de grands services à Cusin' when the latter was the newly appointed Commissioner of the Republic in 1944, without specifying the nature of the services. Gaston Cusin, who had appointed Papon despite the opposition of local Resistance fighters in the Gironde, thought the trial was unjust.

This surprisingly strong reluctance by the Gaullists to see Papon condemned reminded people that the Gaullist position on Vichy was not unproblematic. The General himself never spoke publicly in criticism of the Statuts des Juifs. He was more concerned with the Occupation than with the deportation and fate of Jews. Above all, de Gaulle was eager to unify the country. For him Vichy had not legally existed; its acts were null and void. His ordinance of 9 August 1944 stated that the first act of re-establishing republican government was the declaration that 'the form of government of France is and remains the Republic. In law it has never ceased to exist.' On taking power in 1944, he could therefore retain most of the Vichy officials, including Papon as a new prefect. While President of the Fifth Republic, de Gaulle appointed as his three Prime Ministers people who had been Vichy officials for a time or non-resisters: Michel Debré, member of the Conseil d'État until 1943; Georges Pompidou, teacher in Paris throughout the war; and Maurice Couve de Murville, diplomat and official in the Finance Ministry until November 1942.

Noticeably, both of the two leading politicians at the time of the Papon trial, neither of whom were adults during the war, were critical of Vichy. Chirac was the first President of the Fifth Republic to be publicly critical of the French past. Lionel Jospin, the socialist Prime Minister, held that the trial was justified because it threw light on an illegitimate state and on the inhuman acts of a misled (devoyé) state. Was France looking its past in the face?

The Unresolved Case of Bousquet

If one person is now seen as symbolically illustrating both the role of senior officials in Vichy in serving and operating the machinery of government in an orderly fashion, and also the disabused reaction in recent years to the regime, it is Réne Bousquet, the handsome, elegant, ambitious, insincere careerist, 'un fort joli garçon', in the spiteful words of Joseph Barthélemy.[13] By a trick of fate and turn of events he found bewildering, his career, continuously successful and monetarily rewarding, ended in abject humiliation and death by assassination.

Coming from a middle-class background in Montauban, the son of a radical-socialist lawyer, Bousquet began his precocious career in the prefectoral body of France in 1930 when at the age of twenty he became chief of staff (*chef de cabinet*) of the local prefect of Tarn-et-Garonne. The next year he received a gold medal and the Légion d'Honneur for his brave rescue of people who were drowning. Sympathetic to centre-left politics in pre-war France, friendly with Roger Salengro, the socialist Minister of the Interior, and a protégé of Pierre Laval, the ambitious Bousquet advanced rapidly before and during the war in the official hierarchy.

In September 1940, aged thirty-one, Bousquet was appointed by Pétain to be prefect in the Marne district, one of the 166 appointments in the prefectoral corps, many of whom had served the Third Republic. He was then the youngest prefect in the country. A year later, he was promoted to regional prefect of Champagne. Paradoxically, he had broken the record of Jean Moulin, the legendary hero of the Resistance, who had been the youngest prefect in 1937 at the age of thirty-eight. Their destinies were to be totally different.

Two roads diverged; both could not be travelled. Why did Bousquet accept the positions of prefect and follow the wrong path? At his trial in 1949 he repeated his formula of 1940: he wanted to maintain the sovereignty of France, to reorganise the administration, to provide food for the population. He had approved, if in careful, equivocal and somewhat elliptical fashion, the policy of 'Franco-German collaboration as Marshal Pétain defines it'. This collaboration included vigilance in tracking down and repressing communist activities. A number of communists were arrested by the French police at his instigation as prefect and handed over to the Germans to be shot: the exponent of 'French national sovereignty' was sacrificing Frenchmen to the German police by collaboration.

After Pierre Laval returned to power in April 1942, Bousquet was appointed in Vichy as secretary-general, head, of the national police, a position he held until December 1943, with control of the police in both zones of the country. He envisaged himself as making a sacrifice to keep right-wing extremists from coming to power. As head of the police he was to deal with and collaborate with the German agencies and individuals responsible for security and maintenance of order in France, and with implementation of the discriminatory measures, exclusion, arrest, internment and deportation of Jews.

Those German agencies were riddled with personal rivalries and friction over jurisdiction. At first the Geheime Feldpolizei (GFP), under the Military Command, and the Feldgendarmerie (Field Police) were responsible for security of German troops. In 1942 the GFP was transferred to the Sicherheitspolizei (Security Police), led by Helmut Knochen from 1940 to 1944, eager to carry out the Final Solution against Jews in France. With only 2200 men the Sicherheitspolizei was totally dependent on French police to preserve order.

Knochen's approach was shared by Theodor Dannecker, who had worked for Reinhard Heydrich and was a protégé of Adolf Eichmann. Dannecker, in Paris from August 1940 until July 1942, when he quarrelled with Knochen, his superior, and was replaced by Heinz Roethke, had as his chief priority the strict application of anti-Semitic measures, insistence on deportations and creation of anti-Semitic organisations and propaganda. Dannecker organised the first large arrest of Jews in the 11th *arrondissement* of Paris in May 1941. In March 1942 he accompanied the first convoy from France to Auschwitz.

A less extreme position was that of Karl Oberg, head of the German police in occupied France, and a protégé of Heydrich. Oberg stopped the shooting of hostages for attacks on German soldiers in France, and was primarily concerned with maintaining order in France and preventing a rupture with Vichy. It was Oberg who negotiated agreements with Bousquet over the use of French police, on whom the fulfilment of German demands depended. From these negotiations with Oberg and other German officials came the participation of France in the Final Solution. The brilliant French civil servant became the accomplice of the executioner.

Three weeks after taking office, Bousquet on 6 May 1942 met in Paris with Heydrich, head of the RSHA Reichssicherheitshauptamt (Reich Security Office), Oberg and Knochen, and soon was to meet with Himmler. In the discussions on impending deportation of Jews from France, and on the role of French police, Bousquet brought up the question of whether foreign Jews in camps in the unoccupied zone might be included together with those in the occupied zone. French police would collaborate with their German counterparts in the struggle against the common enemy, and would act as independent executors of orders.

Negotiations between Bousquet and Oberg over the next two months dealt with variations on this basic theme. At the crucial meeting on 2 July 1942, agreement was reached that French police could act autonomously, that they would arrest and help deport foreign Jews from the occupied zone, and later from the unoccupied zone. Bousquet suggested a new census of Jews that would distinguish between French and foreign Jews.[14] He also proposed a new committee to deal with the Jewish question, directed by the CGQJ but on which he and his delegate, Leguay, would have leading roles.

The infamous bargain had been made. The French police would act against Jews, resisters and 'enemies of the Reich'; in return, Germany recognised the 'independence' of the French in these actions. For the moment, the question of arrest of French Jews was in abeyance. The French police would arrest foreign Jews in Paris and would deliver 10,000 foreign Jews from the unoccupied zone, but they would not arrest French citizens, at least not at first.

Vichy agreed that foreign Jews would be deported from both zones. These Jews, in Laval's filthy language 'déchets expédiés', would be sent so that French Jews could be saved. To salve any collective conscience of the Vichy ministers, they were assured that the destination of the deported was 'a state in eastern Europe'.

Bousquet directed the round-ups of the foreign Jews in the Vél d'Hiv in Paris on 16 July 1942 and in the unoccupied zone during 26–8 August, and their transfer to deportation camps. Bousquet assured Oberg that he wanted an effective collaboration in common interests, that he would support the German security services and work closely with local heads of the German police, and that he preferred arrests of Jews in one mass round-up rather than several smaller ones that would permit Jews to escape, hide or flee to neighbouring neutral countries.[15]

In July and August 1942 about 10,000 foreign Jews were arrested by French police in the unoccupied zone as well as the over 13,000 in the Vél d'Hiv in Paris. One of Bousquet's most callous acts was his secret telegram of 18 August 1942 to prefects ordering them to annul the provisions allowing certain categories of Jewish children to be exempted from the police round-ups; he pressed for deportation of those under eighteen.[16] Another of his brutal messages was sent on 22 August 1942 to regional prefects to crush all resistance, to intensify police operations to bring Jews together, and to prevent them from escaping so that their areas would be totally freed of foreign Jews.[17] Sanctions would be taken against officials who did not implement these policies, who were passive or who closed their eyes to evasions. Bousquet dismissed criticism. To Pastor Boegner, head of the Protestant Church, who saw him and Laval in Vichy on 11 September 1942 and brought up the issue of Jewish children being deported, he replied in terms of 'reasons of state'.[18] To silence criticism by clerics, he threatened to eliminate state subsidies for parochial schools.

On the other hand, Bousquet was praised by German authorities. A telegram to Berlin from Ambassador Abetz said, 'General von Stülpnagel commented on the help given by the French police.'

Himmler agreed with Oberg that 'Bousquet was a precious collaborator in the cadre of police collaboration.'[19] Himmler was impressed by the personality of Bousquet, who would be a dangerous adversary if he were in the opposite camp. The French police would be regarded as executors of the orders of the occupation authorities.[20] In Limoges they were put at the disposal of the SS commander.

To carry out his tasks, Bousquet negotiated with Oberg to obtain sufficient weapons. He continued his war against the Resistance, hunted Jews and pressed Laval unsuccessfully to promulgate a decree denaturalising Jews who had acquired French nationality since 1927. He also personally took charge of the French police in the large round-up in Marseille and was present while the methodical destruction of part of the city was taking place between 22 and 24 January 1943. He presided over an operation by 10,000 French police; a celebrated photograph shows Bousquet, smiling and elegant as always, in the company of SS officials, including the head of the German police in the area, and Vichy administrators. All Jews, French or foreign, were arrested in systematic fashion.[21] Bousquet's tenure as police chief was concluded at the end of December 1943, partly because of German pressure to have him dismissed out of concern about his increasing reluctance to implement their policies, and partly because of internal friction with Darnand, who replaced him in the position. The friction arose when a friend of both Bousquet and Laval was assassinated; Darnand freed the killers after Bousquet found and arrested them. He and his family left France in June 1944 with the help of Oberg for temporary exile in Germany.

At his trial in 1949 Bousquet displayed his usual cleverness. When charged, among other accusations, with collaborating in the policy of racial persecution, which otherwise could not have been pursued in France by the Germans without much more difficulty, he replied, with his clever, sordid word-play, that if he upheld that policy it would be as if 'la corde soutient le pendu' (the rope supported the hanged man); the truth was it was collaboration 'du paratonnerre et de la foudre' (the lightning rod and the lightning). Bousquet was not tried for crimes against humanity since no French law was pertinent on the issue until 1964, and thus the question of arrest and deportation of Jews was not central to his case in 1949.[22]

In the High Court in 1949, Bousquet was convicted of 'national indignité' and sentenced to five years of national degradation, loss of civil rights. The sentence was immediately commuted because of Bousquet's 'acts of resistance'; François Mitterrand was to call him a 'man of exceptional standing'. The first amnesty for those found guilty of collaboration had been announced by Mitterrand as Minister of

Information at the time. Bousquet regretted nothing and admitted he would do the same thing if he were in the same situation again. He had got the Germans to acknowledge that the French police was an autonomous body. He had always acted in the interests of and was a servant of the state.

After his minor setback, Bousquet flourished in the business world. He was the typical, solid, respectable upper-class resident of the 16th *arrondissement* in Paris. He became a senior executive in the Banque d'Indochine and served on the board of Banque Indo-Suez and a dozen other corporate boards and newspapers. In 1958 he ran for parliament, having obtained a year earlier from the Conseil d'État an annulment of his exclusion from the Légion d'Honneur. He lost his race but became the *éminence grise* of the influential regional daily *La Dépêche du Midi*, sitting on its administrative board. The paper enthusiastically supported in 1965 the first presidential bid of Mitterrand, who afterwards referred to Bousquet as a friend who 'a rendu des services', and explained that life is not black or white; it is 'gris clair et gris foncé'.[23] Few at the time realised he could have been referring to himself as much as to Bousquet.

The forgotten past of Bousquet came to light in an explosive interview with Louis Darquier de Pellepoix in *L'Express* in 1978, indicating the central role of the former police chief in the deportation of Jews for a year and a half. By chance, indictments of other individuals were taking place at this time. German war criminals, such as Kurt Lischka, former head of the SiPo-SD in Paris, Herbert Hagen, head of the SiPo-SD in Bordeaux, and Ernst Heinrichsohn, aide to Dannecker and Rothke, were all brought to justice.

In 1979 the lawyer and activist Serge Klarsfeld filed a legal complaint against Jean Leguay, and he was indicted, the first French citizen to be charged with crimes against humanity. Jean Leguay had followed Bousquet in junior positions in his prefectures, before being appointed as Bousquet's delegate in the occupied zone. He served as intermediary between Bousquet and the German authorities, and as liaison with the prefects in that zone. In the post-war period, Leguay had worked for French companies in Britain and the United States. Justice worked slowly; after ten years of indictment and collection of evidence by the courts, no trial had taken place before Leguay died of cancer in July 1989.

In that year Klarsfeld filed a complaint against Bousquet also for crimes against humanity, after making public accusations against him six years earlier. Legal attempts to delay any trial were successful for a while. However, in November 1990 the Indictments Division of the Court of Appeals in Paris declared itself competent to deal with the

Bousquet case. After rejection of his appeal in January 1991, Bousquet was finally indicted that year after eight years of investigation. Before the case could come to trial, Bousquet was assassinated on 8 June 1993 by a right-wing individual. The killer was a seemingly deranged writer, who had previously tried to kill Barbie in May 1987, who spoke of his divine 'errance' and who was diagnosed as subject to 'narcissistic psychosis'.[24]

As with the case of Leguay, the mills of justice against Bousquet ground exceedingly slowly. In the case of Bousquet, however, it seems plausible that he was being protected, probably by President François Mitterrand. Bousquet had partly financed Mitterrand's visit to China in 1960 and had supported the latter's presidential bid in 1965. When Mitterrand made the general comment that new trials concerning the events of Vichy would do more damage to 'national reconciliation' in a divided nation than 'a tardy justice meted out to a few old men for acts committed half a century ago', he did not mention that one of those 'old men' was his dinner partner.[25]

Bousquet is now a symbol of the hidden face of collaboration, that of senior officials, prefects, magistrates, police chiefs. He was not the frightful Barbie, the villainous Touvier, the pliant Papon refusing to acknowledge responsibility. Bousquet was not an example of the 'banality of evil', whatever that phrase means; he was the state, serving it and wielding a significant part of its administrative machinery. He served the state, and he facilitated the Holocaust.

Bousquet may have harboured anti-Semitic and xenophobic views, as Klarsfeld suggests, but he was not an ideological anti-Semite. He may not even have approved the anti-Jewish measures of Vichy, but he never expressed disapproval of them and from his appointment as police chief on 18 April 1942 he implemented them and was as responsible as anyone in the government and administration for complicity in crimes against humanity. His role in allowing the French police to participate in the arrest and deportation of innocent people may have, as he later argued, been essential for harmonious relations with Germany, but it is a lasting disgrace for France.

Bousquet portrayed himself, and was seen by friends, as intelligent, dynamic, a good administrator and competent technician, pragmatic, efficient, successful in everything he touched. A republican of the centre-left, he remained faithful to radical associates, even Freemasons. He served the state in Vichy, as in the Third Republic, without truly approving the National Revolution. He was courteous and dignified in dealings with the German occupiers.

Yet this was only part of the complex Bousquet. His place in history rests on his approval of most of the over 75,000 Jewish deportations.

From his early career onwards, he was always a manoeuvrer, rejecting extremes, adapting in an assured, even megalomanic fashion in the quest to exercise power. He was the cold, calculating collaborator. His price for 'French national sovereignty' was the sacrifice of innocent Jews.[26]

Many had hoped that Vichy's policies and actions would be revealed in the trials of those active during the regime. To some extent, the trials of Touvier and Papon, and the indictment of Bousquet, individuals at the centre of judicial investigation, illustrate the different levels of complicity and responsibility for war crimes and crimes against humanity. Touvier was a fascist, a willing collaborator and an unscrupulous war criminal. Bousquet and Papon were respectable senior civil servants who claimed they were defending and protecting the French people from the occupying power.

Yet it is plain that the trials did not in themselves lead to an authoritative judgement on the actions of Vichy France. Many actions of Vichy, including those against members of the Resistance, were not raised. Valuable though trials for crimes against humanity and war crimes are to clarify the historical record, to caution against extreme and inhumane ideologies and to uphold international principles of justice, they did not determine the guilt or innocence of an entire regime. A moral victory was won by conviction of Touvier and Papon, but the debate about Vichy was not settled.

CHAPTER 12

SERVANTS OF THE
STATE AND THE LAW

At the start of the Second World War, about 700,000 civilian officials, including 440,000 full-time career people, 100,000 occasional auxiliary officials and the rest categorised as workers, were part of the highly diversified French central administrative structure. Though not monolithic and though generalisations on the matter must be treated with caution, the body of officials as a whole generally reflected a politically moderate position, marked, as Baruch suggests, more by radicalism, of the French republican kind, than by the spirit of the right-wing Action Française, and more prone to attitudes of xenophobia than to any strong anti-Semitism.

The disturbing question is why so many of this highly intelligent and well-educated group of functionaries, grounded in honourable republican principles, readily abandoned those principles and accepted and applied policies of exclusion and repression and anti-Semitic regulations with minimal opposition or concern. Like other groups in the country, the functionaries were affected by the war and by the defeat of France in 1940. About 26,000 officials were POWs. Almost all of the 3400 Jewish officials were dismissed from public service. By spring 1941 some 5000 officials, including Freemasons, communists and Gaullists as well as Jews, had been dismissed. Changes were evident. Officialdom now reflected a more right-wing Vichy political outlook. In addition, some senior officials and technocrats were transformed into political ministers. Yves Bouthillier, *inspecteur de finance*, senior official in the Treasury Department, became minister there for two years and then went to the Cour des Comptes. Jérôme Carcopino, classicist and university rector, became Minister of Education.

The senior traditional bureaucracy made the administrative machinery run and also dispensed power. These officials were the necessary cogs in the machine, the highly competent and efficacious people who served the Vichy regime loyally, virtually without dissent, with some exceptions, in implementing orders. Freed from the political parliamentary control that some found objectionable in the Third

Republic, the officials were crucial in the new authoritarian regime. Individuals such as Maurice Lagrange, in the secretariat of the Vice-President of the Council of Ministers; Jean-Pierre Ingrand, delegated to Paris by the Minister of the Interior; Jean Giroud, *maître des requêtes* at the Conseil d'État, who became director of legislation at the CGQJ; all were generally unknown to the public but played a vital role. Because of the accusations against him and the indictments starting in the late 1970s, René Bousquet, head of the national police in Vichy from April 1942 until December 1943, has become the best known of the administrative elite group.

Before his appointment Bousquet had been a *départemental* prefect. Originating in the years of Napoleon, the prefects of France, whose operating premises – authority, order, hierarchy – were those on which the authoritarian Vichy state was based, had their powers extended with the suspension of elected general councils in the *départements* and the ending of the national legislature that might exercise parliamentary control over them. Through a series of laws from October 1940 onwards, their powers were reinforced in many areas. They could dissolve the municipal councils, name mayors of communes with fewer than 10,000 people, supervise the discriminations placed on Jews, assign them to residences and to administrative internments, and execute anti-Semitic measures and policies, such as arrangements for deportation.

To ensure conformity, purges were made in the corps of prefects: by the end of August 1940 only twenty-seven remained in the posts to which they had been appointed during the Third Republic. Within a year of the creation of Vichy, of the people working in the offices of the prefectures over 270 had been dismissed or transferred.[2] Though the prefectoral corps supposedly exemplified stability, considerable turnover occurred. During the Vichy years over 220 prefects were appointed to administer the then ninety-seven *départements* in France. Those who remained in office were regarded as politically acceptable to the German occupiers or as collaborators.

Like the rest of the senior administration and the country as a whole, not all prefects were in fact collaborators. Some were active or discreet or passive resisters. Most familiar in the first group was Jean Moulin, who resigned from his post as prefect at Chartres before becoming de Gaulle's representative in France. Other heroic figures included Édouard Bonnefoy, regional prefect at Lyon, and Alfred Golliard, prefect of the Jura, deported and killed in August 1944.[3] Most prefects were prudent, fulfilling their functions and, with few exceptions, taking the oath of loyalty to Pétain, the head of state, which was extended to them in January 1941. Some were notorious collaborators. Among the worst of these were Angelo Chiappe in Orléans, Pierre Le Baube in

Amiens, Georges Reige in Caen, Jacques Morane, regional prefect in the Loiret, and Fernand Carles in the Nord. Prefects on both sides paid a price. Of those who were critical of collaboration, thirty-six prefects and deputy prefects were killed, either by deportation or in the Resistance; another thirty-five who were deported returned to France in 1945. Of the collaborators, at Liberation many were punished or purged; only twenty were kept in their positions.

The senior officials in the administration were generally not Pétainists or advocates of any ideology or of anti-Semitic positions. They exemplified neutrality, legality and continuity of the state institutions. Some may have aided individual Jews, but few protested in any way against the discriminatory legislation and persecution of Jews. This elite group of senior administrators was in essence a political entity, the engine of the new French State. Their behaviour varied to some extent depending on the issues, timing of the events, changing political leaders, and the extent of their commitment or genuine sympathy with Vichy policies. In particular, behaviour altered in April 1942 with the return to power of Pierre Laval, who was cynical about the 'Révolution Nationale' and was ever ready to make deals.

In the last year of Vichy, faced by mounting problems, the STO, increasing friction between the administrators and the regular police, and the Milice, and by Allied victories against the Germans, some administrators became more cautious and more passive, and even turned towards resistance. Some officials played a 'double game', staying in touch with resisters while remaining at their posts. Others, such as Maurice Couve de Murville, who worked in the Ministry of Finance from September 1940 until March 1943, joined first General Giraud in North Africa, and then de Gaulle. A number of officials fall into the category of *Vichysto-résistant*, people who went from collaboration to resistance partly out of career motivation.

After Liberation, dossiers of some 300,000 public officials, about 1 per cent of the French population, were looked at for possible misdeeds. About 60 per cent were shelved, and three quarters of the other 125,000 were condemned in some fashion. Between 22,000 and 28,000 officials were subjected to some sentence, but most of the administrative elite suffered no punishment.

Administrative behaviour, a pot-pourri of accommodations, can be viewed as being derived from a variety of motivations: submission to political power; hope of professional advancement; career opportunism; authoritarian or patrician style; delight in exercising power unrestrained by elected politicians; and efficient contribution to the administrative machine. Official loyalty was to the principles and practices of order, hierarchy and authority rather than to democratic values. Above all, obedience. Very few officials refused to take the oath of loyalty to Pétain in 1941. Even admitting that the Jewish question was not central for many of them, that anti-Semitic sentiments were not uncommon, and that exclusion of Jews was not entirely distasteful to some of them, it is still striking that not one prefect or sub-prefect resigned because of the round-ups of Jews, and few made more than mild critical comment.

The Culture of Obedience

The long tradition or 'culture' of obedience in French administration, the tradition of following instructions without asking questions, is the most convincing explanation of the behaviour of the officials. If challenge emerged from officials, it resulted from meddling in the administrative system by political personalities in Vichy, not from ideological opposition on the part of administrators. A kind of professional conscience present in all administrative units lay behind the diligence of officials in implementing the destruction of the Jews in France.[4]

This attention to duty and professionalism is noticeable in the actions of officials of the French railroads, the Sociéte Nationale des Chemins de Fer (SNCF), in making the convoys – the trains transporting Jews from the unoccupied zone and deporting them from France – run on time.[5] The SNCF was paid per victim, per kilometre for this transport by cattle cars; as late as August 1944 it was still billing for its deportation services. Its contribution to civilised behaviour was to clean and disinfect the cars after transport.

Professionalism, along the lines of the building by British soldiers of the bridge over the River Kwai, as depicted in the film of the same name, can become an irrational juggernaut, causing people to carry out iniquitous activity in the most efficient way possible, insisting all the time on autonomy. For the French, this meant asserting the principle of national sovereignty. The price paid for this assertion was employing administrators and police to collaborate with the Germans in assisting the Final Solution in the Shoah.

This assertion of national sovereignty was made at great cost to the moral fibre of officials. Pressure from the German occupiers was exerted in many ways, but Vichy was not a captive state on which orders were imposed from the occupiers in any unconditional way. The anti-Semitic policies that were put in place resulted from French initiatives and actions, influenced by the xenophobia and the anti-Semitism that were part of French political culture. The Vél d'Hiv round-up, as Prime Minister Jospin said on 20 July 1997, was agreed to and organised by French authorities. In preparing the two Statuts des Juifs, Alibert and Vallat had little or no contact with German authorities.

Administrators acted on the basis of laws in a professional manner, with dispassionate coldness rather than with ideological passion. Professional administrators, bolstered by advice from the Conseil d'État and professors of law, applied state anti-Semitism in excluding Jews from official positions without making openly anti-Semitic statements, except on occasion. This was not negotiable; it was law. Raul Hilberg, discussing German officials, made the same point: there was nothing personal in their participation in genocide, only performance of duty.[6] Yet an inherent anti-Semitism was present in the French senior administration, with the identification of 'Jew' with 'foreigner' and the conclusion that 'Jew' was not part of the French national community or of the state.

Already by the early Vichy law of 17 July 1940, public officials had to be French citizens born of a French father. The two Statuts des Juifs of October 1940 and June 1941, and consequent decrees, breaking with the republican legal order, led to the removal of Jews, with a few exceptions, from 'public functions' and from the professions, including the legal profession. Though some confusion arose about the exact meaning of 'functions publiques', officials applied the Statuts. Maurice Lagrange, the influential senior figure, called at an interministerial conference of officials on 12 December 1940 for a strict interpretation of the first Statut des Juifs. Those officials then elaborated the exact functions forbidden to Jews.[7]

The central issue remains. Why did these senior officials remain in their posts? Why did they obey and implement measures and actions so discriminatory in nature, so contrary to the republican ideals and values in which they were trained? Why did they adapt so readily to the new order, and to what degree were they obliged to do so?

Unconsciously, senior officials passed from protection of the state against 'enemies', among whom Jews stood first, to serving the state by participating in anti-Semitic policies. 'Reasonable' anti-Semitism was appropriate according to the mindset of well-brought-up administrators, not the violence of Nazis. The characteristic attitude of the well-brought-up and well-connected elite was that shown by Marcel Ribière, prefect of the Alpes-Maritimes, brother-in-law of former minister Pierre-Étienne Flandin and member of the Conseil d'État. Many Jews had sought refuge in his region in southern France. He declared that it would be in the highest public interest if Jews were forbidden access to his region; at the very least, a camp in which they could be interned should be set up. 'Nine times out of ten, Jews will be at the bottom of the black market, Gaullist propaganda, anti-government activity.' They were too numerous, too wealthy, flaunting their 'luxe'.

A more restrained view by General de La Porte du Theil, head of the

Chantiers de la Jeunesse, remarked that Jews were barely permeable to the work of moral education of the youth group and that nothing good could result from their presence, which would only be a source of inconvenience. They wanted to dodge their military obligations. Jérôme Carcopino, Minister of Education, organising the educational system, thought a 'barrier had to be put between Jews and public offices'.[8]

Beyond the normal bureaucratic structure were the new administrative bodies set up by Vichy, the most important of which, for this analysis, was the Commissariat Général aux Questions Juives (CGQJ), the virtual ministry of anti-Semitism. It was established on 29 March 1941 under pressure from the German authorities, which had threatened to set up, under their auspices, an agency concerned with application of anti-Semitic legislation in the occupied zone.

Xavier Vallat was not the choice that the Germans would have preferred, but Vichy appointed the head of the Légion to be general commissioner of the new body. Almost immediately the mission of the CGQJ was enlarged on 19 May 1941. It not only proposed all measures to implement government legislation on the state of Jews in their civil, political and legal capacity; it was also now to oversee the necessary co-ordination among the different government departments in applying the diverse aspects of the legislation.

Vallat went about his task methodically, implementing both the law of 11 April 1941 excluding Jews from military positions, and the second Statut of 2 June, which redefined 'Jew'; he also carried out the newly required census, and the elimination of Jews from almost all positions. A document of 2 April 1942 from Vallat's office reported that 3422 Jewish officials had been excluded from the administration, 2910 after the October 1940 Statut and 512 after the June 1941 Statut. Of the total, 2699 had worked in the unoccupied zone, and 753 in the occupied zone. The highest figures were for the army and the Ministries of Finance, Education and Labour.

The CGQJ tracked down any possible influence or authority susceptible of being exercised by Jews, and any position in which they might threaten the state. These threats included Jewish toll collectors, sellers of lottery tickets and funeral bearers, as well as members of boards of hospitals and charity organisations. With the change in general commissioner in May 1942 from Vallat with his 'state anti-Semitism' to Darquier de Pellepoix, the racist anti-Semite, the implementation of the measures and the hunt for Jews became even more emphatic.

The CGQJ had over 1000 employees who were not subject to the same rules as regular officials, came from a less elevated educational and social background and were a more prejudiced and anti-Semitic group than the traditional core of officials. Traditional bureaucrats naturally resented the CGQJ employees, with whom some friction ensued; yet supervisory officials did not ostracise them, but sent recommendations for policy to them and provided generous budgetary resources for them.

Obviously, regular administrative officials differed in their eagerness to consider and to implement anti-Semitic measures. They were likely to be less extreme than members of the CGQJ, whose policy proposals and ardour they sometimes tried to temper. Yet, no evidence is available of any rejection by an official of the principle or the implementation of anti-Semitic measures, and rarely of any opposition to the regime itself.

The stark reality is that not one ambassador, not one head or deputy head of the secretariat of a minister, not one of the highly placed *inspecteurs des finances* joined de Gaulle in London before the end of 1940. The spirit of resistance, as Michel Debré later wittily said, was confined to the banks of the Allier, the Vichy river, until 1943. The officials submitted to their new political masters with little twinge of conscience.

Obedience is a compelling quality for officials, but so is honour. Obstruction and resistance were both possible. Files could have been lost or misplaced, false papers could have been fabricated, information could have been leaked, orders could have been diverted, and train arrangements for convoys could have been delayed. Some officials carried out these actions or joined the Resistance. Police in Nancy in the occupied zone saved nearly 300 Jews by warning of impending arrests; Joseph Rivalland, former police chief and regional prefect of Marseille, refused to deliver hostages and was removed from his position in January 1943; François Bloch-Lainé, *inspecteur des finances*, resigned; Gilbert Lesage, head of the social service for foreigners in Vichy, saved children. Others warned guerrilla units or supplied information to Allied networks.[9]

However, most officials faithfully served the state, administering and preparing the new laws, but betraying republican principles that they were originally appointed to uphold. They acquiesced in the abolition of the Third Republic and the principle of legal equality; they facilitated collaboration with Germany; they implemented the discriminatory measures. Bureaucratic formalism was the *modus operandi*, not an ethic of responsibility.

The Legal Profession

Shakespeare's character Bassanio in *The Merchant of Venice* remarks in a disillusioned way about the legal profession:

In law, what plea so tainted and corrupt
But, being seasoned with a gracious voice,
Obscures the show of evil?

With the outpouring by Vichy of discriminatory measures against
Jews, a new branch of law was born.[10] In little over a year in 1940–1,
168 laws and regulations were issued. In addition, thousands of official
regulations came from circulars, administrative rules made by prefects,
mayors, police and gendarmerie forces, and edicts from the Council of
Ministers, individual ministerial departments and the CGQJ. Over
three-quarters of all the laws and regulations over the whole Vichy
period were adopted before the Germans took over the unoccupied
zone in November 1942. Unofficially, rules came from business,
commercial and professional organisations. Touching on all activities
and professions, the official and unofficial regulations embraced the
gamut of the judicial system: civil, commercial, real estate and penal
law.

The new branch of law was accepted or, at minimum, not
challenged by the legal profession: jurists, lawyers and law professors.
At best, the anti-Semitic laws were received by the different parts of
the profession with scientific detachment.[11] Law reviews had a section
'Juifs' between 'Juge de paix' and 'Justice militaire'. Dissertations were
written in law schools on the 'quality of the Jew'. The Conseil d'État
created in 1941 a commission of the Statut des Juifs under its Vice-
President, Alfred Porché.

The discriminatory legislation was not developed in the law schools
as such, but the most important, the two Statuts des Juifs, emanated
from distinguished law professors. The Statut of 3 October 1940 was
largely the work of Raphaël Alibert, professor of constitutional law,
maître des requêtes in the Conseil d'État 1923–34, and Minister of
Justice in 1940. The second, on 2 June 1941, was highly influenced by
Joseph Barthélemy, one of the foremost constitutionalists in the 1930s,
who was Minister of Justice in 1941, and who led the proceedings
against Léon Blum in the Riom trial in April 1942.

The essence and contents of the new laws were never criticised
except in minutiae, since Jews were regarded, even more than other
naturalised peoples, as not capable of assimilation in France.
Consequently, the laws were more rigorously applied, and were more
extensively implemented, towards Jews than towards other former
foreigners. For this reason Jews were excluded from public service in
the 'national interest'. Jews were described as not having 'certain
political suitability' for these positions.[12] Over and over again, the
same arguments were made to justify legal discriminatory practices,

from definition of 'Jew' to deportation: elimination of Jewish influence in the national economy; public interest; removal of ethnic foreigners from administration; unassimilability of Jews; their troublesome nature.

The new laws did not spring fully developed like Athena from the head of Zeus. The idea was widespread before, during and after the war that a 'Jewish problem' existed. The intellectual climate of the pre-war years fostered the publication of about 600 works on Jewish issues and on foreigners in the five years before 1939. Between 1934 and 1945 almost a thousand anti-Semitic works were published on Jews. Contributions came from major lions in the literary world – Céline, Bernanos – from spurious academic treatises, from priests, journalists and right-wing polemicists. A disproportionate and baffling obsession with anti-Semitism had appeared.

The legal profession was not immune from this obsession. Overt anti-Semitism in the judicial system was evident in a practical way, and latent anti-Semitism was confessed after the war. Jacques Charpentier, head of the Paris Bar, explained in 1949 that a 'Jewish problem' existed in the Bar, as well as a coincidence between the politics of Vichy and the professional interests of lawyers and their willingness to accept the idea of strong power.[13]

Examples of discrimination make this clear. In 1934 a delay of ten years was imposed before a naturalised person could practise law. The Bar readily implemented the Vichy law of 10 September 1940 which barred those who did not have 'French nationality ... being born of a French father' from practising. No Jew was elected to the Conseil de l'Ordre, the administrative body of the Paris Bar, in 1939 when twenty-five members were selected; by contrast, the anti-Semite Vallat had been elected in 1936.[14] No Jew was chosen to head the Paris Bar; the distinguished Pierre Masse, to be murdered in Auschwitz, was turned down in 1933. After the war, the Bar refused to consider reparations for Jews banned during Vichy from practising law.

Yet the anti-Semitic current in the juridical world is only part of the explanation of its behaviour and its acceptance of the new law. What is noticeable is the absence of virulent hostility to Jews in the juridical literature. The approach was neutral and objective, not militant or ideological. For the jurists the promulgated law must be accepted and applied, though contradictions and imperfections in it should be discussed, without enthusiastic adherence to political anti-Semitism.

One commentator has called this 'legal positivism', obeying and implementing law, regardless of content, when it is presented in proper juridical form.[15] This attitude of obedience to the law and cool neutral discussion was early exhibited in the now famous, long article on the Statuts des Juifs by Maurice Duverger, who did not criticise them.[16] In two court cases, in 1968 and 1988, which Duverger brought against his critics, he argued that his work was a neutral commentary on laws that, like all other laws, needed explication. He was the 'conscientious jurist' providing the first synthesis of the new legal texts in a serious law review, comment without criticism, and with an air, or pretence, of neutrality and objectivity. Carefully using rhetorical devices such as the indefinite pronoun or impersonal form in his writing, Duverger kept his personal agreement with or support of the legislation vague.

Exegesis of anti-Semitic laws and regulations, through its very tone of detachment and virtual absence of critical comment, resulted in racist and anti-Semitic language becoming 'naturalised', and conferred respectability on the legislation. Legal ostracism of Jews became normal: Jews were held to be different from the 'Aryan race' and their exclusion was therefore appropriate.

The new laws had their own terminology, their own specialisation, their own doctrinal disputes over the new categories: 'influence atavique'; 'métis juif'; 'Jewish race'; Aryanisation of property. The question of who 'belonged to the Jewish race' divided lawyers for four years.[17] Much would follow from the decision: removal of businesses and their placement in 'Aryan' hands; the appointment of temporary administrators for property; the role of those trustees; the matter of which particular courts had jurisdiction over the matter.

What remained unsaid was that the new law was a perversion of essential principles protecting individuals and ensuring legal equality. A system of discriminatory legislation, based on ethnic and religious identity, was built into the law and applied in the regular functioning of public authorities. The zealous executors of inhuman commands were not, as Primo Levi said, 'the hangmen, monsters, but ordinary people, officials'. The extraordinary, the exorbitant character of the anti-Semitic law was integrated into common, ordinary law. The law was empirical, not normative.

This general question of the nature of law has given rise to unresolved intellectual disputes. Must a law be in accordance with basic accepted moral values to be regarded as law, or is law valid because it stems from the will of the wielder of power?[18] Was legal positivism, through its rejection of natural law constraints on the making and application of law, a factor in the acceptance of anti-Semitic regulations? Did the extraordinary plasticity of legal rhetoric and the immersion of judges in their professional culture make them oblivious to the human consequences of their decisions?[19] Can the legal profession be blamed for doing its duty, usually without personal animus against Jews or any personal gain, and perhaps even with some regret?[20] Whatever the answer to these difficult, controversial questions, it is apparent that in Vichy no challenge based on moral values or some form of natural law emerged. Court cases, some of which were decided positively for Jewish appellants, were on technical aspects of the legislation, which again meant acceptance of the validity of that legislation. Sadly, even the victims appeared before the courts to seek redress, as if 'normal' law were being applied.[21]

They had some, limited, success in this redress. Relief was provided regarding treatment of illegitimate children and Jewish tenants. In the first matter, the courts protected the rights of the children if an uncertainty existed about one of the parents being a Jew. In the second, Jewish tenants could obtain reductions of rent if their inability to pay resulted from 'a circumstance of war'. Some courts allowed such reductions. A double conclusion can be drawn. The courts could protect Jews in the cases they brought. By the same token, they acquiesced in anti-Semitic legislation in all other situations.

Jurists, of course, differed in the degree to which they supported the new laws and in their willingness to play a role in formulating them. Some, hitherto regarded as expositors of the republican legal system, accepted official positions. Reputable jurists with no trace of virulent anti-Semitism or particular hostility to Jews, put themselves at the service of Vichy. Georges Ripert, dean of the Faculty of Law in Paris, became an official in the Ministry of Public Instruction and Youth in 1940. Roger Bonnard, dean of the Faculty of Law in Bordeaux, was an enthusiastic supporter of Pétain, of Vichy and of 'ardent and passionate collaboration'.[22] Joseph Barthélemy, professor of law in Paris, a Catholic intellectual who had protested before the war against Nazi anti-Semitism, became the second Vichy Minister of Justice, holding the post for two years, signing the second Statut des Juifs of 2 June 1941, setting up the 'special courts', excluding Jews from the magistracy, and proposing in February 1941 a *numerus clausus* for university students.[23] Georges Burdeau, law professor, discussing the Statut des Juifs in his influential textbook, wrote that it authenticated the fact regarding Jews that 'given their ethnic characteristics, their reactions, they are unassimilable ... they must be outside the French community'.[24]

Beyond those who served the regime were those in the legal profession who were neutral, whose attitude was detached, who dealt with the law in abstraction, not content. Not a single critical commentary appeared on the Statuts des Juifs. Nor did anyone express reservation about the legality or legitimacy of the new laws that broke with the juridical tradition in which the legal profession was trained.[25] Few spoke of guarantees of equal protection of the laws, property rights and *ex post facto* laws.[26] Few resisted, as did Pierre-Henri Teitgen, François de Menthon and René Capitant.

Not only was the magistracy barred to Jews; the legal profession, with rare exceptions, stood silent when their Jewish colleagues were endangered. And Jewish lawyers were the object of anti-Semitic measures early on. During the round-ups of 20–3 August 1941, when 4232 Jews were arrested by the French police in Paris, forty-two lawyers were among them, forty from the Court of Appeal and two from the Conseil d'État and the Cour de Cassation.

The only modification to the normal, republican court system consisted of special courts set up to try suspected communists, anarchists and 'terrorists'. Otherwise the regular court system functioned, technically applying and interpreting the new law. The new legal texts stemmed from the legitimacy endowed on Pétain by the *plein pouvoirs* of 10 July 1940. Those powers allowed a new legalism to exist, essentially on the principle of *lex posterior priori derogat*, a departure from republican law.[27] The new laws also controverted the traditional French system in which the burden of proof for criminal and other charges was put on the state. In Vichy, the burden for contesting whether one was a 'Jew' or could retain property rights fell on the individual.

The different agencies of Vichy were all involved to varying degrees in formulating and implementing the new laws. Article IV of the second Statut des Juifs of June 1941, for example, stated, 'Jews cannot exercise a liberal profession ... except according to the limits and conditions that will be set by decrees of the Conseil d'État.' The Statut itself resulted from collaborative effort by the Council of Ministers, the Minister of Justice, Barthélemy, other individual ministers and the CGQJ. Differences arose between the ordinary courts and the CGQJ on definition of a Jew and 'the Jewish race', and thus on the property issue. For the CGQJ, proof of adherence to another religion was not enough to determine non-adherence to the Jewish religion. Judgements on individual cases also varied between the agencies, in their interpretation of exceptions from the stringent rules. By the October 1940 Statut, public offices might still be held by Jews if they were veterans of the First World War, or decorated with the military medal of the Légion d'Honneur. Phraseology in the June 1941 Statut provided for exceptions for those who had rendered 'exceptional services' to the French state, or whose family had lived in France 'for at least five generations and rendered the state exceptional services'.

The Counseil d'État

The role of the Conseil d'État, 'the old guard of the Palais Royal', during Vichy is revealing.[28] Part administrative, part judicial, the role was crucial in examining, assessing and helping implement discriminatory legislation. Some of its members even played a part in that legislation and repressive activity. Alibert, so influential in the first anti-Semitic measures, had been a member of the Conseil in 1916, left it six years later, and rejoined it in 1941. Georges Dayras, *maître des requêtes* at the Conseil, was Secretary-General at the Ministry of Justice for almost all the Vichy years. Jean-Pierre Ingrand, delegate in Paris of the Ministry of the Interior, played two roles as co-ordinator of relations with the German occupiers and as guardian of the French administration. He worked closely with Bousquet, in the occupied zone; belatedly in late 1943 he protested against the arrest of French Jews. Jean-Marie Roussel presided over the commission for revision of naturalisation of citizens. Alfred Porché, Vice-President of the Conseil, chaired the committee to examine entry into the public administration, and was involved in the fruitless efforts to formulate a new constitution. André Ripert was on the Conseil de Justice Politique, created at the same time as the special sections of the court.[29]

The Conseil d'État became one of the chief bodies advising on legislation according to the law of 18 December 1940. Thus it played a major role in sanctioning and giving approval to anti-Semitic law. In the stilted language of Article 19 of that law, the Conseil 'participates in the production of law as mandated by the Constitution. It prepares and writes the texts requested of it and gives its opinion concerning the projects established by the government.' Pétain called the members of the Conseil his advisers, helping in the development and drafting of legislation, and in those matters he considered convenient to consult it. The Conseil took an oath to Pétain, swearing fidelity to his person, thus establishing a personal allegiance between Pétain and senior officials, and legitimising the authority of the regime. It was also directly linked to political ministers: by a law of December 1940 the general secretaries of ministers were allowed to sit in general meetings of the Conseil.

As a body it may not have been consulted on the formulation of laws of exclusion, disqualification and nationality, but some of its members, attached to *cabinets* of ministers, helped in drafting and implementing those laws. Primarily, the role of the Conseil was interpretation, calling attention to desirable changes in regulations in the general interest, and acting on them. It decided on the decrees issued by public and professional bodies to enforce the *numerus clausus* for Jews. Among other matters, it approved exemptions allowed by the laws, regulated the nominations of the temporary administrators of Jewish property, decided on removal of Jews from official positions, and gave advice on existing and prospective projects. Much of this activity radiated around the central question, definition of a 'Jew'. Though the proceedings on exemptions were sometimes protracted, very few were granted.

The Conseil had no problem defining Jews in its own midst and profession. Seventeen Jews, including presidents of two of the five sections, were excluded from membership. The Conseil de l'Ordre, the special group attached to the Conseil d'État and to the Cour de Cassation, considered that individuals who could not prove their French origin should be removed from the Bar. All lawyers had to certify their French nationality. The Conseil also chose which Jews were 'eminent' and therefore allowed to remain as lawyers. The subcommittee set up by the Conseil d'État on the Statuts des Juifs clarified who was a Jew; most decisions affirmed the rulings of the CGQJ, denying litigants who sought exemption.[30] The legal profession, of course, did not collaborate in the extermination of Jews, but it gave legitimacy to anti-Semitic legislation, accepting the idea of Jews as a separate people who should be excluded from public positions and the magistracy.[31]

No opposition to discrimination came from the leaders of the legal profession, not on the many regulations, the exclusion or the *numerus clausus*. They did not oppose the imposition on Jewish lawyers of the *numerus clausus* of 2 per cent of the total of non-Jewish lawyers inscribed at the Bar of each jurisdiction. The decree of 16 July 1941 imposing this restriction was applied without protest. It applied to the whole range of the profession: lawyers, notaries, auctioneers, legal counsel and translators. The usual exceptions were made: war veterans, those wounded in the war, those recognised as having eminent quality in their professional service.

The judicial system exemplified conformity, both compliance and obedience. All but one of the 294 magistrates took the oath of loyalty to Pétain. The whole legal system – courts, *avocats*, *avoués* – with only few exceptions, accepted and helped produce the new law. Anti-Semitism became legitimate in successive stages of definition, discrimination, exclusion, spoliation and deportation. First, individual liberties, of conscience, occupation, property and commerce, were flouted. Then, civic personality was ended. Jurists accepted the new categories of incapacity founded on race and religion, categories that led to extermination. Anti-Semitism had metamorphosised from prejudice and unofficial violence to positive law, to adoption by officials and law schools.

Should the profession and judges have accepted and applied unjust laws? One excuse is that the legal regime in Vichy was a continuation of the past, that the regime was established in a legal vote, not by a *coup d'état*, that the judicial and administrative institutions remained in place, and therefore that obedience to the law and to the rulers was appropriate. This is not a convincing argument, not only because it is a specious defence of behaviour wholly contrary to republican tradition, but also because it does not acknowledge the possibility of resignation by officials and legal personnel. Many jurists had been appointed and promoted in the Third Republic, some by the Popular Front government of 1936.[32] They and the legal profession as a whole were not forced to collaborate in the Vichy system. Defence counsel for Léon Blum and the others on trial in Riom in 1942 argued with skill and without censorship and succeeded in getting the trial shelved to some extent, even though Pétain had declared the defendants guilty before it began. The example of these lawyers was not followed in any other direct protest against the discriminatory laws. Instead, the rationale for performing distasteful tasks was 'professionalism'. This misguided pride in doing the job as well as possible became an end in itself, an ethical debasement that led to an excess of French zeal.[33]

The zeal of Vichy officials sometimes surprised, and was sometimes found excessive and too rigid by, the Germans. Surprise came early with the Statut of October 1940, which defined Jews by race, a concept absent in the German ordinance of September 1940. The second Statut in June 1941 was also harsher than German law, including in the definition of Jews those coming from mixed marriages who had wed others from mixed marriages, and limiting the date to 25 June 1940 to assert non-Jewishness. Belonging to the 'Jewish race' was associated with grandparents who belonged to the 'Jewish religion'. The Germans understood that the Vichy formula was more extreme than their own. In December 1941 they agreed with Vichy that in principle French regulations against the Jews would be substituted for the German ones. The broader Vichy definition was adopted by the Germans in 'all doubtful cases'.[34]

Yet the Germans sometimes found Vichy too rigid in those doubtful cases. Roethke reprimanded the CGQJ for not automatically accepting the testimony of Catholic priests affirming baptism of an alleged Jew. The Germans were also less willing to accept the Vichy definition of individuals of mixed marriages and mixed heritages as Jews.[35] Even Eichmann thought that 'Jews in mixed marriages are not presently deportable.'[36] In the Vél d'Hiv round-up the German opinion was that, of people in mixed marriages, only the stateless spouse should be arrested. The Germans wanted more flexibility as well; on another issue, they asked Vichy, which had banned Jews from working as street labourers, to allow them to do this work in the Tunis area since construction was needed.

What were judges to do? It is likely that many of them did not personally approve of the exclusion of Jews from public posts. Should they apply the new laws or resign? If they stayed, should they apply the laws flexibly? If they were too flexible, would their decisions be challenged on appeal, which might hinder their careers?[37] Parenthetically, the role of the *notaires* was a significant demonstration of restraint. Many delayed or blocked the Aryanisation process by advising clients not to be involved in buying Jewish property or businesses, believing they would be subjected to endless litigation.[38]

Some change in attitude within the legal profession came in 1942, when for the first time in May, the Conseil de l'Ordre of the Paris Bar refused to give information about Jewish colleagues. Later, in October, the Council expressed regret about the treatment of fourteen Jewish lawyers. At Liberation some jurists paid the penalty for participation in Vichy. About 170 magistrates of a total of 3000 were punished. One hundred had sat in special repressive jurisdictions, six from the Cour de Cassation and nine from the Paris Court of Appeals.

Yet in the unequal justice meted out after Liberation, officials and professionals were punished less than others. About 120 magistrates were suspended, but since they were needed in the post-war world, the suspension was ended in 1945. In the administrative world too, retribution was uneven. It was highest for officials in the Ministries of the Interior, because of that ministry's repression of resisters, Information because of the availability of written records, and Veterans, Colonies and the Army. It was lowest in Agriculture, Public Works and Transport. Purges were also high in the teaching establishment, including university professors, and the postal service; in all some 28,000 officials were penalised.

The Co-operative Police

In recent years when 'memory' has become a battleground on which discussion of the role of Vichy officials can be waged, the issue of police behaviour has joined that of many others for examination. Should the memory of police officials, who died in obedience to the Vichy regime, be honoured or should only those who co-operated with the Resistance, thus breaking the law, be respected?[39]

In his moving book *The Spanish Testament*, Arthur Koestler confessed that 'the shrug of a policeman's shoulders has remained more deeply engraved on my memory than the screams of the tortured'.[40] The French police, with few exceptions, went beyond shrugs to participate actively in depriving people of their personal freedom and in the process leading them to extermination. Their crucial role in carrying out the arrests and deportations was explained by the need to ensure that the maintenance of public order was in French hands.

The police, and other administrative officials, went far beyond Article 3 of the armistice agreement of June 1940, which called for co-operation with the Germans in 'a correct manner'.[41] They implemented with technical efficiency all the ordinances of both the German occupiers and Vichy. They carried out the October 1940 census and the consequent interning of foreign Jews; they implemented the discriminatory economic measures, increasing in severity as time went on; they carried out actions to compel the banning of radios for Jews on 13 August 1941 and soon the surrender of bicycles by Jews to the police; they carried out orders to disconnect telephones in Jewish residences and not allow Jews to use public telephones; they enforced the curfew from 8 p.m. to 6 a.m. imposed on 7 February 1942.

In the *département* of the Seine, the prefect of police ordered that Jews could not change their domicile without notifying the police commission within twenty-four hours. On 2 January 1942 all Jews, except foreigners protected by their country of origin and veterans, had to present themselves for a new census. This census and the previous one in 1940 became the sheets of music on which the instruments of arrest and brutality were played.[42] In March 1942, the prefect of police ordered a new census of all Jewish children aged under fifteen. On 9 November 1942 foreign Jews were forbidden to leave the towns of their residence.

On 4 March 1942 Adolf Eichmann decided to impose the distinctive badge, the yellow star, on Jews in western Europe; this was rapidly enforced in the occupied zone of France in June by the French police. Vichy declined to impose the badge in the unoccupied zone; instead, on 11 December 1942, it took a decision, applicable in both zones, that identity cards and ration books would henceforth be stamped with the word 'Juif'. The German decision to impose the badge had unintended consequences as some non-Jews mocked the order by wearing stars of different kinds as an ornament and by offering seats in the metro to Jewish wearers of the star in Paris. The German response was to impose a new rule that Jews using the metro and local trains could only travel in the last carriage. A further ordinance of 15 July 1942 forbade Jews from frequenting public places and shops except between 3 and 4 p.m.; non-Jews were forbidden to make a purchase for Jews at any other time. The list of forbidden places included restaurants, theatres, cinemas, music halls, public telephones, markets, baths, museums, libraries, exhibitions, historic châteaux, sports activities and public gardens.

All these prohibitions were enforced by the French police as well as by German security forces. The police also controlled publication of anti-German materials, forbade the taking of photographs in the open, censored broadcast transmissions; and guarded the demarcation line between the zones. Without their crucial role in the arrest and deportation of Jews, many thousands would have remained alive. Among them were French citizens who were arrested together with foreign Jews. Arresting foreign Jews was a mark of French sovereignty. Arrest of French Jews was a more contentious issue, on which Vichy sometimes wavered but acquiesced, especially if some compromise could be found.

The German occupiers soon realised that the co-operation of the French police and gendarmerie would enable them to impose their policies in the occupied zone and that their interests were being safeguarded. On 30 January 1941 Lischka wrote that it was convenient to leave the regulations to the French to prevent any reaction by the French people against the Germans.[43] The German commander, Stülpnagel, commented at the same time that the French police continued to do good work without weakness.[44]

The crucial fact, which has to be the basis for evaluation of the role of the police, is the presence in France of only 2000 Germans available for police work, as both Knochen and Oberg acknowledged at trials in September 1954.[45] Without the French police, gendarmerie and justice system, Knochen said, he could not have done his job. Indeed, the French had a well-organised, formidable force of about 120,000 men, including 44,000 gendarmes, 20,000 mobile police and 30,000 in Paris, which had a separate prefecture of police. The effectiveness of the force was increased by the appointment of the brilliant administrator, René Bousquet, as its head in April 1942, and by changes in its structure and organisational activities.[46] The law of 23 April 1941 had set up a new structure under the Ministry of the Interior assisted by the secretary-general of the police with three units having different functions: public security for the urban police; the regular police; and general intelligence. Three division commanders directed each of the services.[47]

Further change came with the ambitious Bousquet. Centralisation was extended to all towns with over 10,000 inhabitants. Recruitment of policemen and security inspectors was made regional, not municipal. Regional prefects, positions which had been established in April 1941 to co-ordinate administration in a larger area, were given more authority and made responsible for police activities in their areas as well as for the maintenance of order and economic issues. They were assisted by a superintendent of police, who executed orders and application of anti-Semitic and collaborationist policies.

At the same time as the restructuring of the police took place, a new unit was added, the Groupes Mobiles de Réserve (GMR), consisting of about 20,000 men, an elite corps, which would be used against Jews and members of the Resistance, and which was at the disposal of the regional prefects and the *intendants* of police. In addition to the regular police units, others were specifically created to deal with the anti-Semitic measures. The Commissariat Général aux Questions Juives (CGQJ), responsible for preparing regulations concerning Jews, for supervising the sale or liquidation of Jewish property, and for appointment of temporary administrators of Jewish property, could intervene in the activities of governmental ministries and could employ the police for its purposes.

The police function of the CGQJ created problems. The Germans had already intervened to set up a special unit of their own attached to the CGQJ. SS officers had occupied an office in the Paris prefecture of police since January 1941, to establish contact between the Gestapo and the Paris police under Commissioner Jean François. A major advantage of this contact for the Germans was access to the card file of 150,000 Jews kept in the prefecture, and the use of interpreters provided by the prefect. The interpreters, who were also inspectors, increased in number, remained members of the police force but worked essentially for the Gestapo. In November 1941 these inspectors were transferred to a newly created unit, the Police des Questions Juives (PQJ), linked with the CGQJ and attached to the Ministry of the Interior. Part of the functions of the PQJ was to deal with Jewish questions on a national basis, and part to deal with the Paris area. The PQJ was concerned with infractions of the law committed by Jews, enforcing the regulations applicable to Jews only, and keeping the national police informed. The PQJ thus maintained close contact with the national police and the CGQJ. It informed police units of suspect activities of Jews. It was not, however, an admirable body. Composed of volunteers eager not only to hunt Jews but also to enrich themselves, its members made searches, interrogations and arbitrary arrests, and carefully searched the baggage of people in Drancy, confiscating jewellery and stealing money. It became an auxiliary police force, of men without uniforms, an anti-Jewish police unit.

Bousquet, the head of the national police, disliked the PQJ as a competing agency, eager to share his power. He responded by setting up a special section in the Inspection Générale des Services de Police Judicaire to deal with Jewish issues. Each regional police office now had a renamed Section des Affaires Politiques for these issues. Bousquet was also anxious to prevent Darquier, head of the CGQJ, from intruding on his power. He was equally concerned that the Gestapo had approved the creation of the PQJ because it would signify German intrusion on his power as well. Bousquet's concern was justified; in February 1942, Dannecker reported that the PQJ had become 'an elite group and models for future French recruits to the anti-Jewish police. Our [SS] service is completely confident of its influence on the anti-Jewish police in the occupied zone.'[48]

Yet, even the Germans became disturbed by the corruption of the inspectors of the PQJ. It was ended in July 1942, but re-emerged in altered form as the Section d'Enquête et de Contrôle (SEC) in October 1942, directly attached to the CGQJ. Its powers were fewer than those of its predecessor. It could make arrests, but had to hand over the people arrested to the regular police. From January 1944 until Liberation, the anti-Jewish police were under the Secretary-General for the Maintenance of Order, Joseph Darnand, and the Milice. By this time all members of the police force were mercenaries of the Gestapo. In 1944 forty times more Frenchmen than Germans were working for the German police.[49]

The restructuring of the police in April and May 1941 brought in other units. One was the special brigades, composed of volunteers, located in each police commissariat. Their essential function was to search out and arrest those responsible for anti-national propaganda, escaped prisoners, defaulters from the STO, and Jews.[50] Making up about 10 per cent of the effective police commissariat and eager to make arrests, they stalked metro stations looking for suspects.

Though these other units played a role in anti-Semitic activity, the main responsibility for enforcing anti-Semitic legislation was carried by the national and municipal police. The prefecture of police in Paris was active in implementing coercive measures against the Jews. One office, under Commissioner François, collected census information and gave it to the Gestapo. It kept the index of Jews and their property up to date. This card-file index, containing 150,000 names with different colours for French and foreign Jews, administered by André Tulard in the office run by François, was indispensable for the arrest of well-known Jews in December 1941.

The most grievous activity of the Paris prefecture of police was in organising the different round-ups of Jews and arranging for their deportation, and for supervising administration of the internment camps, especially Drancy. It made about 20,000 arrests, and was responsible for almost all the deportations. François' office was a vital part of the anti-Semitic process; he was an ardent collaborator with the Gestapo and his office actively collaborated in the policy of racial persecution. Another unit of the prefecture, under Commissioner Permilleux, not only helped organise the round-ups but also put checkpoints on public highways to capture individual Jews who had escaped. According to one estimate, it was responsible for 35,000 arrests.[51]

Many of the arrangements between Bousquet and the German police chief, Karl Oberg, hinged on the use of the French police. A bargain was made. The French police was autonomous and could act independently, but it would act in close collaboration with the Germans. By the accords of August 1942 and April 1943, the French police would be responsible for all operations, except responses to attacks on Germans. The arrested would be tried in French courts. By the accord of July 1942, Bousquet agreed to arrest and deport foreign Jews. Germany later agreed not to deport French Jews without the consent of Vichy. This agreement, however, was disregarded, as were other Vichy agreements not to arrest French Jews.

Bousquet never paid the penalty for his infamous behaviour in any trial. Nor did other police officials suffer any serious penalty. Amédée Bussière, prefect of the Paris police from May 1942 until the liberation of Paris in August 1944, was condemned after the war to life imprisonment in 1946 but was released in 1951. The cases of about 4000 police officers were examined; 1900 of them were penalised, most for a brief time. Another 196 were condemned by the courts; a few were shot by Resistance fighters.

CHAPTER 13

THE CHURCHES
AND ANTI-SEMITISM

The attitude of the Catholic Church in France, as in other countries, on the question of Jews, or on other issues, cannot be considered in isolation from the position and policies of the Vatican. The wartime conduct of Pope Pius XII has become a matter of acute controversy.[1] Even if the appellation 'Hitler's Pope' is immoderate, questions must be raised in reference to his refusal to speak out forcefully in criticism of Hitler; his silence on the Holocaust when he was well informed of the true nature of Nazi policies; his apparent discouragement of early signs of Catholic protest against the Nazis; and his failure to make any public statement, though he did send some private messages, when on 16 October 1943, 365 SS police and Waffen-SS rounded up over 1250 Jews in Rome, a few yards from the Vatican: 1060 of these Jews were deported to Auschwitz, where only fifteen of them survived.

The Pope, the former Cardinal Eugenio Pacelli, assistant secretary and then secretary of state at the Vatican in the 1930s, signed the concordat with the Nazi government in 1933, thereby accepting the dissolution of Catholic groups in Germany in return for Vatican control over the German bishops and over religious matters of the Catholic Church throughout the country. Earlier, as papal nuncio in Munich at the end of the First World War, Pacelli had expressed, in surprisingly strong private letters, his distaste for Jews, an antipathy that can be regarded as anti-Semitism. On becoming Pope in 1939, he refused to publish the encyclical against Nazi anti-Semitism, 'Humani Generis Unitas', which his predecessor Pius XI had asked to be prepared. Did anti-Semitism play a decisive role in the silence of Pius XII about the extermination of the Jews? The Vatican archives on the war period are still closed and thus no definitive conclusion can yet be drawn about Pius XII.

However, the German archives, which are open, do not reveal any serious correspondence between the Pope and the Nazi government: from this evidence one can argue either that the Pope was exercising caution or that he was genuinely not assisting the Nazis. The Pope was worried that the Nazis might use German Catholics as hostages. He was also concerned with the 'Bolshevik menace', a greater danger for him than Nazism. In addition, he could not have been unaware, even if he was not enthusiastic about it, that about 7000 Jews were hidden by religious groups in Rome in the 150 religious institutions protected by the Vatican.

On Christmas Day 1942, the Pope spoke of 'hundreds of thousands of innocent people put to death or doomed to slow extinction, sometimes merely because of their race or descent'. Reporting on this, the British Ambassador to the Vatican, Francis d'Arcy Osborne, wrote on 31 December 1942 that 'To me he claimed that he had condemned the Jewish persecution. I could not dissent from this, though the condemnation is inferential and not specific, and comes at the end of a long dissertation on social problems.'[2]

The condemnation could easily have been specific. Mgr Konrad Gröber, Archbishop of Freiburg, informed the Pope on 14 June 1942 of the massacres of Jews by the Einsatzgruppen in the east, and Mgr Wilhelm Berning, Bishop of Osnabrück, wrote in some notes on 5 February 1942 that 'the plan for the total elimination of Jews is clearly in force'.

Angelo Guiseppe Roncalli, the Apostolic delegate in Turkey and Greece from 1935 to 1944 and the future Pope John XXIII, in letters and in his diary, made even more striking comments.[3] In his diary he wrote on 10 October 1941 that during a 45-minute audience with the Pope about dealings with Germans, Pius XII had asked him 'if his silence about the behaviour of Nazism was judged harshly' (Mi chiese se il suo silenzio circa il contegno del nazismo non è giudicato male).[4] In a letter of May 1943, Roncalli wrote of hearing the sighs of Jews and his pity for them and intentions to help them: 'they are the kinsmen and countrymen of Jesus. May the Divine Saviour come to their help.'[5] Roncalli himself had tried to help when he wrote to papal nuncio, Archbishop Valeri, bypassing the secretary of state in the Vatican, asking him to help the Jews of Perpignan in France, 'this little caravan of Jews'. He was doubtful about success, but 'it does no harm to try to help these poor people'.[6] Roncalli's act of writing directly to Valeri rather than through the usual diplomatic channel of the Vatican carries the implication that he realised the Pope would not be sympathetic to the plea for such help. He concluded, 'it could be that good Providence may hold in reserve some unthought-of form for us to intervene on behalf of these poor people'.

The Vatican has never formally commented on its wartime role. In the changing climate of the 1990s it did issue its first statement touching indirectly on the issue. On 16 March 1998 the Vatican

Commission for religious relations with the Jews issued a document, 'We Remember: A Reflection on the Shoah', with an introduction by Pope John Paul II. The Pope described the Shoah as a 'crime' and 'an indelible stain on the history of the century'. The document refers to a 'horrible genocide', of which people must be conscious, including the Church, 'by reason of her very close bonds of spiritual kinship with the Jewish people and her remembrance of the injustices of the past'. The document reiterated the words of the Second Vatican Council in *Nostra Aetate* of 28 October 1965, which 'deplores the hatred, persecutions, and displays of anti-Semitism directed against the Jews at any time and in any form and from any source'.

The March 1998 statement, in distinguishing between two concepts, anti-Judaism and anti-Semitism, suggested that the Church had not promoted the latter but that the Nazi persecution of the Jews was 'made easier by the anti-Jewish prejudices imbedded in some Christian minds and hearts'.

The French Catholic Church was more forthright when on 30 September 1997, in a ceremony at the site of the Drancy camp, the French bishops criticised the behaviour of the Church during the Vichy years. Archbishop Olivier de Berranger of Seine-Saint Denis read a Declaration of Repentance, confessing that the Church's 'silence was a mistake ... We beg for the pardon of God, and we ask the Jewish people to hear this word of repentance.' He acknowledged that a public statement by the Church 'might have forestalled an irreparable catastrophe'. He admitted that 'the vast majority of church officials, bound up in loyalism and docility that went far beyond traditional obedience to the established powers, stuck to an attitude of conformism, caution and abstention, dictated in part by fear of reprisals against charitable works and Catholic youth movements'. The Declaration also admitted:

> the primary role if not direct, then indirect, played by the constantly repeated anti-Jewish stereotypes wrongly perpetuated among Christians in the historic process that led to the Holocaust ... The poisonous plant of hatred of the Jews had deformed mentalities, putting consciences to sleep, and diminishing the capacity for resistance to the diabolic anti-Semitism of the Nazis. In the face of the persecution of Jews, especially the multi-faceted anti-Semitic laws passed by Vichy, silence was the rule, and words in favour of the victims the exception.

The Declaration spoke of the impact that a public statement might have had in Vichy. Its own statement certainly had an immediate impact. It was followed by apologies for their behaviour during Vichy by a number of professional groups, including doctors, lawyers and the police. The Order of Physicians, with 180,000 French doctors, apologised for the role it had played and for its silence when Jews were banned from practising medicine.

It was Cardinal Albert Decourtray, Archbishop of Lyon from 1981 to 1993, who first proposed an apology by Church bishops. Soon after his appointment he paid official visits to scenes of Jewish tragedy, especially Izieu, the site of the crime of Touvier, who had been protected by part of the Church. After Touvier's arrest in 1989, Cardinal Decourtray set up a committee of historians to examine the actions of the Church.

Silence was a mistake. Fifty years later it was broken, though some reactionaries such as the *intégristes*, including the Bishop of Versailles, Jean-Charles Thomas, refused to admit that the Church had been wrong. The mainstream Catholic hierarchy concurred about the link between the Holocaust and the Catholic 'teaching of contempt', a term coined by Jules Isaac, the French Jewish historian, to define the Church's traditional attitude to the Jews, an attitude which over the centuries included not simply vituperative language, but also crusades, massacres and inquisitions.[7]

The Church and Vichy

The mainstream Catholic view during Vichy was that Jews as a community resisted assimilation. Ecclesiastical authorities did not object to the anti-Jewish legislation in principle, but asked only that it respect the 'rules of justice and charity', though these rules were left undefined. They did approve of legislation on other issues emanating in 1940, especially on youth and the family, and the appointment of good Catholics, Pierre Goutet, Jeanne Aubert, Émile Mithout and Louis Lafont, to deal with these matters. No wonder that on 2 October 1940 the Archbishop of Aix-en-Provence, Mgr du Bois de la Villerabel, instructed his priests to support the Vichy leaders unreservedly, especially 'the illustrious Marshal'. In those early days, Vichy was seen as the legal and legitimate government of France. There was also no doubt of the strong support of Pétain by the Catholic hierarchy.[8]

The French Catholic Church was not monolithic, but was almost wholly supportive of the Vichy regime and was, for the most part, silent about the enactment of anti-Semitic legislation, at least for the first two years. Individual clerics who took a stand, either supporting collaboration with Vichy and the Germans, or encouraging protest and resistance, were not numerous. More public protests were made by the Church after the summer of 1942, but by that time over 40,000 Jews had been deported to their death. Even when protests were made, as with Mgr Delay, Bishop of Marseille, they were often accompanied by remarks that even if the anti-Semitic laws were too harsh, there was a genuine Jewish problem in France. At the other extreme, the help given to Touvier in hiding and protecting him showed that a minority of the Church approved of collaboration; the help for Touvier revealed the considerable autonomy of the religious orders, abbots and priests included in that minority.

While acknowledging some diversity of this kind, the acceptance and support of Vichy by the Church was typified in a famous early statement of 19 November 1940 by Cardinal Gerlier: 'Pétain is France, France today is Pétain.' Only a rare voice, such as that of the Jesuit Father Gaston Fessard, on 15 December 1940 was heard in protest against the early discriminatory measures against Jews. A year later, in November 1941, Fessard published the first clandestine *Cahier du Témoignage Chrétien* under the title 'France, prends garde de perdre ton âme'. Bishops were Pétainists by inclination and by interest.[9] In general, they supported the regime and its policies to a greater degree than did the Protestant Church.

This Catholic Church support stemmed from a number of factors. First was the general principle of obedience to the regime and its leader. The Assembly of Cardinals and Archbishops (ACA) at a meeting on 15 January 1941 in Paris in the occupied zone pledged complete loyalty to the established power of the government of France. A similar statement was issued by the archbishops in the unoccupied zone in Lyon on 6 February 1941. Mgr Caillot, Bishop of Grenoble, congratulated 'the providential man who is the Marshal' for his attacks on Freemasons and on 'that other power, equally evil, of the *métèques*, of whom the Jews were the most conspicuous'.

The attitude of the Catholic Church and its endorsement of the Vichy government were reiterated on many occasions. An intriguing explanation was given by François Mauriac: 'A Catholic, and especially a priest, and still more a bishop, and above all a cardinal would be reluctant not to consider as legitimate a government to which a papal nuncio was accredited ... For the Catholic hierarchy, the presence of a nuncio precludes debate.'[10] At its worst, disapproval of Pétain might constitute a state of sin. It might also lead to internal divisions, anarchy, insurrection or civil war. A papal nuncio, Archbishop Valerio Valeri, was indeed accredited to Vichy, and the regime in its turn sent Léon Berard, former Minister of Education and senator, as Ambassador to the Vatican. In recognising the validity of the regime, bishops at the beginning declared that Pétain was 'the legitimate authority'.[11] However, not wanting to be completely identified with the regime, the

Church in the declaration of the ACA in January 1941 used a more nuanced phrase, calling Vichy 'le pouvoir établi'.[12]

This language was repeated on 24 July 1941 when the ACA declared 'its sincere and complete loyalty to the established power' (or *de facto* power), though this did not mean deifying the individual (Pétain) who personified that power. The terminology did differ from time to time. On 4 October 1941, Cardinal Gerlier went back to the old formula, speaking of the necessary obedience of French citizens to legitimate authority.[13]

Yet in general the formula had changed. Explicit reference to the 'legitimacy' of Vichy was replaced by *de facto* government. At the important meeting of the ACA on 24 July 1941, the hierarchy, pledging support for the regime, declared that they wanted sincere and complete loyalty, *sans inféodation* (without obligation), towards *le pouvoir établi* (the *de facto* government).

The Church and Vichy joined in a coincidence on social issues: against divorce, against atheism, agreement on the need for religious education of youth, regret over the moral decline of the country. The heralded values of Vichy, *Travail, Famille, Patrie*, were those of the Church. The adversaries of the Church – Freemasons, communists, the secular – were 'enemies' of Vichy, the promoter of Christian Catholic civilisation. Pétain would rescue France from godlessness, end the separation of Church and State, reinstate Catholic education in the public schools and uphold the family and family values.[14] General values basic to Pétain, such as hierarchy and authority, were those of the Church, as was antipathy to materialism, individualism and parliamentarianism. Vichy social laws were founded on Catholic teaching.[15] In addition, the Catholic hierarchy saw Jews as responsible to a large extent for the destruction of a homogeneous religious culture through the influx of foreigners.

Some pious hypocrisy or statistical mischief was at work here. France may be the eldest daughter of the Church, but piety is not and had not been for some time a marked characteristic of French people, especially the working class. As early as 1826 the Papal Nuncio believed that only one-eighth of the population of Paris were practising Christians.[16] Only about a quarter of French Catholics attended Sunday mass regularly, and less than a third at Easter in pre-war France.[17] The war in 1940 heightened religious observance, but this was a temporary phenomenon.[18] Pétain's own religious sensibilities were, as his personal secretary delicately put it, 'peu nuancés'.[19] In a fashion similar to the irreligious Charles Maurras, who had been excommunicated in 1926, the Marshal saw religion as politically essential for social stability.

Whatever else it was, Vichy was not a clerical system. However, some Catholics were prominent in the early days: General Weygand, Minister of Defence; Raphaël Alibert, Minister of Justice until January 1941; Pierre Caziot, Minister of Agriculture until April 1942; André Lavagne, of the Conseil d'État, in charge of religious affairs for Pétain. Catholics were influential in the Légion Française des Combattants; its director, François Valentin, was Catholic. Xavier Vallat was secretary-general of the veterans' organisation; Jacques Chevalier at Education; Georges Lamirand at the Youth Movement; Henri Dhavernas at Scouts. Many were nominated to the National Council; others were appointed to local offices.

It is noticeable that no senior ecclesiastic occupied an official government position; appointments of clergy to such posts was held to be incompatible with sacerdotal functions. In addition, other prominent officials were known to be anti-clerical, even if nominally Catholic: they included Laval, Darlan and Paul Baudouin, Minister of Foreign Affairs for a few months in 1940. It was ironically the secular Laval who was the interlocutor in the famous conversation with Stalin in Moscow in May 1935. The French leader asked if the Soviet leader could 'do something to encourage religion and Catholics in Russia. It would help me so much with the Pope.' Stalin replied, 'The Pope! How many divisions has he got?'[20]

Both the Church and Vichy were equally happy about the end of the Third Republic. For Pétain it was responsible for the defeat of France; for the Church it had created a laic society. Both had as a high priority the fight against communism; for the Church the Statuts des Juifs were of less importance than the struggle against the masons and communists.[21] The Catholic Church, like so many French citizens, saw Pétain as a saviour, the providential man, who would again rescue the country from disaster. Not unrelated to this view was the fact that fifty-one of the ninety-six Catholic prelates had fought in the First World War.[22] Cardinal Liénart, Bishop of Lille, had served courageously in that war and had been decorated in 1917 by Pétain himself.

The Catholic Church blamed the republican educational system for leading to the military defeat of France. The extremist Mgr Durieux, Archbishop of Chambéry in July 1940, believed that God would only return to assist France if secularism was ended.[23] Ignored was the reality that about one-fifth of elementary students and one-third of secondary students attended Catholic schools. In a well-known article, Pétain called for a reformed educational system in which religious values were stressed.[24] The Catholic Church hierarchy expected, but was only partly to be satisfied by, what appeared to be a coincidence of views on educational changes. In general, Catholic leaders wanted among other things the catechism to be taught in schools, subsidies for parochial schools, an end to restrictions on religious orders (thus allowing their members to teach), and the elimination or minimising of organisations unfavourable to religious education.[25] They also held that Jews should not teach Christian children, just as they should not be judges or participate in the legislative process of a Christian state.[26]

The Church leaders wanted anti-clerical bias to be removed from textbooks, the sexes to be segregated in school, and the teaching of morality based on religion. The Church hierarchy not only wanted parochial rather than lay education, but also wanted restitution of Church property, which had been confiscated in 1905.

The first three Ministers of Education in office in Vichy between 17 June 1940 and 13 December 1940, all Catholics, reflected to different degrees the Church's views on education.[27] Jacques Chevalier, godson of Pétain and fervent supporter of the Marshal, on becoming minister on 14 December 1940, introduced changes favoured by the Church. The extreme nature of these changes, however, led to a stormy reaction and his speedy removal. His successor as minister in February 1941, Jérôme Carcopino, academic and moderate Catholic, restored the traditional neutrality of the state schools. The high point of educational clericalism passed. Education became more secularly oriented; Vichy had not provided the Church with the desired solution to the schools question.

Vichy acted on the assumption that the attitude of the Catholic Church was one of approbation. Would Church warnings or disapproval of Vichy's intentions have prevented implementation of its anti-Semitic policies? Certainly Vichy was anxious to know the Vatican's view of the proposed Statut of October 1940. Léon Berard, Vichy's Ambassador to the Holy See, after conversations with Vatican officials, reported back to Pétain on 2 September 1941 that 'there was nothing in [the proposed Statut] that can give rise to criticism by the Holy See'. The Vatican did not intend to quarrel 'with us over the Jewish Statut'. The Vatican only requested that no provisions on marriage be added to the Statut, and that the precepts of justice and charity be considered in the application of the law.[28] This report indicated cautious approval of the legislation. Yet at the same time, at his meeting with Pétain on 26 September 1941, Archbishop Valeri, the Vatican's representative, pointed out the problems resulting from the anti-Jewish legislation. In spite of this ambiguity or lack of clarity in relation to Jewish regulations, the Vatican continued to give its blessing to Vichy.[29] Bérard reported on 18 January 1943 that Pius XII had warmly praised the work of the Marshal and took a keen interest in government actions that were a sign of the fortunate renewal of religious life in France.[30]

The record of the Catholic Church is mixed in relation to persecution of the Jews. The Church welcomed the anti-Semitic measures, but mildly protested against the more extreme. Mostly it was silent or ambivalent; it also changed its perspective as events unfolded and time went on.[31] An interesting example of ambivalent Church leadership is Bishop Delay of Marseille. He had welcomed Pétain in his city in 1940, called on his flock to obey the Marshal, spoke of the necessary union of French people, pointed out the danger of too many foreigners. Yet, in a pastoral letter of 4 September 1942, he wrote of 'the sad cry of Christian conscience' disturbed by the measures taken against 'the Jewish race' and foreigners. If there really is a 'Jewish question', the laws of the state have limits. He criticised the mass arrests of innocent people, who perhaps were being sent to their death, and suggested that the sacred laws of morality and the essential rights of the individual and the family, rights that came down from God, were being violated. Charity and simple humanity were lacking.

Why did the leaders of the Church stay loyal to the regime? The oldest among them remembered the battles with secular persons in power in 1905. All were delighted by the appointment of Catholics to political positions – the first time since 1879 that so many were appointed. None of the Church leaders were Nazis or Fascists, and only a small number were collaborators, welcoming and giving aid to the German occupiers. They were hostile to communism, and called for moral renovation and Christianisation of the country. Wanting order and stability, they denounced the Resistance as 'terrorism' or 'banditry'. Belief in the Marshal entailed obedience to Vichy legislation and actions, though personal conscience about the continuing persecution began to intrude on this attitude as time went on. Most clerics were more interested in pastoral than political affairs, and above all in maintaining and strengthening the institutions of the Church. To protest, or to advise protest and defiance, might mean paying a high price, personally and institutionally.[32]

Yet differences between the Catholic Church hierarchy and the Vichy regime did emerge on a number of issues: the Charter of Labour; the STO; the power acquired by and the ruthlessness of the Milice in 1944. The bishops were divided over Vichy labour policy, wanting to maintain the existence of the Christian trade union, the CFTC, while the government wanted to subsume all trade unions into a single overall group. The Church hierarchy wanted to maintain its own youth organisations while Vichy wanted to amalgamate all youth groups into one mass movement. Some bishops, recognising the general hostility towards the STO, the forced requisition of French workers, were critical of it. The convoluted advice of Cardinal Liénart is interesting: 'I do not say it is a duty of conscience to accept compulsory labour service ... One can therefore evade it without sinning.'[33]

The increasing arrests and deportations of Jews, French as well as foreign, caused some changes in attitude starting in mid 1942: public criticism by six bishops in the still unoccupied zone, private letters by the ACA to Vichy leaders, and fostering aid to and rescue of Jews by Catholic groups.[34] Cardinal Gerlier, no friend of the Jews and still equivocal, began to see Vichy policy as lacking justice and charity. Yet if more concern was now being shown about the round-ups and physical violence, little mention was made of the forms of discrimination imposed on Jews since the beginning of the regime.

Few of the Catholic hierarchy were outright collaborators. One of them, Canon Polimann, was appointed to the National Council, which was supposed to, but did not, draft a new constitution. Only two bishops, Cardinal Alfred Baudrillart and Mgr Dutoit, Bishop of Arras, can be regarded as practitioners of collaboration.[35]

The Cardinals of France

Baudrillart, one of four cardinals at the time, rector of the Catholic Institute in Paris since 1907, was eighty-one years old in 1940. He was a clerical anti-Semite and even more a fanatical anti-communist. Obsessed by fear of a revolution in France, he urged a crusade against communism, called on Pétain to ally with Germany, and called Hitler noble and inspiring. He supported the Legion of Volunteers against Bolshevism (the Légion des Volontaires) as a member of its Honour Committee, and was a patron of the Groupe Collaboration led by Châteaubriant. In a celebrated article in June 1941 in the journal *Toute la Vie*, he wrote of the common noble enterprise led by Germany and of the holy fraternity between the peoples of Europe. His brochure *Choisir, Vouloir, Obéir* was a call for obedience to the regime. Baudrillart was a great admirer of Pétain about whom he wrote a book. Equally, he spoke in his *carnets* of 'the traitor de Gaulle' and 'the miserable de Gaulle'. He died in 1942, apparently of advanced senility.

Mgr Dutoit was one of those in the Church who regarded resisters as bandits, and Allied bombing raids as acts of terrorism. In the new atmosphere of Europe he called for *rapprochement* with Germany and reconciliation of the peoples of the two countries. The most notorious clerical collaborator was Jean Mayol de Lupé, who had no diocese, but acted as chaplain to the Légion des Volontaires; he appeared by the side of Jacques Doriot in German officer uniform at the Vél d'Hiv and won the Iron Cross.[36]

The heritage of this collaborationist group was apparent forty years after the war. In 1992 Cardinal Decourtray, Archbishop of Lyon, set up a committee of respected historians chaired by Réné Rémond to inquire into the Touvier case. Its report made clear the extent of the logistical support given Touvier by that part of the Church which was sympathetic to Vichy; those clerics can essentially be called collaborators. The support continued from the end of the war until Touvier's final arrest in a priory in Nice in May 1989. This support resulted not from any collective decision by the Church hierarchy, but from the convergence of individual behaviour by many people through interconnected channels of an extensive network of priests and religious institutions, particularly in the region of Chambéry.

The network included members of the secretariat of the Archbishop of Lyon, especially Mgr Duquaire, former secretary of Cardinal Gerlier; Catholic Help; Pax Christi; the papal secretariat of the episcopate; and even Cardinal Villot, the Vatican secretary of state. Members of the network had previously called for a complete amnesty and a pardon for Touvier. His most fervent supporters and protectors were the Chevaliers de Saint-Marie, extreme right-wing activists, nationalists, counter-revolutionaries and anti-Semites, with close links to the group of traditionalist priests, the *intégristes*, the Order of the Knights of Notre Dame. These groups were followers of Mgr Lefebvre, who broke with Rome because of opposition to reforms made by the Church after Vatican II. Some in this network saw Touvier as representative of the counter-revolution, some argued that the Church should correct the incorrect judgements of the state against Touvier, some that the justice of God was superior to the law of the state.

The most flagrant case of aid to anti-Semites and collaborators by part of the Church was that of Touvier, but others who played an unholy role in Vichy were later protected by religious institutions and personnel, abroad as well as in France.[37] Raphaël Alibert, former Minister of Justice, took refuge with the Cistercians. Marcel Déat was hidden by priests and died, a converted ex-leftist, ex-rightist, in a convent in Turin in 1955. Georges Dumoulin of the RNP, condemned to death *in absentia*, hid in a convent, as did Joseph Darnand until he was arrested by the British in Italy.

The three Cardinals of France, other than Baudrillart, were less uncompromising than he in their support and enthusiasm for Vichy policies. Cardinal Emmanuel Suhard, Archbishop of Paris and formerly Archbishop of Reims, wrote of his loyalty 'in conformity with traditional Church doctrine'. To show loyalty he appeared, together with Cardinal Gerlier, with Pétain and Laval at a military parade in Vichy on 29 October 1942. Suhard punished two clergymen in his diocese for delivering false baptism certificates to rescue Jews.[38] He was primarily concerned with Christian education of youth and the re-Christianisation of France.[39] Suhard supported Vichy and the German war effort because of his hatred of communism. Ever prudent, he refused to join the National Council in February 1941 when he was nominated to it; instead he sent his chief aide, Mgr Beaussart.[40] Suhard was an accommodator; his aide was a convinced collaborator. Beaussart in November 1941 declared that collaboration was the only reasonable course for France and for the Church.[41]

Nevertheless, Suhard did protest against the worst abuses of the regime. On 22 July 1942, after the Vél d'Hiv, he delivered a letter to the Marshal on behalf of the ACA, which had just met, expressing its emotion at 'the massive arrests of Israelites' and at the harsh treatment inflicted on them. Suhard stressed the 'imprescriptible rights of the human person' and called for pity for the immense sufferings, especially of mothers and children.[42] The text was not made public but was distributed to the clergy. Was a new language being used to speak to power? Suhard's accommodation continued. In June 1943 he wrote to Pétain: 'More than ever France needs you. With spirits in such disarray, it needs a voice to tell it which direction to follow.'[43]

Suhard unwisely took part in two masses in Notre Dame in Paris. On 27 August 1942 he was present for the ceremony honouring the memory of the members of the Legion of Volunteers who had died in eastern Europe fighting for Germany. Even more ill-advisedly, he was involved in the funeral mass, a state occasion, for Philippe Henriot, the notorious collaborator, in June 1944. Two months later, in a celebration for the Liberation of France on 26 August, he was excluded from the cathedral by de Gaulle.

Cardinal Achille Liénart, Bishop of Lille, was a more cautious prelate. Coming from a working-class background, he became prominent in 1928 when he supported Catholic trade unionists in their dispute with textile producers. He was troubled by the laic tendencies of many in France and spoke of the need for Catholic teaching to help them overcome these tendencies. Though not friendly to the Germans, Liénart did not speak out against the Occupation. Indeed a German officer, who was a half-French non-Nazi, protected Jews in the Nord and Pas-de-Calais area to a greater extent than did the Cardinal. Liénart was silent on Jewish issues, though he did speak privately to Pétain after the Vél d'Hiv. His loyalty to Pétain lasted to the very end. After the Marshal's trial and sentence in 1945, Liénart pressed for Pétain's rehabilitation and headed a national committee to free him.[44]

The most complex and equivocating individual in the Church elite was Cardinal Pierre-Marie Gerlier, the elegant and self-confident Archbishop of Lyon and primate of the Gauls. He had been an officer and a prisoner of war in the First World War, and maintained friendship with Pétain as a fellow soldier. Gerlier was a former member of the Paris Bar, and was thus familiar with Jewish fellow lawyers. He was also a brilliant speaker. In contrast to the prudent Suhard, Gerlier was emblematic of the *combattant* Church. Strongly anti-Nazi, Gerlier remained a supporter of Pétain, compliant with Vichy's policies, a pillar of the regime. It was he who on 19 November 1940 said, 'Pétain c'est la France et la France aujourd'hui, c'est Pétain.' At the meeting of the ACA on 31 August 1940, which discussed the forthcoming Statut of October, Gerlier raised no objection to it, or to the state which was reconstituting the country.

Some of his attitude stemmed from personal matters; he claimed that his family had been ruined by the collapse of the Union Générale bank, with which Jews were involved, and so he was aware of 'the enormous harm done by Jews to France'.[45] He also complained of Blum's evil influence in the 1930s. Yet Gerlier was also critical, in his circumspect manner, of the round-ups and deportations of Jews. He intervened on behalf of some Jewish veterans of the First World War and protested against the harsh treatment of deportees. He considered it a victory that Jews being transferred from the unoccupied zone to the deportation transit camp in the north, on one particular occasion, were sent in third-class cars rather than cattle trucks.[46]

Gerlier felt pressure from many sides. The ACA and Suhard in Paris had made a critical statement on 22 July 1942 of the arrests in the occupied zone. The Chief Rabbi Jacob Kaplan sent him a message on 17 August 1942 asking for help to prevent the deportation of those whom the Germans 'wanted exterminated'.[47] Gerlier met with pastor Boegner the next day. Militants of Amitíe Chrétienne and representatives of the Nîmes Committee pressed for a public statement. Gerlier opted for a private letter to Pétain of August 1942. He wrote of the 'very painful measures' being taken in the unoccupied zone, as well as in the occupied zone, against Jews: this treatment violated 'the essential rights of all human beings and the basic rule of charity'.[48]

Gerlier's pastoral letter of 6 September 1942 was more forthright. Speaking of the sad scenes of the deportations and of the cruel dispersion of families where no circumstance was taken into consideration, neither age, nor illness, nor feebleness, he called for increasing the 'protest of our conscience'. The new order could not be built on violence and hatred. He protected a number of Jewish children sought by the police when the prefect in Lyon came to take them from his residence.[49] His aide, Father Chaillet, hid several hundred Jews in monasteries and farms. Pastoral letters called on Catholics to assist Jews.[50]

A flattering comment on Gerlier came from the intrepid researcher Serge Klarsfeld: 'It is to Cardinal Gerlier ... that is owed, more than to any other person, the abrupt slowdown of the massive police co-operation given by Vichy to the Gestapo.'[51] Whether Gerlier deserves such credit is arguable. He was careful in his September letter to preface his criticism of 'the execution of the deportation measures now progressing against the Jews' with the statement, 'We do not forget that the French government has a problem to solve and we measure the difficulties which the government must face.' Yet almost certainly these statements by Gerlier and other members of the episcopate put pressure on the government and influenced public opinion.[52] Many were now conscious of the drama confronting the Christian conscience, a turning point, as Catholics became aware of the rafles in 1942, the inhumane internments and the deportations to certain death.[53]

Nevertheless, troubled conscience and internal personal anguish did not produce courageous lions. The ACA as a body did not dissent from the deportation of foreigners and recently naturalised Jews; after the Vél d'Hiv it did raise some issues with Pétain, but privately. At its meeting on 21 July 1942 the majority of the ACA, including Suhard and Liénart, decided against public protest.[54] A minority went beyond private, secret protestations to Pétain and government ministers, and went public. The most prominent of these senior ecclesiastics were three archbishops, Saliège in Toulouse, Moussaron in Albi, and Gerlier in Lyon, and two bishops, Théas in Montauban and Delay in Marseille. Saliège, in a letter of 2 June 1942 to the Chief Rabbi of Toulouse, had already expressed his sympathy for Jewish suffering.

Cardinal Jules-Gerard Saliège, Archbishop of Toulouse, an individual who was partly paralysed and suffered from a speech defect, and who was to be recognised as 'righteous among the nations' by Yad Vashem in 1969, was the first of the four cardinals to protest against the persecution of Jews. In November 1941, troubled by the miserable conditions for Jews in the detention camps of south-western France, near his diocese, Saliège wrote privately to Vichy authorities about its Jewish policies. After learning of the deportations from the camps at Noé and Récébédou of 450 Jews in August 1942, Saliège went public.

He wrote a pastoral letter to be read in churches the next Sunday, 23 August 1942, without comment. In spite of attempts by Léopold Chéneaux de Leyritz, the regional prefect of the Haute-Garonne *département*, to prevent it, the letter was duly read in 400 churches. The main thrust was protest against the sad spectacle of people being deported, members of a family being separated from one another and sent to an unknown destination. Saliège continued strongly: 'Why does the right of sanctuary no longer exist in our churches? Why are we defeated? ... The Jews are real men and women. Foreigners are real men and women. They cannot be abused without limit ... They are part of the human species. They are our brothers like so many others.'[55] Laval asked the Vatican, unsuccessfully, to retire Saliège. Instead, the Cardinal's letter, known as the 'Bombe Saliège', became a manifesto, a call to arms to limit anti-Semitic policies, to hide Jews, particularly children, and to co-ordinate activities to save Jews by Church institutions.

Even more forthright was Mgr Pierre-Marie Théas, Bishop of Montauban, who protested a week later than Saliège in an episcopal letter against the persecution and the barbarous savagery shown to the Jews in Paris. All men, Aryan or not, were brothers because they were created by the same God. The anti-Semitic measures were a breach of human dignity, a violation of the most sacred rights of individuals and of families. He called for 'a real and lasting peace founded on justice and charity'.[56] Read in churches on Sunday, 30 August 1942, three days after the events at Vénissieux and the deportation of Jews from Lyon, the letter of Théas was one of the turning points in the Catholic hierarchy's development of a more critical attitude to Vichy. Théas not only denounced the 'barbarous savagery' used against Jews, but also blessed those who had been executed by the Germans for resistance, encouraged people to default on the Service du Travail Obligatoire and condemned atrocities committed by occupation troops. He was arrested in June 1944 and interned at Compiègne. A milder form of protest was made by Mgr Paul Roeder, Bishop of Beauvais, who appeared wearing full pontificals to register for the census of Jews because one of his ancestors was Jewish.

Church Concern

Not all Catholic prelates can be typed as prudent or cautious. Both organisationally and individually, protests against the persecution of Jews started in 1941 and began increasing in 1942, in both a public and clandestine form. Church institutions and personnel began helping

Jews, sheltering refugees and children in monasteries and convents, and undertaking clandestine activities such as forging documents, certificates of birth, baptism and marriage, ration books, identity cards and driver's licences. As Mauriac wrote, they saved the honour of French Catholics.[57] Vichy, disturbed by this display of honour, ordered the arrest of all priests who were sheltering Jews; about 120 were arrested and deported.

Some less elevated clerics can be inscribed on an honour roll of righteousness; others remain unheralded. Mgr Rémond, Bishop of Nice, saved a number, perhaps as many as 500, of Jewish children by facilitating false certificates of baptism. Many Jews owe their lives to Father Roger Braun, who hid them in a religiously run house in Limoges. Abbé Robert Sialh saved some thirty children in Lille.

Some Catholic organisations, particularly Amitié Chrétienne, engaged in processes to relieve and rescue children, setting up a secret network in the unoccupied zone. Admirable, sometimes heroic, figures emerged. Father Glasberg, Germaine Ribière, Mgr Théas and Mgr Pic are illustrative of this group. Mgr Théas opened doors of institutions in his diocese to those seeking asylum. Mgr Pic provided false identity papers and ration cards. Lower clergy, nuns and Catholic laity also provided false papers.[58] Father Piperot in Sainte-Baume, and Father de Parceval in Marseille hid Jews in schools and convents.

Father Marie-Bénoit, a Capuchin, had been a soldier and wounded at Verdun in the First World War, and was in Marseille in a monastery in 1940. There he organised a rescue operation, forging documents and smuggling Jews into Spain and Switzerland. After the Nazis occupied the south of France in November 1942, Father Marie-Bénoit persuaded General Lospinoso, Italian Commissioner of Jewish Affairs, to allow Jews to enter the Italian zone, in the Côte d'Azur and the Haute-Savoie.

After an audience with Pius XII in June 1943, resulting from German protests about his activities, Marie-Bénoit negotiated with the Spanish government to repatriate all French Jews of Spanish ancestry; about 2500 were saved in this way. His negotiations with the Italian and Allied governments to transfer the 50,000 Jews still in the south of France to North Africa broke down when the Germans entered the Italian zone in September 1943. He was courageous to the end of the war. On 26 April 1966 Yad Vashem in Jerusalem recognised him as 'Righteous among the nations'.

L'Amitié Chrétienne (AC), an ecumenical body, jointly founded by Catholics and Protestants in Lyon in 1941, provided material assistance for families in need, tried to get the internees liberated from the camps, provided social services, set up houses for children and then dispersed them in religious institutions, and engaged in clandestine activity, especially fabricating false papers. Associated with the AC were clerical as well as lay figures. The most prominent of the Catholics were the Abbé Glasberg, the Jesuit, Father Chaillet, and a laywoman, Germaine Ribière. The active Protestants included Pastor Roland de Pury and Marc Boegner.

In mid-1942 the *Cahiers du Témoignage Chrétien*, a clandestine review, prepared and circulated pamphlets in both zones of France; the most important of these were *Antisémites*, which was distributed with over 20,000 copies, *Silence and Complicity*, *J'Accuse* and *Fraternité*. The first pamphlet appeared as mentioned with a famous article, 'France, prends garde de perdre ton âme', written by Father Gaston Fessard. The declared aim of the journal was 'spiritual resistance', defined as taking a stand against anti-Christian and racialist ideology.[59]

Two priests, Father Chaillet and Father Lubac, were part of the small group involved with the *Cahiers*. Father Chaillet not only published a series of pamphlets arguing for resistance to Nazism, but also helped Jews and families of Resistance members. He was arrested in January 1943 for not disclosing where he had hidden a group of Jewish children. By the end of the war Chaillet had hidden about 1800 Jews in monasteries and farms.

Father Lubac appealed for Christians to help the persecuted. The right of asylum had become a duty to provide asylum. If a life was to be saved, 'I open my door.' Some Catholic organisations did, within a short time, respond to that appeal in Toulouse, Lyon, Clermont-Ferrand, Annecy and Avon. Some rescuers paid a penalty. Abbé Bourcier, who provided a safe house in a presbytery of a church in Villeurbanne near Lyon, was shot by the Germans in 1944. The Bishop of Clermont-Ferrand was deported.

Other theologians were encouraged by the more critical attitudes of senior clerics and by the clandestine *Cahiers du Témoignage Chrétien* to issue and distribute publications of their own, as did the Sulpician, Louis Richard, in Lyon, and to set up networks to save Jews.[60] Some of the rescue networks were organised by clerics who have become legendary. Father Louis Favre put refugee children disguised as pupils in his class in the seminary at Ville-la-Grand near the Swiss border. He was arrested by the Gestapo, tortured and shot in July 1944. The Pères de Notre Dame de Sion, led by Father Charles Devaux, organised shelters from which Jews would be transferred to individual homes, convents and monasteries: he may have saved about 450 children and 500 adults.

A now familiar individual, because of the sympathetic portrait of him in the film *Au Revoir, les Enfants* by Louis Malle, is Father Jacques, a Carmelite priest and headmaster of the Petit Collège d'Avon. As the film shows, he enrolled three Jewish students with changed names in his school, and offered refuge to other Jews, to resisters and to those escaping the STO. Arrested and imprisoned, he died of pneumonia in the slave camp at Gusen in June 1945, ironically a few days after the camp was liberated.

Curiously, the attempts to rescue Jews increased but the number of public protests by the Church did not. At Liberation the episcopate was criticised for this lack of courage; requests were made by the incoming authorities for removal of twenty-one of the eighty-seven bishops. Only five of them, including the extremist Bishop of Arras, were in fact removed.[61]

The Protestant Response

At the very beginning of Vichy the small Protestant community, overwhelmed as was the rest of the population by the defeat of France, was inclined to acquiesce in the coming to power of Marshal Pétain. A minority even supported the new regime. Rear-Admiral Charles Platon, a hero of the Dunkirk evacuation of troops in June 1940, became Minister of the Colonies in September 1940; a fervent collaborator and virulent supporter of discriminatory policies, he was executed by the Resistance in August 1944. Other Protestants, the Sully group, manifested monarchist and extreme right-wing views. René Gillouin, an essayist who was critical of concepts of individualism and rationalism, became an adviser to Pétain and was close to him until May 1942, though increasingly troubled by the anti-Semitism of the regime, as his letter to Pétain of 29 August 1941 showed. The Protestant Gillouin wrote that the Edict of Nantes, a stain on the glory of Louis XIV, would be 'une bergerie', a mere pastoral, compared to Pétain's anti-Jewish laws. Nevertheless, his post-war memoirs are entitled 'I was the friend of Marshal Pétain'.

The Protestant leader, Marc Boegner, was himself equivocal about Vichy at first, reflecting the ambivalence of Protestant opinion in 1940 and 1941. He spoke of Pétain as the noble 'vieillard'. Meeting the Marshal on 13 September 1940, Boegner thanked him for his fight against alcoholism and divorce, and his support of the family, public morality and youth. By the end of 1941 Boegner, now concerned about the possible clericalism and the anti-republicanism of Vichy, and above all the increasing anti-Semitism, began changing his opinion.

Protestants were more conscious and concerned than was the

Catholic Church in general about the continuing Vichy discrimination. The small Protestant music was sensibly different from the Catholic symphony.[62] It was vocal earlier and more intensely and widely expressed. The Protestants published Cardinal Saliège's Easter letter of 1941 with its identification of the God of Abraham as the true God. Catholic help for the Jews came from a minority and was marginal; Protestant help might involve a whole community, as in the area of the Cévennes mountains to which Jews fled.[63]

Remembering their own history of being persecuted as Huguenots, in Nîmes, Uzès and Alès in France, Protestants, though careful and loyal to the regime, were more disturbed than were the Catholics about the fate of Jews.[64] Though the Protestant leaders had supported Pétain at the beginning of Vichy and expressed confidence in him as the man of order, they were aware that the anti-Semitic measures would result in cruel ordeals and poignant injustices for fellow human beings who were members of a minority group.

The dominant Protestant leader was Marc Boegner, President of the Fédération Protestante de France, and of the National Council of the Reformed Church of France. He had also joined the official National Council of Vichy in January 1941, which he thought might be a vehicle for re-Christianisation of the country. With his conscience aroused earlier than other leaders, he soon expressed criticism of the measures against Jews, if at first in a guarded manner.

In two letters in March 1941, one on the 26th to the Chief Rabbi of France, Isaiah Schwartz, and the other to the government leader Admiral Darlan, Boegner wrote of the sadness of Protestants as a result of the government measures and actions which affected French Jews who had lived in France for generations. Yet at the same time Boegner, in a fashion similar to that of the Catholic prelates, wrote of the grave problem posed for the country by the massive immigration of a large number of foreigners, Jewish and others, and by hasty and unjustified naturalisations.[65] Nevertheless, his letters, the first of which, to Schwartz, was circulated in the occupied zone, were the first visible sign of an indignant Christian conscience.[66]

After the Vél d'Hiv and other round-ups and the continuing deportations, Boegner in a stronger letter to Pétain of 20 August 1942 wrote of the terrible fate awaiting the Jews who had been delivered to the Germans. No French person could remain unmoved by events occurring in concentration and internment camps.[67] It is noticeable that Boegner was now concerned with foreign as well as French Jews, the men and women who for political and religious reasons had fled to France and who were being deported under inhuman conditions. Absolutely different methods must be ordered in the treatment of foreigners of the Jewish race, whether baptised or not. The Churches must protest against the trampling underfoot of respect for the human personality.

The National Committee of the Reformed Church expressed anguish in its message of 22 September 1942, read in churches on 4 October, about broken families, children separated from mothers, the right of asylum and pity forgotten, respect for the person transgressed, and helpless people delivered to a tragic fate. This message had resulted from Boegner's bringing together sixty-two pastors at Mialet on 6 September 1942 to recommend assistance for Jews. His meetings with Laval three days later and with Bousquet on 11 September were less successful.[68]

Le Chambon-sur-Lignon is not the only place in France that rescued Jews who were being hunted, but it is now seen as the most celebrated place of refuge and has an honoured place in the record of righteous behaviour. In the plateau of Vivarnais-Lignon, Protestant ministers and their followers in all twelve parishes of the area actively saved Jews in their own operations. The rescue network in Le Chambon was exceptional. Remote, inaccessible at that time, set on steep hills that made transport difficult, this small village in south-eastern France provided shelter for some 5000 Jews who passed through it in three years. In the whole of France, Protestants accounted for less than 1 cent of the population; in Le Chambon they were 90 per cent. Perhaps remembering the revocation of the Edict of Nantes in 1685 and the persecution of their Huguenot ancestors, they risked their lives to provide help for the newly persecuted.

Some persecuted Jews found permanent shelter in the hills around Le Chambon; others remained there temporarily until they could escape. The village set up a number of houses as refuges where Jews, especially young children, were fed, clothed, educated and protected. Some of the houses were strategically located, one on a slope from which the roads could be seen for many miles. The police used another to warn other houses of an impending raid. Religious groups, especially CIMADE, Quakers and the Red Cross, financed seven of the houses. The Secours Suisse arranged two farm schools for older children. The Cévenole School, which André Trocmé founded, whose students were mostly Jewish, had about 350 pupils. Other boarding houses sheltered adolescent refugees.

The spiritual leader of Le Chambon was Pastor André Trocmé of Franco-German parents; his wife had an Italian–Russian background. On arrival in the village in 1934 he founded a private coed school, based on concepts of non-violence, internationalism and peace. Trocmé refused to take the oath of loyalty to Pétain and also to ring

his church bell in honour of the Marshal. In answer to the Vichy
authorities, who knew of his rescue of Jews and demanded he stop it,
Trocmé replied: 'These people came here for help and for shelter. I am
their shepherd ... I do not know what a Jew is. I know only human
beings.'

A deeply pious Calvinist and a pacifist at the outbreak of the war,
Trocmé organised a kind of Gandhian non-obedience and non-violent
resistance to Vichy and to the Germans. Le Chambon, discussed in
Phillip Hallie's moving book, obeyed both the positive (love thy
neighbour) and the negative (thou shalt not kill) ethics of the Hebrew
bible.[69] Trocmé and some helpers were arrested but released after a few
weeks; they then hid from the Germans. His cousin Daniel Trocmé,
equally courageous, was arrested by the Germans and sent to Majdanek,
where he died.

One interesting coincidence is the fact that Albert Camus lived in
Le Chambon between 1942 and 1943 while writing *The Plague*. One
character in the novel argues, 'There was only one resource, to fight
the plague.' Perhaps the plague was the Final Solution. In spite of the
protests, aid and rescue undertaken for Jews by a minority of Catholics
and Protestants, the plague raged on. Indeed, Camus ends his book
with the warning that 'the plague bacillus never dies or vanishes
entirely'.

The Declaration of Repentance of 30 September 1997 by the
Catholic Church implicitly acknowledged that the French Catholic
hierarchy strongly supported Vichy and was clear that it was culpably,
if not completely, silent about the regime's anti-Semitic laws. This
harsh, objective self-judgement is not seriously mitigated by knowing
that a minority of the hierarchy was unhappy about and even
occasionally condemned the most extreme measures, the massive
round-ups of Jews starting in 1942. Nor is it undermined by
appreciation of the aid, shelter and rescue operations by Christian
organisations, and devout individuals who saved hundreds, perhaps
thousands, of Jews, especially children.

Catholic leaders, in the same way as so many French people,
applauded the coming to power of Pétain and the establishment of
Vichy as a desirable response to the débâcle of French defeat. For the
leaders it was retribution for a republic that had disobeyed divine laws;
it was necessary to recreate the *union sacrée* of the First World War,
and an ally in the struggle against the 'enemies' that church and state
had in common.

It is clear that for the Church, 'the Jewish question' did not have
high priority. It prudently avoided taking positions about the regime
and its actions that might risk divisions among the faithful. The

Church hierarchy was not universally anti-Semitic, but it was sufficiently prejudiced to raise little or no objection to the anti-Jewish laws that sought to exclude Jews from the life of France. In this it reflected the anti-Judaism views held by a majority of the faithful. The best that can be said for the hierarchy is that it may have been self-deceived by illusions of French national sovereignty and the supposed requirements of French national interest in dealing with Jews. The worst is that it was silent.

CONCLUSION

The villainy you teach me, I will execute,
and it shall go hard but I will better the instruction.

What more appropriate commentary, made even more compelling in that the words are those of Shylock, can be made on the French State, Vichy France, on its policies and political activity, on its implementation and initiation of discriminatory legislation and actions, on its collaboration and accommodations with Nazi Germany, by both governmental and non-governmental personnel, on the degree of complicity of officials and citizens in the Holocaust? Vichy's policies and actions, both official and non-official, were not dictated by Nazi Germany, nor were they mere imitations of those of the occupiers. They were choices, and sometimes the choices were more extreme and discriminatory than the German ordinances and regulations.

For some years after the war it seemed that, of the 40 million French people alive at that time, 40 million were Pétainists or Maréchalists, and 40 million were Gaullists. Black and white are not the colours to use for a portrait of Vichy. Wartime France was not a country of heroic resisters, risking life and liberty, gallantly defying Nazi demands or attempting, subtly or otherwise, to sabotage them. In spite of the myth, cultivated by the media and Paris intellectuals in the post-war years, the Resistance movement was small and operational mostly in 1943 to 1944. Courageous defiance of the occupiers or the Vichy regime was not evident in those years at the Café des Deux Magots or the Café de Flore: it appeared at the Liberation, or the day after.

Yet nor was France only a land of infamous collaborators and facilitators of anti-Semitic persecution. France remained a divided country. Most citizens, especially at the beginning of the Vichy years, were passive or opportunistic, uninvolved in the crimes and atrocities taking place in their country, but also not unduly perturbed by them. Some, though disliking foreigners and anti-Nazi refugees and holding generally xenophobic beliefs, were still troubled by the increasing degree of persecution. Nevertheless, they remained convinced of the need for the Pétainist regime, which had replaced the democratic republic with which they were disillusioned, and which they viewed as preserving the unity of France, maintaining order and discipline and renovating internal affairs. Some wanted France to play a role in the new German European order.

It is tempting, but unwarranted, to portray Vichy in the style of a chiaroscuro painting, especially since the French courts, in their decisions in the Touvier and Papon cases, fifty years after the wartime events, left an imperfect image or one lacking precise clarity in regard to both the character of the Vichy regime and the degree of its autonomy from or subservience to the policies and demands of Nazi Germany. At his trial in 1997–8, Maurice Papon compounded the problem by asserting in a bizarre interjection that history, like science, was fluid matter and difficult to comprehend.[1] Beyond Papon, the dilemma exists of how, or whether it is at all possible, to relate acceptable moral values and codes of conduct to individual or group behaviour in extreme situations.

The trial of Papon showed that he was not a synecdoche for France. It did not have the same purpose or the same result as the trial of the monstrous Adolf Eichmann. Prime Minister David Ben-Gurion of Israel wanted Eichmann captured in Argentina where he was hiding in 1960 and brought to trial in Jerusalem. Ben-Gurion was less interested in punishment of the man Eichmann than in illustrating simultaneously the pernicious nature of the SS official, the Nazi policy of the Final Solution, the Holocaust and the virulent anti-Semitism in Europe.[2] Through memories and historical analysis, carefully prepared from the German archives, Israeli jurists merged the particular and the universal, using Eichmann to clarify the horrors of the Nazi regime.

Judgement on Vichy, imperfect though it was, started even before the war was over with purges of suspected collaborators, including many women, for their sexual relations with members of the occupying forces. These purges were the result of both judicial and summary procedures, aimed at those accused of treason and collaboration with the enemy. To legalise future punishment General de Gaulle, who was still in August 1943 outside France, established a purge committee. Inside France the National Council of the Resistance issued a charter on 15 March 1944 which called not only for the re-establishment of the Republic and restoration of universal suffrage and civil liberties, but also the punishment of traitors and collaborators.[3] The first major figure who was punished for collaboration was Pierre Pucheu, Minister of the Interior from July 1941 to April 1942, who had left Vichy for North Africa; he was tried in a military court there, and executed in March 1944.

Differences over the purges were immediately evident. De Gaulle, both before and after he became head of the new provisional government of France in August 1944, wanted the purges to take place in a regular fashion through the courts and government ministries, based on the recognised laws, written and customary, of the state and according to the accepted codes of conduct of the community. The internal disorganisation in the country and the independent activity of local resistance groups and vigilantes prevented the desired legal procedures from being enforced. Instead, summary procedures at times took the form of civil war with mob violence, lynchings in a number of towns, including Annecy and Annemasse, of people such as General Barthélemy, President of the Légion des Combattants, and some special purge courts. Some 2000 alleged collaborators were executed in Paris. In extra-judicial proceedings, about 6000 executions took place before and 4000 after Liberation.

If they differed on the method and nature of punishment, these implementers of justice all agreed that purges were necessary, that collaborators, pro-Nazi police and officials had harmed the country and were still a threat. At the local level many were animated by motives of revenge for torture inflicted during the Vichy regime and for personal and national humiliation suffered.[4] Some looked on the purges as the essential preparation for a new and better future.

The provisional French government, eager to establish its legitimacy on taking power in August 1944, set three principles on which punishment for activities during the Vichy years would be based. The penal code as it existed on 16 June 1940 would apply to those who had engaged in propaganda on behalf of the enemy or joined an enemy organisation; in particular, Article 75 of the code forbade consorting with or helping the activities of the enemy. Secondly, juries in trials would be drawn from members of the Resistance. Thirdly, the new crime of 'national *indignité*' was introduced, with a punishment of 'national degradation', loss of civil rights, exclusion from office in professional organisations, the civil service, banking and journalism, and loss of rank in the armed forces.

A hierarchy of judicial bodies examined the charges. The High Court of Justice tried the most prominent ministers and officials, including Pétain and Laval. The 125 Courts of Justice in the *départements* had twenty-seven regional courts and seventeen in Paris. About 100 Chambres Civiques examined those accused of 'unworthy conduct', those belonging to a collaborationist organisation or writing in support of the enemy or of collaboration; they had only one penalty, that of national degradation, from five years to life.

The High Court, which functioned until 1949, judged 108 cases, pronouncing eight death penalties, including one on Pétain but asking that it not be carried out because of his age. Only three of the death penalties were executed: Pierre Laval, Fernand de Brinon, Vichy's Ambassador in Paris to the German authorities, and Joseph Darnand, head of the Milice.

The Courts of Justice, which functioned until 1947, examined 311,000 dossiers submitted to them. About 60 per cent were shelved and the other 125,000 were judged, of whom 76 per cent were found guilty. The courts sentenced 2853 of those standing trial to death; 1303 of these individuals were pardoned. Another 3910 were sentenced to death *in absentia*. Over 38,000 received a prison sentence for collaboration. The Chambres Civiques condemned 46,145 to national degradation; 3184 of these were suspended. In addition, a considerable number, over 60,000, were put in 'administrative internment'. About 15,000 individuals fled to Germany.

Most of the condemned were amnestied between 1947 and 1953, and most never served a full sentence or were put to death. In all, 768 of the 6763 sentenced to death were executed. De Gaulle's policy was to commute many of the sentences and the death penalties in an attempt to reconcile those who had aided Vichy. He was primarily concerned with punishing those 'whose personal and spontaneous action had caused the death of other Frenchmen or directly aided the enemy'.[5] However, local communities were unhappy both about the pardon of some active collaborators and about who should be honoured. The total number of those punished in this way before and after Liberation through these irregular proceedings was about 10,000.[6]

Between 22,000 and 28,000 officials were penalised or dismissed. Most of the serious penalties were for officials in the Ministries of the Interior, Information and Communications, Veterans and Colonies. In 1945, 372 of the 500 officials in Information were penalised, and seventy-seven of the 231 senior officials in Interior were removed. About 10 per cent of the French *magistrature*, including a quarter of the members of the senior staff of the Conseil d'État, were removed or suspended. Among other senior officials, one regional prefect and five *intendants* of police (senior officials of a regional force) were condemned to death. University professors were not condemned to such a dire fate, but they were punished to a greater degree than secondary school teachers. In the cultural area, some of the press were purged, and two writers, Brasillach and Jean Luchaire of *Nouveaux Temps*, were executed. Some film directors and performers, notably Arletty, Ginette Leclerc and Henri-Georges Clouzot, were banned from working for a time.

Charges were more difficult to prove, and fewer cases were brought, against economic leaders who claimed, in a usually specious defence, that by working or pretending to work for the enemy, they were pressured by the Germans or were really saving their workers or their industrial plant from being removed to Germany. The directors of the four large banks, the Crédit Lyonnais, the Comptoir National d'Escompte, the Société Générale and the Banque Nationale pour le Commerce et l'Industrie did not pay any considerable penalty for their collaboration. Nor did officials of the Ministry of Industrial Production, who were punished to a lesser degree than those at Interior or Information. Only some 10 per cent of cases of those involved in the economic area involved some punishment. The notable cases were Renault and Berliet, which were nationalised, the latter for a time, and their owners punished for aiding and providing intelligence to the enemy.

Justice was imperfect in another important way. Judges and prosecutors had held similar positions in Vichy. It took six months before the prosecutor at the Riom trial was obliged to retire from his position on the Cour de Cassation.

The new national Gaullist government was subject, as were so many regional governments in the country, to tension between the desire to punish offenders during Vichy and the need to create a national unity. To hasten procedures, the government introduced the summary process for withdrawing the right to vote from the accused without trying them fully on the charge of 'national *indignité*'. The machinery of the early purge trials took too long to get going and worked too slowly.[7] Sentences were uneven; François Mauriac spoke of the proceedings as 'the new lottery'. The lottery ended quickly. In 1951 amnesty for 'national *indignité*' was introduced; two years later national degradation was ended.

France was divided and ambivalent about purging those who betrayed France on the one hand, and the need for re-establishing public order, civil harmony and the end of divisiveness on the other. The Cold War drew attention away from wartime deeds. All of these factors induced courts to exercise clemency.

The purge was unequal in time and in space, and was incomplete. Above all, those senior officials involved in the Final Solution were not judged for their participation in it. The charge of crimes against humanity was not incorporated into French law until 1964 and then was made imprescriptible. Not until 1979 was the first indictment on this charge, that against Jean Leguay, brought against a Vichy official. France had not totally discredited agents of Vichy even then, nor had many major collaborators and persecutors of Jews been brought to justice. Most of those who had participated in anti-Jewish discriminatory activities escaped serious penalty.

What verdict, then, can be rendered on the Vichy regime and the French population? Consensus on the assessment of the actions and policies of the political leaders and officials in fostering anti-Semitic discrimination and complicity in the Holocaust is more likely to be reached than a conclusion about the people as a whole. It is now apparent that discrimination and complicity, and above all silence and indifference towards the atrocities, were not confined to a small number. A parallel might be drawn with the much discussed and still controversial issue of the 'ordinary men' of the Reserve Police Battalion 101 in Nazi Germany.[8] The haunting question remains of why 500 middle-aged reservists from Hamburg, only a quarter of whom were members of the Nazi Party, who were drafted into the 'Order Police' in May 1941, who were not fanatical SS men and who could have refused orders without punishment, nevertheless were willing to kill or have deported to their death over 80,000 Jews starting in the spring of 1942. One can wonder about French people, as about the Germans, what the motivation was for carrying out these infamous acts: conditioning by propaganda and the general political and social environment; peer pressure; becoming accustomed to persecution as normal; career ambition; the habit of obedience; or anti-Semitic prejudices that saw Jews as outsiders who could be properly removed from the community – all of these factors entered into motivations for supporting anti-Semitic measures. Did conformity to political and social expectations combined with character flaws in individuals dehumanise so many to the point of disregarding normal restraints and customary forms of civilised conduct?

Edmund Burke was right when he wrote: 'I do not know the method of drawing up an indictment against a whole people.' The record of the French people is mixed: mercenary, subservient, heroic, cautious, opportunistic, genuinely admiring of the conqueror, eager for France to play a new role in a new Europe. Few can doubt that Vichy was a squalid period in French history, a reminder of the ease with which, even in a short time, evil can be done by some individuals. Yet, judgement is necessarily related to periodisation, to the changing events and to the opportunities for action or evasion, though it does not and should not prevent moral condemnation where appropriate.

How many of the French population of millions can be considered collaborators, traitors to France, partisans of Nazism, participants in the extermination of Jews and perpetrators of evil deeds? In the literary field of ideological collaboration and anti-Semitism, Brasillach remains the symbolic malefactor, being sentenced to death and executed, as was the less renowned Luchaire. The unpunished cowardly Céline in June 1944 went to the German Embassy in Paris to get travel documents to escape from France, presumably reminding the Germans of his brave remarks in calling for the extermination of Jews. The 'heroic' Simone de Beauvoir worked for a time on a cultural programme for Radio Nationale in occupied Paris. Her companion, Jean-Paul Sartre, happily replaced a dismissed Jewish professor of philosophy. The well-known publisher Bernard Grasset boasted that he was endorsed by the occupation authorities.[9] His colleague Robert Denoël, partly financed by Germany, published 'only' eleven pro-Nazi books.

Economic collaboration, as we have seen, was on a considerable scale, involving a large number of business and commercial enterprises and leaders of industry, few of whom, apart from Renault and Berliet, were punished after the war. The Germans would have had a much more difficult time without the businessmen of Lyon, the Paris Gas Company and the Paris Metropolitan Rail Company, which repaired military transport for Germany and helped transport German troops to the Normandy front. Countless individuals of both sexes engaged in personal, social and cultural interaction with the occupiers.

The Church hierarchy on the whole welcomed the isolation of Jews, which it saw as agents of modernism, from the rest of the community. On the deportations and exterminations they were almost completely silent in spite of all the evidence. Mgr Roncalli, still apostolic delegate in Turkey and Greece, wrote on 8 July 1943 to Deputy Secretary of State Montini in the Vatican referring to 'the millions of Jews sent to and executed in Poland'. Valeri, papal nuncio in Vichy, informed Maglione, the Vatican secretary of state, on 7 August 1942 that the fact that the sick and the old were being deported excluded 'the idea of making use of them for labour'.[10]

In his desire to create a national unity, vital to rebuilding France but possibly requiring a touch of amnesia, de Gaulle in his New Year's speech at the end of 1944 asked, 'Who of us has never made a mistake? Who of us has nothing with which to reproach himself?' Understandable though de Gaulle's political objective may have been, his position implicitly encouraged evasion of responsibility for actions during the war, and was a factor in allowing disagreeable orders and unjust laws to go unpunished. Because de Gaulle retained elites that he thought necessary for reconstruction of the country, powerful figures, ministers, senior officials, prefects and members of the secretarial *cabinets* escaped serious punishment and went on to successful careers in both public and private organisations. Pinay, Couve de Murville, Gaillard, Chaban-Delmas and Debré had important careers as prime ministers and ministers in the Fourth and Fifth Republics.

The French courts have not yet rendered full or unqualified judgement on the Vichy regime and personnel, or dealt satisfactorily with crimes against humanity, and now, with the passage of time and deaths of individuals who could be brought to justice, they are unlikely to do so.

Pétain himself, explaining his policy of collaboration on 30 October 1940 after his meeting with Hitler at Montoire, said: 'It is I that history will judge.' He and those who acted for and aided the Vichy regime must now also be judged for the policies, not only of collaboration, but also of persecution and crimes against humanity. Even recognising that the behaviour of Vichy personnel and of the French population in general cannot be seen as binary in character and that a simple dichotomy does violence to the complex reality, judgement must weigh the conflicting arguments. On one side is the prosecutorial accusation that the Vichy government was actively involved in complicity with and was co-author of or participated in a policy of genocide.

On the other side is the defence that Vichy, reacting to the defeat of France in 1940, tried to prevent, nationally and locally, subordination of the country to the German occupiers. State collaboration was thus explained by the desire to obtain a good place, a front-row seat, in the European New Order to be created by Germany, by eagerness to maintain the political sovereignty and territorial integrity of France, by affirming the national interest, and by laying the basis for the National Revolution that would replace the despised republican system. Part of the price to be paid for political sovereignty was the persecution and deportation of Jews.

From Verdun to Montoire was a crooked path for Pétain. The guardians of the laws and of the government of Vichy were, in Plato's words, 'only seemingly and not really guardians'. They did 'turn the State upside down ... [and] they alone have the power of giving order and happiness to the State'. A starting point for examination of the 'state turned upside down' might be the Vichy laws which removed restraints on the exercise of political power, avoided responsibility for actions, unjustly accused opponents and persecuted innocent people, charging them with betrayal. By Constitutional Act no. 5 of 30 July 1940 and a law of the same day, a Supreme Court of Justice was set up to judge ministers, former ministers and their immediate subordinates, civilian or military, who could be charged with betraying the duties of their office.

Constitutional Act no. 7 of 27 January 1941 gave the head of state judicial power, the power of pronouncing penal sentences. He could investigate and punish 'any betrayal of the duties of office'. Under this power a Council of Political Justice was set up by decree of 29 September 1941, a consultative body to give advice to the head of state about implementing Act no. 7. The Council quickly reported on 15 October that leading figures of the Third Republic, Daladier, Blum, Reynaud, Mandel and Gamelin should be detained in a military prison for an indefinite period; the report was accepted and implemented the next day.

Within a week, court proceedings against the imprisoned individuals began; eventually a trial was held in Riom in March 1942. For Vichy the trial was worse than a crime; it was a mistake. For Blum, charged with the others as being responsible for the war, it was a shining moment in his illustrious career. Luminous, skilful, eloquent, his speech in court on 11 March was a glowing defence of political and social democracy: 'We were not some monstrous excrescence in the history of this country ... we were a people's government: we were in the tradition of this country, in the tradition of the French Revolution.'[11] Blum's eloquence caused Hitler on 15 March to denounce the trial, which was suspended indefinitely on 14 April.

The contrast between Blum's courageous, incandescent statement of fundamental principles of liberty and equality and his acceptance of responsibility for his actions as Socialist leader and Prime Minister in the Third Republic, and Pétain's flaccid refusal, at his trial in July–August 1945, to acknowledge his role, is illuminating. By his own account, at no point was Pétain a leader. Persecutions took place in spite of him. He was rectifying the deficiencies of the Third Republic (he forgot he had been Minister of War in 1934). He was opposed to Jews being forced to wear the yellow star. The real torturers were Darquier, Darnand and the Milice; in fact he waited until 6 August 1944, a few days before the end of Vichy, and after everyone had long been aware of the outrages of 'the political police', to write to Laval saying that 'for several months many reports have called my attention to the harmful activity of the Milice'.

A recent commentary on President Franklin D. Roosevelt's complex character strikingly fits that of Pétain, at least on the Jewish question: 'At the core of him a curious icy coldness ... enabling him to bear with equanimity, if not wholly without guilt feelings, human suffering he might have prevented – even suffering he sometimes, and sometimes quite needlessly, directly imposed.'[12]

How says the defence? The creation of the Vichy state and the assigning of unconventional power to Pétain were essential to guarantee national order and hold a divided and humiliated nation together. The Vichy leaders were misunderstood patriots. The times were extreme, and German power was close by; one cannot judge actions in that period because we can never come to terms with it or even fully comprehend it.[13] Many in Vichy were playing a double game, pretending to be collaborators but in reality helping the Anglo-American forces and providing aid to the Resistance. Orders had to be obeyed; Papon claimed to be only a 'porte-plume', simply signing texts presented to him. Officials could not be held responsible for actions that were based on policies and decisions determined by others, or imposed by the Germans. Officials conformed, to some extent were politicised technicians, and worked on the basis of the Bridge over the River Kwai syndrome, doing the best job possible without questioning the objective of the work. Moral responsibility cannot be equated with penal responsibility. France would play a prominent role in the New Europe. Catholic values were being reinserted into the social and educational framework of the country. Enemies of France, Jews, communists, Freemasons, would be eliminated.

If Vichy sacrificed a high proportion of foreign Jews living in its territory, it did try, with some limited success, to save French Jews and to protect them because they were citizens, if not because they were Jews. Jews, after all, were said by many who were not even rabid anti-Semites to be a real social problem, as anti-Semitic literature suggested. If Vichy did engage in and initiate discriminatory legislation and actions against Jews, with some exceptions the government did not favour, support or encourage deportation or extermination. In any case, for apologists, Vichy did not know the destination or fate of the deported Jews, whom it said were being 'relocated' in eastern Europe.

The heavy charge against Vichy is the imposition of great suffering on innocent people through policies that betrayed France. Betrayal of the legitimate Third Republic in an atmosphere poisoned by humiliating defeat, a mixture of persuasion, intimidation, corruption, fear and deception.[14] Betrayal of the principles of liberty, equality and fraternity inherited from the French Republic. Betrayal of a democratic political and social system based, if imperfectly, on civil liberties, personal freedoms, legal equality, universal suffrage and careers open to talent, and replacing it with an unelected, authoritarian new political system, explicitly rejecting the separation of powers that Montesquieu thought was essential for a desirable polity. Betrayal of the British ally by a unilateral armistice that broke the treaty arrangement between the two countries. Betrayal of national sovereignty and national interest by collaboration in countless ways with Nazi Germany, including military assistance and logistical support for Nazi forces fighting Britain in the Middle East.

The charge against Vichy, neglected for so long in post-war France, is inhumane treatment of minorities whom it held undesirable; violation of the rights of those minorities and of political opponents of Vichy and Germany; devising a code of anti-Semitic law that was accepted and implemented by the administrative and legal professions and which at some points 'bettered the instruction' of Nazi Germany; and participation in the Final Solution. Vichy was responsible for both the civil death of Jews – by legal exclusion from the French community, by removal from economic life, by spoliation and Aryanisation – and their physical death by internment and deportation.

The key issue in judgement and the cardinal quality lacking in the personnel and defenders of Vichy is moral responsibility for public actions. At his trial Maurice Papon, the embodiment of administrative continuity, argued that there were no crises of confidence or conscience when one obeyed the orders of the government. He ignored the decision of the Nuremberg Tribunal, which rejected obedience to orders as an alibi for criminal acts. It is pertinent to ask, at what point does submission to authority end and responsibility of the individual begin?[15] Uncritical acceptance of orders, acquiescence in discriminatory policies, sacrifice of ethical principles and customary practices on the altar of pragmatic politics of collaboration and accommodation, all led Vichy officials and personnel to perform infamous deeds, to tolerate and even initiate acts of persecution, to remain in office and carry out these acts when they could have refused to carry out orders or could have resigned their posts. Few, if any, of the officials and personnel involved in Vichy – Pétain, Papon, Bousquet, Mitterrand, Darquier, Vallat – expressed any regret or remorse for their actions or doubted they had acted properly in their various roles in excluding and eliminating Jews from French life. Intellectual inquiry can appreciate the complexities of the times, the dilemmas for and the internal and external pressures on French people, the extenuating circumstances, the lack of certitude about motivations of individuals and, continuing in the present, the genuine self-induced or inauthentic amnesia about the past. Yet understanding does not necessitate forgiveness.

FATE OF SOME OF
THE COLLABORATORS

Raphaël Alibert (1887–1963): Condemned to death *in absentia* on 7 March 1947; lived in exile in Belgium; amnestied in 1959.

Joseph Barthélemy (1874–1945): Arrested in October 1944, imprisoned, died in hospital on 30 March 1945.

René Bousquet (1909–1993): Sentenced to five years of national degradation in June 1949, immediately removed; prosperous business career; indicted for crimes against humanity in 1991; assassinated in June 1993.

Yves Bouthillier (1901–1977): Sentenced by High Court to three years in prison in 1947; amnestied; worked in private banking sector.

Robert Brasillach (1909–1945): Executed, after trial, on 6 February 1945.

Fernand de Brinon (1885–1947): Left France for Germany in 1944; arrested in Bavaria in May 1945; condemned to death by French High Court of Justice and executed on 15 April 1947.

Amédée Bussière: Sentenced in 1946 to life imprisonment for intelligence with the enemy; released in 1951.

Jérôme Carcopino (1881–1970) High Court in July 1947 decided no case against him because of his services to the Resistance as head of the École Normale Supérieure.

Louis-Ferdinand Céline (1894–1961): Sentenced *in absentia* to one year in prison; arrested in 1951; collected writings published in the *Pléiade* in 1960.

Alphonse de Châteaubriant (1877–1951): Left France for Germany, and then for the Tyrol, where he died in 1951.

François Darlan (1881–1942): Left Vichy for Algeria, autumn 1942; assassinated there on 24 December 1942.

Joseph Darnand (1897–1845): In September 1944 left France for Sigmaringen; tried to hide in Italian religious institutions; condemned to death by High Court of Justice; executed on 10 October 1945.

Louis Darquier (1897–1980): Left France for Spain in 1944; condemned to death *in absentia* 1947, but not extradited, and died in Spain.

Marcel Déat (1894–1955): Left France for Sigmaringen in 1944, and then for Italy in 1945; hid in a religious institution in Turin; died on 5 January 1955, after he was converted.

Jacques Doriot (1898–1945): Left France for Germany in August 1944; worked with Germans to 'liberate' France, 1944–5; killed in an automobile accident on 22 February 1945.

Drieu La Rochelle (1893–1945): Committed suicide on 15 March 1945.

Pierre Étienne Flandin (1889–1958): Left France for Algeria; imprisoned in 1944, but no charge brought; High Court sentenced him to five years of 'national *indignité*', quickly removed.

Philippe Henriot (1889–1944): Assassinated by the Resistance in June 1944.

Pierre Laval (1883–1945): Left France for Belfort and then for Sigmaringen, September 1944; refused entry by Switzerland and Spain, fled to Austria; condemned to death by French High Court of Justice; executed on 15 October 1945.

Jean Leguay (1909–1989): At Liberation suspended from his position as a prefect; left for the United States where he worked for a time in chemicals and cosmetics; returned to France, worked in private sector, indicated in 1978 for crimes against humanity: no trial; died on 3 July 1989.

François Lehideux (1904–1998): Arrested and imprisoned at Liberation; released provisionally in 1946; court decided no case against him, February 1949; post-war prosperous business career.

Bernard Ménétrel (1906–1947): Accompanied Pétain to Sigmaringen in 1944; imprisoned at Fresnes from May 1945 to January 1946; died in 1947 in an automobile accident.

Maurice Papon (1910–): After Liberation, prominent public career; accused by newspaper in 1981 of crimes against humanity; special honour jury investigated his Resistance credentials; indicted in 1983 and again in 1991 for crimes against humanity; trial 1997–April 1998; convicted of complicity in arrests and internments; sentenced to ten years in prison. Released from prison by French appeals court on 18 September, 2002, due to 'poor health'.

Philippe Pétain (1856–1951): Left Vichy for Sigmaringen in August 1944, then to Switzerland in April 1945; returned to France, tried by High Court and sentenced to death in August 1945 but not executed; imprisoned in Île d'Yeu; died in July 1951.

Lucien Rebatet (1903–1972): Left France for Germany in August 1944, then for Austria where he was arrested; condemned to death by the Court of Justice of the Seine, not executed, but placed in prison until freed in July 1952.

André Tulard (1899–1967): No punishment.

Xavier Vallat (1891–1972): Imprisoned at the time of Liberation in Fresnes; condemned by High Court in December 1947 to ten years in prison.

SELECT BIBLIOGRAPHY

The literature on Vichy is now voluminous in both French and English. For convenience this list of works helpful for the present study is divided into pertinent categories.

General Works on the Vichy Regime

Atkin, Nicholas. *Pétain* (London: Longman, 1998).

Azéma, Jean-Pierre. *1940, L'Année Terrible* (Paris: Seuil, 1990).

Azéma, Jean-Pierre and François Bédarida, eds. *La France des Années Noires*, 2 vols, rev. edn (Paris: Seuil, 2000).

Azéma, Jean-Pierre and François Bédarida, eds. *La Régime de Vichy et les Français* (Paris: Fayard, 1992).

Azéma, Jean-Pierre and Olivier Wieviorka. *Vichy 1940–1944* (Paris: Perrin, 1997).

Baruch, Marc-Olivier. *La Régime de Vichy* (Paris: La Découverte, 1996).

Burrin, Philippe. *La France à l'Heure Allemande: 1940–1944* (Paris: Seuil, 1995); trans. Janet Lloyd, *France under the Germans: Collaboration and Compromise* (New York: New Press, 1996).

Cointet, Jean-Paul. *Pierre Laval* (Paris: Fayard, 1993).

Cointet, Jean-Paul. *Histoire de Vichy* (Paris: Plon, 1995).

Cointet, Michèle. *Vichy Capitale 1940–1944: Vérités et Légendes* (Paris: Perrin, 1993).

Conan, Eric and Henry Rousso. *Vichy, un Passé qui ne Passe Pas* (Paris: Fayard, 1994).

Delperrié de Bayac, Jacques. *Le Royaume du Maréchal: Histoire de la Zone Libre* (Paris: Laffont, 1975).

Ferro, Marc. *Pétain* (Paris: Hachette, 1990).

Giolitto, Pierre. *Histoire de la Milice* (Paris: Perrin, 1997).

Griffiths, Richard. *Pétain: a Biography of Marshal Philippe Pétain of Vichy* (New York: Doubleday, 1972).

Hoffmann, Stanley. *Decline or Renewal? France since the 1930s* (New York: Viking, 1974).

Hoffmann, Stanley. *In Search of France* (Cambridge, MA: Harvard University Press, 1963).

Jaeckel, Eberhard. *La France dans l'Europe de Hitler*, trans. Denis Meunier

(Paris: Fayard, 1968).

Kupferman, Fred. *Laval, 1883–1945* (Paris: Flammarion, 1983).

Laborie, Pierre. *L'Opinion Française sous Vichy* (Paris: Seuil, 2001).

Laborie, Pierre. *Les Français des Années Troubles* (Paris: Desclée de Brouwer, 2001).

Lottman, Herbert R. *Pétain: Hero or Traitor: The Untold Story* (New York: Morrow, 1985).

Melton, George, E. *Darlan: Admiral and Statesman of France, 1881–1942* (Westport, CT: Praeger, 1998).

Ousby, Ian. *Occupation: The Ordeal of France 1940–1944* (New York: St Martin's Press, 1998).

Paxton, Robert O. *Vichy France: Old Guard and New Order, 1940–1944* (New York: Knopf, 1972).

Paxton, Robert O. *Parades and Politics at Vichy: the French Officer Corps Under Marshal Pétain* (Princeton, NJ: Princeton University Press, 1966).

Peschanksi, Denis. *Vichy 1940–1944: Contrôle et Exclusion* (Brussels: Editions Complexe, 1997).

Rajsfus, Maurice. *La Police de Vichy: Les Forces de l'Ordre Françaises au Service de la Gestapo 1940–1944* (Paris: Le Cherche Midi, 1995).

Rousso, Henry. *The Vichy Syndrome: History and Memory in France since 1944*, trans. Authur Goldhammer (Cambridge, MA: Harvard University Press, 1991).

Rousso, Henry. *La Hantise du Passé* (Paris: Les Éditions Textuel, 1998).

Warner, Geoffrey. *Pierre Laval and the Eclipse of France* (London: Eyre and Spottiswoode, 1968).

Policies of Vichy

Andrieu, Claire. *La Banque sous l'Occupation* (Paris: Fondation Nationale des Sciences Politiques, 1990).

Cointet, Jean-Paul. *La Légion Française des Combattants* (Paris: Albin Michel, 1995).

Delperrié de Bayac, Jacques. *Histoire de la Milice, 1918–1945* (Paris: Fayard, 1994).

Fishman, Sarah, et al. eds. *France at War: Vichy and the Historians* (New York: Berg, 2000).

Gervereau, Laurent and Denis Peschanski, eds. *La Propagande sous Vichy, 1940–1944* (Paris: Bibliothéque de Documentation Internationale Contemporaine, 1990).

Halls, W. D. *Politics, Society and Christianity in Vichy France* (Oxford: Berg, 1995).

Halls, W. D. *The Youth of Vichy France* (Oxford: Clarendon Press, 1981).

Kuisel, Richard F. *Capitalism and the State in Modern France* (Cambridge: Cambridge UniversityPress, 1981).

Mattéoli Commission Report (Paris: La Documentation Française, 2000).

Milward, Alan S. *The New Order and the French Economy* (Oxford: Clarendon Press, 1970).

Rochebrune, de, Renaud and Jean-Claude Hazera, *Les Patrons sous l'Occupation* (Paris: Odile Jacob, 1995).

Rossignol, Dominique. *Histoire de la Propagande en France de 1940 à 1944: L'Utopie Pétain* (Paris: Presses Universitaires de France, 1991).

Verheyde, Philippe. *Les Mauvais Comptes de Vichy: L'Aryanisation des Enterprises Juives* (Paris: Perrin, 1999).

Vinen, Richard. *The Politics of French Business, 1936–1945* (Cambridge: Cambridge University Press, 1991).

Wormser, Olivier. *Les Origines Doctrinales de la 'Révolution Nationale', Vichy 10 Juillet 1940–31 March 1941* (Paris: Plon, 1971).

Fascism and Vichy

Belot, Robert. *Lucien Rebatet, un Itinéraire Fasciste* (Paris: Seuil, 1994).

Brunet, Jean-Paul. *Jacques Doriot, du Communisme au Fascisme* (Paris: Balland, 1986).

Burrin, Philippe. *Fascisme, Nazisme, Autoritarisme* (Paris: Seuil, 2000).

Burrin, Philippe. *La Dérive Fasciste, Doriot, Déat, Bergery* (Paris: Seuil, 1986).

Carroll, David. *French Literary Fascism: Nationalism, Antisemitism and the Ideology of Culture* (Princeton, NJ: Princeton University Pres, 1995).

Cointet, Jean-Paul. *Marcel Déat* (Paris: Perrin, 1998).

Milza, Pierre. *Fascisme Français, Passé et Présent* (Paris: Flammarion, 1987).

Nobécourt, Jacques. *Le Colonel de La Rocque (1885–1946) ou les Pièges du Nationalisme Chrétien* (Paris: Fayard, 1996).

Paxton, Robert. *French Peasant Fascism: Henry Dorgères's Greenshirts and the Crises of French Agriculture, 1929–1939* (New York: Oxford University Press, 1997).

Payne, Stanley G. *A History of Fascism, 1914–1945* (Madison, WI: University of Wisconsin Press, 1995).

Soucy, Robert. *French Fascism: The Second Wave, 1933–1939* (New Haven, CT: Yale University Press, 1995).

Sternhell, Zeev. *Neither Right nor Left: Fascist Ideology in France*, trans. David Maisel (Princeton, NJ: Princeton University Press, 1986).

Weber, Eugen. *Action Française: Royalism and Reaction in Twentieth Century France* (Stanford, CA: Stanford University Press, 1962).

Jews in France

Albert, Phyllis Cohen. *The Modernization of French Jewry: Consistory and Community in the Nineteenth Century* (Hanover, NH: University Press of New England, 1977).

Albert, Phyllis and Frances Malino, eds. *Essays in Modern Jewish History* (New Brunswick, NJ: Rutgers University Press, 1982).

Benbassa, Esther. *Histoire des Juifs en France* (Paris: Seuil, 1997), trans. M. B. DeBevoise, *The Jews of France: a History from Antiquity to the Present* (Princeton, NK: Princeton University Press, 1999).

Berkovitz, Jay R. *The Shaping of Jewish Identity in Nineteenth-century France* (Detroit, MI: Wayne State University Press, 1989).

Birnbaum, Pierre. *Les Fous de la République: Histoire Politique des Juifs d'État de Gambetta à Vichy* (Paris: Fayard, 1992); trans. Jane Todd, *The Jews of the Republic: A Political History of State Jews from Gambetta to Vichy* (Stanford, CA: Stanford University Press, 1996).

Birnbaum, Pierre. *Antisemitism in France: A Political History from Léon Blum to the Present* (Oxford: Blackwell, 1992).

Birnbaum, Pierre. *'La France aux Français': Histoire des Haines Nationalistes* (Paris: Seuil, 1993).

Caron, Vicki. *Uneasy Asylum: France and the Jewish Refugee Crisis, 1933–1942* (Stanford, CA: Stanford University Press, 1999).

Caron, Vicki. *Between France and Germany: The Jews of Alsace-Lorraine, 1871–1918* (Stanford, CA: Stanford University Press, 1988).

Green, Nancy. *The Pletzl of Paris: Jewish Immigrant Workers in the Belle Epoque* (New York: Holmes and Meir, 1986).

Hertzberg, Arthur. *The French Enlightenment and the Jews* (New York: Columbia University Press, 1968).

Hyman, Paula E. *The Jews of Modern France* (Berkeley, CA: University of California Press, 1998).

Katz, Jacob. *From Prejudice to Destruction* (Cambridge, MA: Harvard University Press, 1980).

Malino, Frances and Bernard Wasserstein, eds. *The Jews in Modern France* (Hanover, NH: University Press of New England, 1985).

Marrus, Michael. *The Politics of Assimilation: The French Jewish Community at the Time of the Dreyfus Affair (Oxford: Clarendon Press, 1980).*

Millman, Richard. *La Question Juive entre les Deux Guerres* (Paris: Armand Colin, 1992).

Schor, Ralph. *L'Antisémitisme en France pendant les Années Trente: Prélude à Vichy* (Brussels: Éditions Complexe, 1992).

Schwarzfuchs, Simon. *Aux Prises avec Vichy: Histoire Politique des Juifs de France 1940–1944* (Paris: Calmann-Lévy, 1998).

Vidal-Nacquet, Pierre. *Assassins of Memory: Essays on the Denial of the Holocaust;* trans. Jeffrey Mehlman (New York: Columbia University Press, 1992).

Vidal-Naquet, Pierre. *The Jews: History, Memory, and the Past*, trans. David A. Curtis (New York: Columbia University Press, 1996).

Weinberg, David. *A Community on Trial: The Jews of Paris in the 1930s* (Chicago, IL: University of Chicago Press, 1977).

Wilson, Stephen. *Ideology and Experience: Antisemitism at the Time of the Dreyfus Affair* (Rutherford, NJ: Fairleigh Dickinson University Press, 1982).

Jews During the War

Abitbol, Michael. *The Jews of North Africa during the Second World War* (Detroit, MI: Wayne State University Press, 1989).

Adler, Jacques. *The Jews of Paris and the Final Solution: Communal Response and Internal Conflicts, 1940–1944* (New York: Oxford University Press, 1987).

Billig, Joseph. *Le Commissariat Général aux Questions Juives, 1941–1944*, 3 vols (Paris: Éditions du Centre, 1955).

Brayard, Florent, ed. *Le Génocide des Juifs entre Procès et Histoire 1943–2000* (Paris: Éditions Complexe, 2000).

Cohen, Asher. *Persécutions et Sauvetages: Juifs et Français Sous l'Occupation et Sous Vichy* (Paris: Cerf, 1993).

Cohen, Richard (Yerachmiel). *The Burden of Conscience: French Jewish Leadership during the Holocaust* (Bloomington, IN: Indiana University Press, 1987).

Courtois, Stéphane and Adam Rayski: *Qui Savait Quoi? L'Extermination des Juifs* (Paris: La Découverte, 1987).

Felman, Shoshana and Dori Laub. *Testimony: Crises of Witnessing in Literature, Psychoanalysis, and History* (New York: Routledge, 1992).

Grynberg, Anne. *Les Camps de la Honte: Les Internés Juifs des Camps Français, 1939–1944* (Paris: La Découverte, 1999).

Hallie, Philip. *Lest Innocent Blood be Shed: The Story of the Village of Le Chambon and How Goodness Happened There* (New York: Harper and Row, 1979).

Kaspi, André. *Les Juifs Pendant L'Occupation* (Paris: Seuil, 1991).

Klarsfeld, Serge. *Vichy–Auschwitz: Le Rôle de Vichy dans la Solution Finale de la Question Juive en France, 1942.* (Paris: Fayard, 1983).

Klarsfeld, Serge. *Le Calendrier de la Persécution des Juifs en France, 1940–1944* (Paris: FFDJF, 1983).

Lambert, Raymond-Raoul. *Carnet d'un Témoin, 1940–1943*, ed. Richard Cohen (Paris: Fayard, 1985).

Lazare, Lucien. *Rescue as Resistance: How Jewish Organizations Fought the Holocaust in France*, trans. Jeffrey M. Green (New York: Columbia University Press, 1996).

Lévy, Claude and Paul Tillard. *Betrayal at the Vél d'Hiv*, trans. Inea Bushnaq (New York: Hill and Wang, 1969).

Lochak, Danièle. A number of articles in *Le Genre Humain*, 1989, 1994, 1996.

Marrus, Michael R. and Robert O. Paxton. *Vichy France and the Jews* (New York: Basic Books, 1981).

Oppetit, Christian, ed. *Marseille, Vichy et les Nazis: Le Temps des Rafles, la Déportation des Juifs* (Marseille: Amicale des Déportés d'Auschwitz et des Camps de Haute-Silésie, 1993).

Peschanski, Denis. *Vichy 1940–1944: Contrôle et Exclusion* (Brussels: Editions Complexe, 1997).

Poznanski, Renée. *Être Juif en France Pendant la Second Guerre Mondiale* (Paris: Hachette, 1994).

Rajsfus, Maurice. *La Police de Vichy: Les Forces de l'Ordre Françaises au Service de la Gestapo, 1940–1944* (Paris: Le Cherche Midi, 1995).

Rajsfus, Maurice. *Jeudi Noir: 50 Ans Après la Rafle du 16 Juillet 1942: Récit-Document* (Levallois-Perret: Manya, 1992).

Rajsfus, Maurice. *Drancy: Un Camp de Concentration Très Ordinaire, 1941–1944* (Paris: Manya, 1991).

Rayski, Adam. *Le Choix des Juifs sous Vichy: Entre Soumission et Résistance* (Paris: Éditions la Découverte, 1992).

Ryan, Donna. *The Holocaust and the Jews of Marseilles: The Enforcement of Antisemitic Policies in Vichy France* (Urbana, IL: University of Illinois Press, 1996).

Singer, Claude. *Vichy, l'Université et les Juifs: Les Silences et la Mémoire* (Paris: Belles Lettres, 1992).

Wellers, Georges, André Kaspi and Serge Klarsfeld. *La France et la Question Juive, 1940–1944* (Paris: Messinger, 1981).

Wieviorka, Annette. *Déportation et Génocide: Entre la Mémoire et l'Oubli* (Paris: Plon, 1992).

Zuccotti, Susan. *The Holocaust, the French and the Jews* (New York: Basic Books, 1993).

Collaborators and Post-War Trials

Azéma, Jean-Pierre. *La Collaboration, 1940–1944* (Paris: Presses Universitaires de France, 1975).

Boulanger, Gérard. *Maurice Papon, un Technocrate dans la Collaboration* (Paris: Seuil, 1994).

Bruno, Jean and Frédéric de Monicault. *L'Affaire Papon: Bordeaux 1942–1944* (Paris: Tallandier, 1997).

Cohen-Grillet, Philippe. *Maurice Papon, de la Collaboration aux Assises* (Paris: Le Bord de L'Eau, 1997).

Cointet-Labrousse, Michèle. *Vichy et le Fascisme* (Brussels: Editions Complexe, 1987).

Comte, Bernard. *Une Utopie Combattante: L'École des Cadres d'Uriage, 1940–1942* (Paris: Fayard, 1991).

Conan, Eric. *Le Procès Papon: Un Journal d'Audience* (Paris: Gallimard, 1998).

Dumay, Jean-Michel. *Le Procès de Maurice Papon: La Chronique de Jean-Michel Dumay*, for *Le Monde* (Paris: Fayard, 1998).

Froment, Pascale. *René Bousquet* (Paris: Stock, 1994).

Golsan, Richard J. *Vichy's Afterlife: History and Counterhistory in Post-war France* (Lincoln, NB: University of Nebraska Press, 2000).

Golsan, Richard J., ed. *Memory, the Holocaust, and French Justice: The Bousquet and Touvier Affairs* (Hanover, NH: University Press of New England, 1996).

Gordon, Bertram M. *Collaborationism in France during the Second World War* (Ithaca, NY: Cornell UniversityPress, 1980).

Hellman, John. *The Knight-Monks of Vichy France: Uriage, 1940–1945*, 2nd edn (Montreal: McGill-Queen's University Press, 1997).

Hirschfeld, Gerhard and Patrick Marsh, eds. *Collaboration in France: Politics and Culture during the Nazi Occupation, 1940–1944* (Oxford: Berg, 1989).

Jankowski, Paul. *Communism and Collaboration: Simon Sabiani and Politics in Marseille 1919–1944* (New Haven, CT: Yale University Press, 1989).

Novick, Peter. *The Resistance Versus Vichy: The Purge of Collaborators in Liberated France* (New York: Columbia University Press, 1968).

Ory, Pascal. *Les Collaborateurs, 1940–1945* (Paris: Seuil, 1976).

Peschanski, Denis *et al. Collaboration and Resistance: Images of Life in Vichy France, 1940–1944*, trans. Lory Frankel (New York, Abrams, 2000).

Rousso, Henry. *La Collaboration* (Paris: Éditions MA, 1987).

Schneidermann, Daniel. *L'Étrange Procès* (Paris: Fayard, 1998).

Slitinsky, Michel. *Procès Papon, le Devoir de Justice* (Paris: L'Aube, 1997).

Veillon, Dominique. *La Collaboration: Textes et Débats* (Paris: Livre de Poche, 1984).

Vinen, Richard. *The Politics of French Business, 1936–1945* (Cambridge: Cambridge University Press, 1991).

Violet, Bernard. *Le Dossier Papon* (Paris: Flammarion, 1997).

Webster, Paul. *Pétain's Crime: The Full Story of French Collaboration in the Holocaust* (Chicago, IL: Dee, 1991).

Administration and Legal Profession

Badinter, Robert. *Un Antisémitisme Ordinaire: Vichy et les Avocats Juifs (1940–1944)* (Paris: Fayard, 1997).

Baruch, Marc Olivier. *Servir l'État Français: L'Administration en France de 1940 à 1944* (Paris: Fayard, 1997).

Bloch-Lainé, François and Claude Gruson. *Hauts Fonctionnaires sous l'Occupation* (Paris: Odile Jacob, 1996).

Gros, Dominique. *Juger sous Vichy: Le Genre Humain* (Paris: Seuil, 1996).

Lochak, Danièle. 'La Doctrine sous Vichy ou les Mésaventures du Positivisme', *Les Usages Sociaux du Droit* (Paris: CURAPP, PUF, 1989).

Lochak, Danièle. 'Le Conseil d'État sous Vichy et le Consiglio di Stato Sous le Fascisme', *Le Droit Administratif en Mutation* (Paris: PUF, 1993).

Lochak, Danièle. 'Écrire, se taire', in *Le Genre Humain* no. 31, May 1996.

Rémy, Dominique, *Les Lois de Vichy*, 2nd edn (Paris: Éditions Romillat, 1992).

Weisberg, Richard H. *Vichy, Law and the Holocaust in France* (New York: New York University Press, 1996).

Cultural Activity

Added, Serge. *Le Théâtre dans les Années Vichy* (Paris: Ramsay, 1992).

Bazin, André. *French Cinema of the Occupation and Resistance: The Birth of a Critical Esthetic* (New York: Ungar, 1981).

Bertin-Maghit, Jean-Pierre. *Le Cinéma sous l'Occupation* (Paris: Orban, 1989).

Bertrand Dorleac, Laurence. *L'Art de la Défaite* (Paris: Seuil, 1993).

Château, Rene. *Le Cinéma Français sous l'Occupation, 1940–1944* (Paris: Éditions Château, 1995).

Colombat, André. *The Holocaust in French Film* (Metuchen: Scarecrow Press, 1993).

Cone, Michèle. *Artists Under Vichy: A Case of Prejudice and Persecution* (Princeton, NJ: Princeton University Press, 1992).

Ehrlich, Evelyn. *French Filmmaking under the German Occupation* (New York: Columbia UniversityPress, 1985).

Faure, Christian. *Le Projet Culturel de Vichy: Folklore et Révolution Nationale 1940–1944* (Lyon: Presses Universitaires de Lyon, 1989).

Feliciano, Hector. *The Lost Museum: The Nazi Conspiracy to Steal the World's Greatest Works of Art* (New York: Basic Books, 1997).

Greene, Naomi. *Landscapes of Loss: The National Past in Postwar French Cinema* (Princeton, NJ: Princeton University Press, 1999).

Hollier, Denis. *Absent without Leave: French Literature under the Threat of War* (Cambridge, MA: Harvard University Press, 1997).

Joubert, Marie-Agnes, *La Comédie-Française sous l'Occupation* (Paris: Tallandier, 1998).

Kaplan, Alice. *Reproductions of Banality: Fascism, Literature and French Intellectual Life* (Minneapolis, MN: University of Minnesota Press, 1986).

Langer, Lawrence L. *The Age of Atrocity: Death in Modern Literature* (Boston, MA: Beacon Press, 1978).

Loiseaux, Gérard. *La Littérature de la Défaite et de la Collaboration* (Paris: Publications de la Sorbonne, 1984).

Martinoir, Francine de. *La Littérature Occupée: Les Années de Guerre, 1939–1945* (Paris: Hatier, 1995).

Morris, Alan. *Collaboration and Resistance Reviewed: Writers and the 'Mode Rétro' in Post-Gaullist France* (New York: Berg, 1992).

Rioux, Jean-Pierre, ed. *La Vie Culturelle sous Vichy* (Brussels: Complexe, 1990).

Suleiman, Susan S. *Risking Who One Is: Encounters with Contemporary Art and Literature* (Cambridge, MA: Harvard University Press, 1994).

Taguieff, Pierre-André, Grégoire Kauffmann and Michaël Lenoire. *L'Antisémitisme de Plume 1940–1944: Études et Documents* (Paris: Berg, 1999).

The Churches

Boegner, Philippe, ed. *Carnets du Pasteur Boegner, 1940–1945* (Paris: Fayard, 1992).

Chadwick, Owen. *Britain and the Vatican during the Second World War* (New York: Cambridge University Press, 1986).

Cointet, Michèle. *L'Église sous Vichy, 1940–1945* (Paris: Perrin, 1998).

Drapac, Vesna. *War and Religion: Catholics in the Churches of Occupied Paris* (Washington, DC: Catholic University of America Press, 1998).

Duquesne, Jacques. *Les Catholiques Français sous l'Occupation* (Paris: Grasset, 1966), reissue (Paris: Seuil, 1986).

Fouilloux, Étienne. *Les Chrétiens Français entre Crise et Libération, 1937–1947* (Paris: Seuil, 1997).

Halls, Wilfred D. *Politics, Society and Christianity in Vichy France* (Oxford: Berg, 1995).

Kaplan, Alice. *The Collaborator: The Trial and Execution of Robert Brasillach* (Chicago, IL: University of Chicago Press, 2000).

Morley, John F. *Vatican Diplomacy and the Jews during the Holocaust, 1939–1943* (New York: Ktav, 1980).

Rémond, René, Jean-Pierre Azéma and François Bedarida. *Paul Touvier et l'Église* (Paris: Fayard, 1992).

Resistance and Civil War

Bertin, Célia. *Femmes sous l'Occupation* (Paris: Stock, 1993).

Hallie, Philip. *Lest Innocent Blood Be Shed: The Story of the Village of Le Chambon and How Goodness Happened There* (New York: Harper and Row, 1979).

Kedward, H. R. *In Search of the Maquis: Rural Resistance in Southern France, 1942–1944* (Oxford: Clarendon Press, 1993).

Kedward, H. R. *Resistance in Vichy France: A Study of Ideas and Motivation in the Southern Zone 1940–1942* (Oxford: Oxford University Press, 1978).

Kedward, H. R. and Roger Austin, eds. *Vichy France and the Resistance* (Totowa, NJ: Barnes and Noble, 1985).

Kedward, H. R. and Nancy Wood. *The Liberation of France: Image and Event* (Oxford: Berg, 1995).

Latour, Anny. *The Jewish Resistance in France* (New York: Holocaust Library, 1981).

Lazare, Lucien. *Rescue as Resistance: How Jewish Organizations Fought the Holocaust in France* (New York: Columbia University Press, 1996).

Marino, Andy. *American Pimpernel: The Man Who Saved the Artists on Hitler's Death List* (London: Hutchinson, 1999).

Pollard, Miranda. *Reign of Virtue: Mobilizing Gender in Vichy France* (Chicago, IL: University of Chicago Press, 1998).

Sweets, John F. *The Politics of Resistance in France, 1940–1944* (De Kalb, IL: Northern Illinois University Press, 1976).

Sweets, John F. *Choices in Vichy France: The French under Nazi Occupation* (New York: Oxford University Press, 1986).

Todorov, Tsvetan. *A French Tragedy: Scenes of Civil War, Summer 1944* (Hanover, NH: University Press of New England, 1996).

Veillon, Dominique. *Le Franc-Tireur: Un Journal Clandestin, Un Mouvement de Résistance 1940–1944* (Paris: Flammarion, 1977).

Weitz, Margaret Collins. *Sisters in the Resistance: How Women Fought to Free France* (New York: Wiley, 1995).

Some Pertinent Memoirs

Antelme, Robert. *L'Espèce Humaine* (Paris: Gallimard, 1957).

Aubrac, Lucie. *Outwitting the Gestapo*, trans. Konrad Bieber (Lincoln, NB: University of Nebraska Press, 1993).

Baudouin, Paul. *Neuf Mois au Gouvernement* (Paris: La Table Ronde, 1948).

Barthélemy, Joseph. *Ministre de la Justice, Vichy 1941–1943: Mémoires* (Paris: Pygmalion, 1989).

Bellos, David. *Georges Perec: A Life in Words* (Boston, MA: Godine, 1993).

Cayrol, Jean. *Alerte aux Ombres* (Paris: Seuil, 1997).

Cretzmeyer, Stacy. *Your Name is Renée. Ruth's Story as a Hidden Child* (Brunswick, ME: Biddle, 1994).

Delbo, Charlotte. *Auschwitz et Après* (Paris: Éditions de Minuit, 1971).

Fittko, Lisa. *Le Chemin des Pyrénées: Souvenirs 1940–1941* (Paris: Sell, 1987).

Fry, Varian. *Surrender on Demand* (New York: Random House, 1945).

Gold, Mary Jayne. *Crossroads Marseilles, 1940* (Garden City, NY: Doubleday, 1980).

Grunberg, Albert. *Journal d'un Coiffeur Juif à Paris sous l'Occupation* (Paris: L'Atelier, 2001).

Hanin, Roger. *Lettre à un Ami Mystérieux* (Paris: Grasset, 2001).

Kahn, Annette. *Why My Father Died: A Daughter Confronts Her Family's Past at the Trial of Klaus Barbie*, trans. Anna Concogni (New York: Summit Press, 1991).

Kofman, Sarah. *Rue Ordener, Rue Labat* (Paris: Éditions Galilée, 1994).

Levendel, Isaac. *Not the Germans Alone: A Son's Search for the Truth of Vichy* (Evanston, IL: Northwestern University Press, 1999).

Moulin de Labarthè, Henri du. *Le Temps des Illusions: Souvenirs Juillet 1940–Avril 1942* (Geneva, 1946).

Semprun, Jorge. *Literature or Life*, trans. Linda Coverdale (New York: Viking, 1997).

Wellers, Georges. *Un Juif sous Vichy* (Paris: Éditions Tiresias, 1991).

Wiesel, Elie. *And the Sea is Never Full: Memoirs 1969–* (New York: Knopf, 1999).

Zeitoun, Sabine. *Les Enfants qu'il Fallait Sauver* (Paris: Michel, 1989).

Fiction and Vichy

Céline, Louis-Ferdinand. *D'un Château l'Autre* (Paris: Gallimard, 1957).

Duras, Marguerite. *La Douleur* (Paris: POL, 1985).

Dutourd, Jean. *The Best Butter*, trans. Robin Chancellor (New York: Simon and Schuster, 1955).

Faulks, Sebastian. *Charlotte Gray* (New York: Random House, 1998).

Hodeir, André. *Musikant* (Paris: Seuil, 1987).

Joffo, Joseph. *Un Sac de Billes* (London: Routledge, 1989).

Lambron, Marc. *1941* (Paris: Grasset, 1997).

Modiano, Patrick. *La Place de L'Étoile* (Paris: Gallimard, 1968).

Modiano, Patrick. *La Ronde de Nuit* (Paris: Gallimard, 1969).

Modiano, Patrick. *Dora Bruder* (Paris: Gallimard, 1997).

Moore, Brian. *The Statement* (London: Bloomsbury, 1995).

Semprun, Jorge. *Le Grand Voyage* (Paris: Gallimard, 1963).

Films Relating to Vichy

L'Accompagnatrice, directed by Claude Miller, 1992.

Une Affaire de Femmes, directed by Claude Chabrol, 1998.

Au Revoir les Enfants, directed by Louis Malle, 1987.

Le Chagrin et la Pitié, directed by Marcel Ophuls, 1969.

Le Chambon: La Colline aux Mille Enfants, directed by Jean-Louis Lorenzi, 1994.

Le Dernier Métro, directed by François Truffaut, 1980.

Entre Nous, directed by Diane Kurys, 1993.

Eye of Vichy, directed by Claude Chabrol, 1996.

Un Héros Très Discret, directed by Jacques Audiard, 1998.

Hiroshima, Mon Amour, directed by Alain Resnais, 1959.

Hotel Terminus: The Life and Times of Klaus Barbie, directed by Marcel Ophuls, 1998.

Les Jeux Interdits, directed by René Clements, 1952.

Lacombe, Lucien, directed by Louis Malle, 1975.

Lucie Aubrac, directed by Claude Berri, 1997.

Monsieur Klein, directed by Joseph Losey, 1976.

Shoah, directed by Claude Lanzmann, 1986.

Terrorists in Retirement, a documentary, 1984.

Uranus, directed by Claude Berri, 1991.

Weapons of the Spirit, directed by Pierre Sauvage, 1988.

NOTES

Introduction

[1] Among recent writings on this theme are Philippe Burrin, *Fascisme, Nazisme, Authoritarisme* (Paris: Seuil, 2000); Eric Conan and Henry Rousso, *Vichy, un Passé qui ne Passe Pas* (Paris: Fayard, 1994); Jean-Marc Varaut, *Plaidoirie devant la Cour d'Assises de la Gironde au Procès de Marluice Papon, Fonctionnaire sous l'Occupation* (Paris: Plon, 1998); Jean-Pierre Azéma and Olivier Wieviorka, *Vichy 1940–1944* (Paris: Perrin, 1997); Philipe Burrin, *La France à l'Heure Allemande* (Paris: Seuil, 1995); Jean-Pierre Azéma and François Bédarida, eds, *La France des Années Noires* (Paris: Seuil, 1993).

[2] Lucette Valensi, 'Présence du Passé, Lenteur de l'Histoire: Vichy, l'Occupation, les Juifs', *Annales: Economies, Sociétés, Civilisations*, 48(3), May–June 1993, pp. 491–500.

[3] The note to *The Ethics of Aristotle* (Harmondsworth: Penguin, 1961), p. 173.

[4] Raymond Aron, *The Committed Observer: Le Spectateur Engagé*, interviews with Jean-Louis Missika and Dominique Wolton (Chicago, IL: Regnery, 1983), p. 95.

[5] Burrin, op. cit., pp. 274, 280; Henry Rousso, *The Vichy Syndrome: History and Memory in France since 1944* (Cambridge, MA: Harvard University Press, 1991); Serge Klarsfeld and Henry Rousso, 'Histoire et Justice', *Esprit*, 181 (1992), p 16–37.

[6] Sarah Farmer, *Martyred Village: Commemorating the 1944 Massacre at Oradour-sur-Glane* (Berkeley, CA: University of California Press, 1999); Pascal Maysounave, *Oradour, Plus près de la Vérité* (Paris: Souny, 1996).

[7] Burrin, op. cit., pp. 307–10.

[8] Henry Rousso, 'Juger le Passé? Justice et Histoire en France', in Florent Brayard, ed., *Le Génocide des Juifs entre Procès et Histoire 1943–2000* (Paris: Éditions Complexe, 2000), pp. 270–3.

[9] Naomi Greene, *Landscapes of Loss: The National Past in Post-war French Cinema* (Princeton, NJ: Princeton University Press, 1999), p. 36.

[10] Jean-Michel Dumay, *Le Procès de Maurice Papon* (Paris: Fayard, 1998), pp. 55–9, 60–3; Eric Conan, *Le Procès Papon: Un Journal d'Audience* (Paris: Gallimard, 1998), pp. 35, 38–9.

[11] Pierre Vidal-Naquet, *Les Assassins de la Mémoire. 'Un Eichmann de Papier' et Autres Essais sur le Révisionnisme* (Paris: La Découverte, 1987); Deborah E. Lipstadt, *Denying the Holocaust: The Growing Assault on Truth and Memory* (New York: Free Press, 1993), pp. 9–10. The main works of the Holocaust deniers are Robert Faurisson, *Mémoire en Défense contre Ceux Qui M'Accusent de Falsifier l'Histoire* (Paris: La

Vieille Taupe, 1980); Paul Rassinier, *Debunking the Genocide Myth: A Study of the Nazi Concentration Camps and the Alleged Extermination of European Jewry* (Los Angeles: Noontide Press, 1978); Roger Garaudy, *Les Mythes Fondateurs de la Politique Israélienne* (Paris: Samiszdat, 1996).

[12] Robert Paxton, *Vichy France: Old Guard and New Order, 1940–1944* (New York: Columbia University Press, 1982 edn); Eberhard Jäckel, *La France dans l'Europe de Hitler* (Paris: Fayard, 1968).

[13] Michael R. Marrus and Robert O. Paxton, *Vichy France and the Jews* (New York: Basic Books, 1980).

[14] Renée Poznanski, 'Vichy et les Juifs: Des Marges de l'Histoire au Coeur de son Écriture', in Jean-Pierre Azéma and François Bédarida, eds, *Le Régime de Vichy et les Français* (Paris: Fayard, 1992), p. 57.

[15] Henry Rousso, 'The Historian, a Site of Memory', in Sarah Fishman *et al.*, eds, *France at War: Vichy and the Historians* (New York: Berg, 2000), p. 295.

[16] Michael Marrus, 'Vichy France and the Jews: After Fifteen Years', in Fishman, p. 38.

[17] Yehuda Bauer, 'In Search of a Definition of Antisemitism', in Michael Brown, ed., *Approaches to Antisemitism* (New York: American Jewish Committee, 1994), p. 20.

[18] Pierre Nora, ed., *Realms of Memory: Rethinking the French Past*, 3 vols (New York: Columbia University Press, 1996); Saul Friedlander, *Memory, History and the Extermination of the Jews of Europe* (Bloomington, IN: Indiana University Press, 1993).

[19] Serge Klarsfeld, *French Children of the Holocaust: A Memorial* (New York: New York University Press, 1996).

[20] Henry Rousso, in Fishman, p. 292.

[21] Philippe Burrin, 'Vichy' in Nora, *Realms*, vol. 1, p. 182.

[22] Robert Aron, *The Vichy Regime, 1940–1944*, trans. Georgette Elgey (London: Putnam, 1958).

[23] Jäckel, op. cit., pp. 142–3, 176, 292–3.

[24] Robert Frank, 'La Mémoire Empoisonnée', in Jean-Pierre Azéma and François Bédarida, eds, *La France des Années Noires*, vol. 2 (Paris: Seuil, 2000), pp. 541–76.

[25] Jean-Pierre Azéma, *La Collaboration 1940–1944* (Paris: Presses Universitaires de France, 1975); Jean-Pierre Azéma and François Bédarida, eds, *Vichy et les Français: Révolution Nationale* (Paris: Fayard, 1992); Marc Ferro, *Pétain* (Paris: Fayard, 1987).

[26] Jean-François Sirinelli, *Deux Intellectuels dans Leur Siècle: Sartre et Aron* (Paris: Fayard, 1995); Gilbert Joseph, *Une Si Douce Occupation: Simone de Beauvoir et Jean-Paul Sartre* (Paris: Albin Michel, 1991); compare with Louis Parrot, *L'Intelligence en Guerre, Panorama de la Pensée Française dans la Clandestinité* (Paris: La Jeune Parque, 1945).

[27] Robert Aron, *The Vichy Regime, 1940–1944*, pp. 207–8, 263–4.

[28] Stanley Hoffman, 'Vichy Studies in France: Before and after Paxton', in Fishman, pp. 49–57.

[29] Henry Rousso, *The Vichy Syndrome*, p. 304.

Chapter 1: The Jews of France

[1] William C. Jordan, *The French Monarchy and the Jews: From Philip Augustus to the Late Capetians* (Philadelphia, PA: University of Pennsylvania Press, 1989), pp. 29–30, 56–7, 246.

[2] Esther Benbassa, *Histoire des Juifs en France* (Paris: Seuil, 1997), pp. 82–4.

[3] Frances Malino, *The Sephardic Jews of Bordeaux* (Tuscaloosa: University of Alabama Press, 1978).

[4] Esther Benbassa, *The Jews of France*, trans. M. B. DeBevoise (Princeton, NJ: Princeton University Press, 1999), p. 71; Arthur Hertzberg, *The French Enlightenment and the Jews* (New York: Columbia University Press, 1968), p. 136.

[5] Pierre Birnbaum, 'Between Social and Political Assimilation: Remarks on the History of Jews in France', in P. Birnbaum and Ira Katznelson, eds, *Paths of Emancipation: Jews, States and Citizenship* (Princeton, NJ: Princeton University Press, 1995), pp. 94–127.

[6] Jay R. Berkovitz, *The Shaping of Jewish Identity in Nineteenth-century France* (Detroit, MI: Wayne State University Press, 1989), p. 59.

[7] Bernhard Blumenkranz and Albert Soboul, eds, *Les Juifs et la Révolution Française* (Toulouse: Privat, 1976), pp. 10–11.

[8] Vicki Caron, *Between France and Germany: The Jews of Alsace-Lorraine, 1871–1918* (Stanford, CA: Stanford University Press, 1988), pp. 187–94.

[9] Jacob Katz, *Out of the Ghetto* (Cambridge, MA: Harvard University Press, 1973), p. 72.

[10] Paula E. Hyman, *The Emancipation of the Jews of Alsace: Acculturation and Tradition in the Nineteenth Century* (New Haven, CT: Yale University Press, 1991), p. 156.

[11] Berkovitz, pp. 128–49.

[12] Speech of Joseph Reinach on 29 January 1891 in the Chamber of Deputies, quoted in Pierre Birnbaum, *Les Fous de la République* (Paris: Fayard, 1992), p. 13.

[13] Paula E. Hyman, *From Dreyfus to Vichy: The Remaking of French Jewry, 1906–1939* (New York: Columbia University Press, 1979), pp. 115–18.

[14] Nancy Green, *The Pletzl of Paris: Jewish Immigrant Workers in the Belle Époque* (New York: Holmes and Meier, 1986).

[15] Emile Durkheim, *Textes 2. Religion, morale*, p. 252, quoted in Dominique Schnapper, *Jewish Identities in France: An Analysis of Contemporary French Jewry* (Chicago, IL: University of Chicago Press, 1983), p. 171.

[16] David H. Weinberg, *A Community on Trial: The Jews of Paris in the 1930s* (Chicago, IL: University of Chicago Press, 1977), p. 18.

[17] Birnbaum, *Antisemitism in France* (Oxford: Blackwell, 1992), pp. 42–4.

[18] Marc Bloch, *Strange Defeat*, p. 3.

[19] Vicki Caron, 'Fools for Love of the Republic?', *AJS*, 24(1), 1999, pp. 101–2.

[20] M. Goldmann, *Darius Milhaud: Un Musicien Heureux*, p. 70 in Schnapper, p. 108.

[21] Joel Colton, *Léon Blum: Humanist in Politics* (New York: Knopf, 1966), p. 43.

[22] Birnbaum, *Jewish Destinies: Citizenship, State and Community in Modern France*, trans. Arthur Goldhammer (New York: Hill and Wang, 2000), p. 19.

[23] Pierre Birnbaum, 'Grégoire, Dreyfus, Drancy, and the rue Copernic: Jews at the Heart of French History', in Nora, vol. 1, p. 389.

[24] Ronald Schechter, 'Translating the "Marseillaise": Biblical Republicanism and the Emancipation of Jews in Revolutionary France', *Past and Present*, 14(3), May 1994, pp. 108–9.

[25] Napoleon, speeches of 30 April and 7 May 1806, and letter to his brother Jerome, King of Westphalia, 6 March 1808.

[26] Paula E. Hyman, *The Jews of Modern France* (Berkeley, CA: University of California Press, 1998), p. 52.

[27] David Vital, *A People Apart: The Jews in Europe, 1789–1939* (New York: Oxford University Press, 1999), pp. 58–9.

[28] Hyman, *The Jews*, p. 43.

[29] Phyllis Cohen Albert, *The Modernization of French Jewry: Consistory and Community in the Nineteenth Century* (Hanover, NH: University Press of New England for Brandeis University, 1977), pp. 57–60.

[30] Michael Graetz, *Les Juifs en France au XIXe Siècle: De la Révolution Française à l'Alliance Israélite Universelle* (Paris: Seuil, 1989), p. 11.

[31] Pierre Birnbaum, *Les Fous*, pp. 8–9.

[32] Philippe E. Landau, *Les Juifs de France et la Grand Guerre: Un Patriotisme Républicain 1914–1941* (Paris: Éditions du CNRS, 1999), p 261.

[33] Birnbaum, *Les Fous*, p. 187.

[34] Pierre Vidal-Naquet, *Mémoires, la Brisure et l'Attente, 1930–1955* (Paris: Seuil/La Découverte, 1995), pp. 130–2.

[35] Lucien Lazare, *Rescue as Resistance: How Jewish Organizations Fought the Holocaust in France* (New York: Columbia University Press, 1996), p. 12.

[36] Pierre Vidal-Naquet, *Les Juifs, la Mémoire et le Présent* (Paris: Maspero, 1981), p. 104; Paula Hyman, *From Dreyfus to Vichy*, p. 117.

[37] Weinberg, p. 76.

[38] Weinberg, p. 85.

[39] Caron, p. 320.

[40] Birnbaum, *Jews*, p. 367.

[41] Weinberg, p. 88.

Chapter 2: Anti-Semitism in France

[1] Zeev Sternhell, *Neither Right Nor Left: Fascist Ideology in France* (Berkeley, CA: University of California Press, 1986). Originally, *Ni Droite ni Gauche: L'Idéologie Fasciste en France* (Paris: Seuil, 1983); Sternhell *et al.*, *The Birth of Fascist Ideology: From Cultural Rebellion to Political Revolution* (Princeton, NJ: Princeton University Press, 1994).

[2] Pierre Birnbaum, *Jewish Destinies*, p. viii.

[3] Vicki Caron, 'The Antisemitic Revival in France in the 1930s: The Socioeconomic Dimension Reconsidered', *Journal of Modern History*, 70(1), 1998, pp. 24–73.

[4] Anthony P. Adamthwaite, *Grandeur and Misery: France's Bid for Power in Europe, 1914–1940* (London: Arnold, 1995); Ernest R. May, *Strange Victory: Hitler's Conquest of France* (New York: Hill and Wang, 2000).

[5] Eugene Weber, *The Hollow Years: France in the 1930s* (New York: Norton, 1994); Omer Bartov, 'Martyrs' Vengeance: Memory, Trauma, and Fear of War in France, 1918–1940', in Joel Blatt, ed., *The French Defeat of 1940: Reassessments* (Providence, RI: Berghahn Books, 1998), pp. 56–7.

[6] Antoine Prost, 'Monuments to the Dead', in Nora, vol. 2, pp. 325, 328; Annette Becker, *La Guerre et la Foi: De la Mort à la Mémoire, 1914–1930* (Paris: Colin, 1994).

[7] Marc Bloch, *Strange Defeat* (London: Oxford University Press, 1949), pp. 134–49.

[8] Carole Fink, 'Marc Bloch and the Drôle de Guerre: Prelude to the "Strange Defeat"', in Blatt, p. 53.

[9] Pierre Birnbaum, 'Grégoire, Dreyfus, Drancy, and the rue Copernic: Jews at the Heart of French History', pp. 382–3.

[10] Pierre Birnbaumn *Antisemitism in France*, pp. 200–2.

[11] Ernest Renan, *Histoire Générale et Système Comparé des Langues Sémitiques* (Paris: Calmann-Lévy, 1901), Book 5, pp. 473–90.

[12] Stephen Wilson, *Ideology and Experience: Antisemitism in France at the Time of the Dreyfus Affair* (Rutherford: Fairleigh Dickinson University Press, 1982), p. 597.

[13] George Steiner, *No Passion Spent: Essays 1978–1996* (London: Faber and Faber, 1996), p. 229.

[14] Eric Cahm, *The Dreyfus Affair in French Society and Politics* (New York: Longman, 1994), p. 163; Maurice Agulhon, *French Republic, 1879–1992* (Oxford: Blackwell, 1993), p. 93.

[15] Nancy Fitch, 'Mass Culture, Mass Parliamentary Politics, and Modern Antisemitism in the Dreyfus Affair in Rural France', *American Historical Review*, 97(1), 1992, p. 92.

[16] Among some recent books are Stephen Wilson, *Ideology and Experience: Antisemitism in France at the Time of the Dreyfus Affair* (Rutherford, NJ: Fairleigh Dickinson University Press, 1980); Jean-Denis Bredin, *L'Affaire Dreyfus: La Vérité en Marche* (Paris: Imprimerie Nationale, 1992); Bredin, *The Affair: The Case of Alfred Dreyfus* (New York: Brazillier, 1986); Michel Winock, *L'Affaire Dreyfus* (Paris, Seuil, 1998); Winock, *Nationalism, Antisemitism, and Fascism in France* (Stanford, CA: Stanford University Press, 1998); Pierre Birnbaum, *Le Moment Antisémite: Un Tour de la France en 1898* (Paris: Fayard, 1998); Michael Burns, *Dreyfus: A Family Affair, 1789–1945* (New York: HarperCollins, 1991).

[17] Richard Griffiths, *The Use of Abuse: The Polemics of the Dreyfus Affair and Its Aftermath* (New York: Berg, 1991), pp. 4–5.

[18] Birnbaum, *Antisemitism in France*, pp. 89, 112.

[19] Birnbaum, ibid., pp. 86–7.

[20] Edouard Drumont, *La Libre Parole*, 3 November 1894.

[21] Maurice Barrès, 'L'Education Nationale', *Le Journal*, 30 October 1899.

[22] Maurice Barrès, *Scènes et Doctrines du Nationalisme* (Paris: Juven, 1902), I, p. 61.

[23] Maurice Barrès, 'L'État de la Question', *Le Journal*, 4 October 1898.

[24] Michael Curtis, *Three against the Third Republic: Sorel, Barrès, and Maurras* (Princeton, NJ: Princeton University Press, 1959), pp. 214–17.

[25] Quoted in Birnbaum, *Antisemitism*, p. 235.

[26] Birnbaum, p. 237, quoting *L'Action Française*, 9 April 1935, 14 May 1936 and 16 May 1936.

[27] Birnbaum, p. 237, quoting Victor Nguyen, *L'Idée de Race dans la Pensée Politique Français Contemporaine*, p. 146.

[28] Zeev Sternhell, 'The Roots of Popular Antisemitism in the Third Republic', in Frances Malino and Bernard Wasserstein, eds, *The Jews in Modern France* (Hanover, NH: University Press of New England, 1985), p. 133.

[29] Edmund Silberner, *Sozialisten zur Judenfrage: Ein Beitrag zur Geschichte des Sozialismus von Anfang des 19 Jahrhunderts bis 1914* (Berlin: Colloquium Verlag, 1962).

[30] Michael Burns, *Rural Society and French Politics: Boulangism and the Dreyfus Affair, 1886–1900* (Princeton, NJ: Princeton University Press, 1984), pp. 6, 140.

[31] Pierre Birnbaum, *Le Moment Antisémite*, chs 4 and 5.

[32] Nancy Fitch, *AHR*, p. 57.

[33] Stephen Wilson, 'Le Monument Henry: La Structure de l'Antisémitisme en France, 1898–1899', *Annales, Economies, Sociétés, Civilisations*, 32(1), 1977, pp. 265–91.

[34] Berkovitz, pp. 240, 260.

[35] André Latreille *et al.*, *Histoire du Catholicisme en France* (Paris: Spes, 1962), vol. 3, p. 491.

[36] Charles Péguy, *La Revue Blanche*, 15 September 1899.

[37] Introduction by Michel Drouin to the republication of Georges Clemenceau's *L'Iniquité* (Paris: Mémoire du Livre, 2001).

[38] Jacques Nobécourt, *Le Colonel de La Rocque (1885–1946) Ou les Pièges du Nationalisme Chrétien* (Paris: Fayard, 1996); Robert Soucy, *French Fascism: The Second Wave, 1933–1939* (New Haven, CT: Yale University Press, 1995); René Rémond, *Les Droits en France* (Paris: Aubier Montaigne, 1982).

[39] Kevin Passmore, 'The Croix de Feu: Bonapartism, National Populism or Fascism', *French History*, 9(l), 1995, pp. 67–92. The phrase is taken from Roger Griffin, *The Nature of Fascism* (London: Pinter, 1991).

[40] Soucy, pp. 119, 158.

[41] Robert D. Paxton, *French Peasant Fascism: Henry Dorgère's Greenshirts and the Crises of French Agriculture, 1929–1939* (New York: Oxford University Press, 1997).

[42] Philippe Burrin, *La Dérive Fasciste: Dotiot, Déat, Bergery: 1933–1945* (Paris: Seuil, 1986).

[43] Zeev Sternhell, Mario Sznajder and Maia Asheri, *Naissance de l'Idéologie Fasciste* (Paris: Fayard, 1989), p. 340.

[44] Soucy, pp. 56–7.

[45] Michèle Cointet, *L'Église sous Vichy, 1940–1945: La Repentance en Question* (Paris: Perrin, 1998), p. 191; Laurent Joly, *Xavier Vallat: Du Nationisme Chrétien à*

Antisémitisme de l'État, 1891–1972 (Paris: Grasset, 2000).

[46] Pierre Birnbaum, *Les Fous de la République* (Paris: Fayard, 1992), pp. 209–10.

[47] Joel Colton, *Léon Blum*, p. 340.

[48] Paxton, *Vichy France*, p. 178.

[49] Paul Webster, *Pétain's Crime: The Full Story of French Collaboration in the Holocaust* (Chicago, IL: Dee, 1991), p. 104.

[50] Birnbaum, *Antisemitism*, p. 171.

[51] Ralph Schor, *L'Antisémitisme en France pendant les Années Trente: Prélude à Vichy* (Brussels: Éditions Complexe, 1992), p. 44.

[52] André Gide, *Journal I, 1887–1925* (Paris: Gallimard, 1996), pp. 762–4; Pierre-André Taguieff, Grégoire Kauffman and Michael Lenoire, *L'Antisémitisme de Plume 1940–1944: Études et Documents* (Paris: Berg International, 1999), p. 20.

[53] Vicki Caron, 'The Antisemitic Revival in France in the 1930s: The Socioeconomic Dimension Reconsidered', and Caron, 'Prelude to Vichy: France and the Jewish Refugees in the Era of Appeasement', *Journal of Contemporary History*, 20(1), 1985, pp. 157–76.

[54] Gérard Noiriel, *Les Origines Républicains de Vichy* (Paris: Hachette Littératures, 1999).

Chapter 3: Vichy: the French State

[1] Ernest R. May, *Strange Victory: Hitler's Conquest of France* (New York: Hill and Wang, 2000); Marc Bloch, *Strange Defeat*.

[2] Ian Ousby, *Occupation: The Ordeal of France 1940–1944* (New York: St Martin's Press, 1998), p. 53.

[3] Public Records Office, Kew Gardens, FO 371/24311.

[4] Paul Baudouin, *Neuf Mois au Gouvernement* (Paris: La Table Ronde, 1948), p. 31.

[5] Martin Blinkhorn, *Fascism and the Right in Europe, 1919–1945* (New York: Longman, 2000), p. 90.

[6] Marshal Pétain's speeches of 10 July 1940 and 10 October 1940 in *Discours aux Français: 17 Juin 1940–20 Août 1944* (Paris: Albin Michel, 1989), pp. 68, 88.

[7] Helen McPhail, *The Long Silence: Civilian Life under the German Occupation of Northern France, 1914–1918* (New York: Tauris, 1999).

[8] Ted Morgan, *An Uncertain Hour: The French, the Germans, the Jews, the Barbie Trial, and the City of Lyon, 1940–1945* (New York: Morrow, 1990), p. 86.

[9] Pascal Ory, 'Why Be So Cruel? Some Modest Proposals to Cure the Vichy Syndrome', in Fishman, p. 277.

[10] Charles Maurras, *Le Petit Marseillais*, 9 February 1941.

[11] Olivier Wieviorka, *Les Orphelins de La République: Destinées des Députés et Sénateurs Français, 1940–1945* (Paris: Seuil, 2001).

[12] Wanda VanDusen, 'Portrait of a National Fetish: Gertrude Stein's "Introduction to The Speeches of Maréchal Pétain" ', *Modernism/Modernity*, 3(3), 1996, pp. 69–96.

[13] Pétain, speeches of 13 June 1940; 25 June 1940; 11 October 1940; 20 December 1940; 25 December 1940; 21 April 1941; 25 May 1941; 17 July 1941; 12 August 1941.

[14] Isser Woloch, *Napoleon and His Collaborators: The Making of a Dictatorship* (New York: Norton, 2001), pp. 10–12.

[15] Joseph Barthélemy, *Ministre de la Justice: Vichy 1941–1943: Mémoires* (Paris: Pygmalion/Gérard Watelet, 1989), p. 34.

[16] Jean-Pierre Azéma, *1940, L'Année Terrible* (Paris: Seuil, 1990), pp. 234, 263–4.

[17] Maurice Martin du Gard, *La Chronique de Vichy, 1940–1944* (Paris: Flammarion, 1948), p. 85.

[18] Ian Kershaw, *'Hitler Myth': Image and Reality in the Third Reich* (New York: Oxford University Press, 1987), pp. 2–5, 257–9.

[19] Pétain's speeches of 13 August 1940, 9 October 1940, 24 December 1940, in *Discours*, pp. 78, 85, 103.

[20] Nicholas Atkin, *Pétain* (New York: Longman, 1998), p. 104; Milton Dank, *The French against the French: Collaboration and Resistance* (New York: Lippincott, 1974), p. 28.

[21] Article 1 of Constitutional Act no. 7, 27 January 1941.

[22] Atkins, p. 156; Pétain's secretary, Henri du Moulin de Labarthète, *Le Temps des Illusions: Souvenirs Juillet 1940–Avril 1942* (Geneva: Éditions du Cheval Ailé, 1946), p. 95.

[23] Pétain's speech 11 May 1941, in *Discours*, p. 131.

[24] PRO, FO 371/24311.

[25] René Rémond, *Les Droites en France* (Paris: Aubier, 1982).

[26] Zeev Sternhell, *Ni Droite Ni Gauche*; also Jacob Talmon, *The Rise of Totalitarian Democracy* (Boston, MA: Beacon Press, 1952).

[27] Michel Winock, *Nationalism, Antisemitism and Fascism in France* (Stanford, CA: Stanford University Press, 1998).

[28] Thierry Maulnier, *La France, la Guerre et la Paix* (Lyon: Lardanchet, 1942), p. 98.

[29] Ernst Nolte, *Three Faces of Fascism: Action Française, Italian Fascism, National Socialism* (New York: Holt, Rinehart and Winston, 1965).

[30] Roger Bouderon, 'Was the Vichy Regime Fascist?', in John C. Cairns, ed., *Contemporary France: Illusion, Conflict and Regeneration* (New York: New Viewpoints, 1978), p. 213.

[31] Among other works on this theme are Robert Soucy, *French Fascism: The Second Wave*; Arno J. Mayer, *The Persistence of the Old Regime: Europe to the Great War* (New York: Pantheon, 1981).

[32] Richard F. Kuisel, 'Technocrats and Public Economic Policy', in Cairns, pp. 228–53.

[33] Yves Chalas, *Vichy et l'Imaginaire Totalitaire* (Arles: Actes Sud, 1985), pp. 31–2.

[34] Ian Kershaw, *Hitler: 1889–1936: Hubris* (London: Allen Lane, 1998), pp. 85–6; Kershaw, *The Nazi Dictatorship*, 4th edn (New York: Oxford University Press, 2000), pp. 5, 69–83, 149.

[35] Helena Pinto Janeiro, 'Salazar et Les Trois France, 1940–1944'; *Vingtième Siècle* (62), 1999, pp. 39–50.

[36] Alfred Rocco introducing the bill on corporations in the Italian Chamber of Deputies, January 1934.

[37] Antonio Salazar, speech of 26 May 1934, in Michael Derrick, *The Portugal of Salazar* (London: Paladin, 1938), pp. 148–9.

[38] Stanley Hoffmann, *Decline or Renewal? France since the 1930s* (New York: Viking Press, 1974), pp. 26-44; Denis Peschanski, 'Vichy Singular and Plural', in Fishman, pp. 107–24.

[39] Yves Durand, *La France dans la Deuxième Guerre Mondiale, 1939–1945* (Paris: Colin 1993); André Encrevé and Jacques Poujol, eds, *Les Protestants Français pendant la Seconde Guerre Mondiale* (Paris: Société de L'Histoire du Protestantisme Française, 1994); Xavier de Montclos, ed., *Églises et Chrétiens dans la IIe Guerre Mondiale* (Lyon: Presses Universitaires de Lyon, 1978–1982).

[40] Alain Decaux, *Morts pour Vichy: Darlan, Pucheu, Pétain, Laval* (Paris: Perrin, 2000), pp. 155–6.

[41] Barthélemy, p. 44.

[42] Philip Whitcomb, trans., *France during the German Occupation, 1940–1944: A Collection of 292 Statements on the Governments of Maréchal Pétain and Pierre Laval* (Stanford, CA: Stanford University Press, 1958–9), vol. II, pp. 626–9.

[43] Barthélemy, p. 620.

[44] Peschanski, 'Vichy Singular and Plural', in Fishman, p. 121.

[45] Atkin, p. 102.

[46] Pétain, speech of 12 August, 1941, *Discours*, p. 104.

[47] Decaux, p. 296.

[48] Michèle Cointet, *Le Conseil National de Vichy: Vie Politique et Réforme de l'État en Régime Autoritaire 1940–1944* (Paris: Aux Amateurs de Livres, 1989).

[49] George E. Melton, *Darlan: Admiral and Statesman of France, 1881–1942* (Westport, CT: Praeger, 1998), pp. 85–6.

[50] Richard Griffiths, *Marshal Pétain* (London: Constable, 1970), p. 284.

[51] Pétain, speech of 12 August 1941, in *Discours*, pp. 164–72.

[52] Atkin, p. 104.

[53] Letter of General Karl Oberg, quoted in Klarsfeld, *Vichy–Auschwitz*, p. 282.

[54] Marc Olivier Baruch, *Servir L'État Français: L'Administration en France de 1940 à 1944* (Paris: Fayard, 1997).

[55] Barthélemy, pp 244–8.

[56] Charles de Gaulle, *Mémories de Guerre: L'Appel, 1940–1942* (Paris: Plon, 1954), p. 1; Maurice Agulhon, *De Gaulle: Histoire, Symbole, Mythe* (Paris: Plon, 2000).

[57] Pétain, speeches of 20 June 1940, 20 April 1941 and 8 July 1941.

[58] Limore Yagil, *'L'Homme Nouveau' et la Révolution Nationale de Vichy, 1940–1944* (Villeneuve d'Ascq: Presses Universitaires du Septentrion, 1977), p. 11.

[59] Jorge Semprun, commenting on Heidegger's writing, in *Literature or Life* (New York: Viking, 1997), p. 92.

[60] Jean-Michel Barreau, 'Vichy, Idéologue de l'École', *Revue d'Histoire Moderne et Contemporaire*, October–December 1991, pp. 590–616.

[61] Roderick Kedward and Roger Austin, eds, *Vichy France and the Resistance: Culture*

and Ideology (Totowa, NJ: Barnes and Noble, 1985), pp. 22–3, 32.

[62] Pétain, 'Message to the Mothers of France, 25 May 1941', in *Discours*, pp. 133–4.

[63] Miranda Pollard, 'Vichy and Abortion: Policing the Body and the New Moral Order in Everyday Life', in Fishman, p. 201.

[64] Linda Clark, 'Higher-ranking Women Civil Servants and the Vichy Regime: Firing and Hirings, Collaboration and Resistance', *French History* 13(3), 1999, pp. 332–59.

[65] Hanna Diamond, *Women and the Second World War in France, 1939–1949: Choices and Constraints* (London: Longman, 1999), p. 34.

[66] Christian Faure, *Le Project Culturel de Vichy: Folklore et Révolution Nationale 1940–1944* (Lyon: Presses Universitaires de Lyon, 1989).

[67] Charles Rearick, *The French in Love and War: Popular Culture in the Era of the World Wars* (New Haven, CT: Yale University Press, 1997), pp. 225, 250–2, 276–7.

[68] Bertram M. Gordon, 'The Countryside and the City: Some Notes on the Collaboration Model during the Vichy Period', in Fishman, p. 149.

[69] Pétain, *Discours*, pp. 60, 104.

[70] Steven Zdatny, 'Collaboration or Resistance? French Hairdressers and Vichy's Labour Charter', *Contemporary European History*, 5(3), 1996, pp. 371–99.

[71] Limore Yagil, ' "Jeunesse de France et d'Outre-mer" et la Vision de l'Homme Nouveau dans la France, 1940–1944', *Guerres Mondiales et Conflits Contemporains*, 40(158), 1990, pp. 93–104.

[72] Quoted in Jean-Louis Gay-Lescot, *Sport et Éducation sous Vichy* (Lyon: Presses Universitaires de Lyon, 1991).

[73] Vincent Giroud, 'Transition to Vichy: The Case of Georges Pelorson', *Modernism/Modernity* 7(2), 2000, pp. 221–48.

[74] Emmanuel Mounier, *Emmanuel Mounier et sa Génération: Lettres, Carnets et Inédits*, ed. Paulette Mounier-Leclercq (Saint-Maur: Parole et Silence, 2000).

[75] John Hellman, *The Knight-Monks of Vichy France: Uriage, 1940–1945*, 2nd ed, (Liverpool: Liverpool University Press, 1997); Bernard Comte, *Une Utopie Combatttante: L'École des Cadres d'Uriage, 1940–1942* (Paris: Fayard, 1991).

[76] Introduction by P. A. Brooke to Joseph Joffo, *Un Sac de Billes* (New York: Routledge, 1989), p. 6.

[77] Pierre Giolitto, *Histoire de la Milice* (Paris: Perrin, 1997).

[78] Jacques Delperrié de Bayac, *Histoire de la Milice, 1918–1945* (Paris: Fayard, 1969).

[79] Renée Poznanski *Être Juif en France pendant la Seconde Guerre Mondiale* (Paris: Hachette, 1994), p. 646.

[80] Tzvetan Todorov, *A French Tragedy: Scenes of Civil War, Summer 1944* (Hanover: University Press of New England, 1996), pp. 107–8.

[81] François-René Nans, *Philippe Henriot* (Paris: Bouillon, 1996).

Chapter 4: The new anti-Semitic legal system

[1] Zeev Sternhell, '1880–1940: Un Statut des Juifs dans le Programme de la Droite Antisémite Française', *Monde Juif*, 47(1941), 1991, pp. 3–8; Denis Peschanski, 'Les

Statuts des Juifs du 3 October 1940 et du 2 Juin 1941', *Monde Juif*, 47(1941), 1991, pp. 9–20.

[2] Susan Zuccotti, *The Holocaust, the French, and the Jews* (New York: Basic Books, 1993), p. 207; Serge Klarsfeld, *Vichy–Auschwitz: 1943–1944*, pp. 180–1.

[3] Joseph Billig, 'La Condition des Juifs en France', *Revue d'Histoire de la Deuxième Guerre Mondiale*, 6(24), 1956, pp. 23–55.

[4] Dominique Gros, 'Peut-on Parler d'un Droit Antisémite?', in *Le Droit Antisémite de Vichy* (Paris: Seuil, 1996), p. 41.

[5] Jean-Louis Halperin, 'La Législation de Vichy Relative aux Avocats et aux Droits de la Défense', *Revue Historique*, 286(1), 1991, pp. 143–56.

[6] Danièle Lochak, 'Écrire, se taire ... Réflexions sur la Doctrine Antisémite de Vichy', in *Le Genre Humain*, no. 30–1, May 1996, p. 256.

[7] Maurice Duverger, 'La Situation des Fonctionnaires depuis la Révolution de 1940', *Revue de Droit Public*, 1941 pp. 277–539; and *Le Monde*, 22 and 23 October 1988, and 20 November 1988.

[8] Ted Morgan, p. 121.

[9] Robert Badinter, *Un Antisémitisme Ordinaire: Vichy et les Avocats Juifs, 1940–1944* (Paris: Fayard, 1997).

[10] Joseph Barthélemy, p. 311.

[11] Danièle Lochak, 'La Doctrine sous Vichy ou les mésaventures du positivisme', in *Les Usages sociaux du Droit*, CURAP (Paris: PUF, 1989), pp. 282–5.

Chapter 5: From definition to detention

[1] Birnbaum, *The Jews of the Republic*, p. 340.

[2] Paul Baudouin, *Neuf Mois au Gouvernement*, p. 366.

[3] Henri du Moulin de la Barthète, *Le Temps des Illusions*, p. 280.

[4] Philip Whitcomb, trans., *France during the German Occupation, 1940–1944*, vol. II, p. 628.

[5] Yehuda Bauer, *Rethinking the Holocaust* (New Haven, CT: Yale University Press, 2001).

[6] Laurence Rosengart, 'L'Évolution de la Définition Raciale de Juif sous le Régime de Vichy', *Monde Juif*, 47(141), 1991 pp. 30–43.

[7] Michel Abitbol, *Le Passé d'une Discorde: Juifs et Arabes du VIIe Siècle à nos Jours* (Paris: Perrin, 1999), p. 367.

[8] CDJC LXXV, p. 278.

[9] Dannecker, in Klarsfeld, *Vichy–Auschwitz*, p. 225.

[10] Darquier, in Klarsfeld, *Vichy–Auschwitz*, p. 423.

[11] Duverger, p. 319.

[12] Gerard Noiriel, *Les Origines Républicaines de Vichy*.

[13] David Pryce-Jones, 'Paris during the German Occupation', in Gerhard Hirschfeld and Patrick Marsh, eds, *Collaboration in France: Politics and Culture during the*

Nazi Occupation, 1940–1944 (Oxford: Berg, 1989), pp. 15–31.

[14] Isaac Levendel, *Not the Germans Alone: A Son's Search for the Truth of Vichy* (Evanston, IL: Northwestern University Press, 1999), p. 28.

[15] Letter of Dr Zeitschel, quoted in Klarsfeld, p. 221.

[16] The two terms 'Acquired French nationality' and 'naturalised' are not synonymous: see Bernard Laguerre, 'Les Dénaturalisés de Vichy, 1940–1948', *Vingtième Siècle*, no. 20, October–December 1988, pp. 3–15; Catherine Kessedjian, 'Le Juif Déchu de la Nationalité Française', in Dominique Gros, ed., *Le Droit Antisémite sous Vichy* (Paris: Seuil, *Le Genre Humain*, no. 30/31, 1996), and Kessedjian, 'Les Dénaturalisés de Vichy', *Vingtième Siècle*, no. 20, october–December 1988, pp. 3–16.

[17] Maurice Rajsfus, *La Police de Vichy: Les Forces de l'Ordre Français au Service de la Gestapo 1940–1944* (Paris: Le Cherche Midi, 1995), p. 184.

[18] Vicki Caron, *Uneasy Asylum: France and the Jewish Refugee Crisis* (Stanford, CA: Stanford University Press, 1999), pp. 335–8.

Chapter 6: The Aryanisation process

[1] Marguerite Blocaille-Boutelet, 'L'Aryanisations des Biens', in Dominique Gros, ed., *Le Droit Antisémite de Vichy* (Paris: Seuil, 1996), p. 243.

[2] Claire Andrieu, 'L'Aryanisation et les Finances Extérieures', in Dominique Gros, pp. 267–301.

[3] Henry Rousso, 'L'Aryanisation Économique, Vichy, l'Occupant et la Spoliation des Juifs', *Yod*, no. 15–16, 1982.

[4] Antoine Prost et al., *Aryanisation Économique et Restitutions* (Paris: Mission d'Étude sur la Spoliation des Juifs de France, 2000), p. 32.

[5] Joseph Billig, *Le Commissariat Général aux Questions Juives, 1941–1944* (Paris: Éditions du Centre, 1955), III, pp. 238–9.

[6] Henry Rousso, 'L'Économie: Pénurie et Modernisation', in Jean-Pierre Azéma and François Bédarida, *La France des Années Noires*, rev. edn, vol. I (Paris: Seuil, 2000), p. 468.

[7] Joseph Billig, I, p. 77.

[8] Jean Laloum, *Les Juifs dans la Banlieue Parisienne des Années 20 aux Années 50* (Paris: CNRS, 1998), p. 346.

[9] Billig, III, pp. 62–3.

[10] André Kaspi, *Les Juifs Pendant l'Occupation* (Paris: Seuil, 1991), p. 115.

[11] Billig, I, pp. 61–2.

[12] Philippe Verheyde, *Les Mauvais Comptes de Vichy: l'Aryanisation des Entreprises Juives* (Paris: Perrin, 1999).

[13] Richard Weisberg, *Vichy Law and the Holocaust in France* (New York: New York University Press, 1996), p. 255.

[14] Verheyde, p. 321.

[15] Joseph Barthélemy, pp. 313–14.

[16] Marrus and Paxton, p. 104.

[17] This figure is an official one. Rousso in 'L'Aryanisation Économique, Vichy, l'Occupant et la Spoliation des Juifs', *Yod*, no 15–16 1982, gives the figure as 10,500.

[18] Jean Laloum, p. 140.

[19] Prost, pp. 24–5.

[20] Verheyde, p. 321.

[21] Its full name was *Direction de l'Enregistrement, des Domainies et du Timbre*, but it was usually referred to as Direction des Domaines, management department of the 'Domaines' authority.

[22] Renaud de Rochebrune and Jean-Claude Hazera, *Les Patrons sous l'Occupation* (Paris: Odile Jacob, 1997), pp. 699–702.

[23] Claire Andrieu, ed., *La Spoliation Financière*, vol. I (Paris: Mission d'Étude sur la Spoliation des Juifs de France, La Documentation Française, 2000), p. 23.

[24] Raymond Sarraute and P. Tager, *Les Juifs sous l'Occupation* (Paris: Éditions du Centre, 1945, republished 1982), pp. 50–6.

[25] Billig, III, p. 107.

[26] *La Spoliation Financière*, p. 38.

[27] Billig, III, p. 112; Jacques Adler, *The Jews of Paris and the Final Solution: Communal Response and Internal Conflicts, 1940–1944* (New York: Oxford University Press, 1987), pp. 25–6.

[28] Jacques Sabille, *Les Juifs de Tunisie sous Vichy et sous l'Occupation* (Paris: Éditions du Centre, 1954), pp. 94, 115–22.

[29] Claire Andrieu, ed., *La Spoliation Financière*, vol. I, pp. 59–61.

[30] Sabille, pp. 118–19.

[31] Sarraute and Tager, p. 166.

[32] Verheyde, p. 339.

[33] Sarraute and Tager, p. 35.

[34] Léon Poliakov, *Brévaire de la Haine: Le IIIe Reich et les Juifs* (Paris: Calmann-Lévy, 1951, reprinted 1979), p. 81; Richard Z. Chesnoff, *Pack of Thieves: How Hitler and Europe Plundered the Jews and Committed the Greatest Theft in History* (New York: Doubleday, 1999), pp. 137–9.

[35] Billig, III, pp. 213, 216.

[36] Trial of the Major War Criminals before the International Military Tribunal, Nuremberg, VI, pp. 560–1.

[37] Hector Feliciano, *The Lost Museum: The Nazi Conspiracy to Steal the World's Greatest Works of Art* (New York: Basic Books, 1997).

[38] David Diamant, *Le Billet Vert* (Paris: Édition Renouveau, 1977).

[39] Billig, I, pp. 202–6, 294–309; II, pp. 9–142.

[40] Georges Wellers, *L'Étoile Jaune à l'Heure de Vichy: De Drancy à Auschwitz* (Paris: Fayard, 1973), pp. 185–219.

[41] Isaac Levendel, *Not the Germans Alone: A Son's Search for the Truth of Vichy* (Evanston, IL: Northwestern University Press, 1999), p. 218.

[42] Claire Andrieu, *La Banque sous l'Occupation: Paradoxe de l'Histoire d'une Profession* (Paris: Presses de la Fondation Nationale des Sciences Politiques, 1990), pp. 278–9.

[43] Rochebrune and Hazera, II, pp. 710–12.

[44] Billig, III, p. 224.

[45] Sarraute, p. 47.

[46] Andrieu, *La Banque*, pp. 235–6.

[47] Raymond Aron, *Mémoires* (Paris: Julliard, 1983), p. 91.

Chapter 7: Detention by Vichy

[1] Michael Marrus, 'Vichy before Vichy: Antisemitic Currents in France during the 1930s', *Bulletin of the Wiener Library*: 33(51–2), 1980, pp. 13–20.

[2] Claude Lévy and Paul Tillard, *Betrayal at the Vél d'Hiv* (New York: Hill and Wang, 1969), p. 148.

[3] Arthur Koestler, *Scum of the Earth* (New York: Macmillan, 1941), pp. 94–6.

[4] Sarah Farmer, 'Out of the Picture: Foreign Labor in Wartime France', in Fishman, pp. 250–2; Joffo, p. 15.

[5] Marrus, 'Vichy before Vichy'; Caron, 'Prelude to Vichy', *Journal of Contemporary History*, 20, 1985, pp. 157–76.

[6] Eric Malo, 'Le Camp de Noé de 1941 à 1944', *Annales du Midi*, 100(183), 1988, pp. 337–52; Christian Eggers, 'L'Internement sous Toutes ses Formes: Approche d'une Vue d'Ensemble du Système d'Internement dans la Zone de Vichy', *Monde Juif*, 51(153), 1995, pp. 7–75.

[7] Anne Grynberg, 'Les Camps de Sud de la France: de l'Internement à la Déportation', *Annales* 48(3), 1993, pp. 557–66; Grynberg, *Les Camps de la Honte: Les Internés Juifs des Camps Français, 1939–1944* (Paris: La Découverte, 1999).

[8] Zuccotti, *The Holocaust*, p. 301 f. 32; Thalmann, *Annales*, p. 598.

[9] Levy and Tillard, p. 148.

[10] Ibid., p. 293.

[11] George Wellers, *L'Étoile Jaune à l'Heure de Vichy*; Wellers, *Un Juif sous Vichy*; Maurice Rajsfus, *Drancy, un Camp de Concentration Très Ordinaire, 1941–1944* (Paris: Manya, 1991).

[12] Zucotti, p. 115.

[13] Yehuda Bauer, *Rethinking the Holocaust*, p. 233.

[14] Grynberg, *Les Camps de la Honte*, p. 311.

[15] Zuccotti, pp. 67–8.

[16] Lazare, p. 121.

[17] Z 5766/821/17.

[18] FO 371/32056.

[19] Albert Memmi, *La Statue de Sel* (Paris: Gallimard, 1966).

[20] Martin Thornas, *The French Empire at War, 1940–1945* (Manchester: Manchester University Press, 1998), p. 239; Christine Levisse-Touzé, *L'Afrique du Nord dans la Guerre, 1939–1945* (Paris: Albin Michel, 1998).

[21] Michel Abitbol *Le Passe d'une Discorde: Juifs et Arabes: Du VIIe Siècle à nos Jours* (Paris: Perrin, 1999), pp. 286–8, 364–6.

[22] H. Z. (J. W.) Hirschberg, *A History of the Jews in North Africa*, vol. II (Leiden: Brill, 1981), p. 139.

[23] Webster, p. 156.

[24] *Foreign Relations of the United States: Conferences at Casablanca*, 1943, pp. 608–11.

[25] Hirschberg, p. 325.

[26] Sabine Zeitoun, *Ces Enfants qu'il Fallait Sauver* (Paris: Michel, 1989), p 77.

[27] Lazare, p. 160.

Chapter 8: Persecution

[1] Michel Abitbol, *The Jews of North Africa during the Second World War*, trans. Catherine T. Zentellis (Detroit, MI: Wayne State University Press, 1989), p. 7.

[2] Darquier, speeches at Municipal Council of Paris, June 1936, and at Salle Wagram, Paris, 11 March 1937.

[3] *Le Petit Parisien*, 1 February 1943.

[4] Raoul Hilberg, *The Politics of Memory* (Chicago, IL: Dee, 1996), p. 76.

[5] Michael Marrus, 'Vichy France and the Jews: After Fifteen Years', in Fishman, pp. 40–42; Marrus, 'Coming to Terms with Vichy', *Holocaust and Genocide Studies*, 9(1)', spring 1995, p. 32.

[6] Pierre Assouline, *Jean Jardin, une Éminence Grise* (Paris: Balland, 1986).

[7] Serge Klarsfeld, 'Archives du Quai d'Orsay', *Monde Juif*, 49(146), 1993, pp. 22–33.

[8] Memo of Donald A. Lowrie, 10 August 1942, in Klarsfeld, *Vichy–Auschwitz*, p. 325.

[9] Rousso, *Vichy Syndrome*, pp. 139–44.

[10] Robert O. Paxton, 'La Spécificité de la Persécution des Juifs en France en 1942', *Annales*, 48(3), 1993, pp. 605–19; Serge Klarsfeld and Henry Rousso, 'Histoire et Justice: Debat entre Klarsfeld et Rousso', *Esprit*, 181, 1992, pp. 16–37.

[11] Tzvetan Todorov, *The Fragility of Goodness: Why Bulgaria's Jews Survived the Holocaust* (London: Weidenfeld and Nicolson, 2001), p. 30.

[12] Primo Levi, *Moments of Reprieve*, trans. Ruth Feldman (New York: Summit, 1986), p. 127; *The Periodic Table*, trans. Raymond Rosenthal (New York: Knopf, 1996), p. 221.

[13] Carl Friedrich and Z. K. Brezinksi, *Totalitarian Dictatorship and Autocracy*, rev. edn by Friedrich (New York: Praeger, 1967); Michael Curtis, *Totalitarianism* (New Brunswick, NJ: Transaction, 1979).

[14] Brian R. Sullivan and Philip Cannistraro, *Il Duce's Other Woman* (New York: Morrow, 1992); Dan V. Segre, *Memoirs of a Fortunate Jew: An Italian Story* (Bethesda: Adler and Adler, 1987).

[15] Primo Levi, *Survival in Auschwitz: The Nazi Assault on Humanity*, trans. Stuart Woolf (New York: Collier, 1959).

[16] Susan Zuccotti, *Under His Very Windows: The Vatican and the Holocaust in Italy* (New Haven, CT: Yale University Press, 2000), p. 129.

[17] Meir Michaelis, *Mussolini and the Jews: German–Italian Relations and the Jewish Question in Italy, 1922–1945* (Oxford: Clarendon Press, 1978), pp. 318–19.

[18] Daniel Carpi, *Between Mussolini and Hitler: The Jews and the Italian Authorities in France and Tunisia* (Hanover, NH: University Press of New England, 1994), pp. 12–15, 83–84.

[19] Serge Klarsfeld, 'Le Jeu de Vichy entre les Italiens et les Allemands', *Monde Juif*, 49(149), 1993, pp 74–83.

[20] Lazare, *Rescue as Resistance*, p. 225.

[21] Michaelis, p. 317.

[22] Léon Poliakov and Jacques Sabille, *Jews under the Italian Occupation* (New York: Fertig, 1983), pp. 60-3.

[23] Morgan, *An Uncertain Hour*, p. 181; Lazare, p. 225.

[24] Poliakov and Sabille, pp. 125–6.

[25] Serge Klarsfeld, 'Juillet–Septembre 1942. Les Divergences dans l'Appareil Policier Nazi et la Réalisation de la Solution Finale en France', *Annales*, 48(3), 1993, pp. 545–55.

[26] Otto Abetz, *Histoire d'une Politique Franco-allemande: Mémoires d'un Ambassadeur* (Paris: Stock, 1953).

[27] Maurice Rajsfus, *La Police de Vichy*, p. 94; CDJC, LXXV, p. 81.

[28] Rajsfus, p. 73.

[29] Rita Thalmann, 'La Traque des Juifs dans le Contexte de la "mise au pas" de la France', *Annales*, 48(3), 1993, pp. 595–604.

[30] Dannecker, note on conversation with Darquier, 15 June 1942, quoted in Webster, p. 108.

[31] Rajsfus, p. 84.

[32] Morgan, p. 155.

[33] Lévy and Tillard, pp. 16–19.

[34] Renée Poznanski, *Être Juif en France*, p. 383.

[35] Serge Klarsfeld, *Vichy–Auschwitz*, I, p. 329.

[36] Annette Kahn, *Why My Father Died: a Daughter Confronts Her Family's Past at the Trial of Klaus Barbie*, trans. Anna Cancogni (New York: Summit, 1991), p. 102.

[37] Vicki Caron, *Uneasy Asylum*, p. 339.

[38] Darquier, 23 July 1942, in Klarsfeld, p. 281.

[39] Knochen report to Adolf Eichmann at Eichmann's trial, 0-33-02.

[40] Anne Grynberg, *Les Camps*, p. 559.

[41] FO 371/32056.

[42] Klarsfeld, I, p. 343.

[43] Klarsfeld, I, pp. 339–40.

[44] Morgan, p. 165.

[45] Leventhal, pp 256–7.

[46] Ernst Papanek, *Out of the Fire* (New York: Morrow, 1975), p. 250.

[47] CDJC, CXCIV, p. 30; Klarsfeld, p. 414.

[48] CDJC, XXVC, p. 213.

[49] Donna F. Ryan, *The Holocaust and the Jews of Marseille: The Enforcement of Antisemitic Policies in Vichy France* (Urban, IL: University of Illinois Press, 1996), p. 193.

[50] Ahlrich Meyer, ed., *Marseille 1942–1944: Le Régard de l'Occupant* (Bremen: Édition Temmen, 1999), pp.167, 171.

[51] Christian Oppetit, ed., *Marseille, Vichy et les Nazis: Le Temps des Rafles, la Déportation des Juifs* (Marseille: Amicale des Déportés d'Auschwitz, 1993); Gérard Guicheteau, Marseille 1943: *La Fin du Vieux Port* (Marseille: Daniel, 1973).

[52] CDJC, CCCLXIV, p. 7.

[53] Webster, p. 106.

[54] CDJC, XXV, p. 288.

[55] Rajsfus, *La Police de Vichy*, p. 139.

[56] Webster, p. 161.

[57] Poznanski, p. 544.

[58] Lazare, p. 219.

[59] Ibid., p. 156.

[60] Weinberg, p. 213.

[61] Michael R. Marrus and Robert O. Paxton, 'The Nazis and the Jews in Occupied Western Europe, 1940–1944', in Michael R. Marrus, ed., *The Nazi Holocaust: The 'Final Solution' Outside Germany*, no. 4, vol. I (Westport, CT: Meckler, 1989), p. 126; Maxime Steinberg, 'Le Paradoxe Français dans la Solution Finale à l'Ouest', *Annales*, 48(3), 1993, pp. 583–94.

Chapter 9: Response to persecution

[1] Lazare, *Rescue as Resistance*, p. 199.

[2] Lazare, p. 172.

[3] FO 371/32056.

[4] Hillel J. Kieval, 'Legality and Resistance in Vichy France: the Rescue of Jewish Children', *Proceedings of the American Philosophical Society*, 124(5), 1980, pp. 339–66.

[5] Claude Bochurberg, *Entretiens avec Serge Klarsfeld* (Paris: Stock, 1997), p. 22.

[6] Klarsfeld, *Vichy–Auschwitz*, p. 324.

[7] Kieval, p. 345.

[8] *The Children of Chabannes*, directed by Lisa Gossels and Dean Wetherell.

[9] Hyman, *The Jews of Modern France*, p. 182.

[10] Sabine Zeitoun, *Les Enfants qu'il Fallait Sauver* (Paris: Michel, 1989), p. 188.

[11] Margaret Collins Weitz, 'French Women in the Resistance: Rescuing Jews', in Ruby Rohrlich, ed., *Resisting the Holocaust* (New York: Berg, 1998), pp. 185–9.

[12] Varian Fry, *Surrender on Demand* (New York: Random House, 1945); Andy Marino, *American Pimpernel: The Man Who Saved the Artists on Hitler's Death List* (London: Hutchinson, 1999); Lisa Fittko, *Le Chemin des Pyrénées: Souvenirs 1940–1941* (Paris: Sell, 1987).

[13] Mary Jayne Gold, *Crossroads Marseilles, 1940* (Garden City, NY: Doubleday, 1980), p. 396.

[14] Gershom Scholem, *On Jews and Judaism in Crisis: Selected Essays*, ed. Werner J. Dannhauser (New York: Schocken, 1976), p. 301.

[15] Hannah Arendt, *Eichmann in Jerusalem: A Report on the Banality of Evil* (New York: Viking, 1963).

[16] Schor, pp. 286–7.

[17] Raymond-Raoul Lambert, *Carnet d'un Témoin, 1940–1943*, ed. Richard Cohen (Paris: Fayard, 1985), p. 72.

[18] Rabbi Schwartz, 31 August 1940, quoted in Poznanski, p. 118.

[19] Rabbi Schwartz Report, Archives of the General Consistory, AIU, CC-I dossier 4.

[20] Adolphe Caen, treasurer of the Consistorial Association of Parisian Jews to Rabbi Schwartz, August 1940, AIU, CC-36, quoted in Poznanski, p. 118.

[21] R. R. Lambert, p. 85.

[22] Jacques Helbronner at meeting of Consistory at Chamalières on 2 December 1940, AIU, CC-15, quoted in Poznanski, p. 120.

[23] Renée Poznanski, 'The Jews of France and the Statutes of Jews, 1940–1941', *Yad Vashem Studies*, 22, 1992, pp. 115–46.

[24] Caron, *Uneasy Asylum*, pp. 348–9.

[25] Erna Paris, *Unhealed Wounds: France and the Klaus Barbie Affair* (New York: Grove, 1985), p. 73.

[26] Birnbaum, *The Jews of the Republic*, p. 367.

[27] Vicki Caron, 'Loyalties in Conflict: French Jewry and the Refugee Crisis, 1933–1935', *Les Baeck Institute Year Book*, 36, (1991), pp. 305–7; Birnbaum, p. 367.

[28] Paris, p. 73.

[29] Simon Schwarzfuchs, *Aux Prises avec Vichy: Histoire Publique des Juifs de France* (Paris: Calmann-Lévy, 1998), pp. 122–59; Jacques Adler, *The Jews of Paris and the Final Solution*, p. 102.

[30] Zuccotti, p. 63.

[31] Adler, p. 109.

[32] Lévy to Pétain, 4 September 1942.

[33] Adler, p. 132.

[34] Different positions on this point are taken by the critical Maurice Rajsfus, the more moderate critic Jacques Adler and the less critical Richard Cohen.

[35] Lazare, p. 158.

[36] Lazare, p. 150.

[37] Georges Friedmann, *The End of the Jewish People?*, Trans. Eric Mosbacher (Garden City, NY: Anchor, 1968), p. 11.

[38] Kieval, pp. 364–85.

[39] Lazare, p. 279.

[40] David Diamant, *Les Juifs dans la Résistance Française, 1940–1944* (Paris Le Pavillon, 1971); Léon Poliakov, 'Les Différentes Formes de la Résistance Juive en France', in Moshe Kohn, ed., *Jewish Resistance during the Holocaust* (Jerusalem: Yad Vashem, 1971), pp. 524–32.

[41] Philippe Ganier-Raymond, *L'Affiche Rouge* (Paris: Marabout, 1975); Claude Lévy, *Les Parias de la Résistance* (Paris: Calmann-Lévy, 1970); Philippe Robrieux, *L'Affaire Manouchian: Vie et Mort d'un Héros Communiste* (Paris: Fayard, 1986).

Chapter 10: Between the devil and the deep blue sea

[1] Helmuth von Moltke, *Briefe an Freya, 1939–1945*, trans. Beate Ruhm von Oppen (Munich: Beck, 1988), p. 182; George F. Kennan, *Memoirs 1925–1950* (Boston, MA: Little, Brown, 1967), pp. 121–2.

[2] David R. Blumenthal, *The Banality of Good and Evil: Moral Lessons from the Shoah and Jewish Tradition* (Washington, DC: Georgetown University Press, 1999), p. 20.

[3] Stanley Milgram, *Obedience to Authority: An Experimental View* (New York: Harper and Row, 1974), pp. 35, 60–1.

[4] Herbert Kelman and V. L. Hamilton, *Crimes of Obedience* (New Haven, CT: Yale University Press, 1989), pp. 47, 57, 76, 89–91.

[5] John M. Darley and C. Daniel Batson, 'From Jerusalem to Jericho: A Study of Situational and Dispositional Variables in Helping Behaviour', *Journal of Personality and Social Psychology*, 27(1), 1973, pp. 100–8.

[6] Kelman and Hamilton, p. 76.

[7] Milgram, p. 142.

[8] David Pryce-Jones, 'Paris during the German Occupation', in Hirschfeld, p. 30.

[9] In a letter on 1 May 1941 to a friend when looking for a house in southern France, Cousteau wrote: 'There won't be any decent apartments until we have chased these wretched yids who are encumbering us out of the door.'

[10] Donna Ryan, *The Holocaust and the Jews of Marseille*, p. 204.

[11] Phillipe Burrin, *France under the Germans: Collaboration and Compromise*, trans. Janet Lloyd (New York: Norton, 1996), pp. 175–6.

[12] Jean-Pierre Rioux, 'Everyday Culture in Occupied France', in Fishman, *France at War*, p. 221.

[13] Jean-Marc Loubier, *Louis Jouvet, le Patron* (Paris: Ramsay, 2001).

[14] Serge Added, *Le Théâtre dans les Années-Vichy, 1940–1944* (Paris: Ramsay, 1992), pp. 128–9.

[15] Denis Hollier, *Absent without Leave: French Literature under the Threat of War* (Cambridge, MA: Harvard University Press, 1997), p. 21.

[16] Serge Added, 'L'Euphorie Théâtrale dans Paris Occupé', in Jean-Pierre Rioux, ed., *La Vie Culturelle sous Vichy* (Paris: Éditions Complexe, 1990), p. 317.

[17] Marie-Agnes Joubert, *La Comédie-Française sous l'Occupation* (Paris: Tallandier, 1998).

[18] François Garçon, 'Ce Curieux Âge d'Or des Cinéastes Français', in Rioux, pp. 293–311, gives different figures of film production.

[19] Christian Faure, *Le Projet Culturel de Vichy: Folklore et Révolution Nationale 1940–1944*, p. 255; Jean-Pierre Bertin-Maghit, *Le Cinéma sous l'Occupation* (Paris: Orban, 1989).

[20] Lucien Rebatet, *Les Juifs en France*, quoted in Andre Bazin, *French Cinema of the Occupation and Resistance: The Birth of a Critical Esthetic* (New York: Ungar, 1981), p. 13.

[21] Gérard Loiseaux, *La Littérature de la Défaite et de la Collaboration* (Paris: Publications de la Sorbonne, 1984); David Carroll, *French Literary Fascism: Nationalism, Antisemitism and the Ideology of Culture* (Princeton, NJ: Princeton University Press, 1995).

[22] Jean-Paul Sartre, 'Qu'est ce que la Littérature?' *Situations III* (Paris: Gallimard, 1948), pp. 43–61.

[23] Renee Winegarten, 'The Fascist Mentality, Drieu La Rochelle', in Henry A. Turner Jr, ed., *Reappraisals of Fascism* (New York: New Viewpoints, 1975), pp. 215–30.

[24] Simone de Beauvoir, *La Force des Choses* (Paris: Gallimard, 1960), pp. 31–3; and Simone de Beauvoir, quoted in Alice Kaplan, *The Collaborator: The Trial and Execution of Robert Brasillach* (Chicago, IL: University of Chicago Press, 2000), p. 218.

[25] Kaplan, p. 52.

[26] Jean-Paul Sartre, *Situations III* (Paris: Gallimard, 1947), p. 373.

[27] Francine de Martinoir, *La Littérature Occupée: Les Années de Guerre, 1939–1945* (Paris: Hatier, 1995), p. 143.

[28] Philip Watts, *Allegories of the Purge: How Literature Responded to the Postwar Trials of Writers and Intellectuals in France* (Stanford, CA: Stanford University Press, 1998), p. 64.

[29] Gilbert Joseph, *Une Si Douce Occupation* (Paris: Albin Michel, 1991), p. 234.

[30] Simone de Beauvoir, p. 513.

[31] Beauvoir, p. 578; Renee Winegarten, *Simone de Beauvoir: A Critical View* (Oxford: Berg, 1988), pp. 52, 58.

[32] The voluminous book, *L'Antisémitisme de Plume 1940–1944: Études et Documents*, by Pierre-André Taguieff, Grégoire Kauffmann and Michaël Lenoire (Paris: Berg International Editeurs, 1999), provides the details of five different anti-Semitic attitudes in literature.

[33] Olivier Todd, *André Malraux: Une Vie* (Paris: Gallimard, 2001).

[34] John Dixon, 'Manipulators of Vichy Propaganda: A Case Study in Personality', in H. R. Kedward and R. Austin, eds, *Vichy France and the Resistance* (London: Croom Helm, 1995), pp. 51–6.

[35] Herbert Lottman, *The Left Bank: Writers, Artists, and Politics from the Popular Front to the Cold War* (San Francisco, CA: Halo, 1991), p. 160; Pierre Assouline, *Gaston Gallimard: Un Demi-Siècle d'Édition Française* (Paris: Balland, 1984); Pascal Ory, *Les Collaborateurs, 1940–1945* (Paris: Seuil, 1976).

[36] Michèle C. Cone, *Artists Under Vichy* (Princeton, NJ: Princeton University Press, 1992); Cone, *French Modernisms: Perspectives on Art before, during and after Vichy* (New York: Cambridge University Press, 2001); Bernard Noël, *Marseille–NewYork: Une Liaison Surréaliste, 1940–45* (Marseille: André Dimanche, 1985).

[37] Laurence Bertrand-Dorléac, *L'Art de la Défaite 1940–1944* (Paris: Seuil, 1993); Bertrand-Dorléac, *Histoire de l'Art. Paris 1940–1944* (Paris: Publications de la Sorbonne, 1986); Bertrand-Dorléac, 'La Question Artistique et le Régime de Vichy', in Rioux, p. 155.

[38] Cone, *Artists*, p. 65.

[39] Feliciano, pp. 124, 238.

[40] Burrin, pp. 319, 321.

[41] Burrin, p. 314.

[42] Lévy, p. 248.

[43] Ryan, p. 48.

[44] Robert Badinter, *Un Antisémitisme Ordinaire*, pp. 18–22, 58–62.

[45] Richard H. Weisberg, *Vichy Law and the Holocaust in France*, pp. 163–6.

[46] FO 371/49140.

[47] Michael Bar-Zohar, *Bitter Scent: The Case of L'Oréal, Nazis, and the Arab Boycott* (New York: Dutton, 1996), pp. 47–9, 194–205.

[48] Simone de Beauvoir, *The Prime of Life* (New York: Paragon House, 1992), p. 373.

[49] Speech on 23 October 1975 at the Jewish Historical Society of New York, quoted in David S. Wyman, *The Abandonment of the Jews: America and the Holocaust, 1941–1945* (New York: Pantheon, 1984), pp. 313, 337.

[50] Wyman, pp. 99–100, 153.

[51] Burrin, p. 464.

[52] André Halimi, *La Délation sous l'Occupation* (Paris: Alain Moreau, 1983).

[53] H. R. Kedward and R. Austin, eds, *Vichy France and the Resistance*, p. 20.

[54] Margaret Collins Weitz, *Sisters in the Resistance: How Women Fought to Free France, 1940–1945* (New York: Wiley, 1995), pp. 232–3.

[55] Jean-Yves Boursier, ed., *Résistants et Résistance* (Paris: L'Harmattan, 1997), p. 17.

[56] Miranda Pollard, *Reign of Virtue: Mobilizing Gender in Vichy France* (Chicago, IL: University of Chicago Press, 1998); Celia Bertin, *Femmes sous l'Occupation* (Paris: Stock, 1993); Sarah Fishman, *We Will Wait: Wives of French Prisoners of War* (New Haven, CT: University Press, 1991).

[57] The informative works of H. R. Kedwood, *Resistance in Vichy France* (Oxford, IL: Oxford University Press, 1978); *Occupied France: Collaboration and Resistance* (Oxford: Blackwell, 1985); *In Search of the Maquis: Rival Resistance in Southern France, 1942–1944* (Oxford: Oxford University Press, 1993). Also Laurent Douzou, *La Désobéissance: Histoire d'un Mouvement et d'un Journal Clandestins: Libération Sud, 1940–1944* (Paris: Odile Jacob, 1995); Olivier Wieviorka, *Une Certaine Idée de la Résistance: Défense de la France, 1940–1949* (Paris: Seuil, 1996); Laurent Douzou et al., eds, *La Résistance et les Européans du Sud: Pré-Actes* (Aix-en-Provence: UMR Telemme, 1997).

[58] Christine Levisse-Touzé, ed., *Paris 1944: Les Enjeux de la Libération* (Paris: Albin Michel, 1944).

[59] François-Yves Guillin, *Le Général Delestraint: Le Premier Chef de l'Armée Secrète* (Paris: Plon, 1995).

[60] Pierre Laborie, *Les Français des Années Troubles* (Paris: Desclée de Brouwer, 2001), pp. 163–5.

[61] Laborie, pp. 165, 176.

[62] Daniel Cordier, *Jean Moulin: L'Inconnu du Panthéon* (Paris: Lattes, 1989), vol. III.

[63] Jean Lacoutre, *Mitterrand: Une Histoire des Français* (Paris: Seuil, 1998); Catherine Nay, *Le Noir et le Rouge: Ou l'Histoire d'une Ambition* (Paris: Grasset, 1984); Pierre Péan, *Une Jeunesse Française: François Mitterrand, 1934–1947* (Paris: Fayard, 1994).

[64] Ronald Tiersky, *François Mitterrand: The Last French President*, New York: St Martin's Press, 2000), pp. 5–9; Alain Peyrefitte, *C'Était de Gaulle* (Paris: Fayard, 1994), I, pp. 578–81.

[65] Roger Hanin, *Lettres à un Ami Mystérieux* (Paris: Grasset, 2001).

[66] Pierre Bergé, *Inventaire Mitterrand* (Paris: Stock, 2001), p. 31.

[67] Slightly different views on this are in Tiersky, p. 44, Franz-Olivier, *François Mitterrand, une Vie* (Paris: Seuil, 1995), p. 51, and John Laughland, *The Death of Politics: France under Mitterrand* (London: Joseph, 1994), p. 206.

[68] John Hellman, *The Knight-Monks of Vichy France: Uriage, 1940–1945*, 2nd edn (Montreal: McGill-Queen's University Press, 1997), p. 241.

[69] François Mitterrand, 'Pèlerinage en Thuringe: Notes d'un Prisonnier de Guerre', *Revue de l'État Nouveau*, 5 December 1942, pp. 693–7, reprinted in Mitterrand, *Politique Textes et Discours, 1938–1981* (Paris: Fayard, 1981), pp. 21–9.

[70] Bergé, p. 56.

[71] Tiersky, p. 352.

[72] Lacoutre, p. 533.

[73] Elie Wiesel, *And the Sea is Never Full: Memoirs, 1969* (New York: Knopf, 1999), pp. 319–20, 340.

[74] Hanin, p. 135.

[75] Claire Andrieu, 'Réponse d'une Historienne', *Esprit*, no. 207, December 1994, p. 206.

[76] Stanley Hoffmann, 'Collaborationism in France during World War II', *Journal of Modern History*, 40(3), September 1968, pp. 375–6.

[77] Yves Durand, 'Collaboration French Style: A European Perspective', in Fishman, pp. 63–5.

[78] George Orwell, *Collected Essays*, vol. 4 (New York: Harcourt, Brace, 1968), p. 133.

[79] Christian Morgenstern, *The Gallows Songs*, trans., W. D. Snodgrass and Lore Segal (Berkeley, CA: University of California Press, 1967), p. 35.

[80] Eberhard Jäckel, *La France dans l'Europe de Hitler*, trans. Denis Meunier (Paris: Fayard, 1968); Paxton, *Vichy France*, pp. 51–2.

[81] Pétain, *Discours*, pp. 86–94.

[82] Louis-Dominique Girard, *Montoire, Verdun Diplomatique: Le Secret du Maréchal* (Paris: Bonne, 1948).

[83] Jäckel.

[84] Helen McPhail, *The Long Silence: Civilian Life under the German Occupation of Northern France, 1914–1918* (New York: Tauris, 1999); Richard Cobb, *French and Germans, Germans and French* (Hanover, NH: University Press of New England, 1983), pp. 12–32.

[85] Alain Brossat, *Les Tondues: Un Carnival Mode* (Levaillois-Perret: Manya, 1992); Fabrice Virgili, *La France 'Virile': Des Femmes Tondues à la Libération* (Paris: Payot, 2000).

[86] Renaud de Rochebrune and J. C. Hazera, *Les Patrons sous l'Occupation* (Paris: Odile Jacob, 1997), pp. 784–6.

[87] Henry Rousso, 'L'Organisation Industrielle de Vichy', *Revue d'Histoire de la Deuxième Guerre Mondiale*, 29 (116), 1979, pp. 27–44.

[88] Lynne Taylor, *Between Resistance and Collaboration: Popular Protest in Northern France, 1940–1944* (New York: St Martin's Press, 2000).

[89] John F. Sweets, *Choices in Vichy France: The French under Nazi Occupation* (New York: Oxford University Press, 1986), p. 25.

[90] Atkin, *Pétain*, p. 174.

[91] Elie Kedourie, *Arabic Political Memoirs and Other Studies* (London: Cass, 1974), p. 278.

[92] Kedourie, p. 200, quoting Sami al-Jundi (Beirut, 1969).

[93] George Kirk, *The Middle East in the War* (London: Oxford University Press, 1952), p. 93, quoting George London, *L'Amiral Estéva et le Général Dentz devant la Haute Cour de Justice* (Lyon: Bonnefon, 1945), p. 247.

[94] Fritz Grobba, *Männer und Mächte in Orient* (Göttingen: Musterschmidt, 1967), pp. 232–4.

[95] Somerset de Chair, *The Golden Carpet* (New York: Harcourt, Brace, 1945).

[96] Morgan, pp. 92–3.

[97] Sarah Farmer, *Martyred Village: Commemorating the 1944 Massacre at Oradour-sur-Glane* (Berkeley, CA: University of California Press, 1999); Pascal Maysounave, *Oradour, Plus Près de la Vérité* (Paris: Souny, 1996).

[98] Kevin Passmore, *From Liberalism to Fascism: The Right in a French Province, 1928–1939* (New York: Cambridge University Press, 1997).

[99] Jean-Pierre Azéma, 'La Milice', *Vingtième Siécle*, 28 October–December 1990, pp. 83–106; Jacques Delperrié de Bayac, *Histoire de la Milice, 1918-1945* (Paris: Fayard, 1994); Pierre Giolitto, *Histoire de la Milice* (Paris: Perrin, 1997).

[100] Giolitto, pp. 298-300.

[101] Tzvetan Todorov, *A French Tragedy: Scenes of Civil War, Summer 1944* (Hanover, NH: University Press of New England, 1996), pp. 99–105.

[102] Jean-Pierre Azéma, 'Les Enjeux de l'Épuration en France', *French Cultural Studies*, V, 1994, pp. 273–9.

Chapter 11: The judgements of Paris

[1] Henry Rousso, 'Une Justice Impossible: l'Épuration et la Politique Antijuive de Vichy', *Annales*, 48(3), 1993, pp. 745–70.

[2] Serge Klarsfeld, *Le Figaro*, 9 June 1993.

[3] Nancy Wood, 'Memory on Trial in Contemporary France', originally in *History and Memory*, reprinted in Wood, *Vectors of Memory: Legacies of Trauma in Postwar Europe* (Oxford: Berg, 1999), pp. 113–42; Pierre Nora, *Realms of Memory*, pp. XV–XXIV, 1–21.

[4] Alain Finkielkraut, *Remembering in Vain: The Klaus Barbie Trial and Crimes against Humanity* (New York: Columbia University Press, 1992), p. 8.

[5] Katy Hazan, 'Les Répresentations de la Persécution des Juifs dans les Procès de l'Épuration en France', *Monde Juif*, 52(156), 1996, pp. 57–79.

[6] Réne Rémond, *Paul Touvier et l'Église* (Paris: Fayard, 1992).

[7] Eric Conan and Henry Rousso, *Vichy, un Passé qui ne Passe Pas* (Paris: Gallimard, 1996), p. 293.

[8] René Terrisse, *Bordeaux, 1942–1944* (Paris: Perrin, 1993).

[9] Charles-Louis Foulon, *Le Pouvoir en Provence à la Libération: Les Commissaires de la République, 1943–1946* (Paris: Presses de la FNSP, Colin, 1975).

[10] Jean-Luc Einaudi, *La Bataille de Paris: 17 Octobre 1961* (Paris: Seuil, 1991), p. 313.

[11] A very considerable literature by scholars and journalists is now available on the Papon trial. Some of it is bland; some is controversial and polemical. Among the more interesting writings are Gerard Boulanger, *Maurice Papon: Un Technocrate Français dans la Collaboration* (Paris: Seuil, 1994); Philippe Cohen-Grillet, *Maurice Papon: De la Collaboration aux Assises* (Bordeaux: Le Bord de l'Eau, 1997); Eric Conan, *Le Procès Papon: Un Journal d'Audience* (Paris: Gallimard, 1998); Jean-Michel Dumay, *Le Procès de Maurice Papon: La Chronique de Jean-Michel Dumay*, for *Le Monde* (Paris: Fayard, 1998); Richard J. Golsan, ed., *Memory, the Holocaust and French Justice: The Bousquet and Touvier Affairs* (Dartmouth: University Press of New England, 1996); Richard J. Golsan, *The Papon Affair: Memory and Justice on Trial* (London: Routledge, 2000); Bertrand Poirot-Delpech, *Papon: Un Crime de Bureau* (Paris: Stock 1998).

[12] Hannah Arendt, *Eichmann in Jerusalem: A Report on the Banality of Evil* (New York: Viking Press, 1965).

[13] Barthélemy, p. 62.

[14] Lambert, p. 88.

[15] Lévy and Tillard, pp. 138–9.

[16] Klarsfeld, p. 339.

[17] Klarsfeld, p. 348.

[18] Philippe Boegner, ed., *Carnets du Pasteur Boegner 1940-1945* (Paris: Fayard, 1992).

[19] Lambert, p. 153.

[20] Klarsfeld, *Vichy–Auschwitz*, II, pp. 54–5.

[21] Lambert, pp. 206–8.

[22] Richard J. Golsan, *Memory, the Holocaust, and French Justice*, pp. 25–6.

[23] Alain Peyrefitte, *C'est de Gaulle*, III, p. 601.

[24] Richard J. Golsan, 'Memory and Justice Abused: The 1949 Trial of René Bousquet', *Studies in Twentieth Century Literature*, 23(1), 1999, pp. 93–110.

[25] Fréderique Tournier, 'François Mitterrand et l'Affaire Bousquet', *Modern and Contemporary France*, 3(3) 1995, pp. 253–61; Serge Klarsfeld, *Le Figaro*, 9 June 1993.

[26] Jean-Pierre Husson, 'L'Itinéraire d'un Haut Fonctionnaire: René Bousquet', in Jean-Pierre Azéma and François Bédarida, eds, *Vichy et les Français*, pp. 287–301.

Chapter 12: Servants of the state and the law

[1] Marc Olivier Baruch, *Servir l'État Français*, p. 168.

[2] Sonia Mazey and Vincent Wright, 'Les Préfets', in Jean-Pierre Azéma and François Bédarida, *Le Régime de Vichy et les Français* (Paris: Fayard, 1992), p. 276.

[3] Op. cit., p. 281.

[4] Baruch, pp. 31, 456–8, 582–3; François Bloch-Lainé in *Vichy et les Français*, p. 367; Bloch-Lainé and Claude Gruson, *Hauts Fonctionnaires sous l'Occupation* (Paris: Odile Jacob, 1996).

[5] *Une Entreprise Publique dans la Guerre: La SNCF 1939–1945*.

[6] Raul Hilberg, *The Destruction*, p. 884.

[7] Baruch, p. 140.

[8] Baruch p. 152.

[9] Webster, *Pétain's Crime*, p. 135.

[10] Dominique Gros, 'Le Droit Antisémite de Vichy Contre la Tradition Républicaine', in *Juger sous Vichy*, 'Le Genre Humain' (Paris: Seuil, 1996), pp. 17–27; Danièle Lochak, 'La doctrine sous Vichy ou les mésaventures du positivisme', in *Les Usages Sociaux du Droit* (Paris: Presses Universitaires de France, 1989), pp. 252–85; Richard H. Weisberg, *Vichy Law and the Holocaust in France* (New York: New York University Press, 1996).

[11] Marrus-Paxton, p. 139.

[12] Georges Burdeau, *Cours de Droit Constitutionnel* (Paris: LGDJ, 1942), p. 191; Maurice Duverger, 'La Situation des Fonctionnaires depuis la Révolution de 1940', *La Revue du Droit Public*, 1941, pp. 277–332, 417–540; also *Le Monde*, 22 October 1988 and 20 November 1988.

[13] Jacques Charpentier, *Au Service de la Liberté* (Paris: Fayard, 1949), p. 127.

[14] Robert Badinter, *Un Antisémitisme Ordinaire*, p. 22.

[15] Danièle Lochak, 'La Doctrine', in *Les Usages*.

[16] Duverger, 'La Situation', *Revue de Droit Public*, 1941.

[17] Richard Weisberg, *Poethics and other Strategies of Law and Literature* (New York: Columbia University Press, 1992), pp. 148–50.

[18] H. L. A. Hart and Lon Fuller in *Harvard Law Review*, 1, 1958, pp. 593–672.

[19] Richard Weisberg, pp. 174–5.

[20] Ingo Müller, *Hitler's Justice: The Courts of the Third Reich* (Cambridge, MA: Harvard University Press, 1991), p. 297; Raul Hilberg, *The Destination of the European Jews*, vol. 3, pp. 993–1029.

[21] Pascal Ancel, 'La Jurisprudence Civile et Commerciale'; in Gros, p. 366.

[22] Roger Bonnard, *Précis de Droit Administratif*, LGDJ, 1943. He is the author of at least six manuals; Michèle Cointet, 'Les Juristes sous l'Occupation: la Tentation du Pétainisme et le choix de la Résistance', in André Gueslin, ed., *Les Facs sous Vichy* (Clermont-Ferrand: PEUMCUBP, 1994), pp 56–9.

[23] Claude Singer, *Vichy, L'Université et les Juifs: Les Silences et la Mémoire* (Paris: Belles Lettres, 1992), p. 90; Gilles Martinez, 'Joseph Barthélemy et la crise de la Démocratie Libérale', *Vingtième Siècle*, 59, 1998, pp. 28–47.

[24] Georges Burdeau, p. 191, quoted in Badinter, p. 45.

[25] Lochak, *Les Usages*, p. 89.

[26] Weisberg, *Poethics*, p. 157.

[27] Gros, in *Juger sous Vichy*.

[28] Jean Massot, 'Le Conseil d'État', in Azéma and Bédarida, *Vichy et les Français*, p. 312.

[29] Baruch, pp. 94, 399, 405.

[30] Weisberg, p. 191.

[31] Lochak, in *Juger* pp. 32–5.

[32] Alain Bancaud, 'La Haute Magistrature sous Vichy', *Vingtième Siècle*, 49, January–March 1996, pp. 45–62.

[33] Weisberg, *Poethics*, pp. 141–5.

[34] CDJC, XXXI, p. 36, 1 July 1942.

[35] CDJC, CXV, p.83.

[36] Klarsfeld, *Vichy–Auschwitz*, p. 199.

[37] Lochak, 'Le Droit Antisémite de Vichy', *Le Genre Humain*, no. 30–1, May 1996.

[38] Marguerite Blocaille-Boutelet, in Dominique Gros, ed., *Le Droit Antisémite de Vichy* (Paris: Seuil, 1996), p. 261.

[39] Jean-Marc Berlière, 'La Cour du 19 Août 1944: Essai sur la Mémoire Policière', *Crime, Histoire, et Sociétés*, 3(1), 1999, pp. 105–27; Berlière, '1944–1945: L'Épuration de la Police Parisienne', *Vingtième Siècle*, no. 49, January 1996, pp. 63–81.

[40] Arthur Koestler, *Spanish Testament* (London: Gollancz, 1937), pp. 266, 280.

[41] Maurice Rajsfus, *La Police de Vichy: Les Forces de l'Ordre Françaises au Service de la Gestapo, 1940–1944* (Paris: Le Cherche Midi, 1995), p. 41.

[42] Levendel, p. 241.

[43] Denis Peschanski, *Vichy 1940–1944: Contrôle et Exclusion* (Paris: Éditions Complexe, 1997), p. 68.

[44] Rajsfus, p. 47.

[45] CDJC, CCCLXIV.

[46] Jean-Pierre Husson, 'L'Itinéraire d'un Haut Fonctionnaire: René Bousquet', in *Vichy et les Français*, pp. 287–301.

[47] Jacques Delarue, 'La Police', in *Vichy et les Français*, pp. 302–3.

[48] Jean Estèbe, *Les Juifs à Toulouse et en Midi Toulousian au Temps de Vichy* (Toulouse: Presses Universitaires du Mirail, 1996), p. 38.

[49] Lévy, pp. 251–2.

[50] Marcel Hasquenoph, *La Gestapo en France*, in Rajsfus, p. 37.

[51] Stéphane Courtois, Denis Peschanski and Adam Rayski, *Le Sang de l'Étranger, les Immigrés de la MOI dans la Résistance* (Paris: Fayard, 1989), pp. 221–41.

Chapter 13: The Churches and anti-Semitism

[1] John Cornwell, *Hitler's Pope: The Secret History of Pius XII* (New York: Viking, 1999); Susan Zuccotti, *Under His Very Windows: The Vatican and the Holocaust in Italy* (New Haven, CT: Yale University Press, 2000), pp. 306–7.

[2] FO 371/34363.

[3] Peter Hoffman, 'Roncalli in the Second World War: Peace Initiatives, the Greek Famine and the Persecution of the Jews', *Journal of Ecclesiastical History*, 40(1), January 1989.

[4] Alberto Melloni, *Fra Istanbul Atene e la Guerra: La Missione di A. G. Roncalli, 1935–1944* (Genoa: Marietta, 1992), pp. 240–1.

[5] Melloni, p. 279.

[6] Melloni, p. 271. (Ma provare non nuoce. Può darsi che la Provvidenza buona tenga in serbo quelche forrna impensata per noi di intervento a favore di questi poveretti.)

[7] Jules Isaac, *The Teaching of Contempt: Christian Roots of Antisemitism*, trans. Helen Weaver (New York: McGraw-Hill, 1965).

[8] Robert Zaretsky, *Nîmes at War: Religion, Politics, and Public Opinion in the Gard, 1938–1944* (University Park, PA: Penn State Press, 1995), p. 95.

[9] Michèle Cointet, *L'Église sous Vichy 1940–1945* (Paris: Perrin, 1998), p. 371.

[10] François Mauriac, *Le Bâillon Denoué: Après Quatre Ans de Silence* (Paris: Grasset, 1945), p. 105.

[11] Cointet, p. 437.

[12] Atkin, pp. 154–61.

[13] Jacques Duquesne, *Les Catholiques Français sous l'Occupation* (Paris: Grasset, 1996), pp. 112–16.

[14] Omer Bartov, 'The Proof of Ignominy: Vichy France's Past and Presence', *Contemporary European History*, 7(1), March 1998, p. 119.

[15] Vesna Drapac, *War and Religion: Catholics in the Churches of Occupied Paris* (Washington, DC: Catholic University of America Press, 1998), p. 280.

[16] Philip Mansel, *Paris between Empires, 1814–1852* (London: Murray, 2001).

[17] W. D. Halls, *Politics, Society and Christianity in Vichy France* (Oxford: Berg 1995); Drapac, p. 27.

[18] W. D. Halls, 'Catholics, the Vichy Interlude, and after', in Fishman, p. 233.

[19] Moulin de Labarthète, p. 95.

[20] Winston Churchill, *The Gathering Storm* (New York: Houghton Mifflin, 1948), p. 135.

[21] Etienne Fouilloux, *Les Chrétiens Français entre Crise et Libération: 1937–1947* (Paris: Seuil, 1997).

[22] Joffo, *Un Sac de Billes*, p. 20.

[23] Atkin, p. 153.

[24] Pétain, 'L'Éducation Nationale', *La Revue des Deux Mondes*, 15 August 1940.

[25] Atkin, p. 156.

[26] Halls, *Politics*, p. 100.

[27] W. D. Halls, *The Youth of Vichy France* (Oxford: Clarendon Press, 1981), pp. 16–20.

[28] Owen Chadwick, *Britain and the Vatican during the Second World War* (New York: Cambridge University Press, 1986), pp. 134–5.

[29] John F. Morley, *Vatican Diplomacy and the Jews during the Holocaust, 1939-1943* (New York: Ktav, 1980), pp. 52–3.

[30] Léon Poliakov, *Harvest of Hate: The Nazi Program for the Destruction of the Jews of Europe* (Syracuse, NY: Syracuse University Press, 1954), pp. 299–300.

[31] Fouillaux, *Les Chrétiens*, pp. 225–6.

[32] Thomas Kselman, 'Catholicism, Christianity, and Vichy', *French Historical Studies*, 23(3), 2000, pp. 513–30.

[33] Halls, *Politics*, p. 314.

[34] Klarsfeld, *Vichy–Auschwitz*, pp. 106, 330–1; Azéma and Bédarida, pp. 445–6.

[35] Halls, *Politics*, pp. 61–2.

[36] Halls, p. 349.

[37] Cointet, *L'Eglise*, pp. 364–5.

[38] Lazare, p. 210.

[39] Halls, *Youth*, p. 9; Atkins, p. 155.

[40] Renée Bédarida, 'La Hiérarchie Catholique', in Azéma and Bédarida, p. 449.

[41] Burrin, p. 221.

[42] Poznanski, p. 432.

[43] Burrin, p. 224.

[44] Halls, in Fishman, p. 236.

[45] Joffo, p. 20; Kedwood and Austin, p. 77.

[46] Cointet, p. 234.

[47] Poznanski, p. 432.

[48] Morgan, p. 167.

[49] Pinchas E. Lapide, *Three Popes and the Jews* (New York: Hawthorne, 1967), p. 192.

[50] Philip Friedman, *Their Brother's Keepers* (New York: Holocaust Library, 1978), pp. 53–4.

[51] Serge Klarsfeld, *Le Monde*, 3 June 1989.

[52] Asher Cohen, *Persécutions et Sauvetages* (Paris: Cerf, 1993), p. 308.

[53] Cointet, p. 222.

[54] Halls, in Fishman, p. 237.

[55] Pastoral letter of Cardinal Saliège, 23 August 1942, in Klarsfeld, *Vichy–Auschwitz*, p. 355.

[56] Letter of Bishop Théas, 26 August 1942, in Klarsfeld, p. 364.

[57] Léon Poliakov, 'Pope Pius XII and the Nazis', *Jewish Frontier*, April 1964, quoted in Pinchas E. Lapide, *Three Popes and the Jews* (New York: Hawthorne, 1967), p. 361.

[58] Halls, p. 141.

[59] Drapac, p. 12.

[60] Bernard Comte, 'Conscience Catholique et Persécution Antisémite: L'Engagement de Théologiens Lyonnais en 1941–1942', *Annales*, 48(3), 1993, pp. 635–54.

[61] Fouilloux, p. 201.

[62] Fouilloux, p. 10.

[63] Philippe Joutard, *Cévennes, Terre de Refuge 1940–1944*, 2nd edn (Montpellier: Presses du Languedoc: Club Cévenol, 1988), p. 26; Zaretsky, pp. 119, 164.

[64] Robert Zaretsky, 'Old Grudges and Atavistic Hatreds: Catholics and Protestants in the Department of the Gard, 1940–1942', *Historical Reflections*, 17(3), 1991, pp. 233–65.

[65] Georges Wellers, ed., *La France et la Question Juive, 1940–1944* (Paris: Sylvie Messinger, 1981), pp. 149–50; Poznanski, *Être Juif*, p. 139.

[66] Pierre Laborie, *Les Français des Années Troubles* (Paris: Desclée de Brouwer, 2001), p. 196.

[67] Klarsfeld, *Vichy–Auschwitz*, pp. 344–5.

[68] Cointet, *L'Église*, pp. 254–5.

[69] Philip P. Hallie, *Lest Innocent Blood Be Shed: The Story of the Village of Le Chambon and How Goodness Happened There* (New York: Harper and Row, 1979).

Conclusion

[1] Jean-Michel Dumay, *La Chronique, Le Procès de Maurice Papon* (Paris: Fayard, 1998), p. 80.

[2] Martin Gilbert, *Israel: A History* (New York: Morrow, 1998), p. 337; Howard M. Sacher, *A History of Israel from the Rise of Zionism to Our Time* (Oxford: Blackwell, 1977), p. 558.

[3] Claire Andrieu, *Le Programme Commun de la Résistance: Des Idées dans la Guerre* (Paris: Éditions de l'Erudit, 1984), pp. 168–70.

[4] Koreman, p. 93.

[5] Charles de Gaulle, *The Complete War Memoirs*, trans. Jonathan Griffin and Richard Howard (New York: Simon and Schuster, 1964), pp. 790–1; Koreman, p. 291.

[6] Henry Rousso, 'L'Épuration en France: Une Histoire Inachevée', *Vingtième Siècle*, no. 33, January–March 1992, pp. 78–105; Jean-Pierre Azéma, 'Les Enjeux de l'Épuration en France', *French Cultural Studies*, V, 1994, pp. 273–9.

[7] Ambassador Duff Cooper to Anthony Eden, 22 March 1945, FO 371/ 49140; Herbert R. Lottman, *The Purge* (New York: Morrow, 1986), p. 144.

[8] Christopher Browning, *Ordinary Men: Reserve Police Battalion 101 and the Final Solution in Poland* (New York: Harper Collins, 1992); Daniel J. Goldhagen, *Hitler's Willing Executioners: Ordinary Germans and the Holocaust* (New York: Knopf, 1996), pp. 203–38.

[9] Lottman, *The Left Bank*, pp. 160–73.

[10] Zuccotti, pp. 103, 110.

[11] Colton, *Léon Blum*, pp. 406–7.

[12] Kenneth S. Davis, *FDR, The War President, 1940–1943: A History* (New York: Random House, 2000), p. 425.

[13] Richard Mitt, *The Politics of Antisemitic Prejudice: The Waldheim Phenomenon in Austria* (Boulder, CO: Westview, 1992), pp. 249–50.

[14] Lottman, *Pétain*, pp. 175–6.

[15] Milgram, *Submission*, p. 269.

INDEX